Hershman & McFarlane
Children Act Handbook

Hershman & McFarlane
Children Act Handbook

Family Law

Published by
Jordan Publishing Limited
21 St Thomas Street
Bristol BS1 6JS

British Library Cataloguing-in-Publication Data

A catalogue record for this book is available from the British Library.

ISBN   978 1 84661 285 5.

Typeset by Letterpart Ltd, Reigate, Surrey

Printed and bound in Great Britain by CPI Antony Rowe, Chippenham and Eastbourne

PREFACE TO THE FIRST EDITION

In the ten years since the publication of *Children Law and Practice*, one drawback of the layout of the text has been that, in order to have both the commentary and the statutory material at court, it has been necessary for users to carry both volumes of the work with them. This modestly sized handbook is being published in order to ease the physical burden on users by providing core statutory material in a portable supplement.

We hope that this handbook will be a useful addition to the family law library and that the selection that we have made is sufficient to meet both the need for portability and the need to provide essential core material. Any suggestions for additional material are welcome.

The *Children Act Handbook* will be updated each year and issued as part of the subscription package to all *Children Law and Practice* subscribers. In addition, the *Handbook* will be available for sale separately to non-subscribers.

David Hershman and
Andrew McFarlane
August 2001

CONTENTS

Part I
STATUTES

ADOPTION AND CHILDREN ACT 2002

ARRANGEMENT OF SECTIONS

PART 1
ADOPTION

Chapter 1
Introductory

Chapter 3
Placement for Adoption and Adoption Orders

Placement of children by adoption agency for adoption

Placement and adoption: general

PART 1
ADOPTION

Chapter 1
Introductory

1 Considerations applying to the exercise of powers

(1) This section applies whenever a court or adoption agency is coming to a decision relating to the adoption of a child.

(2) The paramount consideration of the court or adoption agency must be the child's welfare, throughout his life.

(3) The court or adoption agency must at all times bear in mind that, in general, any delay in coming to the decision is likely to prejudice the child's welfare.

(4) The court or adoption agency must have regard to the following matters (among others) –

(a)   the child's ascertainable wishes and feelings regarding the decision (considered in the light of the child's age and understanding),

(b)   the child's particular needs,

(c)   the likely effect on the child (throughout his life) of having ceased to be a member of the original family and become an adopted person,

(d)   the child's age, sex, background and any of the child's characteristics which the court or agency considers relevant,

(e)   any harm (within the meaning of the Children Act 1989) which the child has suffered or is at risk of suffering,

(f)   the relationship which the child has with relatives, and with any other person in relation to whom the court or agency considers the relationship to be relevant, including –

    (i)   the likelihood of any such relationship continuing and the value to the child of its doing so,

    (ii)   the ability and willingness of any of the child's relatives, or of any such person, to provide the child with a secure environment in which the child can develop, and otherwise to meet the child's needs,

    (iii)   the wishes and feelings of any of the child's relatives, or of any such person, regarding the child.

(5) In placing the child for adoption, the adoption agency must give due consideration to the child's religious persuasion, racial origin and cultural and linguistic background.

(6) The court or adoption agency must always consider the whole range of powers available to it in the child's case (whether under this Act or the Children Act 1989); and the court must not make any order under this Act unless it considers that making the order would be better for the child than not doing so.

(7) In this section, "coming to a decision relating to the adoption of a child", in relation to a court, includes –

(a)   coming to a decision in any proceedings where the orders that might be made by the court include an adoption order (or the revocation of such an order), a placement order (or the revocation of such an order) or an order under section 26 (or the revocation or variation of such an order),

(b)   coming to a decision about granting leave in respect of any action (other than the initiation of proceedings in any court) which may be taken by an adoption agency or individual under this Act,

but does not include coming to a decision about granting leave in any other circumstances.

(8) For the purposes of this section –

(a)   references to relationships are not confined to legal relationships,

(b)   references to a relative, in relation to a child, include the child's mother and father.

****

Chapter 3
Placement for Adoption and Adoption Orders

Placement of children by adoption agency for adoption

18 Placement for adoption by agencies

(1) An adoption agency may –

(a)   place a child for adoption with prospective adopters, or

(b)   where it has placed a child with any persons (whether under this Part or not), leave the child with them as prospective adopters,

but, except in the case of a child who is less than six weeks old, may only do so under section 19 or a placement order.

(2) An adoption agency may only place a child for adoption with prospective adopters if the agency is satisfied that the child ought to be placed for adoption.

(3) A child who is placed or authorised to be placed for adoption with prospective adopters by a local authority is looked after by the authority.

(4) If an application for an adoption order has been made by any persons in respect of a child and has not been disposed of –

(a)   an adoption agency which placed the child with those persons may leave the child with them until the application is disposed of, but

(b)   apart from that, the child may not be placed for adoption with any prospective adopters.

"Adoption order" includes a Scottish or Northern Irish adoption order.

(5) References in this Act (apart from this section) to an adoption agency placing a child for adoption –

(a)   are to its placing a child for adoption with prospective adopters, and

(b)   include, where it has placed a child with any persons (whether under this Act or not), leaving the child with them as prospective adopters;

and references in this Act (apart from this section) to a child who is placed for adoption by an adoption agency are to be interpreted accordingly.

(6) References in this Chapter to an adoption agency being, or not being, authorised to place a child for adoption are to the agency being or (as the case may be) not being authorised to do so under section 19 or a placement order.

(7) This section is subject to sections 30 to 35 (removal of children placed by adoption agencies).

19 Placing children with parental consent

(1) Where an adoption agency is satisfied that each parent or guardian of a child has consented to the child –

    (a)   being placed for adoption with prospective adopters identified in the consent, or

    (b)   being placed for adoption with any prospective adopters who may be chosen by the agency,

and has not withdrawn the consent, the agency is authorised to place the child for adoption accordingly.

(2) Consent to a child being placed for adoption with prospective adopters identified in the consent may be combined with consent to the child subsequently being placed for adoption with any prospective adopters who may be chosen by the agency in circumstances where the child is removed from or returned by the identified prospective adopters.

(3) Subsection (1) does not apply where –

    (a)   an application has been made on which a care order might be made and the application has not been disposed of, or

    (b)   a care order or placement order has been made after the consent was given.

(4) References in this Act to a child placed for adoption under this section include a child who was placed under this section with prospective adopters and continues to be placed with them, whether or not consent to the placement has been withdrawn.

(5) This section is subject to section 52 (parental etc consent).

20 Advance consent to adoption

(1) A parent or guardian of a child who consents to the child being placed for adoption by an adoption agency under section 19 may, at the same or any subsequent time, consent to the making of a future adoption order.

(2) Consent under this section –

    (a)   where the parent or guardian has consented to the child being placed for adoption with prospective adopters identified in the consent, may be consent to adoption by them, or

    (b)   may be consent to adoption by any prospective adopters who may be chosen by the agency.

(3) A person may withdraw any consent given under this section.

(4) A person who gives consent under this section may, at the same or any subsequent time, by notice given to the adoption agency –

    (a)   state that he does not wish to be informed of any application for an adoption order, or

    (b)   withdraw such a statement.

(5) A notice under subsection (4) has effect from the time when it is received by the adoption agency but has no effect if the person concerned has withdrawn his consent.

(6) This section is subject to section 52 (parental etc consent).

21 Placement orders

(1) A placement order is an order made by the court authorising a local authority to place a child for adoption with any prospective adopters who may be chosen by the authority.

(2) The court may not make a placement order in respect of a child unless –

    (a)   the child is subject to a care order,

    (b)   the court is satisfied that the conditions in section 31(2) of the 1989 Act (conditions for making a care order) are met, or

    (c)   the child has no parent or guardian.

(3) The court may only make a placement order if, in the case of each parent or guardian of the child, the court is satisfied –

    (a)   that the parent or guardian has consented to the child being placed for adoption with any prospective adopters who may be chosen by the local authority and has not withdrawn the consent, or

    (b)   that the parent's or guardian's consent should be dispensed with.

This subsection is subject to section 52 (parental etc consent).

(4) A placement order continues in force until –

    (a)   it is revoked under section 24,

    (b)   an adoption order is made in respect of the child, or

    (c)   the child marries[, forms a civil partnership][1] or attains the age of 18 years.

"Adoption order" includes a Scottish or Northern Irish adoption order.

NOTES

Amendments.[1] Words inserted: Civil Partnership Act 2004, s 79(1), (2).

22 Applications for placement orders

(1) A local authority must apply to the court for a placement order in respect of a child if –

    (a)   the child is placed for adoption by them or is being provided with accommodation by them,

    (b)   no adoption agency is authorised to place the child for adoption,

    (c)   the child has no parent or guardian or the authority consider that the conditions in section 31(2) of the 1989 Act are met, and

    (d)   the authority are satisfied that the child ought to be placed for adoption.

(2) If –

    (a)   an application has been made (and has not been disposed of) on which a care order might be made in respect of a child, or

    (b)   a child is subject to a care order and the appropriate local authority are not authorised to place the child for adoption,

the appropriate local authority must apply to the court for a placement order if they are satisfied that the child ought to be placed for adoption.

(3) If –

    (a)   a child is subject to a care order, and

    (b)   the appropriate local authority are authorised to place the child for adoption under section 19,

the authority may apply to the court for a placement order.

(4) If a local authority –

    (a)   are under a duty to apply to the court for a placement order in respect of a child, or

    (b)   have applied for a placement order in respect of a child and the application has not been disposed of,

the child is looked after by the authority.

(5) Subsections (1) to (3) do not apply in respect of a child –

    (a)   if any persons have given notice of intention to adopt, unless the period of four months beginning with the giving of the notice has expired without them applying for an adoption order or their application for such an order has been withdrawn or refused, or

    (b)   if an application for an adoption order has been made and has not been disposed of.

"Adoption order" includes a Scottish or Northern Irish adoption order.

(6) Where –

    (a)   an application for a placement order in respect of a child has been made and has not been disposed of, and

    (b)   no interim care order is in force,

the court may give any directions it considers appropriate for the medical or psychiatric examination or other assessment of the child; but a child who is of sufficient understanding to make an informed decision may refuse to submit to the examination or other assessment.

(7) The appropriate local authority –

    (a)   in relation to a care order, is the local authority in whose care the child is placed by the order, and

    (b)   in relation to an application on which a care order might be made, is the local authority which makes the application.

23 Varying placement orders

(1) The court may vary a placement order so as to substitute another local authority for the local authority authorised by the order to place the child for adoption.

(2) The variation may only be made on the joint application of both authorities.

24 Revoking placement orders

(1) The court may revoke a placement order on the application of any person.

(2) But an application may not be made by a person other than the child or the local authority authorised by the order to place the child for adoption unless –

   (a)   the court has given leave to apply, and
   (b)   the child is not placed for adoption by the authority.

(3) The court cannot give leave under subsection (2)(*a*) unless satisfied that there has been a change in circumstances since the order was made.

(4) If the court determines, on an application for an adoption order, not to make the order, it may revoke any placement order in respect of the child.

(5) Where –

   (a)   an application for the revocation of a placement order has been made and has not been disposed of, and
   (b)   the child is not placed for adoption by the authority,

the child may not without the court's leave be placed for adoption under the order.

25 Parental responsibility

(1) This section applies while –

   (a)   a child is placed for adoption under section 19 or an adoption agency is authorised to place a child for adoption under that section, or
   (b)   a placement order is in force in respect of a child.

(2) Parental responsibility for the child is given to the agency concerned.

(3) While the child is placed with prospective adopters, parental responsibility is given to them.

(4) The agency may determine that the parental responsibility of any parent or guardian, or of prospective adopters, is to be restricted to the extent specified in the determination.

26 Contact

(1) On an adoption agency being authorised to place a child for adoption, or placing a child for adoption who is less than six weeks old, any provision for

contact under the 1989 Act ceases to have effect [and any contact activity direction relating to contact with the child is discharged][1].

(2) While an adoption agency is so authorised or a child is placed for adoption –

   (a)   no application may be made for any provision for contact under that Act, but

   (b)   the court may make an order under this section requiring the person with whom the child lives, or is to live, to allow the child to visit or stay with the person named in the order, or for the person named in the order and the child otherwise to have contact with each other.

(3) An application for an order under this section may be made by –

   (a)   the child or the agency,

   (b)   any parent, guardian or relative,

   (c)   any person in whose favour there was provision for contact under the 1989 Act which ceased to have effect by virtue of subsection (1),

   (d)   if a residence order was in force immediately before the adoption agency was authorised to place the child for adoption or (as the case may be) placed the child for adoption at a time when he was less than six weeks old, the person in whose favour the order was made,

   (e)   if a person had care of the child immediately before that time by virtue of an order made in the exercise of the High Court's inherent jurisdiction with respect to children, that person,

   (f)   any person who has obtained the court's leave to make the application.

(4) When making a placement order, the court may on its own initiative make an order under this section.

(5) This section does not prevent an application for a contact order under section 8 of the 1989 Act being made where the application is to be heard together with an application for an adoption order in respect of the child.

(6) In this section, ["contact activity direction" has the meaning given by section 11A of the 1989 Act and][1] "provision for contact under the 1989 Act" means a contact order under section 8 of that Act or an order under section 34 of that Act (parental contact with children in care).

NOTES

Amendments. [1] Words inserted: Children and Adoption Act 2006, s 15(1), Sch 2, paras 13, 14.

27 Contact: supplementary

(1) An order under section 26 –

   (a)   has effect while the adoption agency is authorised to place the child for adoption or the child is placed for adoption, but

   (b)   may be varied or revoked by the court on an application by the child, the agency or a person named in the order.

(2) The agency may refuse to allow the contact that would otherwise be required by virtue of an order under that section if –

    (a)   it is satisfied that it is necessary to do so in order to safeguard or promote the child's welfare, and

    (b)   the refusal is decided upon as a matter of urgency and does not last for more than seven days.

(3) Regulations may make provision as to –

    (a)   the steps to be taken by an agency which has exercised its power under subsection (2),

    (b)   the circumstances in which, and conditions subject to which, the terms of any order under section 26 may be departed from by agreement between the agency and any person for whose contact with the child the order provides,

    (c)   notification by an agency of any variation or suspension of arrangements made (otherwise than under an order under that section) with a view to allowing any person contact with the child.

(4) Before making a placement order the court must –

    (a)   consider the arrangements which the adoption agency has made, or proposes to make, for allowing any person contact with the child, and

    (b)   invite the parties to the proceedings to comment on those arrangements.

(5) An order under section 26 may provide for contact on any conditions the court considers appropriate.

28 Further consequences of placement

(1) Where a child is placed for adoption under section 19 or an adoption agency is authorised to place a child for adoption under that section –

    (a)   a parent or guardian of the child may not apply for a residence order unless an application for an adoption order has been made and the parent or guardian has obtained the court's leave under subsection (3) or (5) of section 47,

    (b)   if an application has been made for an adoption order, a guardian of the child may not apply for a special guardianship order unless he has obtained the court's leave under subsection (3) or (5) of that section.

(2) Where –

    (a)   a child is placed for adoption under section 19 or an adoption agency is authorised to place a child for adoption under that section, or

    (b)   a placement order is in force in respect of a child,

then (whether or not the child is in England and Wales) a person may not do either of the following things, unless the court gives leave or each parent or guardian of the child gives written consent.

(3) Those things are –

PART I – Statutes

(a)   causing the child to be known by a new surname, or

(b)   removing the child from the United Kingdom.

(4) Subsection (3) does not prevent the removal of a child from the United Kingdom for a period of less than one month by a person who provides the child's home.

29 Further consequences of placement orders

(1) Where a placement order is made in respect of a child and either –

(a)   the child is subject to a care order, or

(b)   the court at the same time makes a care order in respect of the child,

the care order does not have effect at any time when the placement order is in force.

(2) On the making of a placement order in respect of a child, any order mentioned in section 8(1) of the 1989 Act, and any supervision order in respect of the child, ceases to have effect.

(3) Where a placement order is in force –

(a)   no prohibited steps order, residence order or specific issue order, and

(b)   no supervision order or child assessment order,

may be made in respect of the child.

(4) Subsection (3)(*a*) does not apply in respect of a residence order if –

(a)   an application for an adoption order has been made in respect of the child, and

(b)   the residence order is applied for by a parent or guardian who has obtained the court's leave under subsection (3) or (5) of section 47 or by any other person who has obtained the court's leave under this subsection.

(5) Where a placement order is in force, no special guardianship order may be made in respect of the child unless –

(a)   an application has been made for an adoption order, and

(b)   the person applying for the special guardianship order has obtained the court's leave under this subsection or, if he is a guardian of the child, has obtained the court's leave under section 47(5).

(6) Section 14A(7) of the 1989 Act applies in respect of an application for a special guardianship order for which leave has been given as mentioned in subsection (5)(*b*) with the omission of the words "the beginning of the period of three months ending with".

(7) Where a placement order is in force –

(a)   section 14C(1)(b) of the 1989 Act (special guardianship: parental responsibility) has effect subject to any determination under section 25(4) of this Act,

(b)   section 14C(3) and (4) of the 1989 Act (special guardianship: removal of child from UK etc) does not apply.

****

Placement and adoption: general

52 Parental etc consent

(1) The court cannot dispense with the consent of any parent or guardian of a child to the child being placed for adoption or to the making of an adoption order in respect of the child unless the court is satisfied that –

(a)   the parent or guardian cannot be found or [lacks capacity (within the meaning of the Mental Capacity Act 2005) to give consent][1], or
(b)   the welfare of the child requires the consent to be dispensed with.

(2) The following provisions apply to references in this Chapter to any parent or guardian of a child giving or withdrawing –

(a)   consent to the placement of a child for adoption, or
(b)   consent to the making of an adoption order (including a future adoption order).

(3) Any consent given by the mother to the making of an adoption order is ineffective if it is given less than six weeks after the child's birth.

(4) The withdrawal of any consent to the placement of a child for adoption, or of any consent given under section 20, is ineffective if it is given after an application for an adoption order is made.

(5) "Consent" means consent given unconditionally and with full understanding of what is involved; but a person may consent to adoption without knowing the identity of the persons in whose favour the order will be made.

(6) "Parent" (except in subsections (9) and (10) below) means a parent having parental responsibility.

(7) Consent under section 19 or 20 must be given in the form prescribed by rules, and the rules may prescribe forms in which a person giving consent under any other provision of this Part may do so (if he wishes).

(8) Consent given under section 19 or 20 must be withdrawn –

(a)   in the form prescribed by rules, or
(b)   by notice given to the agency.

(9) Subsection (10) applies if –

(a)   an agency has placed a child for adoption under section 19 in pursuance of consent given by a parent of the child, and
(b)   at a later time, the other parent of the child acquires parental responsibility for the child.

(10) The other parent is to be treated as having at that time given consent in accordance with this section in the same terms as those in which the first parent gave consent.

NOTES

Amendments.[1] Words substituted: Mental Capacity Act 2005, s 67(1), Sch 6, para 45.

****

CHILDREN ACT 1989

ARRANGEMENT OF SECTIONS

PART I
INTRODUCTORY

PART II
ORDERS WITH RESPECT TO CHILDREN IN FAMILY AND OTHER PROCEEDINGS

General

Special guardianship

PART IV
CARE AND SUPERVISION
General

PART V
PROTECTION OF CHILDREN

PART I – Statutes

PART VI
COMMUNITY HOMES

PART VII
VOLUNTARY HOMES AND VOLUNTARY ORGANISATIONS

PART VIII
REGISTERED CHILDREN'S HOMES

PART IX
PRIVATE ARRANGEMENTS FOR FOSTERING CHILDREN

PART X
CHILD MINDING AND DAY CARE FOR YOUNG CHILDREN

PART XA
CHILD MINDING AND DAY CARE FOR CHILDREN IN ...
WALES

PART XI
SECRETARY OF STATE'S SUPERVISORY FUNCTIONS AND
RESPONSIBILITIES

PART I – Statutes

PART XII
MISCELLANEOUS AND GENERAL

Notification of children accommodated in certain establishments

An Act to reform the law relating to children; to provide for local authority services for children in need and others; to amend the law with respect to children's homes, community homes, voluntary homes and voluntary organisations; to make provision with respect to fostering, child minding and day care for young children and adoption; and for connected purposes.
[16 November 1989]

PART I
INTRODUCTORY

1 Welfare of the child

(1) When a court determines any question with respect to –

   (a)   the upbringing of a child; or

   (b)   the administration of a child's property or the application of any income arising from it,

the child's welfare shall be the court's paramount consideration.

(2) In any proceedings in which any question with respect to the upbringing of a child arises, the court shall have regard to the general principle that any delay in determining the question is likely to prejudice the welfare of the child.

(3) In the circumstances mentioned in subsection (4), a court shall have regard in particular to –

   (a)   the ascertainable wishes and feelings of the child concerned (considered in the light of his age and understanding);

(b)   his physical, emotional and educational needs;

(c)   the likely effect on him of any change in his circumstances;

(d)   his age, sex, background and any characteristics of his which the court considers relevant;

(e)   any harm which he has suffered or is at risk of suffering;

(f)   how capable each of his parents, and any other person in relation to whom the court considers the question to be relevant, is of meeting his needs;

(g)   the range of powers available to the court under this Act in the proceedings in question.

(4) The circumstances are that –

(a)   the court is considering whether to make, vary or discharge a section 8 order, and the making, variation or discharge of the order is opposed by any party to the proceedings; or

(b)   the court is considering whether to make, vary or discharge [a special guardianship order or]¹ an order under Part IV.

(5) Where a court is considering whether or not to make one or more orders under this Act with respect to a child, it shall not make the order or any of the orders unless it considers that doing so would be better for the child than making no order at all.

NOTES

Amendments. ¹ Words inserted: Adoption and Children Act 2002, s 115(2), (3).

Definitions. 'A section 8 order': s 8(2); 'child': s 105(1); 'harm': ss 31(9), 105(1); 'the court': s 92(7); 'upbringing': s 105(1).

2 Parental responsibility for children

(1) Where a child's father and mother were married to each other at the time of his birth, they shall each have parental responsibility for the child.

[(1A) Where a child –

(a)   has a parent by virtue of section 42 of the Human Fertilisation and Embryology Act 2008; or

(b)   has a parent by virtue of section 43 of that Act and is a person to whom section 1(3) of the Family Law Reform Act 1987 applies,

the child's mother and the other parent shall each have parental responsibility for the child.]²

(2) Where a child's father and mother were not married to each other at the time of his birth –

(a)   the mother shall have parental responsibility for the child;

(b)   the father [shall have parental responsibility for the child if he has acquired it (and has not ceased to have it)]¹ in accordance with the provisions of this Act.

[(2A) Where a child has a parent by virtue of section 43 of the Human Fertilisation and Embryology Act 2008 and is not a person to whom section 1(3) of the Family Law Reform Act 1987 applies –

    (a)   the mother shall have parental responsibility for the child;

    (b)   the other parent shall have parental responsibility for the child if she has acquired it (and has not ceased to have it) in accordance with the provisions of this Act.][2]

(3) References in this Act to a child whose father and mother were, or (as the case may be) were not, married to each other at the time of his birth must be read with section 1 of the Family Law Reform Act 1987 (which extends their meaning).

(4) The rule of law that a father is the natural guardian of his legitimate child is abolished.

(5) More than one person may have parental responsibility for the same child at the same time.

(6) A person who has parental responsibility for a child at any time shall not cease to have that responsibility solely because some other person subsequently acquires parental responsibility for the child.

(7) Where more than one person has parental responsibility for a child, each of them may act alone and without the other (or others) in meeting that responsibility; but nothing in this Part shall be taken to affect the operation of any enactment which requires the consent of more than one person in a matter affecting the child.

(8) The fact that a person has parental responsibility for a child shall not entitle him to act in any way which would be incompatible with any order made with respect to the child under this Act.

(9) A person who has parental responsibility for a child may not surrender or transfer any part of that responsibility to another but may arrange for some or all of it to be met by one or more persons acting on his behalf.

(10) The person with whom any such arrangement is made may himself be a person who already has parental responsibility for the child concerned.

(11) The making of any such arrangement shall not affect any liability of the person making it which may arise from any failure to meet any part of his parental responsibility for the child concerned.

NOTES

Amendment. [1] Words substituted: Adoption and Children Act 2002, s 111(5). [2] Subsections inserted: Human Fertilisation and Embryology Act 2008, s 56, Sch 6, Pt 1, para 26.

Definitions. 'Child': s 105(1); 'married … at the time of his birth': s 2(3); 'parental responsibility': s 3.

PART I – Statutes

3 Meaning of 'parental responsibility'

(1) In this Act 'parental responsibility' means all the rights, duties, powers, responsibilities and authority which by law a parent of a child has in relation to the child and his property.

(2) It also includes the rights, powers and duties which a guardian of the child's estate (appointed, before the commencement of section 5, to act generally) would have had in relation to the child and his property.

(3) The rights referred to in subsection (2) include, in particular, the right of the guardian to receive or recover in his own name, for the benefit of the child, property of whatever description and wherever situated which the child is entitled to receive or recover.

(4) The fact that a person has, or does not have, parental responsibility for a child shall not affect –

   (a)   any obligation which he may have in relation to the child (such as a statutory duty to maintain the child); or
   (b)   any rights which, in the event of the child's death, he (or any other person) may have in relation to the child's property.

(5) A person who –

   (a)   does not have parental responsibility for a particular child; but
   (b)   has care of the child,

may (subject to the provisions of this Act) do what is reasonable in all the circumstances of the case for the purpose of safeguarding or promoting the child's welfare.

NOTES

Definitions. 'Child': s 105(1); 'parental responsibility': s 3.

4 Acquisition of parental responsibility by father

(1) Where a child's father and mother were not married to each other at the time of his birth [, the father shall acquire parental responsibility for the child if –

   (a)   he becomes registered as the child's father under any of the enactments specified in subsection (1A);
   (b)   he and the child's mother make an agreement (a 'parental responsibility agreement') providing for him to have parental responsibility for the child; or
   (c)   the court, on his application, orders that he shall have parental responsibility for the child.][1]

[(1A) The enactments referred to in subsection (1)(a) are –

   (a)   paragraphs (a), (b) and (c) of section 10(1) and of section 10A(1) of the Births and Deaths Registration Act 1953;

(b)   paragraphs (a), (b)(i) and (c) of section 18(1), and sections 18(2)(b) and 20(1)(a) of the Registration of Births, Deaths and Marriages (Scotland) Act 1965; and

(c)   sub-paragraphs (a), (b) and (c) of Article 14(3) of the Births and Deaths Registration (Northern Ireland) Order 1976.

(1B) The [Secretary of State][4] may by order amend subsection (1A) so as to add further enactments to the list in that subsection.][2]

(2) No parental responsibility agreement shall have effect for the purposes of this Act unless –

(a)   it is made in the form prescribed by regulations made by the Lord Chancellor; and

(b)   where regulations are made by the Lord Chancellor prescribing the manner in which such agreements must be recorded, it is recorded in the prescribed manner.

[(2A) A person who has acquired parental responsibility under subsection (1) shall cease to have that responsibility only if the court so orders.

(3) The court may make an order under subsection (2A) on the application –

(a)   of any person who has parental responsibility for the child, or

(b)   with leave of the court, of the child himself,

subject, in the case of parental responsibility acquired under subsection (1)(c), to section 12(4).][3]

(4) The court may only grant leave under subsection (3)(b) if it is satisfied that the child has sufficient understanding to make the proposed application.

NOTES

Amendments.[1] Words substituted: Adoption and Children Act 2002, s 111(1), (2). [2] Subsections (1A), (1B) inserted: Adoption and Children Act 2002, s 111(1), (3).[3] Subsections (2A), (3) inserted: Adoption and Children Act 2002, s 111(1), (4). [4] Words substituted: SI 2003/3191, arts 3(a), 6, Sch, para 1.

Definitions. 'Child': s 105(1); 'parental responsibility': s 3; 'parental responsibility agreement': s 4(1)(b); 'prescribed': s 105(1); 'the court': s 92(7).

[4ZA Acquisition of parental responsibility by second female parent

(1) Where a child has a parent by virtue of section 43 of the Human Fertilisation and Embryology Act 2008 and is not a person to whom section 1(3) of the Family Law Reform Act 1987 applies, that parent shall acquire parental responsibility for the child if –

(a)   she becomes registered as a parent of the child under any of the enactments specified in subsection (2);

(b)   she and the child's mother make an agreement providing for her to have parental responsibility for the child; or

(c)   the court, on her application, orders that she shall have parental responsibility for the child.

(2) The enactments referred to in subsection (1)(a) are –

(a)   paragraphs (a), (b) and (c) of section 10(1B) and of section 10A(1B) of the Births and Deaths Registration Act 1953;

(b)   paragraphs (a), (b) and (d) of section 18B(1) and sections 18B(3)(a) and 20(1)(a) of the Registration of Births, Deaths and Marriages (Scotland) Act 1965; and

(c)   sub-paragraphs (a), (b) and (c) of Article 14ZA(3) of the Births and Deaths Registration (Northern Ireland) Order 1976.

(3) The Secretary of State may by order amend subsection (2) so as to add further enactments to the list in that subsection.

(4) An agreement under subsection (1)(b) is also a "parental responsibility agreement", and section 4(2) applies in relation to such an agreement as it applies in relation to parental responsibility agreements under section 4.

(5) A person who has acquired parental responsibility under subsection (1) shall cease to have that responsibility only if the court so orders.

(6) The court may make an order under subsection (5) on the application –

(a)   of any person who has parental responsibility for the child; or

(b)   with the leave of the court, of the child himself,

subject, in the case of parental responsibility acquired under subsection (1)(c), to section 12(4).

(7) The court may only grant leave under subsection (6)(b) if it is satisfied that the child has sufficient understanding to make the proposed application.][1]

NOTES

Amendments.[1] Section inserted: Human Fertilisation and Embryology Act 2008, s 56, Sch 6, Pt 1, para 27.

[4A Acquisition of parental responsibility by step-parent

(1) Where a child's parent ('parent A') who has parental responsibility for the child is married to[, or a civil partner of,][2] a person who is not the child's parent ('the step-parent') –

(a)   parent A or, if the other parent of the child also has parental responsibility for the child, both parents may by agreement with the step-parent provide for the step-parent to have parental responsibility for the child; or

(b)   the court may, on the application of the step-parent, order that the step-parent shall have parental responsibility for the child.

(2) An agreement under subsection (1)(a) is also a 'parental responsibility agreement', and section 4(2) applies in relation to such agreements as it applies in relation to parental responsibility agreements under section 4.

(3) A parental responsibility agreement under subsection (1)(a), or an order under subsection (1)(b), may only be brought to an end by an order of the court made on the application –

PART I – Statutes

(a) of any person who has parental responsibility for the child; or

(b) with the leave of the court, of the child himself.

(4) The court may only grant leave under subsection (3)(b) if it is satisfied that the child has sufficient understanding to make the proposed application.][1]

NOTES

Amendments.[1] Section inserted: Adoption and Children Act 2002, s 112.[2] Words inserted: Civil Partnership Act 2004, s 75(1), (2).

5 Appointment of guardians

(1) Where an application with respect to a child is made to the court by any individual, the court may by order appoint that individual to be the child's guardian if –

(a) the child has no parent with parental responsibility for him; or

(b) a residence order has been made with respect to the child in favour of a parent [, guardian or special guardian][1] of his who has died while the order was in force[; or

(c) paragraph (b) does not apply, and the child's only or last surviving special guardian dies.][2]

(2) The power conferred by subsection (1) may also be exercised in any family proceedings if the court considers that the order should be made even though no application has been made for it.

(3) A parent who has parental responsibility for his child may appoint another individual to be the child's guardian in the event of his death.

(4) A guardian of a child may appoint another individual to take his place as the child's guardian in the event of his death[; and a special guardian of a child may appoint another individual to be the child's guardian in the event of his death][2].

(5) An appointment under subsection (3) or (4) shall not have effect unless it is made in writing, is dated and is signed by the person making the appointment or –

(a) in the case of an appointment made by a will which is not signed by the testator, is signed at the direction of the testator in accordance with the requirements of section 9 of the Wills Act 1837; or

(b) in any other case, is signed at the direction of the person making the appointment, in his presence and in the presence of two witnesses who each attest the signature.

(6) A person appointed as a child's guardian under this section shall have parental responsibility for the child concerned.

(7) Where –

(a) on the death of any person making an appointment under subsection (3) or (4), the child concerned has no parent with parental responsibility for him; or

[(5B) A relative of a child is entitled to apply for a residence order with respect to the child if the child has lived with the relative for a period of at least one year immediately preceding the application.]⁵

(6) A person who would not otherwise be entitled (under the previous provisions of this section) to apply for the variation or discharge of a section 8 order shall be entitled to do so if –

(a)   the order was made on his application; or
(b)   in the case of a contact order, he is named in the order.

(7) Any person who falls within a category of person prescribed by rules of court is entitled to apply for any such section 8 order as may be prescribed in relation to that category of person.

[(7A) If a special guardianship order is in force with respect to a child, an application for a residence order may only be made with respect to him, if apart from this subsection the leave of the court is not required, with such leave.]³

(8) Where the person applying for leave to make an application for a section 8 order is the child concerned, the court may only grant leave if it is satisfied that he has sufficient understanding to make the proposed application for the section 8 order.

(9) Where the person applying for leave to make an application for a section 8 order is not the child concerned, the court shall, in deciding whether or not to grant leave, have particular regard to –

(a)   the nature of the proposed application for the section 8 order;
(b)   the applicant's connection with the child;
(c)   any risk there might be of that proposed application disrupting the child's life to such an extent that he would be harmed by it; and
(d)   where the child is being looked after by a local authority –
        (i)   the authority's plans for the child's future; and
        (ii)   the wishes and feelings of the child's parents.

(10) The period of three years mentioned in subsection (5)(b) need not be continuous but must not have begun more than five years before, or ended more than three months before, the making of the application.

NOTES

Amendments.¹ Words substituted: Adoption and Children Act 2002, s 139(1), Sch 3, paras 54, 56(a).² Paragraph inserted: Adoption and Children Act 2002, s 139(1), Sch 3, paras 54, 56(b).³ Subsection inserted: Adoption and Children Act 2002, s 139(1), Sch 3, paras 54, 56(c), (d).⁴ Paragraph inserted: Civil Partnership Act 2004, s 77.⁵ Subsection inserted: Children and Young Persons Act 2008, s 36.

Definitions. 'A section 8 order': s 8(2); 'child': s 105(1); 'child who is looked after by a local authority': s 22(1); 'child of the family': s 105(1); 'contact order': s 8(1); 'family proceedings': s 8(3); 'guardian of a child': s 105(1); 'harm': ss 31(a), 105(1); 'local authority': s 105(1); 'parental responsibility': s 3; 'residence order': s 8(1); 'the court': s 92(7).

11 General principles and supplementary provisions

(1) In proceedings in which any question of making a section 8 order, or any other question with respect to such an order, arises, the court shall (in the light of any rules made by virtue of subsection (2)) –

(a) draw up a timetable with a view to determining the question without delay; and

(b) give such directions as it considers appropriate for the purpose of ensuring, so far as is reasonably practicable, that that timetable is adhered to.

(2) Rules of court may –

(a) specify periods within which specified steps must be taken in relation to proceedings in which such questions arise; and

(b) make other provision with respect to such proceedings for the purpose of ensuring, so far as is reasonably practicable, that such questions are determined without delay.

(3) Where a court has power to make a section 8 order, it may do so at any time during the course of the proceedings in question even though it is not in a position to dispose finally of those proceedings.

(4) Where a residence order is made in favour of two or more persons who do not themselves all live together, the order may specify the periods during which the child is to live in the different households concerned.

(5) Where –

(a) a residence order has been made with respect to a child; and

(b) as a result of the order the child lives, or is to live, with one of two parents who each have parental responsibility for him,

the residence order shall cease to have effect if the parents live together for a continuous period of more than six months.

(6) A contact order which requires the parent with whom a child lives to allow the child to visit, or otherwise have contact with, his other parent shall cease to have effect if the parents live together for a continuous period of more than six months.

(7) A section 8 order may –

(a) contain directions about how it is to be carried into effect;

(b) impose conditions which must be complied with by any person –

    (i) in whose favour the order is made;

    (ii) who is a parent of the child concerned;

    (iii) who is not a parent of his but who has parental responsibility for him; or

    (iv) with whom the child is living,

    and to whom the conditions are expressed to apply;

(c) be made to have effect for a specified period, or contain provisions which are to have effect for a specified period;

(d)   make such incidental, supplemental or consequential provision as the court thinks fit.

NOTES

Definitions. 'A section 8 order': s 8(2); 'child': s 105(1); 'contact order': s 8(1); 'parental responsibility': s 3; 'residence order': s 8(1); 'the court': s 92(7).

[11A Contact activity directions

(1) This section applies in proceedings in which the court is considering whether to make provision about contact with a child by making –

(a)   a contact order with respect to the child, or

(b)   an order varying or discharging a contact order with respect to the child.

(2) The court may make a contact activity direction in connection with that provision about contact.

(3) A contact activity direction is a direction requiring an individual who is a party to the proceedings to take part in an activity that promotes contact with the child concerned.

(4) The direction is to specify the activity and the person providing the activity.

(5) The activities that may be so required include, in particular –

(a)   programmes, classes and counselling or guidance sessions of a kind that –

(i)   may assist a person as regards establishing, maintaining or improving contact with a child;

(ii)   may, by addressing a person's violent behaviour, enable or facilitate contact with a child;

(b)   sessions in which information or advice is given as regards making or operating arrangements for contact with a child, including making arrangements by means of mediation.

(6) No individual may be required by a contact activity direction –

(a)   to undergo medical or psychiatric examination, assessment or treatment;

(b)   to take part in mediation.

(7) A court may not on the same occasion –

(a)   make a contact activity direction, and

(b)   dispose finally of the proceedings as they relate to contact with the child concerned.

(8) Subsection (2) has effect subject to the restrictions in sections 11B and 11E.

(9) In considering whether to make a contact activity direction, the welfare of the child concerned is to be the court's paramount consideration.][1]

NOTES

Amendment.[1] Section inserted: Children and Adoption Act 2006, s 1.

[11B Contact activity directions: further provision

(1) A court may not make a contact activity direction in any proceedings unless there is a dispute as regards the provision about contact that the court is considering whether to make in the proceedings.

(2) A court may not make a contact activity direction requiring an individual who is a child to take part in an activity unless the individual is a parent of the child in relation to whom the court is considering provision about contact.

(3) A court may not make a contact activity direction in connection with the making, variation or discharge of a contact order, if the contact order is, or would if made be, an excepted order.

(4) A contact order with respect to a child is an excepted order if –

    (a)   it is made in proceedings that include proceedings on an application for a relevant adoption order in respect of the child; or

    (b)   it makes provision as regards contact between the child and a person who would be a parent or relative of the child but for the child's adoption by an order falling within subsection (5).

(5) An order falls within this subsection if it is –

    (a)   a relevant adoption order;

    (b)   an adoption order, within the meaning of section 72(1) of the Adoption Act 1976, other than an order made by virtue of section 14 of that Act on the application of a married couple one of whom is the mother or the father of the child;

    (c)   a Scottish adoption order, within the meaning of the Adoption and Children Act 2002, other than an order made –

        (i)   by virtue of section 14 of the Adoption (Scotland) Act 1978 on the application of a married couple one of whom is the mother or the father of the child, or

        (ii)   by virtue of section 15(1)(aa) of that Act; or

    (d)   a Northern Irish adoption order, within the meaning of the Adoption and Children Act 2002, other than an order made by virtue of Article 14 of the Adoption (Northern Ireland) Order 1987 on the application of a married couple one of whom is the mother or the father of the child.

(6) A relevant adoption order is an adoption order, within the meaning of section 46(1) of the Adoption and Children Act 2002, other than an order made –

    (a)   on an application under section 50 of that Act by a couple (within the meaning of that Act) one of whom is the mother or the father of the person to be adopted, or

    (b)   on an application under section 51(2) of that Act.

PART I – Statutes

(7) A court may not make a contact activity direction in relation to an individual unless the individual is habitually resident in England and Wales; and a direction ceases to have effect if the individual subject to the direction ceases to be habitually resident in England and Wales.][1]

NOTES

Amendment.[1] Section inserted: Children and Adoption Act 2006, s 1.

[11C Contact activity conditions

(1) This section applies if in any family proceedings the court makes –

    (a)   a contact order with respect to a child, or

    (b)   an order varying a contact order with respect to a child.

(2) The contact order may impose, or the contact order may be varied so as to impose, a condition (a 'contact activity condition') requiring an individual falling within subsection (3) to take part in an activity that promotes contact with the child concerned.

(3) An individual falls within this subsection if he is –

    (a)   for the purposes of the contact order so made or varied, the person with whom the child concerned lives or is to live;

    (b)   the person whose contact with the child concerned is provided for in that order; or

    (c)   a person upon whom that order imposes a condition under section 11(7)(b).

(4) The condition is to specify the activity and the person providing the activity.

(5) Subsections (5) and (6) of section 11A have effect as regards the activities that may be required by a contact activity condition as they have effect as regards the activities that may be required by a contact activity direction.

(6) Subsection (2) has effect subject to the restrictions in sections 11D and 11E.][1]

NOTES

Amendment.[1] Section inserted: Children and Adoption Act 2006, s 1.

[11D Contact activity conditions: further provision

(1) A contact order may not impose a contact activity condition on an individual who is a child unless the individual is a parent of the child concerned.

(2) If a contact order is an excepted order (within the meaning given by section 11B(4)), it may not impose (and it may not be varied so as to impose) a contact activity condition.

(3) A contact order may not impose a contact activity condition on an individual unless the individual is habitually resident in England and Wales;

and a condition ceases to have effect if the individual subject to the condition ceases to be habitually resident in England and Wales.][1]

NOTES

Amendment.[1] Section inserted: Children and Adoption Act 2006, s 1.

[11E Contact activity directions and conditions: making

(1) Before making a contact activity direction (or imposing a contact activity condition by means of a contact order), the court must satisfy itself as to the matters falling within subsections (2) to (4).

(2) The first matter is that the activity proposed to be specified is appropriate in the circumstances of the case.

(3) The second matter is that the person proposed to be specified as the provider of the activity is suitable to provide the activity.

(4) The third matter is that the activity proposed to be specified is provided in a place to which the individual who would be subject to the direction (or the condition) can reasonably be expected to travel.

(5) Before making such a direction (or such an order), the court must obtain and consider information about the individual who would be subject to the direction (or the condition) and the likely effect of the direction (or the condition) on him.

(6) Information about the likely effect of the direction (or the condition) may, in particular, include information as to –

  (a) any conflict with the individual's religious beliefs;
  (b) any interference with the times (if any) at which he normally works or attends an educational establishment.

(7) The court may ask an officer of the Service or a Welsh family proceedings officer to provide the court with information as to the matters in subsections (2) to (5); and it shall be the duty of the officer of the Service or Welsh family proceedings officer to comply with any such request.

(8) In this section 'specified' means specified in a contact activity direction (or in a contact activity condition).][1]

NOTES

Amendment.[1] Section inserted: Children and Adoption Act 2006, s 1.

[11F Contact activity directions and conditions: financial assistance

(1) The Secretary of State may by regulations make provision authorising him to make payments to assist individuals falling within subsection (2) in paying relevant charges or fees.

(2) An individual falls within this subsection if he is required by a contact activity direction or condition to take part in an activity that promotes contact with a child, not being a child ordinarily resident in Wales.

(3) The National Assembly for Wales may by regulations make provision authorising it to make payments to assist individuals falling within subsection (4) in paying relevant charges or fees.

(4) An individual falls within this subsection if he is required by a contact activity direction or condition to take part in an activity that promotes contact with a child who is ordinarily resident in Wales.

(5) A relevant charge or fee, in relation to an activity required by a contact activity direction or condition, is a charge or fee in respect of the activity payable to the person providing the activity.

(6) Regulations under this section may provide that no assistance is available to an individual unless –

   (a)   the individual satisfies such conditions as regards his financial resources as may be set out in the regulations;
   (b)   the activity in which the individual is required by a contact activity direction or condition to take part is provided to him in England or Wales;
   (c)   where the activity in which the individual is required to take part is provided to him in England, it is provided by a person who is for the time being approved by the Secretary of State as a provider of activities required by a contact activity direction or condition;
   (d)   where the activity in which the individual is required to take part is provided to him in Wales, it is provided by a person who is for the time being approved by the National Assembly for Wales as a provider of activities required by a contact activity direction or condition.

(7) Regulations under this section may make provision –

   (a)   as to the maximum amount of assistance that may be paid to or in respect of an individual as regards an activity in which he is required by a contact activity direction or condition to take part;
   (b)   where the amount may vary according to an individual's financial resources, as to the method by which the amount is to be determined;
   (c)   authorising payments by way of assistance to be made directly to persons providing activities required by a contact activity direction or condition.][1]

NOTES

Amendment.[1] Section inserted: Children and Adoption Act 2006, s 1.

[11G   Contact activity directions and conditions: monitoring

(1) This section applies if in any family proceedings the court –

   (a)   makes a contact activity direction in relation to an individual, or
   (b)   makes a contact order that imposes, or varies a contact order so as to impose, a contact activity condition on an individual.

(2) The court may on making the direction (or imposing the condition by means of a contact order) ask an officer of the Service or a Welsh family proceedings officer –

    (a)   to monitor, or arrange for the monitoring of, the individual's compliance with the direction (or the condition);

    (b)   to report to the court on any failure by the individual to comply with the direction (or the condition).

(3) It shall be the duty of the officer of the Service or Welsh family proceedings officer to comply with any request under subsection (2).][1]

NOTES

Amendment.[1] Section inserted: Children and Adoption Act 2006, s 1.

[11H Monitoring contact

(1) This section applies if in any family proceedings the court makes –

    (a)   a contact order with respect to a child in favour of a person, or

    (b)   an order varying such a contact order.

(2) The court may ask an officer of the Service or a Welsh family proceedings officer –

    (a)   to monitor whether an individual falling within subsection (3) complies with the contact order (or the contact order as varied);

    (b)   to report to the court on such matters relating to the individual's compliance as the court may specify in the request.

(3) An individual falls within this subsection if the contact order so made (or the contact order as so varied) –

    (a)   requires the individual to allow contact with the child concerned;

    (b)   names the individual as having contact with the child concerned; or

    (c)   imposes a condition under section 11(7)(b) on the individual.

(4) If the contact order (or the contact order as varied) includes a contact activity condition, a request under subsection (2) is to be treated as relating to the provisions of the order other than the contact activity condition.

(5) The court may make a request under subsection (2) –

    (a)   on making the contact order (or the order varying the contact order), or

    (b)   at any time during the subsequent course of the proceedings as they relate to contact with the child concerned.

(6) In making a request under subsection (2), the court is to specify the period for which the officer of the Service or Welsh family proceedings officer is to monitor compliance with the order; and the period specified may not exceed twelve months.

(7) It shall be the duty of the officer of the Service or Welsh family proceedings officer to comply with any request under subsection (2).

(8) The court may order any individual falling within subsection (3) to take such steps as may be specified in the order with a view to enabling the officer of the Service or Welsh family proceedings officer to comply with the court's request under subsection (2).

(9) But the court may not make an order under subsection (8) with respect to an individual who is a child unless he is a parent of the child with respect to whom the order falling within subsection (1) was made.

(10) A court may not make a request under subsection (2) in relation to a contact order that is an excepted order (within the meaning given by section 11B(4)).][1]

NOTES

Amendment.[1] Section inserted: Children and Adoption Act 2006, s 2.

[11I   Contact orders: warning notices

Where the court makes (or varies) a contact order, it is to attach to the contact order (or the order varying the contact order) a notice warning of the consequences of failing to comply with the contact order.][1]

NOTES

Amendment.[1] Section inserted: Children and Adoption Act 2006, s 3.

[11J   Enforcement orders

(1) This section applies if a contact order with respect to a child has been made.

(2) If the court is satisfied beyond reasonable doubt that a person has failed to comply with the contact order, it may make an order (an 'enforcement order') imposing on the person an unpaid work requirement.

(3) But the court may not make an enforcement order if it is satisfied that the person had a reasonable excuse for failing to comply with the contact order.

(4) The burden of proof as to the matter mentioned in subsection (3) lies on the person claiming to have had a reasonable excuse, and the standard of proof is the balance of probabilities.

(5) The court may make an enforcement order in relation to the contact order only on the application of –

(a)   the person who is, for the purposes of the contact order, the person with whom the child concerned lives or is to live;
(b)   the person whose contact with the child concerned is provided for in the contact order;
(c)   any individual subject to a condition under section 11(7)(b) or a contact activity condition imposed by the contact order; or
(d)   the child concerned.

(6) Where the person proposing to apply for an enforcement order in relation to a contact order is the child concerned, the child must obtain the leave of the court before making such an application.

(7) The court may grant leave to the child concerned only if it is satisfied that he has sufficient understanding to make the proposed application.

(8) Subsection (2) has effect subject to the restrictions in sections 11K and 11L.

(9) The court may suspend an enforcement order for such period as it thinks fit.

(10) Nothing in this section prevents a court from making more than one enforcement order in relation to the same person on the same occasion.

(11) Proceedings in which any question of making an enforcement order, or any other question with respect to such an order, arises are to be regarded for the purposes of section 11(1) and (2) as proceedings in which a question arises with respect to a section 8 order.

(12) In Schedule A1 –

(a) Part 1 makes provision as regards an unpaid work requirement;
(b) Part 2 makes provision in relation to the revocation and amendment of enforcement orders and failure to comply with such orders.

(13) This section is without prejudice to section 63(3) of the Magistrates' Courts Act 1980 as it applies in relation to contact orders.][1]

NOTES

Amendment.[1] Section inserted: Children and Adoption Act 2006, s 4(1).

[11K Enforcement orders: further provision

(1) A court may not make an enforcement order against a person in respect of a failure to comply with a contact order unless it is satisfied that before the failure occurred the person had been given (in accordance with rules of court) a copy of, or otherwise informed of the terms of –

(a) in the case of a failure to comply with a contact order that was varied before the failure occurred, a notice under section 11I relating to the order varying the contact order or, where more than one such order has been made, the last order preceding the failure in question;
(b) in any other case, a notice under section 11I relating to the contact order.

(2) A court may not make an enforcement order against a person in respect of any failure to comply with a contact order occurring before the person attained the age of 18.

(3) A court may not make an enforcement order against a person in respect of a failure to comply with a contact order that is an excepted order (within the meaning given by section 11B(4)).

(4) A court may not make an enforcement order against a person unless the person is habitually resident in England and Wales; and an enforcement order ceases to have effect if the person subject to the order ceases to be habitually resident in England and Wales.][1]

NOTES

Amendment.[1] Section inserted: Children and Adoption Act 2006, s 4(1).

[11L Enforcement orders: making

(1) Before making an enforcement order as regards a person in breach of a contact order, the court must be satisfied that –

  (a) making the enforcement order proposed is necessary to secure the person's compliance with the contact order or any contact order that has effect in its place;

  (b) the likely effect on the person of the enforcement order proposed to be made is proportionate to the seriousness of the breach of the contact order.

(2) Before making an enforcement order, the court must satisfy itself that provision for the person to work under an unpaid work requirement imposed by an enforcement order can be made in the local justice area in which the person in breach resides or will reside.

(3) Before making an enforcement order as regards a person in breach of a contact order, the court must obtain and consider information about the person and the likely effect of the enforcement order on him.

(4) Information about the likely effect of the enforcement order may, in particular, include information as to –

  (a) any conflict with the person's religious beliefs;

  (b) any interference with the times (if any) at which he normally works or attends an educational establishment.

(5) A court that proposes to make an enforcement order may ask an officer of the Service or a Welsh family proceedings officer to provide the court with information as to the matters in subsections (2) and (3).

(6) It shall be the duty of the officer of the Service or Welsh family proceedings officer to comply with any request under this section.

(7) In making an enforcement order in relation to a contact order, a court must take into account the welfare of the child who is the subject of the contact order.][1]

NOTES

Amendment.[1] Section inserted: Children and Adoption Act 2006, s 4(1).

[11M Enforcement orders: monitoring

(1) On making an enforcement order in relation to a person, the court is to ask an officer of the Service or a Welsh family proceedings officer –

(a)   to monitor, or arrange for the monitoring of, the person's compliance with the unpaid work requirement imposed by the order;

(b)   to report to the court if a report under paragraph 8 of Schedule A1 is made in relation to the person;

(c)   to report to the court on such other matters relating to the person's compliance as may be specified in the request;

(d)   to report to the court if the person is, or becomes, unsuitable to perform work under the requirement.

(2) It shall be the duty of the officer of the Service or Welsh family proceedings officer to comply with any request under this section.][1]

NOTES

Amendment.[1] Section inserted: Children and Adoption Act 2006, s 4(1).

[11N   Enforcement orders: warning notices

Where the court makes an enforcement order, it is to attach to the order a notice warning of the consequences of failing to comply with the order.][1]

NOTES

Amendment.[1] Section inserted: Children and Adoption Act 2006, s 4(1).

[11O   Compensation for financial loss

(1) This section applies if a contact order with respect to a child has been made.

(2) If the court is satisfied that –

(a)   an individual has failed to comply with the contact order, and

(b)   a person falling within subsection (6) has suffered financial loss by reason of the breach,

it may make an order requiring the individual in breach to pay the person compensation in respect of his financial loss.

(3) But the court may not make an order under subsection (2) if it is satisfied that the individual in breach had a reasonable excuse for failing to comply with the contact order.

(4) The burden of proof as to the matter mentioned in subsection (3) lies on the individual claiming to have had a reasonable excuse.

(5) An order under subsection (2) may be made only on an application by the person who claims to have suffered financial loss.

(6) A person falls within this subsection if he is –

(a)   the person who is, for the purposes of the contact order, the person with whom the child concerned lives or is to live;

(b)   the person whose contact with the child concerned is provided for in the contact order;

PART I – Statutes

(c)   an individual subject to a condition under section 11(7)(b) or a contact activity condition imposed by the contact order; or
(d)   the child concerned.

(7) Where the person proposing to apply for an order under subsection (2) is the child concerned, the child must obtain the leave of the court before making such an application.

(8) The court may grant leave to the child concerned only if it is satisfied that he has sufficient understanding to make the proposed application.

(9) The amount of compensation is to be determined by the court, but may not exceed the amount of the applicant's financial loss.

(10) In determining the amount of compensation payable by the individual in breach, the court must take into account the individual's financial circumstances.

(11) An amount ordered to be paid as compensation may be recovered by the applicant as a civil debt due to him.

(12) Subsection (2) has effect subject to the restrictions in section 11P.

(13) Proceedings in which any question of making an order under subsection (2) arises are to be regarded for the purposes of section 11(1) and (2) as proceedings in which a question arises with respect to a section 8 order.

(14) In exercising its powers under this section, a court is to take into account the welfare of the child concerned.][1]

NOTES

Amendment.[1] Section inserted: Children and Adoption Act 2006, s 5.

[11P Orders under section 11O(2): further provision

(1) A court may not make an order under section 11O(2) requiring an individual to pay compensation in respect of a failure by him to comply with a contact order unless it is satisfied that before the failure occurred the individual had been given (in accordance with rules of court) a copy of, or otherwise informed of the terms of –

(a)   in the case of a failure to comply with a contact order that was varied before the failure occurred, a notice under section 11I relating to the order varying the contact order or, where more than one such order has been made, the last order preceding the failure in question;
(b)   in any other case, a notice under section 11I relating to the contact order.

(2) A court may not make an order under section 11O(2) requiring an individual to pay compensation in respect of a failure by him to comply with a contact order where the failure occurred before the individual attained the age of 18.

PART I – Statutes

(3) A court may not make an order under section 11O(2) requiring an individual to pay compensation in respect of a failure by him to comply with a contact order that is an excepted order (within the meaning given by section 11B(4)).][1]

NOTES

Amendment.[1] Section inserted: Children and Adoption Act 2006, s 5.

12 Residence orders and parental responsibility

(1) Where the court makes a residence order in favour of the father of a child it shall, if the father would not otherwise have parental responsibility for the child, also make an order under section 4 giving him that responsibility.

[(1A) Where the court makes a residence order in favour of a woman who is a parent of a child by virtue of section 43 of the Human Fertilisation and Embryology Act 2008 it shall, if that woman would not otherwise have parental responsibility for the child, also make an order under section 4ZA giving her that responsibility.][4]

(2) Where the court makes a residence order in favour of any person who is not the parent or guardian of the child concerned that person shall have parental responsibility for the child while the residence order remains in force.

(3) Where a person has parental responsibility for a child as a result of subsection (2), he shall not have the right –

    (a) ...[1]
    (b) to agree, or refuse to agree, to the making of an adoption order, or an order under [section 84 of the Adoption and Children Act 2002][2], with respect to the child; or
    (c) to appoint a guardian for the child.

(4) Where subsection (1) [or (1A)][4] requires the court to make an order under section 4 [or 4ZA][4] in respect of the [parent][4] of a child, the court shall not bring that order to an end at any time while the residence order concerned remains in force.

[(5) ...[5]

(6) ...[5]][3]

NOTES

Amendments.[1] Paragraph repealed: Adoption and Children Act 2002, s 139(1), (3), Sch 3, paras 54, 57(a), Sch 5.[2] Words substituted: Adoption and Children Act 2002, s 139(1), (3), Sch 3, paras 54, 57(b).[3] Subsections inserted: Adoption and Children Act 2002, s 114(1).[4] Subsection inserted, words inserted and word substituted: Human Fertilisation and Embryology Act 2008, s 56, Sch 6, Pt 1, para 28.[5] Subsections repealed: Children and Young Persons Act 2008, ss 36, 42, Sch 4.

Definitions. 'Child': s 105(1); 'guardian of a child': s 105(1); 'parental responsibility': s 3; 'residence order': s 8(1); 'the court': s 92(7).

13 Change of child's name or removal from jurisdiction

(1) Where a residence order is in force with respect to a child, no person may –

(a)   cause the child to be known by a new surname; or

(b)   remove him from the United Kingdom;

without either the written consent of every person who has parental responsibility for the child or the leave of the court.

(2) Subsection (1)(b) does not prevent the removal of a child, for a period of less than one month, by the person in whose favour the residence order is made.

(3) In making a residence order with respect to a child the court may grant the leave required by subsection (1)(b), either generally or for specified purposes.

NOTES

Definitions. 'Child': s 105(1); 'parental responsibility': s 3; 'residence order': s 8(1); 'the court': s 92(7).

14 Enforcement of residence orders

(1) Where –

(a)   a residence order is in force with respect to a child in favour of any person; and

(b)   any other person (including one in whose favour the order is also in force) is in breach of the arrangements settled by that order,

the person mentioned in paragraph (a) may, as soon as the requirement in subsection (2) is complied with, enforce the order under section 63(3) of the Magistrates' Courts Act 1980 as if it were an order requiring the other person to produce the child to him.

(2) The requirement is that a copy of the residence order has been served on the other person.

(3) Subsection (1) is without prejudice to any other remedy open to the person in whose favour the residence order is in force.

NOTES

Definitions. 'Child': s 105(1); 'residence order': s 8(1).

[Special guardianship

14A Special guardianship orders

(1) A 'special guardianship order' is an order appointing one or more individuals to be a child's 'special guardian' (or special guardians).

(2) A special guardian –

(a)   must be aged eighteen or over; and

(b)   must not be a parent of the child in question,

and subsections (3) to (6) are to be read in that light.

(3) The court may make a special guardianship order with respect to any child on the application of an individual who –

(a)   is entitled to make such an application with respect to the child; or

(b)   has obtained the leave of the court to make the application,

or on the joint application of more than one such individual.

(4) Section 9(3) applies in relation to an application for leave to apply for a special guardianship order as it applies in relation to an application for leave to apply for a section 8 order.

(5) The individuals who are entitled to apply for a special guardianship order with respect to a child are –

(a)   any guardian of the child;

(b)   any individual in whose favour a residence order is in force with respect to the child;

(c)   any individual listed in subsection (5)(b) or (c) of section 10 (as read with subsection (10) of that section);

(d)   a local authority foster parent with whom the child has lived for a period of at least one year immediately preceding the application[;

(e)   a relative with whom the child has lived for a period of at least one year immediately preceding the application][2].

(6) The court may also make a special guardianship order with respect to a child in any family proceedings in which a question arises with respect to the welfare of the child if –

(a)   an application for the order has been made by an individual who falls within subsection (3)(a) or (b) (or more than one such individual jointly); or

(b)   the court considers that a special guardianship order should be made even though no such application has been made.

(7) No individual may make an application under subsection (3) or (6)(a) unless, before the beginning of the period of three months ending with the date of the application, he has given written notice of his intention to make the application –

(a)   if the child in question is being looked after by a local authority, to that local authority, or

(b)   otherwise, to the local authority in whose area the individual is ordinarily resident.

(8) On receipt of such a notice, the local authority must investigate the matter and prepare a report for the court dealing with –

(a)   the suitability of the applicant to be a special guardian;

(b)   such matters (if any) as may be prescribed by the Secretary of State; and

(c)   any other matter which the local authority consider to be relevant.

(9) The court may itself ask a local authority to conduct such an investigation and prepare such a report, and the local authority must do so.

PART I – Statutes

(10) The local authority may make such arrangements as they see fit for any person to act on their behalf in connection with conducting an investigation or preparing a report referred to in subsection (8) or (9).

(11) The court may not make a special guardianship order unless it has received a report dealing with the matters referred to in subsection (8).

(12) Subsections (8) and (9) of section 10 apply in relation to special guardianship orders as they apply in relation to section 8 orders.

(13) This section is subject to section 29(5) and (6) of the Adoption and Children Act 2002.][1]

NOTES

Amendments.[1] Section inserted: Adoption and Children Act 2002, s 115(1). [2] Paragraph inserted: Children and Young Persons Act 2008, s 38.

[14B   Special guardianship orders: making

(1) Before making a special guardianship order, the court must consider whether, if the order were made –

- (a)   a contact order should also be made with respect to the child, ...[2]
- (b)   any section 8 order in force with respect to the child should be varied or discharged.
- [(c)   where a contact order made with respect to the child is not discharged, any enforcement order relating to that contact order should be revoked, and
- (d)   where a contact activity direction has been made as regards contact with the child and is in force, that contact activity direction should be discharged][2]

(2) On making a special guardianship order, the court may also –

- (a)   give leave for the child to be known by a new surname;
- (b)   grant the leave required by section 14C(3)(b), either generally or for specified purposes.][1]

NOTES

Amendments.[1] Section inserted: Adoption and Children Act 2002, s 115(1).[2] Word repealed and paragraphs inserted: Children and Adoption Act 2006, s 15, Sch 2, paras 7, 8, Sch 3.

[14C   Special guardianship orders: effect

(1) The effect of a special guardianship order is that while the order remains in force –

- (a)   a special guardian appointed by the order has parental responsibility for the child in respect of whom it is made; and
- (b)   subject to any other order in force with respect to the child under this Act, a special guardian is entitled to exercise parental responsibility to the exclusion of any other person with parental responsibility for the child (apart from another special guardian).

(2) Subsection (1) does not affect –

(a) the operation of any enactment or rule of law which requires the consent of more than one person with parental responsibility in a matter affecting the child; or

(b) any rights which a parent of the child has in relation to the child's adoption or placement for adoption.

(3) While a special guardianship order is in force with respect to a child, no person may –

(a) cause the child to be known by a new surname; or

(b) remove him from the United Kingdom,

without either the written consent of every person who has parental responsibility for the child or the leave of the court.

(4) Subsection (3)(b) does not prevent the removal of a child, for a period of less than three months, by a special guardian of his.

(5) If the child with respect to whom a special guardianship order is in force dies, his special guardian must take reasonable steps to give notice of that fact to –

(a) each parent of the child with parental responsibility; and

(b) each guardian of the child,

but if the child has more than one special guardian, and one of them has taken such steps in relation to a particular parent or guardian, any other special guardian need not do so as respects that parent or guardian.

(6) This section is subject to section 29(7) of the Adoption and Children Act 2002.][1]

NOTES

Amendments.[1] Section inserted: Adoption and Children Act 2002, s 115(1).

[14D Special guardianship orders: variation and discharge

(1) The court may vary or discharge a special guardianship order on the application of –

(a) the special guardian (or any of them, if there are more than one);

(b) any parent or guardian of the child concerned;

(c) any individual in whose favour a residence order is in force with respect to the child;

(d) any individual not falling within any of paragraphs (a) to (c) who has, or immediately before the making of the special guardianship order had, parental responsibility for the child;

(e) the child himself; or

(f) a local authority designated in a care order with respect to the child.

(2) In any family proceedings in which a question arises with respect to the welfare of a child with respect to whom a special guardianship order is in force,

the court may also vary or discharge the special guardianship order if it considers that the order should be varied or discharged, even though no application has been made under subsection (1).

(3) The following must obtain the leave of the court before making an application under subsection (1) –

    (a)   the child;

    (b)   any parent or guardian of his;

    (c)   any step-parent of his who has acquired, and has not lost, parental responsibility for him by virtue of section 4A;

    (d)   any individual falling within subsection (1)(d) who immediately before the making of the special guardianship order had, but no longer has, parental responsibility for him.

(4) Where the person applying for leave to make an application under subsection (1) is the child, the court may only grant leave if it is satisfied that he has sufficient understanding to make the proposed application under subsection (1).

(5) The court may not grant leave to a person falling within subsection (3)(b)(c) or (d) unless it is satisfied that there has been a significant change in circumstances since the making of the special guardianship order.][1]

NOTES

Amendments.[1] Section inserted: Adoption and Children Act 2002, s 115(1).

[14E   Special guardianship orders: supplementary

(1) In proceedings in which any question of making, varying or discharging a special guardianship order arises, the court shall (in the light of any rules made by virtue of subsection (3)) –

    (a)   draw up a timetable with a view to determining the question without delay; and

    (b)   give such directions as it considers appropriate for the purpose of ensuring, so far as is reasonably practicable, that the timetable is adhered to.

(2) Subsection (1) applies also in relation to proceedings in which any other question with respect to a special guardianship order arises.

(3) The power to make rules in subsection (2) of section 11 applies for the purposes of this section as it applies for the purposes of that.

(4) A special guardianship order, or an order varying one, may contain provisions which are to have effect for a specified period.

(5) Section 11(7) (apart from paragraph (c)) applies in relation to special guardianship orders and orders varying them as it applies in relation to section 8 orders.][1]

NOTES

Amendments.[1] Section inserted: Adoption and Children Act 2002, s 115(1).

[14F Special guardianship support services

(1) Each local authority must make arrangements for the provision within their area of special guardianship support services, which means –

(a)   counselling, advice and information; and
(b)   such other services as are prescribed,

in relation to special guardianship.

(2) The power to make regulations under subsection (1)(b) is to be exercised so as to secure that local authorities provide financial support.

(3) At the request of any of the following persons –

(a)   a child with respect to whom a special guardianship order is in force;
(b)   a special guardian;
(c)   a parent;
(d)   any other person who falls within a prescribed description,

a local authority may carry out an assessment of that person's needs for special guardianship support services (but, if the Secretary of State so provides in regulations, they must do so if he is a person of a prescribed description, or if his case falls within a prescribed description, or if both he and his case fall within prescribed descriptions).

(4) A local authority may, at the request of any other person, carry out an assessment of that person's needs for special guardianship support services.

(5) Where, as a result of an assessment, a local authority decide that a person has needs for special guardianship support services, they must then decide whether to provide any such services to that person.

(6) If –

(a)   a local authority decide to provide any special guardianship support services to a person, and
(b)   the circumstances fall within a prescribed description,

the local authority must prepare a plan in accordance with which special guardianship support services are to be provided to him, and keep the plan under review.

(7) The Secretary of State may by regulations make provision about assessments, preparing and reviewing plans, the provision of special guardianship support services in accordance with plans and reviewing the provision of special guardianship support services.

(8) The regulations may in particular make provision –

(a)   about the type of assessment which is to be carried out, or the way in which an assessment is to be carried out;
(b)   about the way in which a plan is to be prepared;
(c)   about the way in which, and the time at which, a plan or the provision of special guardianship support services is to be reviewed;

(d)   about the considerations to which a local authority are to have regard in carrying out an assessment or review or preparing a plan;

(e)   as to the circumstances in which a local authority may provide special guardianship support services subject to conditions (including conditions as to payment for the support or the repayment of financial support);

(f)   as to the consequences of conditions imposed by virtue of paragraph (e) not being met (including the recovery of any financial support provided);

(g)   as to the circumstances in which this section may apply to a local authority in respect of persons who are outside that local authority's area;

(h)   as to the circumstances in which a local authority may recover from another local authority the expenses of providing special guardianship support services to any person.

(9) A local authority may provide special guardianship support services (or any part of them) by securing their provision by –

(a)   another local authority; or

(b)   a person within a description prescribed in regulations of persons who may provide special guardianship support services,

and may also arrange with any such authority or person for that other authority or that person to carry out the local authority's functions in relation to assessments under this section.

(10) A local authority may carry out an assessment of the needs of any person for the purposes of this section at the same time as an assessment of his needs is made under any other provision of this Act or under any other enactment.

(11) Section 27 (co-operation between authorities) applies in relation to the exercise of functions of a local authority under this section as it applies in relation to the exercise of functions of a local authority under Part 3.][1]

NOTES

Amendments.[1] Section inserted: Adoption and Children Act 2002, s 115(1).

[14G

...[2]][1]

NOTES

Amendments.[1] Section inserted: Adoption and Children Act 2002, s 115(1).[2] Section repealed: Health and Social Care (Community Health and Standards) Act 2003, ss 117(2), 196, Sch 14, Pt 2.

Financial relief

15 Orders for financial relief with respect to children

(1) Schedule 1 (which consists primarily of the re-enactment, with consequential amendments and minor modifications, of provisions of

[section 6 of the Family Law Reform Act 1969][1], the Guardianship of Minors Acts 1971 and 1973, the Children Act 1975 and of sections 15 and 16 of the Family Law Reform Act 1987) makes provision in relation to financial relief for children.

(2) The powers of a magistrates' court under section 60 of the Magistrates' Courts Act 1980 to revoke, revive or vary an order for the periodical payment of money [and the power of a clerk of a magistrates' court to vary such an order][2] shall not apply in relation to an order made under Schedule 1.

NOTES

Amendments.[1] Words inserted: Courts and Legal Services Act 1990, s 116, Sch 16, para 10(1).[2] Words inserted: Maintenance Enforcement Act 1991, s 11(1), Sch 2, para 10.

Family assistance orders

16 Family assistance orders

(1) Where, in any family proceedings, the court has power to make an order under this Part with respect to any child, it may (whether or not it makes such an order) make an order requiring –

(a)   [an officer of the Service][1] [or a Welsh family proceedings officer][2] to be made available; or

(b)   a local authority to make an officer of the authority available,

to advise, assist and (where appropriate) befriend any person named in the order.

(2) The persons who may be named in an order under this section ('a family assistance order') are –

(a)   any parent [, guardian or special guardian][3] of the child;

(b)   any person with whom the child is living or in whose favour a contact order is in force with respect to the child;

(c)   the child himself.

(3) No court may make a family assistance order unless –

(a)   ...[4]

(b)   it has obtained the consent of every person to be named in the order other than the child.

(4) A family assistance order may direct –

(a)   the person named in the order; or

(b)   such of the persons named in the order as may be specified in the order,

to take such steps as may be so specified with a view to enabling the officer concerned to be kept informed of the address of any person named in the order and to be allowed to visit any such person.

[(4A) If the court makes a family assistance order with respect to a child and the order is to be in force at the same time as a contact order made with respect to the child, the family assistance order may direct the officer concerned to give advice and assistance as regards establishing, improving and maintaining contact to such of the persons named in the order as may be specified in the order.][4]

(5) Unless it specifies a shorter period, a family assistance order shall have effect for a period of [twelve months][4] beginning with the day on which it is made.

[(6) If the court makes a family assistance order with respect to a child and the order is to be in force at the same time as a section 8 order made with respect to the child, the family assistance order may direct the officer concerned to report to the court on such matters relating to the section 8 order as the court may require (including the question whether the section 8 order ought to be varied or discharged).][4]

(7) A family assistance order shall not be made so as to require a local authority to make an officer of theirs available unless –

(a)   the authority agree; or
(b)   the child concerned lives or will live within their area.

(8), (9) ...[1]

NOTES

Amendments.[1] Words substituted or subsections omitted: Criminal Justice and Court Services Act 2000, s 74, Sch 7, paras 87, 89, Sch 8.[2] Words inserted: Children Act 2004, s 40, Sch 3, paras 5, 7.[3] Words substituted: Adoption and Children Act 2002, s 139(1), Sch 3, paras 54, 58.[4] Paragraph repealed, subsections inserted and substituted, and words substituted: Children and Adoption Act 2006, ss 6(1)–(5), 15(2), Sch 3.

Definitions. 'A section 8 order': s 8(2); 'child': s 105(1); 'contact order': s 8(1); 'family assistance order': s 16(2); 'family proceedings': s 8(3); 'guardian of a child': s 105(1); 'local authority': s 105(1); 'the court': s 92(7).

[16A Risk assessments

(1) This section applies to the following functions of officers of the Service or Welsh family proceedings officers –

(a)   any function in connection with family proceedings in which the court has power to make an order under this Part with respect to a child or in which a question with respect to such an order arises;
(b)   any function in connection with an order made by the court in such proceedings.

(2) If, in carrying out any function to which this section applies, an officer of the Service or a Welsh family proceedings officer is given cause to suspect that the child concerned is at risk of harm, he must –

(a)   make a risk assessment in relation to the child, and
(b)   provide the risk assessment to the court.

(3) A risk assessment, in relation to a child who is at risk of suffering harm of a particular sort, is an assessment of the risk of that harm being suffered by the child.][1]

NOTES

Amendments.[1] Section inserted: Children and Adoption Act 2006, s 7.

PART III
LOCAL AUTHORITY SUPPORT FOR CHILDREN AND FAMILIES

Provision of services for children and their families

17 Provision of services for children in need, their families and others

(1) It shall be the general duty of every local authority (in addition to the other duties imposed on them by this Part) –

   (a)   to safeguard and promote the welfare of children within their area who are in need; and

   (b)   so far as is consistent with that duty, to promote the upbringing of such children by their families,

by providing a range and level of services appropriate to those children's needs.

(2) For the purpose principally of facilitating the discharge of their general duty under this section, every local authority shall have the specific duties and powers set out in Part 1 of Schedule 2.

(3) Any service provided by an authority in the exercise of functions conferred on them by this section may be provided for the family of a particular child in need or for any member of his family, if it is provided with a view to safeguarding or promoting the child's welfare.

(4) The [appropriate national authority][7] may by order amend any provision of Part I of Schedule 2 or add any further duty or power to those for the time being mentioned there.

[(4A) Before determining what (if any) services to provide for a particular child in need in the exercise of functions conferred on them by this section, a local authority shall, so far as is reasonably practicable and consistent with the child's welfare –

   (a)   ascertain the child's wishes and feelings regarding the provision of those services; and

   (b)   give due consideration (having regard to his age and understanding) to such wishes and feelings of the child as they have been able to ascertain.][6]

(5) Every local authority –

   (a)   shall facilitate the provision by others (including in particular voluntary organisations) of services which *the authority have power* [it is a function of the authority][9] to provide by virtue of this section, or section 18, 20, [23 [22A to 22C][9], 23B to 23D, 24A or 24B][3]; and

(b)   may make such arrangements as they see fit for any person to act on their behalf in the provision of any such service.

(6) The services provided by a local authority in the exercise of functions conferred on them by this section may include [providing accommodation and][4] giving assistance in kind or, *in exceptional circumstances,*[10] in cash.

(7) Assistance may be unconditional or subject to conditions as to the repayment of the assistance or of its value (in whole or in part).

(8) Before giving any assistance or imposing any conditions, a local authority shall have regard to the means of the child concerned and of each of his parents.

(9) No person shall be liable to make any repayment of assistance or of its value at any time when he is in receipt of income support [under][5] [Part VII of the Social Security Contributions and Benefits Act 1992][1][, of any element of child tax credit other than the family element, of working tax credit][5] [or of an income-based jobseeker's allowance][2].

(10) For the purposes of this Part a child shall be taken to be in need if –

(a)   he is unlikely to achieve or maintain, or to have the opportunity of achieving or maintaining, a reasonable standard of health or development without the provision for him of services by a local authority under this Part;
(b)   his health or development is likely to be significantly impaired, or further impaired, without the provision for him of such services; or
(c)   he is disabled,

and 'family', in relation to such a child, includes any person who has parental responsibility for the child and any other person with whom he has been living.

(11) For the purposes of this Part, a child is disabled if he is blind, deaf or dumb or suffers from mental disorder of any kind or is substantially and permanently handicapped by illness, injury or congenital deformity or such other disability as may be prescribed; and in this Part –

'development' means physical, intellectual, emotional, social or behavioural development; and
'health' means physical or mental health.

[(12) The Treasury may by regulations prescribe circumstances in which a person is to be treated for the purposes of this Part (or for such of those purposes as are prescribed) as in receipt of any element of child tax credit other than the family element or of working tax credit][, of an income-based jobseeker's allowance or of an income-related employment and support allowance][8].

NOTES

Amendments.[1] Words substituted: Disability Living Allowance and Disability Working Allowance Act 1991, s 7(2), Sch 3, Pt II, para 13.[2] Words substituted: Social Security (Consequential Provisions) Act 1992, s 4, Sch 2, para 108.[3] Words substituted: Children (Leaving Care) Act 2000, s 7(1), (2).[4] Words inserted: Adoption and Children Act 2002, s 116(1). [5] Words substituted and subsection inserted: Tax Credits Act 2002, s 47, Sch 3, paras 15 and 16.[6] Subsection inserted: Children Act 2004, s 53(1).[7] Words substituted: Children and Young Persons Act 2008, s 39, Sch 3, paras 1, 2.[8] Words inserted: Welfare Reform Act 2007, s 28(1), Sch 3, para 6(1), (2). [9] Words in italics substituted by words in square brackets in relation to England: Children and Young Persons Act 2008, s 8(2), Sch 1, para 1. [10] Words in italics repealed in relation to England: Children and Young Persons Act 2008, ss 24, 42, Sch 4.

Definitions. 'Child': s 105(1); 'child in need': s 17(10); 'development': s 17(11); 'disabled': s 17(11); 'family': s 17(10); 'functions': s 105(1); 'health': s 17(11); 'local authority': s 105(1); 'parental responsibility': s 3; 'prescribed': s 105(1); 'service': s 105(1); 'upbringing': s 105(1); 'voluntary organisation': s 105(1).

[17A Direct payments

(1) The [appropriate national authority][3] may by regulations make provision for and in connection with requiring or authorising the responsible authority in the case of a person of a prescribed description who falls within subsection (2) to make, with that person's consent, such payments to him as they may determine in accordance with the regulations in respect of his securing the provision of the service mentioned in that subsection.

(2) A person falls within this subsection if he is –

   (a)   a person with parental responsibility for a disabled child,
   (b)   a disabled person with parental responsibility for a child, or
   (c)   a disabled child aged 16 or 17,

and a local authority ('the responsible authority') have decided for the purposes of section 17 that the child's needs (or, if he is such a disabled child, his needs) call for the provision by them of a service in exercise of functions conferred on them under that section.

(3) Subsections (3) to (5) and (7) of section 57 of the 2001 Act shall apply, with any necessary modifications, in relation to regulations under this section as they apply in relation to regulations under that section.

(4) Regulations under this section shall provide that, where payments are made under the regulations to a person falling within subsection (5) –

   (a)   the payments shall be made at the rate mentioned in subsection (4)(a) of section 57 of the 2001 Act (as applied by subsection (3)); and
   (b)   subsection (4)(b) of that section shall not apply.

(5) A person falls within this subsection if he is –

   (a)   a person falling within subsection (2)(a) or (b) and the child in question is aged 16 or 17, or
   (b)   a person who is in receipt of income support, ...[2] under Part 7 of the Social Security Contributions and Benefits Act 1992[, of any element of child tax credit other than the family element, of working tax credit][2] [, of an income-based jobseeker's allowance or of an income-related employment and support allowance][3].

(6) In this section –

'the 2001 Act' means the Health and Social Care Act 2001;

'disabled' in relation to an adult has the same meaning as that given by section 17(11) in relation to a child;

'prescribed' means specified in or determined in accordance with regulations under this section (and has the same meaning in the provisions of the 2001 Act mentioned in subsection (3) as they apply by virtue of that subsection).][1]

NOTES

Amendments.[1] Section inserted: Carers and Disabled Children Act 2000, s 7(1); and subsequently substituted: Health and Social Care Act 2001, s 58 (applies to England only).[2] Words repealed or inserted: Tax Credits Act 2002, s 47, Sch 3, s 60, paras 15, 17, Sch 6.[3] Words substituted: Children and Young Persons Act 2008, ss 28(1), 39, Sch 3, paras 1, 3, 6(1), (3).

Definitions. 'Accommodation': s 22(2); 'child': s 105(1); 'local authority': s 105(1).

[17B   Vouchers for persons with parental responsibility for disabled children

(1) The Secretary of State may by regulations make provision for the issue by a local authority of vouchers to a person with parental responsibility for a disabled child.

(2) "Voucher" means a document whereby, if the local authority agrees with the person with parental responsibility that it would help him care for the child if the person with parental responsibility had a break from caring, that person may secure the temporary provision of services for the child under section 17.

(3) The regulations may, in particular, provide –

   (a)   for the value of a voucher to be expressed in terms of money, or of the delivery of a service for a period of time, or both;

   (b)   for the person who supplies a service against a voucher, or for the arrangement under which it is supplied, to be approved by the local authority;

   (c)   for a maximum period during which a service (or a service of a prescribed description) can be provided against a voucher.][1]

NOTES

Amendments. [1] Section inserted in relation to England: Carers and Disabled Children Act 2000, s 7(1).

Definitions. 'child': s 105(1); 'disabled': s 17(11); 'local authority': s 105(1); 'parental responsibility': s 3.

18   Day care for pre-school and other children

(1) Every local authority shall provide such day care for children in need within their area who are –

   (a)   aged five or under; and

   (b)   not yet attending schools,

as is appropriate.

PART I – Statutes

(2) A local authority [in Wales][1] may provide day care for children within their area who satisfy the conditions mentioned in subsection (1)(a) and (b) even though they are not in need.

(3) A local authority may provide facilities (including training, advice, guidance and counselling) for those –

(a)   caring for children in day care; or
(b)   who at any time accompany such children while they are in day care.

(4) In this section 'day care' means any form of care or supervised activity provided for children during the day (whether or not it is provided on a regular basis).

(5) Every local authority shall provide for children in need within their area who are attending any school such care or supervised activities as is appropriate –

(a)   outside school hours; or
(b)   during school holidays.

(6) A local authority [in Wales][1] may provide such care or supervised activities for children within their area who are attending any school even though those children are not in need.

(7) In this section 'supervised activity' means an activity supervised by a responsible person.

NOTES

Amendments. Words inserted: Childcare Act 2006, s 103(1), Sch 2, para 4.

Definitions. 'Child': s 105(1); 'child in need': s 17(10); 'day care': s 18(4); 'local authority': s 105(1); 'school': s 105(1); 'supervised activity': s 18(7).

19

...[1]

NOTES

Amendments.[1] Section repealed: Education Act 2002, s 149(2).

Provision of accommodation for children

20 Provision of accommodation for children: general

(1) Every local authority shall provide accommodation for any child in need within their area who appears to them to require accommodation as a result of –

(a)   there being no person who has parental responsibility for him;
(b)   his being lost or having been abandoned; or
(c)   the person who has been caring for him being prevented (whether or not permanently, and for whatever reason) from providing him with suitable accommodation or care.

(2) Where a local authority provide accommodation under subsection (1) for a child who is ordinarily resident in the area of another local authority, that other local authority may take over the provision of accommodation for the child within –

(a)   three months of being notified in writing that the child is being provided with accommodation; or

(b)   such other longer period as may be prescribed.

(3) Every local authority shall provide accommodation for any child in need within their area who has reached the age of sixteen and whose welfare the authority consider is likely to be seriously prejudiced if they do not provide him with accommodation.

(4) A local authority may provide accommodation for any child within their area (even though a person who has parental responsibility for him is able to provide him with accommodation) if they consider that to do so would safeguard or promote the child's welfare.

(5) A local authority may provide accommodation for any person who has reached the age of sixteen but is under twenty-one in any community home which takes children who have reached the age of sixteen if they consider that to do so would safeguard or promote his welfare.

(6) Before providing accommodation under this section, a local authority shall, so far as is reasonably practicable and consistent with the child's welfare –

(a)   ascertain the child's wishes [and feelings][1] regarding the provision of accommodation; and

(b)   give due consideration (having regard to his age and understanding) to such wishes [and feelings][1] of the child as they have been able to ascertain.

(7) A local authority may not provide accommodation under this section for any child if any person who –

(a)   has parental responsibility for him; and

(b)   is willing and able to –

(i)   provide accommodation for him; or

(ii)   arrange for accommodation to be provided for him,

objects.

(8) Any person who has parental responsibility for a child may at any time remove the child from accommodation provided by or on behalf of the local authority under this section.

(9) Subsections (7) and (8) do not apply while any person –

(a)   in whose favour a residence order is in force with respect to the child; ...[2]

[(aa) who is a special guardian of the child; or][3]

(b)   who has care of the child by virtue of an order made in the exercise of the High Court's inherent jurisdiction with respect to children, agrees to the child being looked after in accommodation provided by or on behalf of the local authority.

(10) Where there is more than one such person as is mentioned in subsection (9), all of them must agree.

(11) Subsections (7) and (8) do not apply where a child who has reached the age of sixteen agrees to being provided with accommodation under this section.

NOTES

Amendments.[1] Words inserted: Children Act 2004, s 53(2).[2] Word repealed: Adoption and Children Act 2002, s 139(1), (3), Sch 3, paras 54, 59, Sch 5.[3] Paragraph inserted: Adoption and Children Act 2002, s 139(1), (3), Sch 3, paras 54, 59.

Definitions. 'Child': s 105(1); 'child in need': s 17(10); 'community home': s 53(1); 'local authority': s 105(1); 'ordinary residence': s 105(6); 'parental responsibility': s 3; 'prescribed': s 105(1); 'residence order': s 8(1).

21 Provision of accommodation for children in police protection or detention or on remand, etc

(1) Every local authority shall make provision for the reception and accommodation of children who are removed or kept away from home under Part V.

(2) Every local authority shall receive, and provide accommodation for, children –

(a) in police protection whom they are requested to receive under section 46(3)(f);

(b) whom they are requested to receive under section 38(6) of the Police and Criminal Evidence Act 1984;

(c) who are –

    (i) on remand under [...[7] section][4] 23(1) of the Children and Young Persons Act 1969; ...[7]

    [(ia) remanded to accommodation provided by or on behalf of a local authority by virtue of paragraph 4 of Schedule 1 or paragraph 6 of Schedule 8 to the Powers of Criminal Courts (Sentencing) Act 2000 (breach etc of referral orders and reparation orders);][7]

    [(ii) remanded to accommodation provided by or on behalf of a local authority by virtue of paragraph 21 of Schedule 2 to the Criminal Justice and Immigration Act 2008 (breach etc of youth rehabilitation orders); ...[8]

    [(iia) remanded to accommodation provided by or on behalf of a local authority by virtue of paragraph 10 of the Schedule to the Street Offences Act 1959 (breach of orders under section 1(2A) of that Act)][8]

    (iii) the subject of a youth rehabilitation order imposing a local authority residence requirement or a youth rehabilitation order with fostering,][7]

and with respect to whom they are the designated authority.

[(2A) In subsection (2)(c)(iii), the following terms have the same meanings as in Part 1 of the Criminal Justice and Immigration Act 2008 (see section 7 of that Act) –

'local authority residence requirement';
'youth rehabilitation order';
'youth rehabilitation order with fostering'.][7]

(3) Where a child has been –

(a)   removed under Part V; or
(b)   detained under section 38 of the Police and Criminal Evidence Act 1984,

and he is not being provided with accommodation by a local authority or in a hospital vested in the Secretary of State[, the Welsh Ministers][6] [or a Primary Care Trust][3] [or otherwise made available pursuant to arrangements made by a [[Local Health Board][5]][2]][1] [or a Primary Care Trust][3], any reasonable expenses of accommodating him shall be recoverable from the local authority in whose area he is ordinarily resident.

NOTES

Amendments.[1] Words inserted: National Health Service and Community Care Act 1990, s 66(1), Sch 36, para 1.[2] Words substituted: Health Authorities Act 1995, s 2(1), Sch 1, Pt III, para 118(1), (3).[3] Words inserted: Health Act 1999 (Supplementary, Consequential etc Provisions) Order 2000, SI 2000/90.[4] Words substituted: Powers of Criminal Courts (Sentencing) Act 2000, s 165(1), Sch 9, para 126. [5] Words substituted: SI 2007/961.[6] Children and Young Persons Act 2008, s 39, Sch 3, paras 1, 5.[7] Words repealed, paragraphs inserted and substituted, and subsection inserted: Criminal Justice and Immigration Act 2008, ss 6(2), (3), 149, Sch 4, Pt 1, paras 33, 34(1)–(3), Pt 2, para 105, Sch 28, Pt 1. [8] Word omitted and paragraph inserted: Policing and Crime Act 2009, s 112, Sch 7, Pt 3, para 21, Sch 8, Pt 2.

Definitions. 'Accommodation': s 22(2); 'child': s 105(1); 'hospital': s 105(1); 'local authority': s 105(1); 'police protection': s 46(2); 'supervision order': s 31(11).

Duties of local authorities in relation to children looked after by them

22 General duty of local authority in relation to children looked after by them

(1) In this Act, any reference to a child who is looked after by a local authority is a reference to a child who is –

(a)   in their care; or
(b)   provided with accommodation by the authority in the exercise of any functions (in particular those under this Act) which [are social services functions within the meaning of][1] the Local Authority Social Services Act 1970 [, apart from functions under sections [17][3] 23B and 24B][2].

(2) In subsection (1) 'accommodation' means accommodation which is provided for a continuous period of more than 24 hours.

(3) It shall be the duty of a local authority looking after any child –

(a)   to safeguard and promote his welfare; and

(b)   to make such use of services available for children cared for by their own parents as appears to the authority reasonable in his case.

[(3A) The duty of a local authority under subsection (3)(a) to safeguard and promote the welfare of a child looked after by them includes in particular a duty to promote the child's educational achievement.][4]

(4) Before making any decision with respect to a child whom they are looking after, or proposing to look after, a local authority shall, so far as is reasonably practicable, ascertain the wishes and feelings of –

(a)   the child;
(b)   his parents;
(c)   any person who is not a parent of his but who has parental responsibility for him; and
(d)   any other person whose wishes and feelings the authority consider to be relevant,

regarding the matter to be decided.

(5) In making any such decision a local authority shall give due consideration –

(a)   having regard to his age and understanding, to such wishes and feelings of the child as they have been able to ascertain;
(b)   to such wishes and feelings of any person mentioned in subsection (4)(b) to (d) as they have been able to ascertain; and
(c)   to the child's religious persuasion, racial origin and cultural and linguistic background.

(6) If it appears to a local authority that it is necessary, for the purposes of protecting members of the public from serious injury, to exercise their powers with respect to a child whom they are looking after in a manner which may not be consistent with their duties under this section, they may do so.

(7) If the [appropriate national authority][5] considers it necessary, for the purpose of protecting members of the public from serious injury, to give directions to a local authority with respect to the exercise of their powers with respect to a child whom they are looking after, [the appropriate national authority][5] may give such directions to [the local authority][5].

(8) Where any such directions are given to an authority they shall comply with them even though doing so is inconsistent with their duties under this section.

NOTES

Amendments.[1] Words substituted: Local Government Act 2000, s 107, Sch 5, para 19.[2] Words inserted: Children (Leaving Care) Act 2000, s 2(2).[3] Reference inserted: Adoption and Children Act 2002, s 116(2).[4] Subsection inserted: Children Act 2004, s 52.[5] Words substituted: Children and Young Persons Act 2008, s 39, Sch 3, paras 1, 6.

Definitions. 'Accommodation': s 22(2); 'child': s 105(1); 'child who is looked after by a local authority': s 22(1); 'functions': s 105(1); 'local authority': s 105(1); 'parental responsibility': s 3; 'service': s 105(1).

PART I – Statutes

[22A Provision of accommodation for children in care

When a child is in the care of a local authority, it is their duty to provide the child with accommodation.][1]

NOTES

Amendments. [1] Section substituted together with ss 22B–22F for s 23 in relation to England: Children and Young Persons Act 2008, s 8(1).

Definitions. 'Accommodation': s 22(2); 'child': s 105(1); 'local authority': s 105(1).

[22B Maintenance of looked after children

It is the duty of a local authority to maintain a child they are looking after in other respects apart from the provision of accommodation.][1]

NOTES

Amendments. [1] Section substituted together with ss 22A, 22C–22F for s 23 in relation to England: Children and Young Persons Act 2008, s 8(1).

Definitions. 'Accommodation': s 22(2); 'child': s 105(1); 'local authority': s 105(1).

[22C Ways in which looked after children are to be accommodated and maintained

(1) This section applies where a local authority are looking after a child ('C').

(2) The local authority must make arrangements for C to live with a person who falls within subsection (3) (but subject to subsection (4)).

(3) A person ('P') falls within this subsection if –

    (a)   P is a parent of C;

    (b)   P is not a parent of C but has parental responsibility for C; or

    (c)   in a case where C is in the care of the local authority and there was a residence order in force with respect to C immediately before the care order was made, P was a person in whose favour the residence order was made.

(4) Subsection (2) does not require the local authority to make arrangements of the kind mentioned in that subsection if doing so –

    (a)   would not be consistent with C's welfare; or

    (b)   would not be reasonably practicable.

(5) If the local authority are unable to make arrangements under subsection (2), they must place C in the placement which is, in their opinion, the most appropriate placement available.

(6) In subsection (5) 'placement' means –

    (a)   placement with an individual who is a relative, friend or other person connected with C and who is also a local authority foster parent;

    (b)   placement with a local authority foster parent who does not fall within paragraph (a);

(c) placement in a children's home in respect of which a person is registered under Part 2 of the Care Standards Act 2000; or

(d) subject to section 22D, placement in accordance with other arrangements which comply with any regulations made for the purposes of this section.

(7) In determining the most appropriate placement for C, the local authority must, subject to the other provisions of this Part (in particular, to their duties under section 22) –

(a) give preference to a placement falling within paragraph (a) of subsection (6) over placements falling within the other paragraphs of that subsection;

(b) comply, so far as is reasonably practicable in all the circumstances of C's case, with the requirements of subsection (8); and

(c) comply with subsection (9) unless that is not reasonably practicable.

(8) The local authority must ensure that the placement is such that –

(a) it allows C to live near C's home;

(b) it does not disrupt C's education or training;

(c) if C has a sibling for whom the local authority are also providing accommodation, it enables C and the sibling to live together;

(d) if C is disabled, the accommodation provided is suitable to C's particular needs.

(9) The placement must be such that C is provided with accommodation within the local authority's area.

(10) The local authority may determine –

(a) the terms of any arrangements they make under subsection (2) in relation to C (including terms as to payment); and

(b) the terms on which they place C with a local authority foster parent (including terms as to payment but subject to any order made under section 49 of the Children Act 2004).

(11) The appropriate national authority may make regulations for, and in connection with, the purposes of this section.

(12) In this Act 'local authority foster parent' means a person who is approved as a local authority foster parent in accordance with regulations made by virtue of paragraph 12F of Schedule 2.]¹

NOTES

Amendments. ¹ Section substituted together with ss 22A, 22B, 22D–22F for s 23 in relation to England and, for certain purposes, in relation to Wales: Children and Young Persons Act 2008, s 8(1).

Definitions. 'Accommodation': s 22(2); 'child': s 105(1); 'local authority': s 105(1); 'looked after by a local authority': s 22(1); 'parental responsibility': s 3.

PART I – Statutes

[22D Review of child's case before making alternative arrangements for accommodation

(1) Where a local authority are providing accommodation for a child ('C') other than by arrangements under section 22C(6)(d), they must not make such arrangements for C unless they have decided to do so in consequence of a review of C's case carried out in accordance with regulations made under section 26.

(2) But subsection (1) does not prevent a local authority making arrangements for C under section 22C(6)(d) if they are satisfied that in order to safeguard C's welfare it is necessary –

(a)   to make such arrangements; and
(b)   to do so as a matter of urgency.]¹

NOTES

Amendments. ¹ Section substituted together with ss 22A–22C, 22E, 22F for s 23 in relation to England: Children and Young Persons Act 2008, s 8(1).

Definitions. 'Accommodation': s 22(2); 'child': s 105(1); 'local authority': s 105(1).

[22E Children's homes provided by appropriate national authority.

Where a local authority place a child they are looking after in a children's home provided, equipped and maintained by an appropriate national authority under section 82(5), they must do so on such terms as that national authority may from time to time determine.]

NOTES

Amendments. ¹ Section substituted together with ss 22A–22D, 22F for s 23 in relation to England: Children and Young Persons Act 2008, s 8(1).

Definitions. 'Accommodation': s 22(2); 'child': s 105(1); 'children's home': s 23; 'local authority': s 105(1).

[22F Regulations as to children looked after by local authorities

Part 2 of Schedule 2 has effect for the purposes of making further provision as to children looked after by local authorities and in particular as to the regulations which may be made under section 22C(11).]¹

NOTES

Amendments. ¹ Section substituted together with ss 22A–22E for s 23: Children and Young Persons Act 2008, s 8(1).

[22G General duty of local authority to secure sufficient accommodation for looked after children

(1) It is the general duty of a local authority to take steps that secure, so far as reasonably practicable, the outcome in subsection (2).

(2) The outcome is that the local authority are able to provide the children mentioned in subsection (3) with accommodation that –

(a)   is within the authority's area; and
(b)   meets the needs of those children.

(3) The children referred to in subsection (2) are those –

(a)   that the local authority are looking after,
(b)   in respect of whom the authority are unable to make arrangements under section 22C(2), and
(c)   whose circumstances are such that it would be consistent with their welfare for them to be provided with accommodation that is in the authority's area.

(4) In taking steps to secure the outcome in subsection (2), the local authority must have regard to the benefit of having –

(a)   a number of accommodation providers in their area that is, in their opinion, sufficient to secure that outcome; and
(b)   a range of accommodation in their area capable of meeting different needs that is, in their opinion, sufficient to secure that outcome.

(5) In this section "accommodation providers" means –

local authority foster parents; and
children's homes in respect of which a person is registered under Part 2 of the Care Standards Act 2000.]¹

NOTES

Amendments. ¹ Section inserted in relation to England: Children and Young Persons Act 2008, s 9.

Definitions. 'Accommodation': s 22(2); 'children's home': s 23;'local authority': s 105(1); 'local authority foster parents': s 22C(12).

[23 Provision of accommodation and maintenance by local authority for children whom they are looking after

(1) It shall be the duty of any local authority looking after a child –

(a)   when he is in their care, to provide accommodation for him; and
(b)   to maintain him in other respects apart from providing accommodation for him.

(2) A local authority shall provide accommodation and maintenance for any child whom they are looking after by –

(a)   placing him (subject to subsection (5) and any regulations made by the [appropriate national authority]⁴) with –
(i)   a family;
(ii)   a relative of his; or
(iii)   any other suitable person,
on such terms as to payment by the authority and otherwise as the authority may determine [(subject to section 49 of the Children Act 2004)]³;

[(aa) maintaining him in an appropriate children's home;

(b)–(e) ...]²

(f)   making such other arrangements as –
  (i)   seem appropriate to them; and
  (ii) comply with any regulations made by the [appropriate national authority][4].

[(2A) Where under subsection (2)(aa) a local authority maintains a child in a home provided, equipped and maintained by the [appropriate national authority][4] under section 82(5), it shall do so on such terms as [that national authority][4] may from time to time determine.][2]

(3) Any person with whom a child has been placed under subsection (2)(a) is referred to in this Act as a local authority foster parent unless he falls within subsection (4).

(4) A person falls within this subsection if he is –

(a)   a parent of the child;
(b)   a person who is not a parent of the child but who has parental responsibility for him; or
(c)   where the child is in care and there was a residence order in force with respect to him immediately before the care order was made, a person in whose favour the residence order was made.

(5) Where a child is in the care of a local authority, the authority may only allow him to live with a person who falls within subsection (4) in accordance with regulations made by the [appropriate national authority][4].

[(5A) For the purposes of subsection (5) a child shall be regarded living with a person if he stays with that person for a continuous period of more than 24 hours.][1]

(6) Subject to any regulations made by the [appropriate national authority][4] for the purposes of this subsection, any local authority looking after a child shall make arrangements to enable him to live with –

(a)   a person falling within subsection (4); or
(b)   a relative, friend or other person connected with him,

unless that would not be reasonably practicable or consistent with his welfare.

(7) Where a local authority provide accommodation for a child whom they are looking after, they shall, subject to the provisions of this Part and so far as is reasonably practicable and consistent with his welfare, secure that –

(a)   the accommodation is near his home; and
(b)   where the authority are also providing accommodation for a sibling of his, they are accommodated together.

(8) Where a local authority provide accommodation for a child whom they are looking after and who is disabled, they shall, so far as is reasonably practicable, secure that the accommodation is not unsuitable to his particular needs.

(9) Part II of Schedule 2 shall have effect for the purposes of making further provision as to children looked after by local authorities and in particular as to the regulations that may be made under subsections (2)(a) and (f) and (5).

[(10) In this Act –

'appropriate children's home' means a children's home in respect of which a person is registered under Part II of the Care Standards Act 2000; and 'children's home' has the same meaning as in that Act.][2][5]

NOTES

Amendments.[1] Subsection inserted: Courts and Legal Services Act 1990, s 116, Sch 16, para 12(2).[2] Paragraph (aa) substituted for paras (b)–(e) and subsections inserted: Care Standards Act 2000, s 116, Sch 4, para 14(3).[3] Words inserted: Children Act 2004, s 49(3).[4] Words substituted: Children and Young Persons Act 2008, s 39, Sch 3, paras 1, 7.[5] Section substituted by ss 22A–22F in relation to England: Children and Young Persons Act 2008, s 8(1).

Definitions. 'Care order': s 8(1); 'child': s 105(1); 'child who is looked after by a local authority': s 22(1); 'community home': s 53(1); 'disabled': s 17(11); 'family': s 17(10); 'local authority': s 105(1); 'local authority foster parent': s 23(3); 'parental responsibility': s 3; 'relative': s 105(1); 'residence order': s 8(1); 'voluntary home': s 60(3).

[Visiting

23ZA Duty of local authority to ensure visits to, and contact with, looked after children and others

(1) This section applies to –

(a)   a child looked after by a local authority;
(b)   a child who was looked after by a local authority but who has ceased to be looked after by them as a result of prescribed circumstances.

(2) It is the duty of the local authority –

(a)   to ensure that a person to whom this section applies is visited by a representative of the authority ('a representative');
(b)   to arrange for appropriate advice, support and assistance to be available to a person to whom this section applies who seeks it from them.

(3) The duties imposed by subsection (2) –

(a)   are to be discharged in accordance with any regulations made for the purposes of this section by the appropriate national authority;
(b)   are subject to any requirement imposed by or under an enactment applicable to the place in which the person to whom this section applies is accommodated.

(4) Regulations under this section for the purposes of subsection (3)(a) may make provision about –

(a)   the frequency of visits;
(b)   circumstances in which a person to whom this section applies must be visited by a representative; and
(c)   the functions of a representative.

(5) In choosing a representative a local authority must satisfy themselves that the person chosen has the necessary skills and experience to perform the functions of a representative.][1]

NOTES

Amendments. [1] Section and preceding cross-heading inserted in relation to England and, for certain purposes, in relation to Wales: Children and Young Persons Act 2008, s 15.

[23ZB Independent visitors for children looked after by a local authority

(1) A local authority looking after a child must appoint an independent person to be the child's visitor if –

    (a)   the child falls within a description prescribed in regulations made by the appropriate national authority; or

    (b)   in any other case, it appears to them that it would be in the child's interests to do so.

(2) A person appointed under this section must visit, befriend and advise the child.

(3) A person appointed under this section is entitled to recover from the appointing authority any reasonable expenses incurred by that person for the purposes of that person's functions under this section.

(4) A person's appointment as a visitor in pursuance of this section comes to an end if –

    (a)   the child ceases to be looked after by the local authority;

    (b)   the person resigns the appointment by giving notice in writing to the appointing authority; or

    (c)   the authority give him notice in writing that they have terminated it.

(5) The ending of such an appointment does not affect any duty under this section to make a further appointment.

(6) Where a local authority propose to appoint a visitor for a child under this section, the appointment shall not be made if –

    (a)   the child objects to it; and

    (b)   the authority are satisfied that the child has sufficient understanding to make an informed decision.

(7) Where a visitor has been appointed for a child under this section, the local authority shall terminate the appointment if –

    (a)   the child objects to its continuing; and

    (b)   the authority are satisfied that the child has sufficient understanding to make an informed decision.

(8) If the local authority give effect to a child's objection under subsection (6) or (7) and the objection is to having anyone as the child's visitor, the authority does not have to propose to appoint another person under subsection (1) until the objection is withdrawn.

(9) The appropriate national authority may make regulations as to the circumstances in which a person is to be regarded for the purposes of this section as independent of the appointing authority.]¹

NOTES

Amendments. ¹ Section inserted in relation to England and, for certain purposes, in relation to Wales: Children and Young Persons Act 2008, s 16(1).

Advice and assistance for certain children [and young persons]¹

[23A The responsible authority and relevant children

(1) The responsible local authority shall have the functions set out in section 23B in respect of a relevant child.

(2) In subsection (1) 'relevant child' means (subject to subsection (3)) a child who –

  (a)   is not being looked after by any local authority;
  (b)   was, before last ceasing to be looked after, an eligible child for the purposes of paragraph 19B of Schedule 2; and
  (c)   is aged sixteen or seventeen.

(3) The [appropriate national authority]² may prescribe –

  (a)   additional categories of relevant children; and
  (b)   categories of children who are not to be relevant children despite falling within subsection (2).

(4) In subsection (1) the 'responsible local authority' is the one which last looked after the child.

(5) If under subsection (3)(a) the [appropriate national authority]² prescribes a category of relevant children which includes children who do not fall within subsection (2)(b) (for example, because they were being looked after by a local authority in Scotland), [the appropriate national authority]² may in the regulations also provide for which local authority is to be the responsible local authority for those children.]¹

NOTES

Amendments.¹ Section inserted: Children (Leaving Care) Act 2000, s 2(4).² Words substituted: Children and Young Persons Act 2008, s 39, Sch 3, paras 1, 8.

[23B Additional functions of the responsible authority in respect of relevant children

(1) It is the duty of each local authority to take reasonable steps to keep in touch with a relevant child for whom they are the responsible authority, whether he is within their area or not.

(2) It is the duty of each local authority to appoint a personal adviser for each relevant child (if they have not already done so under paragraph 19C of Schedule 2).

(3) It is the duty of each local authority, in relation to any relevant child who does not already have a pathway plan prepared for the purposes of paragraph 19B of Schedule 2 –

    (a)   to carry out an assessment of his needs with a view to determining what advice, assistance and support it would be appropriate for them to provide him under this Part; and

    (b)   to prepare a pathway plan for him.

[*(4) The local authority may carry out such an assessment at the same time as any assessment of his needs is made under any enactment referred to in sub-paragraphs (a) to (c) of paragraph 3 of Schedule 2, or under any other enactment.*

(5) The [appropriate national authority]² may by regulations make provision as to assessments for the purposes of subsection (3).

(6) The regulations may in particular make provision about –

    (a)   who is to be consulted in relation to an assessment;

    (b)   the way in which an assessment is to be carried out, by whom and when;

    (c)   the recording of the results of an assessment;

    (d)   the considerations to which the local authority are to have regard in carrying out an assessment.

(7) [The local authority]² shall keep the pathway plan under regular review.]³

(8) The responsible local authority shall safeguard and promote the child's welfare and, unless they are satisfied that his welfare does not require it, support him by –

    (a)   maintaining him;

    (b)   providing him with or maintaining him in suitable accommodation; and

    (c)   providing support of such other descriptions as may be prescribed.

(9) Support under subsection (8) may be in cash.

(10) The [appropriate national authority]² may by regulations make provision about the meaning of 'suitable accommodation' and in particular about the suitability of landlords or other providers of accommodation.

(11) If the local authority have lost touch with a relevant child, despite taking reasonable steps to keep in touch, they must without delay –

    (*a*)   consider how to re-establish contact; and

    (*b*)   take reasonable steps to do so,

and while the child is still a relevant child must continue to take such steps until they succeed.

(12) Subsections (7) to (9) of section 17 apply in relation to support given under this section as they apply in relation to assistance given under that section.

(13) Subsections (4) and (5) of section 22 apply in relation to any decision by a local authority for the purposes of this section as they apply in relation to the decisions referred to in that section.]¹

NOTES

Amendments.¹ Section inserted: Children (Leaving Care) Act 2000, s 2(4).² Words substituted: Children and Young Persons Act 2008, s 39, Sch 3, paras 1, 9.³ Subsections (4)–(7) repealed in relation to England: Children and Young Persons Act 2008, ss 22(1), 42, Sch 4.

[23C Continuing functions in respect of former relevant children

(1) Each local authority shall have the duties provided for in this section towards –

    (a)   a person who has been a relevant child for the purposes of section 23A (and would be one if he were under eighteen), and in relation to whom they were the last responsible authority; and

    (b)   a person who was being looked after by them when he attained the age of eighteen, and immediately before ceasing to be looked after was an eligible child,

and in this section such a person is referred to as a 'former relevant child'.

(2) It is the duty of the local authority to take reasonable steps –

    (a)   to keep in touch with a former relevant child whether he is within their area or not; and

    (b)   if they lose touch with him, to re-establish contact.

(3) It is the duty of the local authority –

    (a)   to continue the appointment of a personal adviser for a former relevant child; and

    (b)   to continue to keep his pathway plan under regular review.

(4) It is the duty of the local authority to give a former relevant child –

    (a)   assistance of the kind referred to in section 24B(1), to the extent that his welfare requires it;

    (b)   assistance of the kind referred to in section 24B(2), to the extent that his welfare and his educational or training needs require it;

    (c)   other assistance, to the extent that his welfare requires it.

(5) The assistance given under subsection (4)(c) may be in kind or, in exceptional circumstances, in cash.

[(5A) It is the duty of the local authority to pay the relevant amount to a former relevant child who pursues higher education in accordance with a pathway plan prepared for that person.

(5B) The appropriate national authority may by regulations –

    (a)   prescribe the relevant amount for the purposes of subsection (5A);

    (b)   prescribe the meaning of 'higher education' for those purposes;

    (c)   make provision as to the payment of the relevant amount;

PART I – Statutes

(d)   make provision as to the circumstances in which the relevant amount (or any part of it) may be recovered by the local authority from a former relevant child to whom a payment has been made.

(5C) The duty set out in subsection (5A) is without prejudice to that set out in subsection (4)(b).][2]

(6) Subject to subsection (7), the duties set out in subsections (2), (3) and (4) subsist until the former relevant child reaches the age of twenty-one.

(7) If the former relevant child's pathway plan sets out a programme of education or training which extends beyond his twenty-first birthday –

(a)   the duty set out in subsection (4)(b) continues to subsist for so long as the former relevant child continues to pursue that programme; and

(b)   the duties set out in subsections (2) and (3) continue to subsist concurrently with that duty.

(8) For the purposes of subsection (7)(a) there shall be disregarded any interruption in a former relevant child's pursuance of a programme of education or training if the local authority are satisfied that he will resume it as soon as is reasonably practicable.

(9) Section 24B(5) applies in relation to a person being given assistance under subsection (4)(b) [or who is in receipt of a payment under subsection (5A)][3] as it applies in relation to a person to whom section 24B(3) applies.

(10) Subsections (7) to (9) of section 17 apply in relation to assistance given under this section as they apply in relation to assistance given under that section.][1]

NOTES

Amendments.[1] Section inserted: Children (Leaving Care) Act 2000, s 2(4).[2] Subsections inserted in relation to England and, for certain purposes, in relation to Wales: Children and Young Persons Act 2008, s 21(1), (2). [3] Words inserted in relation to England: Children and Young Persons Act 2008, s 21(1), (3).

[23CA Further assistance to pursue education or training

(1) This section applies to a person if –

(a)   he is under the age of twenty-five or of such lesser age as may be prescribed by the appropriate national authority;

(b)   he is a former relevant child (within the meaning of section 23C) towards whom the duties imposed by subsections (2), (3) and (4) of that section no longer subsist; and

(c)   he has informed the responsible local authority that he is pursuing, or wishes to pursue, a programme of education or training.

(2) It is the duty of the responsible local authority to appoint a personal adviser for a person to whom this section applies.

(3) It is the duty of the responsible local authority –

(a) to carry out an assessment of the needs of a person to whom this section applies with a view to determining what assistance (if any) it would be appropriate for them to provide to him under this section; and

(b) to prepare a pathway plan for him.

(4) It is the duty of the responsible local authority to give assistance of a kind referred to subsection (5) to a person to whom this section applies to the extent that his educational or training needs require it.

(5) The kinds of assistance are –

(a) contributing to expenses incurred by him in living near the place where he is, or will be, receiving education or training; or

(b) making a grant to enable him to meet expenses connected with his education and training.

(6) If a person to whom this section applies pursues a programme of education or training in accordance with the pathway plan prepared for him, the duties of the local authority under this section (and under any provision applicable to the pathway plan prepared under this section for that person) subsist for as long as he continues to pursue that programme.

(7) For the purposes of subsection (6), the local authority may disregard any interruption in the person's pursuance of a programme of education or training if they are satisfied that he will resume it as soon as is reasonably practicable.

(8) Subsections (7) to (9) of section 17 apply to assistance given to a person under this section as they apply to assistance given to or in respect of a child under that section, but with the omission in subsection (8) of the words "and of each of his parents".

(9) Subsection (5) of section 24B applies to a person to whom this section applies as it applies to a person to whom subsection (3) of that section applies.

(10) Nothing in this section affects the duty imposed by subsection (5A) of section 23C to the extent that it subsists in relation to a person to whom this section applies; but the duty to make a payment under that subsection may be taken into account in the assessment of the person's needs under subsection (3)(a).

(11) In this section "the responsible local authority" means, in relation to a person to whom this section applies, the local authority which had the duties provided for in section 23C towards him.][1]

NOTES

Amendments. [1] Section inserted in relation to England: Children and Young Persons Act 2008, s 22(2).

Definitions. 'responsible local authority': s 23CA(11).

[Personal advisers and pathway plans

23D Personal advisers

(1) The [appropriate national authority][2] may by regulations require local authorities to appoint a personal adviser for children or young persons of a prescribed description who have reached the age of sixteen but not the age of [twenty-five][3] who are not –

(a)   children who are relevant children for the purposes of section 23A;
(b)   the young persons referred to in section 23C; or
(c)   the children referred to in paragraph 19C of Schedule 2[; or
(d)   persons to whom section 23CA applies][3].

(2) Personal advisers appointed under or by virtue of this Part shall (in addition to any other functions) have such functions as the [appropriate national authority][2] prescribes.][1]

NOTES

Amendments.[1] Cross-heading and section inserted: Children (Leaving Care) Act 2000, s 3.[2] Words substituted: Children and Young Persons Act 2008, s 39, Sch 3, paras 1, 10.[3] Words substituted, and paragraph and preceding word inserted: Children and Young Persons Act 2008, s 23(1).

[23E Pathway plans

(1) In this Part, a reference to a 'pathway plan' is to a plan setting out –

(a)   in the case of a plan prepared under paragraph 19B of Schedule 2 –
    (i)   the advice, assistance and support which the local authority intend to provide a child under this Part, both while they are looking after him and later; and
    (ii)   when they might cease to look after him; and
(b)   in the case of a plan prepared under section 23B [or 23CA][4], the advice, assistance and support which the local authority intend to provide under this Part,

and dealing with such other matters (if any) as may be prescribed.

[(1A) A local authority may carry out an assessment under section 23B(3) or 23CA(3) of a person's needs at the same time as any assessment of his needs is made under –

(a)   the Chronically Sick and Disabled Persons Act 1970;
(b)   Part 4 of the Education Act 1996 (in the case of an assessment under section 23B(3));
(c)   the Disabled Persons (Services, Consultation and Representation) Act 1986; or
(d)   any other enactment.

(1B) The appropriate national authority may by regulations make provision as to assessments for the purposes of section 23B(3) or 23CA.

(1C) Regulations under subsection (1B) may in particular make provision about –

(a) who is to be consulted in relation to an assessment;
(b) the way in which an assessment is to be carried out, by whom and when;
(c) the recording of the results of an assessment;
(d) the considerations to which a local authority are to have regard in carrying out an assessment.

(1D) A local authority shall keep each pathway plan prepared by them under section 23B or 23CA under review.][3]

(2) The [appropriate national authority][2] may by regulations make provision about pathway plans and their review.][1]

NOTES

Amendments.[1] Section inserted: Children (Leaving Care) Act 2000, s 3.[2] Words in square brackets substituted: Children and Young Persons Act 2008, s 39, Sch 3, paras 1, 11.[3] Subsections inserted in relation to England and ,for certain purposes, in relation to Wales: Children and Young Persons Act 2008, s 22(3), (5). [4] Words inserted in relation to England: Children and Young Persons Act 2008, s 22(3), (4).

[24 Persons qualifying for advice and assistance

[(1) In this Part 'a person qualifying for advice and assistance' means a person to whom subsection (1A) or (1B) applies.

(1A) This subsection applies to a person –

(a) who has reached the age of sixteen but not the age of twenty-one;
(b) with respect to whom a special guardianship order is in force (or, if he has reached the age of eighteen, was in force when he reached that age); and
(c) who was, immediately before the making of that order, looked after by a local authority.

(1B) This subsection applies to a person to whom subsection (1A) does not apply, and who –

(a) is under twenty-one; and
(b) at any time after reaching the age of sixteen but while still a child was, but is no longer, looked after, accommodated or fostered.][3]

(2) In [subsection (1B)(b)][4], 'looked after, accommodated or fostered' means –

(a) looked after by a local authority;
(b) accommodated by or on behalf of a voluntary organisation;
(c) accommodated in a private children's home;
(d) accommodated for a consecutive period of at least three months –
    (i) by any [Local Health Board][6], Special Health Authority [or Primary Care Trust or by a local authority in the exercise of education functions][8], or
    (ii) in any care home or independent hospital or in any accommodation provided by a National Health Service trust [or an NHS foundation trust][2]; or
(e) privately fostered.

(3) Subsection (2)(d) applies even if the period of three months mentioned there began before the child reached the age of sixteen.

(4) In the case of a person qualifying for advice and assistance by virtue of subsection (2)(a), it is the duty of the local authority which last looked after him to take such steps as they think appropriate to contact him at such times as they think appropriate with a view to discharging their functions under sections 24A and 24B.

(5) In each of sections 24A and 24B, the local authority under the duty or having the power mentioned there ('the relevant authority') is –

[(za) in the case of a person to whom subsection (1A) applies, a local authority determined in accordance with regulations made by the [appropriate national authority][7];][5]

(a) in the case of a person qualifying for advice and assistance by virtue of subsection (2)(a), the local authority which last looked after him; or

(b) in the case of any other person qualifying for advice and assistance, the local authority within whose area the person is (if he has asked for help of a kind which can be given under section 24A or 24B).][1]

NOTES

Amendments.[1] Section and words in cross-heading inserted: Children (Leaving Care) Act 2000, ss 2(3), 4(1). [2] Words inserted: Health and Social Care (Community Health and Standards) Act 2003, s 34, Sch 4, paras 75, 76.[3] Subsection substituted: Adoption and Children Act 2002, s 139(1), Sch 3, paras 54, 60(a).[4] Words substituted: Adoption and Children Act 2002, s 139(1), Sch 3, paras 54, 60(b).[5] Paragraph inserted: Adoption and Children Act 2002, s 139(1), Sch 3, paras 54, 60(c).[6] Words substituted: SI 2007/961.[7] Words substituted: Children and Young Persons Act 2008, s 39, Sch 3, paras 1, 12.[8] Words substituted: SI 2010/1158.

[24A Advice and assistance

(1) The relevant authority shall consider whether the conditions in subsection (2) are satisfied in relation to a person qualifying for advice and assistance.

(2) The conditions are that –

(a) he needs help of a kind which they can give under this section or section 24B; and

(b) in the case of a person [to whom section 24(1A) applies, or to whom section 24(1B) applies and][3] who was not being looked after by any local authority, they are satisfied that the person by whom he was being looked after does not have the necessary facilities for advising or befriending him.

(3) If the conditions are satisfied –

(a) they shall advise and befriend him if [he is a person to whom section 24(1A) applies, or he is a person to whom section 24(1B) applies and][4] he was being looked after by a local authority or was accommodated by or on behalf of a voluntary organisation; and

(b) in any other case they may do so.

(4) Where as a result of this section a local authority are under a duty, or are empowered, to advise and befriend a person, they may also give him assistance.

(5) The assistance may be in kind [and, in exceptional circumstances, assistance may be given –

    (a)   by providing accommodation, if in the circumstances assistance may not be given in respect of the accommodation under section 24B, or

    (b)   in cash][2].

(6) Subsections (7) to (9) of section 17 apply in relation to assistance given under this section or section 24B as they apply in relation to assistance given under that section.][1]

NOTES

Amendments.[1] Section inserted: Children (Leaving Care) Act 2000, s 4(1).[2] Words substituted: Adoption and Children Act 2002, s 116(3).[3] Words inserted: Adoption and Children Act 2002, s 139(1), Sch 3, paras 54, 61(a).[4] Words inserted: Adoption and Children Act 2002, s 139(1), Sch 3, paras 54, 61(b).

[24B Employment, education and training

(1) The relevant local authority may give assistance to any person who qualifies for advice and assistance by virtue of [section 24(1A) or][2] section 24(2)(a) by contributing to expenses incurred by him in living near the place where he is, or will be, employed or seeking employment.

(2) The relevant local authority may give assistance to a person to whom subsection (3) applies by –

    (a)   contributing to expenses incurred by the person in question in living near the place where he is, or will be, receiving education or training; or

    (b)   making a grant to enable him to meet expenses connected with his education or training.

(3) This subsection applies to any person who –

    (a)   is under *twenty-four* [twenty-five][4]; and

    (b)   qualifies for advice and assistance by virtue of [section 24(1A) or][2] section 24(2)(a), or would have done so if he were under twenty-one.

(4) Where a local authority are assisting a person under subsection (2) they may disregard any interruption in his attendance on the course if he resumes it as soon as is reasonably practicable.

(5) Where the local authority are satisfied that a person to whom subsection (3) applies who is in full-time further or higher education needs accommodation during a vacation because his term-time accommodation is not available to him then, they shall give him assistance by –

    (a)   providing him with suitable accommodation during the vacation; or

    (b)   paying him enough to enable him to secure such accommodation himself.

(6) The [appropriate national authority][3] may prescribe the meaning of 'full-time', 'further education', 'higher education' and 'vacation' for the purposes of subsection (5).][1]

NOTES

Amendments.[1] Section inserted: Children (Leaving Care) Act 2000, s 4(1).[2] Words inserted: Adoption and Children Act 2002, s 139(1), Sch 3, paras 54, 62.[3] Words substituted: Children and Young Persons Act 2008, s 39, Sch 3, paras 1, 13. [4] Words in square brackets substituted for those in italics in relation to England: Children and Young Persons Act 2008, s 23(2).

[24C Information

(1) Where it appears to a local authority that a person –

    (a)   with whom they are under a duty to keep in touch under section 23B, 23C or 24; or

    (b)   whom they have been advising and befriending under section 24A; or

    (c)   to whom they have been giving assistance under section 24B,

proposes to live, or is living, in the area of another local authority, they must inform that other authority.

(2) Where a child who is accommodated –

    (a)   by a voluntary organisation or in a private children's home;

    (b)   by any [Local Health Board][3], Special Health Authority [or Primary Care Trust or by a local authority in the exercise of education functions][4]; or

    (c)   in any care home or independent hospital or any accommodation provided by a National Health Service trust [or an NHS foundation trust][2],

ceases to be so accommodated, after reaching the age of sixteen, the organisation, authority or (as the case may be) person carrying on the home shall inform the local authority within whose area the child proposes to live.

(3) Subsection (2) only applies, by virtue of paragraph (*b*) or (*c*), if the accommodation has been provided for a consecutive period of at least three months.

[(4) In a case where a child was accommodated by a local authority in the exercise of education functions, subsection (2) applies only if the local authority who accommodated the child are different from the local authority within whose area the child proposes to live.][4]][1]

NOTES

Amendments.[1] Section inserted: Children (Leaving Care) Act 2000, s 4(1). [2] Words inserted: Health and Social Care (Community Health and Standards) Act 2003, s 34, Sch 4, paras 75, 77.[3] Words substituted: SI 2007/961.[4] Words substituted and subsection inserted: SI 2010/1158.

[24D Representations: sections 23A to 24B

(1) Every local authority shall establish a procedure for considering representations (including complaints) made to them by –

(a) a relevant child for the purposes of section 23A or a young person falling within section 23C;

(b) a person qualifying for advice and assistance; or

(c) a person falling within section 24B(2),

about the discharge of their functions under this Part in relation to him.

[(1A) Regulations may be made by the [appropriate national authority]³ imposing time limits on the making of representations under subsection (1).]²

(2) In considering representations under subsection (1), a local authority shall comply with regulations (if any) made by the [appropriate national authority]³ for the purposes of this subsection.]¹

NOTES

Amendments.¹ Section inserted: Children (Leaving Care) Act 2000, s 5.² Subsection inserted: Adoption and Children Act 2002, s 117(1).³ Words substituted: Children and Young Persons Act 2008, s 39, Sch 3, paras 1, 14.

Secure accommodation

25 Use of accommodation for restricting liberty

(1) Subject to the following provisions of this section, a child who is being looked after by a local authority may not be placed, and, if placed, may not be kept, in accommodation provided for the purpose of restricting liberty ('secure accommodation') unless it appears –

(a) that –
    (i)   he has a history of absconding and is likely to abscond from any other description of accommodation; and
    (ii) if he absconds, he is likely to suffer significant harm; or

(b) that if he is kept in any other description of accommodation he is likely to injure himself or other persons.

(2) The [appropriate national authority]² may by regulations –

(a) specify a maximum period –
    (i)   beyond which a child may not be kept in secure accommodation without the authority of the court; and
    (ii) for which the court may authorise a child to be kept in secure accommodation;

(b) empower the court from time to time to authorise a child to be kept in secure accommodation for such further period as the regulations may specify; and

(c) provide that applications to the court under this section shall be made only by local authorities.

(3) It shall be the duty of a court hearing an application under this section to determine whether any relevant criteria for keeping a child in secure accommodation are satisfied in his case.

(4) If a court determines that any such criteria are satisfied, it shall make an order authorising the child to be kept in secure accommodation and specifying the maximum period for which he may be so kept.

(5) On any adjournment of the hearing of an application under this section, a court may make an interim order permitting the child to be kept during the period of the adjournment in secure accommodation.

(6) No court shall exercise the powers conferred by this section in respect of a child who is not legally represented in that court unless, having been informed of his right to apply for [representation funded by the Legal Services Commission as part of the Community Legal Service or Criminal Defence Service][1] and having had the opportunity to do so, he refused or failed to apply.

(7) The [appropriate national authority][2] may by regulations provide that –

   (a)   this section shall or shall not apply to any description of children specified in the regulations;
   (b)   this section shall have effect in relation to children of a description specified in the regulations subject to such modifications as may be so specified;
   (c)   such other provisions as may be so specified shall have effect for the purpose of determining whether a child of a description specified in the regulations may be placed or kept in secure accommodation.

(8) The giving of an authorisation under this section shall not prejudice any power of any court in England and Wales or Scotland to give directions relating to the child to whom the authorisation relates.

(9) This section is subject to section 20(8).

NOTES

Amendments.[1] Words substituted: Access to Justice 1999, s 24, Sch 4, para 45.[2] Words substituted: Children and Young Persons Act 2008, s 39, Sch 3, paras 1, 15.

Definitions. 'Child': s 105(1); 'child who is looked after by a local authority': s 22(1); 'harm': ss 31(9), 105(1); 'local authority': s 105(1); 'secure accommodation': s 25(1); 'significant harm': ss 31(9), (10), 105(1); 'the court': s 92(7).

[Independent reviewing officers

25A Appointment of independent reviewing officer

(1) If a local authority are looking after a child, they must appoint an individual as the independent reviewing officer for that child's case.

(2) The initial appointment under subsection (1) must be made before the child's case is first reviewed in accordance with regulations made under section 26.

(3) If a vacancy arises in respect of a child's case, the local authority must make another appointment under subsection (1) as soon as is practicable.

(4) An appointee must be of a description prescribed in regulations made by the appropriate national authority.]

NOTES

Amendment. [1] Section and preceding cross-heading inserted in relation to England and, for the purpose of making regulations under subs (4), in relation to Wales: Children and Young Persons Act 2008, s 10(1).

[25B Functions of the independent reviewing officer

(1) The independent reviewing officer must –

(a)   monitor the performance by the local authority of their functions in relation to the child's case;

(b)   participate, in accordance with regulations made by the appropriate national authority, in any review of the child's case;

(c)   ensure that any ascertained wishes and feelings of the child concerning the case are given due consideration by the local authority;

(d)   perform any other function which is prescribed in regulations made by the appropriate national authority.

(2) An independent reviewing officer's functions must be performed –

(a)   in such manner (if any) as may be prescribed in regulations made by the appropriate national authority; and

(b)   having regard to such guidance as that authority may issue in relation to the discharge of those functions.

(3) If the independent reviewing officer considers it appropriate to do so, the child's case may be referred by that officer to –

(a)   an officer of the Children and Family Court Advisory and Support Service; or

(b)   a Welsh family proceedings officer.

(4) If the independent reviewing officer is not an officer of the local authority, it is the duty of the authority –

(a)   to co-operate with that individual; and

(b)   to take all such reasonable steps as that individual may require of them to enable that individual's functions under this section to be performed satisfactorily.]

NOTES

Amendment. [1] Section and preceding cross-heading inserted in relation to England and, for the purpose of making regulations under subss (1)(b), (d), (2)(a), in relation to Wales: Children and Young Persons Act 2008, s 10(1).

[25C Referred cases

(1) In relation to children whose cases are referred to officers under section 25B(3), the Lord Chancellor may by regulations –

(a)   extend any functions of the officers in respect of family proceedings (within the meaning of section 12 of the Criminal Justice and Court Services Act 2000) to other proceedings;

(b)   require any functions of the officers to be performed in the manner prescribed by the regulations.

(2) The power to make regulations in this section is exercisable in relation to functions of Welsh family proceedings officers only with the consent of the Welsh Ministers.][1]

NOTES

Amendment. [1] Section inserted in relation to England: Children and Young Persons Act 2008, s 10(2).

Supplemental

26 Review of cases and inquiries into representations

(1) The [appropriate national authority][6] may make regulations requiring the case of each child who is being looked after by a local authority to be reviewed in accordance with the provisions of the regulations.

(2) The regulations may, in particular, make provision –

(a)   as to the manner in which each case is to be reviewed;

(b)   as to the considerations to which the local authority are to have regard in reviewing each case;

(c)   as to the time when each case is first to be reviewed and the frequency of subsequent reviews;

(d)   requiring the authority, before conducting any review, to seek the views of –

    (i)   the child;

    (ii)   his parents;

    (iii)   any person who is not a parent of his but who has parental responsibility for him; and

    (iv)   any other person whose views the authority consider to be relevant,

including, in particular, the views of those persons in relation to any particular matter which is to be considered in the course of the review;

(e)   requiring the authority ...[1], in the case of a child who is in their care [–

    (i)   to keep the section 31A plan for the child under review and, if they are of the opinion that some change is required, to revise the plan, or make a new plan, accordingly;

    (ii)   to consider][1] whether an application should be made to discharge the care order;

(f)   requiring the authority ...[1], in the case of a child in accommodation provided by the authority [–

    (i)   if there is no plan for the future care of the child, to prepare one,

    (ii)   if there is such a plan for the child, to keep it under review and, if they are of the opinion that some change is required, to revise the plan or make a new plan, accordingly,

(iii) to consider][1] whether the accommodation accords with the requirements of this Part;

(g) requiring the authority to inform the child, so far as is reasonably practicable, of any steps he may take under this Act;

(h) requiring the authority to make arrangements, including arrangements with such other bodies providing services as it considers appropriate, to implement any decision which they propose to make in the course, or as a result, of the review;

(i) requiring the authority to notify details of the result of the review and of any decision taken by them in consequence of the review to –

   (i) the child;

   (ii) his parents;

   (iii) any person who is not a parent of his but who has had parental responsibility for him; and

   (iv) any other person whom they consider ought to be notified;

(j) requiring the authority to monitor the arrangements which they have made with a view to ensuring that they comply with the regulations;

[(k) *for the authority to appoint a person in respect of each case to carry out in the prescribed manner the functions mentioned in subsection (2A) and any prescribed function*][1, 7].

[*(2A) The functions referred to in subsection (2)(k) are –*

  (a) participating in the review of the case in question,

  (b) monitoring the performance of the authority's functions in respect of the review,

  (c) referring the case to an officer of the Children and Family Court Advisory and Support Service [or a Welsh family proceedings officer][2]*, if the person appointed under subsection (2)(k) considers it appropriate to do so.*

(2B) A person appointed under subsection (2)(k) must be a person of a prescribed description.

(2C) In relation to children whose cases are referred to officers under subsection (2A)(c), the Lord Chancellor may by regulations –

  (a) extend the functions of the officers in respect of family proceedings (within the meaning of section 12 of the Criminal Justice and Court Services Act 2000) to other proceedings;

  (b) require any functions of the officers to be performed in the manner prescribed by the regulations.][1]

[(2D) The power to make regulations in subsection (2C) is exercisable in relation to functions of Welsh family proceedings officers only with the consent of the [Welsh Ministers][6]*.]*[2, 7]

(3) Every local authority shall establish a procedure for considering any representations (including any complaint) made to them by –

  (a) any child who is being looked after by them or who is not being looked after by them but is in need;

(b)   a parent of his;
(c)   any person who is not a parent of his but who has parental responsibility for him;
(d)   any local authority foster parent;
(e)   such other person as the authority consider has a sufficient interest in the child's welfare to warrant his representations being considered by them,

about the discharge by the authority of any of their [qualifying functions][3] in relation to the child.

[(3A) The following are qualifying functions for the purposes of subsection (3) –

(a)   functions under this Part,
(b)   such functions under Part 4 or 5 as are specified by the [appropriate national authority][6] in regulations.

(3B) The duty under subsection (3) extends to representations (including complaints) made to the authority by –

(a)   any person mentioned in section 3(1) of the Adoption and Children Act 2002 (persons for whose needs provision is made by the Adoption Service) and any other person to whom arrangements for the provision of adoption support services (within the meaning of that Act) extend,
(b)   such other person as the authority consider has sufficient interest in a child who is or may be adopted to warrant his representations being considered by them,

about the discharge by the authority of such functions under the Adoption and Children Act 2002 as are specified by the [appropriate national authority][6] in regulations.][4]

[(3C) The duty under subsection (3) extends to any representations (including complaints) which are made to the authority by –

(a)   a child with respect to whom a special guardianship order is in force,
(b)   a special guardian or a parent of such a child,
(c)   any other person the authority consider has a sufficient interest in the welfare of such a child to warrant his representations being considered by them, or
(d)   any person who has applied for an assessment under section 14F(3) or (4),

about the discharge by the authority of such functions under section 14F as may be specified by the [appropriate national authority][6] in regulations.][5]

(4) The procedure shall ensure that at least one person who is not a member or officer of the authority takes part in –

(a)   the consideration; and
(b)   any discussions which are held by the authority about the action (if any) to be taken in relation to the child in the light of the consideration.

[but this subsection is subject to subsection (5A).]⁴

[(4A) Regulations may be made by the [appropriate national authority]⁶ imposing time limits on the making of representations under this section.]⁴

(5) In carrying out any consideration of representations under this section a local authority shall comply with any regulations made by the [appropriate national authority]⁶ for the purpose of regulating the procedure to be followed.

[(5A) Regulations under subsection (5) may provide that subsection (4) does not apply in relation to any consideration or discussion which takes place as part of a procedure for which provision is made by the regulations for the purpose of resolving informally the matters raised in the representations.]⁴

(6) The [appropriate national authority]⁶ may make regulations requiring local authorities to monitor the arrangements that they have made with a view to ensuring that they comply with any regulations made for the purposes of subsection (5).

(7) Where any representation has been considered under the procedure established by a local authority under this section, the authority shall –

(a) have due regard to the findings of those considering the representation; and

(b) take such steps as are reasonably practicable to notify (in writing) –
   (i) the person making the representation;
   (ii) the child (if the authority consider that he has sufficient understanding); and
   (iii) such other persons (if any) as appear to the authority to be likely to be affected,
   of the authority's decision in the matter and their reasons for taking that decision and of any action which they have taken, or propose to take.

(8) Every local authority shall give such publicity to their procedure for considering representations under this section as they consider appropriate.

NOTES

Amendments.¹ Subsections and paragraph inserted, and words inserted or repealed: Adoption and Children Act 2002, s 118.² Words and subsection inserted: Children Act 2004, s 40, Sch 3, paras 5, 8.³ Words substituted: Adoption and Children Act 2002, s 117(2), (3).⁴ Subsections and words inserted: Adoption and Children Act 2002, s 117(2), (4), (5).⁵ Subsection inserted: Health and Social Care (Community Health and Standards) Act 2003, s 117(1).⁶ Words substituted: Children and Young Persons Act 2008, s 39, Sch 3, paras 1, 16. ⁷ Paragraph (2)(k) and subsections (2A)–(2D) repealed in relation to England: Children and Young Persons Act 2008, ss 10(3), 42, Sch 4.

Definitions. 'Accommodation': s 22(2); 'care order': s 31(11); 'child': s 105(1); 'child in need': s 17(10); 'child who is looked after by the local authority': s 22(1); 'functions': s 105(1); 'local authority': s 105(1); 'local authority foster parent': s 23(3); 'parental responsibility': s 3.

[...²]¹

NOTES

Amendments.[1] Section prospectively inserted: Health and Social Care (Community Health and Standards) Act 2003, s 116(1), from a date to be appointed.[2] Section repealed: Education and Inspections Act 2006, ss 157, 184, Sch 14, paras 9, 10, Sch 18, Pt 5.

[26ZB Representations: further consideration (Wales)

(1) The [Welsh Ministers][2] may by regulations make provision for the further consideration of representations which have been considered by a local authority in Wales under section 24D or section 26.

(2) The regulations may in particular make provision –

(a)   for the further consideration of a representation by an independent panel established under the regulations;
(b)   about the procedure to be followed on the further consideration of a representation;
(c)   for the making of recommendations about the action to be taken as the result of a representation;
(d)   about the making of reports about a representation;
(e)   about the action to be taken by the local authority concerned as a result of the further consideration of a representation;
(f)   for a representation to be referred back to the local authority concerned for reconsideration by the authority.

(3) The regulations may require –

(a)   the making of a payment, in relation to the further consideration of a representation under this section, by any local authority in respect of whose functions the representation is made;
(b)   any such payment to be –
(i)   made to such person or body as may be specified in the regulations;
(ii)   of such amount as may be specified in, or calculated or determined under, the regulations; and
(c)   for an independent panel to review the amount chargeable under paragraph (a) in any particular case and, if the panel thinks fit, to substitute a lesser amount.

(4) The regulations may also –

(a)   provide for different parts or aspects of a representation to be treated differently;
(b)   require the production of information or documents in order to enable a representation to be properly considered;
(c)   authorise the disclosure of information or documents relevant to a representation to a person or body who is further considering a representation under the regulations;

and any such disclosure may be authorised notwithstanding any rule of common law that would otherwise prohibit or restrict the disclosure.][1]

NOTES

Amendments.[1] Section inserted: Health and Social Care (Community Health and Standards) Act 2003, s 116(2).[2] Words substituted: Children and Young Persons Act 2008, s 39, Sch 3, paras 1, 17.

[26A Advocacy services

(1) Every local authority shall make arrangements for the provision of assistance to –

    (a)   persons who make or intend to make representations under section 24D; and

    (b)   children who make or intend to make representations under section 26.

(2) The assistance provided under the arrangements shall include assistance by way of representation.

[(2A) The duty under subsection (1) includes a duty to make arrangements for the provision of assistance where representations under section 24D or 26 are further considered under section …[3] 26ZB.][2]

(3) The arrangements –

    (a)   shall secure that a person may not provide assistance if he is a person who is prevented from doing so by regulations made by the [appropriate national authority][4]; and

    (b)   shall comply with any other provision made by the regulations in relation to the arrangements.

(4) The [appropriate national authority][4] may make regulations requiring local authorities to monitor the steps that they have taken with a view to ensuring that they comply with regulations made for the purposes of subsection (3).

(5) Every local authority shall give such publicity to their arrangements for the provision of assistance under this section as they consider appropriate.][1]

NOTES

Amendments.[1] Section inserted: Adoption and Children Act 2002, s 119.[2] Subsection inserted in relation to Wales: Health and Social Care (Community Health and Standards) Act 2003, s 116(3).[3] Words repealed: Education and Inspections Act 2006, ss 157, 184, Sch 14, paras 9, 11, Sch 18, Pt 5.[4] Words substituted: Children and Young Persons Act 2008, s 39, Sch 3, paras 1, 18.

27 Co-operation between authorities

(1) Where it appears to a local authority that any authority …[1] mentioned in subsection (3) could, by taking any specified action, help in the exercise of any of their functions under this Part, they may request the help of that other authority …[1], specifying the action in question.

(2) An authority whose help is so requested shall comply with the request if it is compatible with their own statutory or other duties and obligations and does not unduly prejudice the discharge of any of their functions.

(3) The [authorities][2] are –

(a)   any local authority;

(b)   ...[9]

(c)   any local housing authority;

(d)   any [[Local Health Board][7], Special Health Authority][4] [, Primary Care Trust][5] [, National Health Service trust or NHS foundation trust][6]; and

(e)   any person authorised by the [appropriate national authority][8] for the purposes of this section.

(4)   ...[3]

NOTES

Amendments.[1] Words repealed: Courts and Legal Services Act 1990, ss 116, 125(7), Sch 16, para 14(a), Sch 20.[2] Words substituted or inserted: Courts and Legal Services Act 1990, s 116, Sch 16, para 14(b).[3] Subsection repealed: Education Act 1993, s 307, Sch 19, para 147.[4] Words substituted: Health Authorities Act 1995, s 2(1), Sch 1, Pt III, para 118(1), (5).[5] Words inserted: Health Act 1999 (Supplementary, Consequential etc Provisions) Order 2000, SI 2000/90.[6] Words inserted: Health and Social Care (Community Health and Standards) Act 2003, s 34, Sch 4, paras 75, 78.[7] Words substituted: SI 2007/961.[8] Words substituted: Children and Young Persons Act 2008, s 39, Sch 3, paras 1, 19.[9] Paragraph repealed: SI 2010/1158.

Definitions. 'Child'; 'functions'; 'health authority'; 'local authority'; 'local education authority'; 'local housing authority'; 'Primary Care Trust'; 'special educational needs': s 105(1).

28 Consultation with local education authorities

...[1]

NOTES

Amendments.[1] Section repealed: SI 2010/1158.

Definitions. 'Appropriate local education authority': s 28(4); 'child': s 105(1); 'child who is looked after by a local authority': s 22(1); 'local authority': s 105(1); 'local education authority': s 105(1); 'special educational needs': s 105(1).

29 Recoupment of cost of providing services etc

(1) Where a local authority provide any service under section 17 or 18, other than advice, guidance or counselling, they may recover from a person specified in subsection (4) such charge for the service as they consider reasonable.

(2) Where the authority are satisfied that that person's means are insufficient for it to be reasonably practicable for him to pay the charge, they shall not require him to pay more than he can reasonably be expected to pay.

(3) No person shall be liable to pay any charge under subsection (1) [for a service provided under section 17 or section 18(1) or (5)][8] at any time when he is in receipt of income support [under][10] [Part VII of the Social Security Contributions and Benefits Act 1992][3][, of any element of child tax credit other than the family element, of working tax credit][10][, of an income-based jobseeker's allowance or of an income-related employment and support allowance][14].

[(3A) No person shall be liable to pay any charge under subsection (1) for a service provided under section 18(2) or (6) at any time when he is in receipt of income support under Part VII of the Social Security and Benefits Act 1992[, of an income-based jobseeker's allowance or of an income-related employment and support allowance][14].][7]

[(3B) No person shall be liable to pay any charge under subsection (1) for a service provided under section 18(2) or (6) at any time when –

    (a)   he is in receipt of guarantee state pension credit under section 1(3)(a) of the State Pension Credit Act 2002, or

    (b)   he is a member of a [couple][12] (within the meaning of that Act) the other member of which is in receipt of guarantee state pension credit.][11]

(4) The persons are –

    (a)   where the service is provided for a child under sixteen, each of his parents;

    (b)   where it is provided for a child who has reached the age of sixteen, the child himself; and

    (c)   where it is provided for a member of the child's family, that member.

(5) Any charge under subsection (1) may, without prejudice to any other method of recovery, be recovered summarily as a civil debt.

(6) Part III of Schedule 2 makes provision in connection with contributions towards the maintenance of children who are being looked after by local authorities and consists of the re-enactment with modifications of provisions in Part V of the Child Care Act 1980.

(7) Where a local authority provide any accommodation under section 20(1) for a child who was (immediately before they began to look after him) ordinarily resident within the area of another local authority, they may recover from that other authority any reasonable expenses incurred by them in providing the accommodation and maintaining him.

(8) Where a local authority provide accommodation under section 21(1) or (2)(a) or (b) for a child who is ordinarily resident within the area of another local authority and they are not maintaining him in –

    (a)   a community home provided by them;

    (b)   a controlled community home; or

    (c)   a hospital vested in the Secretary of State[, the Welsh Ministers][15] [or a Primary Care Trust][6], [or any other hospital made available pursuant to arrangements made by [a Strategic Health Authority,][9] a [[Local Health Board][13]][4]][1] [or a Primary Care Trust][6],

they may recover from that other authority any reasonable expenses incurred by them in providing the accommodation and maintaining him.

(9) [Except where subsection (10) applies,][8] where a local authority comply with any request under section 27(2) in relation to a child or other person who is not ordinarily resident within their area, they may recover from the local authority in whose area the child or person is ordinarily resident any [reasonable expenses][2] incurred by them in respect of that person.

[(10) Where a local authority ('authority A') comply with any request under section 27(2) from another local authority ('authority B') in relation to a child or other person –

    (a)   whose responsible authority is authority B for the purposes of section 23B or 23C; or

    (b)   whom authority B are advising or befriending or to whom they are giving assistance by virtue of section 24(5)(a),

authority A may recover from authority B any reasonable expenses incurred by them in respect of that person.][8]

NOTES

Amendments.[1] Words inserted: National Health Service and Community Care Act 1990, s 66(1), Sch 9, para 36(3).[2] Words substituted: Courts and Legal Services Act 1990, s 116, Sch 16, para 15.[3] Words substituted: Social Security (Consequential Provisions) Act 1992, s 4, Sch 2, para 108.[4] Words substituted: Health Authorities Act 1995, s 2(1), Sch 1, Pt III, para 118(1), (6).[5] Words inserted: Jobseekers Act 1995, s 41(4), Sch 2, para 19.[6] Words inserted: Health Act 1999 (Supplementary, Consequential etc Provisions) Order 2000, SI 2000/90.[7] Words and subsection inserted: Local Government Act 2000, s 103.[8] Words and subsection inserted: Children (Leaving Care) Act 2000, s 7(3).[9] Words inserted: National Health Service Reform and Health Care Professions Act 2002 (Supplementary, Consequential etc Provisions) Regulations 2002, SI 2002/2469, reg 4, Sch 1, para 16(1), (2).[10] Word substituted: Tax Credits Act 2002, s 47, Sch 3, paras 15, 18.[11] Subsection inserted: State Pension Credit Act 2002, s 14, Sch 2, Pt 3, para 30.[12] Word substituted: Civil Partnership Act 2004 (Overseas Relationships and Consequential, etc Amendments) Order 2005, SI 2005/3129, art 4(4), Sch 4, para 9.[13] Words substituted: SI 2007/961.[14] Words substituted: Welfare Reform Act 2007, s 28(1), Sch 3, para 6(1), (4).[15] Words inserted: Children and Young Persons Act 2008, s 39, Sch 3, paras 1, 20.

Definitions. 'Child': s 105(1); 'child who is looked after by a local authority': s 22(1); 'community home': s 53(1); 'controlled community home': s 53(4); 'hospital': s 105(1); 'local authority': s 105(1); 'ordinary residence': s 105(6); 'service': s 105(1).

30 Miscellaneous

(1) Nothing in this Part shall affect any duty imposed on a local authority by or under any other enactment.

(2) Any question arising under section 20(2), 21(3) or 29(7) to (9) as to the ordinary residence of a child shall be determined by agreement between the local authorities concerned or, in default of agreement, by the [determining authority][1].

[(2A) For the purposes of subsection (2) 'the determining authority' is –

    (a)   in a case where all the local authorities concerned are in Wales, the Welsh Ministers;

    (b)   in any other case, the Secretary of State.

(2B) In a case where –

    (a)   the determining authority is the Secretary of State, and

    (b)   one or more of the local authorities concerned are in Wales,

the Secretary of State must consult the Welsh Ministers before making a determination for the purposes of subsection (2).][1]

(3) ...²

(4) The [appropriate national authority]¹ may make regulations for determining, as respects any [education]² functions specified in the regulations, whether a child who is being looked after by a local authority is to be treated, for purposes so specified, as a child of parents of sufficient resources or as a child of parents without resources.

NOTES

Amendments.¹ Words substituted and subsections inserted: Children and Young Persons Act 2008, s 39, Sch 3, paras 1, 21.² Subsection repealed and word substituted: SI 2010/1158.

Definitions. 'Child who is looked after by a local authority': s 22(1); 'functions': s 105(1); 'local authority': s 105(1); 'local education authority': s 105(1); 'ordinary residence': s 105(6).

[30A Meaning of appropriate national authority

In this Part 'the appropriate national authority' means –

    (a)   in relation to England, the Secretary of State; and
    (b)   in relation to Wales, the Welsh Ministers.]¹

NOTES

Amendment.¹ Section inserted: Children and Young Persons Act 2008, s 39, Sch 3, paras 1, 22.

PART IV
CARE AND SUPERVISION

General

31 Care and supervision orders

(1) On the application of any local authority or authorised person, the court may make an order –

    (a)   placing the child with respect to whom the application is made in the care of a designated local authority; or
    (b)   putting him under the supervision of a designated local authority ...².

(2) A court may only make a care order or supervision order if it is satisfied –

    (a)   that the child concerned is suffering, or is likely to suffer, significant harm; and
    (b)   that the harm, or likelihood of harm, is attributable to –
        (i)   the care given to the child, or likely to be given to him if the order were not made, not being what it would be reasonable to expect a parent to give to him; or
        (ii)   the child's being beyond parental control.

(3) No care order or supervision order may be made with respect to a child who has reached the age of seventeen (or sixteen, in the case of a child who is married).

[(3A) No care order may be made with respect to a child until the court has considered a section 31A plan.]⁴

(4) An application under this section may be made on its own or in any other family proceedings.

(5) The court may –

(a)   on an application for a care order, make a supervision order;
(b)   on an application for a supervision order, make a care order.

(6) Where an authorised person proposes to make an application under this section he shall –

(a)   if it is reasonably practicable to do so; and
(b)   before making the application,

consult the local authority appearing to him to be the authority in whose area the child concerned is ordinarily resident.

(7) An application made by an authorised person shall not be entertained by the court if, at the time when it is made, the child concerned is –

(a)   the subject of an earlier application for a care order, or supervision order, which has not been disposed of; or
(b)   subject to –
    (i)   a care order or supervision order;
    [(ii)   a youth rehabilitation order within the meaning of Part 1 of the Criminal Justice and Immigration Act 2008; or][5]
    (iii)   a supervision requirement within the meaning of [Part II of the Children (Scotland) Act 1995][1].

(8) The local authority designated in a care order must be –

(a)   the authority within whose area the child is ordinarily resident; or
(b)   where the child does not reside in the area of a local authority, the authority within whose area any circumstances arose in consequence of which the order is being made.

(9) In this section –

'authorised person' means –
    (a)   the National Society for the Prevention of Cruelty to Children and any of its officers; and
    (b)   any person authorised by order of the Secretary of State to bring proceedings under this section and any officer of a body which is so authorised;

'harm' means ill-treatment or the impairment of health or development [including, for example, impairment suffered from seeing or hearing the ill-treatment of another][3];

'development' means physical, intellectual, emotional, social or behavioural development;

'health' means physical or mental health; and

'ill-treatment' includes sexual abuse and forms of ill-treatment which are not physical.

(10) Where the question of whether harm suffered by a child is significant turns on the child's health or development, his health or development shall be compared with that which could reasonably be expected of a similar child.

(11) In this Act –

'a care order' means (subject to section 105(1)) an order under subsection (1)(a) and (except where express provision to the contrary is made) includes an interim care order made under section 38; and

'a supervision order' means an order under subsection (1)(b) and (except where express provision to the contrary is made) includes an interim supervision order made under section 38.

NOTES

Amendments.[1] Words substituted: Children (Scotland) Act 1995, s 105(4), Sch 4, para 48(1), (2).[2] Words omitted: Criminal Justice and Court Services Act 2000, ss 74, 75, Sch 7, paras 87, 90, Sch 8.[3] Words inserted: Adoption and Children Act 2002, s 120.[4] Subsection inserted: Adoption and Children Act 2002, s 121(1).[5] Paragraph substituted: Criminal Justice and Immigration Act 2008, s 6(2), Sch 4, Pt 1, paras 33, 35.

Definitions. 'Authorised person': s 31(9); 'care order': ss 31(11), 105(1); 'child': s 105(1); 'designated local authority': s 31(8); 'development': s 31(9); 'family proceedings': s 8(3); 'harm': s 31(9); 'health': s 31(9); 'ill-treatment': s 31(9); 'local authority': s 105(1); 'ordinary residence': s 105(6); 'significant harm': s 31(10); 'supervision order': s 31(11); 'the court': s 92(7).

[31A Care orders: care plans

(1) Where an application is made on which a care order might be made with respect to a child, the appropriate local authority must, within such time as the court may direct, prepare a plan ('a care plan') for the future care of the child.

(2) While the application is pending, the authority must keep any care plan prepared by them under review and, if they are of the opinion some change is required, revise the plan, or make a new plan, accordingly.

(3) A care plan must give any prescribed information and do so in the prescribed manner.

(4) For the purposes of this section, the appropriate local authority, in relation to a child in respect of whom a care order might be made, is the local authority proposed to be designated in the order.

(5) In section 31(3A) and this section, references to a care order do not include an interim care order.

(6) A plan prepared, or treated as prepared, under this section is referred to in this Act as a 'section 31A plan'.][1]

Amendments.[1] Section inserted: Adoption and Children Act 2002, s 121(2).

32 Period within which application for order under this Part must be disposed of

(1) A court hearing an application for an order under this Part shall (in the light of any rules made by virtue of subsection (2)) –

(a)   draw up a timetable with a view to disposing of the application without delay; and

(b)   give such directions as it considers appropriate for the purpose of ensuring, so far as is reasonably practicable, that that timetable is adhered to.

(2) Rules of court may –

(a)   specify periods within which specified steps must be taken in relation to such proceedings; and

(b)   make other provision with respect to such proceedings for the purpose of ensuring, so far as is reasonably practicable, that they are disposed of without delay.

NOTES

Definition. 'The court': s 92(7).

Care orders

33 Effect of care order

(1) Where a care order is made with respect to a child it shall be the duty of the local authority designated by the order to receive the child into their care and to keep him in their care while the order remains in force.

(2) Where –

(a)   a care order has been made with respect to a child on the application of an authorised person; but

(b)   the local authority designated by the order was not informed that that person proposed to make the application,

the child may be kept in the care of that person until received into the care of the authority.

(3) While a care order is in force with respect to a child, the local authority designated by the order shall –

(a)   have parental responsibility for the child; and

(b)   have the power (subject to the following provisions of this section) to determine the extent to which [a parent or guardian of the child]
       [(i)   a parent, guardian or special guardian of the child; or
       (ii)   a person who by virtue of section 4A has parental responsibility for the child,][1]
       may meet his parental responsibility for him.

(4) The authority may not exercise the power in subsection (3)(b) unless they are satisfied that it is necessary to do so in order to safeguard or promote the child's welfare.

(5) Nothing in subsection (3)(b) shall prevent [a person mentioned in that provision who has care of the child][1] from doing what is reasonable in all the circumstances of the case for the purpose of safeguarding or promoting his welfare.

(6) While a care order is in force with respect to a child, the local authority designated by the order shall not –

    (a)   cause the child to be brought up in any religious persuasion other than that in which he would have been brought up if the order had not been made; or

    (b)   have the right –

        [(i)   to consent or refuse to consent to the making of an application with respect to the child under section 18 of the Adoption Act 1976;][2]

        (ii)   to agree or refuse to agree to the making of an adoption order, or an order under [section 84 of the Adoption and Children Act 2002][3], with respect to the child; or

        (iii)   to appoint a guardian for the child.

(7) While a care order is in force with respect to a child, no person may –

    (a)   cause the child to be known by a new surname; or

    (b)   remove him from the United Kingdom,

without either the written consent of every person who has parental responsibility for the child or the leave of the court.

(8) Subsection (7)(b) does not –

    (a)   prevent the removal of such a child, for a period of less than one month, by the authority in whose care he is; or

    (b)   apply to arrangements for such a child to live outside England and Wales (which are governed by paragraph 19 of Schedule 2).

(9) The power in subsection (3)(b) is subject (in addition to being subject to the provisions of this section) to any right, duty, power, responsibility or authority which [a person mentioned in that provision][3] has in relation to the child and his property by virtue of any other enactment.

NOTES

Amendments.[1] Words substituted: Adoption and Children Act 2002, s 139(1), Sch 3, paras 54, 63(a), (b).[2] Subparagraph repealed: Adoption and Children Act 2002, s 139(1), Sch 3, paras 54, 63(c)(i).[3] Words substituted: Adoption and Children Act 2002, s 139(1), Sch 3, paras 54, 63(c)(ii), (d).

Definitions. 'Authorised person': s 31(9); 'care order': ss 31(11), 105(1); 'designated local authority': s 31(8); 'guardian of the child': s 105(1); 'local authority': s 105(1); 'parental responsibility': s 3; 'the court': s 92(7).

34 Parental contact etc with children in care

(1) Where a child is in the care of a local authority, the authority shall (subject to the provisions of this section) allow the child reasonable contact with –

(a)   his parents;

(b)   any guardian [or special guardian]¹ of his;

[(ba) any person who by virtue of section 4A has parental responsibility for him;]¹

(c)   where there was a residence order in force with respect to the child immediately before the care order was made, the person in whose favour the order was made; and

(d)   where, immediately before the care order was made, a person had care of the child by virtue of an order made in the exercise of the High Court's inherent jurisdiction with respect to children, that person.

(2) On an application made by the authority or the child, the court may make such order as it considers appropriate with respect to the contact which is to be allowed between the child and any named person.

(3) On an application made by –

(a)   any person mentioned in paragraphs (a) to (d) of subsection (1); or

(b)   any person who has obtained the leave of the court to make the application,

the court may make such order as it considers appropriate with respect to the contact which is to be allowed between the child and that person.

(4) On an application made by the authority or the child, the court may make an order authorising the authority to refuse to allow contact between the child and any person who is mentioned in paragraphs (a) to (d) of subsection (1) and named in the order.

(5) When making a care order with respect to a child, or in any family proceedings in connection with a child who is in the care of a local authority, the court may make an order under this section, even though no application for such an order has been made with respect to the child, if it considers that the order should be made.

(6) An authority may refuse to allow the contact that would otherwise be required by virtue of subsection (1) or an order under this section if –

(a)   they are satisfied that it is necessary to do so in order to safeguard or promote the child's welfare; and

(b)   the refusal –

(i)   is decided upon as a matter of urgency; and

(ii) does not last for more than seven days.

(7) An order under this section may impose such conditions as the court considers appropriate.

(8) The Secretary of State may by regulations make provision as to –

(a)   the steps to be taken by a local authority who have exercised their powers under subsection (6);

(b)   the circumstances in which, and conditions subject to which, the terms of any order under this section may be departed from by agreement between the local authority and the person in relation to whom the order is made;

(c)   notification by a local authority of any variation or suspension of arrangements made (otherwise than under an order under this section) with a view to affording any person contact with a child to whom this section applies.

(9) The court may vary or discharge any order made under this section on the application of the authority, the child concerned or the person named in the order.

(10) An order under this section may be made either at the same time as the care order itself or later.

(11) Before making a care order with respect to any child the court shall –

(a)   consider the arrangements which the authority have made, or propose to make, for affording any person contact with a child to whom this section applies; and

(b)   invite the parties to the proceedings to comment on those arrangements.

NOTES

Amendments.[1] Words and paragraph inserted: Adoption and Children Act 2002, s 139(1), Sch 3, paras 54, 64(a), (b).

Definitions. 'Care order': ss 31(11), 105(1); 'child': s 105(1); 'family proceedings': s 8(3); 'guardian of a child': s 105(1); 'local authority': s 105(1); 'residence order': s 8(1); 'the court': s 92(7).

Supervision orders

35 Supervision orders

(1) While a supervision order is in force it shall be the duty of the supervisor –

(a)   to advise, assist and befriend the supervised child;

(b)   to take such steps as are reasonably necessary to give effect to the order; and

(c)   where –

(i)   the order is not wholly complied with; or

(ii)   the supervisor considers that the order may no longer be necessary,

to consider whether or not to apply to the court for its variation or discharge.

(2) Parts I and II of Schedule 3 make further provision with respect to supervision orders.

NOTES

Definitions. 'Supervised child', 'supervisor': s 105(1); 'supervision order': s 31(11); 'the court': s 92(7).

PART I – Statutes

36 Education supervision orders

(1) On the application of any [local authority][4], the court may make an order putting the child with respect to whom the application is made under the supervision of a designated [local authority][4].

(2) In this Act 'an education supervision order' means an order under subsection (1).

(3) A court may only make an education supervision order if it is satisfied that the child concerned is of compulsory school age and is not being properly educated.

(4) For the purposes of this section, a child is being properly educated only if he is receiving efficient full-time education suitable to his age, ability and aptitude and any special educational needs he may have.

(5) Where a child is –

(a)   the subject of a school attendance order which is in force under [section 437 of the Education Act 1996][2] and which has not been complied with; or

[(b)   is not attending regularly within the meaning of section 444 of that Act –

(i)   a school at which he is a registered pupil,

(ii)   any place at which education is provided for him in the circumstances mentioned in subsection (1) of section 444ZA of that Act, or

(iii)   any place which he is required to attend in the circumstances mentioned in subsection (2) of that section][3],

then, unless it is proved that he is being properly educated, it shall be assumed that he is not.

(6) An education supervision order may not be made with respect to a child who is in the care of a local authority.

(7) The [local authority][4] designated in an education supervision order must be –

(a)   the authority within whose area the child concerned is living or will live; or

(b)   where –

(i)   the child is a registered pupil at a school; and

(ii)   the authority mentioned in paragraph (a) and the authority within whose area the school is situated agree,

the latter authority.

(8) Where a [local authority][4] propose to make an application for an education supervision order they shall, before making the application, consult the ...[1] appropriate local authority [if different][4].

(9) The appropriate local authority is –

(a) in the case of a child who is being provided with accommodation by, or on behalf of, a local authority, that authority; and

(b) in any other case, the local authority within whose area the child concerned lives, or will live.

(10) Part III of Schedule 3 makes further provision with respect to education supervision orders.

NOTES

Amendments.[1] Words repealed: Education Act 1993, s 307, Sch 19, para 149, Sch 21, Part II.[2] Words substituted: Education Act 1996, s 582(1), Sch 37, para 85.[3] Paragraph substituted: Education Act 2005, s 117, Sch 18, para 1.[4] Words substituted and inserted: SI 2010/1158.

Definitions. 'Appropriate local authority': s 36(9); 'child': s 105(1); 'education supervision order': s 36(2); 'local authority': s 105(1); 'local education authority': s 105(1); 'properly educated': s 36(4); 'registered pupil': s 105(1); 'school': s 105(1); 'special educational needs': s 105(1); 'the court': s 92(7).

Powers of court

37 Powers of court in certain family proceedings

(1) Where, in any family proceedings in which a question arises with respect to the welfare of any child, it appears to the court that it may be appropriate for a care or supervision order to be made with respect to him, the court may direct the appropriate authority to undertake an investigation of the child's circumstances.

(2) Where the court gives a direction under this section the local authority concerned shall, when undertaking the investigation, consider whether they should –

(a) apply for a care order or for a supervision order with respect to the child;

(b) provide services or assistance for the child or his family; or

(c) take any other action with respect to the child.

(3) Where a local authority undertake an investigation under this section, and decide not to apply for a care order or supervision order with respect to the child concerned, they shall inform the court of –

(a) their reasons for so deciding;

(b) any service or assistance which they have provided, or intend to provide, for the child and his family; and

(c) any other action which they have taken, or propose to take, with respect to the child.

(4) The information shall be given to the court before the end of the period of eight weeks beginning with the date of the direction, unless the court otherwise directs.

(5) The local authority named in a direction under subsection (1) must be –

(a) the authority in whose area the child is ordinarily resident; or

(b)   where the child [is not ordinarily resident]¹ in the area of a local authority, the authority within whose area any circumstances arose in consequence of which the direction is being given.

(6) If, on the conclusion of any investigation or review under this section, the authority decide not to apply for a care order or supervision order with respect to the child –

(a)   they shall consider whether it would be appropriate to review the case at a later date; and

(b)   if they decide that it would be, they shall determine the date on which that review is to begin.

NOTES

Amendments.¹ Words substituted: Courts and Legal Services Act 1990, s 116, Sch 16, para 16.

Definitions. 'Appropriate authority': s 37(5); 'care order': ss 31(11), 105(1); 'child': s 105(1); 'family proceedings': s 8(3); 'local authority': s 105(1); 'ordinary residence': s 105(6); 'supervision order': s 31(11); 'the court': s 92(7).

38 Interim orders

(1) Where –

(a)   in any proceedings on an application for a care order or supervision order, the proceedings are adjourned; or

(b)   the court gives a direction under section 37(1),

the court may make an interim care order or an interim supervision order with respect to the child concerned.

(2) A court shall not make an interim care order or interim supervision order under this section unless it is satisfied that there are reasonable grounds for believing that the circumstances with respect to the child are as mentioned in section 31(2).

(3) Where, in any proceedings on an application for a care order or supervision order, a court makes a residence order with respect to the child concerned, it shall also make an interim supervision order with respect to him unless satisfied that his welfare will be satisfactorily safeguarded without an interim order being made.

(4) An interim order made under or by virtue of this section shall have effect for such period as may be specified in the order, but shall in any event cease to have effect on whichever of the following events first occurs –

(a)   the expiry of the period of eight weeks beginning with the date on which the order is made;

(b)   if the order is the second or subsequent such order made with respect to the same child in the same proceedings, the expiry of the relevant period;

(c)   in a case which falls within subsection (1)(a), the disposal of the application;

(d)   in a case which falls within subsection (1)(b), the disposal of an application for a care order or supervision order made by the authority with respect to the child;

(e)   in a case which falls within subsection (1)(b) and in which –

    (i)   the court has given a direction under section 37(4), but

    (ii)   no application for a care order or supervision order has been made with respect to the child,

the expiry of the period fixed by that direction.

(5) In subsection (4)(b) 'the relevant period' means –

(a)   the period of four weeks beginning with the date on which the order in question is made; or

(b)   the period of eight weeks beginning with the date on which the first order was made if that period ends later than the period mentioned in paragraph (a).

(6) Where the court makes an interim care order, or interim supervision order, it may give such directions (if any) as it considers appropriate with regard to the medical or psychiatric examination or other assessment of the child; but if the child is of sufficient understanding to make an informed decision he may refuse to submit to the examination or other assessment.

(7) A direction under subsection (6) may be to the effect that there is to be –

(a)   no such examination or assessment; or

(b)   no such examination or assessment unless the court directs otherwise.

(8) A direction under subsection (6) may be –

(a)   given when the interim order is made or at any time while it is in force; and

(b)   varied at any time on the application of any person falling within any class of person prescribed by rules of court for the purposes of this subsection.

(9) Paragraphs 4 and 5 of Schedule 3 shall not apply in relation to an interim supervision order.

(10) Where a court makes an order under or by virtue of this section it shall, in determining the period for which the order is to be in force, consider whether any party who was, or might have been, opposed to the making of the order was in a position to argue his case against the order in full.

NOTES

Definitions. 'Care order': s 31(11); 'child': s 105(1); 'relevant period': s 38(5); 'residence order': s 8(1); 'supervision order': s 31(11); 'the court': s 92(7).

[38A Power to include exclusion requirement in interim care order

(1) Where –

PART I – Statutes

(a)   on being satisfied that there are reasonable grounds for believing that the circumstances with respect to a child are as mentioned in section 31(2)(a) and (b)(i), the court makes an interim care order with respect to a child, and

(b)   the conditions mentioned in subsection (2) are satisfied,

the court may include an exclusion requirement in the interim care order.

(2) The conditions are –

(a)   that there is reasonable cause to believe that, if a person ('the relevant person') is excluded from a dwelling-house in which the child lives, the child will cease to suffer, or cease to be likely to suffer, significant harm, and

(b)   that another person living in the dwelling-house (whether a parent of the child or some other person) –

(i)   is able and willing to give to the child the care which it would be reasonable to expect a parent to give him, and

(ii)   consents to the inclusion of the exclusion requirement.

(3) For the purposes of this section an exclusion requirement is any one or more of the following –

(a)   a provision requiring the relevant person to leave a dwelling-house in which he is living with the child,

(b)   a provision prohibiting the relevant person from entering a dwelling-house in which the child lives, and

(c)   a provision excluding the relevant person from a defined area in which a dwelling-house in which the child lives is situated.

(4) The court may provide that the exclusion requirement is to have effect for a shorter period than the other provisions of the interim care order.

(5) Where the court makes an interim care order containing an exclusion requirement, the court may attach a power of arrest to the exclusion requirement.

(6) Where the court attaches a power of arrest to an exclusion requirement of an interim care order, it may provide that the power of arrest is to have effect for a shorter period than the exclusion requirement.

(7) Any period specified for the purposes of subsection (4) or (6) may be extended by the court (on one or more occasions) on an application to vary or discharge the interim care order.

(8) Where a power of arrest is attached to an exclusion requirement of an interim care order by virtue of subsection (5), a constable may arrest without warrant any person whom he has reasonable cause to believe to be in breach of the requirement.

(9) Sections 47(7), (11) and (12) and 48 of, and Schedule 5 to, the Family Law Act 1996 shall have effect in relation to a person arrested under subsection (8) of this section as they have effect in relation to a person arrested under section 47(6) of that Act.

(10) If, while an interim care order containing an exclusion requirement is in force, the local authority have removed the child from the dwelling-house from which the relevant person is excluded to other accommodation for a continuous period of more than 24 hours, the interim care order shall cease to have effect in so far as it imposes the exclusion requirement.][1]

NOTES

Amendments.[1] Section inserted: Family Law Act 1996, s 52, Sch 6, para 1.

[38B Undertakings relating to interim care orders

(1) In any case where the court has power to include an exclusion requirement in an interim care order, the court may accept an undertaking from the relevant person.

(2) No power of arrest may be attached to any undertaking given under subsection (1).

(3) An undertaking given to a court under subsection (1) –

(a)   shall be enforceable as if it were an order of the court, and

(b)   shall cease to have effect if, while it is in force, the local authority have removed the child from the dwelling-house from which the relevant person is excluded to other accommodation for a continuous period of more than 24 hours.

(4) This section has effect without prejudice to the powers of the High Court and county court apart from this section.

(5) In this section 'exclusion requirement' and 'relevant person' have the same meaning as in section 38A.][1]

NOTES

Amendments.[1] Section inserted: Family Law Act 1996, s 52, Sch 6, para 1.

39 Discharge and variation etc of care orders and supervision orders

(1) A care order may be discharged by the court on the application of –

(a)   any person who has parental responsibility for the child;

(b)   the child himself; or

(c)   the local authority designated by the order.

(2) A supervision order may be varied or discharged by the court on the application of –

(a)   any person who has parental responsibility for the child;

(b)   the child himself; or

(c)   the supervisor.

(3) On the application of a person who is not entitled to apply for the order to be discharged, but who is a person with whom the child is living, a supervision order may be varied by the court in so far as it imposes a requirement which affects that person.

[(3A) On the application of a person who is not entitled to apply for the order to be discharged, but who is a person to whom an exclusion requirement contained in the order applies, an interim care order may be varied or discharged by the court in so far as it imposes the exclusion requirement.

(3B) Where a power of arrest has been attached to an exclusion requirement of an interim care order, the court may, on the application of any person entitled to apply for the discharge of the order so far as it imposes the exclusion requirement, vary or discharge the order in so far as it confers a power of arrest (whether or not any application has been made to vary or discharge any other provision of the order).][1]

(4) Where a care order is in force with respect to a child the court may, on the application of any person entitled to apply for the order to be discharged, substitute a supervision order for the care order.

(5) When a court is considering whether to substitute one order for another under subsection (4) any provision of this Act which would otherwise require section 31(2) to be satisfied at the time when the proposed order is substituted or made shall be disregarded.

NOTES

Amendments.[1] Subsections inserted: Family Law Act 1996, s 52, Sch 6, para 2.

Definitions. 'Care order': ss 31(11), 105(1); 'child': s 105(1); 'local authority': s 105(1); 'supervision order': s 31(11); 'supervisor': s 105(1); 'the court': s 92(7).

40 Orders pending appeals in cases about care or supervision orders

(1) Where –

    (a)   a court dismisses an application for a care order; and

    (b)   at the time when the court dismisses the application, the child concerned is the subject of an interim care order,

the court may make a care order with respect to the child to have effect subject to such directions (if any) as the court may see fit to include in the order.

(2) Where –

    (a)   a court dismisses an application for a care order, or an application for a supervision order; and

    (b)   at the time when the court dismisses the application, the child concerned is the subject of an interim supervision order,

the court may make a supervision order with respect to the child to have effect subject to such directions (if any) as the court may see fit to include in the order.

(3) Where a court grants an application to discharge a care order or supervision order, it may order that –

    (a)   its decision is not to have effect; or

    (b)   the care order, or supervision order, is to continue to have effect but subject to such directions as the court sees fit to include in the order.

(4) An order made under this section shall only have effect for such period, not exceeding the appeal period, as may be specified in the order.

(5) Where –

(a) an appeal is made against any decision of a court under this section; or
(b) any application is made to the appellate court in connection with a proposed appeal against that decision,

the appellate court may extend the period for which the order in question is to have effect, but not so as to extend it beyond the end of the appeal period.

(6) In this section 'the appeal period' means –

(a) where an appeal is made against the decision in question, the period between the making of that decision and the determination of the appeal; and
(b) otherwise, the period during which an appeal may be made against the decision.

NOTES

Definitions. 'Appeal period': s 40(6); 'care order': ss 31(11), 105(1); 'child': s 105(1); 'the court': s 92(7).

[Representation of child][2]

41 Representation of child and of his interests in certain proceedings

(1) For the purpose of any specified proceedings, the court shall appoint [an officer of the Service][2] [or a Welsh family proceedings officer][3] for the child concerned unless satisfied that it is not necessary to do so in order to safeguard his interests.

(2) The [officer of the Service][2] [or Welsh family proceedings officer][3] shall –

(a) be appointed in accordance with rules of court; and
(b) be under a duty to safeguard the interests of the child in the manner prescribed by such rules.

(3) Where –

(a) the child concerned is not represented by a solicitor; and
(b) any of the conditions mentioned in subsection (4) is satisfied,

the court may appoint a solicitor to represent him.

(4) The conditions are that –

(a) no [officer of the Service][2] [or Welsh family proceedings officer][3] has been appointed for the child;
(b) the child has sufficient understanding to instruct a solicitor and wishes to do so;
(c) it appears to the court that it would be in the child's best interests for him to be represented by a solicitor.

(5) Any solicitor appointed under or by virtue of this section shall be appointed, and shall represent the child, in accordance with rules of court.

(6) In this section 'specified proceedings' means any proceedings –

(a) on an application for a care order or supervision order;

(b) in which the court has given a direction under section 37(1) and has made, or is considering whether to make, an interim care order;

(c) on an application for the discharge of a care order or the variation or discharge of a supervision order;

(d) on an application under section 39(4);

(e) in which the court is considering whether to make a residence order with respect to a child who is the subject of a care order;

(f) with respect to contact between a child who is the subject of a care order and any other person;

(g) under Part V;

(h) on an appeal against –

    (i) the making of, or refusal to make, a care order, supervision order or any order under section 34;

    (ii) the making of, or refusal to make, a residence order with respect to a child who is the subject of a care order; or

    (iii) the variation or discharge, or refusal of an application to vary or discharge, an order of a kind mentioned in sub-paragraph (i) or (ii);

    (iv) the refusal of an application under section 39(4);

    (v) the making of, or refusal to make, an order under Part V; or

[(hh) on an application for the making or revocation of a placement order (within the meaning of section 21 of the Adoption and Children Act 2002);][5]

(i) which are specified for the time being, for the purposes of this section, by rules of court.

[(6A) The proceedings which may be specified under subsection (6)(i) include (for example) proceedings for the making, varying or discharging of a section 8 order.][4]

(7)–(9) ...[2]

(10) Rules of court may make provision as to –

(a) the assistance which any [officer of the Service][2] [or Welsh family proceedings officer][3] may be required by the court to give to it;

(b) the consideration to be given by any [officer of the Service][2] [or Welsh family proceedings officer][3], where an order of a specified kind has been made in the proceedings in question, as to whether to apply for the variation or discharge of the order;

(c) the participation of [officers of the Service][2] [or Welsh family proceedings officers][3] in reviews, of a kind specified in the rules, which are conducted by the court.

(11) Regardless of any enactment or rule of law which would otherwise prevent it from doing so, the court may take account of –

(a)   any statement contained in a report made by [an officer of the Service]² [or a Welsh family proceedings officer]³ who is appointed under this section for the purpose of the proceedings in question; and

(b)   any evidence given in respect of the matters referred to in the report,

in so far as the statement or evidence is, in the opinion of the court, relevant to the question which the court is considering.

[(12) ...²]¹

NOTES

Amendments.¹ Subsection inserted: Courts and Legal Services Act 1990, s 116, Sch 16, para 17.² Words substituted or omitted: Criminal Justice and Court Services Act 2000, ss 74, 75, Sch 7, paras 87, 91, Sch 8.³ Words inserted: Children Act 2004, s 40, Sch 3, paras 5, 9.⁴ Subsection inserted: Adoption and Children Act 2002, s 122(1)(b).⁵ Paragraph inserted: Adoption and Children Act 2002, s 122(1)(a).

Definitions. 'Care order': ss 31(11), 105(1); 'child': s 105(1); 'local authority': s 105(1); 'residence order': s 8(1); 'specified proceedings': s 41(6); 'supervision order': s 31(11); 'the court': s 92(7).

42 [Right of officer of the Service to have access to local authority records]⁵

(1) Where [an officer of the Service]⁵ [or Welsh family proceedings officer]⁷ has been appointed [under section 41]⁵ he shall have the right at all reasonable times to examine and take copies of –

(a)   any records of, or held by, a local authority [or an authorised person]¹ which were compiled in connection with the making, or proposed making, by any person of any application under this Act with respect to the child concerned; ...²

(b)   any ...² records of, or held by, a local authority which were compiled in connection with any functions which [are social services functions within the meaning of]⁶ the Local Authority Social Services Act 1970, so far as those records relate to that child [; or

(c)   any records of, or held by, an authorised person which were compiled in connection with the activities of that person, so far as those records relate to that child.]³

(2) Where [an officer of the Service]⁵ [or Welsh family proceedings officer]⁷ takes a copy of any record which he is entitled to examine under this section, that copy or any part of it shall be admissible as evidence of any matter referred to in any –

(a)   report which he makes to the court in the proceedings in question; or

(b)   evidence which he gives in those proceedings.

(3) Subsection (2) has effect regardless of any enactment or rule of law which would otherwise prevent the record in question being admissible in evidence.

[(4) In this section 'authorised person' has the same meaning as in section 31.]⁴

NOTES

Amendments.¹ Words inserted: Courts and Legal Services Act 1990, s 116, Sch 16, para 18(2). ² Words repealed: Courts and Legal Services Act 1990, s 125(7), Sch 20.³ Words inserted: Courts and

Legal Services Act 1990, s 116, Sch 16, para 18(3).[4] Words inserted: Courts and Legal Services Act 1990, s 116, Sch 16, para 18(4).[5] Words substituted: Criminal Justice and Court Services Act 2000, s 74, Sch 7, paras 87, 92.[6] Words substituted: Local Government Act 2000, s 107, Sch 5, para 20.[7] Words inserted: Children Act 2004, s 40, Sch 3, paras 5, 10.

Definitions. 'Child': s 105(1); 'functions': s 105(1); 'local authority': s 105(1).

PART V
PROTECTION OF CHILDREN

43 Child assessment orders

(1) On the application of a local authority or authorised person for an order to be made under this section with respect to a child, the court may make the order if, but only if, it is satisfied that –

    (a)   the applicant has reasonable cause to suspect that the child is suffering, or is likely to suffer, significant harm;

    (b)   an assessment of the state of the child's health or development, or of the way in which he has been treated, is required to enable the applicant to determine whether or not the child is suffering, or is likely to suffer, significant harm; and

    (c)   it is unlikely that such an assessment will be made, or be satisfactory, in the absence of an order under this section.

(2) In this Act 'a child assessment order' means an order under this section.

(3) A court may treat an application under this section as an application for an emergency protection order.

(4) No court shall make a child assessment order if it is satisfied –

    (a)   that there are grounds for making an emergency protection order with respect to the child; and

    (b)   that it ought to make such an order rather than a child assessment order.

(5) A child assessment order shall –

    (a)   specify the date by which the assessment is to begin; and

    (b)   have effect for such period, not exceeding 7 days beginning with that date, as may be specified in the order.

(6) Where a child assessment order is in force with respect to a child it shall be the duty of any person who is in a position to produce the child –

    (a)   to produce him to such person as may be named in the order; and

    (b)   to comply with such directions relating to the assessment of the child as the court thinks fit to specify in the order.

(7) A child assessment order authorises any person carrying out the assessment, or any part of the assessment, to do so in accordance with the terms of the order.

(8) Regardless of subsection (7), if the child is of sufficient understanding to make an informed decision he may refuse to submit to a medical or psychiatric examination or other assessment.

(9) The child may only be kept away from home –

    (a)   in accordance with directions specified in the order;

    (b)   if it is necessary for the purposes of the assessment; and

    (c)   for such period or periods as may be specified in the order.

(10) Where the child is to be kept away from home, the order shall contain such directions as the court thinks fit with regard to the contact that he must be allowed to have with other persons while away from home.

(11) Any person making an application for a child assessment order shall take such steps as are reasonably practicable to ensure that notice of the application is given to –

    (a)   the child's parents;

    (b)   any person who is not a parent of his but who has parental responsibility for him;

    (c)   any other person caring for the child;

    (d)   any person in whose favour a contact order is in force with respect to the child;

    (e)   any person who is allowed to have contact with the child by virtue of an order under section 34; and

    (f)   the child,

before the hearing of the application.

(12) Rules of court may make provision as to the circumstances in which –

    (a)   any of the persons mentioned in subsection (11); or

    (b)   such other person as may be specified in the rules,

may apply to the court for a child assessment order to be varied or discharged.

(13) In this section 'authorised person' means a person who is an authorised person for the purposes of section 31.

NOTES

Definitions. 'Authorised person': s 43(13); 'child': s 105(1); 'child assessment order': s 43(2); 'contact order': s 8(1); 'emergency protection order': s 44(4); 'harm': s 31(9); 'local authority': s 105(1); 'parental responsibility': s 3; 'significant harm': s 31(10); 'the court': s 92(7).

44 Orders for emergency protection of children

(1) Where any person ('the applicant') applies to the court for an order to be made under this section with respect to a child, the court may make the order if, but only if, it is satisfied that –

    (a)   there is reasonable cause to believe that the child is likely to suffer significant harm if –

        (i)   he is not removed to accommodation provided by or on behalf of the applicant; or

(ii)   he does not remain in the place in which he is then being accommodated;

(b)   in the case of an application made by a local authority –

(i)   enquiries are being made with respect to the child under section 47(1)(b); and

(ii)   those enquiries are being frustrated by access to the child being unreasonably refused to a person authorised to seek access and that the applicant has reasonable cause to believe that access to the child is required as a matter of urgency; or

(c)   in the case of an application made by an authorised person –

(i)   the applicant has reasonable cause to suspect that a child is suffering, or is likely to suffer, significant harm;

(ii)   the applicant is making enquiries with respect to the child's welfare; and

(iii)   those enquiries are being frustrated by access to the child being unreasonably refused to a person authorised to seek access and the applicant has reasonable cause to believe that access to the child is required as a matter of urgency.

(2) In this section –

(a)   'authorised person' means a person who is an authorised person for the purposes of section 31; and

(b)   'a person authorised to seek access' means –

(i)   in the case of an application by a local authority, an officer of the local authority or a person authorised by the authority to act on their behalf in connection with the enquiries; or

(ii)   in the case of an application by an authorised person, that person.

(3) Any person –

(a)   seeking access to a child in connection with enquiries of a kind mentioned in subsection (1); and

(b)   purporting to be a person authorised to do so,

shall, on being asked to do so, produce some duly authenticated document as evidence that he is such a person.

(4) While an order under this section ('an emergency protection order') is in force it –

(a)   operates as a direction to any person who is in a position to do so to comply with any request to produce the child to the applicant;

(b)   authorises –

(i)   the removal of the child at any time to accommodation provided by or on behalf of the applicant and his being kept there; or

(ii)   the prevention of the child's removal from any hospital, or other place, in which he was being accommodated immediately before the making of the order; and

(c)   gives the applicant parental responsibility for the child.

(5) Where an emergency protection order is in force with respect to a child, the applicant –

   (a)   shall only exercise the power given by virtue of subsection (4)(b) in order to safeguard the welfare of the child;

   (b)   shall take, and shall only take, such action in meeting his parental responsibility for the child as is reasonably required to safeguard or promote the welfare of the child (having regard in particular to the duration of the order); and

   (c)   shall comply with the requirements of any regulations made by the Secretary of State for the purposes of this subsection.

(6) Where the court makes an emergency protection order, it may give such directions (if any) as it considers appropriate with respect to –

   (a)   the contact which is, or is not, to be allowed between the child and any named person;

   (b)   the medical or psychiatric examination or other assessment of the child.

(7) Where any direction is given under subsection (6)(b), the child may, if he is of sufficient understanding to make an informed decision, refuse to submit to the examination or other assessment.

(8) A direction under subsection (6)(a) may impose conditions and one under subsection (6)(b) may be to the effect that there is to be –

   (a)   no such examination or assessment; or

   (b)   no such examination or assessment unless the court directs otherwise.

(9) A direction under subsection (6) may be –

   (a)   given when the emergency protection order is made or at any time while it is in force; and

   (b)   varied at any time on the application of any person falling within any class of person prescribed by rules of court for the purposes of this subsection.

(10) Where an emergency protection order is in force with respect to a child and –

   (a)   the applicant has exercised the power given by subsection (4)(b)(i) but it appears to him that it is safe for the child to be returned; or

   (b)   the applicant has exercised the power given by subsection (4)(b)(ii) but it appears to him that it is safe for the child to be allowed to be removed from the place in question,

he shall return the child or (as the case may be) allow him to be removed.

(11) Where he is required by subsection (10) to return the child the applicant shall –

   (a)   return him to the care of the person from whose care he was removed; or

   (b)   if that is not reasonably practicable, return him to the care of –

PART I – Statutes

(i)   a parent of his;

(ii)   any person who is not a parent of his but who has parental responsibility for him; or

(iii)   such other person as the applicant (with the agreement of the court) considers appropriate.

(12) Where the applicant has been required by subsection (10) to return the child, or to allow him to be removed, he may again exercise his powers with respect to the child (at any time while the emergency protection order remains in force) if it appears to him that a change in the circumstances of the case makes it necessary for him to do so.

(13) Where an emergency protection order has been made with respect to a child, the applicant shall, subject to any direction given under subsection (6), allow the child reasonable contact with –

(a)   his parents;

(b)   any person who is not a parent of his but who has parental responsibility for him;

(c)   any person with whom he was living immediately before the making of the order;

(d)   any person in whose favour a contact order is in force with respect to him;

(e)   any person who is allowed to have contact with the child by virtue of an order under section 34; and

(f)   any person acting on behalf of any of those persons.

(14) Wherever it is reasonably practicable to do so, an emergency protection order shall name the child; and where it does not name him it shall describe him as clearly as possible.

(15) A person shall be guilty of an offence if he intentionally obstructs any person exercising the power under subsection (4)(b) to remove, or prevent the removal of, a child.

(16) A person guilty of an offence under subsection (15) shall be liable on summary conviction to a fine not exceeding level 3 on the standard scale.

NOTES

Definitions. 'Authorised person': s 44(2); 'child': s 105(1); 'contact order': s 8(1); 'emergency protection order': s 44(4); 'harm': s 31(9); 'hospital': s 105(1); 'local authority': s 105(1); 'parental responsibility': s 3; 'person authorised to seek access': s 44(2); 'significant harm': s 31(10); 'the applicant': s 44(1); 'the court': s 92(7).

[44A Power to include exclusion requirement in emergency protection order

(1) Where –

(a)   on being satisfied as mentioned in section 44(1)(a), (b) or (c), the court makes an emergency protection order with respect to a child, and

(b)   the conditions mentioned in subsection (2) are satisfied,

PART I – Statutes

the court may include an exclusion requirement in the emergency protection order.

(2) The conditions are –

(a)   that there is reasonable cause to believe that, if a person ('the relevant person') is excluded from a dwelling-house in which the child lives, then –
  (i)   in the case of an order made on the ground mentioned in section 44(1)(a), the child will not bc likely to suffer significant harm, even though the child is not removed as mentioned in section 44(1)(a)(i) or does not remain as mentioned in section 44(1)(a)(ii), or
  (ii)   in the case of an order made on the ground mentioned in paragraph (b) or (c) of section 44(1), the enquiries referred to in that paragraph will cease to be frustrated, and
(b)   that another person living in the dwelling-house (whether a parent of the child or some other person) –
  (i)   is able and willing to give to the child the care which it would be reasonable to expect a parent to give him, and
  (ii)   consents to the inclusion of the exclusion requirement.

(3) For the purposes of this section an exclusion requirement is any one or more of the following –

(a)   a provision requiring the relevant person to leave a dwelling-house in which he is living with the child,
(b)   a provision prohibiting the relevant person from entering a dwelling-house in which the child lives, and
(c)   a provision excluding the relevant person from a defined area in which a dwelling-house in which the child lives is situated.

(4) The court may provide that the exclusion requirement is to have effect for a shorter period than the other provisions of the order.

(5) Where the court makes an emergency protection order containing an exclusion requirement, the court may attach a power of arrest to the exclusion requirement.

(6) Where the court attaches a power of arrest to an exclusion requirement of an emergency protection order, it may provide that the power of arrest is to have effect for a shorter period than the exclusion requirement.

(7) Any period specified for the purposes of subsection (4) or (6) may be extended by the court (on one or more occasions) on an application to vary or discharge the emergency protection order.

(8) Where a power of arrest is attached to an exclusion requirement of an emergency protection order by virtue of subsection (5), a constable may arrest without warrant any person whom he has reasonable cause to believe to be in breach of the requirement.

(9) Sections 47(7), (11) and (12) and 48 of, and Schedule 5 to, the Family Law Act 1996 shall have effect in relation to a person arrested under subsection (8) of this section as they have effect in relation to a person arrested under section 47(6) of that Act.

(10) If, while an emergency protection order containing an exclusion requirement is in force, the applicant has removed the child from the dwelling-house from which the relevant person is excluded to other accommodation for a continuous period of more than 24 hours, the order shall cease to have effect in so far as it imposes the exclusion requirement.][1]

NOTES

Amendments.[1] Section inserted: Family Law Act 1996, s 52, Sch 6, para 3.

[44B   Undertakings relating to emergency protection orders

(1) In any case where the court has power to include an exclusion requirement in an emergency protection order, the court may accept an undertaking from the relevant person.

(2) No power of arrest may be attached to any undertaking given under subsection (1).

(3) An undertaking given to a court under subsection (1) –

   (a)   shall be enforceable as if it were an order of the court, and

   (b)   shall cease to have effect if, while it is in force, the applicant has removed the child from the dwelling-house from which the relevant person is excluded to other accommodation for a continuous period of more than 24 hours.

(4) This section has effect without prejudice to the powers of the High Court and county court apart from this section.

(5) In this section 'exclusion requirement' and 'relevant person' have the same meaning as in section 44A.][1]

NOTES

Amendments.[1] Section inserted: Family Law Act 1996, s 52, Sch 6, para 3.

45   Duration of emergency protection orders and other supplemental provisions

(1) An emergency protection order shall have effect for such period, not exceeding eight days, as may be specified in the order.

(2) Where –

   (a)   the court making an emergency protection order would, but for this subsection, specify a period of eight days as the period for which the order is to have effect; but

   (b)   the last of those eight days is a public holiday (that is to say, Christmas Day, Good Friday, a bank holiday or a Sunday), the court may specify a period which ends at noon on the first later day which is not such a holiday.

(3) Where an emergency protection order is made on an application under section 46(7), the period of eight days mentioned in subsection (1) shall begin with the first day on which the child was taken into police protection under section 46.

(4) Any person who –

    (a)   has parental responsibility for a child as the result of an emergency protection order; and

    (b)   is entitled to apply for a care order with respect to the child,

may apply to the court for the period during which the emergency protection order is to have effect to be extended.

(5) On an application under subsection (4) the court may extend the period during which the order is to have effect by such period, not exceeding seven days, as it thinks fit, but may do so only if it has reasonable cause to believe that the child concerned is likely to suffer significant harm if the order is not extended.

(6) An emergency protection order may only be extended once.

(7) Regardless of any enactment or rule of law which would otherwise prevent it from doing so, a court hearing an application for, or with respect to, an emergency protection order may take account of –

    (a)   any statement contained in any report made to the court in the course of, or in connection with, the hearing; or

    (b)   any evidence given during the hearing,

which is, in the opinion of the court, relevant to the application.

(8) Any of the following may apply to the court for an emergency protection order to be discharged –

    (a)   the child;

    (b)   a parent of his;

    (c)   any person who is not a parent of his but who has parental responsibility for him; or

    (d)   any person with whom he was living immediately before the making of the order.

[(8A) On the application of a person who is not entitled to apply for the order to be discharged, but who is a person to whom an exclusion requirement contained in the order applies, an emergency protection order may be varied or discharged by the court in so far as it imposes the exclusion requirement.

(8B) Where a power of arrest has been attached to an exclusion requirement of an emergency protection order, the court may, on the application of any person entitled to apply for the discharge of the order so far as it imposes the exclusion requirement, vary or discharge the order in so far as it confers a power of arrest (whether or not any application has been made to vary or discharge any other provision of the order).][2]

(9) ...[5]

[(10) No appeal may be made against –

(a)   the making of, or refusal to make, an emergency protection order;
(b)   the extension of, or refusal to extend, the period during which such an order is to have effect;
(c)   the discharge of, or refusal to discharge, such an order; or
(d)   the giving of, or refusal to give, any direction in connection with such an order.][1]

(11) Subsection (8) does not apply –

(a)   where the person who would otherwise be entitled to apply for the emergency protection order to be discharged –
(i)   was given notice (in accordance with rules of court) of the hearing at which the order was made; and
(ii)   was present at that hearing; or
(b)   to any emergency protection order the effective period of which has been extended under subsection (5).

(12) A court making an emergency protection order may direct that the applicant may, in exercising any powers which he has by virtue of the order, be accompanied by a registered medical practitioner, registered nurse or [registered midwife][4], if he so chooses.

[(13) The reference in subsection (12) to a registered midwife is to such a midwife who is also registered in the Specialist Community Public Health Nurses' Part of the register maintained under article 5 of the Nursing and Midwifery Order 2001.][3]

NOTES

Amendments.[1] Words substituted: Courts and Legal Services Act 1990, s 116, Sch 16, para 19.[2] Subsections inserted: Family Law Act 1996, s 52, Sch 6, para 4.[3] Subsection inserted: SI 2004/1771.[4] Words substituted: Nursing and Midwifery Order 2001 [*sic*], SI 2002/253, art 54(3), Sch 5, para 10(a).[5] Subsection repealed: Children and Young Persons Act 2008, ss 30, 42, Sch 4.

Definitions. 'Bank holiday': s 105(1); 'care order': ss 31(11), 105(1); 'child': s 105(1); 'emergency protection order': s 44(4); 'harm': s 31(9); 'parental responsibility': s 3; 'significant harm': s 31(10); 'the court': s 92(7).

46 Removal and accommodation of children by police in cases of emergency

(1) Where a constable has reasonable cause to believe that a child would otherwise be likely to suffer significant harm, he may –

(a)   remove the child to suitable accommodation and keep him there; or
(b)   take such steps as are reasonable to ensure that the child's removal from any hospital, or other place, in which he is then being accommodated is prevented.

(2) For the purposes of this Act, a child with respect to whom a constable has exercised his powers under this section is referred to as having been taken into police protection.

(3) As soon as is reasonably practicable after taking a child into police protection, the constable concerned shall –

   (a)   inform the local authority within whose area the child was found of the steps that have been, and are proposed to be, taken with respect to the child under this section and the reasons for taking them;
   (b)   give details to the authority within whose area the child is ordinarily resident ('the appropriate authority') of the place at which the child is being accommodated;
   (c)   inform the child (if he appears capable of understanding) –
      (i)   of the steps that have been taken with respect to him under this section and of the reasons for taking them; and
      (ii)   of the further steps that may be taken with respect to him under this section;
   (d)   take such steps as are reasonably practicable to discover the wishes and feelings of the child;
   (e)   secure that the case is inquired into by an officer designated for the purposes of this section by the chief officer of the police area concerned; and
   (f)   where the child was taken into police protection by being removed to accommodation which is not provided –
      (i)   by or on behalf of a local authority; or
      (ii)   as a refuge, in compliance with the requirements of section 51, secure that he is moved to accommodation which is so provided.

(4) As soon as is reasonably practicable after taking a child into police protection, the constable concerned shall take such steps as are reasonably practicable to inform –

   (a)   the child's parents;
   (b)   every person who is not a parent of his but who has parental responsibility for him; and
   (c)   any other person with whom the child was living immediately before being taken into police protection,

of the steps that he has taken under this section with respect to the child, the reasons for taking them and the further steps that may be taken with respect to him under this section.

(5) On completing any inquiry under subsection (3)(e), the officer conducting it shall release the child from police protection unless he considers that there is still reasonable cause for believing that the child would be likely to suffer significant harm if released.

(6) No child may be kept in police protection for more than 72 hours.

PART I – Statutes

(7) While a child is being kept in police protection, the designated officer may apply on behalf of the appropriate authority for an emergency protection order to be made under section 44 with respect to the child.

(8) An application may be made under subsection (7) whether or not the authority know of it or agree to its being made.

(9) While a child is being kept in police protection –

(a)   neither the constable concerned nor the designated officer shall have parental responsibility for him; but

(b)   the designated officer shall do what is reasonable in all the circumstances of the case for the purpose of safeguarding or promoting the child's welfare (having regard in particular to the length of the period during which the child will be so protected).

(10) Where a child has been taken into police protection, the designated officer shall allow –

(a)   the child's parents;

(b)   any person who is not a parent of the child but who has parental responsibility for him;

(c)   any person with whom the child was living immediately before he was taken into police protection;

(d)   any person in whose favour a contact order is in force with respect to the child;

(e)   any person who is allowed to have contact with the child by virtue of an order under section 34; and

(f)   any person acting on behalf of any of those persons,

to have such contact (if any) with the child as, in the opinion of the designated officer, is both reasonable and in the child's best interests.

(11) Where a child who has been taken into police protection is in accommodation provided by, or on behalf of, the appropriate authority, subsection (10) shall have effect as if it referred to the authority rather than to the designated officer.

NOTES

Definitions. 'Appropriate authority': s 46(3)(b); 'child': s 105(1); 'contact order': s 8(1); 'designated officer': s 46(3)(e); 'emergency protection order': s 44(4); 'harm': s 31(9); 'hospital': s 105(1); 'local authority': s 105(1); 'ordinary residence': s 105(6); 'police protection': s 46(2); 'significant harm': s 31(10).

47 Local authority's duty to investigate

(1) Where a local authority –

(a)   are informed that a child who lives, or is found, in their area –
       (i)   is the subject of an emergency protection order; or
       (ii)   is in police protection; ...[8]
       [(iii) ...[8]][2]

(b)   have reasonable cause to suspect that a child who lives, or is found, in their area is suffering, or is likely to suffer, significant harm,

the authority shall make, or cause to be made, such enquiries as they consider necessary to enable them to decide whether they should take any action to safeguard or promote the child's welfare.

[...[8]][2]

(2) Where a local authority have obtained an emergency protection order with respect to a child, they shall make, or cause to be made, such enquiries as they consider necessary to enable them to decide what action they should take to safeguard or promote the child's welfare.

(3) The enquiries shall, in particular, be directed towards establishing –

(a)   whether the authority should make any application to the court, or exercise any of their other powers under this Act [or section 11 of the Crime and Disorder Act 1998 (child safety orders)][2], with respect to the child;
(b)   whether, in the case of a child –
     (i)   with respect to whom an emergency protection order has been made; and
     (ii)   who is not in accommodation provided by or on behalf of the authority,
     it would be in the child's best interests (while an emergency protection order remains in force) for him to be in such accommodation; and
(c)   whether, in the case of a child who has been taken into police protection, it would be in the child's best interests for the authority to ask for an application to be made under section 46(7).

(4) Where enquiries are being made under subsection (1) with respect to a child, the local authority concerned shall (with a view to enabling them to determine what action, if any, to take with respect to him) take such steps as are reasonably practicable –

(a)   to obtain access to him; or
(b)   to ensure that access to him is obtained, on their behalf, by a person authorised by them for the purpose,

unless they are satisfied that they already have sufficient information with respect to him.

(5) Where, as a result of any such enquiries, it appears to the authority that there are matters connected with the child's education which should be investigated, they shall consult [the local authority (as defined in section 579(1) of the Education 1996), if different, specified in subsection (5ZA).

(5ZA) The local authority referred to in subsection (5) is –

(a)   the local authority who –
     (i)   maintain any school at which the child is a pupil, or

(i)   make arrangements for the provision of education for the child otherwise than at school pursuant to section 19 of the Education Act 1996, or

(b)in a case where the child is a pupil at a school which is not maintained by a local authority, the local authority in whose area the school is situated.][7]

[(5A) For the purposes of making a determination under this section as to the action to be taken with respect to a child, a local authority shall, so far as is reasonably practicable and consistent with the child's welfare –

(a)   ascertain the child's wishes and feelings regarding the action to be taken with respect to him; and

(b)   give due consideration (having regard to his age and understanding) to such wishes and feelings of the child as they have been able to ascertain.][5]

(6) Where, in the course of enquiries made under this section –

(a)   any officer of the local authority concerned; or

(b)   any person authorised by the authority to act on their behalf in connection with those enquiries –

(i)   is refused access to the child concerned; or

(ii)   is denied information as to his whereabouts,

the authority shall apply for an emergency protection order, a child assessment order, a care order or a supervision order with respect to the child unless they are satisfied that his welfare can be satisfactorily safeguarded without their doing so.

(7) If, on the conclusion of any enquiries or review made under this section, the authority decide not to apply for an emergency protection order, a care order, a child assessment order or a supervision order they shall –

(a)   consider whether it would be appropriate to review the case at a later date; and

(b)   if they decide that it would be, determine the date on which that review is to begin.

(8) Where, as a result of complying with this section, a local authority conclude that they should take action to safeguard or promote the child's welfare they shall take that action (so far as it is both within their power and reasonably practicable for them to do so).

(9) Where a local authority are conducting enquiries under this section, it shall be the duty of any person mentioned in subsection (11) to assist them with those enquiries (in particular by providing relevant information and advice) if called upon by the authority to do so.

(10) Subsection (9) does not oblige any person to assist a local authority where doing so would be unreasonable in all the circumstances of the case.

(11) The persons are –

(a)   any local authority;

(b)   ...[7]

(c)   any local housing authority;

(d)   any [[Local Health Board][6], Special Health Authority][1][, Primary Care Trust][3][, National Health Service trust or NHS foundation trust][4]; and

(e)   any person authorised by the Secretary of State for the purposes of this section.

(12) Where a local authority are making enquiries under this section with respect to a child who appears to them to be ordinarily resident within the area of another authority, they shall consult that other authority, who may undertake the necessary enquiries in their place.

NOTES

Amendments.[1] Words substituted: Health Authorities Act 1995, s 2(1), Sch 1, Pt III, para 118(1), (7).[2] Words inserted: Crime and Disorder Act 1998, ss 15(4), 119, Sch 8, para 69.[3] Words inserted: Health Act 1999 (Supplementary, Consequential etc Provisions) Order 2000, SI 2000/90. [4] Words substituted: Health and Social Care (Community Health and Standards) Act 2003, s 34, Sch 4, paras 75, 79.[5] Subsection inserted: Children Act 2004, s 53(3).[6] Words substituted: SI 2007/961.[7] Words and subsection substituted and paragraph repealed: SI 2010/1158.[8] Paragraph and word repealed: Policing and Crime Act 2009, s 112(2), Sch 8, Pt 13.

Definitions. 'Care order': s 31(11); 'child': s 105(1); 'child assessment order': s 43(2); 'emergency protection order': s 44(4); 'harm': s 31(9); 'health authority': s 105(1); 'local authority': s 105(1); 'local education authority': s 105(1); 'local housing authority': s 105(1); 'ordinary residence': s 105(6); 'police protection': s 46(2); 'significant harm': s 31(10); 'supervision order': s 31(11); 'the court': s 92(7).

48 Powers to assist in discovery of children who may be in need of emergency protection

(1) Where it appears to a court making an emergency protection order that adequate information as to the child's whereabouts –

(a)   is not available to the applicant for the order; but

(b)   is available to another person,

it may include in the order a provision requiring that other person to disclose, if asked to do so by the applicant, any information that he may have as to the child's whereabouts.

(2) No person shall be excused from complying with such a requirement on the ground that complying might incriminate him or his spouse [or civil partner][3] of an offence; but a statement or admission made in complying shall not be admissible in evidence against either of them in proceedings for any offence other than perjury.

(3) An emergency protection order may authorise the applicant to enter premises specified by the order and search for the child with respect to whom the order is made.

(4) Where the court is satisfied that there is reasonable cause to believe that there may be another child on those premises with respect to whom an emergency protection order ought to be made, it may make an order authorising the applicant to search for that other child on those premises.

(5) Where –

(a)   an order has been made under subsection (4);

(b)   the child concerned has been found on the premises; and

(c)   the applicant is satisfied that the grounds for making an emergency protection order exist with respect to him,

the order shall have effect as if it were an emergency protection order.

(6) Where an order has been made under subsection (4), the applicant shall notify the court of its effect.

(7) A person shall be guilty of an offence if he intentionally obstructs any person exercising the power of entry and search under subsection (3) or (4).

(8) A person guilty of an offence under subsection (7) shall be liable on summary conviction to a fine not exceeding level 3 on the standard scale.

(9) Where, on an application made by any person for a warrant under this section, it appears to the court –

(a)   that a person attempting to exercise powers under an emergency protection order has been prevented from doing so by being refused entry to the premises concerned or access to the child concerned; or

(b)   that any such person is likely to be so prevented from exercising any such powers,

it may issue a warrant authorising any constable to assist the person mentioned in paragraph (a) or (b) in the exercise of those powers, using reasonable force if necessary.

(10) Every warrant issued under this section shall be addressed to, and executed by, a constable who shall be accompanied by the person applying for the warrant if –

(a)   that person so desires; and

(b)   the court by whom the warrant is issued does not direct otherwise.

(11) A court granting an application for a warrant under this section may direct that the constable concerned may, in executing the warrant, be accompanied by a registered medical practitioner, registered nurse or [registered midwife][2] if he so chooses.

[(11A) The reference in subsection (11) to a registered midwife is to such a midwife who is also registered in the Specialist Community Public Health Nurses' Part of the register maintained under article 5 of the Nursing and Midwifery Order 2001.][1]

(12) An application for a warrant under this section shall be made in the manner and form prescribed by rules of court.

(13) Wherever it is reasonably practicable to do so, an order under subsection (4), an application for a warrant under this section and any such warrant shall name the child; and where it does not name him it shall describe him as clearly as possible.

NOTES

Amendments.[1] Words substituted and subsection inserted: SI 2004/1771.[2] Words substituted: Nursing and Midwifery Order 2001 [*sic*], SI 2002/253, art 54(3), Sch 5, para 10(b).[3] Words inserted: Civil Partnership Act 2004, s 261(1), Sch 27, para 130.

Definitions. 'Child': s 105(1); 'emergency protection order': s 44(4); 'the applicant': s 44(1); 'the court': s 92(7).

49 Abduction of children in care etc

(1) A person shall be guilty of an offence if, knowingly and without lawful authority or reasonable excuse, he –

    (a)   takes a child to whom this section applies away from the responsible person;

    (b)   keeps such a child away from the responsible person; or

    (c)   induces, assists or incites such a child to run away or stay away from the responsible person.

(2) This section applies in relation to a child who is –

    (a)   in care;

    (b)   the subject of an emergency protection order; or

    (c)   in police protection,

and in this section 'the responsible person' means any person who for the time being has care of him by virtue of the care order, the emergency protection order, or section 46, as the case may be.

(3) A person guilty of an offence under this section shall be liable on summary conviction to imprisonment for a term not exceeding six months, or to a fine not exceeding level 5 on the standard scale, or to both.

NOTES

Definitions. 'Care order': ss 31(11), 105(1); 'child': s 105(1); 'emergency protection order': s 44(4); 'police protection': s 46(2); 'responsible person': s 49(2).

50 Recovery of abducted children etc

(1) Where it appears to the court that there is reason to believe that a child to whom this section applies –

    (a)   has been unlawfully taken away or is being unlawfully kept away from the responsible person;

    (b)   has run away or is staying away from the responsible person; or

    (c)   is missing,

the court may make an order under this section ('a recovery order').

(2) This section applies to the same children to whom section 49 applies and in this section 'the responsible person' has the same meaning as in section 49.

(3) A recovery order –

    (a)   operates as a direction to any person who is in a position to do so to produce the child on request to any authorised person;

(b)   authorises the removal of the child by any authorised person;

(c)   requires any person who has information as to the child's whereabouts to disclose that information, if asked to do so, to a constable or an officer of the court;

(d)   authorises a constable to enter any premises specified in the order and search for the child, using reasonable force if necessary.

(4) The court may make a recovery order only on the application of –

(a)   any person who has parental responsibility for the child by virtue of a care order or emergency protection order; or

(b)   where the child is in police protection, the designated officer.

(5) A recovery order shall name the child and –

(a)   any person who has parental responsibility for the child by virtue of a care order or emergency protection order; or

(b)   where the child is in police protection, the designated officer.

(6) Premises may only be specified under subsection (3)(d) if it appears to the court that there are reasonable grounds for believing the child to be on them.

(7) In this section –

'an authorised person' means –
   (a)   any person specified by the court;
   (b)   any constable;
   (c)   any person who is authorised –
      (i)   after the recovery order is made; and
      (ii)   by a person who has parental responsibility for the child by virtue of a care order or an emergency protection order,
   to exercise any power under a recovery order; and

'the designated officer' means the officer designated for the purposes of section 46.

(8) Where a person is authorised as mentioned in subsection (7)(c) –

(a)   the authorisation shall identify the recovery order; and

(b)   any person claiming to be so authorised shall, if asked to do so, produce some duly authenticated document showing that he is so authorised.

(9) A person shall be guilty of an offence if he intentionally obstructs an authorised person exercising the power under subsection (3)(b) to remove a child.

(10) A person guilty of an offence under this section shall be liable on summary conviction to a fine not exceeding level 3 on the standard scale.

(11) No person shall be excused from complying with any request made under subsection (3)(c) on the ground that complying with it might incriminate him or his spouse [or civil partner][1] of an offence; but a statement or admission made in complying shall not be admissible in evidence against either of them in proceedings for an offence other than perjury.

PART I – Statutes

(12) Where a child is made the subject of a recovery order whilst being looked after by a local authority, any reasonable expenses incurred by an authorised person in giving effect to the order shall be recoverable from the authority.

(13) A recovery order shall have effect in Scotland as if it had been made by the Court of Session and as if that court had had jurisdiction to make it.

(14) In this section 'the court', in relation to Northern Ireland, means a magistrates' court within the meaning of the Magistrates' Courts (Northern Ireland) Order 1981.

NOTES

Amendments.[1] Words inserted: Civil Partnership Act 2004, s 261(1), Sch 27, para 131.

Definitions. 'Authorised person': s 50(7); 'care order': s 31(11); 'child': s 105(1); 'child who is looked after by a local authority': s 22(1); 'emergency protection order': s 44(4); 'local authority': s 105(1); 'parental responsibility': s 3; 'police protection': s 46(2); 'recovery order': s 50(1); 'responsible person': s 49(2); 'the court': s 92(7); 'the designated officer': s 50(7).

51 Refuges for children at risk

(1) Where it is proposed to use a voluntary home or [private][2] children's home to provide a refuge for children who appear to be at risk of harm, the Secretary of State may issue a certificate under this section with respect to that home.

(2) Where a local authority or voluntary organisation arrange for a foster parent to provide such a refuge, the Secretary of State may issue a certificate under this section with respect to that foster parent.

(3) In subsection (2) 'foster parent' means a person who is, or who from time to time is, a local authority foster parent or a foster parent with whom children are placed by a voluntary organisation.

(4) The Secretary of State may by regulations –

(a) make provision as to the manner in which certificates may be issued;
(b) impose requirements which must be complied with while any certificate is in force; and
(c) provide for the withdrawal of certificates in prescribed circumstances.

(5) Where a certificate is in force with respect to a home, none of the provisions mentioned in subsection (7) shall apply in relation to any person providing a refuge for any child in that home.

(6) Where a certificate is in force with respect to a foster parent, none of those provisions shall apply in relation to the provision by him of a refuge for any child in accordance with arrangements made by the local authority or voluntary organisation.

(7) The provisions are –

(a) section 49;
[(b) sections 82 (recovery of certain fugitive children) and 83 (harbouring) of the Children (Scotland) Act 1995, so far as they apply in relation to anything done in England and Wales;][1]

(c)   section 32(3) of the Children and Young Persons Act 1969 (compelling, persuading, inciting or assisting any person to be absent from detention, etc), so far as it applies in relation to anything done in England and Wales;

(d)   section 2 of the Child Abduction Act 1984.

NOTES

Amendments.[1] Subsection substituted: Children (Scotland) Act 1995, s 105(4), Sch 4, para 48(1), (3).[2] Word substituted: Care Standards Act 2000, s 116, Sch 4, para 14.

Definitions. 'Child': s 105(1); 'foster parent': s 51(3); 'harm': s 31(9); 'local authority': s 105(1); 'local authority foster parent': s 23(3); 'prescribed': s 105(1); 'voluntary home': s 60(3); 'voluntary organisation': s 105(1).

52 Rules and regulations

(1) Without prejudice to section 93 or any other power to make such rules, rules of court may be made with respect to the procedure to be followed in connection with proceedings under this Part.

(2) The rules may in particular make provision –

(a)   as to the form in which any application is to be made or direction is to be given;

(b)   prescribing the persons who are to be notified of –
   (i)   the making, or extension, of an emergency protection order; or
   (ii)   the making of an application under section 45(4) or (8) or 46(7); and

(c)   as to the content of any such notification and the manner in which, and person by whom, it is to be given.

(3) The Secretary of State may by regulations provide that, where –

(a)   an emergency protection order has been made with respect to a child;

(b)   the applicant for the order was not the local authority within whose area the child is ordinarily resident; and

(c)   that local authority are of the opinion that it would be in the child's best interests for the applicant's responsibilities under the order to be transferred to them,

that authority shall (subject to their having complied with any requirements imposed by the regulations) be treated, for the purposes of this Act, as though they and not the original applicant had applied for, and been granted, the order.

(4) Regulations made under subsection (3) may, in particular, make provision as to –

(a)   the considerations to which the local authority shall have regard in forming an opinion as mentioned in subsection (3)(c); and

(b)   the time at which responsibility under any emergency protection order is to be treated as having been transferred to a local authority.

NOTES

Definitions. 'Child': s 105(1); 'emergency protection order': s 44(4); 'local authority': s 105(1); 'ordinary residence': s 105(6).

PART VI
COMMUNITY HOMES

53 Provision of community homes by local authorities

(1) Every local authority shall make such arrangements as they consider appropriate for securing that homes ('community homes') are available –

(a)   for the care and accommodation of children looked after by them; and

(b)   for purposes connected with the welfare of children (whether or not looked after by them),

and may do so jointly with one or more other local authorities.

(2) In making such arrangements, a local authority shall have regard to the need for ensuring the availability of accommodation –

(a)   of different descriptions; and

(b)   which is suitable for different purposes and the requirements of different descriptions of children.

(3) A community home may be a home –

(a)   provided, [equipped, maintained and (subject to subsection (3A)) managed][1] by a local authority; or

(b)   provided by a voluntary organisation but in respect of which a local authority and the organisation –

(i)   propose that, in accordance with an instrument of management, the [equipment, maintenance and (subject to subsection (3B)) management][1] of the home shall be the responsibility of the local authority; or

(ii)   so propose that the management, equipment and maintenance of the home shall be the responsibility of the voluntary organisation.

[(3A) A local authority may make arrangements for the management by another person of accommodation provided by the local authority for the purpose of restricting the liberty of children.

(3B) Where a local authority are to be responsible for the management of a community home provided by a voluntary organisation, the local authority may, with the consent of the body of managers constituted by the instrument of management for the home, make arrangements for the management by another person of accommodation provided for the purpose of restricting the liberty of children.][1]

(4) Where a local authority are to be responsible for the management of a community home provided by a voluntary organisation, the authority shall designate the home as a controlled community home.

(5) Where a voluntary organisation are to be responsible for the management of a community home provided by the organisation, the local authority shall designate the home as an assisted community home.

(6) Schedule 4 shall have effect for the purpose of supplementing the provisions of this Part.

NOTES

Amendments.[1] Words or subsections inserted: Criminal Justice and Public Order Act 1994, s 22.

Definitions. 'Assisted community home': s 53(5); 'child': s 105(1); 'child who is looked after by the local authority': s 22(1); 'community home': s 53(1); 'controlled community home': s 53(4); 'local authority': s 105(1); 'voluntary organisation': s 105(1).

54

...[1]

NOTES

Amendments.[1] Section repealed: Care Standards Act 2000, s 117, Sch 6.

55 Determination of disputes relating to controlled and assisted community homes

(1) Where any dispute relating to a controlled community home arises between the local authority specified in the home's instrument of management and –

    (a)   the voluntary organisation by which the home is provided; or

    (b)   any other local authority who have placed, or desire or are required to place, in the home a child who is looked after by them,

the dispute may be referred by either party to the Secretary of State for his determination.

(2) Where any dispute relating to an assisted community home arises between the voluntary organisation by which the home is provided and any local authority who have placed, or desire to place, in the home a child who is looked after by them, the dispute may be referred by either party to the Secretary of State for his determination.

(3) Where a dispute is referred to the Secretary of State under this section he may, in order to give effect to his determination of the dispute, give such directions as he thinks fit to the local authority or voluntary organisation concerned.

(4) This section applies even though the matter in dispute may be one which, under or by virtue of Part II of Schedule 4, is reserved for the decision, or is the responsibility, of –

    (a)   the local authority specified in the home's instrument of management; or

    (b)   (as the case may be) the voluntary organisation by which the home is provided.

(5) Where any trust deed relating to a controlled or assisted community home contains provision whereby a bishop or any other ecclesiastical or denominational authority has power to decide questions relating to religious instruction given in the home, no dispute which is capable of being dealt with in accordance with that provision shall be referred to the Secretary of State under this section.

(6) In this Part 'trust deed', in relation to a voluntary home, means any instrument (other than an instrument of management) regulating –

    (a)   the maintenance, management or conduct of the home; or

    (b)   the constitution of a body of managers or trustees of the home.

NOTES

Definitions. 'Assisted community home': s 53(5); 'child': s 105(1); 'child who is looked after by a local authority': s 22(1); 'community home': s 53(1); 'controlled community home': s 53(4); 'local authority': s 105(1); 'trust deed': s 55(6); 'voluntary home': s 60(3); 'voluntary organisation': s 105(1).

56 Discontinuance by voluntary organisation of controlled or assisted community home

(1) The voluntary organisation by which a controlled or assisted community home is provided shall not cease to provide the home except after giving to the Secretary of State and the local authority specified in the home's instrument of management not less than two years' notice in writing of their intention to do so.

(2) A notice under subsection (1) shall specify the date from which the voluntary organisation intend to cease to provide the home as a community home.

(3) Where such a notice is given and is not withdrawn before the date specified in it, the home's instrument of management shall cease to have effect on that date and the home shall then cease to be a controlled or assisted community home.

(4) Where a notice is given under subsection (1) and the home's managers give notice in writing to the Secretary of State that they are unable or unwilling to continue as its managers until the date specified in the subsection (1) notice, the Secretary of State may by order –

    (a)   revoke the home's instrument of management; and

    (b)   require the local authority who were specified in that instrument to conduct the home until –

        (i)   the date specified in the subsection (1) notice; or

        (ii)   such earlier date (if any) as may be specified for the purposes of this paragraph in the order,

    as if it were a community home provided by the local authority.

(5) Where the Secretary of State imposes a requirement under subsection (4)(b) –

PART I – Statutes

(a)   nothing in the trust deed for the home shall affect the conduct of the home by the local authority;

(b)   the Secretary of State may by order direct that for the purposes of any provision specified in the direction and made by or under any enactment relating to community homes (other than this section) the home shall, until the date or earlier date specified as mentioned in subsection (4)(b), be treated as a controlled or assisted community home;

(c)   except in so far as the Secretary of State so directs, the home shall until that date be treated for the purposes of any such enactment as a community home provided by the local authority; and

(d)   on the date or earlier date specified as mentioned in subsection (4)(b) the home shall cease to be a community home.

NOTES

Definitions. 'Assisted community home': s 53(5); 'community home': s 53(1); 'controlled community home': s 53(4); 'local authority': s 105(1); 'trust deed': s 55(6); 'voluntary organisation': s 105(1).

57 Closure by local authority of controlled or assisted community home

(1) The local authority specified in the instrument of management for a controlled or assisted community home may give –

(a)   the Secretary of State; and
(b)   the voluntary organisation by which the home is provided,

not less than two years' notice in writing of their intention to withdraw their designation of the home as a controlled or assisted community home.

(2) A notice under subsection (1) shall specify the date ('the specified date') on which the designation is to be withdrawn.

(3) Where –

(a)   a notice is given under subsection (1) in respect of a controlled or assisted community home;
(b)   the home's managers give notice in writing to the Secretary of State that they are unable or unwilling to continue as managers until the specified date; and
(c)   the managers' notice is not withdrawn,

the Secretary of State may by order revoke the home's instrument of management from such date earlier than the specified date as may be specified in the order.

(4) Before making an order under subsection (3), the Secretary of State shall consult the local authority and the voluntary organisation.

(5) Where a notice has been given under subsection (1) and is not withdrawn, the home's instrument of management shall cease to have effect on –

(a)   the specified date; or
(b)   where an earlier date has been specified under subsection (3), that earlier date,

and the home shall then cease to be a community home.

NOTES

Definitions. 'Assisted community home': s 53(5); 'controlled community home': s 53(4); 'community home': s 53(1); 'local authority': s 105(1); 'the specified date': s 57(2); 'voluntary organisation': s 105(1).

58 Financial provisions applicable on cessation of controlled or assisted community home or disposal etc of premises

(1) Where –

(a) the instrument of management for a controlled or assisted community home is revoked or otherwise ceases to have effect under section . . .[3] 56(3) or (4)(a) or 57(3) or (5); or

(b) any premises used for the purposes of such a home are (at any time after 13th January 1987) disposed of, or put to use otherwise than for those purposes,

the proprietor shall become liable to pay compensation ('the appropriate compensation') in accordance with this section.

(2) Where the instrument of management in force at the relevant time relates –

(a) to a controlled community home; or

(b) to an assisted community home which, at any time before the instrument came into force, was a controlled community home,

the appropriate compensation is a sum equal to that part of the value of any premises which is attributable to expenditure incurred in relation to the premises, while the home was a controlled community home, by the authority who were then the responsible authority.

(3) Where the instrument of management in force at the relevant time relates –

(a) to an assisted community home; or

(b) to a controlled community home which, at any time before the instrument came into force, was an assisted community home,

the appropriate compensation is a sum equal to that part of the value of the premises which is attributable to the expenditure of money provided by way of grant under section 82, section 65 of the Children and Young Persons Act 1969 or section 82 of the Child Care Act 1980.

(4) Where the home is, at the relevant time, conducted in premises which formerly were used as an approved school or were an approved probation hostel or home, the appropriate compensation is a sum equal to that part of the value of the premises which is attributable to the expenditure –

(a) of sums paid towards the expenses of the managers of an approved school under section 104 of the Children and Young Persons Act 1933; . . .[2]

(b)   of sums paid under section 51(3)(c) of the Powers of Criminal Courts Act 1973 [or section 20(1)(c) of the Probation Service Act 1993][1] in relation to expenditure on approved probation hostels or homes [; or

(c)   of sums paid under section 3, 5 or 9 of the Criminal Justice and Court Services Act 2000 in relation to expenditure on approved premises (within the meaning of Part I of that Act).][2]

(5) The appropriate compensation shall be paid –

(a)   in the case of compensation payable under subsection (2), to the authority who were the responsible authority at the relevant time; and

(b)   in any other case, to the Secretary of State.

(6) In this section –

'disposal' includes the grant of a tenancy and any other conveyance, assignment, transfer, grant, variation or extinguishment of an interest in or right over land, whether made by instrument or otherwise;

'premises' means any premises or part of premises (including land) used for the purposes of the home and belonging to the proprietor;

'the proprietor' means –

(a)   the voluntary organisation by which the home is, at the relevant time, provided; or

(b)   if the premises are not, at the relevant time, vested in that organisation, the persons in whom they are vested;

'the relevant time' means the time immediately before the liability to pay arises under subsection (1); and

'the responsible authority' means the local authority specified in the instrument of management in question.

(7) For the purposes of this section an event of a kind mentioned in subsection (1)(b) shall be taken to have occurred –

(a)   in the case of a disposal, on the date on which the disposal was completed or, in the case of a disposal which is effected by a series of transactions, the date on which the last of those transactions was completed;

(b)   in the case of premises which are put to different use, on the date on which they first begin to be put to their new use.

(8) The amount of any sum payable under this section shall be determined in accordance with such arrangements –

(a)   as may be agreed between the voluntary organisation by which the home is, at the relevant time, provided and the responsible authority or (as the case may be) the Secretary of State; or

(b)   in default of agreement, as may be determined by the Secretary of State.

(9) With the agreement of the responsible authority or (as the case may be) the Secretary of State, the liability to pay any sum under this section may be discharged, in whole or in part, by the transfer of any premises.

(10) This section has effect regardless of –

(a) anything in any trust deed for a controlled or assisted community home;

(b) the provisions of any enactment or instrument governing the disposition of the property of a voluntary organisation.

NOTES

Amendments.[1] Words inserted: Probation Service Act 1993, s 32, Sch 3, para 9(2).[2] Word omitted or words inserted: Criminal Justice and Court Services Act 2000, ss 74, 75, Sch 7, paras 87, 93, Sch 8.[3] Word repealed: Care Standards Act 2000, s 117, Sch 6.

Definitions. 'Appropriate compensation': s 58(1)–(4); 'assisted community home': s 53(5); 'community home': s 53(1); 'controlled community home': s 53(4); 'disposal': s 58(6); 'local authority': s 105(1); 'premises': s 58(6); 'the proprietor': s 58(6); 'the relevant time': s 58(6); 'the responsible authority': s 58(6); 'trust deed': s 55(6); 'voluntary organisation': s 105(1).

PART VII
VOLUNTARY HOMES AND VOLUNTARY ORGANISATIONS

59 Provision of accommodation by voluntary organisations

(1) Where a voluntary organisation provide accommodation for a child, they shall do so by –

(a) placing him (subject to subsection (2)) with –
(i)   a family;
(ii) a relative of his; or
(iii) any other suitable person,
on such terms as to payment by the organisation and otherwise as the organisation may determine [(subject to section 49 of the Children Act 2004)][2];

[(aa) maintaining him in *an appropriate children's home* [a children's home in respect of which a person is registered under Part 2 of the Care Standards Act 2000][5];

(b)–(e) ...][1]

(f) making such other arrangements (subject to subsection (3)) as seem appropriate to them.

[(1A) Where under subsection (1)(aa) a *local authority* [voluntary organisation][5] maintains a child in a home provided, equipped and maintained by [an appropriate national authority][3] under section 82(5), it shall do so on such terms as [that national authority][3] may from time to time determine.][1]

(2) The [appropriate national authority][3] may make regulations as to the placing of children with foster parents by voluntary organisations *and the regulations may, in particular, make provision which (with any necessary modifications) is similar to the provision that may be made under section 23(2)(f).*[4]

(3) The [appropriate national authority][3] may make regulations as to the arrangements which may be made under subsection (1)(f) *and the regulations*

may in particular make provision which (with any necessary modifications) is similar to the provision that may be made under section 23(2)(f).[4]

[(3A) Regulations under subsection (2) or (3) may in particular make provision which (with any necessary modifications) is similar to that which may be made under section 22C by virtue of any of paragraphs 12B, 12E and 12F of Schedule 2.][4]

(4) The [appropriate national authority][3] may make regulations requiring any voluntary organisation who are providing accommodation for a child –

   (a)   to review his case; and
   (b)   to consider any representations (including any complaint) made to them by any person falling within a prescribed class of person,

in accordance with the provisions of the regulations.

(5) Regulations under subsection (4) may in particular make provision which (with any necessary modifications) is similar to the provision that may be made under section 26.

[(5A) Regulations under subsection (4) may, in particular –

   (a)   apply with modifications any provision of section 25A or 25B;
   (b)   make provision which (with any necessary modifications) is similar to any provision which may be made under section 25A, 25B or 26.][4]

(6) Regulations under subsections (2) to (4) may provide that any person who, without reasonable excuse, contravenes or fails to comply with a regulation shall be guilty of an offence and liable on summary conviction to a fine not exceeding level 4 on the standard scale.

[(7) In this Part 'appropriate national authority' means –

   (a)   in relation to England, the Secretary of State; and
   (b)   in relation to Wales, the Welsh Ministers.][3]

NOTES

Amendments.[1] Paragraph (aa) substituted for paras (b)–(e) and subsection inserted: Care Standards Act 2000, s 116, Sch 4, para 14(8).[2] Words inserted: Children Act 2004, s 49(4).[3] Words substituted and subsection inserted: Children and Young Persons Act 2008, s 39, Sch 3, paras 1, 23. [4] Words in italics omitted, subsection (3A) inserted and subsection (5A) substituted for (5) in relation to England: Children and Young Persons Act 2008, s 8(2), Sch 1, paras 2(1), (4)–(7). [5] Words in italics substituted by words in square brackets in relation to England: Children and Young Persons Act 2008, s 8(2), Sch 1, para 2(1)–(3).

Definitions. 'Child': s 105(1); 'community home': s 53(1); 'relative': s 105(1); 'voluntary home': s 60(2); 'voluntary organisation': s 105(1).

60 [Voluntary homes][1]

(1), (2) …[2]

[(3) In this Act 'voluntary home' means a children's home which is carried on by a voluntary organisation but does not include a community home.][1]

(4) Schedule 5 shall have effect for the purpose of supplementing the provisions of this Part.

NOTES

Amendments.[1] Section heading and subsection substituted: Care Standards Act 2000, s 116, Sch 4, para 14(1), (9).[2] Subsections repealed: Care Standards Act 2000, s 117, Sch 6.

Definitions. 'Child': s 105(1); 'community home': s 53(1); 'health service hospital': s 105(1); 'mental nursing home': s 105(1); 'nursing home': s 105(1); 'residential care home': s 105(1); 'school': s 105(1); 'voluntary home': s 60(3); 'voluntary organisation': s 105(1).

61 Duties of voluntary organisations

(1) Where a child is accommodated by or on behalf of a voluntary organisation, it shall be the duty of the organisation –

    (a)   to safeguard and promote his welfare;

    (b)   to make such use of the services and facilities available for children cared for by their own parents as appears to the organisation reasonable in his case; and

    (c)   to advise, assist and befriend him with a view to promoting his welfare when he ceases to be so accommodated.

(2) Before making any decision with respect to any such child the organisation shall, so far as is reasonably practicable, ascertain the wishes and feelings of –

    (a)   the child;

    (b)   his parents;

    (c)   any person who is not a parent of his but who has parental responsibility for him; and

    (d)   any other person whose wishes and feelings the organisation consider to be relevant,

regarding the matter to be decided.

(3) In making any such decision the organisation shall give due consideration –

    (a)   having regard to the child's age and understanding, to such wishes and feelings of his as they have been able to ascertain;

    (b)   to such other wishes and feelings mentioned in subsection (2) as they have been able to ascertain; and

    (c)   to the child's religious persuasion, racial origin and cultural and linguistic background.

NOTES

Definitions. 'Child': s 105(1); 'parental responsibility': s 3; 'voluntary organisation': s 105(1).

62 Duties of local authorities

(1) Every local authority shall satisfy themselves that any voluntary organisation providing accommodation –

    (a)   within the authority's area for any child; or

    (b)   outside that area for any child on behalf of the authority, are satisfactorily safeguarding and promoting the welfare of the children so provided with accommodation.

(2) Every local authority shall arrange for children who are accommodated within their area by or on behalf of voluntary organisations to be visited, from time to time, in the interests of their welfare.

(3) The [appropriate national authority]³ may make regulations –

    (a)   requiring every child who is accommodated within a local authority's area, by or on behalf of a voluntary organisation, to be visited by an officer of the authority –
        (i)   in prescribed circumstances; and
        (ii)   on specified occasions or within specified periods; and
    (b)   imposing requirements which must be met by any local authority, or officer of a local authority, carrying out functions under this section.

(4) Subsection (2) does not apply in relation to community homes.

(5) Where a local authority are not satisfied that the welfare of any child who is accommodated by or on behalf of a voluntary organisation is being satisfactorily safeguarded or promoted they shall –

    (a)   unless they consider that it would not be in the best interests of the child, take such steps as are reasonably practicable to secure that the care and accommodation of the child is undertaken by –
        (i)   a parent of his;
        (ii)   any person who is not a parent of his but who has parental responsibility for him; or
        (iii) a relative of his; and
    (b)   consider the extent to which (if at all) they should exercise any of their functions with respect to the child.

(6) Any person authorised by a local authority may, for the purpose of enabling the authority to discharge their duties under this section –

    (a)   enter, at any reasonable time, and inspect any premises in which children are being accommodated as mentioned in subsection (1) or (2);
    (b)   inspect any children there;
    (c)   require any person to furnish him with such records of a kind required to be kept by regulations made under [section 22 of the Care Standards Act 2000]¹ [or section 20 of the Health and Social Care Act 2008]⁴ (in whatever form they are held), or allow him to inspect such records, as he may at any time direct.

(7) Any person exercising the power conferred by subsection (6) shall, if asked to do so, produce some duly authenticated document showing his authority to do so.

(8) Any person authorised to exercise the power to inspect records conferred by subsection (6) –

(a) shall be entitled at any reasonable time to have access to, and inspect and check the operation of, any computer and any associated apparatus or material which is or has been in use in connection with the records in question; and

(b) may require –

(i) the person by whom or on whose behalf the computer is or has been so used; or

(ii) any person having charge of, or otherwise concerned with the operation of, the computer, apparatus or material,

to afford him such assistance as he may reasonably require.

(9) Any person who intentionally obstructs another in the exercise of any power conferred by subsection (6) or (8) shall be guilty of an offence and liable on summary conviction to a fine not exceeding level 3 on the standard scale.

[(10) This section does not apply in relation to any voluntary organisation which is an institution within the further education sector, as defined in section 91 of the Further and Higher Education Act 1992, or a school.][2]

NOTES

Amendments.[1] Words substituted: Care Standards Act 2000, s 116, Sch 4, para 14(10).[2] Subsection inserted: Care Standards Act 2000, s 105(5).[3] Words substituted: Children and Young Persons Act 2008, s 39, Sch 3, paras 1, 24.[4] Words inserted: SI 2010/813.

Definitions. 'Child': s 105(1); 'community home': s 53(1); 'functions', 'local authority': s 105(1); 'parental responsibility': s 3; 'prescribed', 'relative', 'voluntary organisation': s 105(1).

PART VIII
REGISTERED CHILDREN'S HOMES

63 [Private children's homes etc][2]

(1)–(10) ...[1]

(11) Schedule 6 shall have effect with respect to [private][2] children's homes.

(12) Schedule 7 shall have effect for the purpose of setting out the circumstances in which a person may foster more than three children without being treated [, for the purposes of this Act and the Care Standards Act 2000,][2] as carrying on a children's home.

NOTES

Amendments.[1] Subsections repealed: Care Standards Act 2000, s 117, Sch 6.[2] Section heading substituted and words inserted: Care Standards Act 2000, s 116, Sch 4, para 14(1), (11).

Definitions. 'A privately fostered child': s 66(1); 'child': s 105(1); 'children's home': s 23; 'community home': s 53(1); 'health service hospital': s 105(1); 'independent school', 'mental nursing home', 'nursing home': s 105(1); 'parental responsibility': s 3; 'relative', 'residential care home', 'school': s 105(1); 'voluntary home': s 60(3); 'voluntary organisation': s 105(1).

64 Welfare of children in children's homes

(1) Where a child is accommodated in a [private][1] children's home, it shall be the duty of the person carrying on the home to –

(a)   safeguard and promote the child's welfare;

(b)   make such use of the services and facilities available for children cared for by their own parents as appears to that person reasonable in the case of the child; and

(c)   advise, assist and befriend him with a view to promoting his welfare when he ceases to be so accommodated.

(2) Before making any decision with respect to any such child the person carrying on the home shall, so far as is reasonably practicable, ascertain the wishes and feelings of –

(a)   the child;

(b)   his parents;

(c)   any other person who is not a parent of his but who has parental responsibility for him; and

(d)   any person whose wishes and feelings the person carrying on the home considers to be relevant,

regarding the matter to be decided.

(3) In making any such decision the person concerned shall give due consideration –

(a)   having regard to the child's age and understanding, to such wishes and feelings of his as he has been able to ascertain;

(b)   to such other wishes and feelings mentioned in subsection (2) as he has been able to ascertain; and

(c)   to the child's religious persuasion, racial origin and cultural and linguistic background.

(4) Section 62, except subsection (4), shall apply in relation to any person who is carrying on a [private][1] children's home as it applies in relation to any voluntary organisation.

NOTES

Amendments.[1] Word inserted: Care Standards Act 2000, s 116, Sch 4, para 14(12).

Definitions. 'Child': s 105(1); 'children's home': s 23; 'parental responsibility': s 3; 'voluntary organisation': s 105(1).

65 Persons disqualified from carrying on, or being employed in, children's homes

(1) A person who is disqualified (under section 68) from fostering a child privately shall not carry on, or be otherwise concerned in the management of, or have any financial interest in, a children's home unless he has –

(a)   disclosed to [the appropriate authority][1] the fact that he is so disqualified; and

(b)   obtained [its][1] written consent.

(2) No person shall employ a person who is so disqualified in a children's home unless he has –

(a)   disclosed to [the appropriate authority][1] the fact that that person is so disqualified; and

(b)   obtained [its][1] written consent.

(3) Where [the appropriate authority refuses to give its consent under this section, it][1] shall inform the applicant by a written notice which states –[2]

(a)   the reason for the refusal;

[(b)   the applicant's right to appeal under section 65A against the refusal to the [First-tier Tribunal][4]][1]; and

(c)   the time within which he may do so.

(4) Any person who contravenes subsection (1) or (2) shall be guilty of an offence and liable on summary conviction to imprisonment for a term not exceeding six months or to a fine not exceeding level 5 on the standard scale or to both.

(5) Where a person contravenes subsection (2) he shall not be guilty of an offence if he proves that he did not know, and had no reasonable grounds for believing, that the person whom he was employing was disqualified under section 68.

[(6) In this section and section 65A 'appropriate authority' means–

(a)   in relation to England, [[Her Majesty's Chief Inspector of Education, Children's Services and Skills][3]][2]; and

(b)   in relation to Wales, the National Assembly for Wales.][1]

NOTES

Amendments.[1] Words substituted and subsection inserted: Care Standards Act 2000, s 116, Sch 4, para 14(13). [2] Words substituted: Health and Social Care (Community Health and Standards) Act 2003, s 147, Sch 9, para 10(1), (2).[3] Words substituted: Education and Inspections Act 2006, s 157, Sch 14, paras 9, 12.[4] Words substituted: SI 2008/2833.

Definitions. 'Child': s 105(1); 'children's home': s 23; 'responsible authority': Sch 6, para 3(1); 'to foster a child privately': s 66(1)(b).

[65A Appeal against refusal of authority to give consent under section 65

(1) An appeal against a decision of an appropriate authority under section 65 shall lie to the [First-tier Tribunal][2].

(2) On an appeal the Tribunal may confirm the authority's decision or direct it to give the consent in question.][1]

NOTES

Amendments.[1] Section inserted: Care Standards Act 2000, s 116, Sch 4, para 14(14).[2] Words substituted: SI 2008/2833.

PART IX
PRIVATE ARRANGEMENTS FOR FOSTERING CHILDREN

66 Privately fostered children

(1) In this Part –

(a)   'a privately fostered child' means a child who is under the age of sixteen and who is cared for, and provided with accommodation [in their own home][1] by, someone other than –
    (i)   a parent of his;
    (ii)   a person who is not a parent of his but who has parental responsibility for him; or
    (iii) a relative of his; and

(b)   'to foster a child privately' means to look after the child in circumstances in which he is a privately fostered child as defined by this section.

(2) A child is not a privately fostered child if the person caring for and accommodating him –

(a)   has done so for a period of less than 28 days; and
(b)   does not intend to do so for any longer period.

(3) Subsection (1) is subject to –

(a)   the provisions of section 63; and
(b)   the exceptions made by paragraphs 1 to 5 of Schedule 8.

(4) In the case of a child who is disabled, subsection (1)(a) shall have effect as if for 'sixteen' there were substituted 'eighteen'.

[(4A) The Secretary of State may by regulations make provision as to the circumstances in which a person who provides accommodation to a child is, or is not, to be treated as providing him with accommodation in the person's own home.][1]

(5) Schedule 8 shall have effect for the purposes of supplementing the provision made by this Part.

NOTES

Amendments.[1] Words and subsection inserted: Care Standards Act 2000, s 116, Sch 4, para 14(1), (15).

Definitions. 'Child': s 105(1); 'disabled': s 17(11); 'parental responsibility': s 3; 'privately fostered child': s 66(1); 'relative': s 105(1); 'to foster a child privately': s 66(1).

67 Welfare of privately fostered children

(1) It shall be the duty of every local authority to satisfy themselves that the welfare of children who are [or are proposed to be][1] privately fostered within their area is being [or will be][1] satisfactorily safeguarded and promoted and to secure that such advice is given to those [concerned with][1] them as appears to the authority to be needed.

(2) The Secretary of State may make regulations –

(a)   requiring every child who is privately fostered within a local authority's area to be visited by an officer of the authority –
    (i)   in prescribed circumstances; and
    (ii)   on specified occasions or within specified periods; and

(b)   imposing requirements which are to be met by any local authority, or officer of a local authority, in carrying out functions under this section.

[(2A) Regulations under subsection (2)(b) may impose requirements as to the action to be taken by a local authority for the purposes of discharging their duty under subsection (1) where they have received notification of a proposal that a child be privately fostered.]¹

(3) Where any person who is authorised by a local authority [for the purpose]¹ has reasonable cause to believe that –

(a)   any privately fostered child is being accommodated in premises within the authority's area; or

(b)   it is proposed to accommodate any such child in any such premises,

he may at any reasonable time inspect those premises and any children there.

(4) Any person exercising the power under subsection (3) shall, if so required, produce some duly authenticated document showing his authority to do so.

(5) Where a local authority are not satisfied that the welfare of any child who is [or is proposed to be]¹ privately fostered within their area is being [or will be]¹ satisfactorily safeguarded or promoted they shall –

(a)   unless they consider that it would not be in the best interests of the child, take such steps as are reasonably practicable to secure that the care and accommodation of the child is undertaken by –
    (i)   a parent of his;
    (ii)   any person who is not a parent of his but who has parental responsibility for him; or
    (iii)   a relative of his; and
(b)   consider the extent to which (if at all) they should exercise any of their functions under this Act with respect to the child.

[(6) The Secretary of State may make regulations requiring a local authority to monitor the way in which the authority discharge their functions under this Part (and the regulations may in particular require the authority to appoint an officer for that purpose).]¹

NOTES

Amendments.¹ Words inserted or substituted and subsections inserted: Children Act 2004, s 44.

Definitions. 'Child': s 105(1); 'functions': s 105(1); 'local authority': s 105(1); 'parental responsibility': s 3; 'prescribed': s 105(1); 'privately fostered child': s 66(1); 'relative': s 105(1).

68 Persons disqualified from being private foster parents

(1) Unless he has disclosed the fact to the appropriate local authority and obtained their written consent, a person shall not foster a child privately if he is disqualified from doing so by regulations made by the Secretary of State for the purposes of this section.

(2) The regulations may, in particular, provide for a person to be so disqualified where –

(a)   an order of a kind specified in the regulations has been made at any time with respect to him;

(b)   an order of a kind so specified has been made at any time with respect to any child who has been in his care;

(c)   a requirement of a kind so specified has been imposed at any time with respect to any such child, under or by virtue of any enactment;

(d)   he has been convicted of any offence of a kind so specified, or ...[1] discharged absolutely or conditionally for any such offence;

(e)   a prohibition has been imposed on him at any time under section 69 or under any other specified enactment;

(f)   his rights and powers with respect to a child have at any time been vested in a specified authority under a specified enactment.

[(2A) A conviction in respect of which a probation order was made before 1st October 1992 (which would not otherwise be treated as a conviction) is to be treated as a conviction for the purposes of subsection (2)(d).][1]

(3) Unless he has disclosed the fact to the appropriate local authority and obtained their written consent, a person shall not foster a child privately if –

(a)   he lives in the same household as a person who is himself prevented from fostering a child by subsection (1); or

(b)   he lives in a household at which any such person is employed.

[(3A) A person shall not foster a child privately if –

(a)   he is barred from regulated activity relating to children (within the meaning of section 3(2) of the Safeguarding Vulnerable Groups Act 2006); or

(b)   he lives in the same household as a person who is barred from such activity.][2]

(4) Where an authority refuse to give their consent under this section, they shall inform the applicant by a written notice which states –

(a)   the reason for the refusal;

(b)   the applicant's right under paragraph 8 of Schedule 8 to appeal against the refusal; and

(c)   the time within which he may do so.

(5) In this section –

'the appropriate authority' means the local authority within whose area it is proposed to foster the child in question; and

'enactment' means any enactment having effect, at any time, in any part of the United Kingdom.

NOTES

Amendments.[1] Words repealed and subsection inserted: Criminal Justice Act 2003, ss 304, 332, Sch 32, Pt 1, paras 59, 60, Sch 37, Pt 7.[2] Subsection inserted: Safeguarding Vulnerable Groups Act 2006, s 63(1), Sch 9, Pt 2, para 12.

Definitions. 'Appropriate authority': s 68(5); 'child': s 105(1); 'enactment': s 68(5); 'local authority': s 105(1); 'to foster a child privately': s 66(1).

69 Power to prohibit private fostering

(1) This section applies where a person –

(a) proposes to foster a child privately; or

(b) is fostering a child privately.

(2) Where the local authority for the area within which the child is proposed to be, or is being, fostered are of the opinion that –

(a) he is not a suitable person to foster a child;

(b) the premises in which the child will be, or is being, accommodated are not suitable; or

(c) it would be prejudicial to the welfare of the child for him to be, or continue to be, accommodated by that person in those premises,

the authority may impose a prohibition on him under subsection (3).

(3) A prohibition imposed on any person under this subsection may prohibit him from fostering privately –

(a) any child in any premises within the area of the local authority; or

(b) any child in premises specified in the prohibition;

(c) a child identified in the prohibition, in premises specified in the prohibition.

(4) A local authority who have imposed a prohibition on any person under subsection (3) may, if they think fit, cancel the prohibition –

(a) of their own motion; or

(b) on an application made by that person,

if they are satisfied that the prohibition is no longer justified.

(5) Where a local authority impose a requirement on any person under paragraph 6 of Schedule 8, they may also impose a prohibition on him under subsection (3).

(6) Any prohibition imposed by virtue of subsection (5) shall not have effect unless –

(a) the time specified for compliance with the requirement has expired; and

(b) the requirement has not been complied with.

(7) A prohibition imposed under this section shall be imposed by notice in writing addressed to the person on whom it is imposed and informing him of –

(a) the reason for imposing the prohibition;

(b) his right under paragraph 8 of Schedule 8 to appeal against the prohibition; and

(c) the time within which he may do so.

NOTES

Definitions. 'Child': s 105(1); 'local authority': s 105(1); 'to foster a child privately': s 66(1).

70 Offences

(1) A person shall be guilty of an offence if –

(a)   being required, under any provision made by or under this Part, to give any notice or information –

(i)   he fails without reasonable excuse to give the notice within the time specified in that provision; or

(ii)   he fails without reasonable excuse to give the information within a reasonable time; or

(iii)   he makes, or causes or procures another person to make, any statement in the notice or information which he knows to be false or misleading in a material particular;

(b)   he refuses to allow a privately fostered child to be visited by a duly authorised officer of a local authority;

(c)   he intentionally obstructs another in the exercise of the power conferred by section 67(3);

(d)   he contravenes section 68;

(e)   he fails without reasonable excuse to comply with any requirement imposed by a local authority under this Part;

(f)   he accommodates a privately fostered child in any premises in contravention of a prohibition imposed by a local authority under this Part;

(g)   he knowingly causes to be published, or publishes, an advertisement which he knows contravenes paragraph 10 of Schedule 8.

(2) Where a person contravenes section 68(3), he shall not be guilty of an offence under this section if he proves that he did not know, and had no reasonable ground for believing, that any person to whom section 68(1) applied was living or employed in the premises in question.

(3) A person guilty of an offence under subsection (1)(a) shall be liable on summary conviction to a fine not exceeding level 5 on the standard scale.

(4) A person guilty of an offence under subsection (1)(b), (c) or (g) shall be liable on summary conviction to a fine not exceeding level 3 on the standard scale.

(5) A person guilty of an offence under subsection (1)(d) or (f) shall be liable on summary conviction to imprisonment for a term not exceeding six months, or to a fine not exceeding level 5 on the standard scale, or to both.

(6) A person guilty of an offence under subsection (1)(e) shall be liable on summary conviction to a fine not exceeding level 4 on the standard scale.

(7) If any person who is required, under any provision of this Part, to give a notice fails to give the notice within the time specified in that provision,

proceedings for the offence may be brought at any time within six months from the date when evidence of the offence came to the knowledge of the local authority.

(8) Subsection (7) is not affected by anything in section 127(1) of the Magistrates' Courts Act 1980 (time limit for proceedings).

NOTES

Definitions. 'Child': s 105(1); 'local authority': s 105(1); 'privately fostered child': s 66(1).

PART X
CHILD MINDING AND DAY CARE FOR YOUNG CHILDREN

...[1]

NOTES

Amendments.[1] Part X repealed in relation to England and Wales: Care Standards Act 2000, s 79(5).

[PART XA[1]
CHILD MINDING AND DAY CARE FOR CHILDREN IN ...[2] WALES

NOTES

Amendment. [1] Part XA repealed in relation to Wales: Children and Families (Wales) Measure 2010, s 73, Sch 2 (with transitional provisions and savings, SI 2010/2582, Schs 2, 3).[2] Words omitted: Childcare Act 2006, s 103, Sch 2, para 5, Sch 3, Pt 2.

Introductory

[79A Child minders and day care providers

(1) This section and section 79B apply for the purposes of this Part.

(2) 'Act as a child minder' means (subject to the following subsections) look after one or more children under the age of eight on domestic premises for reward; and 'child minding' shall be interpreted accordingly.

(3) A person who –

    (a)   is the parent, or a relative, of a child;
    (b)   has parental responsibility for a child;
    (c)   is a local authority foster parent in relation to a child;
    (d)   is a foster parent with whom a child has been placed by a voluntary organisation; or
    (e)   fosters a child privately,

does not act as a child minder when looking after that child.

(4) Where a person –

    (a)   looks after a child for the parents ('P1'), or
    (b)   in addition to that work, looks after another child for different parents ('P2'),

and the work consists (in a case within paragraph (a)) of looking after the child wholly or mainly in P1's home or (in a case within paragraph (b)) of looking after the children wholly or mainly in P1's home or P2's home or both, the work is not to be treated as child minding.

(5) In subsection (4), 'parent', in relation to a child, includes –

(a)   a person who is not a parent of the child but who has parental responsibility for the child;

(b)   a person who is a relative of the child.

(6) 'Day care' means care provided at any time for children under the age of eight on premises other than domestic premises.

(7) This Part does not apply in relation to a person who acts as a child minder, or provides day care on any premises, unless the period, or the total of the periods, in any day which he spends looking after children or (as the case may be) during which the children are looked after on the premises exceeds two hours.

(8) In determining whether a person is required to register under this Part for child minding, any day on which he does not act as a child minder at any time between 2 am and 6 pm is to be disregarded.][1]

NOTES

Amendments. [1] Part XA repealed in relation to Wales: Children and Families (Wales) Measure 2010, s 73, Sch 2 (with transitional provisions and savings, SI 2010/2582, Schs 2, 3).

[79B   Other definitions, etc

(1) ...[5]

[(2) In this Act 'the Assembly' means the National Assembly for Wales.][5]

(3) A person is qualified for registration for child minding if –

(a)   he, and every other person looking after children on any premises on which he is or is likely to be child minding, is suitable to look after children under the age of eight;

(b)   every person living or employed on the premises in question is suitable to be in regular contact with children under the age of eight;

(c)   the premises in question are suitable to be used for looking after children under the age of eight, having regard to their condition and the condition and appropriateness of any equipment on the premises and to any other factor connected with the situation, construction or size of the premises; and

(d)   he is complying with regulations under section 79C and with any conditions imposed [under this Part][2].

(4) A person is qualified for registration for providing day care on particular premises if –

[(a)   he has made adequate arrangements to ensure that –

      (i)   every person (other than himself and the responsible individual) looking after children on the premises is suitable to look after children under the age of eight; and

      (ii)   every person (other than himself and the responsible individual) living or working on the premises is suitable to be in regular contact with children under the age of eight;

    (b)   the responsible individual –

      (i)   is suitable to look after children under the age of eight, or

      (ii)   if he is not looking after such children, is suitable to be in regular contact with them;][3]

    (c)   the premises are suitable to be used for looking after children under the age of eight, having regard to their condition and the condition and appropriateness of any equipment on the premises and to any other factor connected with the situation, construction or size of the premises; and

    (d)   he is complying with regulations under section 79C and with any conditions imposed [under this Part][2].

(5) For the purposes of subsection [(4)(a)][3] a person is not treated as working on the premises in question if –

    (a)   none of his work is done in the part of the premises in which children are looked after; or

    (b)   he does not work on the premises at times when children are looked after there.

[(5ZA) For the purposes of subsection (4), 'the responsible individual' means –

    (a)   in a case of one individual working on the premises in the provision of day care, that person;

    (b)   in a case of two or more individuals so working, the individual so working who is in charge.][3]

[(5A) Where, for the purposes of determining a person's qualification for registration under this Part –

    (a)   [the Assembly][5] requests any person ('A') to consent to the disclosure to the authority by another person ('B') of any information relating to A which is held by B and is of a prescribed description, and

    (b)   A does not give his consent (or withdraws it after having given it),

[the Assembly][5] may, if regulations so provide and it thinks it appropriate to do so, regard A as not suitable to look after children under the age of eight, or not suitable to be in regular contact with such children.][1]

(6) 'Domestic premises' means any premises which are wholly or mainly used as a private dwelling and 'premises' includes any area and any vehicle.

[(7) 'Regulations' means regulations made by the Assembly.][5]

(8) ...[6]

(9) Schedule 9A (which supplements the provisions of this Part) shall have effect.][7]

Part I   Statutes

NOTES

Amendments.[1] Subsection inserted: Education Act 2002, s 152, Sch 13, para 1.[2] Words substituted: Children Act 2004, s 48, Sch 4, paras 1, 2.[3] Subsection inserted and paragraphs and words substituted: Children Act 2004, s 48, Sch 4, paras 1, 6.[4] Words substituted: Education and Inspections Act 2006, s 157, Sch 14, paras 9, 13.[5] Subsections repealed and substituted and words substituted: Childcare Act 2006, s 103, Sch 2, paras 6, 7, Sch 3, Pt 2.[6] Subsection repealed: SI 2008/2833. [7] Part XA repealed in relation to Wales: Children and Families (Wales) Measure 2010, s 73, Sch 2 (with transitional provisions and savings, SI 2010/2582, Schs 2, 3).

Regulations

[79C Regulations etc governing child minders and day care providers

(1) ...[1]

(2) The Assembly may make regulations governing the activities of registered persons who act as child minders, or provide day care, on premises in Wales.

(3) The regulations under this section may deal with the following matters (among others) –

(a)   the welfare and development of the children concerned;
(b)   suitability to look after, or be in regular contact with, children under the age of eight;
(c)   qualifications and training;
(d)   the maximum number of children who may be looked after and the number of persons required to assist in looking after them;
(e)   the maintenance, safety and suitability of premises and equipment;
(f)   the keeping of records;
(g)   the provision of information.

(4), (5) ...[1]

(6) If the regulations require any person (other than [the Assembly][1]) to have regard to or meet factors, standards and other matters prescribed by or referred to in the regulations, they may also provide for any allegation that the person has failed to do so to be taken into account –

(a)   by [the Assembly][1] in the exercise of its functions under this Part, or
(b)   in any proceedings under this Part.

(7) Regulations may provide –

(a)   that a registered person who without reasonable excuse contravenes, or otherwise fails to comply with, any requirement of the regulations shall be guilty of an offence; and
(b)   that a person guilty of the offence shall be liable on summary conviction to a fine not exceeding level 5 on the standard scale.][2]

NOTES

Amendments.[1] Subsections repealed and words substituted: Childcare Act 2006, s 103, Sch 2, paras 6, 8, Sch 3, Pt 2. [2] Part XA repealed in relation to Wales: Children and Families (Wales) Measure 2010, s 73, Sch 2 (with transitional provisions and savings, SI 2010/2582, Schs 2, 3).

Registration

[79D Requirement to register

[(1) No person shall act as a child minder in Wales unless he is registered under this Part for child minding by the Assembly.][1]

(2) Where it appears to [the Assembly][1] that a person has contravened subsection (1), the authority may serve a notice ('an enforcement notice') on him.

(3) An enforcement notice shall have effect for a period of one year beginning with the date on which it is served.

(4) If a person in respect of whom an enforcement notice has effect contravenes subsection (1) without reasonable excuse ...[1], he shall be guilty of an offence.

(5) No person shall provide day care on any premises [in Wales][1] unless he is registered under this Part for providing day care on those premises by [the Assembly][1].

(6) If any person contravenes subsection (5) without reasonable excuse, he shall be guilty of an offence.

(7) A person guilty of an offence under this section shall be liable on summary conviction to a fine not exceeding level 5 on the standard scale.][2]

NOTES

Amendments.[1] Subsection substituted, and words substituted and inserted: Childcare Act 2006, s 103(1), Sch 2, paras 6, 9, Sch 3, Pt 2. [2] Part XA repealed in relation to Wales: Children and Families (Wales) Measure 2010, s 73, Sch 2 (with transitional provisions and savings, SI 2010/2582, Schs 2, 3).

[79E Applications for registration

(1) A person who wishes to be registered under this Part shall make an application to [the Assembly][2].

(2) The application shall –

  (a) give prescribed information about prescribed matters;
  (b) give any other information which [the Assembly][2] reasonably requires the applicant to give
  [(c) be accompanied by the prescribed fee][1].

(3) Where a person provides, or proposes to provide, day care on different premises, he shall make a separate application in respect of each of them.

(4) Where [the Assembly][2] has sent the applicant notice under section 79L(1) of its intention to refuse an application under this section, the application may not be withdrawn without the consent of the authority.

(5) A person who, in an application under this section, knowingly makes a statement which is false or misleading in a material particular shall be guilty of an offence and liable, on summary conviction, to a fine not exceeding level 5 on the standard scale.][3]

NOTES

Amendments.[1] Paragraph inserted: Children Act 2004, s 48, Sch 4, paras 1, 3(1).[2] Words substituted: Childcare Act 2006, s 103(1), Sch 2, para 6.[3] Part XA repealed in relation to Wales: Children and Families (Wales) Measure 2010, s 73, Sch 2 (with transitional provisions and savings, SI 2010/2582, Schs 2, 3).

[79F   Grant or refusal of registration

(1) If, on an application [under section 79E][1] by a person for registration for child minding –

   (a)   [the Assembly][3] is of the opinion that the applicant is, and will continue to be, qualified for registration for child minding (so far as the conditions of section 79B(3) are applicable); ...[2]
   (b)   ...[2]

[the Assembly][3] shall grant the application; otherwise, it shall refuse it.

(2) If, on an application [under section 79E][1] by any person for registration for providing day care on any premises –

   (a)   [the Assembly][3] is of the opinion that the applicant is, and will continue to be, qualified for registration for providing day care on those premises (so far as the conditions of section 79B(4) are applicable); ...[2]
   (b)   ...[2]

[the Assembly][3] shall grant the application; otherwise, it shall refuse it.

(3) An application may, as well as being granted subject to any conditions [the Assembly][3] thinks necessary or expedient for the purpose of giving effect to regulations under section 79C, be granted subject to any other conditions [the Assembly][3] thinks fit to impose.

(4) [The Assembly][3] may as it thinks fit vary or remove any condition to which the registration is subject or impose a new condition.

(5) Any register kept by [the Assembly][3] of persons who act as child minders or provide day care shall be open to inspection by any person at all reasonable times.

(6) A registered person who without reasonable excuse contravenes, or otherwise fails to comply with, any condition imposed on his registration shall be guilty of an offence.

(7) A person guilty of an offence under subsection (6) shall be liable on summary conviction to a fine not exceeding level 5 on the standard scale.][4]

PART I – Statutes

NOTES

Amendments.[1] Words inserted: Children Act 2004, s 48, Sch 4, paras 1, 3(2)(a).[2] Words or paragraphs repealed: Children Act 2004, ss 48, 64, Sch 4, paras 1, 3(2)(b), Sch 5, Pt 2.[3] Words substituted: Childcare Act 2006, s 103(1), Sch 2, para 6. [4] Part XA repealed in relation to Wales: Children and Families (Wales) Measure 2010, s 73, Sch 2 (with transitional provisions and savings, SI 2010/2582, Schs 2, 3).

[79G Cancellation of registration

(1) [The Assembly][3] may cancel the registration of any person if –

(a)   in the case of a person registered for child minding, [the Assembly][3] is of the opinion that the person has ceased or will cease to be qualified for registration for child minding;

(b)   in the case of a person registered for providing day care on any premises, [the Assembly][3] is of the opinion that the person has ceased or will cease to be qualified for registration for providing day care on those premises,

or if [a fee][2] which is due from the person has not been paid.

(2) Where a requirement to make any changes or additions to any services, equipment or premises has been imposed on a registered person ...[1], his registration shall not be cancelled on the ground of any defect or insufficiency in the services, equipment or premises if –

(a)   the time set for complying with the requirements has not expired; and

(b)   it is shown that the defect or insufficiency is due to the changes or additions not having been made.

(3) Any cancellation under this section must be in writing.][4]

NOTES

Amendments.[1] Words repealed: Children Act 2004, ss 48, 64, Sch 4, paras 1, 2(2), Sch 5, Pt 2.[2] Words substituted: Children Act 2004, s 48, Sch 4, paras 1, 4(1).[3] Words substituted: Childcare Act 2006, s 103(1), Sch 2, para 6. [4] Part XA repealed in relation to Wales: Children and Families (Wales) Measure 2010, s 73, Sch 2 (with transitional provisions and savings, SI 2010/2582, Schs 2, 3).

[79H Suspension of registration

(1) Regulations may provide for the registration of any person for acting as a child minder or providing day care to be suspended for a prescribed period by [the Assembly][2] in prescribed circumstances.

(2) Any regulations made under this section shall include provision conferring on the person concerned a right of appeal to the [First-tier][3] Tribunal against suspension.

[(3) ...[2]

(4) A person registered under this Part for child minding by the Assembly shall not act as a child minder in Wales at a time when that registration is so suspended.

(5) A person registered under this Part for providing day care on any premises shall not provide day care on those premises at any time when that registration is so suspended.

(6) If any person contravenes subsection (3), (4) or (5) without reasonable excuse, he shall be guilty of an offence and liable on summary conviction to a fine not exceeding level 5 on the standard scale.]¹]⁴

NOTES

Amendments.¹ Subsections inserted: Education Act 2002, s 152, Sch 13, para 2.² Words substituted and subsection repealed: Childcare Act 2006, s 103, Sch 2, paras 6, 10, Sch 3, Pt 2.³ Words inserted: SI 2008/2833. ⁴ Part XA repealed in relation to Wales: Children and Families (Wales) Measure 2010, s 73, Sch 2 (with transitional provisions and savings, SI 2010/2582, Schs 2, 3).

[79J Resignation of registration

(1) A person who is registered for acting as a child minder or providing day care may by notice in writing to [the Assembly]¹ resign his registration.

(2) But a person may not give a notice under subsection (1) –

(a)   if [the Assembly]¹ has sent him a notice under section 79L(1) of its intention to cancel the registration, unless the authority has decided not to take that step; or

(b)   if [the Assembly]¹ has sent him a notice under section 79L(5) of its decision to cancel the registration and the time within which an appeal may be brought has not expired or, if an appeal has been brought, it has not been determined.]²

NOTES

Amendments.¹ Words substituted: Childcare Act 2006, s 103(1), Sch 2, para 6. ² Part XA repealed in relation to Wales: Children and Families (Wales) Measure 2010, s 73, Sch 2 (with transitional provisions and savings, SI 2010/2582, Schs 2, 3).

[79K Protection of children in an emergency

(1) If, in the case of any person registered [under this Part]¹ for acting as a child minder or providing day care –

(a)   [the Assembly]¹ applies to a justice of the peace for an order –
    (i)   cancelling the registration;
    (ii)   varying or removing any condition to which the registration is subject; or
    (iii) imposing a new condition; and

(b)   it appears to the justice that a child who is being, or may be, looked after by that person, or (as the case may be) in accordance with the provision for day care made by that person, is suffering, or is likely to suffer, significant harm,

the justice may make the order.

(2) The cancellation, variation, removal or imposition shall have effect from the time when the order is made.

(3) An application under subsection (1) may be made without notice.

(4) An order under subsection (1) shall be made in writing.

(5) Where an order is made under this section, [the Assembly]¹ shall serve on the registered person, as soon as is reasonably practicable after the making of the order –

    (a)   a copy of the order;

    (b)   a copy of any written statement of [the Assembly's]¹ reasons for making the application for the order which supported that application; and

    (c)   notice of any right of appeal conferred by section 79M.

(6) Where an order has been so made, [the Assembly]¹ shall, as soon as is reasonably practicable after the making of the order, notify the local authority in whose area the person concerned acts or acted as a child minder, or provides or provided day care, of the making of the order.]²

NOTES

Amendments.¹ Words inserted and substituted: Childcare Act 2006, s 103(1), Sch 2, paras 6, 11. ² Part XA repealed in relation to Wales: Children and Families (Wales) Measure 2010, s 73, Sch 2 (with transitional provisions and savings, SI 2010/2582, Schs 2, 3).

[79L Notice of intention to take steps

(1) Not less than 14 days before –

    (a)   refusing an application for registration;

    (b)   cancelling a registration;

    (c)   removing or varying any condition to which a registration is subject or imposing a new condition; or

    (d)   refusing to grant an application for the removal or variation of any condition to which a registration is subject,

[the Assembly]¹ shall send to the applicant, or (as the case may be) registered person, notice in writing of its intention to take the step in question.

(2) Every such notice shall –

    (a)   give [the Assembly's]¹ reasons for proposing to take the step; and

    (b)   inform the person concerned of his rights under this section.

(3) Where the recipient of such a notice informs [the Assembly]¹ in writing of his desire to object to the step being taken, [the Assembly]¹ shall afford him an opportunity to do so.

(4) Any objection made under subsection (3) may be made orally or in writing, by the recipient of the notice or a representative.

(5) If [the Assembly]¹, after giving the person concerned an opportunity to object to the step being taken, decides nevertheless to take it, it shall send him written notice of its decision.

(6) A step of a kind mentioned in subsection (1)(b) or (c) shall not take effect until the expiry of the time within which an appeal may be brought under section 79M or, where such an appeal is brought, before its determination.

(7) Subsection (6) does not prevent a step from taking effect before the expiry of the time within which an appeal may be brought under section 79M if the person concerned notifies [the Assembly]¹ in writing that he does not intend to appeal.]²

NOTES

Amendments.¹ Words substituted: Childcare Act 2006, s 103(1), Sch 2, para 6. ² Part XA repealed in relation to Wales: Children and Families (Wales) Measure 2010, s 73, Sch 2 (with transitional provisions and savings, SI 2010/2582, Schs 2, 3).

[79M Appeals

(1) An appeal against –

- (a)   the taking of any step mentioned in section 79L(1); ...¹
- (b)   an order under section 79K, [or
- (c)   a determination made by [the Assembly]² under this Part (other than one falling within paragraph (a) or (b)) which is of a prescribed description,]¹

shall lie to the [First-tier]³ Tribunal.

(2) On an appeal, the [First-tier]³ Tribunal may –

- (a)   confirm the taking of the step or the making of the order [or determination]¹ or direct that it shall not have, or shall cease to have, effect; and
- (b)   impose, vary or cancel any condition.]⁴

NOTES

Amendments.¹ Words repealed and inserted: Education Act 2002, ss 149(2), 152, 215(2), Sch 13, para 3, Sch 22, Pt 3.² Words substituted: Childcare Act 2006, s 103(1), Sch 2, para 6.³ Words inserted: SI 2008/2833. ⁴ Part XA repealed in relation to Wales: Children and Families (Wales) Measure 2010, s 73, Sch 2 (with transitional provisions and savings, SI 2010/2582, Schs 2, 3).

Inspection: England

79N General functions of the Chief Inspector

...¹

NOTES

Amendments.¹ Section repealed: Childcare Act 2006, s 103, Sch 2, para 12, Sch 3, Pt 2.

79P

...¹

NOTES

Amendments.¹ Section repealed: Education Act 2005, ss 53, 123, Sch 7, Pt 1, para 2, Sch 19, Pt 1.

79Q Inspection of provision of child minding and day care in England

...¹

NOTES

Amendments.¹ Section repealed: Childcare Act 2006, s 103, Sch 2, para 12, Sch 3, Pt 2.

79R Reports of inspections

...¹

NOTES

Amendments.¹ Section repealed: Childcare Act 2006, s 103, Sch 2, para 12, Sch 3, Pt 2.

Inspection: Wales

[79S General functions of the Assembly

(1) The Assembly may secure the provision of training for persons who provide or assist in providing child minding or day care, or intend to do so.

(2) In relation to child minding and day care provided in Wales, the Assembly shall have any additional function specified in regulations made by the Assembly; ...¹]²

NOTES

Amendments.¹ Words repealed: Childcare Act 2006, s 103, Sch 2, para 13, Sch 3, Pt 2. ² Part XA repealed in relation to Wales: Children and Families (Wales) Measure 2010, s 73, Sch 2 (with transitional provisions and savings, SI 2010/2582, Schs 2, 3).

[79T Inspection: Wales

(1) The Assembly may at any time require any registered person to provide it with any information connected with the person's activities as a child minder or provision of day care which the Assembly considers it necessary to have for the purposes of its functions under this Part.

(2) The Assembly may by regulations make provision –

(a)   for the inspection of the quality and standards of child minding provided in Wales by registered persons and of day care provided by registered persons on premises in Wales;

(b)   for the publication of reports of the inspections in such manner as the Assembly considers appropriate.

(3) The regulations may provide for the inspections to be organised by –

(a)   the Assembly; or

(b)   Her Majesty's Chief Inspector of Education and Training in Wales, or any other person, under arrangements made with the Assembly.

(4) The regulations may provide for subsections (2) to (4) of section 42A of the School Inspections Act 1996 to apply with modifications in relation to the publication of reports under the regulations.]¹

PART I – Statutes

NOTES

Amendments. ¹ Part XA repealed in relation to Wales: Children and Families (Wales) Measure 2010, s 73, Sch 2 (with transitional provisions and savings, SI 2010/2582, Schs 2, 3).

Supplementary

[79U Rights of entry etc

(1) [Any person authorised for the purposes of this subsection by [the Assembly]³]¹ may at any reasonable time enter any premises in ...³ Wales on which child minding or day care is at any time provided.

(2) Where [a person authorised for the purposes of this subsection by [the Assembly]³]¹ has reasonable cause to believe that a child is being looked after on any premises in contravention of this Part, he may enter those premises at any reasonable time.

[(2A) Authorisation under subsection (1) or (2) –

    (a)   may be given for a particular occasion or period;
    (b)   may be given subject to conditions.]¹

(3) [A person entering premises under this section may (subject to any conditions imposed under subsection (2A)(b)]¹ –

    (a)   inspect the premises;
    (b)   inspect, and take copies of –
        (i)   any records kept by the person providing the child minding or day care; and
        (ii) any other documents containing information relating to its provision;
    (c)   seize and remove any document or other material or thing found there which he has reasonable grounds to believe may be evidence of a failure to comply with any condition or requirement imposed by or under this Part;
    (d)   require any person to afford him such facilities and assistance with respect to matters within the person's control as are necessary to enable him to exercise his powers under this section;
    (e)   take measurements and photographs or make recordings;
    (f)   inspect any children being looked after there, and the arrangements made for their welfare;
    (g)   interview in private the person providing the child minding or day care; and
    (h)   interview in private any person looking after children, or living or working, there who consents to be interviewed.

(4) [Section 58 of the Education Act 2005]² (inspection of computer records for purposes of Part I of that Act) shall apply for the purposes of subsection (3) as it applies for the purposes of Part I of that Act.

(5) ...¹

(6) A person exercising any power conferred by this section shall, if so required, produce some duly authenticated document showing his authority to do so.

(7) It shall be an offence wilfully to obstruct a person exercising any such power.

(8) Any person guilty of an offence under subsection (7) shall be liable on summary conviction to a fine not exceeding level 4 on the standard scale.

(9) In this section –

    ...[1]

'documents' and 'records' each include information recorded in any form.][4]

NOTES

Amendments.[1] Words and subsection inserted, and subsection and definition repealed: Education Act 2002, s 152, Sch 13, para 5.[2] Words substituted: Education Act 2005, s 53, Sch 7, Pt 1, para 6.[3] Words repealed and substituted: Childcare Act 2006, s 103, Sch 2, paras 6, 14, Sch 3, Pt 2. [4] Part XA repealed in relation to Wales: Children and Families (Wales) Measure 2010, s 73, Sch 2 (with transitional provisions and savings, SI 2010/2582, Schs 2, 3).

[79V Function of local authorities

Each local authority [in Wales][1] shall, in accordance with regulations, secure the provision –

    (a)   of information and advice about child minding and day care; and
    (b)   of training for persons who provide or assist in providing child minding or day care.][2]

NOTES

Amendments.[1] Words inserted: Childcare Act 2006, s 103(1), Sch 2, para 15. [2] Part XA repealed in relation to Wales: Children and Families (Wales) Measure 2010, s 73, Sch 2 (with transitional provisions and savings, SI 2010/2582, Schs 2, 3).

Checks on suitability of persons working with children over the age of seven

[79W Requirement for certificate of suitability

(1) This section applies to any person not required to register under this Part who looks after, or provides care for, children [in Wales][1] and meets the following conditions.

References in this section to children are to those under the age of 15 or (in the case of disabled children) 17.

(2) The first condition is that the period, or the total of the periods, in any week which he spends looking after children or (as the case may be) during which the children are looked after exceeds five hours.

(3) The second condition is that he would be required to register under this Part (or, as the case may be, this Part if it were subject to prescribed modifications) if the children were under the age of eight.

Part I   Statutes

(4) Regulations may require a person to whom this section applies to hold a certificate issued by [the Assembly][2] as to his suitability, and the suitability of each prescribed person, to look after children.

(5) The regulations may make provision about –

(a)   applications for certificates;
(b)   the matters to be taken into account by [the Assembly][2] in determining whether to issue certificates;
(c)   the information to be contained in certificates;
(d)   the period of their validity.

(6) The regulations may provide that a person to whom this section applies shall be guilty of an offence –

(a)   if he does not hold a certificate as required by the regulations; or
(b)   if, being a person who holds such a certificate, he fails to produce it when reasonably required to do so by a prescribed person.

(7) The regulations may provide that a person who, for the purpose of obtaining such a certificate, knowingly makes a statement which is false or misleading in a material particular shall be guilty of an offence.

(8) The regulations may provide that a person guilty of an offence under the regulations shall be liable on summary conviction to a fine not exceeding level 5 on the standard scale.][3]

NOTES

Amendments.[1] Words inserted: Childcare Act 2006, s 103(1), Sch 2, para 16.[2] Words substituted: Childcare Act 2006, s 103(1), Sch 2, para 6. [3] Part XA repealed in relation to Wales: Children and Families (Wales) Measure 2010, s 73, Sch 2 (with transitional provisions and savings, SI 2010/2582, Schs 2, 3).

Time limit for proceedings

[79X   Time limit for proceedings

Proceedings for an offence under this Part or regulations made under it may be brought within a period of six months from the date on which evidence sufficient in the opinion of the prosecutor to warrant the proceedings came to his knowledge; but no such proceedings shall be brought by virtue of this section more than three years after the commission of the offence.][1]][2]

NOTES

Amendments.[1] Part inserted: Care Standards Act 2000, s 79(1). [2] Part XA repealed in relation to Wales: Children and Families (Wales) Measure 2010, s 73, Sch 2 (with transitional provisions and savings, SI 2010/2582, Schs 2, 3).

PART XI
SECRETARY OF STATE'S SUPERVISORY FUNCTIONS AND RESPONSIBILITIES

80 Inspection of children's homes etc by persons authorised by Secretary of State

(1) The Secretary of State may cause to be inspected from time to time any –

   (a) [private][4] children's home;

   (b) premises in which a child who is being looked after by a local authority is living;

   (c) premises in which a child who is being accommodated by or on behalf of a [local authority in the exercise of education functions or a][9] voluntary organisation is living;

   (d) premises in which a child who is being accommodated by or on behalf of a [[Local Health Board][8], Special Health Authority][2][, Primary Care Trust][3][, National Health Service trust or NHS foundation trust][6] is living;

   (e) ...[7]

   (f) ...[7]

   (g) premises in which a privately fostered child, or child who is treated as a foster child by virtue of paragraph 9 of Schedule 8, is living or in which it is proposed that he will live;

   (h) premises on which any person is acting as a child minder;

   [(i) *premises with respect to which a person is registered under section 71(1)(b) [or with respect to which a person is registered for providing day care under Part XA][4];*][11]

   (j) [care home or independent hospital used to accommodate children;][4]

   (k) premises which are provided by a local authority and in which any service is provided by that authority under Part III;

   (l) [school or college][5] providing accommodation for any child.

(2) An inspection under this section shall be conducted by a person authorised to do so by the Secretary of State.

(3) An officer of a local authority shall not be authorised except with the consent of that authority.

(4) The Secretary of State may require any person of a kind mentioned in subsection (5) to furnish him with such information, or allow him to inspect such records (in whatever form they are held), relating to –

   (a) any premises to which subsection (1) or, in relation to Scotland, subsection (1)(h) or (i) applies;

   (b) any child who is living in any such premises;

   (c) the discharge by the Secretary of State of any of his functions under this Act;

   (d) the discharge by any local authority of any of their functions under this Act,

as the Secretary of State may at any time direct.

(5) The persons are any –

    (a)   local authority;

    (b)   voluntary organisation;

    (c)   person carrying on a [private]⁴ children's home;

    (d)   proprietor of an independent school [or governing body of any other school]⁵;

  [(da) governing body of an institution designated under section 28 of the Further and Higher Education Act 1992;

  (db) further education corporation;]⁵

  [(dc) sixth form college corporation;]¹⁰

    (e)   person fostering any privately fostered child or providing accommodation for a child on behalf of a local authority, ...⁹ [[Local Health Board]⁸, Special Health Authority]² [, Primary Health Care Trust]³[, National Health Service trust]¹ [, NHS foundation trust]⁶ or voluntary organisation;

    (f)   ...⁹

    (g)   person employed in a teaching or administrative capacity at any educational establishment (whether or not maintained by [a local authority]⁹) at which a child is accommodated on behalf of a local authority ...⁹;

  [*(h)* *person who is the occupier of any premises in which any person acts as a child minder (within the meaning of Part X) or provides day care for young children (within the meaning of that Part);*]¹¹

  [*(hh)* *person who is the occupier of any premises –*

    (i)   *in which any person required to be registered for child minding under Part XA acts as a child minder (within the meaning of that Part); or*

    (ii) *with respect to which a person is required to be registered under that Part for providing day care;*]⁴, ¹¹

    (i)   person carrying on any home of a kind mentioned in subsection (1)(j);

   [(j)   person carrying on a fostering agency.]⁵

(6) Any person inspecting any home or other premises under this section may –

    (a)   inspect the children there; and

    (b)   make such examination into the state and management of the home or premises and the treatment of the children there as he thinks fit.

(7) Any person authorised by the Secretary of State to exercise the power to inspect records conferred by subsection (4) –

    (a)   shall be entitled at any reasonable time to have access to, and inspect and check the operation of, any computer and any associated apparatus or material which is or has been in use in connection with the records in question; and

    (b)   may require –

        (i)   the person by whom or on whose behalf the computer is or has been so used; or

        (ii)   any person having charge of, or otherwise concerned with the operation of, the computer, apparatus or material, to afford him such reasonable assistance as he may require.

(8) A person authorised to inspect any premises under this section shall have a right to enter the premises for that purpose, and for any purpose specified in subsection (4), at any reasonable time.

(9) Any person exercising that power shall, if so required, produce some duly authenticated document showing his authority to do so.

(10) Any person who intentionally obstructs another in the exercise of that power shall be guilty of an offence and liable on summary conviction to a fine not exceeding level 3 on the standard scale.

(11) The Secretary of State may by order provide for subsections (1), (4) and (6) not to apply in relation to such homes, or other premises, as may be specified in the order.

(12) Without prejudice to section 104, any such order may make different provision with respect to each of those subsections.

[(13) In this section –

'college' means an institution within the further education sector as defined
    in section 91 of the Further and Higher Education Act 1992;
'fostering agency' has the same meaning as in the Care Standards Act 2000;
'further education corporation' has the same meaning as in the Further and
    Higher Education Act 1992.
['sixth form college corporation' has the same meaning as in that Act.][10]][5]

NOTES

Amendments.[1] Words inserted: National Health Service and Community Care Act 1990, s 66(1), Sch 9, para 36(4)(b).[2] Words substituted: Health Authorities Act 1995, s 2(1), Sch 1, Pt III, para 118(1), (9).[3] Words inserted: Health Act 1999 (Supplementary, Consequential etc Provisions) Order 2000, SI 2000/90.[4] Paragraph and words inserted or substituted: Care Standards Act 2000, ss 116, 117(2), Sch 4, paras 14(1), (16).[5] Subsection, paragraphs and words inserted or substituted: Care Standards Act 2000, s 109 (applies to England only).[6] Words substituted or inserted: Health and Social Care (Community Health and Standards) Act 2003, s 34, Sch 4, paras 75, 80.[7] Paragraphs repealed: Adoption and Children Act 2002, s 139(1), (3), Sch 3, paras 54, 65, Sch 5.[8] Words substituted: SI 2007/961.[9] Words substituted and repealed, and words and paragraph repealed: SI 2010/1158.[10] Paragraph and definition inserted: SI 2010/1080. [11] Paragraphs omitted in relation to Wales: Children and Families (Wales) Measure 2010, ss 72, 73, Sch 1, paras 5, 6, Sch 2.

Definitions. 'Adoption agency': s 105(1); 'child': s 105(1); 'child minder': s 71(2)(a); 'child who is looked after by a local authority': s 22(1); 'children's home': s 23; 'day care': ss 18, 71(2)(b); 'functions': s 105(1); 'health authority': s 105(1); 'independent school': s 105(1); 'local authority': s 105(1); 'local education authority': s 105(1); 'mental nursing home': s 105(1); 'nursing home': s 105(1); 'privately fostered child': s 105(1); 'residential care home': s 105(1); 'voluntary home': s 60(3); 'voluntary organisation': s 105(1).

81

…[1]

NOTES

Amendments.[1] Section repealed: Inquiries Act 2005, ss 48(1), 49(2), Sch 2, Pt 1, para 12, Sch 3.

PART I – Statutes *(side tab)*

82 Financial support by Secretary of State

(1) The Secretary of State may (with the consent of the Treasury) defray or contribute towards –

   (a)   any fees or expenses incurred by any person undergoing approved child care training;

   (b)   any fees charged, or expenses incurred, by any person providing approved child care training or preparing material for use in connection with such training; or

   (c)   the cost of maintaining any person undergoing such training.

(2) The Secretary of State may make grants to local authorities in respect of expenditure incurred by them in providing secure accommodation in community homes other than assisted community homes.

(3) Where –

   (a)   a grant has been made under subsection (2) with respect to any secure accommodation; but

   (b)   the grant is not used for the purpose for which it was made or the accommodation is not used as, or ceases to be used as, secure accommodation,

the Secretary of State may (with the consent of the Treasury) require the authority concerned to repay the grant, in whole or in part.

(4) The Secretary of State may make grants to voluntary organisations towards –

   (a)   expenditure incurred by them in connection with the establishment, maintenance or improvement of voluntary homes which, at the time when the expenditure was incurred –
      (i)   were assisted community homes; or
      (ii)   were designated as such; or

   (b)   expenses incurred in respect of the borrowing of money to defray any such expenditure.

(5) The Secretary of State may arrange for the provision, equipment and maintenance of homes for the accommodation of children who are in need of particular facilities and services which –

   (a)   are or will be provided in those homes; and

   (b)   in the opinion of the Secretary of State, are unlikely to be readily available in community homes.

(6) In this Part –

   'child care training' means training undergone by any person with a view to, or in the course of –

      (a)   his employment for the purposes of any of the functions mentioned in section 83(9) or in connection with the adoption of children or with the accommodation of children in a [care home or independent hospital][1]; or

PART I – Statutes

(b)   his employment by a voluntary organisation for similar purposes;

'approved child care training' means child care training which is approved by
   the Secretary of State; and
'secure accommodation' means accommodation provided for the purpose of
   restricting the liberty of children.

(7) Any grant made under this section shall be of such amount, and shall be
subject to such conditions, as the Secretary of State may (with the consent of
the Treasury) determine.

NOTES

Amendments.[1] Words substituted: Care Standards Act 2000, s 116, Sch 4, para 14(18).

Definitions. 'Approved child care training': s 82(6); 'assisted community home': s 53(5); 'child':
s 105(1); 'child care training': s 82(6); 'community home': s 53(1); 'functions': s 105(1); 'mental
nursing home': s 105(1); 'nursing home': s 105(1); 'residential care home': s 105(1); 'secure
accommodation': s 82(6); 'voluntary home': s 60(3); 'voluntary organisation': s 105(1).

83 Research and returns of information

(1) The Secretary of State may conduct, or assist other persons in conducting,
research into any matter connected with –

(a)   his functions, or the functions of local authorities, under the
      enactments mentioned in subsection (9);
[(aa) the functions of Local Safeguarding Children Boards;][5]
(b)   the adoption of children; or
(c)   the accommodation of children in a [care home or independent
      hospital][2].

(2) Any local authority may conduct, or assist other persons in conducting,
research into any matter connected with –

(a)   their functions under the enactments mentioned in subsection (9);
[(aa) the functions of Local Safeguarding Children Boards;][5]
(b)   the adoption of children; or
(c)   the accommodation of children in a [care home or independent
      hospital][2].

(3) Every local authority shall, at such times and in such form as the Secretary
of State may direct, transmit to him such particulars as he may require with
respect to –

(a)   the performance by the local authority of all or any of their
      functions –
      (i)   under the enactments mentioned in subsection (9); or
      (ii)   in connection with the accommodation of children in a [care
             home or independent hospital][2]; and
(b)   the children in relation to whom the authority have exercised those
      functions[; and

(c)   the performance by the Local Safeguarding Children Board established by them under the Children Act 2004 of all or any of its functions][5].

(4) Every voluntary organisation shall, at such times and in such form as the Secretary of State may direct, transmit to him such particulars as he may require with respect to children accommodated by them or on their behalf.

[(4A) Particulars required to be transmitted under subsection (3) or (4) may include particulars relating to and identifying individual children.][3]

(5) The Secretary of State may direct the [designated officer for][1] each magistrates' court to which the direction is expressed to relate to transmit –

(a)   to such person as may be specified in the direction; and
(b)   at such times and in such form as he may direct,

such particulars as he may require with respect to proceedings of the court which relate to children.

(6) The Secretary of State shall in each year lay before Parliament a consolidated and classified abstract of the information transmitted to him under subsections (3) to (5).

(7) The Secretary of State may institute research designed to provide information on which requests for information under this section may be based.

(8) The Secretary of State shall keep under review the adequacy of the provision of child care training and for that purpose shall receive and consider any information from or representations made by –

(a)   the Central Council for Education and Training in Social Work;
(b)   such representatives of local authorities as appear to him to be appropriate; or
(c)   such other persons or organisations as appear to him to be appropriate,

concerning the provision of such training.

(9) The enactments are –

(a)   this Act;
(b)   the Children and Young Persons Acts 1933 to 1969;
(c)   section 116 of the Mental Health Act 1983 (so far as it relates to children looked after by local authorities);
[(ca) Part 1 of the Adoption and Children Act 2002;
(cb) the Children Act 2004;
(cc) the Children and Young Persons Act 2008;][5]
(d)   ...[4]

NOTES

Amendments.[1] Words substituted: Courts Act 2003, s 109(1), Sch 8, para 336. [2] Words substituted: Care Standards Act 2000, s 116, Sch 4, para 14(19). [3] Subsection inserted: Children Act 2004, s 54. [4] Paragraph repealed: SI 2005/2078, art 16(1), Sch 3. [5] Paragraphs inserted: Children and Young Persons Act 2008, s 33(1)–(5).

Definitions. 'Child': s 105(1); 'child care training': s 82(6); 'functions': s 105(1); 'local authority': s 105(1); 'mental nursing home': s 105(1); 'nursing home': s 105(1); 'residential care home': s 105(1); 'voluntary organisation': s 105(1).

84 Local authority failure to comply with statutory duty: default power of Secretary of State

(1) If the Secretary of State is satisfied that any local authority has failed, without reasonable excuse, to comply with any of the duties imposed on them by or under this Act he may make an order declaring that authority to be in default with respect to that duty.

(2) An order under subsection (1) shall give the Secretary of State's reasons for making it.

(3) An order under subsection (1) may contain such directions for the purpose of ensuring that the duty is complied with, within such period as may be specified in the order, as appear to the Secretary of State to be necessary.

(4) Any such direction shall, on the application of the Secretary of State, be enforceable by mandamus.

PART XII
MISCELLANEOUS AND GENERAL

Notification of children accommodated in certain establishments

85 Children accommodated by health authorities and local education authorities

(1) Where a child is provided with accommodation by any [[Local Health Board][4], Special Health Authority][2], [Primary Care Trust,][3] [National Health Service trust][1] [or NHS foundation trust or by a local authority in the exercise of education functions][5] ('the accommodating authority') –

(a)   for a consecutive period of at least three months; or
(b)   with the intention, on the part of that authority, of accommodating him for such a period,

the accommodating authority shall notify [the appropriate officer of][6] the responsible authority.

(2) Where subsection (1) applies with respect to a child, the accommodating authority shall also notify [the appropriate officer of][6] the responsible authority when they cease to accommodate the child.

[(2A) In a case where the child is provided with accommodation by a local authority in the exercise of education functions, subsections (1) and (2) apply only if the local authority providing the accommodation is different from the responsible authority.][5]

(3) In this section 'the responsible authority' means –

(a)   the local authority appearing to the accommodating authority to be the authority within whose area the child was ordinarily resident immediately before being accommodated; or

(b)   where it appears to the accommodating authority that a child was not ordinarily resident within the area of any local authority, the local authority within whose area the accommodation is situated.

[(3A) In this section and sections 86 and 86A 'the appropriate officer' means –

(a)   in relation to a local authority in England, their director of children's services; and

(b)   in relation to a local authority in Wales, their lead director for children and young people's services.][6]

(4) Where [the appropriate officer of a local authority has][6] been notified under this section, [the local authority][6] shall –

(a)   take such steps as are reasonably practicable to enable them to determine whether the child's welfare is adequately safeguarded and promoted while he is accommodated by the accommodating authority; and

(b)   consider the extent to which (if at all) they should exercise any of their functions under this Act with respect to the child.

[(5) For the purposes of subsection (4)(b), if the child is not in the area of the local authority, they must treat him as if he were in that area.][6]

NOTES

Amendments.[1] Words inserted: National Health Service and Community Care Act 1990, s 66(1), Sch 9, para 36(5).[2] Words inserted: Health Authorities Act 1995, s 2(1), Sch 1, Pt III, para 118(1), (9).[3] Words inserted: Health Act 1999 (Supplementary, Consequential etc Provisions) Order 2000, SI 2000/90.[4] Words substituted: SI 2007/961.[5] Words substituted and subsection inserted: SI 2010/1158.[6] Words inserted and substituted and subsections inserted: Children and Young Persons Act 2008, s 17(1)–(5).

Definitions. 'Child': s 105(1); 'functions': s 105(1); 'health authority': s 105(1); 'local authority': s 105(1); 'local education authority': s 105(1); 'the accommodating authority': s 85(1); 'the responsible authority': s 85(3).

86 [Children accommodated in care homes or independent hospitals][1]

(1) Where a child is provided with accommodation in any [care home or independent hospital][1] –

(a)   for a consecutive period of at least three months; or

(b)   with the intention, on the part of the person taking the decision to accommodate him, of accommodating him for such period,

the person carrying on [the establishment in question][2] shall notify [the appropriate officer of][2] the local authority within whose area [the establishment][2] is carried on.

(2) Where subsection (1) applies with respect to a child, the person carrying on [the establishment][2] shall also notify [the appropriate officer of][2] that authority when he ceases to accommodate the child in [the establishment][2].

(3) Where [the appropriate officer of a local authority has][2] been notified under this section, [the local authority][2] shall –

(a)   take such steps as are reasonably practicable to enable them to determine whether the child's welfare is adequately safeguarded and promoted while he is accommodated in [the establishment in question][2]; and

(b)   consider the extent to which (if at all) they should exercise any of their functions under this Act with respect to the child.

(4) If the person carrying on any [care home or independent hospital][2] fails, without reasonable excuse, to comply with this section he shall be guilty of an offence.

(5) A person authorised by a local authority may enter any [care home or independent hospital][1] within the authority's area for the purpose of establishing whether the requirements of this section have been complied with.

(6) Any person who intentionally obstructs another in the exercise of the power of entry shall be guilty of an offence.

(7) Any person exercising the power of entry shall, if so required, produce some duly authenticated document showing his authority to do so.

(8) Any person committing an offence under this section shall be liable on summary conviction to a fine not exceeding level 3 on the standard scale.

NOTES

Amendments.[1] Words substituted: Care Standards Act 2000, s 116, Sch 4, para 14(20). [2] Words substituted and inserted: Children and Young Persons Act 2008, s 17(6)–(10).

Definitions. 'Child': s 105(1); 'functions': s 105(1); 'local authority': s 105(1); 'mental nursing home': s 105(1); 'nursing home': s 105(1); 'residential care home': s 105(1).

[86A Visitors for children notified to local authority under section 85 or 86

(1) This section applies if the appropriate officer of a local authority –

(a)   has been notified with respect to a child under section 85(1) or 86(1); and

(b)   has not been notified with respect to that child under section 85(2) or, as the case may be, 86(2).

(2) The local authority must, in accordance with regulations made under this section, make arrangements for the child to be visited by a representative of the authority ("a representative").

(3) It is the function of a representative to provide advice and assistance to the local authority on the performance of their duties under section 85(4) or, as the case may be, 86(3).

(4) Regulations under this section may make provision about –

(a)   the frequency of visits under visiting arrangements;

(b)   circumstances in which visiting arrangements must require a child to be visited; and

(c)   additional functions of a representative.

(5) Regulations under this section are to be made by the Secretary of State and the Welsh Ministers acting jointly.

(6) In choosing a representative a local authority must satisfy themselves that the person chosen has the necessary skills and experience to perform the functions of a representative.

(7) In this section 'visiting arrangements' means arrangements made under subsection (2).][1]

NOTES

Amendment. [1] Section inserted: Children and Young Persons Act 2008, s 18.

87 [Welfare of children in boarding schools and colleges][1]

[(1) Where a school or college provides accommodation for any child, it shall be the duty of the relevant person to safeguard and promote the child's welfare.

(2) Subsection (1) does not apply in relation to a school or college which is a children's home or care home.

(3) Where accommodation is provided for a child by any school or college the appropriate authority shall take such steps as are reasonably practicable to enable them to determine whether the child's welfare is adequately safeguarded and promoted while he is accommodated by the school or college.

(4) Where the [the Chief Inspector for England is][4] of the opinion that there has been a failure to comply with subsection (1) in relation to a child provided with accommodation by a school or [college in England, he shall][4] –

   (a)   in the case of a school other than an independent school or a special school, notify the [local authority][5] for the area in which the school is situated;
   (b)   in the case of a special school which is maintained by a [local authority][5], notify that authority;
   (c)   in any other case, notify the Secretary of State.

(4A) Where the National Assembly for Wales are of the opinion that there has been a failure to comply with subsection (1) in relation to a child provided with accommodation by a school or college [in Wales][4], they shall –

   (a)   in the case of a school other than an independent school or a special school, notify the [local authority][5] for the area in which the school is situated;
   (b)   in the case of a special school which is maintained by a [local authority][5], notify that authority;

(5) Where accommodation is, or is to be, provided for a child by any school or college, a person authorised by the appropriate authority may, for the purpose of enabling that authority to discharge its duty under this section, enter at any time premises which are, or are to be, premises of the school or college.][1]

(6) Any person [exercising]¹ the power conferred by subsection (5) may carry out such inspection of premises, children and records as is prescribed by regulations made by the Secretary of State for the purposes of this section.

(7) Any person exercising that power shall, if asked to do so, produce some duly authenticated document showing his authority to do so.

(8) Any person authorised by the regulations to inspect records –

    (a)   shall be entitled at any reasonable time to have access to, and inspect and check the operation of, any computer and any associated apparatus or material which is or has been in use in connection with the records in question; and

    (b)   may require –

        (i)   the person by whom or on whose behalf the computer is or has been so used; or

        (ii)   any person having charge of, or otherwise concerned with the operation of, the computer, apparatus or material,

    to afford him such assistance as he may reasonably require.

(9) Any person who intentionally obstructs another in the exercise of any power conferred by this section or the regulations shall be guilty of an offence and liable on summary conviction to a fine not exceeding level 3 on the standard scale.

[(9A) Where [the Chief Inspector for England]⁴ or the National Assembly for Wales exercises the power conferred by subsection (5) in relation to a child, [that authority must]⁴ publish a report on whether the child's welfare is adequately safeguarded and promoted while he is accommodated by the school or college.

(9B) Where [the Chief Inspector for England]⁴ or the National Assembly for Wales publishes a report under this section, [that authority must]⁴ –

    (a)   send a copy of the report to the school or college concerned; and

    (b)   make copies of the report available for inspection at its offices by any person at any reasonable time.

(9C) Any person who requests a copy of a report published under this section is entitled to have one on payment of such reasonable fee (if any) as [the Chief Inspector for England]⁴ or the National Assembly for Wales (as the case may be) considers appropriate.]²

[(10) In this section and sections 87A to 87D –

    'the 1992 Act' means the Further and Higher Education Act 1992;
    'appropriate authority' means –

        (a)   in relation to England, [[the Chief Inspector for England]⁴]³;

        (b)   in relation to Wales, the National Assembly for Wales;

    ['the Chief Inspector for England' means Her Majesty's Chief Inspector of Education, Children's Services and Skills;]⁴
    'college' means an institution within the further education sector as defined in section 91 of the 1992 Act;

...[4];

'further education corporation' has the same meaning as in the 1992 Act;
'[local authority][5]' and 'proprietor' have the same meanings as in the Education Act 1996.
['sixth form college corporation' has the same meaning as in the 1992 Act.][6]

(11) In this section and sections 87A and 87D 'relevant person' means –

(a)   in relation to an independent school, the proprietor of the school;
(b)   in relation to any other school, or an institution designated under section 28 of the 1992 Act, the governing body of the school or institution;
(c)   in relation to an institution conducted by a further education corporation [or sixth form college corporation][6], the corporation.

(12) Where a person other than the proprietor of an independent school is responsible for conducting the school, references in this section to the relevant person include references to the person so responsible.][1]

NOTES

Amendments.[1] Subsections and words substituted: Care Standards Act 2000, ss 105, 116, Sch 4, para 14(1), (21).[2] Subsections inserted: Health and Social Care (Community Health and Standards) Act 2003, s 111.[3] Words substituted: Health and Social Care (Community Health and Standards) Act 2003, s 147, Sch 9, para 10(1), (3).[4] Words inserted, substituted and repealed: Education and Inspections Act 2006, s 157, Sch 14, paras 9, 16(1)–(5), Sch 18, Pt 5.[5] Words substituted: SI 2010/1158.[6] Definition and words inserted: SI 2010/1080.

Definitions. 'Child': s 105(1); 'children's home': s 23; 'independent school': s 105(1); 'local authority': s 105(1); 'proprietor': s 87(10); 'residential care home': s 105(1).

[87A   Suspension of duty under section 87(3)

(1) The Secretary of State may appoint a person to be an inspector for the purposes of this section if –

(a)   that person already acts as an inspector for other purposes in relation to schools or colleges to which section 87(1) applies, and
(b)   the Secretary of State is satisfied that the person is an appropriate person to determine whether the welfare of children provided with accommodation by such schools or colleges is adequately safeguarded and promoted while they are accommodated by them.

(2) Where –

(a)   the relevant person enters into an agreement in writing with a person appointed under subsection (1),
(b)   the agreement provides for the person so appointed to have in relation to the school or college the function of determining whether section 87(1) is being complied with, and
(c)   the appropriate authority receive from the person mentioned in paragraph (b) ('the inspector') notice in writing that the agreement has come into effect,

the authority's duty under section 87(3) in relation to the school or college shall be suspended.

(3) Where the appropriate authority's duty under section 87(3) in relation to any school or college is suspended under this section, it shall cease to be so suspended if the appropriate authority receive –

   (a)   a notice under subsection (4) relating to the inspector, or

   (b)   a notice under subsection (5) relating to the relevant agreement.

(4) The Secretary of State shall terminate a person's appointment under subsection (1) if –

   (a)   that person so requests, or

   (b)   the Secretary of State ceases, in relation to that person, to be satisfied that he is such a person as is mentioned in paragraph (b) of that subsection,

and shall give notice of the termination of that person's appointment to the appropriate authority.

(5) Where –

   (a)   the appropriate authority's duty under section 87(3) in relation to any school or college is suspended under this section, and

   (b)   the relevant agreement ceases to have effect,

the inspector shall give to the appropriate authority notice in writing of the fact that it has ceased to have effect.

(6) In this section references to the relevant agreement, in relation to the suspension of the appropriate authority's duty under section 87(3) as regards any school or college, are to the agreement by virtue of which the appropriate authority's duty under that provision as regards that school or college is suspended.]¹

NOTES

Amendments.¹ Section substituted: Care Standards Act 2000, s 106(1).

[87B Duties of inspectors under section 87A

(1) The Secretary of State may impose on a person appointed under section 87A(1) ('an authorised inspector') such requirements relating to, or in connection with, the carrying out under substitution agreements of the function mentioned in section 87A(2)(b) as the Secretary of State thinks fit.

(2) Where, in the course of carrying out under a substitution agreement the function mentioned in section 87A(2)(b), it appears to an authorised inspector that there has been a failure to comply with section 87(1) in the case of a child provided with accommodation by the school [or college]² to which the agreement relates, the inspector shall give notice of that fact –

(3) The powers given by that Act to include requirements in supervision orders shall have effect subject to amendments made by Schedule 12.

NOTES

Amendments.[1] Words substituted: Criminal Justice Act 1991, s 100, Sch 11, para 40(1), (2)(r).

Effect and duration of orders etc

91 Effect and duration of orders etc

(1) The making of a residence order with respect to a child who is the subject of a care order discharges the care order.

(2) The making of a care order with respect to a child who is the subject of any section 8 order discharges that order.

[(2A) Where a contact activity direction has been made as regards contact with a child, the making of a care order with respect to the child discharges the direction.][5]

(3) The making of a care order with respect to a child who is the subject of a supervision order discharges that other order.

(4) The making of a care order with respect to a child who is a ward of court brings that wardship to an end.

(5) The making of a care order with respect to a child who is the subject of a school attendance order made under [section 437 of the Education Act 1996][1] discharges the school attendance order.

[(5A) The making of a special guardianship order with respect to a child who is the subject of –

(a)   a care order; or
(b)   an order under section 34,

discharges that order.][2]

(6) Where an emergency protection order is made with respect to a child who is in care, the care order shall have effect subject to the emergency protection order.

(7) Any order made under section 4(1) [4ZA(1),][6] [4A(1)][3] or 5(1) shall continue in force until the child reaches the age of eighteen, unless it is brought to an end earlier.

(8) Any –

(a)   agreement under section 4[, 4ZA][6] [or 4A][3]; or
(b)   appointment under section 5(3) or (4),

shall continue in force until the child reaches the age of eighteen, unless it is brought to an end earlier.

(9) An order under Schedule 1 has effect as specified in that Schedule.

(10) A section 8 order [other than a residence order][7] shall, if it would otherwise still be in force, cease to have effect when the child reaches the age of sixteen, unless it is to have effect beyond that age by virtue of section 9(6) [...[7]][4].

(11) Where a section 8 order has effect with respect to a child who has reached the age of sixteen, it shall, if it would otherwise still be in force, cease to have effect when he reaches the age of eighteen.

(12) Any care order, other than an interim care order, shall continue in force until the child reaches the age of eighteen, unless it is brought to an end earlier.

(13) Any order made under any other provision of this Act in relation to a child shall, if it would otherwise still be in force, cease to have effect when he reaches the age of eighteen.

(14) On disposing of any application for an order under this Act, the court may (whether or not it makes any other order in response to the application) order that no application for an order under this Act of any specified kind may be made with respect to the child concerned by any person named in the order without leave of the court.

(15) Where an application ('the previous application') has been made for –

(a)   the discharge of a care order;
(b)   the discharge of a supervision order;
(c)   the discharge of an education supervision order;
(d)   the substitution of a supervision order for a care order; or
(e)   a child assessment order,

no further application of a kind mentioned in paragraphs (a) to (e) may be made with respect to the child concerned, without leave of the court, unless the period between the disposal of the previous application and the making of the further application exceeds six months.

(16) Subsection (15) does not apply to applications made in relation to interim orders.

(17) Where –

(a)   a person has made an application for an order under section 34;
(b)   the application has been refused; and
(c)   a period of less than six months has elapsed since the refusal,

that person may not make a further application for such an order with respect to the same child, unless he has obtained the leave of the court.

NOTES

Amendments.[1] Words substituted: Education Act 1996, s 582(1), Sch 37, Pt I, para 90.[2] Subsection inserted: Adoption and Children Act 2002, s 139(a), (3), Sch 3, paras 54, 68(a).[3] Words inserted: Adoption and Children Act 2002, s 139(a), (3), Sch 3, paras 54, 68(b), (c).[4] Words inserted: Adoption and Children Act 2002, s 114(3).[5] Subsection inserted: Children and Adoption Act 2006, s 15(1), Sch 2, paras 7, 9.[6] References inserted: Human Fertilisation and Embryology Act 2008, s 56, Sch 6, Pt 1, para 29.[7] Words inserted or repealed: Children and Young Persons Act 2008, ss 37(3)(a), 42, Sch 4.

PART I – Statutes

Definitions. 'A section 8 order': s 8(2); 'care order': ss 31(11), 105(1); 'child': s 105(1); 'child assessment order': s 43(2); 'education supervision order': s 36(2); 'emergency protection order': s 44(4); 'residence order': s 8(1); 'supervision order': s 31(11); 'the court': s 92(7).

Jurisdiction and procedure etc

92 Jurisdiction of courts

(1) The name 'domestic proceedings', given to certain proceedings in magistrates' courts, is hereby changed to 'family proceedings' and the names 'domestic court' and 'domestic court panel' are hereby changed to 'family proceedings court' and 'family panel', respectively.

(2) Proceedings under this Act shall be treated as family proceedings in relation to magistrates' courts.

(3) Subsection (2) is subject to the provisions of section 65(1) and (2) of the Magistrates' Courts Act 1980 (proceedings which may be treated as not being family proceedings), as amended by this Act.

(4) A magistrates' court shall not be competent to entertain any application, or make any order, involving the administration or application of –

   (a)   any property belonging to or held in trust for a child; or
   (b)   the income of any such property.

(5) The powers of a magistrates' court under section 63(2) of the Act of 1980 to suspend or rescind orders shall not apply in relation to any order made under this Act.

(6) Part I of Schedule 11 makes provision, including provision for the Lord Chancellor to make orders, with respect to the jurisdiction of courts and justices of the peace in relation to –

   (a)   proceedings under this Act; and
   (b)   proceedings under certain other enactments.

(7) For the purposes of this Act 'the court' means the High Court, a county court or a magistrates' court.

(8) Subsection (7) is subject to the provision made by or under Part I of Schedule 11 and to any express provision as to the jurisdiction of any court made by any other provision of this Act.

(9) The Lord Chancellor may[, after consulting the Lord Chief Justice,][1] by order make provision for the principal registry of the Family Division of the High Court to be treated as if it were a county court for such purposes of this Act, or of any provision made under this Act, as may be specified in the order.

(10) Any order under subsection (9) may make such provision as the Lord Chancellor thinks expedient[, after consulting the Lord Chief Justice,][1] for the purpose of applying (with or without modifications) provisions which apply in relation to the procedure in county courts to the principal registry when it acts as if it were a county court.

[(10A) The Lord Chief Justice may nominate a judicial office holder (as defined in section 109(4) of the Constitutional Reform Act 2005) to exercise his functions under subsection (9) or (10).][1]

(11) Part II of Schedule 11 makes amendments consequential on this section.

NOTES

Amendments.[1] Words and subsection inserted: Constitutional Reform Act 2005, s 15(1), Sch 4, Pt 1, paras 203, 205(1)–(4).

Definitions. 'Family panel': s 92(1); 'family proceedings': s 92(2); 'family proceedings court': s 92(1); 'the court': s 92(7).

93 Rules of Court

(1) An authority having power to make rules of court may make such provision for giving effect to –

    (a)   this Act;
    (b)   the provisions of any statutory instrument made under this Act; or
    (c)   any amendment made by this Act in any other enactment,

as appears to that authority to be necessary or expedient.

(2) The rules may, in particular, make provision –

    (a)   with respect to the procedure to be followed in any relevant proceedings (including the manner in which any application is to be made or other proceedings commenced);
    (b)   as to the persons entitled to participate in any relevant proceedings, whether as parties to the proceedings or by being given the opportunity to make representations to the court;
    [(bb)   for children to be separately represented in relevant proceedings,][2]
    (c)   with respect to the documents and information to be furnished, and notices to be given, in connection with any relevant proceedings;
    (d)   applying (with or without modification) enactments which govern the procedure to be followed with respect to proceedings brought on a complaint made to a magistrates' court to relevant proceedings in such a court brought otherwise than on a complaint;
    (e)   with respect to preliminary hearings;
    (f)   for the service outside [England and Wales][1], in such circumstances and in such manner as may be prescribed, of any notice of proceedings in a magistrates' court;
    (g)   for the exercise by magistrates' courts, in such circumstances as may be prescribed, of such powers as may be prescribed (even though a party to the proceedings in question is [or resides][1] outside England and Wales);
    (h)   enabling the court, in such circumstances as may be prescribed, to proceed on any application even though the respondent has not been given notice of the proceedings;
    (i)   authorising a single justice to discharge the functions of a magistrates' court with respect to such relevant proceedings as may be prescribed;

PART I – Statutes

(j)   authorising a magistrates' court to order any of the parties to such relevant proceedings as may be prescribed, in such circumstances as may be prescribed, to pay the whole or part of the costs of all or any of the other parties.

(3) In subsection (2) –

'notice of proceedings' means a summons or such other notice of proceedings as is required; and 'given', in relation to a summons, means 'served';

'prescribed' means prescribed by the rules; and

'relevant proceedings' means any application made, or proceedings brought, under any of the provisions mentioned in paragraphs (a) to (c) of subsection (1) and any part of such proceedings.

(4) This section and any other power in this Act to make rules of court are not to be taken as in any way limiting any other power of the authority in question to make rules of court.

(5) When making any rules under this section an authority shall be subject to the same requirements as to consultation (if any) as apply when the authority makes rules under its general rule making power.

NOTES

Amendments.[1] Words substituted and inserted: Courts and Legal Services Act 1990, s 116, Sch 16, para 22.[2] Paragraph inserted: Adoption and Children Act 2002, s 122(2).

Definitions. 'Notice of proceedings': s 93(3); 'prescribed': s 93(3); 'relevant proceedings': s 93(3); 'the court': s 92(7).

94 Appeals

(1) [Subject to any express provision to the contrary made by or under this Act, an][1] appeal shall lie to [a county court][4] against –

(a)   the making by a magistrates' court of any order under this Act [or the Adoption and Children Act 2002][2]; or

(b)   any refusal by a magistrates' court to make such an order.

(2) Where a magistrates' court has power, in relation to any proceedings under this Act [or the Adoption and Children Act 2002][2], to decline jurisdiction because it considers that the case can more conveniently be dealt with by another court, no appeal shall lie against any exercise by that magistrates' court of that power.

(3) Subsection (1) does not apply in relation to an interim order for periodical payments made under Schedule 1.

(4) On an appeal under this section, [a county court][4] may make such orders as may be necessary to give effect to its determination of the appeal.

(5) Where an order is made under subsection (4) [a county court][4] may also make such incidental or consequential orders as appear to it to be just.

(6) Where an appeal from a magistrates' court relates to an order for the making of periodical payments, [a county court]⁴ may order that its determination of the appeal shall have effect from such date as it thinks fit to specify in the order.

(7) The date so specified must not be earlier than the earliest date allowed in accordance with rules of court made for the purposes of this section.

(8) Where, on an appeal under this section in respect of an order requiring a person to make periodical payments, [a county court]⁴ reduces the amount of those payments or discharges the order –

(a)   it may order the person entitled to the payments to pay to the person making them such sum in respect of payments already made as [the county court]⁴ thinks fit; and

(b)   if any arrears are due under the order for periodical payments, it may remit payment of the whole, or part, of those arrears.

(9) Any order of [a county court]⁴ made on an appeal under this section (other than one directing that an application be re-heard by a magistrates' court) shall, for the purposes –

(a)   of the enforcement of the order; and

(b)   of any power to vary, revive or discharge orders,

be treated as if it were an order of the magistrates' court from which the appeal was brought and not an order of [a county court]⁴.

(10) The Lord Chancellor may[, after consulting the Lord Chief Justice,]³ by order make provision as to the circumstances in which appeals may be made against decisions taken by courts on questions arising in connection with the transfer, or proposed transfer, of proceedings by virtue of any order under paragraph 2 of Schedule 11.

(11) Except to the extent provided for in any order made under subsection (10), no appeal may be made against any decision of a kind mentioned in that subsection.

[(12) The Lord Chief Justice may nominate a judicial office holder (as defined in section 109(4) of the Constitutional Reform Act 2005) to exercise his functions under subsection (10).]³

NOTES

Amendments.¹ Words inserted: Courts and Legal Services Act 1990, s 116, Sch 16, para 23.² Words inserted: Adoption and Children Act 2002, s 100.³ Words and subsection inserted: Constitutional Reform Act 2005, s 15(1), Sch 4, Pt 1, paras 203, 206(1)–(3).⁴ Words substituted: SI 2009/871.

95 Attendance of child at hearing under Part IV or V

(1) In any proceedings in which a court is hearing an application for an order under Part IV or V, or is considering whether to make any such order, the court may order the child concerned to attend such stage or stages of the proceedings as may be specified in the order.

(2) The power conferred by subsection (1) shall be exercised in accordance with rules of court.

(3) Subsections (4) to (6) apply where –

(a)   an order under subsection (1) has not been complied with; or
(b)   the court has reasonable cause to believe that it will not be complied with.

(4) The court may make an order authorising a constable, or such person as may be specified in the order –

(a)   to take charge of the child and to bring him to the court; and
(b)   to enter and search any premises specified in the order if he has reasonable cause to believe that the child may be found on the premises.

(5) The court may order any person who is in a position to do so to bring the child to the court.

(6) Where the court has reason to believe that a person has information about the whereabouts of the child it may order him to disclose it to the court.

NOTES

Definitions. 'Child': s 105(1); 'the court': s 92(7).

96 Evidence given by, or with respect to, children

(1) Subsection (2) applies in any civil proceedings where a child who is called as a witness in any civil proceedings does not, in the opinion of the court, understand the nature of an oath.

(2) The child's evidence may be heard by the court if, in its opinion –

(a)   he understands that it is his duty to speak the truth; and
(b)   he has sufficient understanding to justify his evidence being heard.

(3) The Lord Chancellor may[, with the concurrence of the Lord Chief Justice,]² by order make provision for the admissibility of evidence which would otherwise be inadmissible under any rule of law relating to hearsay.

(4) An order under subsection (3) may only be made with respect to –

(a)   civil proceedings in general or such civil proceedings, or class of civil proceedings, as may be prescribed; and
(b)   evidence in connection with the upbringing, maintenance or welfare of a child.

(5) An order under subsection (3) –

(a)   may, in particular, provide for the admissibility of statements which are made orally or in a prescribed form or which are recorded by any prescribed method of recording;
(b)   may make different provision for different purposes and in relation to different descriptions of court; and

PART I – Statutes

(c)   may make such amendments and repeals in any enactment relating to evidence (other than in this Act) as the Lord Chancellor considers necessary or expedient in consequence of the provision made by the order.

(6) Subsection (5)(b) is without prejudice to section 104(4).

(7) In this section –

['civil proceedings' means civil proceedings, before any tribunal, in relation to which the strict rules of evidence apply, whether as a matter of law or by agreement of the parties, and references to 'the court' shall be construed accordingly;][1] and

'prescribed' means prescribed by an order under subsection (3).

NOTES

Amendments.[1] Definition substituted: Civil Evidence Act 1995, s 15(1), Sch 1, para 16.[2] Words inserted: Constitutional Reform Act 2005, s 15(1), Sch 4, Pt 1, paras 203, 207.

Definitions. 'Child': s 105(1); 'civil proceedings': s 96(7); 'court': s 92(7); 'prescribed': s 96(7); 'upbringing': s 105(1).

97 Privacy for children involved in certain proceedings

(1) Rules made under section 144 of the Magistrates' Courts Act 1980 may make provision for a magistrates' court to sit in private in proceedings in which any powers under this Act [or the Adoption and Children Act 2002][6] may be exercised by the court with respect to any child.

(2) No person shall publish [to the public at large or any section of the public][5] any material which is intended, or likely, to identify –

(a)   any child as being involved in any proceedings before [the High Court, a county court or][4] a magistrates' court in which any power under this Act [or the Adoption and Children Act 2002][6] may be exercised by the court with respect to that or any other child; or

(b)   an address or school as being that of a child involved in any such proceedings.

(3) In any proceedings for an offence under this section it shall be a defence for the accused to prove that he did not know, and had no reason to suspect, that the published material was intended, or likely, to identify the child.

(4) The court or the [Lord Chancellor][3] may, if satisfied that the welfare of the child requires it [and, in the case of the Lord Chancellor, if the Lord Chief Justice agrees][7], by order dispense with the requirements of subsection (2) to such extent as may be specified in the order.

(5) For the purposes of this section –

'publish' includes –
(a)   include in a programme service (within the meaning of the Broadcasting Act 1990);][1] or
(b)   cause to be published; and

'material' includes any picture or representation.

(6) Any person who contravenes this section shall be guilty of an offence and liable, on summary conviction, to a fine not exceeding level 4 on the standard scale.

(7) Subsection (1) is without prejudice to –

(a)   the generality of the rule making power in section 144 of the Act of 1980; or

(b)   any other power of a magistrates' court to sit in private.

(8) [Sections 69 (sittings of magistrates' courts for family proceedings) and 71 (newspaper reports of certain proceedings) of the Act of 1980][2] shall apply in relation to any proceedings [(before a magistrates' court)][4] to which this section applies subject to the provisions of this section.

[(9) The Lord Chief Justice may nominate a judicial office holder (as defined in section 109(4) of the Constitutional Reform Act 2005) to exercise his functions under subsection (4).][7]

NOTES

Amendments.[1] Words substituted: Broadcasting Act 1990, s 203(1), Sch 20, para 53.[2] Words substituted: Courts and Legal Services Act 1990, s 116, Sch 16, para 24.[3] Words substituted: Transfer of Functions (Magistrates' Courts and Family Law) Order 1992, SI 1992/709.[4] Words inserted: Access to Justice Act 1999, s 72.[5] Words inserted: Children Act 2004, s 62(1).[6] Words inserted: Adoption and Children Act 2002, s 101(3).[7] Words and subsection inserted: Constitutional Reform Act 2005, s 15(1), Sch 4, Pt 1, paras 203, 208(1)–(3).

Definitions. 'Child': s 105(1); 'material': s 97(5); 'publish': s 97(5); 'school': s 105(1); 'the court': s 92(7).

98 Self-incrimination

(1) In any proceedings in which a court is hearing an application for an order under Part IV or V, no person shall be excused from –

(a)   giving evidence on any matter; or

(b)   answering any question put to him in the course of his giving evidence,

on the ground that doing so might incriminate him or his spouse [or civil partner][1] of an offence.

(2) A statement or admission made in such proceedings shall not be admissible in evidence against the person making it or his spouse [or civil partner][1] in proceedings for an offence other than perjury.

NOTES

Amendments.[1] Words inserted: Civil Partnership Act 2004, s 261(1), Sch 27, para 132.

99

...[1]

NOTES

Amendments.[1] Section repealed: Access to Justice Act 1999, s 106, Sch 15, Pt I.

100 Restrictions on use of wardship jurisdiction

(1) Section 7 of the Family Law Reform Act 1969 (which gives the High Court power to place a ward of court in the care, or under the supervision, of a local authority) shall cease to have effect.

(2) No court shall exercise the High Court's inherent jurisdiction with respect to children –

(a)   so as to require a child to be placed in the care, or put under the supervision, of a local authority;

(b)   so as to require a child to be accommodated by or on behalf of a local authority;

(c)   so as to make a child who is the subject of a care order a ward of court; or

(d)   for the purpose of conferring on any local authority power to determine any question which has arisen, or which may arise, in connection with any aspect of parental responsibility for a child.

(3) No application for any exercise of the court's inherent jurisdiction with respect to children may be made by a local authority unless the authority have obtained the leave of the court.

(4) The court may only grant leave if it is satisfied that –

(a)   the result which the authority wish to achieve could not be achieved through the making of any order of a kind to which subsection (5) applies; and

(b)   there is reasonable cause to believe that if the court's inherent jurisdiction is not exercised with respect to the child he is likely to suffer significant harm.

(5) This subsection applies to any order –

(a)   made otherwise than in the exercise of the court's inherent jurisdiction; and

(b)   which the local authority is entitled to apply for (assuming, in the case of any application which may only be made with leave, that leave is granted).

NOTES

Definitions. 'Care order': ss 31(11), 105(1); 'child': s 105(1); 'harm': s 31(9); 'local authority': s 105(1); 'parental responsibility': s 3; 'significant harm': s 31(10); 'the court': s 92(7).

101 Effect of orders as between England and Wales and Northern Ireland, the Channel Islands or the Isle of Man

(1) The Secretary of State may make regulations providing –

(a)   for prescribed orders which –
  (i)   are made by a court in Northern Ireland; and
  (ii)   appear to the Secretary of State to correspond in their effect to orders which may be made under any provision of this Act,

PART I – Statutes

to have effect in prescribed circumstances, for prescribed purposes of this Act, as if they were orders of a prescribed kind made under this Act;

(b)   for prescribed orders which –
   (i)   are made by a court in England and Wales; and
   (ii)   appear to the Secretary of State to correspond in their effect to orders which may be made under any provision in force in Northern Ireland,
   to have effect in prescribed circumstances, for prescribed purposes of the law of Northern Ireland, as if they were orders of a prescribed kind made in Northern Ireland.

(2) Regulations under subsection (1) may provide for the order concerned to cease to have effect for the purposes of the law of Northern Ireland, or (as the case may be) the law of England and Wales, if prescribed conditions are satisfied.

(3) The Secretary of State may make regulations providing for prescribed orders which –

(a)   are made by a court in the Isle of Man or in any of the Channel Islands; and

(b)   appear to the Secretary of State to correspond in their effect to orders which may be made under this Act,
   to have effect in prescribed circumstances for prescribed purposes of this Act, as if they were orders of a prescribed kind made under this Act.

(4) Where a child who is in the care of a local authority is lawfully taken to live in Northern Ireland, the Isle of Man or in any of the Channel Islands, the care order in question shall cease to have effect if the conditions prescribed in regulations by the Secretary of State are satisfied.

(5) Any regulations made under this section may –

(a)   make such consequential amendments (including repeals) in –
   (i)   section 25 of the Children and Young Persons Act 1969 (transfers between England and Wales and Northern Ireland); or
   (ii)   section 26 (transfers between England and Wales and Channel Islands or Isle of Man) of that Act,
   as the Secretary of State considers necessary or expedient; and

(b)   modify any provision of this Act, in its application (by virtue of the regulations) in relation to an order made otherwise than in England and Wales.

NOTES

Definitions. 'Care order': ss 31(11), 105(1); 'child': s 105(1); 'local authority': s 105(1); 'prescribed': s 105(1); 'the court': s 92(7).

Search warrants

102 Power of constable to assist in exercise of certain powers to search for children or inspect premises

(1) Where, on an application made by any person for a warrant under this section, it appears to the court –

(a) that a person attempting to exercise powers under any enactment mentioned in subsection (6) has been prevented from doing so by being refused entry to the premises concerned or refused access to the child concerned; or

(b) that any such person is likely to be so prevented from exercising any such powers,

it may issue a warrant authorising any constable to assist that person in the exercise of those powers, using reasonable force if necessary.

(2) Every warrant issued under this section shall be addressed to, and executed by, a constable who shall be accompanied by the person applying for the warrant if –

(a) that person so desires; and

(b) the court by whom the warrant is issued does not direct otherwise.

(3) A court granting an application for a warrant under this section may direct that the constable concerned may, in executing the warrant, be accompanied by a registered medical practitioner, registered nurse or [registered midwife][1] if he so chooses.

[(3A) The reference in subsection (3) to a registered midwife is to such a midwife who is also registered in the Specialist Community Public Health Nurses' Part of the register maintained under article 5 of the Nursing and Midwifery Order 2001.][2]

(4) An application for a warrant under this section shall be made in the manner and form prescribed by rules of court.

(5) Where –

(a) an application for a warrant under this section relates to a particular child; and

(b) it is reasonably practicable to do so,

the application and any warrant granted on the application shall name the child; and where it does not name him it shall describe him as clearly as possible.

(6) The enactments are –

(a) sections 62, 64, 67, 76, 80, 86 and 87;

(b) paragraph 8(1)(b) and (2)(b) of Schedule 3;

(c) ...[3]

NOTES

Amendments.[1] Words substituted: SI 2002/253.[2] Subsection inserted: SI 2004/1771.[3] Paragraph repealed: Adoption and Children Act 2002, s 139(1), (3), Sch 3, paras 54, 69, Sch 5.

Definitions. 'Child': s 105(1); 'the court': s 92(7).

General

103 Offences by bodies corporate

(1) This section applies where any offence under this Act is committed by a body corporate.

(2) If the offence is proved to have been committed with the consent or connivance of or to be attributable to any neglect on the part of any director, manager, secretary or other similar officer of the body corporate, or any person who was purporting to act in any such capacity, he (as well as the body corporate) shall be guilty of the offence and shall be liable to be proceeded against and punished accordingly.

104 Regulations and orders

(1) Any power of the Lord Chancellor[, the Treasury][2][, the Secretary of State or the National Assembly for Wales][4] under this Act to make an order, regulations, or rules, except an order under section …[1] 56(4)(a), 57(3), 84 or 97(4) or paragraph 1(1) of Schedule 4, shall be exercisable by statutory instrument.

(2) Any such statutory instrument, except one made under section [4(1)(b),][3] [4ZA(3),][6] 17(4), 107 or 108(2) [or one containing regulations which fall within subsection (3B) or (3C)][7], shall be subject to annulment in pursuance of a resolution of either House of Parliament.

[(2A) …[8]][5]

[(3A) An order under section 4(1B)[, 4ZA(3)][11] or 17(4) or regulations which fall within subsection (3B) or (3C) shall not be made by the Secretary of State unless a draft of the statutory instrument containing the order or regulations has been laid before, and approved by a resolution of, each House of Parliament.

(3B) Regulations fall within this subsection if they are the first regulations to be made by the Secretary of State in the exercise of the power conferred by section 23C(5B)(b).

(3C) Regulations fall within this subsection if they are the first regulations to be made by the Secretary of State in the exercise of the power conferred by paragraph 6(2) of Schedule 2.][9]

(4) Any statutory instrument made under this Act may –

    (a)   make different provision for different cases;

    (b)   provide for exemptions from any of its provisions; and

    (c)   contain …[10] incidental, supplemental and transitional provisions …[10].

PART I – Statutes

NOTES

Amendments.[1] Word repealed: Care Standards Act 2000, s 117, Sch 6.[2] Words inserted: Tax Credits Act 2002, s 47, Sch 3.[3] Words inserted: Adoption and Children Act 2002, s 111(6).[4] Words substituted: Children and Adoption Act 2006, s 15(1), Sch 2, paras 7, 10(a).[5] Subsection inserted: Children and Adoption Act 2006, s 15(1), Sch 2, paras 7, 10(b).[6] Reference inserted: Human Fertilisation and Embryology Act 2008, s 56, Sch 6, Pt 1, para 30(a).[7] Words inserted: Children and Young Persons Act 2008, s 39, Sch 3, paras 1, 25(1), (2).[8] Subsection repealed: Children and Young Persons Act 2008, ss 39, 42, Sch 3, paras 1, 25(1), (3), Sch 4.[9] Subsections substituted: Children and Young Persons Act 2008, s 39, Sch 3, paras 1, 25(1), (4).[10] Words repealed: Children and Young Persons Act 2008, ss 39, 42, Sch 3, paras 1, 25(1), (5), Sch 4.[11] Reference inserted: SI 2009/1892.

[104A Regulations and orders made by the Welsh Ministers under Part 3 etc

(1) Any power of the Welsh Ministers under Part 3, Part 7 or section 86A to make an order or regulations shall be exercisable by statutory instrument.

(2) Any such statutory instrument, except one made under section 17(4) or one containing regulations which fall within subsection (4) or (5), shall be subject to annulment in pursuance of a resolution of the National Assembly for Wales.

(3) An order under section 17(4) or regulations which fall within subsection (4) or (5) shall not be made by the Welsh Ministers unless a draft of the statutory instrument containing the order or regulations has been laid before and approved by a resolution of the National Assembly for Wales.

(4) Regulations fall within this subsection if they are the first regulations to be made by the Welsh Ministers in the exercise of the power conferred by section 23C(5B)(b).

(5) Regulations fall within this subsection if they are the first regulations to be made by the Welsh Ministers in the exercise of the power conferred by paragraph 6(2) of Schedule 2.][1]

NOTES

Amendments.[1] Section inserted: Children and Young Persons Act 2008, s 39, Sch 3, paras 1, 26.

105 Interpretation

(1) In this Act –

'adoption agency' means a body which may be referred to as an adoption agency by virtue of [section 2 of the Adoption and Children Act 2002][16];
['*appropriate children's home' has the meaning given by section 23;*][12, 29]
'bank holiday' means a day which is a bank holiday under the Banking and Financial Dealings Act 1971;
['care home' has the same meaning as in the Care Standards Act 2000;][12]
'care order' has the meaning given by section 31(11) and also includes any order which by or under any enactment has the effect of, or is deemed to be, a care order for the purposes of this Act; and any reference to a child who is in the care of an authority is a reference to a child who is in their care by virtue of a care order;
'child' means, subject to paragraph 16 of Schedule 1, a person under the age of eighteen;

'child assessment order' has the meaning given by section 43(2);

'child minder' has the meaning given by section 71;

['child of the family', in relation to parties to a marriage, or to two people who are civil partners of each other, means –

    (a)   a child of both of them, and

    (b)   any other child, other than a child placed with them as foster parents by a local authority or voluntary organisation, who has been treated by both of them as a child of their family;][19]

['children's home', has the meaning given by section 23;][12]

['children's home' has the same meaning as it has for the purposes of the Care Standards Act 2000 (see section 1 of that Act);][29]

'community home' has the meaning given by section 53;

['contact activity condition' has the meaning given by section 11C;

'contact activity direction' has the meaning given by section 11A;][22]

'contact order' has the meaning given by section 8(1);

'day care' [*(except in Part XA)*][11, 30] has the same meaning as in section 18;

'disabled', in relation to a child, has the same meaning as in section 17(11);

…[3]

'domestic premises' has the meaning given by section 71(12);

['dwelling-house' includes –

    (a)   any building or part of a building which is occupied as a dwelling;

    (b)   any caravan, house-boat or structure which is occupied as a dwelling; and any yard, garage or outhouse belonging to it and occupied with it;][6]

['education functions' has the meaning given by section 579(1) of the Education Act 1996;][27]

'education supervision order' has the meaning given in section 36;

'emergency protection order' means an order under section 44;

['enforcement order' has the meaning given by section 11J;][22]

'family assistance order' has the meaning given in section 16(2);

'family proceedings' has the meaning given by section 8(3);

'functions' includes powers and duties;

'guardian of a child' means a guardian (other than a guardian of the estate of a child) appointed in accordance with the provisions of section 5;

'harm' has the same meaning as in section 31(9) and the question of whether harm is significant shall be determined in accordance with section 31(10);

[…[20]][3]

'health service hospital' [means a health service hospital within the meaning given by the National Health Service Act 2006 or the National Health Service (Wales) Act 2006][20];

'hospital' [*(except in Schedule 9A)*][12, 30] has the same meaning as in the Mental Health Act 1983, except that it does not include a [hospital at which high security psychiatric services within the meaning of that Act are provided][7];

'ill-treatment' has the same meaning as in section 31(9);

['income-based jobseeker's allowance' has the same meaning as in the Jobseekers Act 1995;][4]

['income-related employment and support allowance' means an income-related allowance under Part 1 of the Welfare Reform Act 2007 (employment and support allowance);][23]

['independent hospital' –

    (a)   in relation to England, means a hospital as defined by section 275 of the National Health Service Act 2006 that is not a health service hospital as defined by that section; and

    (b)   in relation to Wales, has the same meaning as in the Care Standards Act 2000;][28]

'independent school' has the same meaning as in [the Education Act 1996][5];

'local authority' means, in relation to England ...[2], the council of a county, a metropolitan district, a London Borough or the Common Council of the City of London [, in relation to Wales, the council of a county or a county borough][2] and, in relation to Scotland, a local authority within the meaning of section 1(2) of the Social Work (Scotland) Act 1968;

'local authority foster parent' has the same meaning as in section 23(3);

['local authority foster parent' has the meaning given in section 22C(12);][29]

['Local Health Board' means a Local Health Board established under section 11 of the National Health Service (Wales) Act 2006;][21]
...[27]

'local housing authority' has the same meaning as in the Housing Act 1985;
...[12]

['officer of the Service' has the same meaning as in the Criminal Justice and Court Services Act 2000;][9]

'parental responsibility' has the meaning given in section 3;

'parental responsibility agreement' has the meaning given in [sections 4(1)[, 4ZA(4)][24] and 4A(2)][16];

'prescribed' means prescribed by regulations made under this Act;

['private children's home' means a children's home in respect of which a person is registered under Part II of the Care Standards Act 2000 which is not a community home or a voluntary home;][12]

['Primary Care Trust' means a Primary Care Trust established under [section 18 of the National Health Service Act 2006][20];][7]

'privately fostered child' and 'to foster a child privately' have the same meaning as in section 66;

'prohibited steps order' has the meaning given by section 8(1);
...[18]
...[12]

'registered pupil' has the same meaning as in [the Education Act 1996][5];

'relative', in relation to a child, means a grandparent, brother, sister, uncle or aunt (whether of the full blood or half blood or [by marriage or civil partnership)][19] or step-parent;

'residence order' has the meaning given by section 8(1);
...[12]

'responsible person', in relation to a child who is the subject of a supervision order, has the meaning given in paragraph 1 of Schedule 3;

'school' has the same meaning as in [the Education Act 1996][5] or, in relation to Scotland, in the Education (Scotland) Act 1980;

['section 31A plan' has the meaning given by section 31A(6);][17]

'service', in relation to any provision made under Part III, includes any facility;

'signed', in relation to any person, includes the making by that person of his mark;

'special educational needs' has the same meaning as in [the Education Act 1993][5];

['special guardian' and 'special guardianship order' have the meaning given by section 14A;][17]

['Special Health Authority' means a Special Health Authority established under [section 28 of the National Health Service Act 2006 or section 22 of the National Health Service (Wales) Act 2006,][20];][3]

'specific issue order' has the meaning given by section 8(1);

['Strategic Health Authority' means a Strategic Health Authority established under [section 13 of the National Health Service Act 2006][20];][13]

'supervision order' has the meaning given by section 31(11);

'supervised child' and 'supervisor', in relation to a supervision order or an education supervision order, mean respectively the child who is (or is to be) under supervision and the person under whose supervision he is (or is to be) by virtue of the order;

'upbringing', in relation to any child, includes the care of the child but not his maintenance;

'voluntary home' has the meaning given by section 60;

'voluntary organisation' means a body (other than a public or local authority) whose activities are not carried on for profit.

['Welsh family proceedings officer' has the meaning given by section 35 of the Children Act 2004][15].

(2) References in this Act to a child whose father and mother were, or (as the case may be) were not, married to each other at the time of his birth must be read with section 1 of the Family Law Reform Act 1987 (which extends the meaning of such references).

(3) References in this Act to –

(a)   a person with whom a child lives, or is to live, as the result of a residence order; or

(b)   a person in whose favour a residence order is in force,

shall be construed as references to the person named in the order as the person with whom the child is to live.

(4) References in this Act to a child who is looked after by a local authority have the same meaning as they have (by virtue of section 22) in Part III.

(5) References in this Act to accommodation provided by or on behalf of a local authority are references to accommodation so provided in the exercise of

functions [of that or any other local authority which are social services functions within the meaning of][10] the Local Authority Social Services Act 1970.

[*(5A)* *References in this Act to a child minder shall be construed –*

    (a) ...[14]

    (b) *in relation to* ...[25] *Wales, in accordance with section 79A.*][11, 30]

[(5B) *(Applies to Scotland only)*][14]

(6) In determining the 'ordinary residence' of a child for any purpose of this Act, there shall be disregarded any period in which he lives in any place –

    (a)   which is a school or other institution;

    (b)   in accordance with the requirements of a supervision order under this Act ...[26]

[(ba)   in accordance with the requirements of a youth rehabilitation order under Part 1 of the Criminal Justice and Immigration Act 2008; or][26]

    (c)   while he is being provided with accommodation by or on behalf of a local authority.

(7) References in this Act to children who are in need shall be construed in accordance with section 17.

(8) Any notice or other document required under this Act to be served on any person may be served on him by being delivered personally to him, or being sent by post to him in a registered letter or by the recorded delivery service at his proper address.

(9) Any such notice or other document required to be served on a body corporate or a firm shall be duly served if it is served on the secretary or clerk of that body or a partner of that firm.

(10) For the purposes of this section, and of section 7 of the Interpretation Act 1978 in its application to this section, the proper address of a person –

    (a)   in the case of a secretary or clerk of a body corporate, shall be that of the registered or principal office of that body;

    (b)   in the case of a partner of a firm, shall be that of the principal office of the firm; and

    (c)   in any other case, shall be the last known address of the person to be served.

NOTES

Amendments.[1] Words inserted: Registered Homes (Amendment) Act 1991, s 2(6).[2] Words repealed or inserted: Local Government (Wales) Act 1994, Sch 10, para 13, Sch 18.[3] Definitions repealed or substituted: Health Authorities Act 1995, ss 2(1), 5(1), Sch 1, Pt III, para 118(1), (10).[4] Definition inserted: Jobseekers Act 1995, s 41(4), Sch 2, para 19.[5] Words substituted: Education Act 1996, s 582(1), Sch 37, Pt I, para 91.[6] Definition inserted: Family Law Act 1996, s 52, Sch 6, para 5.[7] Definitions inserted or amended: Health Act 1999 (Supplementary, Consequential etc Provisions) Order 2000, SI 2000/90.[8] Words substituted: Powers of Criminal Courts (Sentencing) Act 2000, s 165(1), Sch 9, para 128.[9] Definition inserted: Criminal Justice and Court Services Act 2000, s 74, Sch 7, paras 87, 95.[10] Words substituted: Local Government Act 2000, s 107, Sch 5, para 22.[11] Definition amended and subsection inserted: Care Standards Act 2000, s 116, Sch 4, para 14(1), 23.[12] Definitions and words repealed, inserted and substituted: Care Standards Act 2000, s 116, Sch 4, para 14(23).[13] Definition inserted: National Health Service Reform and Health Care Professions Act 2002 (Supplementary, Consequential etc Provisions) Regulations 2002, SI 2002/2469.[14] Paragraph repealed and subsection inserted: Regulation of Care (Scotland) Act 2001, s 79, Sch 3, para 15.[15] Definition inserted: Children Act 2004, s 40, Sch 3, paras 5, 11.[16] Words substituted: Adoption and Children Act 2002, s 139(1), Sch 3, paras 54, 70(a),(c).[17] Definition inserted: Adoption and Children Act 2002, s 139(1), Sch 3, paras 54, 70(b), (e).[18] Definition repealed: Adoption and Children Act 2002, s 139(1), Sch 3, paras 54, 70(d).[19] Definition and words substituted: Civil Partnership Act 2004, s 75(1), (3), (4).[20] Words repealed and substituted: National Health Service (Consequential Provisions) Act 2006, s 2, Sch 1, paras 124, 125.[21] Definition inserted: SI 2007/961.[22] Definitions inserted: Children and Adoption Act 2006, s 15(1), Sch 2, paras 7, 11.[23] Definition inserted: Welfare Reform Act 2007, s 28(1), Sch 3, para 6(1), (5).[24] Reference inserted: Human Fertilisation and Embryology Act 2008, s 56, Sch 6, Pt 1, para 31.[25] Words repealed: Childcare Act 2006, s 103, Sch 2, para 17, Sch 3, Pt 2.[26] Words repealed and paragraph inserted: Criminal Justice and Immigration Act 2008, ss 6(2), 149, Sch 4, Pt 1, paras 33, 36, Sch 28, Pt 1.[27] Definitions inserted and repealed: SI 2010/1158.[28] Definition 'independent hospital' substituted: SI 2010/813. [29] Definition 'appropriate children's home' repealed and definitions 'children's home' and 'local authority foster parent' in italics substituted by definitions in square brackets in relation to England: Children and Young Persons Act 2008, ss 8(2), 42, Sch 1, para 3, Sch 4. [30] Words in italics omitted and subsection (5A) omitted in relation to Wales: Children and Families (Wales) Measure 2010, ss 72, 73, Sch 1, paras 5, 7, Sch 2.

106 Financial provisions

(1) Any –

(a)   grants made by the Secretary of State under this Act; and

(b)   any other expenses incurred by the Secretary of State under this Act,

shall be payable out of money provided by Parliament.

(2) Any sums received by the Secretary of State under section 58, or by way of the repayment of any grant made under section 82(2) or (4) shall be paid into the Consolidated Fund.

107 Application to the Channel Islands

Her Majesty may by Order in Council direct that any of the provisions of this Act shall extend to any of the Channel Islands with such exceptions and modifications as may be specified in the Order.

108 Short title, commencement, extent, etc

(1) This Act may be cited as the Children Act 1989.

(2) Sections 89 and 96(3) to (7), and paragraph 35 of Schedule 12, shall come into force on the passing of this Act and paragraph 36 of Schedule 12 shall come into force at the end of the period of two months beginning with the day on which this Act is passed but otherwise this Act shall come into force on such date as may be appointed by order made by the Lord Chancellor or the Secretary of State, or by both acting jointly.

(3) Different dates may be appointed for different provisions of this Act in relation to different cases.

(4) The minor amendments set out in Schedule 12 shall have effect.

(5) The consequential amendments set out in Schedule 13 shall have effect.

(6) The transitional provisions and savings set out in Schedule 14 shall have effect.

(7) The repeals set out in Schedule 15 shall have effect.

(8) An order under subsection (2) may make such transitional provisions or savings as appear to the person making the order to be necessary or expedient in connection with the provisions brought into force by the order, including –

    (a)   provisions adding to or modifying the provisions of Schedule 14; and
    (b)   such adaptations –
        (i)   of the provisions brought into force by the order; and
        (ii)   of any provisions of this Act then in force,
        as appear to him necessary or expedient in consequence of the partial operation of this Act.

(9) The Lord Chancellor may by order make such amendments or repeals, in such enactments as may be specified in the order, as appear to him to be necessary or expedient in consequence of any provision of this Act.

(10) This Act shall, in its application to the Isles of Scilly, have effect subject to such exceptions, adaptations and modifications as the Secretary of State may by order prescribe.

(11) The following provisions of this Act extend to Scotland –

...[2]
section 25(8);
section 50(13)
...[2]
section 88;
section 104 (so far as necessary);
section 105 (so far as necessary);
subsections (1) to (3), (8) and (9) and this subsection;
in Schedule 2, paragraph 24;
in Schedule 12, paragraphs 1, 7 to 10, 18, 27, 30(a) and 41 to 44;
in Schedule 13, paragraphs 18 to 23, 32, 46, 47, 50, 57, 62, 63, 68(a) and (b) and 71;
in Schedule 14, paragraphs 1, 33 and 34;
in Schedule 15, the entries relating to –
    (a)   the Custody of Children Act 1891;
    (b)   the Nurseries and Child Minders Regulation Act 1948;
    (c)   section 53(3) of the Children and Young Persons Act 1963;
    (d)   section 60 of the Health Services and Public Health Act 1968;
    (e)   the Social Work (Scotland) Act 1968;
    (f)   the Adoption (Scotland) Act 1978;
    (g)   the Child Care Act 1980;
    (h)   the Foster Children (Scotland) Act 1984;
    (i)   the Child Abduction and Custody Act 1985; and
    (j)   the Family Law Act 1986.

(12) The following provisions of this Act extend to Northern Ireland –

section 101(1)(b), (2) and (5)(a)(i);
subsections (1) to (3), (8) and (9) and this subsection;
in Schedule 2, paragraph 24;
in Schedule 12, paragraphs 7 to 10, 18 and 27;
in Schedule 13, paragraphs 21, 22, 46, 47, 57, 62, 63, 68(c) to (e) and 69 to 71;
in Schedule 14, paragraphs ...[1] 28 to 30 and 38(a); and
in Schedule 15, the entries relating to the Guardianship of Minors Act 1971, the Children Act 1975, the Child Care Act 1980, and the Family Law Act 1986.

NOTES

Amendments.[1] Word repealed: Courts and Legal Services Act 1990, ss 116, 125(7), Sch 16, para 25, Sch 20.[2] Words repealed: Regulation of Care (Scotland) Act 2001, s 80(1), Sch 4.

[SCHEDULE A1
ENFORCEMENT ORDERS

PART 1
UNPAID WORK REQUIREMENT

General

1. Subject to the modifications in paragraphs 2 and 3, Chapter 4 of Part 12 of the Criminal Justice Act 2003 has effect in relation to an enforcement order as it has effect in relation to a community order (within the meaning of Part 12 of that Act).

References to an offender

2. Subject to paragraph 3, references in Chapter 4 of Part 12 of the Criminal Justice Act 2003 to an offender are to be treated as including references to a person subject to an enforcement order.

Specific modifications

3. (1) The power of the Secretary of State by order under section 197(3) to amend the definition of 'responsible officer' and to make consequential amendments includes power to make any amendments of this Part (including further modifications of Chapter 4 of Part 12 of the Criminal Justice Act 2003) that appear to the Secretary of State to be necessary or expedient in consequence of any amendment made by virtue of section 197(3)(a) or (b).

(2) In section 198 (duties of responsible officer) –

  (a) in subsection (1) –
     (i)   at the end of paragraph (a) insert 'and', and
     (ii) omit paragraph (c) and the word 'and' immediately preceding it, and
  (b) after subsection (1) insert –

'(1A) Subsection (1B) applies where –

    (a)   an enforcement order is in force, and

    (b)   an officer of the Children and Family Court Advisory and Support Service or a Welsh family proceedings officer (as defined in section 35 of the Children Act 2004) is required under section 11M of the Children Act 1989 to report on matters relating to the order.

(1B) The officer of the Service or the Welsh family proceedings officer may request the responsible officer to report to him on such matters relating to the order as he may require for the purpose of making a report under section 11M(1)(c) or (d); and it shall be the duty of the responsible officer to comply with such a request.'

(3) In section 199 (unpaid work requirement) –

    (a)   in subsection (2) (minimum and maximum hours of unpaid work) for paragraph (b) substitute –
        '(b) not more than 200.',
    (b)   omit subsections (3) and (4), and
    (c)   in subsection (5) for the words from the beginning to 'of them' substitute 'Where on the same occasion and in relation to the same person the court makes more than one enforcement order imposing an unpaid work requirement'.

(4) In section 200 (obligations of person subject to unpaid work requirement), for subsection (2) substitute –

'(2) Subject to paragraphs 7 and 9 of Schedule A1 to the Children Act 1989, the work required to be performed under an unpaid work requirement imposed by an enforcement order must be performed during a period of twelve months.

(2A) But the period of twelve months is not to run while the enforcement order is suspended under section 11J(9) of the Children Act 1989.'

(5) Section 217 (requirement to avoid conflict with religious beliefs, etc) is omitted.

(6) In section 218 (availability of arrangements in local area), subsection (1) (condition for imposition of unpaid work requirement) is omitted.

(7) Section 219 (provision of copies of relevant order) is omitted.

(8) The power of the Secretary of State to make rules under section 222 in relation to persons subject to relevant orders may also be exercised in relation to persons subject to enforcement orders.

(9) The power of the Secretary of State by order under section 223(1) to amend the provision mentioned in section 223(1)(a) includes power to amend this Part so as to make such modifications of Chapter 4 of Part 12 of the

Criminal Justice Act 2003 as appear to the Secretary of State to be necessary or expedient in consequence of any amendment of the provision mentioned in section 223(1)(a).

PART 2
REVOCATION, AMENDMENT OR BREACH OF ENFORCEMENT ORDER

Power to revoke

4. (1) This paragraph applies where a court has made an enforcement order in respect of a person's failure to comply with a contact order and the enforcement order is in force.

(2) The court may revoke the enforcement order if it appears to the court that –

    (a)   in all the circumstances no enforcement order should have been made,

    (b)   having regard to circumstances which have arisen since the enforcement order was made, it would be appropriate for the enforcement order to be revoked, or

    (c)   having regard to the person's satisfactory compliance with the contact order or any contact order that has effect in its place, it would be appropriate for the enforcement order to be revoked.

(3) The enforcement order may be revoked by the court under sub-paragraph (2) of its own motion or on an application by the person subject to the enforcement order.

(4) In deciding whether to revoke the enforcement order under sub-paragraph (2)(b), the court is to take into account –

    (a)   the extent to which the person subject to the enforcement order has complied with it, and

    (b)   the likelihood that the person will comply with the contact order or any contact order that has effect in its place in the absence of an enforcement order.

(5) In deciding whether to revoke the enforcement order under sub-paragraph (2)(c), the court is to take into account the likelihood that the person will comply with the contact order or any contact order that has effect in its place in the absence of an enforcement order.

Amendment by reason of change of residence

5. (1) This paragraph applies where a court has made an enforcement order in respect of a person's failure to comply with a contact order and the enforcement order is in force.

(2) If the court is satisfied that the person has changed, or proposes to change, his residence from the local justice area specified in the order to another local justice area, the court may amend the order by substituting the other area for the area specified.

(3) The enforcement order may be amended by the court under sub-paragraph (2) of its own motion or on an application by the person subject to the enforcement order.

Amendment of hours specified under unpaid work requirement

6. (1) This paragraph applies where a court has made an enforcement order in respect of a person's failure to comply with a contact order and the enforcement order is in force.

(2) If it appears to the court that, having regard to circumstances that have arisen since the enforcement order was made, it would be appropriate to do so, the court may reduce the number of hours specified in the order (but not below the minimum specified in section 199(2)(a) of the Criminal Justice Act 2003).

(3) In amending the enforcement order under sub-paragraph (2), the court must be satisfied that the effect on the person of the enforcement order as proposed to be amended is no more than is required to secure his compliance with the contact order or any contact order that has effect in its place.

(4) The enforcement order may be amended by the court under sub-paragraph (2) of its own motion or on an application by the person subject to the enforcement order.

Amendment to extend unpaid work requirement

7. (1) This paragraph applies where a court has made an enforcement order in respect of a person's failure to comply with a contact order and the enforcement order is in force.

(2) If it appears to the court that, having regard to circumstances that have arisen since the enforcement order was made, it would be appropriate to do so, the court may, in relation to the order, extend the period of twelve months specified in section 200(2) of the Criminal Justice Act 2003 (as substituted by paragraph 3).

(3) The period may be extended by the court under sub-paragraph (2) of its own motion or on an application by the person subject to the enforcement order.

Warning and report following breach

8. (1) This paragraph applies where a court has made an enforcement order in respect of a person's failure to comply with a contact order.

(2) If the responsible officer is of the opinion that the person has failed without reasonable excuse to comply with the unpaid work requirement imposed by the enforcement order, the officer must give the person a warning under this paragraph unless –

    (a)   the person has within the previous twelve months been given a warning under this paragraph in relation to a failure to comply with the unpaid work requirement, or

PART I – Statutes

    (b)   the responsible officer reports the failure to the appropriate person.

(3) A warning under this paragraph must –

    (a)   describe the circumstances of the failure,
    (b)   state that the failure is unacceptable, and
    (c)   inform the person that, if within the next twelve months he again fails to comply with the unpaid work requirement, the warning and the subsequent failure will be reported to the appropriate person.

(4) The responsible officer must, as soon as practicable after the warning has been given, record that fact.

(5) If –

    (a)   the responsible officer has given a warning under this paragraph to a person subject to an enforcement order, and
    (b)   at any time within the twelve months beginning with the date on which the warning was given, the responsible officer is of the opinion that the person has since that date failed without reasonable excuse to comply with the unpaid work requirement imposed by the enforcement order,

the officer must report the failure to the appropriate person.

(6) A report under sub-paragraph (5) must include a report of the warning given to the person subject to the enforcement order.

(7) The appropriate person, in relation to an enforcement order, is the officer of the Service or the Welsh family proceedings officer who is required under section 11M to report on matters relating to the enforcement order.

(8) 'Responsible officer', in relation to a person subject to an enforcement order, has the same meaning as in section 197 of the Criminal Justice Act 2003 (as modified by paragraph 2).

Breach of an enforcement order

9. (1) This paragraph applies where a court has made an enforcement order ('the first order') in respect of a person's failure to comply with a contact order.

(2) If the court is satisfied beyond reasonable doubt that the person has failed to comply with the unpaid work requirement imposed by the first order, the court may –

    (a)   amend the first order so as to make the requirement more onerous, or
    (b)   make an enforcement order ('the second order') in relation to the person and (if the first order is still in force) provide for the second order to have effect either in addition to or in substitution for the first order.

(3) But the court may not exercise its powers under sub-paragraph (2) if it is satisfied that the person had a reasonable excuse for failing to comply with the unpaid work requirement imposed by the first order.

(4) The burden of proof as to the matter mentioned in sub-paragraph (3) lies on the person claiming to have had a reasonable excuse, and the standard of proof is the balance of probabilities.

(5) The court may exercise its powers under sub-paragraph (2) in relation to the first order only on the application of a person who would be able to apply under section 11J for an enforcement order if the failure to comply with the first order were a failure to comply with the contact order to which the first order relates.

(6) Where the person proposing to apply to the court is the child with respect to whom the contact order was made, subsections (6) and (7) of section 11J have effect in relation to the application as they have effect in relation to an application for an enforcement order.

(7) An application to the court to exercise its powers under sub-paragraph (2) may only be made while the first order is in force.

(8) The court may not exercise its powers under sub-paragraph (2) in respect of a failure by the person to comply with the unpaid work requirement imposed by the first order unless it is satisfied that before the failure occurred the person had been given (in accordance with rules of court) a copy of, or otherwise informed of the terms of, a notice under section 11N relating to the first order.

(9) In dealing with the person under sub-paragraph (2)(a), the court may –

(a) increase the number of hours specified in the first order (but not above the maximum specified in section 199(2)(b) of the Criminal Justice Act 2003, as substituted by paragraph 3);

(b) in relation to the order, extend the period of twelve months specified in section 200(2) of the Criminal Justice Act 2003 (as substituted by paragraph 3).

(10) In exercising its powers under sub-paragraph (2), the court must be satisfied that, taking into account the extent to which the person has complied with the unpaid work requirement imposed by the first order, the effect on the person of the proposed exercise of those powers –

(a) is no more than is required to secure his compliance with the contact order or any contact order that has effect in its place, and

(b) is no more than is proportionate to the seriousness of his failures to comply with the contact order and the first order.

(11) Where the court exercises its powers under sub-paragraph (2) by making an enforcement order in relation to a person who has failed to comply with another enforcement order –

(a) sections 11K(4), 11L(2) to (7), 11M and 11N have effect as regards the making of the order in relation to the person as they have effect as regards the making of an enforcement order in relation to a person who has failed to comply with a contact order;

(b)   this Part of this Schedule has effect in relation to the order so made as if it were an enforcement order made in respect of the failure for which the other order was made.

(12) Sub-paragraph (2) is without prejudice to section 63(3) of the Magistrates' Courts Act 1980 as it applies in relation to enforcement orders.

Provision relating to amendment of enforcement orders

10. Sections 11L(2) to (7) and 11M have effect in relation to the making of an order under paragraph 6(2), 7(2) or 9(2)(a) amending an enforcement order as they have effect in relation to the making of an enforcement order; and references in sections 11L(2) to (7) and 11M to an enforcement order are to be read accordingly.][1]

NOTES

Amendments.[1] Schedule inserted: Children and Adoption Act 2006, s 4(2), Sch 1.

SCHEDULE 1
FINANCIAL PROVISION FOR CHILDREN

Section 15(1)

Orders for financial relief against parents

1. (1) On an application made by a parent[, guardian or special guardian][2] of a child, or by any person in whose favour a residence order is in force with respect to a child, the court may –

(a)   in the case of an application to the High Court or a county court, make one or more of the orders mentioned in sub-paragraph (2);

(b)   in the case of an application to a magistrates' court, make one or both of the orders mentioned in paragraphs (a) and (c) of that sub-paragraph.

(2) The orders referred to in sub-paragraph (1) are –

(a)   an order requiring either or both parents of a child –
(i)   to make to the applicant for the benefit of the child; or
(ii)   to make to the child himself,
such periodical payments, for such term, as may be specified in the order;

(b)   an order requiring either or both parents of a child –
(i)   to secure to the applicant for the benefit of the child; or
(ii)   to secure to the child himself,
such periodical payments, for such term, as may be so specified;

(c)   an order requiring either or both parents of a child –
(i)   to pay to the applicant for the benefit of the child; or
(ii)   to pay to the child himself,
such lump sum as may be so specified;

(d)   an order requiring a settlement to be made for the benefit of the child, and to the satisfaction of the court, of property –

PART I – Statutes

    (i)   to which either parent is entitled (either in possession or in reversion); and

    (ii)   which is specified in the order;

  (e)   an order requiring either or both parents of a child –

    (i)   to transfer to the applicant, for the benefit of the child; or

    (ii)   to transfer to the child himself,

such property to which the parent is, or the parents are, entitled (either in possession or in reversion) as may be specified in the order.

(3) The powers conferred by this paragraph may be exercised at any time.

(4) An order under sub-paragraph (2)(a) or (b) may be varied or discharged by a subsequent order made on the application of any person by or to whom payments were required to be made under the previous order.

(5) Where a court makes an order under this paragraph –

  (a)   it may at any time make a further such order under sub-paragraph (2)(a), (b) or (c) with respect to the child concerned if he has not reached the age of eighteen;

  (b)   it may not make more than one order under sub-paragraph (2)(d) or (e) against the same person in respect of the same child.

(6) On making, varying or discharging a residence order [or a special guardianship order][3] the court may exercise any of its powers under this Schedule even though no application has been made to it under this Schedule.

[(7) Where a child is a ward of court, the court may exercise any of its powers under this Schedule even though no application has been made to it.][1]

NOTES

Amendments.[1] Sub-paragraph added: Courts and Legal Services Act 1990, s 116, Sch 16, para 10(2).[2] Words substituted: Adoption and Children Act 2002, s 139(1), Sch 3, paras 54, 71(a)(i).[3] Words inserted: Adoption and Children Act 2002, s 139(1), Sch 3, paras 54, 71(a)(ii).

Definitions. 'Child': s 105(1); 'parent': Sch 1, para 16(2); 'residence order': s 8(1); 'the court': s 92(7).

Orders for financial relief for persons over eighteen

2. (1) If, on an application by a person who has reached the age of eighteen, it appears to the court –

  (a)   that the applicant is, will be or (if an order were made under this paragraph) would be receiving instruction at an educational establishment or undergoing training for a trade, profession or vocation, whether or not while in gainful employment; or

  (b)   that there are special circumstances which justify the making of an order under this paragraph,

the court may make one or both of the orders mentioned in sub-paragraph (2).

(2) The orders are –

(a)   an order requiring either or both of the applicant's parents to pay to the applicant such periodical payments, for such term, as may be specified in the order;

(b)   an order requiring either or both of the applicant's parents to pay to the applicant such lump sum as may be so specified.

(3) An applicant may not be made under this paragraph by any person if, immediately before he reached the age of sixteen, a periodical payments order was in force with respect to him.

(4) No order shall be made under this paragraph at a time when the parents of the applicant are living with each other in the same household.

(5) An order under sub-paragraph (2)(a) may be varied or discharged by a subsequent order made on the application of any person by or to whom payments were required to be made under the previous order.

(6) In sub-paragraph (3) 'periodical payments order' means an order made under –

(a)   this Schedule;

(b)   ...[1]

(c)   section 23 or 27 of the Matrimonial Causes Act 1973;

(d)   Part I of the Domestic Proceedings and Magistrates' Courts Act 1978,

[(e)   Part 1 or 9 of Schedule 5 to the Civil Partnership Act 2004 (financial relief in the High Court or a county court etc);

(f)   Schedule 6 to the 2004 Act (financial relief in the magistrates' courts etc),][2]

for the making or securing of periodical payments.

(7) The powers conferred by this paragraph shall be exercisable at any time.

(8) Where the court makes an order under this paragraph it may from time to time while that order remains in force make a further such order.

NOTES

Amendments.[1] Words repealed: Child Support Act 1991, s 58(14).[2] Subparagraphs inserted: Civil Partnership Act 2004, s 78(1), (2).

Definitions. 'Periodical payments order': Sch 1, para 2(6); 'the court': s 92(7).

Duration of orders for financial relief

3. (1) The term to be specified in an order for periodical payments made under paragraph 1(2)(a) or (b) in favour of a child may begin with the date of the making of an application for the order in question or any later date [or a date ascertained in accordance with sub-paragraph (5) or (6)][1] but –

(a)   shall not in the first instance extend beyond the child's seventeenth birthday unless the court thinks it right in the circumstances of the case to specify a later date; and

(b)   shall not in any event extend beyond the child's eighteenth birthday.

(2) Paragraph (b) of sub-paragraph (1) shall not apply in the case of a child if it appears to the court that –

(a) the child is, or will be (if an order were made without complying with that paragraph) would be receiving instruction at an educational establishment or undergoing training for a trade, profession or vocation, whether or not while in gainful employment; or

(b) there are special circumstances which justify the making of an order without complying with that paragraph.

(3) An order for periodical payments made under paragraph 1(2)(a) or 2(2)(a) shall, notwithstanding anything in the order, cease to have effect on the death of the person liable to make payments under the order.

(4) Where an order is made under paragraph 1(2)(a) or (b) requiring periodical payments to be made or secured to the parent of a child, the order shall cease to have effect if –

(a) any parent making or securing the payments; and

(b) any parent to whom the payments are made or secured,

live together for a period of more than six months.

[(5) Where –

(a) a maintenance assessment ('the current assessment') is in force with respect to a child; and

(b) an application is made for an order under paragraph 1(2)(a) or (b) of this Schedule for periodical payments in favour of that child –

(i) in accordance with section 8 of the Child Support Act 1991; and

(ii) before the end of the period of 6 months beginning with the making of the current assessment,

the term to be specified in any such order made on that application may be expressed to begin on, or at any time after, the earliest permitted date.

(6) For the purposes of subsection (5) above, 'the earliest permitted date' is whichever is the later of –

(a) the date 6 months before the application is made; or

(b) the date on which the current assessment took effect or, where successive maintenance assessments have been continuously in force with respect to a child, on which the first of those assessments took effect.

(7) Where –

(a) a maintenance assessment ceases to have effect or is cancelled by or under any provision of the Child Support Act 1991, and

(b) an application is made, before the end of the period of 6 months beginning with the relevant date, for an order for periodical payments under paragraph 1(2)(a) or (b) in favour of a child with respect to whom that maintenance assessment was in force immediately before it ceased to have effect or was cancelled, the term to be specified in any such order, or in any interim order under paragraph 9, made on that application may begin with the date on which that maintenance assessment ceased to have effect or, as the case may be, the date with effect from which it was cancelled, or any later date.

(8) In sub-paragraph (7)(b) –

    (a)   where the maintenance assessment ceased to have effect, the relevant date is the date on which it so ceased; and

    (b)   where the maintenance assessment was cancelled, the relevant date is the later of –

        (i)   the date on which the person who cancelled it did so, and

        (ii)   the date from which the cancellation first had effect.][1]

NOTES

Amendments.[1] Words and subparagraphs inserted: Maintenance Orders (Backdating) Order 1993, SI 1993/623.

Matters to which court is to have regard in making orders for financial relief

4. (1) In deciding whether to exercise its powers under paragraph 1 or 2, and if so in what manner, the court shall have regard to all the circumstances including –

    (a)   the income, earning capacity, property and other financial resources which each person mentioned in sub-paragraph (4) has or is likely to have in the foreseeable future;

    (b)   the financial needs, obligations and responsibilities which each person mentioned in sub-paragraph (4) has or is likely to have in the foreseeable future;

    (c)   the financial needs of the child;

    (d)   the income, earning capacity (if any), property and other financial resources of the child;

    (e)   any physical or mental disability of the child;

    (f)   the manner in which the child was being, or was expected to be, educated or trained.

(2) In deciding whether to exercise its powers under paragraph 1 against a person who is not the mother or father of the child, and if so in what manner, the court shall in addition have regard to –

    (a)   whether that person had assumed responsibility for the maintenance of the child, and, if so, the extent to which and basis on which he assumed that responsibility and the length of the period during which he met that responsibility;

    (b)   whether he did so knowing that the child was not his child;

    (c)   the liability of any other person to maintain the child.

(3) Where the court makes an order under paragraph 1 against a person who is not the father of the child, it shall record in the order that the order is made on the basis that the person against whom the order is made is not the child's father.

(4) The persons mentioned in sub-paragraph (1) are –

(a) in relation to a decision whether to exercise its powers under paragraph 1, any parent of the child;

(b) in relation to a decision whether to exercise its powers under paragraph 2, the mother and father of the child;

(c) the applicant for the order;

(d) any other person in whose favour the court proposes to make the order.

[(5) In the case of a child who has a parent by virtue of section 42 or 43 of the Human Fertilisation and Embryology Act 2008, any reference in sub-paragraph (2), (3) or (4) to the child's father is a reference to the woman who is a parent of the child by virtue of that section.][1]

NOTES

Amendments.[1] Subparagraph inserted: Human Fertilisation and Embryology Act 2008, s 56, Sch 6, Pt 1, para 32(1), (2).

Provisions relating to lump sums

5. (1) Without prejudice to the generality of paragraph 1, an order under that paragraph for the payment of a lump sum may be made for the purpose of enabling any liabilities or expenses –

(a) incurred in connection with the birth of the child or in maintaining the child; and

(b) reasonably incurred before the making of the order,

to be met.

(2) The amount of any lump sum required to be paid by an order made by a magistrates' court under paragraph 1 or 2 shall not exceed £1000 or such larger amount as the [Lord Chancellor][1] may[, after consulting the Lord Chief Justice,][2] from time to time by order fix for the purposes of this sub-paragraph.

(3) The power of the court under paragraph 1 or 2 to vary or discharge an order for the making or securing of periodical payments by a parent shall include power to make an order under that provision for the payment of a lump sum by that parent.

(4) The amount of any lump sum which a parent may be required to pay by virtue of sub-paragraph (3) shall not, in the case of an order made by a magistrates' court, exceed the maximum amount that may at the time of the making of the order be required to be paid under sub-paragraph (2), but a magistrates' court may make an order for the payment of a lump sum not exceeding that amount even though the parent was required to pay a lump sum by a previous order under this Act.

(5) An order made under paragraph 1 or 2 for the payment of a lump sum may provide for the payment of that sum by instalments.

PART I – Statutes

(6) Where the court provides for the payment of a lump sum by instalments the court, on an application made either by the person liable to pay or the person entitled to receive that sum, shall have power to vary that order by varying –

    (a)   the number of instalments payable;

    (b)   the amount of any instalment payable;

    (c)   the date on which any instalment becomes payable.

[(7) The Lord Chief Justice may nominate a judicial office holder (as defined in section 109(4) of the Constitutional Reform Act 2005) to exercise his functions under this paragraph.][2]

NOTES

Amendments.[1] Words substituted: Transfer of Functions (Magistrates' Courts and Family Law) Order 1992, SI 1992/709.[2] Words and subparagraph inserted: Constitutional Reform Act 2005, s 15(1), Sch 4, Pt 1, paras 203, 209(1)–(3).

Definitions. 'Child': s 105(1), Sch 1, para 16(1); 'parent': Sch 1, para 16(2); 'the court': s 92(7).

Variation etc of orders for periodical payments

6. (1) In exercising its powers under paragraph 1 or 2 to vary or discharge an order for the making or securing of periodical payments the court shall have regard to all the circumstances of the case, including any change in any of the matters to which the court was required to have regard when making the order.

(2) The power of the court under paragraph 1 or 2 to vary an order for the making or securing of periodical payments shall include power to suspend any provision of the order temporarily and to revive any provision so suspended.

(3) Where on an application under paragraph 1 or 2 for the variation or discharge of an order for the making or securing of periodical payments the court varies the payments required to be made under that order, the court may provide that the payments as so varied shall be made from such date as the court may specify [except that, subject to sub-paragraph (9), the date shall not be][1] earlier than the date of the making of the application.

(4) An application for the variation of an order made under paragraph 1 for the making or securing of periodical payments to or for the benefit of a child may, if the child has reached the age of sixteen, be made by the child himself.

(5) Where an order for the making or securing of periodical payments made under paragraph 1 ceases to have effect on the date on which the child reaches the age of sixteen, or at any time after that date but before or on the date on which he reaches the age of eighteen, the child may apply to the court which made the order for an order for its revival.

(6) If on such an application it appears to the court that –

    (a)   the child is, will be or (if an order were made under this sub-paragraph) would be receiving instruction at an educational establishment or undergoing training for a trade, profession or vocation, whether or not while in gainful employment; or

(b)   there are special circumstances which justify the making of an order under this paragraph,

the court shall have power by order to revive the order from such date as the court may specify, not being earlier than the date of the making of the application.

(7) Any order which is revived by an order under sub-paragraph (5) may be varied or discharged under that provision, on the application of any person by whom or to whom payments are required to be made under the revived order.

(8) An order for the making or securing of periodical payments made under paragraph 1 may be varied or discharged, after the death of either parent, on the application of a guardian [or special guardian]² of the child concerned.

[(9) Where –

(a)   an order under paragraph 1(2)(a) or (b) for the making or securing of periodical payments in favour of more than one child ('the order') is in force;
(b)   the order requires payments specified in it to be made to or for the benefit of more than one child without apportioning those payments between them;
(c)   a maintenance assessment ('the assessment') is made with respect to one or more, but not all, of the children with respect to whom those payments are to be made; and
(d)   an application is made, before the end of the period of 6 months beginning with the date on which the assessment was made, for the variation or discharge of the order,

the court may, in exercise of its powers under paragraph 1 to vary or discharge the order, direct that the variation or discharge shall take effect from the date on which the assessment took effect or any later date.]¹

NOTES

Amendments.¹ Words substituted or subparagraph inserted: Maintenance Orders (Backdating) Order 1993, SI 1993/623.² Words inserted: Adoption and Children Act 2002, s 139(1), Sch 3, paras 54, 71(b).

[Variation of orders for periodical payments etc made by magistrates' courts

6A. (1) Subject to sub-paragraphs (7) and (8), the power of a magistrates' court –

(a)   under paragraph 1 or 2 to vary an order for the making of periodical payments, or
(b)   under paragraph 5(6) to vary an order for the payment of a lump sum by instalments,

shall include power, if the court is satisfied that payment has not been made in accordance with the order, to exercise one of its powers under paragraphs (a) to (d) of section 59(3) of the Magistrates' Courts Act 1980.

(2) In any case where –

PART I – Statutes

(a)   a magistrates' court has made an order under this Schedule for the making of periodical payments or for the payment of a lump sum by instalments, and

(b)   payments under the order are required to be made by any method of payment falling within section 59(6) of the Magistrates' Courts Act 1980 (standing order, etc),

any person entitled to make an application under this Schedule for the variation of the order (in this paragraph referred to as 'the applicant') may apply to [a magistrates' court acting in the same local justice area as the court which made the order]³ for the order to be varied as mentioned in sub-paragraph (3).

(3) Subject to sub-paragraph (5), where an application is made under sub-paragraph (2), [a justices' clerk]³, after giving written notice (by post or otherwise) of the application to any interested party and allowing that party, within the period of 14 days beginning with the date of the giving of that notice, an opportunity to make written representations, may vary the order to provide that payments under the order shall be made [to the designated officer for the court]³.

(4) The clerk may proceed with an application under sub-paragraph (2) notwithstanding that any such interested party as is referred to in sub-paragraph (3) has not received written notice of the application.

(5) Where an application has been made under sub-paragraph (2), the clerk may, if he considers it inappropriate to exercise his power under sub-paragraph (3), refer the matter to the court which, subject to sub-paragraphs (7) and (8), may vary the order by exercising one of its powers under paragraphs (a) to (d) of section 59(3) of the Magistrates' Courts Act 1980.

(6) Subsection (4) of section 59 of the Magistrates' Courts Act 1980 (power of court to order that account be opened) shall apply for the purposes of sub-paragraphs (1) and (5) as it applies for the purposes of that section.

(7) Before varying the order by exercising one of its powers under paragraphs (a) to (d) of section 59(3) of the Magistrates' Courts Act 1980, the court shall have regard to any representations made by the parties to the application.

(8) If the court does not propose to exercise its power [under paragraph (c), (cc) or (d)]² of subsection (3) of section 59 of the Magistrates' Courts Act 1980, the court shall, unless upon representations expressly made in that behalf by the applicant for the order it is satisfied that it is undesirable to do so, exercise its power under paragraph (b) of that subsection.

(9) None of the powers of the court, or of [a justices' clerk]³, conferred by this paragraph shall be exercisable in relation to an order under this Schedule for the making of periodical payments, or for the payment of a lump sum by instalments, which is not a qualifying maintenance order (within the meaning of section 59 of the Magistrates' Courts Act 1980).

(10) In sub-paragraphs (3) and (4) 'interested party', in relation to an application made by the applicant under sub-paragraph (2), means a person

who would be entitled to be a party to an application for the variation of the order made by the applicant under any other provision of this Schedule if such an application were made.][1]

NOTES

Amendments.[1] Paragraph inserted: Maintenance Enforcement Act 1991, s 6.[2] Words substituted: Child Support Act 1991 (Consequential Amendments) Order 1994, SI 1994/731.[3] Words substituted: Courts Act 2003, s 109(1), Sch 8, para 338(1)–(3).

Variation of orders for secured periodical payments after death of parent

7. (1) Where the parent liable to make payments under a secured periodical payments order has died, the persons who may apply for the variation or discharge of the order shall include the personal representatives of the deceased parent.

(2) No application for the variation of the order shall, except with the permission of the court, be made after the end of the period of six months from the date on which representation in regard to the estate of that parent is first taken out.

(3) The personal representatives of a deceased person against whom a secured periodical payments order was made shall not be liable for having distributed any part of the estate of the deceased after the end of the period of six months referred to in sub-paragraph (2) on the ground that they ought to have taken into account the possibility that the court might permit an application for variation to be made after that period by the person entitled to payments under the order.

(4) Sub-paragraph (3) shall not prejudice any power to recover any part of the estate so distributed arising by virtue of the variation of an order in accordance with this paragraph.

(5) Where an application to vary a secured periodical payments order is made after the death of the parent liable to make payments under the order, the circumstances to which the court is required to have regard under paragraph 6(1) shall include the changed circumstances resulting from the death of the parent.

(6) In considering for the purposes of sub-paragraph (2) the question when representation was first taken out, a grant limited to settled land or to trust property shall be left out of account and a grant limited to real estate or to personal estate shall be left out of account unless a grant limited to the remainder of the estate has previously been made or is made at the same time.

(7) In this paragraph 'secured periodical payments order' means an order for secured periodical payments under paragraph 1(2)(b).

NOTES

Definitions. 'Child': s 105(1), Sch 1, para 16(1); 'parent': Sch 1, para 16(2); 'secured periodical payments order': Sch 1, para 7(7); 'the court': s 92(7).

Part I   Statutes

Financial relief under other enactments

8. (1) This paragraph applies where a residence order [or a special guardianship order]¹ is made with respect to a child at a time when there is in force an order ('the financial relief order') made under any enactment other than this Act and requiring a person to contribute to the child's maintenance.

(2) Where this paragraph applies, the court may, on the application of –

(a)   any person required by the financial relief order to contribute to the child's maintenance; or

(b)   any person in whose favour a residence order [or a special guardianship order]¹ with respect to the child is in force,

make an order revoking the financial relief order, or varying it by altering the amount of any sum payable under that order or by substituting the applicant for the person to whom any such sum is otherwise payable under that order.

NOTES

Amendments.¹ Words inserted: Adoption and Children Act 2002, s 139(1), Sch 3, paras 54, 71(c).

Interim orders

9. (1) Where an application is made under paragraph 1 or 2 the court may, at any time before it disposes of the application, make an interim order –

(a)   requiring either or both parents to make such periodical payments, at such times and for such term as the court thinks fit; and

(b)   giving any direction which the court thinks fit.

(2) An interim order made under this paragraph may provide for payments to be made from such date as the court may specify [except that, subject to paragraph 3(5) and (6), the date shall not be]¹ earlier than the date of the making of the application under paragraph 1 or 2.

(3) An interim order made under this paragraph shall cease to have effect when the application is disposed of or, if earlier, on the date specified for the purposes of this paragraph in the interim order.

(4) An interim order in which a date has been specified for the purposes of sub-paragraph (3) may be varied by substituting a later date.

NOTES

Amendments.¹ Words substituted: Maintenance Orders (Backdating) Order 1993, SI 1993/623.

Definitions. 'Child': s 105(1); 'parent': Sch 1, para 16(2); 'residence order': s 8(1); 'the court': s 92(7); 'the financial relief order': Sch 1, para 8(1).

Alteration of maintenance agreements

10. (1) In this paragraph and in paragraph 11 'maintenance agreement' means any agreement in writing made with respect to a child, whether before or after the commencement of this paragraph, which –

(a)   is or was made between the father and mother of the child; and

(b)   contains provision with respect to the making or securing of payments, or the disposition or use of any property, for the maintenance or education of the child,

and any such provisions are in this paragraph, and paragraph 11, referred to as 'financial arrangements'.

(2) Where a maintenance agreement is for the time being subsisting and each of the parties to the agreement is for the time being either domiciled or resident in England and Wales, then, either party may apply for an order under this paragraph.

(3) If the court to which the application is made is satisfied either –

(a)   that, by reason of a change in the circumstances in the light of which any financial arrangements contained in the agreement were made (including a change foreseen by the parties when making the agreement), the agreement should be altered so as to make different financial arrangements; or

(b)   that the agreement does not contain proper financial arrangements with respect to the child,

then that court may by order make such alterations in the agreement by varying or revoking any financial arrangements contained in it as may appear to it to be just having regard to all the circumstances.

(4) If the maintenance agreement is altered by an order under this paragraph, the agreement shall have effect thereafter as if the alteration had been made by agreement between the parties and for valuable consideration.

(5) Where a court decides to make an order under this paragraph altering the maintenance agreement –

(a)   by inserting provision for the making or securing by one of the parties to the agreement of periodical payments for the maintenance of the child; or

(b)   by increasing the rate of periodical payments required to be made or secured by one of the parties for the maintenance of the child,

then, in deciding the term for which under the agreement as altered by the order the payments or (as the case may be) the additional payments attributable to the increase are to be made or secured for the benefit of the child, the court shall apply the provisions of sub-paragraphs (1) and (2) of paragraph 3 as if the order were an order under paragraph 1(2)(a) or (b).

(6) A magistrates' court shall not entertain an application under sub-paragraph (2) unless both the parties to the agreement are resident in England and Wales and .[the court acts in, or is authorised by the Lord Chancellor to act for, a local justice area in which at least one of the parties is resident][1], and shall not have power to make any order on such an application except –

(a)   in a case where the agreement contains no provision for periodical payments by either of the parties, an order inserting provision for the making by one of the parties of periodical payments for the maintenance of the child;

(b)   in a case where the agreement includes provision for the making by one of the parties of periodical payments, an order increasing or reducing the rate of, or terminating, any of those payments.

(7) For the avoidance of doubt it is hereby declared that nothing in this paragraph affects any power of a court before which any proceedings between the parties to a maintenance agreement are brought under any other enactment to make an order containing financial arrangements or any right of either party to apply for such an order in such proceedings.

[(8) In the case of a child who has a parent by virtue of section 42 or 43 of the Human Fertilisation and Embryology Act 2008, the reference in sub-paragraph (1)(a) to the child's father is a reference to the woman who is a parent of the child by virtue of that section.][2]

NOTES

Amendments.[1] Words substituted: Courts Act 2003, s 109(1), Sch 8, para 339.[2] Subparagraph inserted: Human Fertilisation and Embryology Act 2008, s 56, Sch 6, Pt 1, para 32(1), (3).

11. (1) Where a maintenance agreement provides for the continuation, after the death of one of the parties, of payments for the maintenance of a child and that party dies domiciled in England and Wales, the surviving party or the personal representatives of the deceased party may apply to the High Court or a county court for an order under paragraph 10.

(2) If a maintenance agreement is altered by a court on an application under this paragraph, the agreement shall have effect thereafter as if the alteration had been made, immediately before the death, by agreement between the parties and for valuable consideration.

(3) An application under this paragraph shall not, except with leave of the High Court or a county court, be made after the end of the period of six months beginning with the day on which representation in regard to the estate of the deceased is first taken out.

(4) In considering for the purposes of sub-paragraph (3) the question when representation was first taken out, a grant limited to settled land or to trust property shall be left out of account and a grant limited to real estate or to personal estate shall be left out of account unless a grant limited to the remainder of the estate has previously been made or is made at the same time.

(5) A county court shall not entertain an application under this paragraph, or an application for leave to make an application under this paragraph, unless it would have jurisdiction to hear and determine proceedings for an order under section 2 of the Inheritance (Provision for Family and Dependants) Act 1975 in relation to the deceased's estate by virtue of section 25 of the County Courts Act 1984 (jurisdiction under the Act of 1975).

PART I – Statutes

(6) The provisions of this paragraph shall not render the personal representatives of the deceased liable for having distributed any part of the estate of the deceased after the expiry of the period of six months referred to in sub-paragraph (3) on the ground that they ought to have taken into account the possibility that a court might grant leave for an application by virtue of this paragraph to be made by the surviving party after that period.

(7) Sub-paragraph (6) shall not prejudice any power to recover any part of the estate so distributed arising by virtue of the making of an order in pursuance of this paragraph.

NOTES

Definitions. 'Child': s 105(1); 'financial arrangements': Sch 1, para 10(1); 'maintenance agreement': Sch 1, para 10(1); 'the court': s 92(7).

Enforcement of orders for maintenance

12. (1) Any person for the time being under an obligation to make payments in pursuance of any order for the payment of money made by a magistrates' court under this Act shall give notice of any change of address to such person (if any) as may be specified in the order.

(2) Any person failing without reasonable excuse to give such a notice shall be guilty of an offence and liable on summary conviction to a fine not exceeding level 2 on the standard scale.

(3) An order for the payment of money made by a magistrates' court under this Act shall be enforceable as a magistrates' court maintenance order within the meaning of section 150(1) of the Magistrates' Courts Act 1980.

Direction for settlement of instrument by conveyancing counsel

13. Where the High Court or a county court decides to make an order under this Act for the securing of periodical payments or for the transfer or settlement of property, it may direct that the matter be referred to one of the conveyancing counsel of the court to settle a proper instrument to be executed by all necessary parties.

Financial provision for child resident in country outside England and Wales

14. (1) Where one parent of a child lives in England and Wales and the child lives outside England and Wales with –

   (a)   another parent of his;
   (b)   a guardian [or special guardian][1] of his; or
   (c)   a person in whose favour a residence order is in force with respect to the child,

the court shall have power, on an application made by any of the persons mentioned in paragraphs (a) to (c), to make one or both of the orders mentioned in paragraph 1(2)(a) and (b) against the parent living in England and Wales.

(2) Any reference in this Act to the powers of the court under paragraph 1(2) or to an order made under paragraph 1(2) shall include a reference to the powers which the court has by virtue of sub-paragraph (1) or (as the case may be) to an order made by virtue of sub-paragraph (1).

NOTES

Amendments.[1] Words inserted: Adoption and Children Act 2002, s 139(1), Sch 3, paras 54, 71(d).

Local authority contribution to child's maintenance

15. (1) Where a child lives, or is to live, with a person as the result of a residence order, a local authority may make contributions to that person towards the cost of the accommodation and maintenance of the child.

(2) Sub-paragraph (1) does not apply where the person with whom the child lives, or is to live, is a parent of the child or the husband or wife [or civil partner][1] of a parent of the child.

NOTES

Amendments.[1] Words inserted: Civil Partnership Act 2004, s 78(1), (3).

Interpretation

16. (1) In this Schedule 'child' includes, in any case where an application is made under paragraph 2 or 6 in relation to a person who has reached the age of eighteen, that person.

[(2) In this Schedule, except paragraphs 2 and 15, 'parent' includes –

(a)   any party to a marriage (whether or not subsisting) in relation to whom the child concerned is a child of the family, and

(b)   any civil partner in a civil partnership (whether or not subsisting) in relation to whom the child concerned is a child of the family;

and for this purpose any reference to either parent or both parents shall be read as a reference to any parent of his and to all of his parents.][2]

[(3) In this Schedule, 'maintenance assessment' has the same meaning as it has in the Child Support Act 1991 by virtue of section 54 of that Act as read with any regulations in force under that section.][1]

NOTES

Amendments.[1] Words added: Maintenance Orders (Backdating) Order 1993, SI 1993/623.
[2] Subparagraph substituted: Civil Partnership Act 2004, s 78(1), (4).

Definitions. 'Child': s 105(1), Sch 1, para 16(1); 'child of the family': s 105(1); 'local authority': s 105(1); 'parent': Sch 1, para 16(2); 'residence order': s 8(1).

SCHEDULE 2
LOCAL AUTHORITY SUPPORT FOR CHILDREN AND FAMILIES

Sections 17, 23 and 29

PART I
PROVISION OF SERVICES FOR FAMILIES

Identification of children in need and provision of information

1. (1) Every local authority shall take reasonable steps to identify the extent to which there are children in need within their area.

(2) Every local authority shall –

    (a) publish information
        (i) about services provided by them under sections 17, 18, [20, 23B to 23D, 24A and 24B][1]; and
        (ii) where they consider it appropriate, about the provision by others (including, in particular, voluntary organisations) of services which the authority have power to provide under those sections; and

    (b) take such steps as are reasonably practicable to ensure that those who might benefit from the services receive the information relevant to them.

1A. ...[2]

Maintenance of a register of disabled children

2. (1) Every local authority shall open and maintain a register of disabled children within their area.

(2) The register may be kept by means of a computer.

Assessment of children's needs

3. Where it appears to a local authority that a child within their area is in need, the authority may assess his needs for the purposes of this Act at the same time as any assessment of his needs is made under –

    (a) the Chronically Sick and Disabled Persons Act 1970;
    (b) [Part IV of the Education Act 1996][3];
    (c) the Disabled Persons (Services, Consultation and Representation) Act 1986; or
    (d) any other enactment.

Prevention of neglect and abuse

4. (1) Every local authority shall take reasonable steps, through the provision of services under Part III of this Act, to prevent children within their area suffering ill-treatment or neglect.

(2) Where a local authority believe that a child who is at any time within their area –

    (a) is likely to suffer harm; but
    (b) lives or proposes to live in the area of another local authority they shall inform that other local authority.

(3) When informing that other local authority they shall specify –

(a)   the harm that they believe he is likely to suffer; and

(b)   (if they can) where the child lives or proposes to live.

Provision of accommodation in order to protect child

5. (1) Where –

(a)   it appears to a local authority that a child who is living on particular premises is suffering, or is likely to suffer, ill treatment at the hands of another person who is living on those premises; and

(b)   that other person proposes to move from the premises,

the authority may assist that other person to obtain alternative accommodation.

(2) Assistance given under this paragraph may be in cash.

(3) Subsections (7) to (9) of section 17 shall apply in relation to assistance given under this paragraph as they apply in relation to assistance given under that section.

Provision for disabled children

6. [(1)][5] Every local authority shall provide services designed –

(a)   to minimise the effect on disabled children within their area of their disabilities; *and*[5]

(b)   to give such children the opportunity to lead lives which are as normal as possible[; and

(c)   to assist individuals who provide care for such children to continue to do so, or to do so more effectively, by giving them breaks from caring][5].

[(2) The duty imposed by sub-paragraph (1)(c) shall be performed in accordance with regulations made by the appropriate national authority.][4]

Provision to reduce need for care proceedings etc.

7. Every local authority shall take reasonable steps designed –

(a)   to reduce the need to bring –

(i)   proceedings for care or supervision orders with respect to children within their area;

(ii)   criminal proceedings against such children;

(iii)   any family or other proceedings with respect to such children which might lead to them being placed in the authority's care; or

(iv)   proceedings under the inherent jurisdiction of the High Court with respect to children;

(b)   to encourage children within their area not to commit criminal offences; and

(c)   to avoid the need for children within their area to be placed in secure accommodation.

Provision for children living with their families

8. Every local authority shall make such provision as they consider appropriate for the following services to be available with respect to children in need within their area while they are living with their families –

    (a)   advice, guidance and counselling;

    (b)   occupational, social, cultural or recreational activities;

    (c)   home help (which may include laundry facilities);

    (d)   facilities for, or assistance with, travelling to and from home for the purpose of taking advantage of any other service provided under this Act or of any similar service;

    (e)   assistance to enable the child concerned and his family to have a holiday.

[Provision for accommodated children

8A (1) Every local authority shall make provision for such services as they consider appropriate to be available with respect to accommodated children.

(2) 'Accommodated children' are those children in respect of whose accommodation the local authority have been notified under section 85 or 86.

(3) The services shall be provided with a view to promoting contact between each accommodated child and that child's family.

(4) The services may, in particular, include –

    (a)   advice, guidance and counselling;

    (b)   services necessary to enable the child to visit, or to be visited by, members of the family;

    (c)   assistance to enable the child and members of the family to have a holiday together.

(5) Nothing in this paragraph affects the duty imposed by paragraph 10.][6]

Family centres

9. (1) Every local authority shall provide such family centres as they consider appropriate in relation to children within their area.

(2) 'Family centre' means a centre at which any of the persons mentioned in sub-paragraph (3) may –

    (a)   attend for occupational, social, cultural or recreational activities;

    (b)   attend for advice, guidance or counselling; or

    (c)   be provided with accommodation while he is receiving advice, guidance or counselling.

(3) The persons are –

    (a)   a child;

    (b)   his parents;

    (c)   any person who is not a parent of his but who has parental responsibility for him;

PART I – Statutes

(d)   any other person who is looking after him.

Maintenance of the family home

10. Every local authority shall take such steps as are reasonably practicable, where any child within their area who is in need and whom they are not looking after is living apart from his family –

(a)   to enable him to live with his family; or
(b)   to promote contact between him and his family,

if, in their opinion, it is necessary to do so in order to safeguard or promote his welfare.

Duty to consider racial groups to which children in need belong

11. Every local authority shall, in making any arrangements –

(a)   for the provision of day care within their area; or
(b)   designed to encourage persons to act as local authority foster parents,

have regard to the different racial groups to which children within their area who are in need belong.

NOTES

Amendments. [1] Words substituted: Children (Leaving Care) Act 2000, s 7(1), (4). [2] Paragraph repealed: Children Act 2004, s 64, Sch 5, Pt 1. [3] Words substituted: Education Act 1996, s 582(1), Sch 37, Pt I, para 92. [4] Subparagraph inserted in relation to England and, for the purpose of making regulations, in relation to Wales: Children and Young Persons Act 2008, s 25(1), (4). [5] Subsection designated (1), word 'and' in italics omitted and paragraph inserted in relation to England: Children and Young Persons Act, ss 25(1)–(3), 42, Sch 4. [6] Paragraph inserted in relation to England: Children and Young Persons Act 2008, s 19.

Definitions. 'Care order': ss 31(11), 105(1); 'child': s 105(1); 'child in need': s 17(10); 'day care': ss 18(4), 105(1); 'disabled': ss 17(11), 105(1); 'family': s 17(10); 'family centre': Sch 2, para 9(2); 'family proceedings': s 8(3); 'harm': ss 31(9), 105(1); 'ill-treatment': ss 31(9), 105(1); 'local authority': s 105(1); 'local authority foster parent': s 23(3); 'parental responsibility': s 3; 'secure accommodation': s 25(1); 'significant harm': ss 31(10), 105(1); 'supervision order': s 31(11); voluntary organisation': s 105(1).

PART II
CHILDREN LOOKED AFTER BY LOCAL AUTHORITIES

[Regulations as to conditions under which child in care is allowed to live with parent, etc

12A. Regulations under section 22C may, in particular, impose requirements on a local authority as to –

(a)   the making of any decision by a local authority to allow a child in their care to live with any person falling within section 22C(3) (including requirements as to those who must be consulted before the decision is made and those who must be notified when it has been made);
(b)   the supervision or medical examination of the child concerned;

(c)   the removal of the child, in such circumstances as may be prescribed, from the care of the person with whom the child has been allowed to live;

(d)   the records to be kept by local authorities.

Regulations as to placements of a kind specified in section 22C(6)(d)

12B. Regulations under section 22C as to placements of the kind specified in section 22C(6)(d) may, in particular, make provision as to –

(a)   the persons to be notified of any proposed arrangements;

(b)   the opportunities such persons are to have to make representations in relation to the arrangements proposed;

(c)   the persons to be notified of any proposed changes in arrangements;

(d)   the records to be kept by local authorities;

(e)   the supervision by local authorities of any arrangements made.

Placements out of area

12C. Regulations under section 22C may, in particular, impose requirements which a local authority must comply with –

(a)   before a child looked after by them is provided with accommodation at a place outside the area of the authority; or

(b)   if the child's welfare requires the immediate provision of such accommodation, within such period of the accommodation being provided as may be prescribed.

Avoidance of disruption in education

12D. (1) Regulations under section 22C may, in particular, impose requirements which a local authority must comply with before making any decision concerning a child's placement if he is in the fourth key stage.

(2) A child is 'in the fourth key stage' if he is a pupil in the fourth key stage for the purposes of Part 6 or 7 of the Education 2002 (see section 82 and 103 of that Act).

Regulations as to placing of children with local authority foster parents

12E. Regulations under section 22C may, in particular, make provision –

(a)   with regard to the welfare of children placed with local authority foster parents;

(b)   as to the arrangements to be made by local authorities in connection with the health and education of such children;

(c)   as to the records to be kept by local authorities;

(d)   for securing that where possible the local authority foster parent with whom a child is to be placed is –

    (i)   of the same religious persuasion as the child; or

    (ii)   gives an undertaking that the child will be brought up in that religious persuasion;

PART I – Statutes

(e)   for securing the children placed with local authority foster parents, and the premises in which they are accommodated, will be supervised and inspected by a local authority and that the children will be removed from those premises if their welfare appears to require it.

12F. (1) Regulations under section 22C may, in particular, also make provision –

(a)   for securing that a child is not placed with a local authority foster parent unless that person is for the time being approved as a local authority foster parent by such local authority as may be prescribed;

(b)   establishing a procedure under which any person in respect of whom a qualifying determination has been made may apply to the appropriate national authority for a review of that determination by a panel constituted by that national authority.

(2) A determination is a qualifying determination if –

(a)   it relates to the issue of whether a person should be approved, or should continue to be approved, as a local authority foster parent; and

(b)   it is of a prescribed description.

(3) Regulations made by virtue of sub-paragraph (1)(b) may include provision as to –

(a)   the duties and powers of a panel;

(b)   the administration and procedures of a panel;

(c)   the appointment of members of a panel (including the number, or any limit on the number, of members who may be appointed and any conditions for appointment);

(d)   the payment of fees to members of a panel;

(e)   the duties of any person in connection with a review conducted under the regulations;

(f)   the monitoring of any such reviews.

(4) Regulations made by virtue of sub-paragraph (3)(e) may impose a duty to pay to the appropriate national authority such sum as that national authority may determine; but such a duty may not be imposed upon a person who has applied for a review of a qualifying determination.

(5) The appropriate national authority must secure that, taking one financial year with another, the aggregate of the sums which become payable to it under regulations made by virtue of sub-paragraph (4) does not exceed the cost to it of performing its independent review functions.

(6) The appropriate national authority may make an arrangement with an organisation under which independent review functions are performed by the organisation on the national authority's behalf.

(7) If the appropriate national authority makes such an arrangement with an organisation, the organisation is to perform its functions under the arrangement in accordance with any general or special directions given by that national authority.

(8) The arrangement may include provision for payments to be made to the organisation by the appropriate national authority.

(9) Payments made by the appropriate national authority in accordance with such provision shall be taken into account in determining (for the purpose of sub-paragraph (5)) the cost to that national authority of performing its independent review functions.

(10) Where the Welsh Ministers are the appropriate national authority, sub-paragraphs (6) and (8) also apply as if references to an organisation included references to the Secretary of State.

(11) In this paragraph –

'financial year' means a period of twelve months ending with 31st March;
'independent review function' means a function conferred or imposed on a national authority by regulations made by virtue of sub-paragraph (1)(b);
'organisation' includes a public body and a private or voluntary organisation.

12G. Regulations under section 22C may, in particular, also make provision as to the circumstances in which local authorities may make arrangements for duties imposed on them by the regulations to be discharged on their behalf.]⁹

Promotion and maintenance of contact between child and family

15. (1) Where a child is being looked after by a local authority, the authority shall, unless it is not reasonably practicable or consistent with his welfare, endeavour to promote contact between the child and –

   (a)   his parents;
   (b)   any person who is not a parent of his but who has parental responsibility for him; and
   (c)   any relative, friend or other person connected with him.

(2) Where a child is being looked after by a local authority –

   (a)   the authority shall take such steps as are reasonably practicable to secure that
      (i)   his parents; and
      (ii)   any person who is not a parent of his but who has parental responsibility for him,
      are kept informed of where he is being accommodated; and
   (b)   every such person shall secure that the authority are kept informed of his or her address.

(3) Where a local authority ('the receiving authority') take over the provision of accommodation for a child from another local authority ('the transferring authority') under section 20(2) –

   (a)   the receiving authority shall (where reasonably practicable) inform
      (i)   the child's parents; and
      (ii)   any person who is not a parent of his but who has parental responsibility for him;

PART I – Statutes

(b)   sub-paragraph (2)(a) shall apply to the transferring authority, as well as the receiving authority, until at least one such person has been informed of the change; and

(c)   sub-paragraph (2)(b) shall not require any person to inform the receiving authority of his address until he has been so informed.

(4) Nothing in this paragraph requires a local authority to inform any person of the whereabouts of a child if –

(a)   the child is in the care of the authority; and

(b)   the authority has reasonable cause to believe that informing the person would prejudice the child's welfare.

(5) Any person who fails (without reasonable excuse) to comply with sub-paragraph (2)(b) shall be guilty of an offence and liable on summary conviction to a fine not exceeding level 2 on the standard scale.

(6) It shall be a defence in any proceedings under sub-paragraph (5) to prove that the defendant was residing at the same address as another person who was the child's parent or had parental responsibility for the child and had reasonable cause to believe that the other person had informed the appropriate authority that both of them were residing at that address.

Visits to or by children: expenses

16. (1) This paragraph applies where –

(a)   a child is being looked after by a local authority; and

(b)   the conditions mentioned in sub-paragraph (3) are satisfied.

(2) The authority may –

(a)   make payments to –
    (i)   a parent of the child;
    (ii)   any person who is not a parent of his but who has parental responsibility for him; or
    (iii) any relative, friend or other person connected with him,
    in respect of travelling, subsistence or other expenses incurred by that person in visiting the child; or

(b)   make payments to the child, or to any person on his behalf, in respect of travelling, subsistence or other expenses incurred by or on behalf of the child in his visiting –
    (i)   a parent of his;
    (ii)   any person who has parental responsibility for him; or
    (iii) any relative, friend or other person connected with him.

(3) The conditions are that –

(a)   it appears to the authority that the visit in question could not otherwise be made without undue financial hardship; and

(b)   the circumstances warrant the making of the payments.

[Appointment of visitor for child who is not being visited

17. *(1) Where it appears to a local authority in relation to any child that they are looking after that –*

(a) communication between the child and –

(i) a parent of his, or

(ii) any person who is not a parent of his but who has parental responsibility for him,

has been infrequent; or

(b) he has not visited or been visited by (or lived with) any such person during the preceding twelve months,

and that it would be in the child's best interests for an independent person to be appointed to be his visitor for the purposes of this paragraph, they shall appoint such a visitor.

(2) A person so appointed shall –

(a) have the duty of visiting, advising and befriending the child; and

(b) be entitled to recover from the authority who appointed him any reasonable expenses incurred by him for the purposes of his functions under this paragraph.

(3) A person's appointment as a visitor in pursuance of this paragraph shall be determined if –

(a) he gives notice in writing to the authority who appointed him that he resigns the appointment; or

(b) the authority give him notice in writing that they have terminated it.

(4) The determination of such an appointment shall not prejudice any duty under this paragraph to make a further appointment.

(5) Where a local authority propose to appoint a visitor for a child under this paragraph, the appointment shall not be made if –

(a) the child objects to it; and

(b) the authority are satisfied that he has sufficient understanding to make an informed decision.

(6) Where a visitor has been appointed for a child under this paragraph, the local authority shall determine the appointment if –

(a) the child objects to its continuing; and

(b) the authority are satisfied that he has sufficient understanding to make an informed decision.

(7) The [appropriate national authority][8] may make regulations as to the circumstances in which a person appointed as a visitor under this paragraph is to be regarded as independent of the local authority appointing him.][10]

Power to guarantee apprenticeship deeds etc

18. (1) While a child is being looked after by a local authority, or is a person qualifying for advice and assistance, the authority may undertake any obligation by way of guarantee under any deed of apprenticeship or articles of clerkship which he enters into.

(2) Where a local authority have undertaken any such obligation under any deed or articles they may at any time (whether or not they are still looking after the person concerned) undertake the like obligation under any supplemental deed or articles.

Arrangements to assist children to live abroad

19. (1) A local authority may only arrange for, or assist in arranging for, any child in their care to live outside England and Wales with the approval of the court.

(2) A local authority may, with the approval of every person who has parental responsibility for the child arrange for, or assist in arranging for, any other child looked after by them to live outside England and Wales.

(3) The court shall not give its approval under sub-paragraph (1) unless it is satisfied that –

    (a)   living outside England and Wales would be in the child's best interests;

    (b)   suitable arrangements have been, or will be, made for his reception and welfare in the country in which he will live;

    (c)   the child has consented to living in that country; and

    (d)   every person who has parental responsibility for the child has consented to his living in that country.

(4) Where the court is satisfied that the child does not have sufficient understanding to give or withhold his consent, it may disregard sub-paragraph (3)(c) and give its approval if the child is to live in the country concerned with a parent, guardian, [special guardian,][4] or other suitable person.

(5) Where a person whose consent is required by sub-paragraph (3)(d) fails to give his consent, the court may disregard that provision and give its approval if it is satisfied that that person –

    (a)   cannot be found;

    (b)   is incapable of consenting; or

    (c)   is withholding his consent unreasonably.

(6) [Section 85 of the Adoption and Children Act 2002 (which imposes restrictions on taking children out of the United Kingdom)][5] shall not apply in the case of any child who is to live outside England and Wales with the approval of the court given under this paragraph.

(7) Where a court decides to give its approval under this paragraph it may order that its decision is not to have effect during the appeal period.

(8) In sub-paragraph (7) 'the appeal period' means –

(a) where an appeal is made against the decision, the period between the making of the decision and the determination of the appeal; and

(b) otherwise, the period during which an appeal may be made against the decision.

[(9) This paragraph does not apply to a local authority placing a child for adoption with prospective adopters.][6]

[Preparation for ceasing to be looked after

19A. It is the duty of the local authority looking after a child to advise, assist and befriend him with a view to promoting his welfare when they have ceased to look after him.

19B. (1) A local authority shall have the following additional functions in relation to an eligible child whom they are looking after.

(2) In sub-paragraph (1) 'eligible child' means, subject to sub-paragraph (3), a child who –

(a) is aged sixteen or seventeen; and

(b) has been looked after by a local authority for a prescribed period, or periods amounting in all to a prescribed period, which began after he reached a prescribed age and ended after he reached the age of sixteen.

(3) The [appropriate national authority][8] may prescribe –

(a) additional categories of eligible children; and

(b) categories of children who are not to be eligible children despite falling within sub-paragraph (2).

(4) For each eligible child, the local authority shall carry out an assessment of his needs with a view to determining what advice, assistance and support it would be appropriate for them to provide him under this Act –

(a) while they are still looking after him; and

(b) after they cease to look after him,

and shall then prepare a pathway plan for him.

(5) The local authority shall keep the pathway plan under regular review.

(6) Any such review may be carried out at the same time as a review of the child's case carried out by virtue of section 26.

(7) The [appropriate national authority][8] may by regulations make provision as to assessments for the purposes of sub-paragraph (4).

(8) The regulations may in particular provide for the matters set out in section 23B(6).

Personal advisers

19C. A local authority shall arrange for each child whom they are looking after who is an eligible child for the purposes of paragraph 19B to have a personal adviser.][2]

PART I – Statutes

Death of children being looked after by local authorities

20. (1) If a child who is being looked after by a local authority dies, the authority –

    (a)   shall notify the [appropriate national authority][8] [[and (in the case of a local authority in England) Her Majesty's Chief Inspector of Education, Children's Services and Skills][7]][3];

    (b)   shall, so far as is reasonably practicable, notify the child's parents and every person who is not a parent of his but who has parental responsibility for him;

    (c)   may, with the consent (so far as it is reasonably practicable to obtain it) of every person who has parental responsibility for the child, arrange for the child's body to be buried or cremated; and

    (d)   may, if the conditions mentioned in sub-paragraph (2) are satisfied, make payments to any person who has parental responsibility for the child, or any relative, friend or other person connected with the child, in respect of travelling, subsistence or other expenses incurred by that person in attending the child's funeral.

(2) The conditions are that –

    (a)   it appears to the authority that the person concerned could not otherwise attend the child's funeral without undue financial hardship; and

    (b)   that the circumstances warrant the making of the payments.

(3) Sub-paragraph (1) does not authorise cremation where it does not accord with the practice of the child's religious persuasion.

(4) Where a local authority have exercised their power under sub-paragraph (1)(c) with respect to a child who was under sixteen when he died, they may recover from any parent of the child any expenses incurred by them.

(5) Any sums so recoverable shall, without prejudice to any other method of recovery, be recoverable summarily as a civil debt.

(6) Nothing in this paragraph affects any enactment regulating or authorising the burial, cremation or anatomical examination of the body of a deceased person.

NOTES

Amendments.[1] Sub-paragraph added: Courts and Legal Services Act 1990, s 116, Sch 16, para 27.[2] Paragraphs inserted: Children (Leaving Care) Act 2000, s 1.[3] Words inserted: Health and Social Care (Community Health and Standards) Act 2003, s 147, Sch 9, para 10(1), (4).[4] Words inserted: Adoption and Children Act 2002, s 139(1), Sch 3, paras 54, 72(a).[5] Words substituted: Adoption and Children Act 2002, s 139(1), Sch 3, paras 54, 72(b).[6] Subparagraph inserted: Adoption and Children Act 2002, s 139(1), Sch 3, paras 54, 72(c).[7] Words substituted: Education and Inspections Act 2006, s 157, Sch 14, paras 9, 17.[8] Words substituted: Children and Young Persons Act 2008, s 39, Sch 3, paras 1, 27(1), (2).[9] Paras 12A–12G substituted for paras 12–14 as originally enacted: Children and Young Persons Act 2008, s 8(2), Sch 1, para 4. [10] Paragraph repealed in relation to England: Children and Young Persons Act 2008, ss 16(2), 42, Sch 8.

Definitions. 'Child': s 105(1); 'child who is looked after by a local authority': s 22(1); 'functions': s 105(1); 'local authority': s 105(1); 'local authority foster parent': s 23(3); 'parental responsibility':

s 3; 'person qualifying for advice and assistance': s 24(2); 'prescribed': s 105(1); 'relative': s 105(1); 'receiving authority': Sch 2, para 15(3); 'the appeal period': Sch 2, para 19(8); 'the court': s 92(7); 'the transferring authority': Sch 2, para 15(3).

PART III
CONTRIBUTIONS TOWARDS MAINTENANCE OF CHILDREN

Liability to contribute

21. (1) Where a local authority are looking after a child (other than in the cases mentioned in sub-paragraph (7)) they shall consider whether they should recover contributions towards the child's maintenance from any person liable to contribute ('a contributor').

(2) An authority may only recover contributions from a contributor if they consider it reasonable to do so.

(3) The persons liable to contribute are –

    (a)   where the child is under sixteen, each of his parents;

    (b)   where he has reached the age of sixteen, the child himself.

(4) A parent is not liable to contribute during any period when he is in receipt of income support [under]² [Part VII of the Social Security Contributions and Benefits Act 1992]¹[, of any element of child tax credit other than the family element, of working tax credit]²[, of an income-based jobseeker's allowance or of an income-related employment and support allowance]⁴.

(5) A person is not liable to contribute towards the maintenance of a child in the care of a local authority in respect of any period during which the child is *allowed by the authority (under section 23(5)) to live with* [living with, under arrangements made by the authority in accordance with section 22C,]⁵ a parent of his.

(6) A contributor is not obliged to make any contribution towards a child's maintenance except as agreed or determined in accordance with this Part of this Schedule.

(7) The cases are where the child is looked after by a local authority under –

    (a)   section 21;

    (b)   an interim care order;

    (c)   [section 92 of the Powers of Criminal Courts (Sentencing) Act 2000]³.

Agreed contributions

22. (1) Contributions towards a child's maintenance may only be recovered if the local authority have served a notice ('a contribution notice') on the contributor specifying –

    (a)   the weekly sum which they consider that he should contribute; and

    (b)   arrangements for payment.

(2) The contribution notice must be in writing and dated.

(3) Arrangements for payment shall, in particular, include –

(a)   the date on which liability to contribute begins (which must not be earlier than the date of the notice);

(b)   the date on which liability under the notice will end (if the child has not before that date ceased to be looked after by the authority); and

(c)   the date on which the first payment is to be made.

(4) The authority may specify in a contribution notice a weekly sum which is a standard contribution determined by them for all children looked after by them.

(5) The authority may not specify in a contribution notice a weekly sum greater than that which they consider –

(a)   they would normally be prepared to pay if they had placed a similar child with local authority foster parents; and

(b)   it is reasonably practicable for the contributor to pay (having regard to his means).

(6) An authority may at any time withdraw a contribution notice (without prejudice to their power to serve another).

(7) Where the authority and the contributor agree –

(a)   the sum which the contributor is to contribute; and

(b)   arrangements for payment,

(whether as specified in the contribution notice or otherwise) and the contributor notifies the authority in writing that he so agrees, the authority may recover summarily as a civil debt any contribution which is overdue and unpaid.

(8) A contributor may, by serving a notice in writing on the authority, withdraw his agreement in relation to any period of liability falling after the date of service of the notice.

(9) Sub-paragraph (7) is without prejudice to any other method of recovery.

Contribution orders

23. (1) Where a contributor has been served with a contribution notice and has –

(a)   failed to reach any agreement with the local authority as mentioned in paragraph 22(7) within the period of one month beginning with the day on which the contribution notice was served; or

(b)   served a notice under paragraph 22(8) withdrawing his agreement,

the authority may apply to the court for an order under this paragraph.

(2) On such an application the court may make an order ('a contribution order') requiring the contributor to contribute a weekly sum towards the child's maintenance in accordance with arrangements for payment specified by the court.

(3) A contribution order –

(a)   shall not specify a weekly sum greater than that specified in the contribution notice; and

(b)   shall be made with due regard to the contributor's means.

(4) A contribution order shall not –

(a)   take effect before the date specified in the contribution notice; or

(b)   have effect while the contributor is not liable to contribute (by virtue of paragraph 21); or

(c)   remain in force after the child has ceased to be looked after by the authority who obtained the order.

(5) An authority may not apply to the court under sub-paragraph (1) in relation to a contribution notice which they have withdrawn.

(6) Where –

(a)   a contribution order is in force;

(b)   the authority serve another contribution notice; and

(c)   the contributor and the authority reach an agreement under paragraph 22(7) in respect of that other contribution notice,

the effect of the agreement shall be to discharge the order from the date on which it is agreed that the agreement shall take effect.

(7) Where an agreement is reached under sub-paragraph (6) the authority shall notify the court –

(a)   of the agreement; and

(b)   of the date on which it took effect.

(8) A contribution order may be varied or revoked on the application of the contributor or the authority.

(9) In proceedings for the variation of a contribution order, the authority shall specify –

(a)   the weekly sum which, having regard to paragraph 22, they propose that the contributor should contribute under the order as varied; and

(b)   the proposed arrangements for payment.

(10) Where a contribution order is varied, the order –

(a)   shall not specify a weekly sum greater than that specified by the authority in the proceedings for variation; and

(b)   shall be made with due regard to the contributor's means.

(11) An appeal shall lie in accordance with rules of court from any order made under this paragraph.

Enforcement of contribution orders etc

24. (1) A contribution order made by a magistrates' court shall be enforceable as a magistrates' court maintenance order (within the meaning of section 150(1) of the Magistrates' Courts Act 1980).

(2) Where a contributor has agreed, or has been ordered, to make contributions to a local authority, any other local authority within whose area the contributor is for the time being living may –

(a)   at the request of the local authority who served the contribution notice; and

(b)   subject to agreement as to any sum to be deducted in respect of services rendered,

collect from the contributor any contributions due on behalf of the authority who served the notice.

(3) In sub-paragraph (2) the reference to any other local authority includes a reference to –

(a)   a local authority within the meaning of section 1(2) of the Social Work (Scotland) Act 1968; and

(b)   a Health and Social Services Board established under Article 16 of the Health and Personal Social Services (Northern Ireland) Order 1972.

(4) The power to collect sums under sub-paragraph (2) includes the power to –

(a)   receive and give a discharge for any contributions due; and

(b)   (if necessary) enforce payment of any contributions,

even though those contributions may have fallen due at a time when the contributor was living elsewhere.

(5) Any contributions collected under sub-paragraph (2) shall be paid (subject to any agreed deduction) to the local authority who served the contribution notice.

(6) In any proceedings under this paragraph, a document which purports to be –

(a)   a copy of an order made by a court under or by virtue of paragraph 23; and

(b)   certified as a true copy by the [designated officer for][6] the court,

shall be evidence of the order.

(7) In any proceedings under this paragraph, a certificate which –

(a)   purports to be signed by the clerk or some other duly authorised officer of the local authority who obtained the contribution order; and

(b)   states that any sum due to the authority under the order is overdue and unpaid,

shall be evidence that the sum is overdue and unpaid.

Regulations

25. The [appropriate national authority][7] may make regulations –

(a)   as to the considerations which a local authority must take into account in deciding –

(i)   whether it is reasonable to recover contributions; and

(ii)   what the arrangements for payment should be;

(b)   as to the procedures [a local authority][7] must follow in reaching agreements with –

(i)   contributors (under paragraph 22 and 23); and

(ii)   any other local authority (under paragraph 23).

NOTES

Amendments. [1] Words substituted: Social Security (Consequential Provisions) Act 1992, s 4, Sch 2, para 108.[2] Words substituted or inserted: Tax Credits Act 2002, s 47, Sch 3, paras 15, 20.[3] Words substituted: Powers of Criminal Courts (Sentencing) Act 2000, s 165(1), Sch 9, para 131.[4] Words substituted: Welfare Reform Act 2007, s 28(1), Sch 3, para 6(1), (6). [5] Words in italics substituted by words in square brackets in relation to England: Children and Young Persons Act 2008, s 8(2), Sch 1, para 5.[6] Words substituted: Courts Act 2003, s 109(1), Sch 8, para 340.[7] Words substituted: Children and Young Persons Act 2008, s 39, Sch 3, paras 1, 27(1), (5).

Definitions. 'Child': s 105(1); 'child who is looked after by a local authority': s 22(1); 'contribution notice': Sch 2, para 22(1); 'contribution order': Sch 2, para 23(2); 'contributor': Sch 2, para 21(1); 'local authority': s 105(1); 'local authority foster parent': s 23(3); 'signed': s 105(1); 'the court': s 92(7).

SCHEDULE 3
SUPERVISION ORDERS

Sections 35 and 36

PART I
GENERAL

Meaning of 'responsible person'

1. In this Schedule, 'the responsible person', in relation to a supervised child, means –

(a)   any person who has parental responsibility for the child; and

(b)   any other person with whom the child is living.

Power of supervisor to give directions to supervised child

2. (1) A supervision order may require the supervised child to comply with any directions given from time to time by the supervisor which require him to do all or any of the following things –

(a)   to live at a place or places specified in the directions for a period or periods so specified;

(b)   to present himself to a person or persons specified in the directions at a place or places and on a day or days so specified;

(c)   to participate in activities specified in the directions on a day or days so specified.

(2) It shall be for the supervisor to decide whether, and to what extent, he exercises his power to give directions and to decide the form of any directions which he gives.

PART I – Statutes

(3) Sub-paragraph (1) does not confer on a supervisor power to give directions in respect of any medical or psychiatric examination or treatment (which are matters dealt with in paragraphs 4 and 5).

Imposition of obligations on responsible person

3. (1) With the consent of any responsible person, a supervision order may include a requirement –

(a)   that he take all reasonable steps to ensure that the supervised child complies with any direction given by the supervisor under paragraph 2;

(b)   that he take all reasonable steps to ensure that the supervised child complies with any requirement included in the order under paragraph 4 or 5;

(c)   that he comply with any directions given by the supervisor requiring him to attend at a place specified in the directions for the purpose of taking part in activities so specified.

(2) A direction given under sub-paragraph (1)(c) may specify the time at which the responsible person is to attend and whether or not the supervised child is required to attend with him.

(3) A supervision order may require any person who is a responsible person in relation to the supervised child to keep the supervisor informed of his address, if it differs from the child's.

Psychiatric and medical examinations

4. (1) A supervision order may require the supervised child –

(a)   to submit to a medical or psychiatric examination; or

(b)   to submit to any such examination from time to time as directed by the supervisor.

(2) Any such examination shall be required to be conducted –

(a)   by, or under the direction of, such registered medical practitioner as may be specified in the order;

(b)   at a place specified in the order and at which the supervised child is to attend as a non-resident patient; or

(c)   at –

(i)   a health service hospital; or

(ii)   in the case of a psychiatric examination, a hospital [, independent hospital or care home][1],

at which the supervised child is, or is to attend as, a resident patient.

(3) A requirement of a kind mentioned in sub-paragraph (2)(c) shall not be included unless the court is satisfied, on the evidence of a registered medical practitioner, that –

(a)   the child may be suffering from a physical or mental condition that requires, and may be susceptible to, treatment; and

(b) a period as a resident patient is necessary if the examination is to be carried out properly.

(4) No court shall include a requirement under this paragraph in a supervision order unless it is satisfied that –

(a) where the child has sufficient understanding to make an informed decision, he consents to its inclusion; and
(b) satisfactory arrangements have been, or can be, made for the examination.

Psychiatric and medical treatment

5. (1) Where a court which proposes to make or vary a supervision order is satisfied, on the evidence of a registered medical practitioner approved for the purposes of section 12 of the Mental Health Act 1983, that the mental condition of the supervised child –

(a) is such as requires, and may be susceptible to, treatment; but
(b) is not such as to warrant his detention in pursuance of a hospital order under Part III of that Act,

the court may include in the order a requirement that the supervised child shall, for a period specified in the order, submit to such treatment as is so specified.

(2) The treatment specified in accordance with sub-paragraph (1) must be –

(a) by, or under the direction of, such registered medical practitioner as may be specified in the order;
(b) as a non-resident patient at such a place as may be so specified; or
(c) as a resident patient in a hospital [, independent hospital or care home][1].

(3) Where a court which proposes to make or vary a supervision order is satisfied, on the evidence of a registered medical practitioner, that the physical condition of the supervised child is such as requires, and may be susceptible to, treatment, the court may include in the order a requirement that the supervised child shall, for a period specified in the order, submit to such treatment as is so specified.

(4) The treatment specified in accordance with sub-paragraph (3) must be –

(a) by, or under the direction of, such registered medical practitioner as may be specified in the order;
(b) as a non-resident patient at such place as may be so specified; or
(c) as a resident patient in a health service hospital.

(5) No court shall include a requirement under this paragraph in a supervision order unless it is satisfied –

(a) where the child has sufficient understanding to make an informed decision, that he consents to its inclusion; and
(b) that satisfactory arrangements have been, or can be, made for the treatment.

Side note: PART I – Statutes

(6) If a medical practitioner by whom or under whose direction a supervised person is being treated in pursuance of a requirement included in a supervision order by virtue of this paragraph is unwilling to continue to treat or direct the treatment of the supervised child or is of the opinion that –

(a)   the treatment should be continued beyond the period specified in the order;

(b)   the supervised child needs different treatment;

(c)   he is not susceptible to treatment; or

(d)   he does not require further treatment,

the practitioner shall make a report in writing to that effect to the supervisor.

(7) On receiving a report under this paragraph the supervisor shall refer it to the court, and on such a reference the court may make an order cancelling or varying the requirement.

NOTES

Amendments.[1] Words substituted: Care Standards Act 2000, s 116, Sch 4, para 14(24).

Definitions. 'Child': s 105(1); 'health service hospital': s 105(1); 'hospital': s 105(1); 'mental nursing home': s 105(1); 'parental responsibility': s 3; 'supervised child': s 105(1); 'supervision order': s 31(11); 'supervisor': s 105(1); 'the court': s 92(7); 'the responsible person': Sch 3, para 1.

PART II
MISCELLANEOUS

Life of supervision order

6. (1) Subject to sub-paragraph (2) and section 91, a supervision order shall cease to have effect at the end of the period of one year beginning with the date on which it was made.

(2) A supervision order shall also cease to have effect if an event mentioned in section 25(1)(a) or (b) of the Child Abduction and Custody Act 1985 (termination of existing orders) occurs with respect to the child.

(3) Where the supervisor applies to the court to extend, or further extend, a supervision order the court may extend the order for such period as it may specify.

(4) A supervision order may not be extended so as to run beyond the end of the period of three years beginning with the date on which it was made.

7. ...[1]

Information to be given to supervisor etc.

8. (1) A supervision order may require the supervised child –

(a)   to keep the supervisor informed of any change in his address; and

(b)   to allow the supervisor to visit him at the place where he is living.

(2) The responsible person in relation to any child with respect to whom a supervision order is made shall –

    (a)   if asked by the supervisor, inform him of the child's address (if it is known to him); and

    (b)   if he is living with the child, allow the supervisor reasonable contact with the child.

Selection of supervisor

9. (1) A supervision order shall not designate a local authority as the supervisor unless –

    (a)   the authority agree; or

    (b)   the supervised child lives or will live within their area.

(2)–(5) ...[2]

Effect of supervision order on earlier orders

10. The making of a supervision order with respect to any child brings to an end any earlier care or supervision order which –

    (a)   was made with respect to that child; and

    (b)   would otherwise continue in force.

Local authority functions and expenditure

11. (1) The Secretary of State may make regulations with respect to the exercise by a local authority of their functions where a child has been placed under their supervision by a supervision order.

(2) Where a supervision order requires compliance with directions given by virtue of this section, any expenditure incurred by the supervisor for the purposes of the directions shall be defrayed by the local authority designated in the order.

NOTES

Amendments.[1] Paragraph repealed: Courts and Legal Services Act 1990, ss 116, 125(7), Sch 16, para 27, Sch 20.[2] Subparagraphs omitted: Criminal Justice and Court Services Act 2000, ss 74, 75, Sch 7, paras 87, 96, Sch 8.

Definitions. 'Care order': ss 31(11), 105(1); 'child': s 105(1); 'local authority': s 105(1); 'supervised child': s 105(1); 'supervision order': s 31(11); 'supervisor': s 105(1); 'the appropriate authority': Sch 3, para 9(3); 'the responsible person': Sch 3, para 1.

PART III
EDUCATION SUPERVISION ORDERS

Effect of orders

12. (1) Where an education supervision order is in force with respect to a child, it shall be the duty of the supervisor –

    (a)   to advise, assist and befriend, and give directions to –

        (i)   the supervised child; and

        (ii)   his parents;

PART I – Statutes

in such a way as will, in the opinion of the supervisor, secure that he is properly educated;

(b)   where any such directions given to

(i)   the supervised child; or

(ii)   a parent of his,

have not been complied with, to consider what further steps to take in the exercise of the supervisor's powers under this Act.

(2) Before giving any directions under sub-paragraph (1) the supervisor shall, so far as is reasonably practicable, ascertain the wishes and feelings of –

(a)   the child; and

(b)   his parents;

including, in particular, their wishes as to the place at which the child should be educated.

(3) When settling the terms of any such directions, the supervisor shall give due consideration –

(a)   having regard to the child's age and understanding, to such wishes and feelings of his as the supervisor has been able to ascertain; and

(b)   to such wishes and feelings of the child's parents as he has been able to ascertain.

(4) Directions may be given under this paragraph at any time while the education supervision order is in force.

13. (1) Where an education supervision order is in force with respect to a child, the duties of the child's parents under [sections 7 and 444 of the Education Act 1996 (duties to secure education of children and]¹ to secure regular attendance of registered pupils) shall be superseded by their duty to comply with any directions in force under the education supervision order.

(2) Where an education supervision order is made with respect to a child –

(a)   any school attendance order –

(i)   made under [section 437 of the Education Act 1996]¹ with respect to the child; and

(ii)   in force immediately before the making of the education supervision order,

shall cease to have effect; and

(b)   while the education supervision order remains in force, the following provisions shall not apply with respect to the child –

(i)   [section 437]¹ of that Act (school attendance orders);

(ii)   [section 9 of that Act]¹ (pupils to be educated in accordance with wishes of their parents);

(iii)   [sections 411 and 423 of that Act]¹ (parental preference and appeals against admission decisions);

[(c)   a youth rehabilitation order made under Part 1 of the Criminal Justice and Immigration Act 2008 with respect to the child, while the education supervision order is in force, may not include an education requirement (within the meaning of that Part);]³

(d)   any education requirement of a kind mentioned in paragraph (c), which was in force with respect to the child immediately before the making of the education supervision order, shall cease to have effect.

Effect where child also subject to supervision order

14. (1) This paragraph applies where an education supervision order and a supervision order, or [youth rehabilitation order (within the meaning of Part 1 of the Criminal Justice and Immigration Act 2008)][3], are in force at the same time with respect to the same child.

(2) Any failure to comply with a direction given by the supervisor under the education supervision order shall be disregarded if it would not have been reasonably practicable to comply with it without failing to comply with a direction [or instruction][3] given under the other order.

Duration of orders

15. (1) An education supervision order shall have effect for a period of one year, beginning with the date on which it is made.

(2) An education supervision order shall not expire if, before it would otherwise have expired, the court has (on the application of the authority in whose favour the order was made) extended the period during which it is in force.

(3) Such an application may not be made earlier than three months before the date on which the order would otherwise expire.

(4) The period during which an education supervision order is in force may be extended under sub-paragraph (2) on more than one occasion.

(5) No one extension may be for a period of more than three years.

(6) An education supervision order shall cease to have effect on –

(a)   the child's ceasing to be of compulsory school age; or
(b)   the making of a care order with respect to the child;

and sub-paragraphs (1) to (4) are subject to this sub-paragraph.

Information to be given to supervisor etc.

16. (1) An education supervision order may require the child –

(a)   to keep the supervisor informed of any change in his address; and
(b)   to allow the supervisor to visit him at the place where he is living.

(2) A person who is the parent of a child with respect to whom an education supervision order has been made shall –

(a)   if asked by the supervisor, inform him of the child's address (if it is known to him); and
(b)   if he is living with the child, allow the supervisor reasonable contact with the child.

PART I – Statutes

Discharge of orders

17. (1) The court may discharge any education supervision order on the application of –

(a)   the child concerned;

(b)   a parent of his; or

(c)   [the local authority designated in the order][4].

(2) On discharging an education supervision order, the court may direct the local authority within whose area the child lives, or will live, to investigate the circumstances of the child.

Offences

18. (1) If a parent of a child with respect to whom an education supervision order is in force persistently fails to comply with a direction given under the order he shall be guilty of an offence.

(2) It shall be a defence for any person charged with such an offence to prove that –

(a)   he took all reasonable steps to ensure that the direction was complied with;

(b)   the direction was unreasonable; or

(c)   he had complied with –

(i)   a requirement included in a supervision order made with respect to the child; or

(ii)   directions given under such a requirement,

and that it was not reasonably practicable to comply both with the direction and with the requirement or directions mentioned in this paragraph.

(3) A person guilty of an offence under this paragraph shall be liable on summary conviction to a fine not exceeding level 3 on the standard scale.

Persistent failure of child to comply with directions

19. (1) Where a child with respect to whom an education supervision order is in force persistently fails to comply with any direction given under the order, [the local authority designated in the order shall notify the appropriate local authority, if different][4].

(2) Where a local authority have been notified under sub-paragraph (1) they shall investigate the circumstances of the child.

(3) In this paragraph 'the appropriate local authority' has the same meaning as in section 36.

Miscellaneous

20. The Secretary of State may by regulations make provision modifying, or displacing, the provisions of any enactment about education in relation to any child with respect to whom an education supervision order is in force to such extent as appears to the Secretary of State to be necessary or expedient in consequence of the provision made by this Act with respect to such orders.

Interpretation

21. In this part of this Schedule 'parent' has the same meaning as in [the Education Act 1996][1].

NOTES

Amendments. [1] Words substituted: Education Act 1996, s 582(1), Sch 37, Pt I, para 93. [2] Words substituted: Powers of Criminal Courts (Sentencing) Act 2000, s 165(1), Sch 9, para 131. [3] [3] Subparagraph and words substituted, and words inserted: Criminal Justice and Immigration Act 2008, s 6(2), Sch 4, Pt 1, paras 33, 37(1)–(3). [4] Words substituted: SI 2010/1158.

Definitions. 'Care order': ss 31(11), 105(1); 'child': s 105(1); 'education supervision order': s 36(2); 'local education authority': s 105(1); 'parent': Sch 3, para 21; 'supervised child': s 105(1); 'supervision order': s 31(11); 'supervisor': s 105(1); 'the appropriate local authority': Sch 3, para 19(3); 'the court': s 92(7).

SCHEDULE 4
MANAGEMENT AND CONDUCT OF COMMUNITY HOMES

Section 53(6)

PART I
INSTRUMENTS OF MANAGEMENT

Instruments of management for controlled and assisted community homes

1. (1) The Secretary of State may by order make an instrument of management providing for the constitution of a body of managers for any ...[1] home which is designated as a controlled or assisted community home.

(2) Sub-paragraph (3) applies where two or more ...[1] homes are designated as controlled community homes or as assisted community homes.

(3) If –

    (a)   those homes are, or are to be, provided by the same voluntary organisation; and

    (b)   the same local authority is to be represented on the body of managers for those homes,

a single instrument of management may be made by the Secretary of State under this paragraph constituting one body of managers for those homes or for any two or more of them.

(4) The number of persons who, in accordance with an instrument of management, constitute the body of managers for a ...[1] home shall be such number (which must be a multiple of three) as may be specified in the instrument.

(5) The instrument shall provide that the local authority specified in the instrument shall appoint –

(a)   in the case of a ...[1] home which is designated as a controlled community home, two-thirds of the managers; and

(b)   in the case of a ...[1] home which is designated as an assisted community home, one-third of them.

(6) An instrument of management shall provide that the foundation managers shall be appointed, in such manner and by such persons as may be specified in the instrument –

(a)   so as to represent the interests of the voluntary organisation by which the home is, or is to be, provided; and

(b)   for the purpose of securing that
  (i)   so far as is practicable, the character of the home ...[1] will be preserved; and
  (ii)   subject to paragraph 2(3), the terms of any trust deed relating to the home are observed.

(7) An instrument of management shall come into force on such date as it may specify.

(8) If an instrument of management is in force in relation to a ...[1] home the home shall be (and be known as) a controlled community home or an assisted community home, according to its designation.

(9) In this paragraph –

'foundation managers', in relation to a ...[1] home, means those of the managers of the home who are not appointed by a local authority in accordance with sub-paragraph (5); and
'designated' means designated in accordance with section 53.

2. (1) An instrument of management shall contain such provisions as the Secretary of State considers appropriate.

(2) Nothing in the instrument of management shall affect the purposes for which the premises comprising the home are held.

(3) Without prejudice to the generality of sub-paragraph (1), an instrument of management may contain provisions –

(a)   specifying the nature and purpose of the home (or each of the homes) to which it relates;

(b)   requiring a specified number or proportion of the places in that home (or those homes) to be made available to local authorities and to any other body specified in the instrument; and

(c)   relating to the management of that home (or those homes) and the charging of fees with respect to –
  (i)   children placed there; or
  (ii)   places made available to any local authority or other body.

(4) Subject to sub-paragraphs (1) and (2), in the event of any inconsistency between the provisions of any trust deed and an instrument of management, the instrument of management shall prevail over the provisions of the trust deed in so far as they relate to the home concerned.

(5) After consultation with the voluntary organisation concerned and with the local authority specified in its instrument of management, the Secretary of State may by order vary or revoke any provisions of the instrument.

NOTES

Amendments.[1] Words repealed: Courts and Legal Services Act 1990, ss 116, 125(7), Sch 16, para 28, Sch 20.

Definitions. 'Assisted community home': s 53(5); 'child': s 105(1); 'community home': s 53(1); 'controlled community home': s 53(4); 'designated': Sch 4, para 1(9); 'foundation managers': Sch 4, para 1(9); 'local authority': s 105(1); 'trust deed': s 55(6); 'voluntary home': s 60(3); 'voluntary organisation': s 105(1).

PART II
MANAGEMENT OF CONTROLLED AND ASSISTED COMMUNITY HOMES

3. (1) The management, equipment and maintenance of a controlled community home shall be the responsibility of the local authority specified in its instrument of management.

(2) The management, equipment and maintenance of an assisted community home shall be the responsibility of the voluntary organisation by which the home is provided.

(3) In this paragraph –

'home' means a controlled community home or (as the case may be) assisted community home; and
'the managers', in relation to a home, means the managers constituted by its instrument of management; and
'the responsible body', in relation to a home, means the local authority or (as the case may be) voluntary organisation responsible for its management, equipment and maintenance.

(4) The functions of a home's responsible body shall be exercised through the managers [, except in so far as, under section 53(3B), any of the accommodation is to be managed by another person][1].

(5) Anything done, liability incurred or property acquired by a home's managers shall be done, incurred or acquired by them as agents of the responsible body [; and similarly, to the extent that a contract so provides, as respects anything done, liability incurred or property acquired by a person by whom, under section 53(3B), any of the accommodation is to be managed][1].

(6) In so far as any matter is reserved for the decision of a home's responsible body by –

(a) sub-paragraph (8);
(b) the instrument of management;
(c) the service by the body on the managers, or any of them, of a notice reserving any matter,

that matter shall be dealt with by the body and not by the managers.

(7) In dealing with any matter so reserved, the responsible body shall have regard to any representations made to the body by the managers.

(8) The employment of persons at a home shall be a matter reserved for the decision of the responsible body.

(9) Where the instrument of management of a controlled community home so provides, the responsible body may enter into arrangements with the voluntary organisation by which that home is provided whereby, in accordance with such terms as may be agreed

between them and the voluntary organisation, persons who are not in the employment of the responsible body shall undertake duties at that home.

(10) Subject to sub-paragraph (11) –

    (a)   where the responsible body for an assisted community home proposes to engage any person to work at that home or to terminate without notice the employment of any person at that home, it shall consult the local authority specified in the instrument of management and, if that authority so direct, the responsible body shall not carry out its proposal without their consent; and

    (b)   that local authority may, after consultation with the responsible body, require that body to terminate the employment of any person at that home.

(11) Paragraphs (a) and (b) of sub-paragraph (10) shall not apply –

    (a)   in such cases or circumstances as may be specified by notice in writing given by the local authority to the responsible body; and

    (b)   in relation to the employment of any persons or class of persons specified in the home's instrument of management.

(12) The accounting year of the managers of a home shall be such as may be specified by the responsible body.

(13) Before such date in each accounting year as may be so specified, the managers of a home shall submit to the responsible body estimates, in such form as the body may require, of expenditure and receipts in respect of the next accounting year.

(14) Any expenses incurred by the managers of a home with the approval of the responsible body shall be defrayed by that body.

(15) The managers of a home shall keep –

    (a)   proper accounts with respect to the home; and

    (b)   proper records in relation to the accounts.

(16) Where an instrument of management relates to more than one home, one set of accounts and records may be kept in respect of all the homes to which it relates.

NOTES

Amendments.[1] Words inserted: Criminal Justice and Public Order Act 1994, s 22.

Definitions. 'Assisted community home': s 53(5); 'community home': s 53(1); 'controlled community home': s 53(4); 'functions': s 105(1); 'home': Sch 4, para 3(3); 'local authority': s 105(1); 'the managers': Sch 4, para 3(3); 'the responsible body': Sch 4, para 3(3).

PART III
REGULATIONS

4. (1) The Secretary of State may make regulations –

(a)   as to the placing of children in community homes;

(b)–(c) ...[1]

(2), (3) ...[1]

NOTES

Amendments.[1] Paragraphs repealed: Care Standards Act 2000, s 117, Sch 6.

SCHEDULE 5
VOLUNTARY HOMES AND VOLUNTARY ORGANISATIONS

Section 60(4)

PART I
REGISTRATION OF VOLUNTARY HOMES

1.–6. ...[1]

NOTES

Amendments.[1] Part repealed: Care Standards Act 2000, s 117, Sch 6

PART II
REGULATIONS AS TO VOLUNTARY HOMES

Regulations as to conduct of voluntary homes

7. (1) The [appropriate national authority][2] may make regulations –

(a)   as to the placing of children in voluntary homes;
(b)–(c) ...[1]

(2)–(4) ...[1]

8. ...[1]

NOTES

Amendments.[1] Paragraph and sub-paragraphs repealed: Care Standards Act 2000, s 117, Sch 6.[2] Words substituted: Children and Young Persons Act 2008, s 39, Sch 3, paras 1, 28.

SCHEDULE 6
[PRIVATE CHILDREN'S HOMES][1]

Section 63(11)

PART I – Statutes

PART I
REGISTRATION

1.–9. ...[2]

NOTES

Amendments.[1] Heading substituted: Care Standards Act 2000, s 116, Sch 4, para 14(1), (25)(a).[2] Part repealed: Care Standards Act 2000, s 117, Sch 6.

PART II
REGULATIONS

10. (1) The Secretary of State may make regulations –

(a)   as to the placing of children in [private][1] children's homes;

(b)–(c) ...[2]

(2) The regulations may in particular –

(a)–(k) ...[2]

(l)   make provision similar to that made by regulations under section 26.

(3), (4) ...[2]

NOTES

Amendments.[1] Word substituted: Care Standards Act 2000, s 116, Sch 4, para 14(25).[2] Paragraphs and sub-paragraphs repealed: Care Standards Act 2000, s 117, Sch 6.

SCHEDULE 7
FOSTER PARENTS: LIMITS ON NUMBER OF FOSTER CHILDREN

Section 63(12)

Interpretation

1. For the purposes of this Schedule, a person fosters a child if –

(a)   he is a local authority foster parent in relation to the child;
(b)   he is a foster parent with whom the child has been placed by a voluntary organisation; or
(c)   he fosters the child privately.

The usual fostering limit

2. Subject to what follows, a person may not foster more than three children ('the usual fostering limit').

Siblings

3. A person may exceed the usual fostering limit if the children concerned are all siblings with respect to each other.

Exemption by local authority

4. (1) A person may exceed the usual fostering limit if he is exempted from it by the local authority within whose area he lives.

(2) In considering whether to exempt a person, a local authority shall have regard, in particular, to –

  (a)   the number of children whom the person proposes to foster;
  (b)   the arrangements which the person proposes for the care and accommodation of the fostered children;
  (c)   the intended and likely relationship between the person and the fostered children;
  (d)   the period of time for which he proposes to foster the children; and
  (e)   whether the welfare of the fostered children (and of any other children who are or will be living in the accommodation) will be safeguarded and promoted.

(3) Where a local authority exempt a person, they shall inform him by notice in writing –

  (a)   that he is so exempted;
  (b)   of the children, described by name, whom he may foster; and
  (c)   of any condition to which the exemption is subject.

(4) A local authority may at any time by notice in writing –

  (a)   vary or cancel an exemption; or
  (b)   impose, vary or cancel a condition to which the exemption is subject,

and, in considering whether to do so, they shall have regard in particular to the considerations mentioned in sub-paragraph (2).

(5) The Secretary of State may make regulations amplifying or modifying the provisions of this paragraph in order to provide for cases where children need to be placed with foster parents as a matter of urgency.

Effect of exceeding fostering limit

5. (1) A person shall cease to be treated [, for the purposes of this Act and the Care Standards Act 2000][1] as fostering and shall be treated as carrying on a children's home if –

  (a)   he exceeds the usual fostering limit; or
  (b)   where he is exempted under paragraph 4 –
      (i)   he fosters any child not named in the exemption; and
      (ii)   in so doing, he exceeds the usual fostering limit.

(2) Sub-paragraph (1) does not apply if the children concerned are all siblings in respect of each other.

NOTES

Amendments.[1] Words inserted: Care Standards Act 2000, s 116, Sch 4, para 14(26).

PART I – Statutes

Complaints etc

6. (1) Every local authority shall establish a procedure for considering any representations (including any complaint) made to them about the discharge of their functions under paragraph 4 by a person exempted or seeking to be exempted under that paragraph.

(2) In carrying out any consideration of representations under subparagraph (1), a local authority shall comply with any regulations made by the Secretary of State for the purposes of this paragraph.

NOTES

Definitions. 'Child': s 105(1); 'children's home': s 23; 'foster': Sch 7, para 1; 'local authority': s 105(1); 'local authority foster parent': s 23(3); 'the usual fostering limit': Sch 7, para 2; 'voluntary organisation': s 105(1).

SCHEDULE 8
PRIVATELY FOSTERED CHILDREN

Section 66(5)

Exemptions

1. A child is not a privately fostered child while he is being looked after by a local authority.

2. (1) A child is not a privately fostered child while he is in the care of any person –

    (a)   in premises in which any –
        (i)   parent of his;
        (ii)   person who is not a parent of his but who has parental responsibility for him; or
        (iii)   person who is a relative of his and who has assumed responsibility for his care,
        is for the time being living;
    (b)   ...[1]
    (c)   in accommodation provided by or on behalf of any voluntary organisation;
    (d)   in any school in which he is receiving full-time education;
    (e)   in any health service hospital;
    (f)   [in any care home or independent hospital;][2]
    (g)   in any home or institution not specified in this paragraph but provided, equipped and maintained by the Secretary of State.

(2) Sub-paragraph [(1)(c)][1] to (g) does not apply where the person caring for the child is doing so in his personal capacity and not in the course of carrying out his duties in relation to the establishment mentioned in the paragraph in question.

NOTES

Amendments.[1] Sub-paragraph repealed and word substituted: Care Standards Act 2000, s 116, Sch 4, para 14(27).[2] Sub-paragraph substituted: Care Standards Act 2000, s 116, Sch 4, para 14(28).

3. A child is not a privately fostered child while he is in the care of any person in compliance with –

[(a) a youth rehabilitation order made under section 1 of the Criminal Justice and Immigration Act 2008;][2]; or

(b) a supervision requirement within the meaning of [Part II of the Children (Scotland) Act 1995][1].

NOTES

Amendments.[1] Words substituted: Children (Scotland) Act 1995, s 105(4), Sch 4, para 48(1), (5).[2] Subparagraph substituted: Criminal Justice and Immigration Act 2008, s 6(2), Sch 4, Pt 1, paras 33, 38.

4. A child is not a privately fostered child while he is liable to be detained, or subject to guardianship, under the Mental Health Act 1983.

5. A child is not a privately fostered child while [he is placed in the care of a person who proposes to adopt him under arrangements made by an adoption agency within the meaning of –

(a) section 2 of the Adoption and Children Act 2002;

(b) section 1 of the Adoption (Scotland) Act 1978; or

(c) Article 3 of the Adoption (Northern Ireland) Order 1987][1]

[or while he is a child in respect of whom a local authority have functions by virtue of regulations under section 83(6)(b) of the Adoption and Children Act 2002 (which relates to children brought into the United Kingdom for adoption), or corresponding functions by virtue of regulations under section 1 of the Adoption (Intercountry Aspects) Act 1999 (regulations to give effect to Hague Convention on Protection of Children and Co-operation in respect of Intercountry Adoption)][2]

NOTES

Amendments.[1] Words substituted: Adoption and Children Act 2002, s 139(1), Sch 3, paras 54, 73.[2] Words inserted: Children and Adoption Act 2006, s 14(3).

Power of local authority to impose requirements

6. (1) Where a person is fostering any child privately, or proposes to foster any child privately, the appropriate local authority may impose on him requirements as to –

(a) the number, age and sex of the children who may be privately fostered by him;

(b) the standard of the accommodation and equipment to be provided for them;

(c) the arrangements to be made with respect to their health and safety; and

(d) particular arrangements which must be made with respect to the provision of care for them,

PART I – Statutes

and it shall be his duty to comply with any such requirement before the end of such period as the authority may specify unless, in the case of a proposal, the proposal is not carried out.

(2) A requirement may be limited to a particular child, or class of child.

(3) A requirement (other than one imposed under sub-paragraph (1)(a)) may be limited by the authority so as to apply only when the number of children fostered by the person exceeds a specified number.

(4) A requirement shall be imposed by notice in writing addressed to the person on whom it is imposed and informing him of –

(a)   the reason for imposing the requirement;
(b)   his right under paragraph 8 to appeal against it; and
(c)   the time within which he may do so.

(5) A local authority may at any time vary any requirement, impose any additional requirement or remove any requirement.

(6) In this Schedule –

(a)   'the appropriate local authority' means –
    (i)   the local authority within whose area the child is being fostered; or
    (ii)   in the case of a proposal to foster a child, the local authority within whose area it is proposed that he will be fostered; and
(b)   'requirement', in relation to any person, means a requirement imposed on him under this paragraph.

Regulations requiring notification of fostering etc

7. (1) The Secretary of State may by regulations make provision as to –

(a)   the circumstances in which notification is required to be given in connection with children who are, have been or are proposed to be fostered privately; and
(b)   the manner and form in which such notification is to be given.

(2) The regulations may, in particular –

(a)   require any person who is, or proposes to be, involved (whether or not directly) in arranging for a child to be fostered privately to notify the appropriate authority;
(b)   require any person who is –
    (i)   a parent of a child; or
    (ii)   a person who is not a parent of his but who has parental responsibility for a child,
    and who knows that it is proposed that the child should be fostered privately, to notify the appropriate authority;
(c)   require any parent of a privately fostered child, or person who is not a parent of such a child but who has parental responsibility for him, to notify the appropriate authority of any change in his address;

(d)   require any person who proposes to foster a child privately, to notify the appropriate authority of his proposal;

(e)   require any person who is fostering a child privately, or proposes to do so, to notify the appropriate authority of –

(i)   any offence of which he has been convicted;

(ii)   any disqualification imposed on him under section 68; or

(iii) any prohibition imposed on him under section 69;

(f)   require any person who is fostering a child privately, to notify the appropriate authority of any change in his address;

(g)   require any person who is fostering a child privately to notify the appropriate authority in writing of any person who begins, or ceases, to be part of his household;

(h)   require any person who has been fostering a child privately, but has ceased to do so, to notify the appropriate authority (indicating, where the child has died, that that is the reason).

[7A. Every local authority must promote public awareness in their area of requirements as to notification for which provision is made under paragraph 7.][1]

NOTES

Amendments.[1] Paragraph inserted in relation to England: Children Act 2004, s 44(7).

Appeals

8. (1) A person aggrieved by –

(a)   a requirement imposed under paragraph 6;

(b)   a refusal of consent under section 68;

(c)   a prohibition imposed under section 69;

(d)   a refusal to cancel such a prohibition;

(e)   a refusal to make an exemption under paragraph 4 of Schedule 7;

(f)   a condition imposed in such an exemption; or

(g)   a variation or cancellation of such an exemption,

may appeal to the court.

(2) The appeal must be made within fourteen days from the date on which the person appealing is notified of the requirement, refusal, prohibition, condition, variation or cancellation.

(3) Where the appeal is against –

(a)   a requirement imposed under paragraph 6;

(b)   a condition of an exemption imposed under paragraph 4 of Schedule 7; or

(c)   a variation or cancellation of such an exemption,

the requirement, condition, variation or cancellation shall not have effect while the appeal is pending.

(4) Where it allows an appeal against a requirement or prohibition, the court may, instead of cancelling the requirement or prohibition –

(a)   vary the requirement, or allow more time for compliance with it; or

(b)   if an absolute prohibition has been imposed, substitute for it a prohibition on using the premises after such time as the court may specify unless such specified requirements as the local authority had power to impose under paragraph 6 are complied with.

(5) Any requirement or prohibition specified or substituted by a court under this paragraph shall be deemed for the purposes of Part IX (other than this paragraph) to have been imposed by the local authority under paragraph 6 or (as the case may be) section 69.

(6) Where it allows an appeal against a refusal to make an exemption, a condition imposed in such an exemption or a variation or cancellation of such an exemption, the court may –

(a)   make an exemption;

(b)   impose a condition; or

(c)   vary the exemption.

(7) Any exemption made or varied under sub-paragraph (6), or any condition imposed under that sub-paragraph, shall be deemed for the purposes of Schedule 7 (but not for the purposes of this paragraph) to have been made, varied or imposed under that Schedule.

(8) Nothing in sub-paragraph (1)(e) to (g) confers any right of appeal on –

(a)   a person who is, or would be if exempted under Schedule 7, a local authority foster parent; or

(b)   a person who is, or would be if so exempted, a person with whom a child is placed by a voluntary organisation.

Extension of Part IX to certain school children during holidays

9. (1) Where a child under sixteen who is a pupil at a school . . .[1] lives at the school during school holidays for a period of more than two weeks, Part IX shall apply in relation to the child as if –

(a)   while living at the school, he were a privately fostered child; and

(b)   paragraphs [2(1)(c) and (d)][2] and 6 were omitted.

[But this sub-paragraph does not apply to a school which is *an appropriate children's home* [a children's home in respect of which a person is registered under Part 2 of the Care Standards Act 2000][3].][2]

(2) Sub-paragraph (3) applies to any person who proposes to care for and accommodate one or more children at a school in circumstances in which some or all of them will be treated as private foster children by virtue of this paragraph.

(3) That person shall, not less than two weeks before the first of those children is treated as a private foster child by virtue of this paragraph during the holiday in question, give written notice of his proposal to the local authority within whose area the child is ordinarily resident ('the appropriate authority'), stating the estimated number of the children.

(4) A local authority may exempt any person from the duty of giving notice under sub-paragraph (3).

(5) Any such exemption may be granted for a special period or indefinitely and may be revoked at any time by notice in writing given to the person exempted.

(6) Where a child who is treated as a private foster child by virtue of this paragraph dies, the person caring for him at the school shall, not later than 48 hours after the death, give written notice of it –

   (a)   to the appropriate local authority; and

   (b)   where reasonably practicable, to each parent of the child and to every person who is not a parent of his but who has parental responsibility for him.

(7) Where a child who is treated as a foster child by virtue of this paragraph ceases for any other reason to be such a child, the person caring for him at the school shall give written notice of the fact to the appropriate local authority.

NOTES

Amendments.[1] Words repealed: Care Standards Act 2000, s 110.[2] Words inserted and substituted: Care Standards Act 2000, s 116, Sch 4, para 14(27). [3] Words in italics substituted by words in square brackets in relation to England: Children and Young Persons Act 2008, s 8(2), Sch 1, para 6.

Prohibition of advertisements relating to fostering

10. No advertisement indicating that a person will undertake, or will arrange for, a child to be privately fostered shall be published, unless it states that person's name and address.

Avoidance of insurances on lives of privately fostered children

11. A person who fosters a child privately and for reward shall be deemed for the purposes of the Life Assurance Act 1774 to have no interest in the life of the child.

NOTES

Definitions. 'Child': s 105(1); 'child who is looked after by a local authority': s 22(1); 'children's home': s 23; 'health service hospital': s 105(1); 'local authority': s 105(1); 'local authority foster parent': s 23(3); 'local education authority': s 105(1); 'mental nursing home': s 105(1); 'nursing home': s 105(1); 'parental responsibility': s 3; 'privately fostered child': s 66; 'relative': s 105(1); 'requirement': Sch 8, para 6(6); 'residential care home': s 105(1); 'school': s 105(1); 'the appropriate local authority': Sch 8, para 6(6); 'the court': s 92(7); 'to foster a child privately': s 66; 'voluntary organisation': s 105(1).

[Schedule 9 ceases to extend to England and Wales.]

[SCHEDULE 9A¹
CHILD MINDING AND DAY CARE FOR YOUNG CHILDREN [IN WALES]²

NOTES

Amendments. ¹ Schedule 9A repealed in relation to Wales: Children and Families (Wales) Measure 2010, s 73, Sch 2 (with transitional and savings provisions, SI 2010/2582, Schs 2, 3). ² Words inserted: Childcare Act 2006, s 103(1), Sch 2, para 18(1), (2).

[Exemption of certain schools

1. (1) Except in prescribed circumstances, Part XA does not apply to provision of day care within sub-paragraph (2) for any child looked after in –

    (a)   a maintained school;

    (b)   a school assisted by a [local authority]²;

    (c)   a school in respect of which payments are made by …¹ the Assembly under section 485 of the Education Act 1996;

    (d)   an independent school.

(2) The provision mentioned in sub-paragraph (1) is provision of day care made by –

    (a)   the person carrying on the establishment in question as part of the establishment's activities; or

    (b)   a person employed to work at that establishment and authorised to make that provision as part of the establishment's activities.

(3) In sub-paragraph (1) –

'assisted' has the same meaning as in the Education Act 1996;

'maintained school' has the meaning given by section 20(7) of the School Standards and Framework Act 1998.]³

NOTES

Amendments.¹ Words repealed: Childcare Act 2006, s 103, Sch 2, para 18(1), (3), Sch 3, Pt 2.² Words substituted: SI 2010/1158. ³ Schedule 9A repealed in relation to Wales: Children and Families (Wales) Measure 2010, s 73, Sch 2 (with transitional and savings provisions, SI 2010/2582, Schs 2, 3).

[Exemption for other establishments

2. (1) Part XA does not apply to provision of day care within sub-paragraph (2) for any child looked after –

    (a)   in *an appropriate children's home* [a children's home in respect of which a person is registered under Part 2 of the Care Standards Act 2000]³;

    (b)   in a care home;

    (c)   as a patient in a hospital (within the meaning of the Care Standards Act 2000);

    (d)   in a residential family centre.

(2) The provision mentioned in sub-paragraph (1) is provision of day care made by –

(a)   the department, authority or other person carrying on the establishment in question as part of the establishment's activities; or

(b)   a person employed to work at that establishment and authorised to make that provision as part of the establishment's activities.

[**2A.** (1) Part XA does not apply to provision of day care in a hotel, guest house or other similar establishment for children staying in that establishment where –

(a)   the provision takes place only between 6pm and 2 am; and

(b)   the person providing the care is doing so for no more than two different clients at the same time.

(2) For the purposes of sub-paragraph (1)(b), a 'client' is a person at whose request (or persons at whose joint request) day care is provided for a child.]¹]²

NOTES

Amendments. ¹ Paragraph inserted: Children Act 2004, s 48, Sch 4, paras 1, 7. ² Schedule 9A repealed in relation to Wales: Children and Families (Wales) Measure 2010, s 73, Sch 2 (with transitional and savings provisions, SI 2010/2582, Schs 2, 3). ³ Words in italics substituted by words in square brackets: Children and Young Persons Act 2008, s 8(2), Sch 1, para 7.

[Exemption for occasional facilities

3. (1) Where day care is provided on particular premises on less than six days in any year, that provision shall be disregarded for the purposes of Part XA if the person making it has notified [the Assembly]¹ in writing before the first occasion on which the premises concerned are so used in that year.

(2) In sub-paragraph (1) 'year' means the year beginning with the day (after the commencement of paragraph 5 of Schedule 9) on which the day care in question was or is first provided on the premises concerned and any subsequent year.]²

NOTES

Amendments.¹ Words substituted: Childcare Act 2006, s 103(1), Sch 2, para 6. ² Schedule 9A repealed in relation to Wales: Children and Families (Wales) Measure 2010, s 73, Sch 2 (with transitional and savings provisions, SI 2010/2582, Schs 2, 3).

[Disqualification for registration

4. (1) Regulations may provide for a person to be disqualified for registration for child minding or providing day care [in Wales]⁶.

(2) The regulations may, in particular, provide for a person to be disqualified where –

(a)   he is included in the list kept under section 1 of the Protection of Children Act 1999;

[(b) he is subject to a direction under section 142 of the Education Act 2002, given on the grounds that he is unsuitable to work with children [or on grounds relating to his health]⁵]²;

[(ba) he is barred from regulated activity relating to children (within the meaning of section 3(2) of the Safeguarding Vulnerable Groups Act 2006);][7]

(c) an order of a prescribed kind has been made at any time with respect to him;

(d) an order of a prescribed kind has been made at any time with respect to any child who has been in his care;

(e) a requirement of a prescribed kind has been imposed at any time with respect to such a child, under or by virtue of any enactment;

(f) he has at any time been refused registration under Part X or Part XA[, or Part 3 of the Childcare Act 2006,][6] or any prescribed enactment or had any such registration cancelled;

(g) he has been convicted of any offence of a prescribed kind, or has been ...[4] discharged absolutely or conditionally for any such offence;

[(ga) he has been given a caution in respect of any offence of a prescribed kind;][5]

(h) he has at any time been disqualified from fostering a child privately;

(j) a prohibition has been imposed on him at any time under section 69, section 10 of the Foster Children (Scotland) Act 1984 or any prescribed enactment;

(k) his rights and powers with respect to a child have at any time been vested in a prescribed authority under a prescribed enactment.

(3) Regulations may provide for a person who lives –

(a) in the same household as a person who is himself disqualified for registration for child minding or providing day care [in Wales]; or

(b) in a household at which any such person is employed,

to be disqualified for registration for child minding or providing day care [in Wales].

[(3A) Regulations under this paragraph may provide for a person not to be disqualified for registration [(and may in particular provide for a person not to be disqualified for registration for the purposes of sub-paragraphs (4) and (5))][3] by reason of any fact which would otherwise cause him to be disqualified if –

(a) he has disclosed the fact to [the Assembly][6], and

(b) [the Assembly][6] has consented in writing ...[3] and has not withdrawn that consent.][1]

(4) A person who is disqualified for registration for providing day care [in Wales][6] shall not provide day care, or be [directly][3] concerned in the management of ...[3] any provision of day care [in Wales][6].

(5) No person shall employ, in connection with the provision of day care [in Wales][6], a person who is disqualified for registration for providing day care [in Wales][6].

[(6) In this paragraph –

'caution' includes a reprimand or warning within the meaning of section 65 of the Crime and Disorder Act 1998;

'enactment' means any enactment having effect, at any time, in any part of the United Kingdom.]⁵

[(7) A conviction in respect of which a probation order was made before 1st October 1992 (which would not otherwise be treated as a conviction) is to be treated as a conviction for the purposes of this paragraph.]⁴]⁸

NOTES

Amendments.¹ Sub-paragraph inserted: Education Act 2002, s 152, Sch 13, para 6.² Subparagraph substituted: Education Act 2002, s 215(1), Sch 21, para 9.³ Words inserted or repealed in relation to England: Children Act 2004, ss 48, 64, Sch 4, paras 1, 5, 8, Sch 5, Pt 2.⁴ Words repealed and subparagraph inserted: Criminal Justice Act 2003, ss 304, 332, Sch 32, Pt 1, paras 59, 61(1)–(3), Sch 37, Pt 7.⁵ Words and subparagraph inserted, and subparagraph substituted: Childcare Act 2006, s 102(1), (2)(a).⁶ Words inserted and substituted: Childcare Act 2006, s 103(1), Sch 2, paras 6, 18(1), (4).⁷ Subparagraph inserted: Safeguarding Vulnerable Groups Act 2006, s 63(1), Sch 9, Pt 1, para 1. ⁸ Schedule 9A repealed in relation to Wales: Children and Families (Wales) Measure 2010, s 73, Sch 2 (with transitional and savings provisions, SI 2010/2582, Schs 2, 3).

[5. (1) If any person –

   (a)   acts as a child minder [in Wales]¹ at any time when he is disqualified for registration for child minding [in Wales]¹; or

   (b)   contravenes [sub-paragraph (4) or (5)]² of paragraph 4,

he shall be guilty of an offence.

[(2) A person who contravenes sub-paragraph (4) of paragraph 4 shall not be guilty of an offence under this paragraph if –

   (a)   he is disqualified for registration by virtue only of regulations made under sub-paragraph (3) of paragraph 4, and

   (b)   he proves that he did not know, and had no reasonable grounds for believing, that he was living in the same household as a person who was disqualified for registration or in a household in which such a person was employed.]²

(3) Where a person contravenes sub-paragraph (5) of paragraph 4, he shall not be guilty of an offence under this paragraph if he proves that he did not know, and had no reasonable grounds for believing, that the person whom he was employing was disqualified.

(4) A person guilty of an offence under this paragraph shall be liable on summary conviction to imprisonment for a term not exceeding six months, or to a fine not exceeding level 5 on the standard scale, or to both.]³

NOTES

Amendments.¹ Words inserted: Childcare Act 2006, s 103(1), Sch 2, para 18(1), (5).² Words and subparagraph substituted in relation to England: Childcare Act 2006, s 103(1), Sch 2, para 18(1), (5). ³ Schedule 9A repealed in relation to Wales: Children and Families (Wales) Measure 2010, s 73, Sch 2 (with transitional and savings provisions, SI 2010/2582, Schs 2, 3).

[Provision of day care: unincorporated associations

5A. (1) References in Part XA to a person, so far as relating to the provision of day care, include an unincorporated association.

(2) Proceedings for an offence under Part XA which is alleged to have been committed by an unincorporated association must be brought in the name of the association (and not in that of any of its members).

(3) For the purpose of any such proceedings, rules of court relating to the service of documents are to have effect as if the association were a body corporate.

(4) In proceedings for an offence under Part XA brought against an unincorporated association, section 33 of the Criminal Justice Act 1925 and Schedule 3 to the Magistrates' Courts Act 1980 (procedure) apply as they do in relation to a body corporate.

(5) A fine imposed on an unincorporated association on its conviction of an offence under Part XA is to be paid out of the funds of the association.

(6) If an offence under Part XA committed by an unincorporated association is shown –

(a)   to have been committed with the consent or connivance of an officer of the association or a member of its governing body, or

(b)   to be attributable to any neglect on the part of such an officer or member,

the officer or member as well as the association is guilty of the offence and liable to proceeded against and punished accordingly.][1, 2]

NOTES

Amendments.[1] Paragraph inserted: Children Act 2004, s 48, Sch 4, paras 1, 9. [2] Schedule 9A repealed in relation to Wales: Children and Families (Wales) Measure 2010, s 73, Sch 2 (with transitional and savings provisions, SI 2010/2582, Schs 2, 3).

[Certificates of registration

6. (1) If an application for registration is granted, [the Assembly][1] shall give the applicant a certificate of registration.

(2) A certificate of registration shall give prescribed information about prescribed matters.

(3) Where, due to a change of circumstances, any part of the certificate requires to be amended, [the Assembly][1] shall issue an amended certificate.

(4) Where [the Assembly][1] is satisfied that the certificate has been lost or destroyed, the authority shall issue a copy, on payment by the registered person of any prescribed fee.

(5) For the purposes of Part XA, a person is –

(a)   registered for providing child minding [in Wales][1]; or

(b)   registered for providing day care on any premises [in Wales][1],

if a certificate of registration to that effect is in force in respect of him.][2]

NOTES

Amendments.[1] Words substituted and inserted: Childcare Act 2006, s 103(1), Sch 2, paras 6, 18(1), (6). [2] Schedule 9A repealed in relation to Wales: Children and Families (Wales) Measure 2010, s 73, Sch 2 (with transitional and savings provisions, SI 2010/2582, Schs 2, 3).

[...[1] Fees

7. Regulations may require registered persons to pay to [the Assembly][2][, at or by the prescribed times, fees of the prescribed amounts in respect of the discharge by [the Assembly][2] of its functions under Part XA][1].][3]

NOTES

Amendments.[1] Word repealed and words substituted: Children Act 2004, ss 48, 64, Sch 4, paras 1, 4(2), Sch 5, Pt 2.[2] Words substituted: Childcare Act 2006, s 103(1), Sch 2, para 6. [3] Schedule 9A repealed in relation to Wales: Children and Families (Wales) Measure 2010, s 73, Sch 2 (with transitional and savings provisions, SI 2010/2582, Schs 2, 3).

[Co-operation between authorities

8. (1) ...[1]

(2) Where it appears to the Assembly that any local authority in Wales could, by taking any specified action, help in the exercise of any of its functions under Part XA, the Assembly may request the help of that authority specifying the action in question.

(3) An authority whose help is so requested shall comply with the request if it is compatible with their own statutory or other duties and obligations and does not unduly prejudice the discharge of any of their functions.][2][3]

NOTES

Amendments.[1] Subparagraph repealed: Childcare Act 2006, s 103, Sch 2, para 18(1), (7), Sch 3, Pt 2.[2] Schedule inserted: Care Standards Act 2000, s 79(2), Sch 3. [3] Schedule 9A repealed in relation to Wales: Children and Families (Wales) Measure 2010, s 73, Sch 2 (with transitional and savings provisions, SI 2010/2582, Schs 2, 3).

SCHEDULE 10
AMENDMENTS OF ADOPTION LEGISLATION

[not reproduced]

SCHEDULE 11
JURISDICTION

Section 92

PART I
GENERAL

Commencement of proceedings

1. (1) The Lord Chancellor may[, after consulting the Lord Chief Justice,][4] by order specify proceedings under this Act or [the Adoption and Children Act 2002][3] which may only be commenced in –

    (a)   a specified level of court;

    (b)   a court which falls within a specified class of court; or

    (c)   a particular court determined in accordance with, or specified in, the order.

(2) The Lord Chancellor may[, after consulting the Lord Chief Justice,][4] by order specify circumstances in which specified proceedings under this Act or [the Adoption and Children Act 2002][3] (which might otherwise be commenced elsewhere) may only be commenced in –

    (a)   a specified level of court;

    (b)   a court which falls within a specified class of court; or

    (c)   a particular court determined in accordance with, or specified in, the order.

[(2A) Sub-paragraphs (1) and (2) shall also apply in relation to proceedings –

    [(a)   under section 55A of the Family Law Act 1986 (declarations of parentage); or][2]

    (b)   which are to be dealt with in accordance with an order made under section 45 [of the Child Support Act 1991][2] (jurisdiction of courts in certain proceedings under that Act).][1]

(3) The Lord Chancellor may[, after consulting the Lord Chief Justice,][4] by order make provision by virtue of which, where specified proceedings with respect to a child under –

    (a)   this Act;

    (b)   [the Adoption and Children Act 2002][3];

    [(bb) section 20 (appeals) ...[2] of the Child Support Act 1991;][1] or

    (c)   the High Court's inherent jurisdiction with respect to children,

have been commenced in or transferred to any court (whether or not by virtue of an order under this Schedule), any other specified family proceedings which may affect, or are otherwise connected with, the child may, in specified circumstances, only be commenced in that court.

(4) A class of court specified in an order under this Schedule may be described by reference to a description of proceedings and may include different levels of court.

Transfer of proceedings

2. (1) The Lord Chancellor may[, after consulting the Lord Chief Justice,][4] by order provide that in specified circumstances the whole, or any specified part of, specified proceedings to which this paragraph applies shall be transferred to –

    (a)   a specified level of court;

    (b)   a court which falls within a specified class of court; or

    (c)   a particular court determined in accordance with, or specified in, the order.

(2) Any order under this paragraph may provide for the transfer to be made at any stage, or specified stage, of the proceedings and whether or not the proceedings, or any part of them, have already been transferred.

(3) The proceedings to which this paragraph applies are –

   (a)   any proceedings under this Act;

   (b)   any proceedings under [the Adoption and Children Act 2002][3];

   [(ba) any proceedings under section 55A of the Family Law Act 1986][2]

   [(bb) [any proceedings under][2] section 20 (appeals) ...[2] of the Child Support Act 1991;][1]

   (c)   any other proceedings which –

      (i)   are family proceedings for the purposes of this Act, other than proceedings under the inherent jurisdiction of the High Court; and

      (ii) may affect, or are otherwise connected with, the child concerned.

(4) Proceedings to which this paragraph applies by virtue of sub-paragraph (3)(c) may only be transferred in accordance with the provisions of an order made under this paragraph for the purpose of consolidating them with proceedings under –

   (a)   this Act;

   (b)   [the Adoption and Children Act 2002][3]; or

   (c)   the High Court's inherent jurisdiction with respect to children.

(5) An order under this paragraph may make such provision as the Lord Chancellor thinks appropriate[, after consulting the Lord Chief Justice,][4] for excluding proceedings to which this paragraph applies from the operation of any enactment which would otherwise govern the transfer of those proceedings, or any part of them.

Hearings by single justice

3. (1) In such circumstances as the Lord Chancellor may[, after consulting the Lord Chief Justice,][4] by order specify –

   (a)   the jurisdiction of a magistrates' court to make an emergency protection order;

   (b)   any specified question with respect to the transfer of specified proceedings to or from a magistrates' court in accordance with the provisions of an order under paragraph 2,

may be exercised by a single justice.

(2) Any provision made under this paragraph shall be without prejudice to any other enactment or rule of law relating to the functions which may be performed by a single justice of the peace.

General

4. (1) For the purposes of this Schedule –

   (a)   the commencement of proceedings under this Act includes the making of any application under this Act in the course of proceedings (whether or not those proceedings are proceedings under this Act); and

   (b)   there are three levels of court, that is to say the High Court, any county court and any magistrates' court.

(2) In this Schedule 'specified' means specified by an order made under this Schedule.

(3) Any order under paragraph 1 may make provision as to the effect of commencing proceedings in contravention of any of the provisions of the order.

(4) An order under paragraph 2 may make provision as to the effect of a failure to comply with any of the provisions of the order.

(5) An order under this Schedule may –

   (a)   make such consequential, incidental or transitional provision as the Lord Chancellor considers expedient, [after consulting the Lord Chief Justice,][4] including provision amending any other enactment so far as it concerns the jurisdiction of any court or justice of the peace;

   (b)   make provision for treating proceedings which are –

       (i)   in part proceedings of a kind mentioned in paragraph (a) or (b) of paragraph 2(3); and

      (ii)   in part proceedings of a kind mentioned in paragraph (c) of paragraph 2(3),

      as consisting entirely of proceedings of one or other of those kinds, for the purposes of the application of any order made under paragraph 2.

[(6) The Lord Chief Justice may nominate a judicial office holder (as defined in section 109(4) of the Constitutional Reform Act 2005) to exercise his functions under this Part of this Schedule.]

NOTES

Amendments.[1] Words inserted: Child Support Act 1991, s 45(3)–(5).[2] Words inserted, substituted or repealed: Child Support, Pensions and Social Security Act 2000, ss 83, 85, Sch 8, para 10(1)–(3), Sch 9, Part IX.[3] Words substituted: Adoption and Children Act 2002, s 139(1), Sch 3, paras 54, 75.[4] Words and subparagraph inserted: Constitutional Reform Act 2005, s 15(1), Sch 4, Pt 1, paras 203, 210(1)–(2).

Definitions. 'Child': s 105(1); 'class of court': Sch 11, para 1(4); 'emergency protection order': s 44(4); 'family proceedings': s 8(3); 'functions': s 105(1); 'levels of court': Sch 11, para 4(1); 'specified': Sch 11, para 4(2); 'the commencement of proceedings under this Act': Sch 11, para 4(1).

PART II
CONSEQUENTIAL AMENDMENTS

[not reproduced]

SCHEDULE 12
MINOR AMENDMENTS

[not reproduced]

SCHEDULE 13
CONSEQUENTIAL AMENDMENTS

[not reproduced]

SCHEDULE 14
TRANSITIONALS AND SAVINGS

Section 108(6)

Pending Proceedings, etc

1. (1) [Subject to sub-paragraphs (1A) and (4)]¹, nothing in any provision of this Act (other than the repeals mentioned in sub-paragraph (2)) shall affect any proceedings which are pending immediately before the commencement of that provision.

[(1A) Proceedings pursuant to section 7(2) of the Family Law Reform Act 1969 (committal or wards of court to care of local authority) or in the exercise of the High Court's inherent jurisdiction with respect to children which are pending in relation to a child who has been placed or allowed to remain in the care of a local authority shall not be treated as pending proceedings after 13th October 1992 for the purposes of this Schedule if no final order has been made by that date pursuant to section 7(2) of the 1969 Act or in the exercise of the High Court's inherent jurisdiction in respect of the child's care.]¹

(2) The repeals are those of –

   (a)   section 42(3) of the Matrimonial Causes Act 1973 (declaration by court that party to marriage unfit to have custody of children of family); and
   (b)   section 38 of the Sexual Offences Act 1956 (power of court to divest person of authority over girl or boy in cases of incest).

(3) For the purposes of the following provisions of this Schedule, any reference to an order in force immediately before the commencement of a provision of this Act shall be construed as including a reference to an order made after that commencement in proceedings pending before that commencement.

(4) Sub-paragraph (3) is not to be read as making the order in question have effect from a date earlier than that on which it was made.

(5) An order under section 96(3) may make such provision with respect to the application of the order in relation to proceedings which are pending when the order comes into force as the Lord Chancellor considers appropriate.

2. Where, immediately before the day on which Part IV comes into force, there was in force an order under section 3(1) of the Children and Young Persons Act 1963 (order directing a local authority to bring a child or young person before a [youth court]⁶ under section 1 of the Children and Young Persons Act 1969), the order shall cease to have effect on that day.

CUSTODY ORDERS, ETC

Cessation of declarations of unfitness, etc.

3. Where, immediately before the day on which Parts I and II come into force, there was in force –

(a)   a declaration under section 42(3) of the Matrimonial Causes Act 1973 (declaration by court that party to marriage unfit to have custody of children of family); or

(b)   an order under section 38(1) of the Sexual Offences Act 1956 divesting a person of authority over a girl or boy in a case of incest;

the declaration or, as the case may be, the order shall cease to have effect on that day.

The Family Law Reform Act 1987 (c. 42)

Conversion of orders under section 4

4. Where, immediately before the day on which Parts I and II come into force, there was in force an order under section 4(1) of the Family Law Reform Act 1987 (order giving father parental rights and duties in relation to a child), then, on and after that day, the order shall be deemed to be an order under section 4 of this Act giving the father parental responsibility for the child.

Orders to which paragraphs 6 to 11 apply

5. (1) In paragraphs 6 to 11 'an existing order' means any order which –

(a)   is in force immediately before the commencement of Parts I and II;

(b)   was made under any enactment mentioned in sub-paragraph (2);

(c)   determines all or any of the following –

(i)   who is to have custody of a child;

(ii)   who is to have care and control of a child;

(iii)   who is to have access to a child;

(iv)   any matter with respect to a child's education or upbringing; and

(d)   is not an order of a kind mentioned in paragraph 15(1).

(2) The enactments are –

(a)   the Domestic Proceedings and Magistrates' Courts Act 1978;

(b)   the Children Act 1975;

(c)   the Matrimonial Causes Act 1973;

(d)   the Guardianship of Minors Acts 1971 and 1973;

(e)   the Matrimonial Causes Act 1965;

(f)   the Matrimonial Proceedings (Magistrates' Courts) Act 1960.

(3) For the purposes of this paragraph and paragraphs 6 to 11 'custody' includes legal custody and joint as well as sole custody but does not include access.

Parental responsibility of parents

6. (1) Where –

    (a)   a child's father and mother were married to each other at the time of his birth; and

    (b)   there is an existing order with respect to the child,

each parent shall have parental responsibility for the child in accordance with section 2 as modified by sub-paragraph (3).

(2) Where –

    (a)   a child's father and mother were not married to each other at the time of his birth; and

    (b)   there is an existing order with respect to the child,

section 2 shall apply as modified by sub-paragraphs (3) and (4).

(3) The modification is that for section 2(8) there shall be substituted –

    '(8) The fact that a person has parental responsibility for a child does not entitle him to act in a way which would be incompatible with any existing order or any order made under this Act with respect to the child'.

(4) The modifications are that –

    (a)   for the purposes of section 2(2), where the father has custody or care and control of the child by virtue of any existing order, the court shall be deemed to have made (at the commencement of that section) an order under section 4(1) giving him parental responsibility for the child; and

    (b)   where by virtue of paragraph (a) a court is deemed to have made an order under section 4(1) in favour of a father who has care and control of a child by virtue of an existing order, the court shall not bring the order under section 4(1) to an end at any time while he has care and control of the child by virtue of the order.

Persons who are not parents but who have custody or care and control

7. (1) Where a person who is not the parent or guardian of a child has custody or care and control of him by virtue of an existing order, that person shall have parental responsibility for him so long as he continues to have that custody or care and control by virtue of the order.

(2) Where sub-paragraph (1) applies, [Parts I and II and paragraph 15 of Schedule 1][1] shall have effect as modified by this paragraph.

(3) The modifications are that –

    (a)   for section 2(8) there shall be substituted –

    '(8) The fact that a person has parental responsibility for a child does not entitle him to act in a way which would be incompatible with any existing order or with any order made under this Act with respect to the child';

PART I – Statutes

(b)   at the end of section 9(4) there shall be inserted –

'(c)   any person who has custody or care and control of a child by virtue of any existing order'; and

(c)   at the end of section 34(1)(c) there shall be inserted –

'(cc)   where immediately before the care order was made there was an existing order by virtue of which a person had custody or care and control of the child, that person.'

[(d)   for paragraph 15 of Schedule I there shall be substituted –

'**15.** Where a child lives with a person as the result of a custodianship order within the meaning of section 33 of the Children Act 1975, a local authority may make contributions to that person towards the cost of the accommodation and maintenance of the child so long as that person continues to have legal custody of that child by virtue of the order.']¹

Persons who have care and control

8. (1) Sub-paragraphs (2) to (6) apply where a person has care and control of a child by virtue of an existing order, but they shall cease to apply when that order ceases to have effect.

(2) Section 5 shall have effect as if –

(a)   for any reference to a residence order in favour of a parent or guardian there were substituted a reference to any existing order by virtue of which the parent or guardian has care and control of the child; and

(b)   for subsection (9) there were substituted –

'(9) Subsections (1) and (7) do not apply if the existing order referred to in paragraph (b) of those subsections was one by virtue of which a surviving parent of the child also had care and control of him.'

(3) Section 10 shall have effect as if for subsection (5)(c)(i) there were substituted –

'(i)   in any case where by virtue of an existing order any person or persons has or have care and control of the child, has the consent of that person or each of those persons'.

(4) Section 20 shall have effect as if for subsection (9)(a) there were substituted 'who has care and control of the child by virtue of an existing order.'

(5) Section 23 shall have effect as if for subsection (4)(c) there were substituted –

'(c)   where the child is in care and immediately before the care order was made there was an existing order by virtue of which a person had care and control of the child, that person.'

(6) In Schedule 1, paragraphs 1(1) and 14(1) shall have effect as if for the words 'in whose favour a residence order is in force with respect to the child' there were substituted 'who has been given care and control of the child by virtue of an existing order'.

Persons who have access

9. (1) Sub-paragraphs (2) to (4) apply where a person has access by virtue of an existing order.

(2) Section 10 shall have effect as if after subsection (5) there were inserted –

'(5A) Any person who has access to a child by virtue of an existing order is entitled to apply for a contact order.'

(3) Section 16(2) shall have effect as if after paragraph (b) there were inserted

'(bb) any person who has access to the child by virtue of an existing order.'

(4) Sections 43(11), 44(13) and 46(10), shall have effect as if in each case after paragraph (d) there were inserted –

'(dd) any person who has been given access to him by virtue of an existing order.'

Enforcement of certain existing orders

10. (1) Sub-paragraph (2) applies in relation to any existing order which, but for the repeal by this Act of –

(a) section 13(1) of the Guardianship of Minors Act 1971;
(b) section 43(1) of the Children Act 1975; or
(c) section 33 of the Domestic Proceedings and Magistrates' Courts Act 1978,

(provisions concerning the enforcement of custody orders) might have been enforced as if it were an order requiring a person to give up a child to another person.

(2) Where this sub-paragraph applies, the existing order may, after the repeal of the enactments mentioned in sub-paragraph (1)(a) to (c), be enforced under section 14 as if –

(a) any reference to a residence order were a reference to the existing order; and
(b) any reference to a person in whose favour the residence order is in force were a reference to a person to whom actual custody of the child is given by an existing order which is in force.

(3) In sub-paragraph (2) 'actual custody', in relation to a child, means the actual possession of his person.

Discharge of existing orders

11. (1) The making of a residence order or a care order with respect to a child who is the subject of an existing order discharges the existing order.

(2) Where the court makes any section 8 order (other than a residence order) with respect to a child with respect to whom any existing order is in force, the existing order shall have effect subject to the section 8 order.

(3) The court may discharge an existing order which is in force with respect to a child –

(a)   in any family proceedings relating to the child or in which any question arises with respect to the child's welfare; or

(b)   on the application of –

(i)   any parent or guardian of the child;

(ii)   the child himself; or

(iii)   any person named in the order.

(4) A child may not apply for the discharge of an existing order except with the leave of the court.

(5) The power in sub-paragraph (3) to discharge an existing order includes the power to discharge any part of the order.

(6) In considering whether to discharge an order under the power conferred by sub-paragraph (3) the court shall, if the discharge of the order is opposed by any party to the proceedings, have regard in particular to the matters mentioned in section 1(3).

GUARDIANS

Existing guardians to be guardians under this Act

12. (1) Any appointment of a person as guardian of a child which –

(a)   was made –

(i)   under sections 3 to 5 of the Guardianship of Minors Act 1971;

(ii)   under section 38(3) of the Sexual Offences Act 1956; or

(iii)   under the High Court's inherent jurisdiction with respect to children; and

(b)   has taken effect before the commencement of section 5(4),

shall (subject to sub-paragraph (2)) be deemed, on and after the commencement of section 5(4), to be an appointment made and having effect under that section.

(2) Where an appointment of a person as guardian of a child has effect under section 5 by virtue of sub-paragraph (1)(a)(ii), the appointment shall not have effect for a period which is longer than any period specified in the order.

Appointment of guardian not yet in effect

13. Any appointment of a person to be a guardian of a child –

(a)   which was made as mentioned in paragraph 12(1)(a)(i); but

(b)   which, immediately before the commencement of section 5(4), had not taken effect,

shall take effect in accordance with section 5 (as modified, where it applies, by paragraph 8(2)).

Persons deemed to be appointed as guardians under existing wills

14. For the purposes of the Wills Act 1837 and of this Act any disposition by will and testament or devise of the custody and tuition of any child, made before the commencement of section 5(4) and paragraph 1 of Schedule 13, shall be deemed to be an appointment by will of a guardian of the child.

CHILDREN IN CARE

Children in compulsory care

15. (1) Sub-paragraph (2) applies where, immediately before the day on which Part IV comes into force, a person was –

(a) in care by virtue of –
   (i)   a care order under section 1 of the Children and Young Persons Act 1969;
   (ii) a care order under section 15 of that Act, on discharging a supervision order made under section 1 of that Act; or
   (iii) an order or authorisation under section 25 or 26 of that Act;
(b) ...⁵
to be the subject of a care order under the Children and Young Persons Act 1969;
(c) in care –
   (i)   under section 2 of the Child Care Act 1980; or
   (ii) by virtue of paragraph 1 of Schedule 4 to that Act (which extends the meaning of a child in care under section 2 to include children in care under section 1 of the Children Act 1948),
   and a child in respect of whom a resolution under section 3 of the Act of 1980 or section 2 of the Act of 1948 was in force;
(d) a child in respect of whom a resolution had been passed under section 65 of the Child Care Act 1980;
(e) in care by virtue of an order under –
   (i)   section 2(1)(e) of the Matrimonial Proceedings (Magistrates' Courts) Act 1960;
   (ii) section 7(2) of the Family Law Reform Act 1969;
   (iii) section 43(1) of the Matrimonial Causes Act 1973; or
   (iv) section 2(2)(b) of the Guardianship Act 1973;
   (v)   section 10 of the Domestic Proceedings and Magistrates' Courts Act 1978,
(orders having effect for certain purposes as if the child had been received into care under section 2 of the Child Care Act 1980);
(f) in care by virtue of an order made, on the revocation of a custodianship order, under section 36 of the Children Act 1975; ...²
(g) in care by virtue of an order made, on the refusal of an adoption order, under section 26 of the Adoption Act 1976 or any order having effect (by virtue of paragraph 1 of Schedule 2 to that Act) as if made under that section [; or

(h)   in care by virtue of an order of the court made in the exercise of the High Court's inherent jurisdiction with respect to children.]²

(2) Where this sub-paragraph applies, then, on and after the day on which Part IV commences –

(a)   the order or resolution in question shall be deemed to be a care order;
(b)   the authority in whose care the person was immediately before that commencement shall be deemed to be the authority designated in that deemed care order; and
(c)   any reference to a child in the care of a local authority shall include a reference to a person who is the subject of such a deemed care order,

and the provisions of this Act shall apply accordingly, subject to paragraph 16.

Modifications

16. (1) Sub-paragraph (2) only applies where a person who is the subject of a care order by virtue of paragraph 15(2) is a person falling within sub-paragraph (1)(a) ...⁵ of that paragraph.

(2) Where the person would otherwise have remained in care until reaching the age of nineteen, by virtue of –

(a)   section 20(3)(a) or 21(1) of the Children and Young Persons Act 1969;
      ...⁵
(b)   ...⁵

this Act applies as if in section 91(12) for the word 'eighteen' there were substituted 'nineteen'.

(3) ...⁵

[(3A) Where in respect of a child who has been placed or allowed to remain in the care of a local authority pursuant to section 7(2) of the Family Law Reform Act 1969 or in the exercise of the High Court's inherent jurisdiction and the child is still in the care of a local authority, proceedings have ceased by virtue of paragraph 1(1A) to be treated as pending, paragraph 15(2) shall apply on 14th October 1992 as if the child was in care pursuant to an order as specified in paragraph 15(1)(e)(ii) or (h) as the case may be.]¹

(4) [Sub-paragraphs (5) and (6) only apply]³ where a child who is the subject of a care order by virtue of paragraph 15(2) is a person falling within sub-paragraph (1)(e) to [(h)]² of that paragraph.

(5) [Subject to sub-paragraph (6),]³ where a court, on making the order, or at any time thereafter, gave directions under –

[(a)   section 4(4)(a) of the Guardianship Act 1973;
(b)   section 43(5)(a) of the Matrimonial Causes Act 1973; or
(c)   in the exercise of the High Court's inherent jurisdiction with respect to children,]²

as to the exercise by the authority of any powers, those directions shall[, subject to the provisions of section 25 of this Act and of any regulations made under that section,][3] continue to have effect (regardless of any conflicting provision in this Act [other than section 25][3]) until varied or discharged by a court under this sub-paragraph.

[(6) Where directions referred to in sub-paragraph (5) are to the effect that a child be placed in accommodation provided for the purpose of restricting liberty then the directions shall cease to have effect upon the expiry of the maximum period specified by regulations under section 25(2)(a) in relation to children of his description, calculated from 14th October 1991.][3]

Cessation of wardship where ward in care

[**16A.** (1) Where a child who is a ward of court is in care by virtue of –

(a)   an order under section 7(2) of the Family Law Reform Act 1969; or
(b)   an order made in the exercise of the High Court's inherent jurisdiction with respect to children,

he shall, on the day on which Part IV commences, cease to be a ward of court.][2]

[(2) Where immediately before the day on which Part IV commences a child was in the care of a local authority and as the result of an order –

(a)   pursuant to section 7(2) of the Family Law Reform Act 1969; or
(b)   made in the exercise of the High Court's inherent jurisdiction with respect to children,

continued to be in the care of a local authority and was made a ward of court, he shall on the day on which Part IV commences, cease to be a ward of court.

(3) Sub-paragraphs (1) and (2) do not apply in proceedings which are pending.][1]

Children placed with parent etc. while in compulsory care

17. (1) This paragraph applies where a child is deemed by paragraph 15 to be in the care of a local authority under an order or resolution which is deemed by that paragraph to be a care order.

(2) If, immediately before the day on which Part III comes into force, the child was allowed to be under the charge and control of –

(a)   a parent or guardian under section 21(2) of the Child Care Act 1980; or
(b)   a person who, before the child was in the authority's care, had care and control of the child by virtue of an order falling within paragraph 5,

on and after that day the provision made by and under section 23(5) shall apply as if the child had been placed with the person in question in accordance with that provision.

Orders for access to children in compulsory care

18. (1) This paragraph applies to any access order –

(a)   made under section 12C of the Child Care Act 1980 (access orders with respect to children in care of local authorities); and

(b)   in force immediately before the commencement of Part IV

(2) On and after the commencement of Part IV, the access order shall have effect as an order made under section 34 in favour of the person named in the order.

[18A. (1) This paragraph applies to any decision of a local authority to terminate arrangements for access or to refuse to make such arrangements –

(a)   of which notice has been given under, and in accordance with, section 12B of the Child Care Act 1980 (termination of access); and

(b)   which is in force immediately before the commencement of Part IV.

(2) On and after the commencement of Part IV, a decision to which this paragraph applies shall have effect as a court order made under section 34(4) authorising the local authority to refuse to allow contact between the child and the person to whom notice was given under section 12B of the Child Care Act 1980.][3]

19. (1) This paragraph applies where, immediately before the commencement of Part IV, an access order made under section 12C of the Act of 1980 was suspended by virtue of an order made under section 12E of that Act (suspension of access orders in emergencies).

(2) The suspending order shall continue to have effect as if this Act had not been passed.

(3) If –

(a)   before the commencement of Part IV; and

(b)   during the period for which the operation of the access order is suspended,

the local authority concerned made an application for its variation or discharge to an appropriate juvenile court, its operation shall be suspended until the date on which the application to vary or discharge it is determined or abandoned.

Children in voluntary care

20. (1) This paragraph applies where, immediately before the day on which Part III comes into force –

(a)   a child was in the care of a local authority –

(i)   under section 2(1) of the Child Care Act 1980; or

(ii)   by virtue of paragraph 1 of Schedule 4 to that Act (which extends the meaning of references to children in care under section 2 to include references to children in care under section 1 of the Children Act 1948); and

(b)   he was not a person in respect of whom a resolution under section 3 of the Act of 1980 or section 2 of the Act of 1948 was in force.

(2) Where this paragraph applies, the child shall, on and after the day mentioned in sub-paragraph (1), be treated for the purposes of this Act as a child who is provided with accommodation by the local authority under Part III, but he shall cease to be so treated once he ceases to be so accommodated in accordance with the provisions of Part III.

(3) Where –

(a) this paragraph applies; and
(b) the child, immediately before the day mentioned in sub-paragraph (1), was (by virtue of section 21(2) of the Act of 1980) under the charge and control of a person falling within paragraph 17(2)(a) or (b),

the child shall not be treated for the purposes of this Act as if he were being looked after by the authority concerned.

Boarded out children

21. (1) Where, immediately before the day on which Part III comes into force, a child in the care of a local authority –

(a) was –
    (i) boarded out with a person under section 21(1)(a) of the Child Care Act 1980; or
    (ii) placed under the charge and control of a person, under section 21(2) of that Act; and
(b) the person with whom he was boarded out, or (as the case may be) placed, was not a person falling within paragraph 17(2)(a) or (b),

on and after that day, he shall be treated (subject to sub-paragraph (2)) as having been placed with a local authority foster parent and shall cease to be so treated when he ceases to be placed with that person in accordance with the provisions of this Act.

(2) Regulations made under section 23(2)(a) shall not apply in relation to a person who is a local authority foster parent by virtue of sub-paragraph (1) before the end of the period of twelve months beginning with the day on which Part III comes into force and accordingly that person shall for that period be subject –

(a) in a case falling within sub-paragraph (1)(a)(i), to terms and regulations mentioned in section 21(1)(a) of the Act of 1980; and
(b) in a case falling within sub-paragraph (1)(a)(ii), to terms fixed under section 21(2) of that Act and regulations made under section 22A of that Act,

as if that Act had not been repealed by this Act.

Children in care to qualify for advice and assistance

22. Any reference in Part III to a person qualifying for advice and assistance shall be construed as including a reference to a person within the area of the local authority in question who is under twenty-one and who was, at any time after reaching the age of sixteen but while still a child –

- (a)   a person falling within –
  - (i)   any of paragraphs (a) to [(h)]² of paragraph 15(1); or
  - (ii)   paragraph 20(1); or
- (b)   the subject of a criminal care order (within the meaning of paragraph 34).

Emigration of children in care

23. Where –

- (a)   the Secretary of State has received a request in writing from a local authority that he give his consent under section 24 of the Child Care Act 1980 to the emigration of a child in their care; but
- (b)   immediately before the repeal of the Act of 1980 by this Act, he has not determined whether or not to give his consent,

section 24 of the Act of 1980 shall continue to apply (regardless of that repeal) until the Secretary of State has determined whether or not to give his consent to the request.

Contributions for maintenance of children in care

24. (1) Where, immediately before the day on which Part III of Schedule 2 comes into force, there was in force an order made (or having effect as if made) under any of the enactments mentioned in sub-paragraph (2), then, on and after that day –

- (a)   the order shall have effect as if made under paragraph 23(2) of Schedule 2 against a person liable to contribute; and
- (b)   Part III of Schedule 2 shall apply to the order, subject to the modifications in sub-paragraph (3).

(2) The enactments are –

- (a)   section 11(4) of the Domestic Proceedings and Magistrates' Courts Act 1978;
- (b)   section 26(2) of the Adoption Act 1976;
- (c)   section 36(5) of the Children Act 1975;
- (d)   section 2(3) of the Guardianship Act 1973;
- (e)   section 2(1)(h) of the Matrimonial Proceedings (Magistrates' Courts) Act 1960,

(provisions empowering the court to make an order requiring a person to make periodical payments to a local authority in respect of a child in care).

(3) The modifications are that, in paragraph 23 of Schedule 2 –

- (a)   in sub-paragraph (4), paragraph (a) shall be omitted;
- (b)   for sub-paragraph (6) there shall be substituted –

    '(6) Where –

(a)   a contribution order is in force;

(b)   the authority serve a contribution notice under paragraph 22; and

(c)   the contributor and the authority reach an agreement under paragraph 22(7) in respect of the contribution notice,

the effect of the agreement shall be to discharge the order from the date on which it is agreed that the agreement shall take effect'; and

(c)   at the end of sub-paragraph (10) there shall be inserted –
      'and
      (c)   where the order is against a person who is not a parent of the child, shall be made with due regard to –
            (i)   whether that person had assumed responsibility for the maintenance of the child, and, if so, the extent to which and basis on which he assumed that responsibility and the length of the period during which he met that responsibility;
            (ii)   whether he did so knowing that the child was not his child;
            (iii) the liability of any other person to maintain the child.'

SUPERVISION ORDERS

Orders under section 1(3)(b) or 21(2) of the 1969 Act

25. (1) This paragraph applies to any supervision order –

(a)   made –
      (i)   under section 1(3)(b) of the Children and Young Persons Act 1969; or
      (ii)   under section 21(2) of that Act on the discharge of a care order made under section 1(3)(c) of that Act; and

(b)   in force immediately before the commencement of Part IV.

(2) On and after the commencement of Part IV, the order shall be deemed to be a supervision order made under section 31 and –

(a)   any requirement of the order that the child reside with a named individual shall continue to have effect while the order remains in force, unless the court otherwise directs

(b)   any other requirement imposed by the court, or directions given by the supervisor, shall be deemed to have been imposed or given under the appropriate provisions of Schedule 3.

(3) Where, immediately before the commencement of Part IV, the order had been in force for a period of [six months or more][3], it shall cease to have effect at the end of the period of six months beginning with the day on which Part IV comes into force unless –

(a)   the court directs that it shall cease to have effect at the end of a different period (which shall not exceed three years);

(b)   it ceased to have effect earlier in accordance with section 91; or

(c)   it would have ceased to have had effect earlier had this Act not been passed.

(4) Where sub-paragraph (3) applies, paragraph 6 of Schedule 3 shall not apply.

(5) Where, immediately before the commencement of Part IV, the order had been in force for less than six months it shall cease to have effect in accordance with section 91 and paragraph 6 of Schedule 3 unless –

(a)   the court directs that it shall cease to have effect at the end of a different period (which shall not exceed three years); or
(b)   it would have ceased to have had effect earlier had this Act not been passed.

Other supervision orders

26. (1) This paragraph applies to any order for the supervision of a child which was in force immediately before the commencement of Part IV and was made under –

(a)   section 2(1)(f) of the Matrimonial Proceedings (Magistrates' Courts) Act 1960;
(b)   section 7(4) of the Family Law Reform Act 1969;
(c)   section 44 of the Matrimonial Causes Act 1973;
(d)   section 2(2)(a) of the Guardianship Act 1973;
(e)   section 34(5) or 36(3)(b) of the Children Act 1975;
(f)   section 26(1)(a) of the Adoption Act 1976; or
(g)   section 9 of the Domestic Proceedings and Magistrates' Courts Act 1978.

(2) The order shall not be deemed to be a supervision order made under any provision of this Act but shall nevertheless continue in force for a period of one year beginning with the day on which Part IV comes into force unless –

(a)   the court directs that it shall cease to have effect at the end of a lesser period; or
(b)   it would have ceased to have had effect earlier had this Act not been passed.

PLACE OF SAFETY ORDERS

27. (1) This paragraph applies to –

(a)   any order or warrant authorising the removal of a child to a place of safety which –
    (i)   was made, or issued, under any of the enactments mentioned in sub-paragraph (2); and
    (ii) was in force immediately before the commencement of Part IV; and

(b) any interim order made under section 23(5) of the Children and Young Persons Act 1963 or section 28(6) of the Children and Young Persons Act 1969.

(2) The enactments are –

(a) section 40 of the Children and Young Persons Act 1933 (warrant to search for or remove child);

(b) section 28(1) of the Children and Young Persons Act 1969 (detention of child in place of safety);

(c) section 34(1) of the Adoption Act 1976 (removal of protected children from unsuitable surroundings);

(d) section 12(1) of the Foster Children Act 1980 (removal of foster children kept in unsuitable surroundings).

(3) The order or warrant shall continue to have effect as if this Act had not been passed.

(4) Any enactment repealed by this Act shall continue to have effect in relation to the order or warrant so far as is necessary for the purposes of securing that the effect of the order is what it would have been had this Act not been passed.

(5) Sub-paragraph (4) does not apply to the power to make an interim order or further interim order given by section 23(5) of the Children and Young Persons Act 1963 or section 28(6) of the Children and Young Persons Act 1969.

(6) Where, immediately before section 28 of the Children and Young Persons Act 1969 is repealed by this Act, a child is being detained under the powers granted by that section, he may continue to be detained in accordance with that section but subsection (6) shall not apply.

RECOVERY OF CHILDREN

28. The repeal by this Act of subsection (1) of section 16 of the Child Care Act 1980 (arrest of child absent from compulsory care) shall not affect the operation of that section in relation to any child arrested before the coming into force of the repeal.

29. (1) This paragraph applies where –

(a) a summons has been issued under section 15 or 16 of the Child Care Act 1980 (recovery of children in voluntary or compulsory care); and

(b) the child concerned is not produced in accordance with the summons before the repeal of that section by this Act comes into force.

(2) The summons, any warrant issued in connection with it and section 15 or (as the case may be) section 16, shall continue to have effect as if this Act had not been passed.

30. The amendment by paragraph 27 of Schedule 12 of section 32 of the Children and Young Persons Act 1969 (detention of absentees) shall not affect the operation of that section in relation to –

(a)   any child arrested; or

(b)   any summons or warrant issued,

under that section before the coming into force of that paragraph.

VOLUNTARY ORGANISATIONS: PARENTAL RIGHTS RESOLUTIONS

31. (1) This paragraph applies to a resolution –

(a)   made under section 64 of the Child Care Act 1980 (transfer of parental rights and duties to voluntary organisations); and

(b)   in force immediately before the commencement of Part IV.

(2) The resolution shall continue to have effect until the end of the period of six months beginning with the day on which Part IV comes into force unless it is brought to an end earlier in accordance with the provisions of the Act of 1980 preserved by this paragraph.

(3) While the resolution remains in force, any relevant provisions of, or made under, the Act of 1980 shall continue to have effect with respect to it.

(4) Sub-paragraph (3) does not apply to –

(a)   section 62 of the Act of 1980 and any regulations made under that section (arrangements by voluntary organisations for emigration of children); or

(b)   section 65 of the Act of 1980 (duty of local authority to assume parental rights and duties).

(5) Section 5(2) of the Act of 1980 (which is applied to resolutions under Part VI of that Act by section 64(7) of that Act) shall have effect with respect to the resolution as if the reference in paragraph (c) to an appointment of a guardian under section 5 of the Guardianship of Minors Act 1971 were a reference to an appointment of a guardian under section 5 of this Act.

FOSTER CHILDREN

32. (1) This paragraph applies where –

(a)   immediately before the commencement of Part VIII, a child was a foster child within the meaning of the Foster Children Act 1980; and

(b)   the circumstances of the case are such that, had Parts VIII and IX then been in force, he would have been treated for the purposes of this Act as a child who was being provided with accommodation in a children's home and not as a child who was being privately fostered.

(2) If the child continues to be cared for and provided with accommodation as before, section 63(1) and (10) shall not apply in relation to him if –

(a)   an application for registration of the home in question is made under section 63 before the end of the period of three months beginning with the day on which Part VIII comes into force; and

(b)   the application has not been refused or, if it has been refused –
  (i)   the period for an appeal against the decision has not expired; or
  (ii)   an appeal against the refusal has been made but has not been determined or abandoned.

(3) While section 63(1) and (10) does not apply, the child shall be treated as a privately fostered child for the purposes of Part IX.

NURSERIES AND CHILD MINDING

33. (1) Sub-paragraph (2) applies where, immediately before the commencement of Part X, any premises are registered under section 1(1)(a) of the Nurseries and Child-Minders Regulation Act 1948 (registration of premises, other than premises wholly or mainly used as private dwellings, where children are received to be looked after).

(2) During the transitional period, the provisions of the Act of 1948 shall continue to have effect with respect to those premises to the exclusion of Part X.

(3) Nothing in sub-paragraph (2) shall prevent the local authority concerned from registering any person under section 71(1)(b) with respect to the premises.

(4) In this paragraph 'the transitional period' means the period ending with –

(a)   the first anniversary of the commencement of Part X; or
(b)   if earlier, the date on which the local authority concerned registers any person under section 71(1)(b) with respect to the premises.

34. (1) Sub-paragraph (2) applies where, immediately before the commencement of Part X –

(a)   a person is registered under section 1(1)(b) of the Act of 1948 (registration of persons who for reward receive into their homes children under the age of five to be looked after); and
(b)   all the children looked after by him as mentioned in section 1(1)(b) of that Act are under the age of five.

(2) During the transitional period, the provisions of the Act of 1948 shall continue to have effect with respect to that person to the exclusion of Part X.

(3) Nothing in sub-paragraph (2) shall prevent the local authority concerned from registering that person under section 71(1)(a).

(4) In this paragraph 'the transitional period' means the period ending with –

(a)   the first anniversary of the commencement of Part X; or
(b)   if earlier, the date on which the local authority concerned registers that person under section 71(1)(a).

CHILDREN ACCOMMODATED IN CERTAIN ESTABLISHMENTS

35. In calculating, for the purposes of section 85(1)(a) or 86(1)(a), the period of time for which a child has been accommodated any part of that period which fell before the day on which that section came into force shall be disregarded.

CRIMINAL CARE ORDERS

36. (1) This paragraph applies where, immediately before the commencement of section 90(2) there was in force an order ('a criminal care order') made –

    (a)   under section 7(7)(a) of the Children and Young Persons Act 1969 (alteration in treatment of young offenders etc.); or

    (b)   under section 15(1) of that Act, on discharging a supervision order made under section 7(7)(b) of that Act.

(2) The criminal care order shall continue to have effect until the end of the period of six months beginning with the day on which section 90(2) comes into force unless it is brought to an end earlier in accordance with –

    (a)   the provisions of the Act of 1969 preserved by sub-paragraph (3)(a); or

    (b)   this paragraph.

(3) While the criminal care order remains in force, any relevant provisions –

    (a)   of the Act of 1969; and

    (b)   of the Child Care Act 1980,

shall continue to have effect with respect to it.

(4) While the criminal care order remains in force, a court may, on the application of the appropriate person, make –

    (a)   a residence order;

    (b)   a care order or a supervision order under section 31;

    (c)   an education supervision order under section 36 (regardless of subsection (6) of that section); or

    (d)   an order falling within sub-paragraph (5),

and shall, on making any of those orders, discharge the criminal care order.

(5) The order mentioned in sub-paragraph (4)(d) is an order having effect as if it were a supervision order of a kind mentioned in section 12AA of the Act of 1969 (as inserted by paragraph 23 of Schedule 12), that is to say, a supervision order –

    (a)   imposing a requirement that the child shall live for a specified period in local authority accommodation; but

    (b)   in relation to which the conditions mentioned in [subsection (6)][2] of section 12AA are not required to be satisfied.

(6) The maximum period which may be specified in an order made under sub-paragraph (4)(d) is six months and such an order may stipulate that the child shall not live with a named person.

(7) Where this paragraph applies, section 5 of the Rehabilitation of Offenders Act 1974 (rehabilitation periods for particular sentences) shall have effect regardless of the repeals in it made by this Act.

(8) In sub-paragraph (4) 'appropriate person' means –

    (a)   in the case of an application for a residence order, any person (other than a local authority) who has the leave of the court;

    (b)   in the case of an application for an education supervision order, a local education authority; and

    (c)   in any other case, the local authority to whose care the child was committed by the order.

MISCELLANEOUS

Consents under the Marriage Act 1949 (c. 76)

37. (1) In the circumstances mentioned in sub-paragraph (2), section 3 of and Schedule 2 to the Marriage Act 1949 (consents to marry) shall continue to have effect regardless of the amendment of that Act by paragraph 5 of Schedule 12.

(2) The circumstances are that –

    (a)   immediately before the day on which paragraph 5 of Schedule 12 comes into force, there is in force –
        (i)   an existing order, as defined in paragraph 5(1); or
        (ii)   an order of a kind mentioned in paragraph 16(1); and

    (b)   section 3 of and Schedule 2 to the Act of 1949 would, but for this Act, have applied to the marriage of the child who is the subject of the order.

The Children Act 1975 (c. 72)

38. The amendments of other enactments made by the following provisions of the Children Act 1975 shall continue to have effect regardless of the repeal of the Act of 1975 by this Act –

    (a)   section 68(4), (5) and (7) (amendments of section 32 of the Children and Young Persons Act 1969); and

    (b)   in Schedule 3 –
        (i)   paragraph 13 (amendments of Births and Deaths Registration Act 1953);
        (ii)   paragraph 43 (amendment of Perpetuities and Accumulations Act 1964);
        (iii)   paragraphs 46 and 47 (amendments of Health Services and Public Health Act 1968); and
        (iv)   paragraph 77 (amendment of Parliamentary and Other Pensions Act 1972).

PART I – Statutes

The Child Care Act 1980 (c. 5)

39. The amendment made to section 106(2)(a) of the Children and Young Persons Act 1933) by paragraph 26 of Schedule 5 to the Child Care Act 1980 shall continue to have effect regardless of the repeal of the Act of 1980 by this Act.

Legal aid

40. ...[7]

NOTES

Amendments.[1] Words inserted or substituted: SI 1991/1990, amending SI 1991/828.[2] Words repealed, inserted or substituted: Courts and Legal Services Act 1990, ss 116, 125(7), Sch 16, para 33, Sch 20.[3] Words inserted or substituted: Children Act 1989 (Commencement and Transitional Provisions) Order 1991, SI 1991/828, art 4, Sch.[4] References in paras 12, 13 and 14 to 'the commencement of section 5' shall be construed as references to the commencement of sub-ss (1)–(10) and (13) of that section (14 Oct 1991) except in relation to the appointment of a guardian of the estate of any child in which case they shall be construed as a reference to the commencement of sub-ss (11) and (12) of that section (1 Feb 1992): SI 1991/1990, amending SI 1991/828.[5] Words repealed: Armed Forces Act 1991, s 26(2), Sch 3.[6] Words substituted: Criminal Justice Act 1991, s 100, Sch 11, para 40(2)(r).[7] Paragraph repealed: Access to Justice Act 1999, s 106, Sch 15, Pt I.

Definitions. 'A section 8 order': s 8(2); 'actual custody': Sch 14, para 10(3); 'appropriate person': Sch 14, para 36(8); 'care order': ss 31(11), 105(1); 'child': s 105(1); 'children's home': s 23; 'contact order': s 8(1); 'contribution notice': Sch 2, para 22(1); 'contribution order': Sch 2, para 23(2); 'contributor': Sch 2, para 21(1); 'criminal care order': Sch 14, para 36(1); 'custody': Sch 14, para 5(3); 'education supervision order': s 36(2); 'existing order': Sch 14, para 5(1), (2); 'family proceedings': s 8(3); 'local authority': s 105(1); 'local authority foster parent': s 23(3); 'local education authority': s 105(1); 'order in force immediately before the commencement of ... this Act': Sch 14, para (1), (3), (4); 'parental responsibility': s 3; 'privately fostered child': s 66(1); 'residence order': s 8(1); 'supervision order': s 31(11); 'supervisor': s 105(1); 'the transitional period': Sch 14, para 33(4); 'upbringing': s 105(1).

Part II

STATUTORY INSTRUMENTS

PART II – Statutory Instruments

ALLOCATION AND TRANSFER OF PROCEEDINGS ORDER 2008

SI 2008/2836

ARRANGEMENT OF ARTICLES

PART 1
PRELIMINARY

PART 2
STARTING PROCEEDINGS

Section 1
Starting Proceedings in Specified Level of Court

Section 2
Starting Proceedings in Specified Class of County Court

PART 3
TRANSFER OF PROCEEDINGS

Section 1
General

Section 2
Transfer of Proceedings to Specified Level of Court

Section 3
Transfer of Proceedings to a Specified Class of County Court

PART 1
PRELIMINARY

1 Citation, commencement, interpretation and application

(1) This Order may be cited as the Allocation and Transfer of Proceedings Order 2008 and, subject to paragraph (2), shall come into force on 25 November 2008.

(2) Articles 6(a)(i), 9(1) and 20(1), in so far as they apply to section 11J(6) or 11O(7) of, and paragraphs 4 to 7 and 9 of Schedule A1 to, the 1989 Act, shall come into force on the same day as sections 4 and 5 of the Children and Adoption Act 2006 come into force.

(3) In this Order –

'the 1989 Act' means the Children Act 1989;
'the 1996 Act' means the Family Law Act 1996;
'the 2002 Act' means the Adoption and Children Act 2002;
'Convention adoption order' means an adoption order under the 2002 Act which, by virtue of regulations under section 1 of the Adoption (Intercountry Aspects) Act 1999 (regulations giving effect to the Convention), is made as a Convention adoption order;
'proceedings' means, unless the context otherwise requires, proceedings under –

(a) section 55A of the Family Law Act 1986 (declarations of parentage);

(b) the 1989 Act;

(c) section 20 of the Child Support Act 1991 (appeals);

(d) [section 54 of the Human Fertilisation and Embryology Act 2008][1] (parental orders);

(e) Part 4 of the 1996 Act; and

(f) the 2002 Act.

(4) The provisions in this Order apply unless any enactment or rule provides otherwise.

NOTES

Amendments.[1] Words substituted: SI 2010/986.

2 Classes of county court

For the purposes of this Order there are the following classes of county court –

(a) family hearing centres, being those courts against which the word yes appears in column 2 of the table in Schedule 1;

(b) care centres, being those courts against which the word yes appears in column 3 of that table;

(c) adoption centres, being those courts against which the word yes appears in column 4 of that table;

(d) intercountry adoption centres, being those courts against which the word yes appears in column 5 of that table; and

(e) forced marriage county courts, being those courts against which the word yes appears in column 6 of that table.

3 Principal Registry of the Family Division

[(1)][1] The principal registry of the Family Division of the High Court is treated, for the purposes of this Order, as if it were –

(a) a family hearing centre;

(b) a care centre;

(c) an adoption centre;

(d) an intercountry adoption centre; and

(e) a forced marriage county court.

[(2) The principal registry of the Family Division of the High Court is treated as if it were a county court for the purposes of appeals from decisions of a magistrates' court under –

(a) section 94 of the 1989 Act; and

(b) section 61 of the 1996 Act.][1]

NOTES

Amendments.[1] Paragraph renumbered and paragraph inserted: SI 2009/871.

4 Contravention of a provision of this Order

Where proceedings are started or transferred in contravention of a provision of this Order, the contravention does not have the effect of making the proceedings invalid.

PART 2
STARTING PROCEEDINGS

Section 1
Starting Proceedings in Specified Level of Court

5 Proceedings which must be started in a magistrates' court

(1) Proceedings under the following provisions must be started in a magistrates' court –

(a)   section 79K of the 1989 Act (protection of children in an emergency);
(b)   paragraph 23 of Schedule 2 to the 1989 Act (contribution order);
(c)   paragraph 8 of Schedule 8 to the 1989 Act (certain appeals);
(d)   section 23 of the 2002 Act (varying placement order);
(e)   section 50 or 51 of the 2002 Act (adoption order), unless any local authority will be a party to the proceedings or article 6(c) or (d) applies;
(f)   section 20 of the Child Support Act 1991 (appeals) where the proceedings are to be dealt with in accordance with the Child Support Appeals (Jurisdiction of Courts) Order 2002; and
(g)   [section 54 of the Human Fertilisation and Embryology Act 2008][1] (parental orders).

(2) Subject to paragraphs (3) and (4), proceedings under the following provisions must be started in a magistrates' court –

(a)   section 4 of the 1989 Act (acquisition of parental responsibility by father);
(b)   section 4A of the 1989 Act (acquisition of parental responsibility by step-parent);
(c)   section 25 of the 1989 Act (use of accommodation for restricting liberty);
(d)   section 31 of the 1989 Act (care and supervision orders);
(e)   section 33(7) of the 1989 Act (leave to change surname of, or remove from United Kingdom, child in care);
(f)   section 34 of the 1989 Act (parental contact etc. with children in care);
(g)   section 36 of the 1989 Act (education supervision orders);
(h)   section 43 of the 1989 Act (child assessment orders);
(i)   section 44 of the 1989 Act (emergency protection orders);
(j)   section 45 of the 1989 Act (extension, variation or discharge of emergency protection order);
(k)   section 46(7) of the 1989 Act (emergency protection order by police officer);

(l) section 48 of the 1989 Act (powers to assist in discovery of children etc.);

(m) section 50 of the 1989 Act (recovery orders);

(n) section 102 of the 1989 Act (warrant authorising a constable to assist in exercise of certain powers to search for children etc.); and

(o) paragraph 19 of Schedule 2 to the 1989 Act (approval of arrangements to assist child to live abroad).

(3) Proceedings to which paragraph (2) applies which –

(a) concern a child who is the subject of proceedings which are pending in a county court or the High Court; and

(b) arise out of the same circumstances as gave rise to those proceedings

may be started in the court in which those proceedings are pending.

(4) Proceedings under section 4 or 4A of the 1989 Act which are started at the same time as proceedings in a county court or the High Court for an order under section 8 of the 1989 Act (residence, contact and other applications in relation to children) in relation to the same child must be started in the court in which proceedings under section 8 are started.

NOTES

Amendments.[1] Words substituted: SI 2010/986.

6 Proceedings which must be started in a county court

Subject to article 7, proceedings –

(a) brought by an applicant who is under the age of eighteen under –
  (i) section 10(2)(b), 11J(6) or 11O(7) of, or paragraph 9(6) of Schedule A1 to, the 1989 Act (leave of the court to make an application); or
  (ii) Part 4 of the 1996 Act;

(b) under section 43 of the 1996 Act (leave of the court for applications by children under sixteen);

(c) for a Convention adoption order; or

(d) for an adoption order under the 2002 Act where section 83 of that Act (restriction on bringing children in) applies,

must be started in a county court.

7 Proceedings which may be started in the High Court

Subject to articles 5(3) and (4) and 8, proceedings may be started in the High Court only if –

(a) the proceedings are exceptionally complex;

(b) the outcome of the proceedings is important to the public in general; or

(c) there is another substantial reason for the proceedings to be started in the High Court.

PART II – Statutory Instruments

8 Proceedings which must be started in the court where proceedings under the 2002 Act are pending

(1) Where proceedings under section 50 or 51 of the 2002 Act (adoption order) are pending, proceedings concerning the same child under –

- (a) section 29(4)(b) of the 2002 Act (leave to apply for a residence order);
- (b) section 29(5)(b) of the 2002 Act (leave to apply for a special guardianship order);
- (c) section 8 of the 1989 Act where section 28(1)(a) or 29(4)(b) of the 2002 Act applies (leave obtained to make application for a residence order);
- (d) section 14A of the 1989 Act where section 28(1)(b) or 29(5)(b) of the 2002 Act applies (leave obtained to make application for a special guardianship order);
- (e) section 37(a) of the 2002 Act (leave to remove the child); or
- (f) section 47(3) or (5) of the 2002 Act (leave to oppose the making of an adoption order),

must be started in the court in which the proceedings under section 50 or 51 are pending.

(2) Where proceedings under section 22 of the 2002 Act (placement order) are pending, proceedings under section 30(2)(b) of that Act (leave to remove a child from accommodation provided by the local authority) must be started in the court in which the proceedings under section 22 are pending.

(3) Where proceedings under section 42(6) of the 2002 Act (leave to apply for an adoption order) are pending, proceedings under section 38(3)(a) or 40(2)(a) of that Act (leave to remove a child) must be started in the court in which the proceedings under section 42(6) are pending.

Section 2
Starting Proceedings in Specified Class of County Court

9 Starting proceedings under the 1989 Act

(1) Subject to article 8(1)(c) and (d), proceedings under Part 1 or 2 of, or Schedule 1 or paragraphs 4 to 7 or 9 of Schedule A1 to, the 1989 Act which are to be started in a county court must be started in a family hearing centre.

(2) Proceedings under Part 3, 4 or 5 of the 1989 Act which are to be started in a county court must be started in a care centre.

10 Starting proceedings under Part 4A of the 1996 Act

(1) Proceedings under Part 4A of the 1996 Act which are to be started in a county court must be started in a forced marriage county court.

(2) Article 7 applies to proceedings under Part 4A of the 1996 Act as it applies to other proceedings.

11 Starting proceedings under the 2002 Act

(1) Subject to paragraph (2), proceedings under the 2002 Act which are to be started in a county court must be started in an adoption centre.

(2) Proceedings for –

(a)   a Convention adoption order; or

(b)   an adoption order under the 2002 Act where section 83 of that Act applies

which are to be started in a county court must be started in an intercountry adoption centre.

PART 3
TRANSFER OF PROCEEDINGS

Section 1
General

12 Disapplication of enactments about transfer

The proceedings to which this Order applies are excluded from the operation of sections 38 and 39 of the Matrimonial and Family Proceedings Act 1984 (transfer of family proceedings).

13 General rules about transfer of proceedings

(1) When making any decision about the transfer of proceedings under articles 14, 15, 17 and 18 the court must have regard to the need to avoid delay in the proceedings.

(2) Articles 16 and 19 do not apply if the transfer of proceedings would cause the determination of the proceedings to be delayed.

(3) The transfer of proceedings under this Part may be made at any stage of the proceedings and whether or not the proceedings have already been transferred.

Section 2
Transfer of Proceedings to Specified Level of Court

14 Transfer of proceedings from one magistrates' court to another

A magistrates' court (the 'transferring court') may transfer proceedings to another magistrates' court (the 'receiving court') only if the transferring court considers that –

(a)   the transfer will significantly accelerate the determination of the proceedings;

(b)   it is more convenient for the parties or for the child who is the subject of the proceedings for the proceedings to be dealt with by the receiving court; or

PART II – Statutory Instruments

(c)   there is another good reason for the proceedings to be transferred.

15 Transfer of proceedings from magistrates' court to county court

(1) Subject to paragraphs (2) and (3), a magistrates' court may transfer the whole or any part of proceedings to a county court only if the magistrates' court considers that –

(a)   the transfer will significantly accelerate the determination of the proceedings;

(b)   there is a real possibility of difficulty in resolving conflicts in the evidence of witnesses;

(c)   there is a real possibility of a conflict in the evidence of two or more experts;

(d)   there is a novel or difficult point of law;

(e)   there are proceedings concerning the child in another jurisdiction or there are international law issues;

(f)   there is a real possibility that enforcement proceedings may be necessary and the method of enforcement or the likely penalty is beyond the powers of a magistrates' court;

(g)   there is a real possibility that a guardian ad litem will be appointed under rule 9.5 of the Family Proceedings Rules 1991;

(h)   (revoked)[1]

(i)   there is another good reason for the proceedings to be transferred.

(2) Proceedings under any of the provisions mentioned in articles 5(1)(a) to (c) or 5(2)(i) to (l) may not be transferred from a magistrates' court.

(3) Proceedings under section 25 of the 1989 Act (use of accommodation for restricting liberty) may not be transferred from a magistrates' court which is not a family proceedings court within the meaning of section 67 of the Magistrates' Courts Act 1980.

NOTES

Amendments.[1] Paragraph revoked: SI 2011/1045.

16 Transfer of proceedings from county court to magistrates' court

(1) A county court must transfer to a magistrates' court proceedings which were transferred under article 15(1) if the county court considers that none of the criteria in article 15(1) applies.

(2) Subject to articles 5(3) and (4), 6 and 8, a county court must transfer to a magistrates' court proceedings which were started in the county court if the county court considers that none of the criteria in article 15(1)(b) to (i) applies.

17 Transfer of proceedings from one county court to another

Subject to articles 16, 20, 21 and 22 a county court (the 'transferring court') may transfer proceedings to another county court (the 'receiving court') only if the transferring court considers that –

(a)   the transfer will significantly accelerate the determination of the proceedings;

(b)   it is more convenient for the parties or for the child who is the subject of the proceedings for the proceedings to be dealt with by the receiving court;

(c)   the proceedings involve the determination of a question of a kind mentioned in section 59(1) of the 1996 Act and the property in question is situated in the district of the receiving court; or

(d)   there is another good reason for the proceedings to be transferred.

18 Transfer of proceedings from county court to High Court

A county court may transfer proceedings to the High Court only if the county court considers that –

(a)   the proceedings are exceptionally complex;

(b)   the outcome of the proceedings is important to the public in general; or

(c)   there is another substantial reason for the proceedings to be transferred.

19 Transfer of proceedings from High Court

The High Court must transfer to a county court or a magistrates' court proceedings which were started in, or transferred to, the High Court if the High Court considers that none of the criteria in article 18 applies.

Section 3
Transfer of Proceedings to a Specified Class of County Court

20 Transfer of proceedings under the 1989 Act

(1) Where proceedings under Part 1 or 2 of, or Schedule 1 or paragraphs 4 to 7 or 9 of Schedule A1 to, the 1989 Act are to be transferred to a county court, they must be transferred to a family hearing centre.

(2) Where proceedings under Part 3, 4 or 5 of the 1989 Act are to be transferred to a county court, they must be transferred to a care centre.

21 Transfer of proceedings under the 2002 Act

(1) Subject to paragraph (2), where proceedings under the 2002 Act are to be transferred to a county court, they must be transferred to an adoption centre.

(2) Where proceedings for –

(a)   a Convention Adoption Order; or

(b)   an adoption order under the 2002 Act where section 83 of that Act applies,

are to be transferred to a county court, they must be transferred to an intercountry adoption centre.

22 Transfer of proceedings under Part 4A of the 1996 Act

(1) Where proceedings under Part 4A of the 1996 Act are to be transferred to a county court, they must be transferred to a forced marriage county court.

(2) Articles 17 to 19 apply to the transfer of proceedings under Part 4A of the 1996 Act as they apply to the transfer of other proceedings but as if the modification in paragraph (3) were made.

(3) Article 19 is to be read as if 'or a magistrates' court' were omitted.

Section 4
Transfer of Proceedings to Particular Court

23 Transfer of proceedings when arrested for breach of order under Part 4 of the 1996 Act

Where a person is brought before –

(a)   the relevant judicial authority in accordance with section 47(7)(a) of the 1996 Act (arrest for breach of order); or

(b)   a court by virtue of a warrant issued under section 47(9) of the 1996 Act,

and the matter is not then disposed of immediately, the relevant judicial authority or the court may transfer the matter to the relevant judicial authority or court which attached the power of arrest under section 47(2) or (3) of the 1996 Act or which issued the warrant.

24 Transfer of proceedings when arrested for breach of order under Part 4A of the 1996 Act

Where a person is brought before –

(a)   the relevant judge in accordance with section 63I(3) of the 1996 Act (arrest for breach of order); or

(b)   a court by virtue of a warrant issued under section 63J(3) of the 1996 Act,

and the matter is not then disposed of immediately, the relevant judge or the court may transfer the matter to the relevant judge or court which attached the power of arrest under section 63H(2) or (4) of the 1996 Act or which issued the warrant.

PART 4
APPLICATION FOLLOWING REFUSAL TO TRANSFER FROM MAGISTRATES' COURT TO COUNTY COURT AND APPEAL AGAINST TRANSFER TO MAGISTRATES' COURT BY COUNTY COURT

25 Application following refusal to order transfer of proceedings from magistrates' court to county court

(1) Where a magistrates' court refuses to order the transfer of proceedings to a county court under article 15(1), an application may be made for an order transferring proceedings to a county court.

(2) An application under paragraph (1) must be made –

    (a)   in relation to proceedings under the 2002 Act, to an adoption centre;

    (b)   in relation to proceedings under Parts 3, 4 and 5, to a care centre; and

    (c)   in any other case, to a family hearing centre.

(3) In this article, 'proceedings' means the proceedings under the 1989 Act or the 2002 Act and proceedings under section 55A of the Family Law Act 1986 (declarations of parentage).

26 Appeal against transfer of proceedings to magistrates' court by county court

Where a county court orders the transfer of proceedings to a magistrates' court under article 16, an appeal may be made against that decision –

    (a)   where the decision was made by a district judge or deputy district judge of a county court, to a circuit judge; or

    (b)   where the decision was made by a district judge or deputy district judge of the principal registry of the Family Division, to a judge of the Family Division of the High Court.

PART 5
REVOCATIONS, CONSEQUENTIAL AMENDMENTS AND TRANSITIONAL PROVISIONS

27 Revocations

Subject to article 29(2) and (3), the instruments listed in column 1 of the table in Schedule 2 (which have the references listed in column 2) are revoked to the extent indicated in column 3.

28 Consequential amendments

(1) Subject to article 29(4), the Family Proceedings Rules 1991 are amended as follows –

    (a)   in rule 2.39(1) for 'where no such application as is referred to in rule 2.40(1) is pending the', substitute 'The';

    (b)   omit rule 2.40;

PART II – Statutory Instruments

(c)   in rule 3.8(2) omit 'but shall be treated, in the first instance, as an application to the High Court for leave';

(d)   for rule 4.22(2A) substitute –

'(2A) In relation to an appeal to the High Court under section 94, the documents required to be filed by paragraph (2) shall be filed in the district registry, being in the same place as a care centre within the meaning of article 2(b) of the Allocation and Transfer of Proceedings Order 2008, which is nearest to the court below.'; and

(e)   in rule 4.26 after paragraph (5) add –

'(6) Where a local authority makes an application to a magistrates' court for a care or supervision order with respect to the child in relation to whom the direction was given, the local authority must inform the court that gave the direction of the application in writing.'.

(2) Subject to article 29(4), for rule 3A(8) of the Family Proceedings Courts (Matrimonial Proceedings etc) Rules 1991 substitute –

'(8) Subject to any enactment, where an application for an occupation order or a non-molestation order is pending, the court may transfer the proceedings to another court of its own motion or on the application of either party; and any order for transfer shall be made in Form FL417.'.

29 Transitional provisions

(1) This Order applies, so far as practicable, to proceedings started before but not concluded by 25 November 2008.

(2) Where, by reason of paragraph (1), this Order does not apply to particular proceedings which have been started but not concluded before the 25 November 2008, the Children (Allocation of Proceedings) Order 1991 or the Family Law Act 1996 (Part IV) (Allocation of Proceedings) Order 1997, as the case may be, continue to apply to those proceedings.

(3) The Children (Allocation of Proceedings) (Appeals) Order 1991 continues to apply to –

(a)   an appeal started before 25 November 2008; and

(b)   an appeal in proceedings to which the Children (Allocation of Proceedings) Order 1991 still applies by virtue of paragraph (2).

(4) The amendments in article 28 do not apply in relation to proceedings to which the Children (Allocation of Proceedings) Order 1991 or the Family Law Act 1996 (Part IV) (Allocation of Proceedings) Order 1997 still apply by virtue of paragraph (2).

(5) In relation to an appeal in respect of a type of case before the commencement of section 10 of the Child Support, Pensions and Social Security Act 2000 for the purposes of that type of case, the reference to the Child Support Appeals (Jurisdiction of Courts) Order 2002 in article 5(1)(f) is to be read as a reference to the Child Support Appeals (Jurisdiction of Courts) Order 1993.

SCHEDULE 1

Article 2

CLASSES OF COUNTY COURT

Column 1	Column 2	Column 3	Column 4	Column 5	Column 6
County court	Family Hearing Centre	Care Centre	Adop-tion Centre	Inter-coun-try Adop-tion Centre	Forced Marriage county court
Aberystwyth County Court	Yes		Yes		
Accrington County Court	Yes				
Aldershot County Court	Yes				
Altrincham County Court	Yes				
Barnet County Court	Yes				
Barnsley County Court	Yes				
Barnstaple County Court	Yes				
Barrow in Furness County Court	Yes				
Basingstoke County Court	Yes				
Bath County Court	Yes				
Bedford County Court	Yes				
Birkenhead County Court	Yes				
Birmingham County Court	Yes	Yes	Yes	Yes	Yes
Bishop Auckland County Court	Yes				
Blackburn County Court	Yes	Yes	Yes		Yes
Blackpool County Court	Yes				

Column 1	Column 2	Column 3	Column 4	Column 5	Column 6
County court	Family Hearing Centre	Care Centre	Adoption Centre	Inter-country Adoption Centre	Forced Marriage county court
Blackwood County Court	Yes				
Bodmin County Court	Yes				
Bolton County Court	Yes		Yes		
Boston County Court	Yes				
Bournemouth County Court	Yes	Yes	Yes	Yes	
Bow County Court	Yes		Yes		
Bradford County Court	Yes		Yes		Yes
Brecon County Court	Yes				
Brentford County Court	Yes		Yes		
Bridgend County Court	Yes				
Brighton County Court	Yes	Yes	Yes		
Bristol County Court	Yes	Yes	Yes	Yes	Yes
Bromley County Court	Yes		Yes		
Burnley County Court	Yes				
Burton-on-Trent County Court	Yes				
Bury County Court	Yes				
Bury St. Edmunds County Court	Yes				
Caernarfon County Court	Yes	Yes			
Cambridge County Court	Yes	Yes	Yes		

Column 1	Column 2	Column 3	Column 4	Column 5	Column 6
County court	Family Hearing Centre	Care Centre	Adoption Centre	Inter-country Adoption Centre	Forced Marriage county court
Canterbury County Court	Yes	Yes	Yes		
Cardiff County Court	Yes	Yes	Yes	Yes	Yes
Carlisle County Court	Yes	Yes	Yes		
Carmarthen County Court	Yes				
Chelmsford County Court	Yes	Yes	Yes		
Chester County Court	Yes	Yes	Yes	Yes	
Chesterfield County Court	Yes				
Chichester County Court	Yes				
Chorley County Court	Yes				
Clerkenwell & Shoreditch County Court	Yes				
Colchester and Clacton County Court	Yes				
Consett County Court	Yes				
Coventry County Court	Yes	Yes	Yes		
Crewe County Court	Yes				
Croydon County Court	Yes		Yes		
Darlington County Court	Yes				
Dartford County Court	Yes				

Column 1	Column 2	Column 3	Column 4	Column 5	Column 6
County court	Family Hearing Centre	Care Centre	Adoption Centre	Inter-country Adoption Centre	Forced Marriage county court
Derby County Court	Yes	Yes	Yes		Yes
Dewsbury County Court	Yes				
Doncaster County Court	Yes				
Dudley County Court	Yes				
Durham County Court	Yes				
Eastbourne County Court	Yes				
Edmonton County Court	Yes				
Epsom County Court	Yes				
Exeter County Court	Yes	Yes	Yes	Yes	
Gateshead County Court	Yes				
Gloucester County Court	Yes				
Grimsby County Court	Yes				
Guildford County Court	Yes	Yes	Yes		
Halifax County Court	Yes				
Harlow County Court	Yes				
Harrogate County Court	Yes				
Hartlepool County Court	Yes				
Hastings County Court	Yes				

Column 1 County court	Column 2 Family Hearing Centre	Column 3 Care Centre	Column 4 Adoption Centre	Column 5 Inter-country Adoption Centre	Column 6 Forced Marriage county court
Haverfordwest County Court	Yes				
Hereford County Court	Yes				
Hertford County Court	Yes				
Hitchin County Court	Yes				
Horsham County Court	Yes				
Huddersfield County Court	Yes				
Ilford County Court	Yes				
Ipswich County Court	Yes	Yes	Yes		
Keighley County Court	Yes				
Kendal County Court	Yes				
King's Lynn County Court	Yes				
Kingston-upon-Hull County Court	Yes	Yes	Yes		
Kingston-upon-Thames County Court	Yes				
Lambeth County Court	Yes				
Lancaster County Court	Yes	Yes	Yes		
Leeds County Court	Yes	Yes	Yes	Yes	Yes
Leicester County Court	Yes	Yes	Yes		Yes
Leigh County Court	Yes				
Lincoln County Court	Yes	Yes	Yes		

Column 1 County court	Column 2 Family Hearing Centre	Column 3 Care Centre	Column 4 Adoption Centre	Column 5 Inter-country Adoption Centre	Column 6 Forced Marriage county court
Liverpool County Court	Yes	Yes	Yes	Yes	
Llanelli County Court	Yes				
Llangefni County Court	Yes		Yes		
Lowestoft County Court	Yes				
Luton County Court	Yes	Yes	Yes		Yes
Macclesfield County Court	Yes		Yes		
Maidstone County Court	Yes				
Manchester County Court	Yes	Yes	Yes	Yes	Yes
Mansfield County Court	Yes				
Medway County Court	Yes	Yes	Yes		
Merthyr Tydfil County Court	Yes				
Middlesbrough County Court at Teesside Combined Court	Yes	Yes	Yes		Yes
Milton Keynes County Court	Yes	Yes	Yes		
Morpeth County Court	Yes				
Neath County Court	Yes				
...					
Newcastle-upon-Tyne County Court	Yes	Yes	Yes	Yes	Yes

Column 1	Column 2	Column 3	Column 4	Column 5	Column 6
County court	Family Hearing Centre	Care Centre	Adop-tion Centre	Inter-coun-try Adop-tion Centre	Forced Marriage county court
Newport (Gwent) County Court	Yes	Yes	Yes		
Newport (Isle of Wight) County Court	Yes				
Northampton County Court	Yes	Yes	Yes		
North Shields County Court	Yes				
Norwich County Court	Yes	Yes	Yes		
Nottingham County Court	Yes	Yes	Yes	Yes	
Oldham County Court	Yes				
Oxford County Court	Yes	Yes	Yes		
Penrith County Court	Yes				
Penzance County Court	Yes				
Peterborough County Court	Yes	Yes	Yes		
Plymouth County Court	Yes	Yes	Yes		
Pontefract County Court	Yes				
Pontypridd County Court	Yes	Yes	Yes		
Portsmouth County Court	Yes	Yes	Yes	Yes	
Preston County Court	Yes				
Rawtenstall County Court	Yes				

PART II – Statutory Instruments

Column 1	Column 2	Column 3	Column 4	Column 5	Column 6
County court	Family Hearing Centre	Care Centre	Adoption Centre	Intercountry Adoption Centre	Forced Marriage county court
Reading County Court	Yes	Yes	Yes		
Reigate County Court	Yes				
Rhyl County Court	Yes	Yes	Yes		
Romford County Court	Yes		Yes		Yes
Rotherham County Court	Yes				
Runcorn County Court	Yes				
St. Helens County Court	Yes				
Salford County Court	Yes				
Salisbury County Court	Yes				
Scarborough County Court	Yes				
Scunthorpe County Court	Yes				
Sheffield County Court	Yes	Yes	Yes		
Shrewsbury County Court	Yes				
Skipton County Court	Yes				
Slough County Court	Yes				
Southampton County Court	Yes		Yes		
Southend County Court	Yes				
Southport County Court	Yes				

Column 1	Column 2	Column 3	Column 4	Column 5	Column 6
County court	Family Hearing Centre	Care Centre	Adop-tion Centre	Inter-coun-try Adop-tion Centre	Forced Marriage county court
South Shields County Court	Yes				
Stafford County Court	Yes				
Staines County Court	Yes				
Stockport County Court	Yes		Yes		
Stoke-on-Trent County Court	Yes	Yes	Yes		
Sunderland County Court	Yes	Yes	Yes		
Swansea County Court	Yes	Yes	Yes		
Swindon County Court	Yes	Yes	Yes		
Tameside County Court	Yes				
Taunton County Court	Yes	Yes	Yes		
Telford County Court	Yes	Yes	Yes		
Thanet County Court	Yes				
Torquay County Court	Yes				
Trowbridge County Court	Yes				
Truro County Court	Yes	Yes	Yes		
Tunbridge Wells County Court	Yes				
Uxbridge County Court	Yes				
Wakefield County Court	Yes				

PART II – Statutory Instruments

Column 1	Column 2	Column 3	Column 4	Column 5	Column 6
County court	Family Hearing Centre	Care Centre	Adoption Centre	Intercountry Adoption Centre	Forced Marriage county court
Walsall County Court	Yes				
Wandsworth County Court	Yes				
Warrington County Court	Yes	Yes	Yes		
Watford County Court	Yes	Yes	Yes		
Welshpool and Newtown County Court	Yes				
Weston Super Mare County Court	Yes				
Weymouth County Court	Yes				
Whitehaven County Court	Yes				
Wigan County Court	Yes				
Willesden County Court	Yes				Yes
Winchester County Court	Yes				
Wolverhampton County Court	Yes	Yes	Yes		
Woolwich County Court	Yes				
Worcester County Court	Yes	Yes	Yes		
Worthing County Court	Yes				
Wrexham County Court	Yes	Yes	Yes	Yes	
Yeovil County Court	Yes				
York County Court	Yes	Yes	Yes		

NOTES

Amendments.[1] Entry 'Nelson County Court' revoked: SI 2009/3319.

****

PART II – Statutory Instruments

FAMILY PROCEDURE RULES 2010

(SI 2010/2955)

ARRANGEMENT OF RULES

PART 1
OVERRIDING OBJECTIVE

PART 2
APPLICATION AND INTERPRETATION OF THE RULES

PART 3
ALTERNATIVE DISPUTE RESOLUTION: THE COURT'S POWERS

PART 4
GENERAL CASE MANAGEMENT POWERS

PART 6
SERVICE

Chapter 1
Scope of this Part and Interpretation

Chapter 3
Service of Documents other than an Application for a Matrimonial
Order or Civil Partnership Order in the United Kingdom

Chapter 4
Service Out of the Jurisdiction

PART 8
PROCEDURE FOR MISCELLANEOUS APPLICATIONS
Chapter 1
Procedure

Chapter 5
Declarations

Chapter 9
Application for Consent to Marriage of a Child or to Registration of
Civil Partnership of a Child

PART 9
APPLICATIONS FOR A FINANCIAL REMEDY
Chapter 3
Applications for Financial Remedies for Children

PART 12
PROCEEDINGS RELATING TO CHILDREN EXCEPT
PARENTAL ORDER PROCEEDINGS AND PROCEEDINGS FOR
APPLICATIONS IN ADOPTION, PLACEMENT AND RELATED
PROCEEDINGS
Chapter 1
Interpretation and Application of this Part

Chapter 2
General Rules

PART II – Statutory Instruments

Chapter 6
Proceedings under the 1980 Hague Convention, the European
Convention, the Council Regulation, and the 1996 Hague Convention

Section 1
Proceedings under the 1980 Hague Convention or the European
Convention

Section 2
Applications relating to the Council Regulation and the 1996 Hague
Convention

PART II – Statutory Instruments

PART 14
PROCEDURE FOR APPLICATIONS IN ADOPTION, PLACEMENT AND RELATED PROCEEDINGS

PART II – Statutory Instruments

PART 14

PROCEDURE FOR APPLICATIONS IN ADOPTION,
PLACEMENT AND RELATED PROCEEDINGS

PART 16
REPRESENTATION OF CHILDREN AND REPORTS IN PROCEEDINGS INVOLVING CHILDREN

PART II – Statutory Instruments

PART II – Statutory Instruments

PART 31
REGISTRATION OF ORDERS UNDER THE COUNCIL REGULATION, THE CIVIL PARTNERSHIP (JURISDICTION AND RECOGNITION OF JUDGMENTS) REGULATIONS 2005 AND UNDER THE HAGUE CONVENTION 1996

PART 32
REGISTRATION AND ENFORCEMENT OF ORDERS

Chapter 4
Registration and Enforcement of Custody Orders under the 1986 Act

PART II – Statutory Instruments

PART 1
OVERRIDING OBJECTIVE

1.1 The overriding objective

(1) These rules are a new procedural code with the overriding objective of enabling the court to deal with cases justly, having regard to any welfare issues involved.

(2) Dealing with a case justly includes, so far as is practicable –

    (a)   ensuring that it is dealt with expeditiously and fairly;

    (b)   dealing with the case in ways which are proportionate to the nature, importance and complexity of the issues;

    (c)   ensuring that the parties are on an equal footing;

(d)   saving expense; and

(e)   allotting to it an appropriate share of the court's resources, while taking into account the need to allot resources to other cases.

1.2 Application by the court of the overriding objective

The court must seek to give effect to the overriding objective when it –

(a)   exercises any power given to it by these rules; or

(b)   interprets any rule.

1.3 Duty of the parties

The parties are required to help the court to further the overriding objective.

1.4 Court's duty to manage cases

(1) The court must further the overriding objective by actively managing cases.

(2) Active case management includes –

(a)   encouraging the parties to co-operate with each other in the conduct of the proceedings;

(b)   identifying at an early stage –

   (i)   the issues; and

   (ii)   who should be a party to the proceedings;

(c)   deciding promptly –

   (i)   which issues need full investigation and hearing and which do not; and

   (ii)   the procedure to be followed in the case;

(d)   deciding the order in which issues are to be resolved;

(e)   encouraging the parties to use an alternative dispute resolution procedure if the court considers that appropriate and facilitating the use of such procedure;

(f)   helping the parties to settle the whole or part of the case;

(g)   fixing timetables or otherwise controlling the progress of the case;

(h)   considering whether the likely benefits of taking a particular step justify the cost of taking it;

(i)   dealing with as many aspects of the case as it can on the same occasion;

(j)   dealing with the case without the parties needing to attend at court;

(k)   making use of technology; and

(l)   giving directions to ensure that the case proceeds quickly and efficiently.

PART 2
APPLICATION AND INTERPRETATION OF THE RULES

2.1 Application of these Rules

(1) Unless the context otherwise requires, these Rules apply to family proceedings in –

(a)   the High Court;
(b)   a county court; and
(c)   a magistrates' court.

(2) Nothing in these rules is to be construed as –

(a)   purporting to apply to proceedings in a magistrates' court which are not family proceedings within the meaning of section 65 of the Magistrates' Courts Act 1980; or
(b)   conferring upon a magistrate a function which a magistrate is not permitted by statute to perform.

2.2 The glossary

(1) The glossary at the end of these rules is a guide to the meaning of certain legal expressions used in the rules, but is not to be taken as giving those expressions any meaning in the rules which they do not have in the law generally.

(2) Subject to paragraph (3), words in these rules which are included in the glossary are followed by 'GL'.

(3) The word 'service', which appears frequently in the rules, is included in the glossary but is not followed by 'GL'.

2.3 Interpretation

(1) In these rules –

'the 1973 Act' means the Matrimonial Causes Act 1973;
'the 1978 Act' means the Domestic Proceedings and Magistrates' Courts 1978;
'the 1980 Hague Convention' means the Convention on the Civil Aspects of International Child Abduction which was signed at The Hague on 25 October 1980;
'the 1984 Act' means the Matrimonial and Family Proceedings Act 1984;
'the 1986 Act' means the Family Law Act 1986;
'the 1989 Act' means the Children Act 1989;
'the 1990 Act' means the Human Fertilisation and Embryology Act 1990;
'the 1991 Act' means the Child Support Act 1991;
'the 1996 Act' means the Family Law Act 1996;
'the 1996 Hague Convention' means the Convention on Jurisdiction, Applicable Law, Recognition, Enforcement and Co-Operation in Respect of Parental Responsibility and Measures for the Protection of Children;
'the 2002 Act' means the Adoption and Children Act 2002;
'the 2004 Act' means the Civil Partnership Act 2004;
'the 2005 Act' means the Mental Capacity Act 2005;
'the 2008 Act' means the Human Fertilisation and Embryology Act 2008;
'adoption proceedings' means proceedings for an adoption order under the 2002 Act;
'Allocation Order' means any order made by the Lord Chancellor under Part 1 of Schedule 11 to the 1989 Act;

'alternative dispute resolution' means methods of resolving a dispute, including mediation, other than through the normal court process;

'application form' means a document in which the applicant states his intention to seek a court order other than in accordance with the Part 18 procedure;

'application notice' means a document in which the applicant states his intention to seek a court order in accordance with the Part 18 procedure;

'Assembly' means the National Assembly for Wales;

'bank holiday' means a bank holiday under the Banking and Financial Dealings Act 1971 –

    (a)   for the purpose of service of a document within the United Kingdom, in the part of the United Kingdom where service is to take place; and

    (b)   for all other purposes, in England and Wales.

'business day' means any day other than –

    (a)   a Saturday, Sunday, Christmas Day or Good Friday; or

    (b)   a bank holiday;

'care order' has the meaning assigned to it by section 31(11) of the 1989 Act;

'CCR' means the County Court Rules 1981, as they appear in Schedule 2 to the CPR;

'child' means a person under the age of 18 years who is the subject of the proceedings; except that –

    (a)   in adoption proceedings, it also includes a person who has attained the age of 18 years before the proceedings are concluded; and

    (b)   in proceedings brought under the Council Regulation, the 1980 Hague Convention or the European Convention, it means a person under the age of 16 years who is the subject of the proceedings;

'child of the family' has the meaning given to it by section 105(1) of the 1989 Act;

'children and family reporter' means an officer of the Service or a Welsh family proceedings officer who has been asked to prepare a welfare report under section 7(1)(a) of the 1989 Act or section 102(3)(b) of the 2002 Act;

'children's guardian' means –

    (a)   in relation to a child who is the subject of and a party to specified proceedings or proceedings to which Part 14 applies, the person appointed in accordance with rule 16.3(1); and

    (b)   in any other case, the person appointed in accordance with rule 16.4;

    'civil partnership order' means one of the orders mentioned in section 37 of the 2004 Act;

'civil partnership proceedings' means proceedings for a civil partnership order;

'civil partnership proceedings county court' means a county court so designated by the Lord Chancellor under section 36A of the 1984 Act;

PART II – Statutory Instruments

'civil restraint order' means an order restraining a party –

(a)   from making any further applications in current proceedings (a limited civil restraint order);

(b)   from making certain applications in specified courts (an extended civil restraint order); or

(c)   from making any application in specified courts (a general civil restraint order);

'Commission' means the Child Maintenance and Enforcement Commission;

'consent order' means an order in the terms applied for to which the respondent agrees;

'contact order' has the meaning assigned to it by section 8(1) of the 1989 Act;

'the Council Regulation' means Council Regulation (EC) No 2201/2003 of 27 November 2003 on jurisdiction and the recognition and enforcement of judgments in matrimonial matters and in matters of parental responsibility;

'court' means, subject to any rule or other enactment which provides otherwise, the High Court, a county court or a magistrates' court;

(rule 2.5 relates to the power to perform functions of the court.)

'court of trial' means –

(a)   in proceedings under the 1973 Act, a divorce county court designated by the Lord Chancellor as a court of trial pursuant to section 33(1) of the 1984 Act; or

(b)   in proceedings under the 2004 Act, a civil partnership proceedings county court designated by the Lord Chancellor as a court of trial pursuant to section 36A(1)(b) of the 1984 Act; and

(c)   in proceedings under the 1973 Act pending in a divorce county court or proceedings under the 2004 Act pending in a civil partnership proceedings county court, the principal registry is treated as a court of trial having its place of sitting at the Royal Courts of Justice;

'court officer' means –

(a)   in the High Court or in a county court, a member of court staff; and

(b)   in a magistrates' court, the designated officer;

('designated officer' is defined in section 37(1) of the Courts Act 2003.)

'CPR' means the Civil Procedure Rules 1998;

'deputy' has the meaning given in section 16(2)(b) of the 2005 Act;

'designated county court' means a court designated as –

(a)   a divorce county court;

(b)   a civil partnership proceedings county court; or

(c)   both a divorce county court and a civil partnership proceedings county court;

'detailed assessment proceedings' means the procedure by which the amount of costs is decided in accordance with Part 47 of the CPR;

'directions appointment' means a hearing for directions;

'district judge' –

    (a)   in relation to proceedings in the High Court, includes a district judge of the principal registry and in relation to proceedings in a county court, includes a district judge of the principal registry when the principal registry is treated as if it were a county court;

    (b)   in relation to proceedings in a district registry or a county court, means the district judge or one of the district judges of that registry or county court, as the case may be;

'district registry' means –

    (a)   in proceedings under the 1973 Act, any district registry having a divorce county court within its district;

    (b)   in proceedings under the 2004 Act, any district registry having a civil partnership proceedings county court within its district; and

    (c)   in any other case, any district registry having a designated county court within its district;

'divorce county court' means a county court so designated by the Lord Chancellor pursuant to section 33(1) of the 1984 Act, including the principal registry when it is treated as a divorce county court;

'the European Convention' means the European Convention on Recognition and Enforcement of Decisions concerning Custody of Children and on the Restoration of Custody of Children which was signed in Luxembourg on 20 May 1980;

'filing', in relation to a document, means delivering it, by post or otherwise, to the court office;

'financial order' means –

    (a)   an avoidance of disposition order;

    (b)   an order for maintenance pending suit;

    (c)   an order for maintenance pending outcome of proceedings;

    (d)   an order for periodical payments or lump sum provision as mentioned in section 21(1) of the 1973 Act, except an order under section 27(6) of that Act;

    (e)   an order for periodical payments or lump sum provision as mentioned in paragraph 2(1) of Schedule 5 to the 2004 Act, made under Part 1 of Schedule 5 to that Act;

    (f)   a property adjustment order;

    (g)   a variation order;

    (h)   a pension sharing order; or

    (i)   a pension compensation sharing order;

('variation order', 'pension compensation sharing order' and 'pension sharing order' are defined in rule 9.3)

'financial remedy' means –

    (a)   a financial order;

    (b)   an order under Schedule 1 to the 1989 Act;

    (c)   an order under Part 3 of the 1984 Act;

    (d)   an order under Schedule 7 to the 2004 Act;

    (e)   an order under section 27 of the 1973 Act;

    (f)   an order under Part 9 of Schedule 5 to the 2004 Act;

PART II – Statutory Instruments

(g)   an order under section 35 of the 1973 Act;

(h)   an order under paragraph 69 of Schedule 5 to the 2004 Act;

(i)   an order under Part 1 of the 1978 Act;

(j)   an order under Schedule 6 to the 2004 Act;

(k)   an order under section 10(2) of the 1973 Act; or

(l)   an order under section 48(2) of the 2004 Act;

'hearing' includes a directions appointment;

'hearsay' means a statement made, otherwise than by a person while giving oral evidence in proceedings, which is tendered as evidence of the matters stated, and references to hearsay include hearsay of whatever degree;

'inherent jurisdiction' means the High Court's power to make any order or determine any issue in respect of a child, including in wardship proceedings, where it would be just and equitable to do so unless restricted by legislation or case law;

(Practice Direction 12D (Inherent Jurisdiction (including Wardship Proceedings)) provides examples of inherent jurisdiction proceedings.)

'judge', in the High Court or a county court, means, unless the context requires otherwise, a judge, district judge or a person authorised to act as such;

'jurisdiction' means, unless the context requires otherwise, England and Wales and any part of the territorial waters of the United Kingdom adjoining England and Wales;

'justices' clerk' has the meaning assigned to it by section 27(1) of the Courts Act 2003;

'legal representative' means a –

(a)   barrister;

(b)   solicitor;

(c)   solicitor's employee;

(d)   manager of a body recognised under section 9 of the Administration of Justice Act 1985; or

(e)   person who, for the purposes of the Legal Services Act 2007, is an authorised person in relation to an activity which constitutes the conduct of litigation (within the meaning of the Act),

who has been instructed to act for a party in relation to proceedings;

'litigation friend' has the meaning given –

(a)   in relation to a protected party, by Part 15; and

(b)   in relation to a child, by Part 16;

'matrimonial cause' means proceedings for a matrimonial order;

'matrimonial order' means –

(a)   a decree of divorce made under section 1 of the 1973 Act;

(b)   a decree of nullity made on one of the grounds set out in sections 11 or 12 of the 1973 Act;

(c)   a decree of judicial separation made under section 17 of the 1973 Act;

'note' includes a record made by mechanical means;

'officer of the Service' has the meaning given by section 11(3) of the Criminal Justice and Court Services Act 2000;

'order' includes directions of the court;

'order for maintenance pending outcome of proceedings' means an order under paragraph 38 of Schedule 5 to the 2004 Act;

'order for maintenance pending suit' means an order under section 22 of the 1973 Act;

'parental order proceedings' has the meaning assigned to it by rule 13.1;

'parental responsibility' has the meaning assigned to it by section 3 of the 1989 Act;

'placement proceedings' means proceedings for the making, varying or revoking of a placement order under the 2002 Act;

'principal registry' means the principal registry of the Family Division of the High Court;

'proceedings' means, unless the context requires otherwise, family proceedings as defined in section 75(3) of the Courts Act 2003;

'professional acting in furtherance of the protection of children' includes –

    (a) an officer of a local authority exercising child protection functions;

    (b) a police officer who is –

        (i) exercising powers under section 46 of the Act of 1989; or

        (ii) serving in a child protection unit or a paedophile unit of a police force,

    (c) any professional person attending a child protection conference or review in relation to a child who is the subject of the proceedings to which the information regarding the proceedings held in private relates; or

    (d) an officer of the National Society for the Prevention of Cruelty to Children;

'professional legal adviser' means a –

    (a) barrister;

    (b) solicitor;

    (c) solicitor's employee;

    (d) manager of a body recognised under section 9 of the Administration of Justice Act 1985; or

    (e) person who, for the purposes of the Legal Services Act 2007, is an authorised person in relation to an activity which constitutes the conduct of litigation (within the meaning of that Act),

who is providing advice to a party but is not instructed to represent that party in the proceedings;

'property adjustment order' means –

    (a) in proceedings under the 1973 Act, any of the orders mentioned in section 21(2) of that Act;

    (b) in proceedings under the 1984 Act, an order under section 17(1)(a)(ii) of that Act;

    (c) in proceedings under Schedule 5 to the 2004 Act, any of the orders mentioned in paragraph 7(1); or

(d)   in proceedings under Schedule 7 to the 2004 Act, an order for property adjustment under paragraph 9(2) or (3);

'protected party' means a party, or an intended party, who lacks capacity (within the meaning of the 2005 Act) to conduct proceedings;

'reporting officer' means an officer of the Service or a Welsh family proceedings officer appointed to witness the documents which signify a parent's or guardian's consent to the placing of the child for adoption or to the making of an adoption order or a section 84 order;

'risk assessment' has the meaning assigned to it by section 16A(3) of the 1989 Act;

'Royal Courts of Justice', in relation to matrimonial proceedings pending in a divorce county court or civil partnership proceedings pending in a civil partnership proceedings county court, means such place as may be specified in directions given by the Lord Chancellor pursuant to section 42(2)(a) of the 1984 Act;

'RSC' means the Rules of the Supreme Court 1965 as they appear in Schedule 1 to the CPR;

'section 8 order' has the meaning assigned to it by section 8(2) of the 1989 Act;

'section 84 order' means an order made by the High Court under section 84 of the 2002 Act giving parental responsibility prior to adoption abroad;

'section 89 order' means an order made by the High Court under section 89 of the 2002 Act –

(a)   annulling a Convention adoption or Convention adoption order;

(b)   providing for an overseas adoption or determination under section 91 of the 2002 Act to cease to be valid; or

(c)   deciding the extent, if any, to which a determination under section 91 of the 2002 Act has been affected by a subsequent determination under that section;

'Service' has the meaning given by section 11 of the Criminal Justice and Court Services Act 2000;

'the Service Regulation' means Regulation (EC) No. 1393/2007 of the European Parliament and of the Council of 13 November 2007 on the service in the Member States of judicial and extrajudicial documents in civil or commercial matters (service of documents), and repealing Council Regulation (EC) No. 1348/2000, as amended from time to time and as applied by the Agreement made on 19 October 2005 between the European Community and the Kingdom of Denmark on the service of judicial and extrajudicial documents in civil and commercial matters;

'specified proceedings' has the meaning assigned to it by section 41(6) of the 1989 Act and rule 12.27;

'welfare officer' means a person who has been asked to prepare a report under section 7(1)(b) of the 1989 Act;

'Welsh family proceedings officer' has the meaning given by section 35(4) of the Children Act 2004.

(2) In these rules a reference to –

(a) an application for a matrimonial order or a civil partnership order is to be read as a reference to a petition for –
   (i)   a matrimonial order;
   (ii) a decree of presumption of death and dissolution of marriage made under section 19 of the 1973 Act; or
   (iii) a civil partnership order,
   and includes a petition by a respondent asking for such an order;
(b) 'financial order' in matrimonial proceedings is to be read as a reference to 'ancillary relief';
(c) 'matrimonial proceedings' is to be read as a reference to a matrimonial cause or proceedings for an application for a decree of presumption of death and dissolution of marriage made under section 19 of the 1973 Act.

(3) Where these rules apply the CPR, they apply the CPR as amended from time to time.

2.4 Modification of rules in application to serial numbers etc.

If a serial number has been assigned under rule 14.2 or the name or other contact details of a party is not being revealed in accordance with rule 29.1 –

(a) any rule requiring any party to serve any document will not apply; and
(b) the court will give directions about serving any document on the other parties.

2.5 Power to perform functions conferred on the court by these rules and practice directions

(1) Where these rules or a practice direction provide for the court to perform any function then, except where any rule or practice direction, any other enactment or any directions made by the President of the Family Division under section 9 of the Courts and Legal Services Act 1990, provides otherwise, that function may be performed –

(a) in relation to proceedings in the High Court or in a district registry, by any judge or district judge of that Court including a district judge of the principal registry;
(b) in relation to proceedings in a county court, by any judge or district judge including a district judge of the principal registry when the principal registry is treated as if it were a county court; and
(c) in relation to proceedings in a magistrates' court—
   (i)   by any family proceedings court constituted in accordance with sections 66 and 67 of the Magistrates' Courts Act 1980; or
   (ii) by a single justice of the peace who is a member of the family panel in accordance with Practice Direction 2A.

(The Justices' Clerks Rules 2005 make provision for a justices' clerk or assistant clerk to carry out certain functions of a single justice of the peace.)

PART II – Statutory Instruments

(2) A deputy High Court judge and a district judge, including a district judge of the principal registry, may not try a claim for a declaration of incompatibility in accordance with section 4 of the Human Rights Act 1998.

2.6 Powers of the single justice to perform functions under the 1989 Act, the 1996 Act, the 2002 Act and the Childcare Act 2006

(1) A single justice who is a member of the family panel may perform the functions of a magistrates' court –

(a)   where an application without notice is made under sections 10, 44(1), 48(9), 50(4) and 102(1) of the 1989 Act;

(b)   subject to paragraph (2), under sections 11(3) or 38(1) of the 1989 Act;

(c)   under sections 4(3)(b), 4A(3)(b), 4ZA(6)(b), 7, 34(3)(b), 41, 44(9)(b) and (11)(b)(iii), 48(4), 91(15) or (17) or paragraph 11(4) of Schedule 14 of the 1989 Act;

(d)   in accordance with the Allocation Order;

(e)   where an application without notice is made under section 41(2) of the 2002 Act (recovery orders);

(f)   where an application without notice is made for an occupation order or a non molestation order under Part 4 of the 1996 Act; or

(g)   where an application is made for a warrant under section 79 of the Childcare Act 2006;

(2) A single justice of the peace may make an order under section 11(3) or 38(1) of the 1989 Act where –

(a)   a previous such order has been made in the same proceedings;

(b)   the terms of the order sought are the same as those of the last such order made; and

(c)   a written request for such an order has been made and –

    (i)   the other parties and any children's guardian consent to the request and they or their legal representatives have signed the request; or

    (ii)   at least one of the other parties and any children's guardian consent to the request and they or their legal representatives have signed the request, and the remaining parties have not indicated that they either consent to or oppose the making of the order.

(3) The proceedings referred to in paragraph (1)(a), (c) and (d) are proceedings which are prescribed for the purposes of section 93(2)(i) of the 1989 Act.

2.7 Single justice's power to refer to a magistrates' court

Where a single justice –

(a)   is performing the function of a magistrates' court in accordance with rules 2.5(1)(c)(ii) and 2.6(1) and (2); and

(b)   considers, for whatever reason, that it is inappropriate to perform the function, the single justice must refer the matter to a magistrates' court which may perform the function.

2.8 Court's discretion as to where it deals with cases

The court may deal with a case at any place that it considers appropriate.

2.9 Computation of time

(1) This rule shows how to calculate any period of time for doing any act which is specified –

    (a)   by these rules;

    (b)   by a practice direction; or

    (c)   by a direction or order of the court.

(2) A period of time expressed as a number of days must be computed as clear days.

(3) In this rule 'clear days' means that in computing the numbers of days –

    (a)   the day on which the period begins; and

    (b)   if the end of the period is defined by reference to an event, the day on which that event occurs,

are not included.

(4) Where the specified period is 7 days or less and includes a day which is not a business day, that day does not count.

(5) When the period specified –

    (a)   by these rules or a practice direction; or

    (b)   by any direction or order of the court,

for doing any act at the court office ends on a day on which the office is closed, that act will be in time if done on the next day on which the court office is open.

2.10 Dates for compliance to be calendar dates and to include time of day

(1) Where the court makes an order or gives a direction which imposes a time limit for doing any act, the last date for compliance must, wherever practicable –

    (a)   be expressed as a calendar date; and

    (b)   include the time of day by which the act must be done.

(2) Where the date by which an act must be done is inserted in any document, the date must, wherever practicable, be expressed as a calendar date.

(3) Where 'month' occurs in any order, direction or other document, it means a calendar month.

PART II – Statutory Instruments

Practice Direction –
Practice Directions relating to Family Proceedings in force before 6th April 2011 which support the Family Procedure Rules 2010

Introduction and the Existing Practice Directions

1.1 The Family Procedure Rules 2010 ('the FPR 2010') come into force on 6th April 2011.The purpose of this practice direction is to inform court users of the practice directions relating (only) to family proceedings which date from before 6th April 2011 ('existing Practice Directions') but will continue to apply after that date.

1.2 The table in the Annex to this practice direction lists those existing Practice Directions which will continue to apply. The listed existing Practice Directions will apply to family proceedings on and after 6th April 2011 –

    (a)   with the modifications outlined in the Annex (in particular that the numbering of the existing Practice Directions will be as set out in column one of the table in the Annex) and any other modifications necessary in consequence of the FPR 2010 coming into force; and

    (b)   subject to the FPR 2010 and any other practice directions supporting those rules.

Application of Practice Direction 23B of the Civil Procedure Rules 1998

2.1 Paragraphs 1.1, 1.2, 1.4 and 1.5 of CPR Practice Direction 23B apply to applications under Part III of the Family Law Reform Act 1969 for the use of scientific tests to determine parentage. These applications will be made using the procedure in Part 18 of the FPR 2010 (Procedure for Other Applications in Proceedings).

ANNEX

Number	Title	Date	Court	Updated rule references
PD6C	Practice Direction (Disclosure of Addresses by Government Departments) (amending Practice Direction of 13th February 1989) (NB this practice direction does not apply to requests for disclosure from HMRC and related agencies which are covered by 'Disclosure Orders against the Inland Revenue-Guidance from the President's Office (November 2003)'	20 July 1995	High Court, county court and magistrates' court	

Number	Title	Date	Court	Updated rule references
PD7D	Gender Recognition Act 2004	5 April 2005	High Court and county court	
PD12A	Public Law Proceedings Guide to Case Management: April 2010	April 2010	High Court, county court and magistrates' court	
PD12B	The Revised Private Law Programme	April 2010	High Court, county court and magistrates' court	
PD12I	Applications for Reporting Restriction Orders (nb this practice direction applies to information about children and protected parties)	18 March 2005	High Court	
PD12J	Residence and Contact Orders: Domestic Violence and Harm	14 January 2009	High Court, county court and magistrates' court	In paragraph 10, for 'the Family Proceedings Rules 1991, rule 4.17AA and by the Family Proccedings Courts (Children Act 1989) Rules 1991, rule 17AA', substitute, 'rule 12.34 of the Family Procedure Rules 2010'
PD12K	President's Direction (Children Act 1989: Exclusion Requirement)	17 December 1997	High Court, county court and magistrates' court	
PD12L	Children Act 1989:Risk Assessments under Section 16A	3 September 2007	High Court, county court and magistrates' court	
PD12M	Family Assistance Orders: Consultation	3 September 2007	High Court, county court and magistrates' court	

Number	Title	Date	Court	Updated rule references
PD12N	Enforcement of Children Act 1989 Contact Orders: Disclosure of Information to Officers of the National Probation Service (High Court and county court)	6 November 2008	High Court and county court (The Lord Chief Justice issued a Practice Direction on this subject for the magistrates' courts mirroring the one for the High Court and county courts)	
PD12O	Practice Direction (Arrival of Child in England by Air)	18 January 1980	High Court and county court	
PD12P	Registrar's Direction (Removal from jurisdiction: issue of Passports)	15 May 1987	High Court and county court	
PD14A	Who Receives a Copy of the Application Form for Orders in Proceedings		High Court, county court and magistrates' court	In the heading, for 'Part 5,rule 24(1)(b)(ii) of the Family Procedure (Adoption) Rules 2005', substitute 'Part 14, rule 14.6(1)(b)(ii) of the Family Procedure Rules 2010'
PD14B	The First Directions Hearing-Adoptions with a Foreign Element		High Court, county court and magistrates' court	In the heading, for 'Part 5,rule 26(3) of the Family Procedure (Adoption) Rules 2005', substitute 'Part 14, rule 14.8(3) of the Family Procedure Rules 2010'; and in paragraph 2, for 'rule 26(1)', substitute 'rule 14.8(1)'
PD14C	Reports by the Adoption Agency or Local Authority		High Court, county court and magistrates' court	In the heading for 'Part 5,rule 29(3) of the Family Procedure (Adoption) Rules 2005', substitute 'Part 14, rule 14.11(3) of the Family Procedure Rules 2010'

Number	Title	Date	Court	Updated rule references
PD14D	Reports by a Registered Medical Practitioner ('Health Reports')		High Court, county court and magistrates' court	In the heading for 'Part 5,rule 30(2) of the Family Procedure(Adoption) Rules 2005',substitute 'Part 14, rule 14.12(2) of the Family Procedure Rules 2010'; and in paragraph 1.1, for 'rule 30(1)', substitute 'rule 14.12(1)'
PD14E	Communication of Information Relating to the Proceedings		High Court, county court and magistrates' court	In the heading for 'Part 8,rule 78(1)(b) of the Family Procedure (Adoption) Rules 2005', substitute 'Part 14, rule 14.14(b) of the Family Procedure Rules 2010'; and in paragraph 1.1, for 'rule 78', substitute 'rule 14.14'
PD14F	Disclosing Information to an Adopted Adult		High Court, county court and magistrates' court	In the heading for 'Part 8,rule 84(1)(d) of the Family Procedure (Adoption) Rules 2005', substitute 'Part 14, rule 14.18(1)(d) of the Family Procedure Rules 2010'; in paragraphs 1,1 and 1.2, for 'rule 84', substitute 'rule 14.18'; and in paragraph 1.2, for 'rule 17', substitute 'rule 5'
PD27A	Family Proceedings: Court Bundles (Universal Practice to be applied in All Courts other than the Family Proceedings Court)	27 July 2006	High Court and county court	

PART II – Statutory Instruments

Number	Title	Date	Court	Updated rule references
PD27B	Attendance of Media Representatives at Hearings in Family Proceedings (High Court and county courts) (This practice direction should be read as if amended by *Re X (a child) (residence and contact: rights of media attendance)* (2009) EWHC 1728 (Fam) [87])	20 April 2009	High Court and county courts	For references to 'rule 10.28 of the Family Proceedings Rules 1991', substitute 'rule 27.11 of the Family Procedure Rules 2010'; in paragraph 2.2 for 'paragraphs (4) to (6)', substitute 'paragraphs (3) to (5)'; in paragraph 2.3, for 'Part 11 of the Family Proceedings Rules 1991', substitute 'Part 12,Chapter 7 of the Family Procedure Rules 2010 and Practice Direction 12G'; in paragraph 4.2, for 'paragraph (8)',substitute 'paragraph (7)'; in paragraph 4.3, for 'paragraph (3)(f)', substitute 'paragraph 2(f)' and for 'paragraph 3(g)', substitute 'paragraph (2)(g)'; in paragraph 5.1,for paragraph(4), substitute paragraph (3); in paragraph 5.2, for 'paragraph (4)',substitute 'paragraph (3)' and for 'paragraph (4)(a)', substitute 'paragraph 3(a)'; in paragraph 5.3, for 'paragraph 4(a)(iii)', substitute 'paragraph 3(a)(iii)'; in paragraph 5.4, for 'paragraph 4(b)', substitute 'paragraph 3(b)'; and in paragraph 6.1, for 'paragraph (6)' substitute 'paragraph (5)'

Number	Title	Date	Court	Updated rule references
PD27C	Attendance of Media Representatives at Hearings in Family Proceedings (Family Proceedings Court) (This practice direction should be read as if amended by *Re X (a child) (residence and contact: rights of media attendance)* (2009) EWHC 1728 (Fam) at [87]	20 April 2009	Magistrates' courts	In paragraph 1.1, for 'rule 16A of the Family Proceedings Courts (Children Act 1989) Rules 1991 ("the Rules")', substitute 'rule 27.11 of the Family Procedure Rules 2010 ("the Rules")'; in paragraph 2.1, for references to 'rule 16A(2)' where it occurs, substitute 'rule 27.11(1)' and for 'paragraphs (3) to (5) of rule 16A', substitute; 'paragraphs (3) to(5) of rule 27.11'; in paragraph 2.2, for 'rule 16A(2)', substitute 'rule 27.11(1)'; in paragraph 2.3 for 'Part 11C (rules relating to disclosure to third parties)', substitute 'Part 12, Chapter 7 of the Family Procedure Rules 2010 and Practice Direction 12G'; in paragraph 2.4, for 'rule 16A', substitute 'rule 27.11';and in paragraph 4.3, for 'paragraph (1)(f)', substitute 'paragraph 2(f)' and for 'paragraph (1)(g)' substitute ' paragraph 2(g)'
PD29B	Human Rights Act 1998	24 July 2000	High Court, county court and magistrates' court	
PD34B	Practice Note Tracing Payers Overseas	10 February 1976	High Court and county court	

PART II – Statutory Instruments

Practice Direction 2A –
Functions of the Court in the Family Procedure Rules 2010 and Practice Directions which may be Performed by a Single Justice of the Peace

This Practice Direction supplements FPR Part 2, rule 2.5(1)(c)(ii) (Power to perform functions conferred on the court by these rules and practice directions)

1.1 Where the FPR or a practice direction provide for the court to perform any function, that function may be performed by a single justice of the peace who is a member of a family panel except that such a justice cannot perform the functions listed in:

(a) column 2 of Table 1 in accordance with the rules listed in column 1; and

(b) column 2 of Table 2 in accordance with the paragraph of the practice direction listed in column 1.

1.2 For the avoidance of doubt, unless a rule, practice direction or other enactment provides otherwise, a single justice cannot make the decision of a magistrates' court at the final hearing of an application for a substantive order. For example, a single justice cannot make a residence order on notice, placement order, adoption or care order. However, a single justice can discharge the functions of a family proceedings court under the statutory provisions listed in rule 2.6 of the FPR.

Table 1

Rule	Nature of function
4.1(3)(g)	Stay the whole or part of any proceedings or judgment either generally or until a specified date or event.
4.1(3)(l)	Exclude an issue from consideration.
4.1(3)(m)	Dismiss or give a decision on an application after a decision on a preliminary issue.
4.1(4)(a)	When the court makes an order, making that order subject to conditions.
4.1(6)	Varying and revoking an order (other than directions which the court has made).

Rule	Nature of function
4.3(1)	Ability of the court to make orders (other than directions) of its own initiative.
4.4, 4.5 and 4.6	All the powers of a magistrates' court under these rules (power to strike out statement of case, sanctions have effect unless defaulting party obtains relief from sanctions).
8.20(4)	A direction that a child should be made a respondent to the application for a declaration of parentage under section 55A of the Family Law Act 1986, except where the parties consent to the child being made a respondent.
9.11(2)	Direction that a child be separately represented on an application.
9.22	All the powers of a magistrates' court under this rule (relating to proceedings by or against a person outside England and Wales for variation or revocation of orders under section 20 of the 1978 Act or paragraphs 30 to 34 of Schedule 6 to the 2004 Act).
12.3(2)	Where the person with parental responsibility is a child, a direction for that child be made a party, except where the parties consent to that child being made a party.
12.3(3)	Direction that a child be made a party to proceedings or that a child who is a party be removed, except where the parties consent to the child being made a party or to the removal of that party.
12.3(4)	Consequential directions following the addition or removal of a party except where a single justice is able to make such a direction under rule 12.3(2) and (3).

PART II – Statutory Instruments

Rule	Nature of function
12.61(1) and (2)	Considering the transfer of proceedings to the court of another member state, directions in relation to the manner in which parties may make representations and power to deal with question of transfer without a hearing with the consent of parties.
12.64(1)	Exercising court's powers under Article 15 of the Council Regulation or Article 8 of the 1996 Hague Convention.
12.68(1)	Staying the proceedings.
12.68(3)	Giving reasons for the court's decision, making a finding of fact and stating a finding of fact where such a finding has been made.
12.70(1)	Contemplating the placement of a child in another member state.
12.70(3)	Sending request directly to the central authority or other authority having jurisdiction in the other Member State.
12.70(4)	Sending request to Central Authority for England and Wales for onward transmission.
12.70(5)	Considering the documents which should accompany the request.
13.3(3)	Where the person with parental responsibility is a child, a direction for that child be made a party, except where the parties consent to that child being made a party.
13.3(4)	Direction that a child be made a party to proceedings or that a child who is a party be removed, except where the parties consent to the child being made a party or to the removal of that party.

Rule	Nature of function
13.3(5)	Consequential directions following the addition or removal of a party except where a single justice is able to make such a direction under rule 13.3(3) and (4).
13.9(7)	Variation or revocation of direction following transfer, except where a single justice would be able to make the direction in question under rule 13.9(1).
13.15(3)	Determination of the probable date of the child's birth.
13.20(1)	Specifying a later date by which a parental order takes effect.
14.3(2)	Direction that a child be made a respondent, except where the parties consent to the child being made a respondent.
14.3(3)(b)	Direction that a child who is a party be removed, except where the parties consent to the child being made a respondent.
14.3(4)	Consequential directions following the addition or removal of a party except where a single justice is able to make such a direction under rule 14.3(2) and (3)
14.8(3)	Any of the directions listed in PD14B in proceedings for – (a) a Convention adoption order (b) a section 84 order (c) a section 88 direction (d) a section 89 order; or (e) an adoption order where section 83(1) of the 2002 Act applies (restriction on bringing children in)
14.16(8)	Making an adoption order under section 50 of the 2002 Act after personal attendance of one only of the applicants if there are special circumstances.

PART II – Statutory Instruments

Rule	Nature of function
14.16(9)	Not making a placement order unless the legal representative of the applicant attends the final hearing.
14.17(4)	Determination of the probable date of the child's birth.
14.25(1)	Specifying a later date by which an order takes effect.
15.3(1)	Permission to a person to take steps before the protected party has a litigation friend.
15.3(2)	Permission to a party to take steps (where during proceedings a person lacks capacity to continue to conduct proceedings) before the protected party has a litigation friend.
15.3(3)	Making an order that a step taken before a protected party has a litigation friend has effect.
15.6(1)	Making an order appointing a person as a litigation friend.
15.6(6)	Court may not appoint a litigation friend unless it is satisfied that the person complies with the conditions in rule 15.4(3).
15.7	Direction that a person may not act as a litigation friend, termination of an appointment, appointment of a litigation friend in substitution for an existing one.
16.2	Power of court to make a child a party to proceedings if it considers it is in the best interests of the child to do so.
16.6(3)(a)	Permission to a child to conduct proceedings without a children's guardian or litigation friend.

Rule	Nature of function
16.6(6)	Power of the court to grant an application under paragraph (3)(a) or (5) if the court considers that the child has sufficient understanding to conduct the proceedings.
16.6(7)	Power of the court to require the litigation friend or children's guardian to take such part in proceedings (referred to in paragraph (6)) as the court directs.
16.6(8)	Power of the court to revoke permission granted under paragraph (3) in specified circumstances.
16.6(10)	Power of the court, in specified circumstances, to appoint a person to be the child's litigation friend or children's guardian.
16.8(2)	Permission to a person to take steps before the child has a litigation friend.
16.8(3)	Making an order that a step taken before the child has a litigation friend has effect.
16.11(1)	Making an order appointing a person as a litigation friend.
16.12	Direction that a person may not act as a litigation friend, termination of an appointment, appointment of a litigation friend in substitution for an existing one.
16.23(2)	Permission to a person to take steps before the child has a children's guardian.
18.3(1)(c)	Direction that a child be a respondent to an application under Part 18.
18.9(1)(a)	Power of court to deal with a Part 18 application without a hearing.

PART II – Statutory Instruments

Rule	Nature of function
18.12	Power of the court to proceed in absence of a party, except where a single justice has the power to make the relevant order applied for.
19.8(2)	The court's power to require or permit a party to give oral evidence at the hearing.
21.3	Power of court relating to withholding inspection or disclosure of a document.
22.1(2) to (4)	Power to exclude evidence that would otherwise be admissible, power to permit a party to adduce evidence, or to seek to rely on a document, in respect of which that party has failed to comply with requirements of Part 22 and power to limit cross examination.
22.6	Court's powers relating to use at final hearing of witness statements which have been served.
22.12	Power of court to require evidence by affidavit instead of or in addition to a witness statement.
22.15(4)	Permission for a party to amend or withdraw any admission made by that party on such terms as the court thinks just.
22.20(3)(a)	Permission for a witness statement in proceedings in the magistrates' court under Part 9 to be used for a purpose other than the proceedings in which it is served.
24.16(2)	Ordering the issue of a request to a designated court.
24.16(5)	Order for the submission of a request under article 17 of the Taking of Evidence Regulation.

Rule	Nature of function
27.10(1)(b)	Direction that proceedings to which the Rules apply will not be held in private, expect that a single justice may give such a direction in relation to a hearing which that single justice is conducting.
27.11(2)(g)	Power of the court to permit any other person to be present during any hearing, except that a single justice may give such permission in relation to a hearing which that single justice is conducting.
27.11(3)	Direction that persons within rule 27.11(2)(f) shall not attend the proceedings or any part of them.
Part 28	Powers of the court to make costs orders including wasted costs orders under section 145A of the Magistrates' Courts Act 1980.
29.8(1)	Court's opinion that it would be prevented by section 8 or 9 of the Child Support Act 1991 from making an order.
29.8(2)	Court's consideration of the matter without a hearing.
29.8(10)	Power of the court to determine that it would be prevented by sections 8 or 9 of the 1991 Act from making an order, and to dismiss the application.
29.8(11)	The court must give written reasons for its decision.
29.9(2)	Direction that the document will be treated as if it contained the application and directions as the court considers appropriate as to the subsequent conduct of the proceedings.

PART II – Statutory Instruments

Rule	Nature of function
29.13(1)	Direction for a court officer not to serve a copy of an order (other than directions that the single justice has made) to every party affected by it.
29.15	Specifying alternative date for an order to take effect, except an order which the single justice has made.
29.16	Correcting an accidental slip or omission in an order, except where that order was made by a single justice.
Part 30	Any power of the magistrates' court (where it is the lower court) to grant or refuse permission to appeal, except where a single justice has the power to make the order which is subject to the appeal.
31.9	Power for court to stay the proceedings.

Table 2

| Practice Direction: Family Assistance Orders dated 3 September 2007 – Paragraphs 2, 3, and 5 | Under paragraph 2 the court must have obtained the opinion of the appropriate officer about whether it would be in the best interests of the child in question for a family assistance order to be made and, if so, how the family assistance order could operate and for what period.

 Under paragraph 3 the court decides on the category of officer required to be made available under the family assistance order.
 Under paragraph 5 the court must give to the person it proposes to name in the order an opportunity to comment. |

Public Law Proceedings Guide to Case Management: 6th April 2010 – Paragraphs 8.1 to 8.5	Under paragraphs 8.1 to 8.5 determination by the court of issues as to whether an adult party or intended party to proceedings lacks capacity.
Practice Direction: Residence and Contact Orders: Domestic Violence and Harm: 14 January 2009 – Paragraphs 17, 18, 21 to 23, 28 and 29	Under paragraph 17 the court will consider whether a child who is the subject of an application should be made a party to proceedings. Under paragraph 18 the court will consider whether an interim order for residence or contact is in the best interests of the child. Under paragraphs 21–23, 27, 28 and 29 determinations of the court at fact finding hearings, in cases where a finding of domestic violence is made consideration of the conduct of the parents and where there has been a finding of domestic violence court directions or conditions on orders.
Practice Direction: Attendance of Media Representatives at Hearings in Family Proceedings dated 6 April 2009	Generally – court's discretion to exclude media representatives from attending hearings or part of hearings for 'relevant proceedings' as defined in rule 1 of the Family Proceedings Courts (Children Act 1989) Rules 1991 (other than where a Single Justice or Justice's Clerk is conducting the hearing)
PD14B – The First Directions Hearing – adoptions with a Foreign Element – Paragraph 2	Under paragraph 2 the court's consideration of: (a) whether the requirements of the Adoption and Children Act 2002 and the Adoptions with a Foreign Element Regulations 2005 (S.I. 2005/392) appear to have been complied with and, if not, consider whether or not it is appropriate to transfer the case to the High Court;

PART II – Statutory Instruments

	(b) whether all relevant documents are translated into English and, if not, fix a timetable for translating any outstanding documents; (c) whether the applicant needs to file an affidavit setting out the full details of the circumstances in which the child was brought to the United Kingdom, of the attitude of the parents to the application and confirming compliance with the requirements of The Adoptions with a Foreign Element Regulations 2005; and (d) give directions about: (i) the production of the child's passport and visa; (ii) the need for the Official Solicitor and a representative of the Home office to attend future hearings; and (iii) personal service on the parents (via the Central Authority in the case of an application for a Convention Adoption Order) including information about the role of the Official Solicitor and availability of legal aid to be represented within the proceedings; and (e) consider fixing a further directions no later than 6 weeks after the date of the first directions appointment and timetable a date by which the Official Solicitor should file an interim report in advance of that further appointment.
PD15A – Protected Parties – Paragraph 4.2(b)	Under paragraph 4.2(b) court directions on service on protected party.
PD16A – Representation of Children – Paragraphs 6.8 and 7.5	Under paragraph 6.8 the children's guardian must – (a) unless the court otherwise directs, file a written report advising on the interests of the child in accordance with the timetable set by the court; and

	(b) in proceedings to which Part 14 applies, where practicable, notify any person the joining of whom as a party to those proceedings would be likely, in the opinion of the children's guardian, to safeguard the interests of the child, of the court's power to join that person as a party under rule 14.3 and must inform the court
	(i) of any notification;
	(ii) of anyone whom the child's guardian attempted to notify under this paragraph but was unable to contact; and
	(iii) of anyone whom the children's guardian believes may wish to be joined to the proceedings
	Under paragraph 7.5 the court may, at the same time as deciding whether to join the child as a party, consider whether the proceedings should be transferred to another court taking into account the provisions of Part 3 of the Allocation and Transfer of Proceedings Order 2008.
PD18A – Other Applications in Proceedings Paragraphs 4.1 to 4.4(a)	Under paragraph 4.1 on receipt of an application notice containing a request for a hearing, unless the court considers that the application is suitable for consideration without a hearing, the court officer will, if serving a copy of the application notice, notify the applicant of the time and date fixed for the hearing of the application.
	Under paragraph 4.2 on receipt of an application notice containing a request that the application be dealt with without a hearing, the court will decide whether the application is suitable for consideration without a hearing.

PART II – Statutory Instruments

	Under paragraph 4.3 where the court considers that the application is suitable for consideration without a hearing but is not satisfied that it has sufficient material to decide the application immediately it may give directions for the filing of evidence and will inform the applicant and the respondent(s) of its decision.
	Under paragraph 4.4(a) where the court does not consider that the application is suitable for consideration without a hearing it may give directions as to the filing of evidence.
PD22A – Written Evidence – Paragraphs 1.6, 14.1 and 14.2	Under paragraph 1.6 the court may give a direction under rule 22.12 that evidence shall be given by affidavit instead of or in addition to a witness statement on its own initiative; or after any party has applied to the court for such a direction.
	Under paragraph 14.1 where an affidavit, a witness statement or an exhibit to either an affidavit or a witness statement does not comply with Part 22 or PD22A in relation to its form, the court may refuse to admit it as evidence and may refuse to allow the costs arising from its preparation.
	Under paragraph 14.2 permission to file a defective affidavit or witness statement or to use a defective exhibit may be obtained from the court where the case is proceeding.

| PD24A – Witnesses, Depositions and Taking of Evidence in Member States of the European Union – Paragraph 9.1 and 9.6 | Under paragraph 9.1 where a person wishes to take a deposition from a person in another Regulation State, the court where proceedings are taking place may order the issue of a request to the designated court in the Regulation State (rule 24.16(2)). The form of request is prescribed as Form A in the Taking of Evidence Regulation. Under paragraph 9.6 Article 17 permits the court where proceedings are taking place to take evidence directly from a deponent in another Regulation State if the conditions of the article are satisfied. Direct taking of evidence can only take place if evidence is given voluntarily without the need for coercive measures. Rule 24.16(5) provides for the court to make an order for the submission of a request to take evidence directly.

The form of request is Form I annexed to the Taking of Evidence Regulation and rule 24.16(6) makes provision for a draft of this form to be filed by the a party seeking the order. An application for an order under rule 24.16(5) should be by application notice in accordance with Part 18. |

PART II – Statutory Instruments

PART 3
ALTERNATIVE DISPUTE RESOLUTION: THE COURT'S POWERS

3.1 Scope of this Part

(1) This Part contains the court's powers to encourage the parties to use alternative dispute resolution and to facilitate its use.

(2) The powers in this Part are subject to any powers given to the court by any other rule or practice direction or by any other enactment or any powers it may otherwise have.

3.2 Court's duty to consider alternative dispute resolution

The court must consider, at every stage in proceedings, whether alternative dispute resolution is appropriate.

3.3 When the court will adjourn proceedings or a hearing in proceedings

(1) If the court considers that alternative dispute resolution is appropriate, the court may direct that the proceedings, or a hearing in the proceedings, be adjourned for such specified period as it considers appropriate –

(a) to enable the parties to obtain information and advice about alternative dispute resolution; and

(b) where the parties agree, to enable alternative dispute resolution to take place.

(2) The court may give directions under this rule on an application or of its own initiative.

(3) Where the court directs an adjournment under this rule, it will give directions about the timing and method by which the parties must tell the court if any of the issues in the proceedings have been resolved.

(4) If the parties do not tell the court if any of the issues have been resolved as directed under paragraph (3), the court will give such directions as to the management of the case as it considers appropriate.

(5) The court or court officer will –

(a) record the making of an order under this rule; and

(b) arrange for a copy of the order to be served as soon as practicable on the parties.

(6) Where the court proposes to exercise its powers of its own initiative the procedure set out in rule 4.3(2) to (6) applies.

(By rule 4.1(7), any direction given under this rule may be varied or revoked.)

Practice Direction 3A –
Pre-Application Protocol for Mediation Information and Assessment

This Practice Direction supplements FPR Part 3 (Pre-Application Protocol for Mediation Information and Assessment)

Introduction

1.1 This Practice Direction applies where a person is considering applying for an order in family proceedings of a type specified in Annex B (referred to in this Direction as 'relevant family proceedings').

1.2 Terms used in this Practice Direction and the accompanying Pre-action Protocol have the same meaning as in the FPR.

1.3 This Practice Direction is supplemented by the following Annexes –

(i)   Annex A: The Pre-application Protocol ('the Protocol'), which sets out steps which the court will normally expect an applicant to follow before an application is made to the court in relevant family proceedings;

(ii)   Annex B: Proceedings which are 'relevant family proceedings' for the purposes of this Practice Direction; and

(iii)   Annex C: Circumstances in which attendance at a Mediation Information and Assessment Meeting is not expected.

Aims

2.1 The purpose of this Practice Direction and the accompanying Protocol is to –

(a)   supplement the court's powers in Part 3 of the FPR to encourage and facilitate the use of alternative dispute resolution;

(b)   set out good practice to be followed by any person who is considering making an application to court for an order in relevant family proceedings; and

(c)   ensure, as far as possible, that all parties have considered mediation as an alternative means of resolving their disputes.

Rationale

3.1 There is a general acknowledgement that an adversarial court process is not always best suited to the resolution of family disputes, particularly private law disputes between parents relating to children, with such disputes often best resolved through discussion and agreement, where that can be managed safely and appropriately.

3.2 Litigants who seek public funding for certain types of family proceedings are (subject to some exceptions) already required to attend a meeting with a mediator as a pre-condition of receiving public funding.

3.3 There is growing recognition of the benefits of early information and advice about mediation and of the need for those wishing to make an application to court, whether publicly funded or otherwise, to consider alternative means of resolving their disputes, as appropriate.

3.4 In private law proceedings relating to children, the court is actively involved in helping parties to explore ways of resolving their dispute. The Private Law Programme, set out in Practice Direction 12B, provides for a first hearing dispute resolution appointment ('FHDRA'), at which the judge, legal advisor or magistrates, accompanied by an officer from Cafcass (the Children and Family Court Advisory and Support Service), will discuss with parties both the nature of their dispute and whether it could be resolved by mediation or other alternative means and can give the parties information about services which may be available to assist them. The court should also have information obtained through safeguarding checks carried out by Cafcass, to ensure that any agreement between the parties, or any dispute resolution process selected, is in the interests of the child and safe for all concerned.

PART II – Statutory Instruments

3.5 Against that background, it is likely to save court time and expense if the parties take steps to resolve their dispute without pursuing court proceedings. Parties will therefore be expected to explore the scope for resolving their dispute through mediation before embarking on the court process.

The Pre-application Protocol

4.1 To encourage this approach, all potential applicants for a court order in relevant family proceedings will be expected, before making their application, to have followed the steps set out in the Protocol. This requires a potential applicant except in certain specified circumstances, to consider with a mediator whether the dispute may be capable of being resolved through mediation. The court will expect all applicants to have compiled with the Protocol before commencing proceedings and (except where any of the circumstances In Annex C applies) will expect any respondent to have attended a Mediation Information and Assessment Meeting, if invited to do so. If court proceedings are taken, the court will wish to know at the first hearing whether mediation has been considered by the parties. In considering the conduct of any relevant family proceedings, the court will take into account any failure to comply with the Protocol and may refer the parties to a meeting with a mediator before the proceedings continue further.

4.2 Nothing in the Protocol is to be read as affecting the operation of the Private Law Programme, set out in Practice Direction 12B, or the role of the court at the first hearing in any relevant family proceedings.

ANNEX A – THE PRE-APPLICATION PROTOCOL

1 This Protocol applies where a person ('the applicant') is considering making an application to the court for an order in relevant family proceedings.

2 Before an applicant makes an application to the court for an order in relevant family proceedings, the applicant (or the applicant's legal representative) should contact a family mediator to arrange for the applicant to attend an information meeting about family mediation and other forms of alternative dispute resolution (referred to in this Protocol as 'a Mediation Information and Assessment Meeting').

3 An applicant is not expected to attend a Mediation Information and Assessment Meeting where any of the circumstances set out in Annex C applies.

4 Information on how to find a family mediator may be obtained from local family courts, from the Community Legal Advice Helpline – CLA Direct (0845 345 4345) or at www.direct.gov.uk.

5 The applicant (or the applicant's legal representative) should provide the mediator with contact details for the other party or parties to the dispute ('the respondent(s)'), so that the mediator can contact the respondent(s) to discuss that party's willingness and availability to attend a Mediation Information and Assessment Meeting.

6 The applicant should then attend a Mediation Information and Assessment Meeting arranged by the mediator. If the parties are willing to attend together, the meeting may be conducted jointly, but where necessary separate meetings may be held. If the applicant and respondent(s) do not attend a joint meeting, the mediator will invite the respondent(s) to a separate meeting unless any of the circumstances set out in Annex C applies.

7 A mediator who arranges a Mediation Information and Assessment Meeting with one or more parties to a dispute should consider with the party or parties concerned whether public funding may be available to meet the cost of the meeting and any subsequent mediation. Where none of the parties is eligible for, or wishes to seek, public funding, any charge made by the mediator for the Mediation Information and Assessment Meeting will be the responsibility of the party or parties attending, in accordance with any agreement made with the mediator.

8 If the applicant then makes an application to the court in respect of the dispute, the applicant should at the same time file a completed Family Mediation Information and Assessment Form (Form FM1) confirming attendance at a Mediation Information and Assessment Meeting or giving the reasons for not attending.

9 The Form FM1, must be completed and signed by the mediator, and countersigned by the applicant or the applicant's legal representative, where either –

    (a)   the applicant has attended a Mediation Information and Assessment Meeting; or

    (b)   the applicant has not attended a Mediation Information and Assessment Meeting and –

        (i)   the mediator is satisfied that mediation is not suitable because another party to the dispute is unwilling to attend a Mediation Information and Assessment Meeting and consider mediation;

        (ii)   the mediator determines that the case is not suitable for a Mediation Information and Assessment Meeting; or

        (iii)   a mediator has made a determination within the previous four months that the case is not suitable for a Mediation Information and Assessment Meeting or for mediation.

10 In all other circumstances, the Form FM1 must be completed and signed by the applicant or the applicant's legal representative.

11 The form may be obtained from magistrates' courts, county courts or the High Court or from www.direct.gov.uk.

ANNEX B – PROCEEDINGS WHICH ARE 'RELEVANT FAMILY PROCEEDINGS' FOR THE PURPOSES OF THIS PRACTICE DIRECTION

1 Private law proceedings relating to children, except:

    •   proceedings for an enforcement order, a financial compensation order or an order under paragraph 9 or Part 2 of Schedule A1 to the Children Act 1989;

- any other proceedings for enforcement of an order made in private law proceedings; or
- where emergency proceedings have been brought in respect of the same child(ren) and have not been determined.

('Private law proceedings' and 'emergency proceedings' are defined in Rule 12.2)

2 Proceedings for a financial remedy, except:

- Proceedings for an avoidance of disposition order or an order preventing a disposition;
- Proceedings for enforcement of any order made in financial remedy proceedings.

('Financial remedy' is defined in Rule 2.3(1) and 'avoidance of disposition order' and 'order preventing a disposition' are defined in Rule 9.3(1))

ANNEX C – A PERSON CONSIDERING MAKING AN APPLICATION TO THE COURT IN RELEVANT FAMILY PROCEEDINGS IS NOT EXPECTED TO ATTEND A MEDIATION INFORMATION AND ASSESSMENT MEETING BEFORE DOING SO IF ANY OF THE FOLLOWING CIRCUMSTANCES APPLIES:

1 The mediator is satisfied that mediation is not suitable because another party to the dispute is unwilling to attend a Mediation Information and Assessment Meeting and consider mediation.

2 The mediator determines that the case is not suitable for a Mediation Information and Assessment Meeting.

3 A mediator has made a determination within the previous four months that the case is not suitable for a Mediation Information and Assessment Meeting or for mediation.

4 *Domestic abuse*

Any party has, to the applicant's knowledge, made an allegation of domestic violence against another party and this has resulted in a police investigation or the issuing of civil proceedings for the protection of any party within the last 12 months.

5 *Bankruptcy*

The dispute concerns financial issues and the applicant or another party is bankrupt.

6 The parties are in agreement and there is no dispute to mediate.

7 The whereabouts of the other party are unknown to the applicant.

8 The prospective application is for an order in relevant family proceedings which are already in existence and are continuing.

9 The prospective application is to be made without notice to the other party.

10 *Urgency*

The prospective application is urgent, meaning –

(a) there is a risk to the life, liberty or physical safety of the applicant or his or her family or his or her home; or

(b) any delay caused by attending a Mediation Information and Assessment Meeting would cause a risk of significant harm to a child, a significant risk of a miscarriage of justice, unreasonable hardship to the applicant or irretrievable problems in dealing with the dispute (such as an Irretrievable loss of significant evidence).

11 There is current social services involvement as a result of child protection concerns in respect of any child who would be the subject of the prospective application.

12 A child would be a party to the prospective application by virtue of Rule 12.3(1).

13 The applicant (or the applicant's legal representative) contacts three mediators within 15 miles of the applicant's home and none is able to conduct a Mediation Information and Assessment Meeting within 15 working days of the date of contact.

PART 4
GENERAL CASE MANAGEMENT POWERS

4.1 The court's general powers of management

(1) In this Part, 'statement of case' means the whole or part of, an application form or answer.

(2) The list of powers in this rule is in addition to any powers given to the court by any other rule or practice direction or by any other enactment or any powers it may otherwise have.

(3) Except where these rules provide otherwise, the court may –

(a) extend or shorten the time for compliance with any rule, practice direction or court order (even if an application for extension is made after the time for compliance has expired);

(b) make such order for disclosure and inspection, including specific disclosure of documents, as it thinks fit;

(c) adjourn or bring forward a hearing;

(d) require a party or a party's legal representative to attend the court;

(e) hold a hearing and receive evidence by telephone or by using any other method of direct oral communication;

(f) direct that part of any proceedings be dealt with as separate proceedings;

(g) stay(GL) the whole or part of any proceedings or judgment either generally or until a specified date or event;

(h) consolidate proceedings;

(i) hear two or more applications on the same occasion;

(j) direct a separate hearing of any issue;

PART II – Statutory Instruments

    (k)   decide the order in which issues are to be heard;

    (l)   exclude an issue from consideration;

    (m)   dismiss or give a decision on an application after a decision on a preliminary issue;

    (n)   direct any party to file and serve an estimate of costs; and

    (o)   take any other step or make any other order for the purpose of managing the case and furthering the overriding objective.

(Rule 21.1 explains what is meant by disclosure and inspection.)

(4) When the court makes an order, it may –

    (a)   make it subject to conditions, including a condition to pay a sum of money into court; and

    (b)   specify the consequence of failure to comply with the order or a condition.

(5) Where the court gives directions it will take into account whether or not a party has complied with any relevant pre-action protocol[(GL)].

(6) A power of the court under these rules to make an order includes a power to vary or revoke the order.

(7) Any provision in these rules –

    (a)   requiring or permitting directions to be given by the court is to be taken as including provision for such directions to be varied or revoked; and

    (b)   requiring or permitting a date to be set is to be taken as including provision for that date to be changed or cancelled.

(8) The court may not extend the period within which a section 89 order must be made.

4.2 Court officer's power to refer to the court

Where a step is to be taken by a court officer –

    (a)   the court officer may consult the court before taking that step;

    (b)   the step may be taken by the court instead of the court officer.

4.3 Court's power to make order of its own initiative

(1) Except where an enactment provides otherwise, the court may exercise its powers on an application or of its own initiative.

(Part 18 sets out the procedure for making an application.)

(2) Where the court proposes to make an order of its own initiative –

    (a)   it may give any person likely to be affected by the order an opportunity to make representations; and

    (b)   where it does so it must specify the time by and the manner in which the representations must be made.

(3) Where the court proposes –

(a)   to make an order of its own initiative; and

(b)   to hold a hearing to decide whether to make the order,

it must give each party likely to be affected by the order at least 5 days' notice of the hearing.

(4) The court may make an order of its own initiative without hearing the parties or giving them an opportunity to make representations.

(5) Where the court has made an order under paragraph 0 –

(a)   a party affected by the order may apply to have it set aside(GL), varied or stayed(GL); and

(b)   the order must contain a statement of the right to make such an application.

(6) An application under paragraph (5)(a) must be made –

(a)   within such period as may be specified by the court; or

(b)   if the court does not specify a period, within 7 days beginning with the date on which the order was served on the party making the application.

(7) If the High Court or a county court of its own initiative strikes out a statement of case or dismisses an application (including an application for permission to appeal) and it considers that the application is totally without merit –

(a)   the court's order must record that fact; and

(b)   the court must at the same time consider whether it is appropriate to make a civil restraint order.

4.4 Power to strike out a statement of case

(1) Except in proceedings to which Parts 12 to 14 apply, the court may strike out(GL) a statement of case if it appears to the court –

(a)   that the statement of case discloses no reasonable grounds for bringing or defending the application;

(b)   that the statement of case is an abuse of the court's process or is otherwise likely to obstruct the just disposal of the proceedings;

(c)   that there has been a failure to comply with a rule, practice direction or court order; or

(d)   in relation to applications for matrimonial and civil partnership orders and answers to such applications, that the parties to the proceedings consent.

(2) When the court strikes out a statement of case it may make any consequential order it considers appropriate.

(3) Where –

(a)   the court has struck out an applicant's statement of case;

(b)   the applicant has been ordered to pay costs to the respondent; and

PART II – Statutory Instruments

(c)   before paying those costs, the applicant starts another application against the same respondent, arising out of facts which are the same or substantially the same as those relating to the application in which the statement of case was struck out,

the court may, on the application of the respondent, stay$^{(GL)}$ that other application until the costs of the first application have been paid.

(4) Paragraph (1) does not limit any other power of the court to strike out$^{(GL)}$ a statement of case.

(5) If the High Court or a county court strikes out an applicant's statement of case and it considers that the application is totally without merit –

(a)   the court's order must record that fact; and

(b)   the court must at the same time consider whether it is appropriate to make a civil restraint order.

4.5 Sanctions have effect unless defaulting party obtains relief

(1) Where a party has failed to comply with a rule, practice direction or court order, any sanction for failure to comply imposed by the rule, practice direction or court order has effect unless the party in default applies for and obtains relief from the sanction.

(Rule 4.6 sets out the circumstances which the court may consider on an application to grant relief from a sanction.)

(2) Where the sanction is the payment of costs, the party in default may only obtain relief by appealing against the order for costs.

(3) Where a rule, practice direction or court order –

(a)   requires a party to do something within a specified time; and

(b)   specifies the consequence of failure to comply,

the time for doing the act in question may not be extended by agreement between the parties

4.6 Relief from sanctions

(1) On an application for relief from any sanction imposed for a failure to comply with any rule, practice direction or court order the court will consider all the circumstances including –

(a)   the interests of the administration of justice;

(b)   whether the application for relief has been made promptly;

(c)   whether the failure to comply was intentional;

(d)   whether there is a good explanation for the failure;

(e)   the extent to which the party in default has complied with other rules, practice directions, court orders and any relevant pre –action protocol$^{(GL)}$;

(f)   whether the failure to comply was caused by the party or the party's legal representative;

(g) whether the hearing date or the likely hearing date can still be met if relief is granted;

(h) the effect which the failure to comply had on each party; and

(i) the effect which the granting of relief would have on each party or a child whose interest the court considers relevant.

(2) An application for relief must be supported by evidence.

4.7 General power of the court to rectify matters where there has been an error of procedure

Where there has been an error of procedure such as a failure to comply with a rule or practice direction –

(a) the error does not invalidate any step taken in the proceedings unless the court so orders; and

(b) the court may make an order to remedy the error.

4.8 Power of the court to make civil restraint orders

Practice Direction 4B sets out –

(a) the circumstances in which the High Court or a county court has the power to make a civil restraint order against a party to proceedings;

(b) the procedure where a party applies for a civil restraint order against another party; and

(c) the consequences of the court making a civil restraint order.

Practice Direction 4A – Striking Out a Statement of Case

This Practice Direction supplements FPR Part 4, rule 4.4 (Power to strike out a statement of case)

Introduction

1.1 Rule 4.4 enables the court to strike out the whole or part of a statement of case which discloses no reasonable grounds for bringing or defending the application (rule 4.4(1)(a)), or which is an abuse of the process of the court or otherwise likely to obstruct the just disposal of the proceedings (rule 4.4(1)(b)). These powers may be exercised on an application by a party or on the court's own initiative.

1.2 This practice direction sets out the procedure a party should follow to make an application for an order under rule 4.4.

Examples of cases within the rule

2.1 The following are examples of cases where the court may conclude that an application falls within rule 4.4(1)(a) –

(a) those which set,1 out no facts indicating what the application is about;

(b) those which are incoherent and make no sense;

(c)   those which contain a coherent set of facts but those facts, even if true, do not disclose any legally recognisable application against the respondent.

2.2 An application may fall within rule 4.4(1)(b) where it cannot be justified, for example because it is frivolous, scurrilous or obviously ill-founded.

2.3 An answer may fall within rule 4.4(1)(a) where it consists of a bare denial or otherwise sets out no coherent statement of facts.

2.4 A party may believe that it can be shown without the need for a hearing that an opponent's case has no real prospect of success on the facts, or that the case is bound to succeed or fail, as the case may be, because of a point of law (including the construction of a document). In such a case the party concerned may make an application under rule 4.4.

2.5 The examples set out above are intended only as illustrations.

2.6 Where a rule, practice direction or order states 'shall be struck out or dismissed' or 'will be struck out or dismissed' this means that the order striking out or dismissing the proceedings will itself bring the proceedings to an end and that no further order of the court is required.

Applications which appear to fall within rule 4.4(1)(a) or (b)

3.1 A court officer who is asked to issue an application form but believes the application may fall within rule 4.4(1)(a) or (b) should issue the application form, but may then consult the court (under rule 4.2) before returning the form to the applicant or taking any other step to serve the respondent. The court may of its own initiative make an immediate order designed to ensure that the application is disposed of or (as the case may be) proceeds in a way that accords with the rules.

3.2 The court may allow the applicant a hearing before deciding whether to make such an order.

3.3 Orders the court may make include –

(a)   an order that the application be stayed until further order;
(b)   an order that the application form be retained by the court and not served until the stay is lifted;
(c)   an order that no application by the applicant to lift the stay be heard unless the applicant files such further documents (for example a witness statement or an amended application form) as may be specified in the order.

3.4 Where the court makes any such order or, subsequently, an order lifting the stay, it may give directions about the service on the respondent of the order and any other documents on the court file.

3.5 The fact that the court allows an application referred to it by a court officer to proceed does not prejudice the right of any party to apply for any order against the applicant.

Answers which appear to fall within rule 4.4(1)(a) or (b)

4.1 A court officer may similarly consult the court about any document filed which purports to be an answer and which the officer believes may fall within rule 4.4(1)(a) or (b).

4.2 If the court decides that the document falls within rule 4.4(1)(a) or (b) it may on its own initiative make an order striking it out. Where the court does so it may extend the time for the respondent to file a proper answer.

4.3 The court may allow the respondent a hearing before deciding whether to make such an order.

4.4 Alternatively the court may make an order requiring the respondent within a stated time to clarify the answer or to give additional information about it. The order may provide that the answer will be struck out if the respondent does not comply.

4.5 The fact that the court does not strike out an answer on its own initiative does not prejudice the right of the applicant to apply for any order against the respondent.

General provisions

5.1 The court may exercise its powers under rule 4.4(1)(a) or (b) on application by a party to the proceedings or on its own initiative at any time.

5.2 Where the court at a hearing strikes out all or part of a party's statement of case it may enter such judgment for the other party as that party appears entitled to.

Applications for orders under rule 4.4(1)

6.1 Attention is drawn to Part 18 (Procedure for Other Applications in Proceedings) and to the practice direction that supplements it. The practice direction requires all applications to be made as soon as possible.

6.2 While many applications under rule 4.4(1) can be made without evidence in support, the applicant should consider whether facts need to be proved and, if so, whether evidence in support should be filed and served.

Practice Direction 4B –
Civil Restraint Orders

This Practice Direction supplements FPR rule 4.8

Introduction

1.1 This practice direction applies where the court is considering whether to make –

    (a)   a limited civil restraint order;

    (b)   an extended civil restraint order; or

    (c)   a general civil restraint order,

PART II – Statutory Instruments

against a party who has made applications which are totally without merit.

Rules 4.3(7), 4.4(5) and 18.13 provide that where a statement of case or application is struck out or dismissed and is totally without merit, the court order must specify that fact and the court must consider whether to make a civil restraint order. Rule 30.11(5) makes similar provision where the appeal court refuses an application for permission to appeal, strikes out an appellant's notice or dismisses an appeal.

The powers of the court to make civil restraint orders are separate from and do not replace the powers given to the court by section 91(14) of the Children Act 1989.

Limited civil restraint orders

2.1 A limited civil restraint order may be made by a judge of the High Court or a county court where a party has made 2 or more applications which are totally without merit.

2.2 Where the court makes a limited civil restraint order, the party against whom the order is made –

(a)   will be restrained from making any further applications in the proceedings in which the order is made without first obtaining the permission of a judge identified in the order;

(b)   may apply for amendment or discharge of the order, but only with the permission of a judge identified in the order; and

(c)   may apply for permission to appeal the order and if permission is granted, may appeal the order.

2.3 Where a party who is subject to a limited civil restraint order –

(a)   makes a further application in the proceedings in which the order is made without first obtaining the permission of a judge identified in the order, such application will automatically be dismissed –

(i)   without the judge having to make any further order; and

(ii)   without the need for the other party to respond to it; and

(b)   repeatedly makes applications for permission pursuant to that order which are totally without merit, the court may direct that if the party makes any further application for permission which is totally without merit, the decision to dismiss the application will be final and there will be no right of appeal, unless the judge who refused permission grants permission to appeal.

2.4 A party who is subject to a limited civil restraint order may not make an application for permission under paragraphs 2.2(a) or (b) without first serving notice of the application on the other party in accordance with paragraph 2.5.

2.5 A notice under paragraph 2.4 must –

(a)   set out the nature and grounds of the application; and

(b)   provide the other party with at least 7 days within which to respond.

2.6 An application for permission under paragraphs 2.2(a) or (b) –

(a) must be made in writing;

(b) must include the other party's written response, if any, to the notice served under paragraph 2.4; and

(c) will be determined without a hearing.

2.7 An order under paragraph 2.3(b) may only be made by a High Court judge but not a district judge.

2.8 Where a party makes an application for permission under paragraphs 2.2(a) or (b) and permission is refused, any application for permission to appeal –

(a) must be made in writing; and

(b) will be determined without a hearing.

2.9 A limited civil restraint order –

(a) is limited to the particular proceedings in which it is made;

(b) will remain in effect for the duration of the proceedings in which it is made, unless the court orders otherwise; and

(c) must identify the judge or judges to whom an application for permission under paragraphs 2.2(a), 2.2(b) or 2.8 should be made.

Extended civil restraint orders

3.1 An extended civil restraint order may be made by a judge of the High Court but not a district judge where a party has persistently made applications which are totally without merit.

3.2 Unless the court orders otherwise, where the court makes an extended civil restraint order, the party against whom the order is made –

(a) will be restrained from making applications in any court concerning any matter involving or relating to or touching upon or leading to the proceedings in which the order is made without first obtaining the permission of a judge identified in the order;

(b) may apply for amendment or discharge of the order, but only with the permission of a judge identified in the order; and

(c) may apply for permission to appeal the order and if permission is granted, may appeal the order.

3.3 Where a party who is subject to an extended civil restraint order –

(a) makes an application in a court identified in the order concerning any matter involving or relating to or touching upon or leading to the proceedings in which the order is made without first obtaining the permission of a judge identified in the order, the application will automatically be struck out or dismissed –

(i)   without the judge having to make any further order; and

(ii) without the need for the other party to respond to it; and

(b) repeatedly makes applications for permission pursuant to that order which are totally without merit, the court may direct that if the party makes any further application for permission which is totally without

PART II – Statutory Instruments

merit, the decision to dismiss the application will be final and there will be no right of appeal, unless the judge who refused permission grants permission to appeal.

3.4 A party who is subject to an extended civil restraint order may not make an application for permission under paragraphs 3.2(a) or (b) without first serving notice of the application on the other party in accordance with paragraph 3.5.

3.5 A notice under paragraph 3.4 must –

(a)   set out the nature and grounds of the application; and
(b)   provide the other party with at least 7 days within which to respond.

3.6 An application for permission under paragraphs 3.2(a) or (b) –

(a)   must be made in writing;
(b)   must include the other party's written response, if any, to the notice served under paragraph 3.4; and
(c)   will be determined without a hearing.

3.7 An order under paragraph 3.3(b) may only be made by a High Court judge but not a district judge.

3.8 Where a party makes an application for permission under paragraphs 3.2(a) or (b) and permission is refused, any application for permission to appeal –

(a)   must be made in writing; and
(b)   will be determined without a hearing.

3.9 An extended civil restraint order –

(a)   will be made for a specified period not exceeding 2 years;
(b)   must identify the courts in which the party against whom the order is made is restrained from making applications; and
(c)   must identify the judge or judges to whom an application for permission under paragraphs 3.2(a), 3.2(b) or 3.8 should be made.

3.10 The court may extend the duration of an extended civil restraint order, if it considers it appropriate to do so, but the duration of the order must not be extended for a period greater than 2 years on any given occasion.

General civil restraint orders

4.1 A general civil restraint order may be made by a judge of the High Court but not a district judge where, the party against whom the order is made persists in making applications which are totally without merit, in circumstances where an extended civil restraint order would not be sufficient or appropriate.

4.2 Unless the court otherwise orders, where the court makes a general civil restraint order, the party against whom the order is made –

(a)   will be restrained from making any application in any court without first obtaining the permission of a judge identified in the order;
(b)   may apply for amendment or discharge of the order, but only with the permission of a judge identified in the order; and

(c)   may apply for permission to appeal the order and if permission is granted, may appeal the order.

4.3 Where a party who is subject to a general civil restraint order –

(a)   makes an application in any court without first obtaining the permission of a judge identified in the order, the application will automatically be struck out or dismissed –
    (i)   without the judge having to make any further order; and
    (ii)   without the need for the other party to respond to it; and
(b)   repeatedly makes applications for permission pursuant to that order which are totally without merit, the court may direct that if the party makes any further application for permission which is totally without merit, the decision to dismiss that application will be final and there will be no right of appeal, unless the judge who refused permission grants permission to appeal.

4.4 A party who is subject to a general civil restraint order may not make an application for permission under paragraphs 4.2(a) or (b) without first serving notice of the application on the other party in accordance with paragraph 4.5.

4.5 A notice under paragraph 4.4 must –

(a)   set out the nature and grounds of the application; and
(b)   provide the other party with at least 7 days within which to respond.

4.6 An application for permission under paragraphs 4.2(a) or (b) –

(a)   must be made in writing;
(b)   must include the other party's written response, if any, to the notice served under paragraph 4.4; and
(c)   will be determined without a hearing.

4.7 An order under paragraph 4.3(b) may only be made by a High Court judge but not a district judge.

4.8 Where a party makes an application for permission under paragraphs 4. 2(a) or (b) and permission is refused, any application for permission to appeal –

(a)   must be made in writing; and
(b)   will be determined without a hearing.

4.9 A general civil restraint order –

(a)   will be made for a specified period not exceeding 2 years;
(b)   must identify the courts in which the party against whom the order is made is restrained from making applications; and
(c)   must identify the judge or judges to whom an application for permission under paragraphs 4.2(a), 4.2(b) or 4.8 should be made.

4.10 The court may extend the duration of a general civil restraint order, if it considers it appropriate to do so, but he duration of the order must not be extended for a period greater than 2 years on any given occasion.

PART II – Statutory Instruments

General

5.1 The other party or parties to the proceedings may apply for any civil restraint order.

5.2 An application under paragraph 5.1 must be made using the procedure in Part 18 unless the court otherwise directs and the application must specify which type of civil restraint order is sought.

****

PART 6
SERVICE

Chapter 1
Scope of this Part and Interpretation

6.1 Part 6 rules about service apply generally

This Part applies to the service of documents, except where –

    (a)   another Part, any other enactment or a practice direction makes a different provision; or

    (b)   the court directs otherwise.

6.2 Interpretation

In this Part 'solicitor' includes any person who, for the purposes of the Legal Services Act 2007, is an authorised person in relation to an activity which constitutes the conduct of litigation (within the meaning of that Act).

****

Chapter 3
Service of Documents other than an Application for a Matrimonial Order or Civil Partnership Order in the United Kingdom

6.23 Method of service

A document may be served by any of the following methods –

    (a)   personal service, in accordance with rule 6.25;

    (b)   first class post, document exchange or other service which provides for delivery on the next business day, in accordance with Practice Direction 6A;

    (c)   leaving it at a place specified in rule 6.26; or

    (d)   fax or other means of electronic communication in accordance with Practice Direction 6A.

(Rule 6.35 provides for the court to permit service by an alternative method or at an alternative place.)

6.24 Who is to serve

(1) A party to proceedings will serve a document which that party has prepared, or which the court has prepared or issued on behalf of that party, except where –

    (a)   a rule or practice direction provides that the court will serve the document; or

    (b)   the court directs otherwise.

(2) Where a court officer is to serve a document, it is for the court to decide which method of service is to be used.

(3) Where the court officer is to serve a document prepared by a party, that party must provide a copy for the court and for each party to be served.

6.25 Personal service

(1) Where required by another Part, any other enactment, a practice direction or a court order, a document must be served personally.

(2) In other cases, a document may be served personally except where the party to be served has given an address for service under rule 6.26(2)(a).

(3) A document is served personally on an individual by leaving it with that individual.

6.26 Address for service

(1) A party to proceedings must give an address at which that party may be served with documents relating to those proceedings.

(2) Subject to paragraph (4), a party's address for service must be –

    (a)   the business address either within the United Kingdom or any other EEA state of a solicitor acting for the party to be served; or

    (b)   where there is no solicitor acting for the party to be served, an address within the United Kingdom at which the party resides or carries on business.

('EEA state' is defined in Schedule 1 to the Interpretation Act 1978.)

(3) Where there is no solicitor acting for the party to be served and the party does not have an address within the United Kingdom at which that party resides or carries on business, the party must, subject to paragraph (4), give an address for service within the United Kingdom.

(4) A party who –

    (a)   has been served with an application for a matrimonial or civil partnership order outside the United Kingdom; and

    (b)   apart from acknowledging service of the application, does not take part in the proceedings,

need not give an address for service within the United Kingdom.

PART II – Statutory Instruments

(5) Any document to be served in proceedings must be sent, or transmitted to, or left at, the party's address for service unless it is to be served personally or the court orders otherwise.

(6) Where, in accordance with Practice Direction 6A, a party indicates or is deemed to have indicated that they will accept service by fax, the fax number given by that party must be at the address for service.

(7) Where a party indicates in accordance with Practice Direction 6A, that they will accept service by electronic means other than fax, the e-mail address or electronic identification given by that party will be deemed to be at the address for service.

(8) This rule does not apply where an order made by the court under rule 6.35 (service by an alternative method or at an alternative place) specifies where a document may be served.

6.27 Change of address for service

Where the address for service of a party changes, that party must give notice in writing of the change, as soon as it has taken place, to the court and every other party.

6.28 Service of an application form commencing proceedings on children and protected parties

(1) This rule applies to the service of an application form commencing proceedings other than an application for a matrimonial or civil partnership order.

(2) An application form commencing proceedings which would otherwise be served on a child or protected party must be served –

   (a)   where the respondent is a child, in accordance with rule 6.14(1); and
   (b)   where the respondent is a protected party, in accordance with rule 6.14(2).

6.29 Service of other documents on or by children and protected parties where a litigation friend has been or will be appointed

(1) This rule applies to –

   (a)   a protected party; or
   (a)   a child to whom the provisions of rule 16.5 and Chapter 5 of Part 16 apply (litigation friends).

(2) An application for an order appointing a litigation friend where a protected party or child has no litigation friend must be served in accordance with rule 15.8 or rule 16.13 as the case may be.

(3) Any other document which would otherwise be served on or by a child or protected party must be served on or by the litigation friend conducting the proceedings on behalf of the child or protected party.

6.30 Service on or by children where a children's guardian has been or will be appointed under rule 16.4

(1) This rule applies to a child to whom the provisions of rule 16.4 and Chapter 7 apply.

(2) An application for an order appointing a children's guardian where a child has no children's guardian must be served in accordance with rule 16.26.

(3) Any other document which would otherwise be served on or by a child must be served on or by the children's guardian conducting the proceedings on behalf of the child.

6.31 Service on or by children where a children's guardian has been appointed under rule 16.3

(1) This rule applies where a children's guardian has been appointed for a child in accordance with rule 16.3.

(2) Any document which would otherwise be served on the child must be served on –

    (a)   the solicitor appointed by the court in accordance with section 41(3) of the 1989 Act; and

    (b)   the children's guardian.

(3) Any document which would otherwise be served by the child must be served by –

    (a)   the solicitor appointed by the court in accordance with section 41(3) of the 1989 Act or by the children's guardian; or

    (b)   if no solicitor has been appointed as mentioned in paragraph (a), the children's guardian.

6.32 Supplementary provisions relating to service on children and protected parties

(1) The court may direct that a document be served on the protected party or child or on some person other than a person upon whom it would be served under rules 6.28 to 6.31 above.

(2) The court may direct that, although a document has been sent or given to someone other than a person upon whom it should be served under rules 6.28 to 6.31 above, the document is to be treated as if had been properly served.

(3) This rule and rules 6.28 to 6.31 do not apply where the court has made an order under rule 16.6 allowing a child to conduct proceedings without a children's guardian or litigation friend.

6.33 Supplementary provision relating to service on children

(1) This rule applies to proceedings to which Part 12 applies.

(2) Where a rule requires –

PART II – Statutory Instruments

(a)   a document to be served on a party;

(b)   a party to be notified of any matter; or

(c)   a party to be supplied with a copy of a document,

in addition to the persons to be served in accordance with rules 6.28 to 6.32, the persons or bodies mentioned in paragraph (3) must be served, notified or supplied with a copy of a document, as applicable, unless the court directs otherwise.

(3) The persons or bodies referred to in paragraph (2) are –

(a)   such of the following who are appointed in the proceedings –

   (i)   the children's guardian (if the children's guardian is not otherwise to be served);

   (ii)   the welfare officer;

   (iii)   the children and family reporter;

   (iv)   the officer of the Service, Welsh family proceedings officer or local authority officer acting under a duty referred to in rule 16.38; and

(b)   a local authority preparing a report under section 14A(8) or (9) of the 1989 Act.

6.34 Deemed service

A document, other than an application for a matrimonial or civil partnership order, served in accordance with these rules or a practice direction is deemed to be served on the day shown in the following table –

Method of service	*Deemed day of service*
First class post (or other service which provides for delivery on the next business day)	The second day after it was posted, left with, delivered to or collected by the relevant service provider, provided that day is a business day; or, if not, the next business day after that day
Document exchange	The second day after it was left with, delivered to or collected by the relevant service provider, provided that day is a business day; or, if not, the next business day after that day.
Delivering the document to or leaving it at a permitted address	If it is delivered to or left at the permitted address on a business day before 4.30p.m., on that day; or in any other case, on the next business day after that day.
Fax.	If the transmission of the fax is completed on a business day before 4.30p.m., on that day; or, in any other case, the next business day after the day on which it was transmitted.

Method of service	Deemed day of service
Other electronic method.	If the e-mail or other electronic transmission is sent on a business day before 4.30p.m., on that day; or in any other case, on the next business day after the day on which it was sent.
Personal service	If the document is served personally before 4.30p.m. on a business day, on that day; or, in any other case, on the next business day after that day.

(Practice Direction 6A contains examples of how the date of deemed service is calculated.)

6.35 Service by an alternative method or at an alternative place

Rule 6.19 applies to any document in proceedings as it applies to an application for a matrimonial or civil partnership order and reference to the respondent in that rule is modified accordingly.

6.36 Power to dispense with service

The court may dispense with the service of any document which is to be served in proceedings.

6.37 Certificate of service

(1) Where a rule, practice direction or court order requires a certificate of service, the certificate must state the details set out in the following table –

Method of service	Details to be certified
Personal service	Date and time of personal service and method of identifying the person served.
First class post, document exchange or other service which provides for delivery on the next business day.	Date of posting, leaving with, delivering to or collection by the relevant service provider.
Delivery of document to or leaving it at a permitted place.	Date and time when the document was delivered to or left at the permitted place.
Fax.	Date and time of completion of transmission.
Other electronic method	Date and time of sending the email or other electronic transmission.
Alternative method or place permitted by court	As required by the court.

(2) An applicant who is required to file a certificate of service of an application form must do so at or before the earlier of –

(a)   the first directions appointment in; or
(b)   the hearing of,

the proceedings unless a rule or practice direction provides otherwise.

(Rule 17.2 requires a certificate of service to contain a statement of truth.)

6.38 Notification of outcome of service by the court

Where –

(a)   a document to be served by a court officer is served by post or other service which provides for delivery on the next working day; and
(b)   the document is returned to the court,

the court officer will send notification to the party who requested service that the document has been returned.

6.39 Notification of non-service by bailiff

Where –

(a)   the bailiff is to serve a document; and
(b)   the bailiff is unable to serve it,

the court officer must send notification to the party who requested service.

Chapter 4
Service Out of the Jurisdiction

6.40 Scope and interpretation

(1) This Chapter contains rules about –

(a)   service of application forms and other documents out of the jurisdiction; and
(b)   the procedure for service.

('Jurisdiction' is defined in rule 2.3.)

(2) In this Chapter –

'application form' includes an application notice;
'Commonwealth State' means a State listed in Schedule 3 to the British Nationality Act 1981; and
'the Hague Convention' means the Convention on the service abroad of judicial and extra-judicial documents in civil or commercial matters signed at the Hague on November 15, 1965.

6.41 Permission to serve not required

Any document to be served for the purposes of these rules may be served out of the jurisdiction without the permission of the court.

6.42 Period for acknowledging service or responding to application where application is served out of the jurisdiction

(1) This rule applies where, under these rules, a party is required to file –

(a)   an acknowledgment of service; or

(b)   an answer to an application,

and sets out the time period for doing so where the application is served out of the jurisdiction.

(2) Where the applicant serves an application on a respondent in –

(a)   Scotland or Northern Ireland; or

(b)   a Member State or Hague Convention country within Europe,

the period for filing an acknowledgment of service or an answer to an application is 21 days after service of the application.

(3) Where the applicant serves an application on a respondent in a Hague Convention country outside Europe, the period for filing an acknowledgment of service or an answer to an application is 31 days after service of the application.

(4) Where the applicant serves an application on a respondent in a country not referred to in paragraphs (2) and (3), the period for filing an acknowledgment of service or an answer to an application is set out in Practice Direction 6B.

6.43 Method of service – general provisions

(1) This rule contains general provisions about the method of service of an application for a matrimonial or civil partnership order, or other document, on a party out of the jurisdiction.

Where service is to be effected on a party in Scotland or Northern Ireland

(2) Where a party serves an application form or other document on a party in Scotland or Northern Ireland, it must be served by a method permitted by Chapter 2 (and references to 'jurisdiction' in that Chapter are modified accordingly) or Chapter 3 of this Part and rule 6.26(5) applies.

Where service is to be effected on a respondent out of the United Kingdom

(3) Where the applicant wishes to serve an application form, or other document, on a respondent out of the United Kingdom, it may be served by any method –

provided for by –
        rule 6.44 (service in accordance with the Service Regulation);
        rule 6.45 (service through foreign governments, judicial authorities and British Consular authorities); or
        permitted by the law of the country in which it is to be served.

(4) Nothing in paragraph (3) or in any court order authorises or requires any person to do anything which is contrary to the law of the country where the application form, or other document, is to be served.

6.44 Service in accordance with the Service Regulation

(1) This rule applies where the applicant wishes to serve the application form, or other document, in accordance with the Service Regulation.

(2) The applicant must file –

    (a)   the application form or other document;

    (b)   any translation; and

    (c)   any other documents required by the Service Regulation.

(3) When the applicant files the documents referred to in paragraph (2), the court officer will –

    (a)   seal$^{(GL)}$, or otherwise authenticate with the stamp of the court, the copy of the application form; and

    (b)   forward the documents to the Senior Master of the Queen's Bench Division.

(The Service Regulation is annexed to Practice Direction 6B.)

(Article 20(1) of the Service Regulation provides that the Regulation prevails over other provisions contained in any other agreement or arrangement concluded by Member States.)

6.45 Service through foreign governments, judicial authorities and British Consular authorities

(1) Where the applicant wishes to serve an application form, or other document, on a respondent in any country which is a party to the Hague Convention, it may be served –

    (a)   through the authority designated under the Hague Convention in respect of that country; or

    (b)   if the law of that country permits –

        (i)   through the judicial authorities of that country; or

        (ii) through a British Consular authority in that country.

(2) Where the applicant wishes to serve an application form, or other document, on a respondent in any country which is not a party to the Hague Convention, it may be served, if the law of that country so permits –

    (a)   through the government of that country, where that government is willing to serve it; or

    (b)   through a British Consular authority in that country.

(3) Where the applicant wishes to serve an application form, or other document, in –

    (a)   any Commonwealth State which is not a party to the Hague Convention;

    (b)   the Isle of Man or the Channel Islands; or

    (c)   any British Overseas Territory,

the methods of service permitted by paragraphs (1)(b) and (2) are not available and the applicant or the applicant's agent must effect service on a respondent in accordance with rule 6.43 unless Practice Direction 6B provides otherwise.

(4) This rule does not apply where service is to be effected in accordance with the Service Regulation.

(A list of British overseas territories is reproduced in Practice Direction 6B.)

6.46 Procedure where service is to be through foreign governments, judicial authorities and British Consular authorities

(1) This rule applies where the applicant wishes to serve an application form, or other document, under rule 6.45(1) or (2).

(2) Where this rule applies, the applicant must file –

    (a)   a request for service of the application form, or other document, by specifying one or more of the methods in rule 6.45(1) or (2);

    (b)   a copy of the application form or other document;

    (c)   any other documents or copies of documents required by Practice Direction 6B; and

    (d)   any translation required under rule 6.47.

(3) When the applicant files the documents specified in paragraph (2), the court officer will –

    (a)   seal$^{(GL)}$, or otherwise authenticate with the stamp of the court, the copy of the application form or other document; and

    (b)   forward the documents to the Senior Master of the Queen's Bench Division.

(4) The Senior Master will send documents forwarded under this rule –

    (a)   where the application form, or other document, is being served through the authority designated under the Hague Convention, to that authority; or

    (b)   in any other case, to the Foreign and Commonwealth Office with a request that it arranges for the application form or other document to be served.

(5) An official certificate which –

    (a)   states that the method requested under paragraph (2)(a) has been performed and the date of such performance;

    (b)   states, where more than one method is requested under paragraph (2)(a), which method was used; and

    (c)   is made by –

        (i)   a British Consular authority in the country where the method requested under paragraph (2)(a) was performed;

        (ii)   the government or judicial authorities in that country; or

        (iii)   the authority designated in respect of that country under the Hague Convention,

PART II – Statutory Instruments

is evidence of the facts stated in the certificate.

(6) A document purporting to be an official certificate under paragraph (5) is to be treated as such a certificate, unless it is proved not to be.

6.47 Translation of application form or other document

(1) Except where paragraphs (4) and (5) apply, every copy of the application form, or other document, filed under rule 6.45 (service through foreign governments, judicial authorities and British Consular authorities) must be accompanied by a translation of the application form or other document.

(2) The translation must be –

(a) in the official language of the country in which it is to be served; or
(b) if there is more than one official language of that country, in any official language which is appropriate to the place in the country where the application form or other document is to be served.

(3) Every translation filed under this rule must be accompanied by a statement by the person making it that it is a correct translation, and the statement must include that person's name, address and qualifications for making the translation.

(4) The applicant is not required to file a translation of the application form, or other document, filed under rule 6.45 where it is to be served in a country of which English is an official language.

(5) The applicant is not required to file a translation of the application form or other document filed under rule 6.45 where –

(a) the person on whom the document is to be served is able to read and understand English; and
(b) service of the document is to be effected directly on that person.

(This rule does not apply to service in accordance with the Service Regulation which contains its own provisions about the translation of documents.)

6.48 Undertaking to be responsible for expenses of the Foreign and Commonwealth Office

Every request for service filed under rule 6.46 (procedure where service is to be through foreign governments, judicial authorities etc.) must contain an undertaking by the person making the request –

(a) to be responsible for all expenses incurred by the Foreign and Commonwealth Office or foreign judicial authority; and
(b) to pay those expenses to the Foreign and Commonwealth Office or foreign judicial authority on being informed of the amount.

Practice Direction 6A –
Service within the Jurisdiction

This Practice Direction supplements FPR Part 6, Chapters 2 and 3

General Provisions

Scope of this Practice Direction

1.1 This Practice Direction supplements the following provisions of Part 6 –

(a) Chapter 2 (service of the application for a matrimonial order or civil partnership order in the jurisdiction);

(b) Chapter 3 (service of documents other than an application for a matrimonial order or civil partnership order in the United Kingdom); and

(c) rule 6.43(2) in relation to the method of service on a party in Scotland or Northern Ireland.

(Practice Direction B supplementing Part 6 contains provisions relevant to service on a party in Scotland or Northern Ireland, including provisions about the period for responding to an application notice.)

When service may be by document exchange

2.1 Subject to the provisions of rule 6.4 (which provides when an application for a matrimonial or civil partnership order may be served by document exchange) service by document exchange (DX) may take place only where –

(a) the address at which the party is to be served includes a numbered box at a DX; or

(b) the writing paper of the party who is to be served or of the solicitor acting for that party sets out a DX box number; and

(c) the party or the solicitor acting for that party has not indicated in writing that they are unwilling to accept service by DX.

How service is effected by post, an alternative service provider or DX

3.1 Service by post, DX or other service which provides for delivery on the next business day is effected by –

(a) placing the document in a post box;

(b) leaving the document with or delivering the document to the relevant service provider; or

(c) having the document collected by the relevant service provider.

Service by fax or other electronic means

4.1 This paragraph applies to the service of a document other than an application for a matrimonial or civil partnership order and documents in adoption proceedings and parental order proceedings.

4.2 Subject to the provisions of rule 6.26(6) and (7), where a document is to be served by fax or other electronic means –

(a)   the party who is to be served or the solicitor acting for that party must previously have indicated in writing to the party serving –
   (i)   that the party to be served or the solicitor is willing to accept service by fax or other electronic means; and
   (ii)   the fax number, e-mail address or other electronic identification to which it must be sent; and
(b)   the following are to be taken as sufficient written indications for the purposes of paragraph 4.2(a) –
   (i)   a fax number set out on the writing paper of the solicitor acting for the party to be served;
   (ii)   an e-mail address set out on the writing paper of the solicitor acting for the party to be served but only where it is stated that the e-mail address may be used for service; or
   (iii)   a fax number, e-mail address or electronic identification set out on a statement of case or an answer to a claim filed with the court.

4.3 Where a party intends to serve a document by electronic means (other than by fax) that party must first ask the party who is to be served whether there are any limitations to the recipient's agreement to accept service by such means (for example, the format in which documents are to be sent and the maximum size of attachments that may be received).

4.4 Where a document is served by electronic means, the party serving the document need not in addition send or deliver a hard copy.

Service on members of the Regular Forces and United States Air Force

5.1 The provisions that apply to service on members of the regular forces (within the meaning of the Armed Forces Act 2006) and members of the United States Air Force are annexed to this practice direction.

Application for an order for service by an alternative method or at an alternative place

6.1 An application in the High Court or a county court for an order under rule 6.19 may be made without notice.

6.2 Where an application for an order under rule 6.19 is made before the document is served, the application must be supported by evidence stating –

(a)   the reason why an order is sought;
(b)   what alternative method or place is proposed; and
(c)   why the applicant believes that the document is likely to reach the person to be served by the method or at the place proposed.

6.3 Where the application for an order is made after the applicant has taken steps to bring the document to the attention of the person to be served by an alternative method or at an alternative place, the application must be supported by evidence stating –

(a)   the reason why the order is sought;
(b)   what alternative method or alternative place was used;

(c)   when the alternative method or place was used; and

(d)   why the applicant believes that the document is likely to have reached the person to be served by the alternative method or at the alternative place.

6.4 Examples –

(a)   an application to serve by posting or delivering to an address of a person who knows the other party must be supported by evidence that if posted or delivered to that address, the document is likely to be brought to the attention of the other party;

(b)   an application to serve by sending a SMS text message or leaving a voicemail message at a particular telephone number saying where the document is must be accompanied by evidence that the person serving the document has taken, or will take, appropriate steps to ensure that the party being served is using that telephone number and is likely to receive the message.

Applications for an order to dispense with service

7.1 An application in the High Court or a county court for an order under rule 6.36 (power to dispense with service) may be made without notice.

Deemed service of a document other than an application for a matrimonial or civil partnership order

8.1 Rule 6.34 contains provisions about deemed service of a document other than an application for a matrimonial or civil partnership order. Examples of how deemed service is calculated are set out below.

Example 1

8.2 Where the document is posted (by first class post) on a Monday (a business day), the day of deemed service is the following Wednesday (a business day).

Example 2

8.3 Where the document is left in a numbered box at the DX on a Friday (a business day), the day of deemed service is the following Monday (a business day).

Example 3

8.4 Where the document is sent by fax on a Saturday and the transmission of that fax is completed by 4.30p.m. on that day, the day of deemed service is the following Monday (a business day).

Example 4

8.5 Where the document is served personally before 4.30p.m. on a Sunday, the day of deemed service is the next day (Monday, a business day).

PART II – Statutory Instruments

Example 5

8.6 Where the document is delivered to a permitted address after 4.30p.m. on the Thursday (a business day) before Good Friday, the day of deemed service is the following Tuesday (a business day) as the Monday is a bank holiday.

Example 6

8.7 Where the document is posted (by first class post) on a bank holiday Monday, the day of deemed service is the following Wednesday (a business day).

Service of application on children and protected parties

9.1 Rule 16.14(1) and (2) are applied to service of an application form (other than an application for a matrimonial or civil partnership order) commencing proceedings on children and protected parties by rule 6.28. Rule 6.14(7) makes provision as to how an application form must be served where the respondent is a child or protected party. A document served in accordance with rule 6.14(7) must be endorsed with the following notice which is set out in Form D5 –

Important Notice

The contents or purport of this document are to be communicated to the Respondent

[or as the case may be], [full name of Respondent]

if s/he is over 16 [add if the person to be served lacks capacity within the meaning of the Mental Capacity Act 2005 to conduct the proceedings] unless you are satisfied [after consultation with the responsible medical officer within the meaning of the Mental Health Act 1983 or, if s/he is not liable to be detained or subject to guardianship under that Act, his/her medical attendant]* that communication will be detrimental to his/her mental condition].

Provisions relating to Applications for Matrimonial and Civil Partnership Orders

Acknowledgment of service to be sent to applicant

10.1 Where the court office receives an acknowledgment of service the court officer must send a photographic copy of it to the applicant.

Personal service of application by bailiff

11.1 The court will only consider a request for personal service of the application by a bailiff if the address for service is in England and Wales.

11.2 In normal circumstances, a request should only be made if postal service has been attempted. In this case, if –

(a)   a signed acknowledgment of service is not returned to the court within 14 days after posting; and

(b)   the applicant reasonably believes the respondent is still living at the stated address,

the applicant may make a request to the court for personal service by a bailiff.

11.3 A request for personal service by a bailiff should be made in writing to the court officer on the prescribed form and accompanied by the relevant fee. The request should also be accompanied by-

(a)   evidence that postal service has been attempted and failed; or
(b)   if postal service has not been attempted, an explanation as to why postal service is not considered appropriate in the circumstances of the case.

11.4 A request will rarely be granted where the applicant is legally represented and it will be necessary for the representative to show why service by bailiff is required rather than by a process server.

Proof of personal service by bailiff

12.1 Once service of the application has been effected or attempted by the bailiff he must file a certificate of service in the issuing court.

12.2 If the respondent fails to sign and return an acknowledgment of service to the court office and –

(a)   the certificate contains a signature of receipt of the application by the respondent; or
(b)   the identity of the respondent is to be proved by a photograph supplied by the applicant,

the applicant must prove the signature or photograph in the affidavit filed by the applicant under rule 7.19(4).

Service by bailiff in proceedings in the Principal Registry

13.1 This paragraph applies where proceedings which are pending in the Principal Registry of the Family Division are treated as pending in a divorce county court.

13.2 Where a document is to be served by a bailiff it must be sent for service to the Principal Registry for onward transmission to the court officer of the county court in whose district the document is to be served.

Service of application on children and protected parties

14.1 A document served in accordance with rule 6.14(7) must be endorsed with the notice contained in paragraph 9.1.

ANNEX

Service on Members of the Regular Forces

1 The following information is for litigants and legal representatives who wish to serve legal documents in civil proceedings in the courts of England and

PART II – Statutory Instruments

Wales on parties to the proceedings who are (or who, at the material time, were) members of the regular forces (as defined in the Armed Forces Act 2006).

2 The proceedings may take place in the county court or the High Court, and the documents to be served may be claim forms, interim application notices and pre-action application notices. Proceedings for divorce or maintenance and proceedings in the Family Courts generally are subject to special rules as to service which are explained in a practice direction issued by the Senior District Judge of the Principal Registry on 26 June 1979.

  (now see Practice Direction 1 Maintenance Orders: Service Personnel; 2 Disclosure of Addresses [1995] 2 FLR 813.)

3 In this Annex, the person wishing to effect service is referred to as the 'claimant' and the member of the regular forces to be served is referred to as 'the member'; the expression 'overseas' means outside the United Kingdom.

Enquiries as to address

4 As a first step, the claimant's legal representative will need to find out where the member is serving, if this is not already known. For this purpose the claimant's legal representative should write to the appropriate officer of the Ministry of Defence as specified in paragraph 10 below.

5 The letter of enquiry should in every case show that the writer is a legal representative and that the enquiry is made solely with a view to the service of legal documents in civil proceedings.

6 In all cases the letter must give the full name, service number, rank or rate, and Ship, Arm or Trade, Regiment or Corps and Unit or as much of this information as is available. Failure to quote the service number and the rank or rate may result either in failure to identify the member or in considerable delay.

7 The letter must contain an undertaking by the legal representative that, if the address is given, it will be used solely for the purpose of issuing and serving documents in the proceedings and that so far as is possible the legal representative will disclose the address only to the court and not to the claimant or to any other person or body. A legal representative in the service of a public authority or private company must undertake that the address will be used solely for the purpose of issuing and serving documents in the proceedings and that the address will not be disclosed so far as is possible to any other part of the legal representative's employing organisation or to any other person but only to the court. Normally on receipt of the required information and undertaking the appropriate office will give the service address.

8 If the legal representative does not give the undertaking, the only information that will be given is whether the member is at that time serving in England or Wales, Scotland, Northern Ireland or overseas.

9 It should be noted that a member's address which ends with a British Forces Post Office address and reference (BFPO) will nearly always indicate that the member is serving overseas.

10 The letter of enquiry should be addressed as follows –

Royal Navy and Royal Marine Officers, Ratings and Other Ranks
Director Naval Personnel
Fleet Headquarters
MP 3.1
Leach Building
Whale Island
Portsmouth
Hampshire
PO2 8BY

Army Officers and other Ranks –
Army Personnel Centre
Disclosures 1
MP 520
Kentigern House
65 Brown Street
Glasgow
G2 8EX

Royal Air Force Officers and Other Ranks –
Manning 22E
RAF Disclosures
Room 221B
Trenchard Hall
RAF Cranwell
Sleaford
Lincolnshire
NG34 8HB

Assistance in serving documents on members

11 Once the claimant's legal representative has ascertained the member's address, the legal representative may use that address as the address for service by post, in cases where this method of service is allowed by the Civil Procedure Rules. There are, however, some situations in which service of the proceedings, whether in the High Court or in the county court, must be effected personally; in these cases an appointment will have to be sought, through the Commanding Officer of the Unit, Establishment or Ship concerned, for the purpose of effecting service. The procedure for obtaining an appointment is described below, and it applies whether personal service is to be effected by the claimant's legal representative or the legal representative's agent or by a court bailiff, or, in the case of proceedings served overseas (with the leave of the court) through the British Consul or the foreign judicial authority.

12 The procedure for obtaining an appointment to effect personal service is by application to the Commanding Officer of the Unit, Establishment or Ship in which the member is serving. The Commanding Officer may grant permission for the document server to enter the Unit, Establishment or Ship but if this is not appropriate the Commanding Officer may offer arrangements for the member to attend at a place in the vicinity of the Unit, Establishment or Ship in order that the member may be served. If suitable arrangements cannot be

PART II – Statutory Instruments

made the legal representative will have evidence that personal service is impracticable, which may be useful in an application for service by an alternative method or at an alternative place.

General

13 Subject to the procedure outlined in paragraphs 11 and 12, there are no special arrangements to assist in the service of legal documents when a member is outside the United Kingdom. The appropriate office will, however, give an approximate date when the member is likely to return to the United Kingdom.

14 It sometimes happens that a member has left the regular forces by the time an enquiry as to address is made. If the claimant's legal representative confirms that the proceedings result from an occurrence when the member was in the regular forces and the legal representative gives the undertaking referred to in paragraph 7, the last known private address after discharge will normally be provided. In no other case, however, will the Ministry of Defence disclose the private address of a member of the regular forces.

Service on Members of United States Air Force

15 In addition to the information contained in the memorandum of 26 July 1979, and after some doubts having been expressed as to the correct procedure to be followed by persons having civil claims against members of the United States Air Force in England and Wales, the Lord Chancellor's Office (as it was then) issued the following notes for guidance with the approval of the appropriate United States authorities.

16 Instructions have been issued by the United States authorities to the commanding officers of all their units in England and Wales that every facility is to be given for the service of documents in civil proceedings on members of the United States Air Force. The proper course to be followed by a creditor or other person having a claim against a member of the United States Air Force is for that person to communicate with the commanding officer or, where the unit concerned has a legal officer, with the legal officer of the defendant's unit requesting the provision of facilities for the service of documents on the defendant. It is not possible for the United States authorities to act as arbitrators when a civil claim is made against a member of their forces. It is, therefore, essential that the claim should either be admitted by the defendant or judgment should be obtained on it, whether in the High Court or a county court. If a claim has been admitted or judgment has been obtained and the claimant has failed to obtain satisfaction within a reasonable period, the claimant's proper course is then to write to: Office of the Staff Judge Advocate, Headquarters, Third Air Force, R.A.F. Mildenhall, Suffolk, enclosing a copy of the defendant's written admission of the claim or, as the case may be, a copy of the judgment. Steps will then be taken by the Staff Judge Advocate to ensure that the matter is brought to the defendant's attention with a view to prompt satisfaction of the claim.

Practice Direction 6B –
Service out of the Jurisdiction

This Practice Direction supplements FPR Part 6, Chapters 2 and 3

Contents of this Practice Direction

Scope of this Practice Direction	Paragraph 1
Service in other Member States of the European Union	Paragraph 2
Documents to be filed under rule 6.46(2)(c)	Paragraph 3
Service in a Commonwealth State or British Overseas Territory	Paragraph 4
Period for responding to an application form	Paragraph 5
Service of application notices and orders	Paragraph 6
Period for responding to an application notice	Paragraph 7
Further information	Paragraph 8

Scope of this Practice Direction

1.1 This Practice Direction supplements Chapter 4 (service out of the jurisdiction) of Part 6.

> (Practice Direction 6A contains relevant provisions supplementing rule 6.43(2) in relation to the method of service on a party in Scotland or Northern Ireland.)

Service in other Member States of the European Union

2.1 Where service is to be effected in another Member of State of the European Union, the Service Regulation applies.

2.2 The Service Regulation is Regulation (EC) No. 1393/2007 of the European Parliament and of the Council of 13 November 2007 on the service in the Member States of judicial and extrajudicial documents in civil or commercial matters (service of documents), and repealing Council Regulation (EC) no. 1348/2000, as amended from time to time and as applied by the Agreement made on 19 October 2005 between the European Community and the Kingdom of Denmark on the service of judicial and extrajudicial documents in civil and commercial matters.

2.3 The Service Regulation is annexed to this Practice Direction.

PART II – Statutory Instruments

(Article 20(1) of the Service Regulation provides that the Regulation prevails over other provisions contained in bilateral or multilateral agreements or arrangements concluded by the Member of States and in particular Article IV of the protocol to the Brussels Convention of 1968 and the Hague Convention of 15 November 1965)

Documents to be filed under rule 6.46(2)

3.1 A duplicate of –

(a)   the application form or other document to be served under rule 6.45(1) or (2);

(b)   any documents accompanying the application or other document referred to in paragraph (a); and

(c)   any translation required by rule 6.47;

must be provided for each party to be served out of the jurisdiction, together with forms for responding to the application.

3.2 Some countries require legalisation of the document to be served and some require a formal letter of request which must be signed by the Senior Master. Any queries on this should be addressed to the Foreign Process Section (Room E02) at the Royal Courts of Justice.

Service in a Commonwealth State or British Overseas Territory

4.1 The judicial authorities of certain Commonwealth States which are not a party to the Hague Convention require service to be in accordance with rule 6.45(1)(b)(i) and not 6.45(3). A list of such countries can be obtained from the Foreign Process Section (Room E02) at the Royal Courts of Justice.

4.2 The list of British overseas territories is contained in Schedule 6 to the British Nationality Act 1981. For ease of reference these are –

(a)   Anguilla;
(b)   Bermuda;
(c)   British Antarctic Territory;
(d)   British Indian Ocean Territory;
(e)   Cayman Islands;
(f)   Falkland Islands;
(g)   Gibraltar;
(h)   Montserrat;
(i)   Pitcairn, Henderson, Ducie and Oeno Islands;
(j)   St. Helena, Ascension and Tristan da Cunha;
(k)   South Georgia and the South Sandwich Islands;
(l)   Sovereign Base Areas of Akrotiri and Dhekelia;
(m)   Turks and Caicos Islands;
(n)   Virgin Islands.

Period for responding to an application form

5.1 Where rule 6.42 applies, the period within which the respondent must file an acknowledgment of service or an answer to the application is the number of days listed in the Table after service of the application.

5.2 Where an application is served out of the jurisdiction any statement as to the period for responding to the claim contained in any of the forms required by the Family Procedure Rules to accompany the application must specify the period prescribed under rule 6.42.

Service of application notices and orders

6.1 The provisions of Chapter 4 of Part 6 (special provisions about service out of the jurisdiction) also apply to service out of the jurisdiction of an application notice or order.

6.2 Where an application notice is to be served out of the jurisdiction in accordance with Chapter 4 of Part 6 the court must have regard to the country in which the application notice is to be served in setting the date for the hearing of the application and giving any direction about service of the respondent's evidence.

Period for responding to an application notice

7.1 Where an application notice or order is served out of the jurisdiction, the period for responding is 7 days less than the number of days listed in the Table.

Further information

8.1 Further information concerning service out of the jurisdiction can be obtained from the Foreign Process Section, Room E02, Royal Courts of Justice, Strand, London WC2A 2LL (telephone 020 7947 6691).

TABLE

Place or country	Number of days
Afghanistan	23
Albania	25
Algeria	22
Andorra	21
Angola	22
Anguilla	31
Antigua and Barbuda	23
Antilles (Netherlands)	31
Argentina	22

PART II – Statutory Instruments

Place or country	Number of days
Armenia	21
Ascension Island	31
Australia	25
Austria	21
Azerbaijan	22
Azores	23
Bahamas	22
Bahrain	22
Balearic Islands	21
Bangladesh	23
Barbados	23
Belarus	21
Belgium	21
Belize	23
Benin	25
Bermuda	31
Bhutan	28
Bolivia	23
Bosnia and Herzegovina	21
Botswana	23
Brazil	22
British Virgin Islands	31
Brunei	25
Bulgaria	23
Burkina Faso	23
Burma	23
Burundi	22
Cambodia	28

Place or country	Number of days
Cameroon	22
Canada	22
Canary Islands	22
Cape Verde	25
Caroline Islands	31
Cayman Islands	31
Central African Republic	25
Chad	25
Chile	22
China	24
China (Hong Kong)	31
China (Macau)	31
China (Taiwan)	23
China (Tibet)	34
Christmas Island	27
Cocos (Keeling) Islands	41
Colombia	22
Comoros	23
Congo (formerly Congo Brazzaville or French Congo)	25
Congo (Democratic Republic)	25
Corsica	21
Costa Rica	23
Croatia	21
Cuba	24
Cyprus	31
Czech Republic	21
Denmark	21
Djibouti	22

PART II – Statutory Instruments

Place or country	Number of days
Dominica	23
Dominican Republic	23
East Timor	25
Ecuador	22
Egypt	22
El Salvador	25
Equatorial Guinea	23
Eritrea	22
Estonia	21
Ethiopia	22
Falkland Islands and Dependencies	31
Faroe Islands	31
Fiji	23
Finland	24
France	21
French Guyana	31
French Polynesia	31
French West Indies	31
Gabon	25
Gambia	22
Georgia	21
Germany	21
Ghana	22
Gibraltar	31
Greece	21
Greenland	31
Grenada	24
Guatemala	24

Place or country	Number of days
Guernsey	21
Guinea	22
Guinea-Bissau	22
Guyana	22
Haiti	23
Holland (Netherlands)	21
Honduras	24
Hungary	22
Iceland	22
India	23
Indonesia	22
Iran	22
Iraq	22
Ireland (Republic of)	21
Ireland (Northern)	21
Isle of Man	21
Israel	22
Italy	21
Ivory Coast	22
Jamaica	22
Japan	23
Jersey	21
Jordan	23
Kazakhstan	21
Kenya	22
Kiribati	23
Korea (North)	28
Korea (South)	24

PART II – Statutory Instruments

Place or country	Number of days
Kosovo	21
Kuwait	22
Kyrgyzstan	21
Laos	30
Latvia	21
Lebanon	22
Lesotho	23
Liberia	22
Libya	21
Liechtenstein	21
Lithuania	21
Luxembourg	21
Macedonia	21
Madagascar	23
Madeira	31
Malawi	23
Malaysia	24
Maldives	26
Mali	25
Malta	21
Mariana Islands	26
Marshall Islands	32
Mauritania	23
Mauritius	22
Mexico	23
Micronesia	23
Moldova	21
Monaco	21

Place or country	Number of days
Mongolia	24
Montenegro	21
Montserrat	31
Morocco	22
Mozambique	23
Namibia	23
Nauru	36
Nepal	23
Netherlands	21
Nevis	24
New Caledonia	31
New Zealand	26
New Zealand Island Territories	50
Nicaragua	24
Niger (Republic of)	25
Nigeria	22
Norfolk Island	31
Norway	21
Oman (Sultanate of)	22
Pakistan	23
Palau	23
Panama	26
Papua New Guinea	26
Paraguay	22
Peru	22
Philippines	23
Pitcairn, Henderson, Ducie and Oeno Islands	31
Poland	21

Place or country	Number of days
Portugal	21
Portuguese Timor	31
Puerto Rico	23
Qatar	23
Reunion	31
Romania	22
Russia	21
Rwanda	23
Sabah	23
St. Helena	31
St. Kitts and Nevis	24
St. Lucia	24
St. Pierre and Miquelon	31
St. Vincent and the Grenadines	24
Samoa (U.S.A. Territory) (See also Western Samoa)	30
San Marino	21
Sao Tome and Principe	25
Sarawak	28
Saudi Arabia	24
Scotland	21
Senegal	22
Serbia	21
Seychelles	22
Sierra Leone	22
Singapore	22
Slovakia	21
Slovenia	21
Society Islands (French Polynesia)	31

Place or country	Number of days
Solomon Islands	29
Somalia	22
South Africa	22
South Georgia (Falkland Island Dependencies)	31
South Orkneys	21
South Shetlands	21
Spain	21
Spanish Territories of North Africa	31
Sri Lanka	23
Sudan	22
Surinam	22
Swaziland	22
Sweden	21
Switzerland	21
Syria	23
Tajikistan	21
Tanzania	22
Thailand	23
Togo	22
Tonga	30
Trinidad and Tobago	23
Tristan Da Cunha	31
Tunisia	22
Turkey	21
Turkmenistan	21
Turks & Caicos Islands	31
Tuvalu	23
Uganda	22

PART II – Statutory Instruments

Place or country	Number of days
Ukraine	21
United Arab Emirates	22
United States of America	22
Uruguay	22
Uzbekistan	21
Vanuatu	29
Vatican City State	21
Venezuela	22
Vietnam	28
Virgin Islands – U.S.A	24
Wake Island	25
Western Samoa	34
Yemen (Republic of)	30
Zaire	25
Zambia	23
Zimbabwe	22

ANNEX – SERVICE REGULATION (RULE 6.44)

http://www.justice.gov.uk/civil/procrules_fin/contents/form_section_images/
practice_directions/pd6b_pdf_eps/pd6b_ecreg2007.pdf

Practice Direction 6C –
Disclosure of Addresses by Government Departments
13 February 1989 [as amended by Practice Direction
20 July 1995]

This Practice Direction supplements FPR Part 6

The arrangements set out in the Registrar's Direction of 26 April 1988 whereby the court may request the disclosure of addresses by government departments have been further extended. These arrangements will now cover:

(a)   tracing the address of a person in proceedings against whom another person is seeking to obtain or enforce an order for financial provision either for himself or herself or for the children of the former marriage; and, (*b*)   tracing the whereabouts of a child, or the person with whom the child is said to be, in proceedings under the Child Abduction and Custody Act 1985 or in which a [Part I order] is being sought or enforced.

Requests for such information will be made officially by the [district judge]. The request, in addition to giving the information mentioned below, should certify:

1 *In financial provision applications either*

(*a*)   that a financial provision order is in existence, but cannot be enforced because the person against whom the order has been made cannot be traced; or

(*b*)   that the applicant has filed or issued a notice, petition or originating summons containing an application for financial provision which cannot be served because the respondent cannot be traced.

[A "financial provision order" means any of the orders mentioned in s 21 of the Matrimonial Causes Act 1973, except an order under s 27(6) of that Act].

2 *In wardship proceedings* that the child is the subject of wardship proceedings and cannot be traced, and is believed to be with the person whose address is sought.

3 (*deleted*)

The following notes set out the information required by those departments which are likely to be of the greatest assistance to an applicant.

(1) Department of Social Security

The department most likely to be able to assist is the Department of Social Security, whose records are the most comprehensive and complete. The possibility of identifying one person amongst so many will depend on the particulars given. An address will not be supplied by the department unless it is satisfied from the particulars given that the record of the person has been reliably identified.

The applicant or his solicitor should therefore be asked to supply as much as possible of the following information about the person sought:

(i)   National Insurance number;

(ii)   surname;

(iii)   forenames in full;

(iv)   date of birth (or, if not known, approximate age);

(v)   last known address, with date when living there;

(vi)   any other known address(es) with dates;

(vii)   if the person sought is a war pensioner, his war pension and service particulars (if known);

and in applications for financial provision:

(viii) the exact date of the marriage and the wife's forenames.

Enquiries should be sent by the [district judge] to:

Contribution Agency
Special Section A, Room 101B
Longbenton
Newcastle upon Tyne
NE98 1YX

The department will be prepared to search if given full particulars of the person's name and date of birth, but the chances of accurate identification are increased by the provision of more identifying information.

Second requests for records to be searched, provided that a reasonable interval has elapsed, will be met by the Department of Social Security.

Income Support [/Supplementary Benefit]

Where, in the case of applications for financial provision, the wife is or has been in receipt of [income support/supplementary benefit], it would be advisable in the first instance to make enquiries of the manager of the local Social Security office for the area in which she resides in order to avoid possible duplication of enquiries.

(2) [Office for National Statistics]

National Health Service Central Register

[The Office for National Statistics] administers the National Health Service Central Register for the Department of Health. The records held in the Central Register include individuals' names, with dates of birth and National Health Service number, against a record of the Family Practitioner Committee area where the patient is currently registered with a National Health Service doctor. The Central Register does not hold individual patients' addresses, but can advise courts of the last Family Practitioner Committee area registration. Courts can then apply for information about addresses to the appropriate Family Practitioner Committee for independent action.

When application is made for the disclosure of Family Practitioner Committee area registrations from these records the applicant or his solicitor should supply as much as possible of the following information about the person sought:

(i)   National Health Service number;
(ii)   surname;
(iii) forenames in full;
(iv)   date of birth (or, if not known, approximate age);
(v)   last known address;
(vi)   mother's maiden name.

Enquiries should be sent by the [district judge] to:

[The Office for National Statistics]
National Health Service Central Register
Smedley Hydro, Trafalgar Road
Southport
Merseyside PR8 2HH

(3) **Passport Office**

If all reasonable enquiries, including the aforesaid methods, have failed to reveal an address, or if there are strong grounds for believing that the person sought may have made a recent application for a passport, enquiries may be made to the Passport Office. The applicant or his solicitor should provide as much of the following information about the person as possible:

(i)   surname;

(ii)   forenames in full;

(iii) date of birth (or, if not known, approximate age);

(iv)   place of birth;

(v)   occupation;

(vi)   whether known to have travelled abroad, and, if so, the destination and dates;

(vii) last known address, with date living there;

(viii) any other known address(es), with dates.

The applicant or his solicitor must also undertake in writing that information given in response to the enquiry will be used solely for the purpose for which it was requested, ie to assist in tracing the husband in connection with the making or enforcement of a financial provision order or in tracing a child in connection with a [Part 1 order] or wardship proceedings, as the case may be.

Enquiries should be sent to:

The Chief Passport Officer
[UK Passport Agency]
Home Office
Clive House, Petty France
London SW1H 9HD

(4) **Ministry of Defence**

In cases where the person sought is known to be serving or to have recently served in any branch of HM Forces, the solicitor representing the applicant may obtain the address for service of financial provision or [Part I] and wardship proceedings direct from the appropriate service department. In the case of army servicemen, the solicitor can obtain a list of regiments and of the various manning and record offices from the Officer in Charge, Central Manning Support Office, Higher Barracks, Exeter EC4 4ND.

The solicitor's request should be accompanied by a written undertaking that the address will be used for the purpose of service of process in those proceedings and that so far as is possible the solicitor will disclose the address only to the court and not to the applicant or any other person, except in the normal course of the proceedings.

Alternatively, if the solicitor wishes to serve process on the person's commanding officer under the provisions contained in s 101 of the Naval Act 1957, s 153 of the Army Act 1955 and s 153 of the Air Force Act 1955 (all of which as amended by s 62 of the Armed Forces Act 1971) he may obtain that officer's address in the same way.

PART II – Statutory Instruments

Where the applicant is acting in person the appropriate service department is prepared to disclose the address of the person sought, or that of his commanding officer, to a [district judge] on receipt of an assurance that the applicant has given an undertaking that the information will be used solely for the purpose of serving process in the proceedings.

In all cases, the request should include details of the person's full name, service number, rank or rating, and his ship, arm or trade, corps, regiment or unit or as much of this information as is available. The request should also include details of his date of birth, or, if not known, his age, his date of entry into the service and, if no longer serving, the date of discharge, and any other information, such as his last known address. Failure to quote the service number and the rank or rating may result in failure to identify the serviceman or at least in considerable delay.

Enquiries should be addressed as follows:

[(a)	Officers of Royal Navy and Women's Royal Naval Service	The Naval Secretary Room 161 Victory Building HM Naval Base Portsmouth Hants PO1 3LS
	Ratings in the Royal Navy WRNS Ratings QARNNS Ratings	Captain Naval Drafting Centurion Building Grange Road Gosport Hants PO13 9XA
	RN Medical and Dental Officers	The Medical Director General (Naval) Room 114 Victory Building HM Naval Base Portsmouth Hants PO1 3LS
	Naval Chaplains	Director General Naval Chaplaincy Service Room 201 Victory Building HM Naval Base Portsmouth Hants PO1 3LS
(b)	Royal Marine Officers	The Naval Secretary Room 161 Victory Building HM Naval Base Portsmouth Hants PO1 3LS

	Royal Marine Ranks	HQRM (DRORM) West Battery Whale Island Portsmouth Hants PO2 8DX
(*c*)	Army Officers (including WRAC and QARANC)	Army Officer Documentation Office Index Department Room F7 Government Buildings Stanmore Middlesex
	Other Ranks, Army	The Manning and Record Office which is appropriate to the Regiment or Corps
(*d*)	Royal Air Force Officers and Other Ranks Women's Royal Air Force Officers and Other Ranks (including PMRA FNS)	Ministry of Defence RAF Personnel Management 2b1(a) (RAF) Building 248 RAF Innsworth Gloucester GL3 1EZ]

General notes

Records held by other departments are less likely to be of use, either because of their limited scope or because individual records cannot readily be identified. If, however, the circumstances suggest that the address may be known to another department, application may be made to it by the [district judge], all relevant particulars available being given.

When the department is able to supply the address of the person sought to the [district judge], it will be passed on by him to the applicant's solicitor (or, in proper cases, direct to the applicant if acting in person) on an understanding to use it only for the purpose of the proceedings.

Nothing in this practice direction affects the service in matrimonial causes of petitions which do not contain any application for financial provision, etc. The existing arrangements whereby the Department of Social Security will at the request of the solicitor forward a letter by ordinary post to a party's last known address remain in force in such cases.

The Registrar's Direction of 26 April 1988 is hereby revoked.

Issued [in its original form] with the concurrence of the Lord Chancellor.

NOTES
Amendments. FPR PD6C.

****

PART 8
PROCEDURE FOR MISCELLANEOUS APPLICATIONS

Chapter 1
Procedure

8.1 Procedure

Subject to rules 8.13 and 8.24, applications to which this Part applies must be made in accordance with the Part 19 procedure.

****

Chapter 5
Declarations

8.18 Scope of this Chapter

The rules in this Chapter apply to applications made in accordance with –

(a)   section 55 of the 1986 Act (declarations as to marital status) and section 58 of the 2004 Act (declarations as to civil partnership status);
(b)   section 55A of the 1986 Act (declarations of parentage);
(c)   section 56(1)(b) and (2) of the 1986 Act (declarations of legitimacy or legitimation); and
(d)   section 57 of the 1986 Act (declaration as to adoptions effected overseas).

8.19 Where to start proceedings

The application may be made in the High Court or a county court and applications under section 55A of the 1986 Act may also be made in a magistrates' court.

8.20 Who the parties are

(1) In relation to the proceedings set out in column 1 of the following table, column 2 sets out who the respondents to those proceedings will be.

Proceedings	Respondent
Applications for declarations as to marital or civil partnership status.	The other party to the marriage or civil partnership in question or, where the applicant is a third party, both parties to the marriage or civil partnership.
Applications for declarations of parentage.	The person whose parentage is in issue or any person who is or is alleged to be the parent of the person whose parentage is in issue.

Proceedings	Respondent
Applications for declarations of legitimacy or legitimation.	The applicant's father and mother or the survivor of them.
Applications for declarations as to adoption effected overseas.	The person(s) whom the applicant is claiming are or are not the applicant's adoptive parents.

(2) The applicant must include in his application particulars of every person whose interest may be affected by the proceedings and his relationship to the applicant.

(3) The acknowledgment of service filed under rule 19.5 must give details of any other persons the respondent considers should be made a party to the application or be given notice of the application.

(4) Upon receipt of the acknowledgment of service, the court must give directions as to any other persons who should be made a respondent to the application or be given notice of the proceedings.

(5) A person given notice of proceedings under paragraph (4) may, within 21 days beginning with the date on which the notice was served, apply to be joined as a party.

(6) No directions may be given as to the future management of the case under rule 19.9 until the expiry of the notice period in paragraph (5).

8.21 The role of the Attorney General

(1) The applicant must, except in the case of an application for a declaration of parentage, send a copy of the application and all accompanying documents to the Attorney General at least one month before making the application.

(2) The Attorney General may, when deciding whether to intervene in the proceedings, inspect any document filed at court relating to any family proceedings mentioned in the declaration proceedings.

(3) If the court is notified that the Attorney General wishes to intervene in the proceedings, a court officer must send the Attorney General a copy of any subsequent documents filed at court.

(4) The court must, when giving directions under rule 8.20(4), consider whether to ask the Attorney General to argue any question relating to the proceedings.

(5) If the court makes a request to the Attorney General under paragraph (4) and the Attorney General agrees to that request, the Attorney General must serve a summary of the argument on all parties to the proceedings.

PART II – Statutory Instruments

8.22 Declarations of parentage

(1) If the applicant or the person whose parentage or parenthood is in issue, is known by a name other than that which appears in that person's birth certificate, that other name must also be stated in any order and declaration of parentage.

(2) A court officer must send a copy of a declaration of parentage and the application to the Registrar General within 21 days beginning with the date on which the declaration was made.

****

Chapter 9
Application for Consent to Marriage of a Child or to Registration of Civil
Partnership of a Child

8.41 Scope of this Chapter

The rules in this Chapter apply to an application under –

   (a)   section 3 of the Marriage Act 1949; or
   (b)   paragraph 3, 4 or 10 of Schedule 2 to the 2004 Act.

8.42 Child acting without a children's guardian

The child may bring an application without a children's guardian, unless the court directs otherwise.

8.43 Who the respondents are

Where an application follows a refusal to give consent to –

   (a)   the marriage of a child; or
   (b)   a child registering as the civil partner of another person,

every person who has refused consent will be a respondent to the application.

PART 9
APPLICATIONS FOR A FINANCIAL REMEDY

****

Chapter 3
Applications for Financial Remedies for Children

9.10 Application by parent, guardian etc for financial remedy in respect of children

(1) The following people may apply for a financial remedy in respect of a child –

   (a)   a parent, guardian or special guardian of any child of the family;

    (b)   any person in whose favour a residence order has been made with respect to a child of the family, and any applicant for such an order;

    (c)   any other person who is entitled to apply for a residence order with respect to a child;

    (d)   a local authority, where an order has been made under section 31(1)(a) of the 1989 Act placing a child in its care;

    (e)   the Official Solicitor, if appointed the children's guardian of a child of the family under rule 16.24; and

    (f)   a child of the family who has been given permission to apply for a financial remedy.

(2) In this rule 'residence order' has the meaning given to it by section 8(1) of the 1989 Act.

9.11 Children to be separately represented on certain applications

(1) Where an application for a financial remedy includes an application for an order for a variation of settlement, the court must, unless it is satisfied that the proposed variation does not adversely affect the rights or interests of any child concerned, direct that the child be separately represented on the application.

(2) On any other application for a financial remedy the court may direct that the child be separately represented on the application.

(3) Where a direction is made under paragraph (1) or (2), the court may if the person to be appointed so consents, appoint –

    (a)   a person other than the Official Solicitor; or

    (b)   the Official Solicitor,

to be a children's guardian and rule 16.24(5) and (6) and rules 16.25 to 16.28 apply as appropriate to such an appointment.

****

PART 12
PROCEEDINGS RELATING TO CHILDREN EXCEPT PARENTAL ORDER PROCEEDINGS AND PROCEEDINGS FOR APPLICATIONS IN ADOPTION, PLACEMENT AND RELATED PROCEEDINGS

Chapter 1
Interpretation and Application of this Part

12.1 Application of this Part

(1) The rules in this Part apply to –

    (a)   emergency proceedings;

    (b)   private law proceedings;

    (c)   public law proceedings;

PART II – Statutory Instruments

(d)   proceedings relating to the exercise of the court's inherent jurisdiction (other than applications for the court's permission to start such proceedings);

(e)   proceedings relating to child abduction and the recognition and enforcement of decisions relating to custody under the European Convention;

(f)   proceedings relating to the Council Regulation or the 1996 Hague Convention in respect of children; and

(g)   any other proceedings which may be referred to in a practice direction.

(Part 18 sets out the procedure for making an application for permission to bring proceedings.)

(Part 31 sets out the procedure for making applications for recognition and enforcement of judgments under the Council Regulation or the 1996 Hague Convention.)

(2)   The rules in Chapter 7 of this Part also apply to family proceedings which are not within paragraph (1) but which otherwise relate wholly or mainly to the maintenance or upbringing of a minor.

12.2 Interpretation

In this Part –

'the 2006 Act' means the Childcare Act 2006;

'advocate' means a person exercising a right of audience as a representative of, or on behalf of, a party;

'care proceedings' means proceedings for a care order under section 31(1)(a) of the 1989 Act;

'Case Management Order' means an order in the form referred to in Practice Direction 12A which may contain such of the provisions listed in that practice direction as may be appropriate to the proceedings;

'child assessment order' has the meaning assigned to it by section 43(2) of the 1989 Act;

'contact activity condition' has the meaning assigned to it by section 11C(2) of the 1989 Act;

'contact activity direction' has the meaning assigned to it by section 11A(3) of the 1989 Act;

'contribution order' has the meaning assigned to it by paragraph 23(2) of Schedule 2 to the 1989 Act;

'education supervision order' has the meaning assigned to it by section 36(2) of the 1989 Act;

'emergency proceedings' means proceedings for –

(a)   the disclosure of information as to the whereabouts of a child under section 33 of the 1986 Act;

(b)   an order authorising the taking charge of and delivery of a child under section 34 of the 1986 Act;

(c)   an emergency protection order;

(d) an order under section 44(9)(b) of the 1989 Act varying a direction in an emergency protection order given under section 44(6) of that Act;

(e) an order under section 45(5) of the 1989 Act extending the period during which an emergency protection order is to have effect;

(f) an order under section 45(8) of the 1989 Act discharging an emergency protection order;

(g) an order under section 45(8A) of the 1989 Act varying or discharging an emergency protection order in so far as it imposes an exclusion requirement on a person who is not entitled to apply for the order to be discharged;

(h) an order under section 45(8B) of the 1989 Act varying or discharging an emergency protection order in so far as it confers a power of arrest attached to an exclusion requirement;

(i) warrants under sections 48(9) and 102(1) of the 1989 Act and under section 79 of the 2006 Act; or

(j) a recovery order under section 50 of the 1989 Act;

'emergency protection order' means an order under section 44 of the 1989 Act;

'enforcement order' has the meaning assigned to it by section 11J(2) of the 1989 Act;

'financial compensation order' means an order made under section 11O(2) of the 1989 Act;

'interim order' means an interim care order or an interim supervision order referred to in section 38(1) of the 1989 Act;

'private law proceedings' means proceedings for –

(a) a section 8 order except a residence order under section 8 of the 1989 Act relating to a child who is the subject of a care order;

(b) a parental responsibility order under sections 4(1)(c), 4ZA(1)(c) or 4A(1)(b) of the 1989 Act or an order terminating parental responsibility under sections 4(2A), 4ZA(5) or 4A(3) of that Act;

(c) an order appointing a child's guardian under section 5(1) of the 1989 Act or an order terminating the appointment under section 6(7) of that Act;

(d) an order giving permission to change a child's surname or remove a child from the United Kingdom under sections 13(1) or 14C(3) of the 1989 Act;

(e) a special guardianship order except where that order relates to a child who is subject of a care order;

(f) an order varying or discharging such an order under section 14D of the 1989 Act;

(g) an enforcement order;

(h) a financial compensation order;

(i) an order under paragraph 9 of Schedule A1 to the 1989 Act following a breach of an enforcement order;

(j) an order under Part 2 of Schedule A1 to the 1989 Act revoking or amending an enforcement order; or

(k)   an order that a warning notice be attached to a contact order;

'public law proceedings' means proceedings for –

(a)   a residence order under section 8 of the 1989 Act relating to a child who is the subject of a care order;

(b)   a special guardianship order relating to a child who is the subject of a care order;

(c)   a secure accommodation order under section 25 of the 1989 Act;

(d)   a care order, or the discharge of such an order under section 39(1) of the 1989 Act;

(e)   an order giving permission to change a child's surname or remove a child from the United Kingdom under section 33(7) of the 1989 Act;

(f)   a supervision order under section 31(1)(b) of the 1989 Act, the discharge or variation of such an order under section 39(2) of that Act, or the extension or further extension of such an order under paragraph 6(3) of Schedule 3 to that Act;

(g)   an order making provision regarding contact under section 34(2) to (4) of the 1989 Act or an order varying or discharging such an order under section 34(9) of that Act;

(h)   an education supervision order, the extension of an education supervision order under paragraph 15(2) of Schedule 3 to the 1989 Act, or the discharge of such an order under paragraph 17(1) of Schedule 3 to that Act;

(i)   an order varying directions made with an interim care order or interim supervision order under section 38(8)(b) of the 1989 Act;

(j)   an order under section 39(3) of the 1989 Act varying a supervision order in so far as it affects a person with whom the child is living but who is not entitled to apply for the order to be discharged;

(k)   an order under section 39(3A) of the 1989 Act varying or discharging an interim care order in so far as it imposes an exclusion requirement on a person who is not entitled to apply for the order to be discharged;

(l)   an order under section 39(3B) of the 1989 Act varying or discharging an interim care order in so far as it confers a power of arrest attached to an exclusion requirement;

(m)   the substitution of a supervision order for a care order under section 39(4) of the 1989 Act;

(n)   a child assessment order, or the variation or discharge of such an order under section 43(12) of the 1989 Act;

(o)   an order permitting the local authority to arrange for any child in its care to live outside England and Wales under paragraph 19(1) of Schedule 2 to the 1989 Act;

(p)   a contribution order, or revocation of such an order under paragraph 23(8) of Schedule 2 to the 1989 Act;

(q)   an appeal under paragraph 8(1) of Schedule 8 to the 1989 Act;

'special guardianship order' has the meaning assigned to it by section 14A(1) of the 1989 Act;

'supervision order' has the meaning assigned to it by section 31(11) of the 1989 Act;

'supervision proceedings' means proceedings for a supervision order under section 31(1)(b) of the 1989 Act;

'warning notice' means a notice attached to an order pursuant to section 8(2) of the Children and Adoption Act 2006.

(The 1980 Hague Convention, the 1996 Hague Convention, the Council Regulation, and the European Convention are defined in rule 2.3.)

Chapter 2
General Rules

12.3 Who the parties are

(1) In relation to the proceedings set out in column 1 of the following table, column 2 sets out who may make the application and column 3 sets out who the respondents to those proceedings will be.

Proceedings for	*Applicants*	*Respondents*
A parental responsibility order (section 4(1)(c), 4ZA(1)(c), or section 4A(1)(b) of the 1989 Act).	The child's father; the step parent; or the child's parent (being a woman who is a parent by virtue of section 43 of the Human Fertilisation and Embryology Act 2008 and who is not a person to whom section 1(3) of the Family Law Reform Act 1987 applies) (sections 4(1)(c), 4ZA(1)(c) and 4A(1)(b) of the 1989 Act).	Every person whom the applicant believes to have parental responsibility for the child; where the child is the subject of a care order, every person whom the applicant believes to have had parental responsibility immediately prior to the making of the care order; in the case of an application to extend, vary or discharge an order, the parties to the proceedings leading to the order which it is sought to have extended, varied or discharged; in the case of specified proceedings, the child.

PART II – Statutory Instruments

Proceedings for	Applicants	Respondents
An order terminating a parental responsibility order or agreement (section 4(2A), 4ZA(5) or section 4A(3) of the 1989 Act).	Any person who has parental responsibility for the child; or with the court's permission, the child (section 4(3), 4ZA(6) and section 4A(3) of the 1989 Act).	As above.
An order appointing a guardian (section 5(1) of the 1989 Act).	An individual who wishes to be appointed as guardian (section 5(1) of the 1989 Act).	As above.
An order terminating the appointment of a guardian (section 6(7) of the 1989 Act).	Any person who has parental responsibility for the child; or with the court's permission, the child (section 6(7) of the 1989 Act).	As above.
A section 8 order.	Any person who is entitled to apply for a section 8 order with respect to the child (section 10(4) to (7) of the 1989 Act); or with the court's permission, any person (section 10(2)(b) of the 1989 Act).	As above.
An enforcement order (section 11J of the 1989 Act).	A person who is, for the purposes of the contact order, a person with whom the child concerned lives or is to live; any person whose contact with the child concerned is provided for in the contact order;	The person the applicant alleges has failed to comply with the contact order.

Proceedings for	Applicants	Respondents
	any individual subject to a condition under section 11(7)(b) of the 1989 Act or a contact activity condition imposed by a contact order; or with the court's permission, the child (section 11J(5) of the 1989 Act).	
A financial compensation order (section 11O of the 1989 Act).	Any person who is, for the purposes of the contact order, a person with whom the child concerned lives or is to live; any person whose contact with the child concerned is provided for in the contact order; any individual subject to a condition under section 11(7)(b) of the 1989 Act or a contact activity condition imposed by a contact order; or with the court's permission, the child (section 11O(6) of the 1989 Act).	The person the applicant alleges has failed to comply with the contact order.
An order permitting the child's name to be changed or the removal of the child from the United Kingdom (section 13(1), 14C(3) or 33(7) of the 1989 Act).	Any person (section 13(1), 14C(3), 33(7) of the 1989 Act).	As for a parental responsibility order.

Proceedings for	Applicants	Respondents
A special guardianship order (section 14A of the 1989 Act).	Any guardian of the child; any individual in whose favour a residence order is in force with respect to the child; any individual listed in subsection (5)(b) or (c) of section 10 (as read with subsection (10) of that section) of the 1989 Act; a local authority foster parent with whom the child has lived for a period of at least one year immediately preceding the application; or any person with the court's permission (section 14A(3) of the 1989 Act) (more than one such individual can apply jointly (section 14A(3) and (5) of that Act)).	As above, and if a care order is in force with respect to the child, the child.
Variation or discharge of a special guardianship order (section 14D of the 1989 Act).	The special guardian (or any of them, if there is more than one); any individual in whose favour a residence order is in force with respect to the child; the local authority designated in a care order with respect to the child;	As above.

Proceedings for	Applicants	Respondents
	any individual within section 14D(1)(d) of the 1989 Act who has parental responsibility for the child; the child, any parent or guardian of the child and any step-parent of the child who has acquired, and has not lost, parental responsibility by virtue of section 4A of that Act with the court's permission; or any individual within section 14D(1)(d) of that Act who immediately before the making of the special guardianship order had, but no longer has, parental responsibility for the child with the court's permission.	

Proceedings for	Applicants	Respondents
A secure accommodation order (section 25 of the 1989 Act).	The local authority which is looking after the child; or the Health Authority, Primary Care Trust, National Health Service Trust established under section 25 of the National Health Service Act 2006 or section 18(1) of the National Health Service (Wales) Act 2006, National Health Service Foundation Trust or any local authority providing accommodation for the child (unless the child is looked after by a local authority).	As above.
A care or supervision order (section 31 of the 1989 Act).	Any local authority; the National Society for the Prevention of Cruelty to Children and any of its officers (section 31(1) of the 1989 Act); or any authorised person.	As above.
An order varying directions made with an interim care or interim supervision order (section 38(8)(b) of the 1989 Act).	The parties to proceedings in which directions are given under section 38(6) of the 1989 Act; or any person named in such a direction.	As above.

Proceedings for	Applicants	Respondents
An order discharging a care order (section 39(1) of the 1989 Act).	Any person who has parental responsibility for the child; the child; or the local authority designated by the order (section 39(1) of the 1989 Act).	As above.
An order varying or discharging an interim care order in so far as it imposes an exclusion requirement (section 39(3A) of the 1989 Act).	A person to whom the exclusion requirement in the interim care order applies who is not entitled to apply for the order to be discharged (section 39(3A) of the 1989 Act).	As above.
An order varying or discharging an interim care order in so far as it confers a power of arrest attached to an exclusion requirement (section 39(3B) of the 1989 Act).	Any person entitled to apply for the discharge of the interim care order in so far as it imposes the exclusion requirement (section 39(3B) of the 1989 Act).	As above.
An order substituting a supervision order for a care order (section 39(4) of the 1989 Act).	Any person entitled to apply for a care order to be discharged under section 39(1) (section 39(4) of the 1989 Act).	As above.
A child assessment order (section 43(1) of the 1989 Act).	Any local authority; the National Society for the Prevention of Cruelty to Children and any of its officers; or	As above.

Proceedings for	Applicants	Respondents
	any person authorised by order of the Secretary of State to bring the proceedings and any officer of a body who is so authorised (section 43(1) and (13) of the 1989 Act).	
An order varying or discharging a child assessment order (section 43(12) of the 1989 Act).	The applicant for an order that has been made under section 43(1) of the 1989 Act; or the persons referred to in section 43(11) of the 1989 Act (section 43(12) of that Act).	As above.
An emergency protection order (section 44(1) of the 1989 Act).	Any person (section 44(1) of the 1989 Act).	As for a parental responsibility order.
An order extending the period during which an emergency protection order is to have effect (section 45(4) of the 1989 Act).	Any person who – has parental responsibility for a child as the result of an emergency protection order; and is entitled to apply for a care order with respect to the child (section 45(4) of the 1989 Act).	As above.
An order discharging an emergency protection order (section 45(8) of the 1989 Act).	The child; a parent of the child; any person who is not a parent of the child but who has parental responsibility for the child; or	As above.

Proceedings for	Applicants	Respondents
	any person with whom the child was living before the making of the emergency protection order (section 45(8) of the 1989 Act).	
An order varying or discharging an emergency protection order in so far as it imposes the exclusion requirement (section 45(8A) of the 1989 Act).	A person to whom the exclusion requirement in the emergency protection order applies who is not entitled to apply for the emergency protection order to be discharged (section 45(8A) of the 1989 Act).	As above.
An order varying or discharging an emergency protection order in so far as it confers a power of arrest attached to an exclusion requirement (section 45(8B) of the 1989 Act).	Any person entitled to apply for the discharge of the emergency protection order in so far as it imposes the exclusion requirement (section 45(8B) of the 1989 Act).	As above.
An emergency protection order by the police (section 46(7) of the 1989 Act).	The officer designated officer for the purposes of section 46(3)(e) of the 1989 Act (section 46(7) of the 1989 Act).	As above.

Proceedings for	Applicants	Respondents
A warrant authorising a constable to assist in exercise of certain powers to search for children and inspect premises (section 48 of the 1989 Act).	Any person attempting to exercise powers under an emergency protection order who has been or is likely to be prevented from doing so by being refused entry to the premises concerned or refused access to the child concerned (section 48(9) of the 1989 Act).	As above.
A warrant authorising a constable to assist in exercise of certain powers to search for children and inspect premises (section 102 of the 1989 Act).	Any person attempting to exercise powers under the enactments mentioned in section 102(6) of the 1989 Act who has been or is likely to be prevented from doing so by being refused entry to the premises concerned or refused access to the child concerned (section 102(1) of that Act).	As above.
An order revoking an enforcement order (paragraph 4 of Schedule A1 to the 1989 Act).	The person subject to the enforcement order.	The person who was the applicant for the enforcement order; and where the child was a party to the proceedings in which the enforcement order was made, the child.

Proceedings for	Applicants	Respondents
An order amending an enforcement order (paragraphs 5 to 7 of Schedule A1 to the 1989 Act).	The person subject to the enforcement order.	The person who was the applicant for the enforcement order. (Rule 12.33 makes provision about applications under paragraph 5 of Schedule A1 to the 1989 Act.)
An order following breach of an enforcement order (paragraph 9 of Schedule A1 to the 1989 Act).	Any person who is, for the purposes of the contact order, the person with whom the child lives or is to live; any person whose contact with the child concerned is provided for in the contact order; any individual subject to a condition under section 11(7)(b) of the 1989 Act or a contact activity condition imposed by a contact order; or with the court's permission, the child (paragraph 9 of Schedule A1 to the 1989 Act).	The person the applicant alleges has failed to comply with the unpaid work requirement imposed by an enforcement order; and where the child was a party to the proceedings in which the enforcement order was made, the child.
An order permitting the local authority to arrange for any child in its care to live outside England and Wales (Schedule 2, paragraph 19(1), to the 1989 Act).	The local authority (Schedule 2, paragraph 19(1), to the 1989 Act).	As for a parental responsibility order.
A contribution order (Schedule 2, paragraph 23(1), to the 1989 Act).	The local authority (Schedule 2, paragraph 23(1), to the 1989 Act).	As above and the contributor.

Proceedings for	Applicants	Respondents
An order revoking a contribution order (Schedule 2, paragraph 23(8), to the 1989 Act).	The contributor; or the local authority.	As above.
An order relating to contact with the child in care and any named person (section 34(2) of the 1989 Act) or permitting the local authority to refuse contact (section 34(4) of that Act).	The local authority; or the child (section 34(2) or 34(4) of the 1989 Act).	As above; and the person whose contact with the child is the subject of the application.
An order relating to contact with the child in care (section 34(3) of the 1989 Act).	The child's parents; any guardian or special guardian of the child; any person who by virtue of section 4A of the 1989 Act has parental responsibility for the child; a person in whose favour there was a residence order in force with respect to the child immediately before the care order was made; a person who by virtue of an order made in the exercise of the High Court's inherent jurisdiction with respect to children had care of the child immediately before the care order was made (section 34(3)(a) of the 1989 Act); or	As above; and the person whose contact with the child is the subject of the application.

Proceedings for	Applicants	Respondents
	with the court's permission, any person (section 34(3)(b) of that Act).	
An order varying or discharging an order for contact with a child in care under section 34 (section 34((9) of the 1989 Act).	The local authority; the child; or any person named in the order (section 34(9) of the 1989 Act).	As above; and the person whose contact with the child is the subject of the application.
An education supervision order (section 36 of the 1989 Act).	Any local authority (section 36(1) of the 1989 Act).	As above; and the child.
An order varying or discharging a supervision order (section 39(2) of the 1989 Act).	Any person who has parental responsibility for the child; the child; or the supervisor (section 39(2) of the 1989 Act).	As above; and the supervisor.
An order varying a supervision order in so far as it affects the person with whom the child is living (section 39(3) of the 1989 Act).	The person with whom the child is living who is not entitled to apply for the order to be discharged (section 39(3) of the 1989 Act).	As above; and the supervisor.
An order varying a direction under section 44(6) of the 1989 Act in an emergency protection order (section 44(9)(b) of that Act).	The parties to the application for the emergency protection order in respect of which it is sought to vary the directions; the children's guardian; the local authority in whose area the child is ordinarily resident; or any person who is named in the directions.	As above, and the parties to the application for the order in respect of which it is sought to vary the directions; any person who was caring for the child prior to the making of the order; and any person whose contact with the child is affected by the direction which it is sought to have varied.

PART II – Statutory Instruments

Proceedings for	Applicants	Respondents
A recovery order (section 50 of the 1989 Act).	Any person who has parental responsibility for the child by virtue of a care order or an emergency protection order; or where the child is in police protection the officer designated for the purposes of section 46(3)(e) of the 1989 Act (section 50(4) of the 1989 Act).	As above; and the person whom the applicant alleges to have effected or to have been or to be responsible for the taking or keeping of the child.
An order discharging an education supervision order (Schedule 3, paragraph 17(1), to the 1989 Act).	The child concerned; a parent of the child; or the local authority concerned (Schedule 3, paragraph 17(1), to the 1989 Act).	As above; and the local authority concerned; and the child.
An order extending an education supervision order (Schedule 3, paragraph 15(2), to the 1989 Act).	The local authority in whose favour the education supervision order was made (Schedule 3, paragraph 15(2), to the 1989 Act).	As above; and the child.
An appeal under paragraph (8) of Schedule 8 to the 1989 Act.	A person aggrieved by the matters listed in paragraph 8(1) of Schedule 8 to the 1989 Act.	The appropriate local authority.
An order for the disclosure of information as to the whereabouts of a child under section 33 of the 1986 Act.	Any person with a legitimate interest in proceedings for an order under Part 1 of the 1986 Act; or	Any person alleged to have information as to the whereabouts of the child.

Proceedings for	Applicants	Respondents
	a person who has registered an order made elsewhere in the United Kingdom or a specified dependent territory.	
An order authorising the taking charge of and delivery of a child under section 34 of the 1986 Act.	The person to whom the child is to be given up under section 34(1) of the 1986 Act.	As above; and the person who is required to give up the child in accordance with section 34(1) of the 1986 Act.
An order relating to the exercise of the court's inherent jurisdiction (including wardship proceedings).	A local authority (with the court's permission); any person with a genuine interest in or relation to the child; or the child (wardship proceedings only).	The parent or guardian of the child; any other person who has an interest in or relationship to the child; and the child (wardship proceedings only and with the court's permission as described at rule 12.37).
A warrant under section 79 of the 2006 Act authorising any constable to assist Her Majesty's Chief Inspector for Education, Children's Services and Skills in the exercise of powers conferred on him by section 77 of the 2006 Act.	Her Majesty's Chief Inspector for Education, Children's Services and Skills.	Any person preventing or likely to prevent Her Majesty's Chief Inspector for Education, Children's Services and Skills from exercising powers conferred on him by section 77 of the 2006 Act.

PART II – Statutory Instruments

Proceedings for	Applicants	Respondents
An order in respect of a child under the 1980 Hague Convention.	Any person, institution or body who claims that a child has been removed or retained in breach of rights of custody or claims that there has been a breach of rights of access in relation to the child.	The person alleged to have brought the child into the United Kingdom; the person with whom the child is alleged to be; any parent or guardian of the child who is within the United Kingdom and is not otherwise a party; any person in whose favour a decision relating to custody has been made if that person is not otherwise a party; and any other person who appears to the court to have sufficient interest in the welfare of the child.
An order concerning the recognition and enforcement of decisions relating to custody under the European Convention.	Any person who has a court order giving that person rights of custody in relation to the child.	As above.
An application for the High Court to request transfer of jurisdiction under Article 15 of the Council Regulation or Article 9 of the 1996 Hague Convention (rule 12.65).	Any person with sufficient interest in the welfare of the child and who would be entitled to make a proposed application in relation to that child, or who intends to seek the permission of the court to make such application if the transfer is agreed.	As directed by the court in accordance with rule 12.65.

Proceedings for	Applicants	Respondents
An application under rule 12.71 for a declaration as to the existence, or extent, of parental responsibility under Article 16 of the 1996 Convention.	Any interested person including a person who holds, or claims to hold, parental responsibility for the child under the law of another State which subsists in accordance with Article 16 of the 1996 Hague Convention following the child becoming habitually resident in a territorial unit of the United Kingdom	Every person whom the applicant believes to have parental responsibility for the child; any person whom the applicant believes to hold parental responsibility for the child under the law of another State which subsists in accordance with Article 16 of the 1996 Hague Convention following the child becoming habitually resident in a territorial unit of the United Kingdom; and where the child is the subject of a care order, every person whom the applicant believes to have had parental responsibility immediately prior to the making of the care order
A warning notice.	The person who is, for the purposes of the contact order, the person with whom the child concerned lives or is to live; the person whose contact with the child concerned is provided for in the contact order;	Any person who was a party to the proceedings in which the contact order was made. (Rule 12.33 makes provision about applications for warning notices).

PART II – Statutory Instruments

Proceedings for	Applicants	Respondents
	any individual subject to a condition under section 11(7)(b) of the 1989 Act or a contact activity condition imposed by the contact order; or with the court's permission, the child.	

(2) The court will direct that a person with parental responsibility be made a party to proceedings where that person requests to be one.

(3) Subject to rule 16.2, the court may at any time direct that –

(a)   any person or body be made a party to proceedings; or

(b)   a party be removed.

(4) If the court makes a direction for the addition or removal of a party under this rule, it may give consequential directions about –

(a)   the service of a copy of the application form or other relevant documents on the new party;

(b)   the management of the proceedings.

(5) In this rule –

'a local authority foster parent' has the meaning assigned to it by section 23(3) of the 1989 Act; and

'care home', 'independent hospital', 'local authority' and 'Primary Care Trust' have the meanings assigned to them by section 105 of the 1989 Act.

(Part 16 contains the rules relating to the representation of children.)

12.4   Notice of proceedings to person with foreign parental responsibility

(1) This rule applies where a child is subject to proceedings to which this Part applies and –

(a)   a person holds or is believed to hold parental responsibility for the child under the law of another State which subsists in accordance with Article 16 of the 1996 Hague Convention following the child becoming habitually resident in a territorial unit of the United Kingdom; and

(b)   that person is not otherwise required to be joined as a respondent under rule 12.3.

(2) The applicant shall give notice of the proceedings to any person to whom the applicant believes paragraph (1) applies in any case in which a person whom the applicant believed to have parental responsibility under the 1989 Act would be a respondent to those proceedings in accordance with rule 12.3.

(3) The applicant and every respondent to the proceedings shall provide such details as they possess as to the identity and whereabouts of any person they believe to hold parental responsibility for the child in accordance with paragraph (1) to the court officer, upon making, or responding to the application as appropriate.

(4) Where the existence of a person who is believed to have parental responsibility for the child in accordance with paragraph (1) only becomes apparent to a party at a later date during the proceedings, that party must notify the court officer of those details at the earliest opportunity.

(5) Where a person to whom paragraph (1) applies receives notice of proceedings, that person may apply to the court to be joined as a party using the Part 18 procedure.

12.5 What the court will do when the application has been issued

When the proceedings have been issued the court will consider –

    (a)   setting a date for –
        (i)   a directions appointment;
        (ii)   in private law proceedings, a First Hearing Dispute Resolution Appointment;
        (iii)   in care and supervision proceedings and in so far as practicable other public law proceedings, the First Appointment; or
        (iv)   the hearing of the application or an application for an interim order,
        and if the court sets a date it will do so in accordance with rule 12.13 and Practice Directions 12A and 12B;
    (b)   giving any of the directions listed in rule 12.12 or, where Chapter 6, section 1 applies, rule 12.48; and
    (c)   doing anything else which is set out in Practice Directions 12A or 12B or any other practice direction.

(Practice Directions 12A and 12B supplementing this Part set out details relating to the First Hearing Dispute Resolution Appointment and the First Appointment.)

12.6 Children's guardian, solicitor and reports under section 7 of the 1989 Act

As soon as practicable after the issue of proceedings or the transfer of the proceedings to the court, the court will –

    (a)   in specified proceedings, appoint a children's guardian under rule 16.3(1) unless –
        (i)   such an appointment has already been made by the court which made the transfer and is subsisting; or
        (ii)   the court considers that such an appointment is not necessary to safeguard the interests of the child;
    (b)   where section 41(3) of the 1989 Act applies, consider whether a solicitor should be appointed to represent the child, and if so, appoint a solicitor accordingly;

PART II – Statutory Instruments

(c)   consider whether to ask an officer of the service or a Welsh family proceedings officer for advice relating to the welfare of the child;

(d)   consider whether a report relating to the welfare of the child is required, and if so, request such a report in accordance with section 7 of the 1989 Act.

(Part 16 sets out the rules relating to representation of children.)

12.7 What a court officer will do

(1) As soon as practicable after the issue of proceedings the court officer will return to the applicant the copies of the application together with the forms referred to in Practice Direction 5A.

(2) As soon as practicable after the issue of proceedings or the transfer of proceedings to the court or at any other stage in the proceedings the court officer will –

(a)   give notice of any hearing set by the court to the applicant; and

(b)   do anything else set out in Practice Directions 12A or 12B or any other practice direction.

12.8 Service of the application

The applicant will serve –

(a)   the application together with the documents referred to in Practice Direction 12C on the persons referred to and within the time specified in that Practice Direction; and

(b)   notice of any hearing set by the court on the persons referred to in Practice Direction 12C at the same time as serving the application.

12.9 Request for transfer from magistrates' court to county court or to another magistrates' court

(1) In accordance with the Allocation Order, a magistrates' court may order proceedings before the court (or any part of them) to be transferred to another magistrates' court or to a county court.

(2) Where any request to transfer proceedings to another magistrates' court or to a county court is refused, the court officer will send a copy of the written record of the reasons for refusing the transfer to the parties.

12.10 Procedure following refusal of magistrates' court to order transfer

(1) Where a request under rule 12.9 to transfer proceedings to a county court in accordance with the provisions of the Allocation Order is refused, a party to the proceedings may apply to a county court for an order transferring proceedings from the magistrates' court.

(2) Such an application must be made in accordance with Part 18 and the Allocation Order.

12.11 Transfer of proceedings from one court to another court

Where proceedings are transferred from one court to another court in accordance with the provisions of the Allocation Order, the court officer from the transferring court will notify the parties of any order transferring the proceedings.

12.12 Directions

(1) This rule does not apply to proceedings under Chapter 6 of this Part.

(2) At any stage in the proceedings, the court may give directions about the conduct of the proceedings including –

- (a) the management of the case;
- (b) the timetable for steps to be taken between the giving of directions and the final hearing;
- (c) the joining of a child or other person as a party to the proceedings in accordance with rules 12.3(2) and (3);
- (d) the attendance of the child;
- (e) the appointment of a children's guardian or of a solicitor under section 41(3) of the 1989 Act;
- (f) the appointment of a litigation friend;
- (g) the service of documents;
- (h) the filing of evidence including experts' reports; and
- (i) the exercise by an officer of the Service, Welsh family proceedings officer or local authority officer of any duty referred to in rule 16.38(1).

(3) Paragraph (4) applies where –

- (a) an officer of the Service or a Welsh family proceedings officer has filed a report or a risk assessment as a result of exercising a duty referred to in rule 16.38(1)(a); or
- (b) a local authority officer has filed a report as a result of exercising a duty referred to in rule 16.38(1)(b).

(4) The court may –

- (a) give directions setting a date for a hearing at which that report or risk assessment will be considered; and
- (b) direct that the officer who prepared the report or risk assessment attend any such hearing.

(5) The court may exercise the powers in paragraphs (2) and (4) on an application or of its own initiative.

(6) Where the court proposes to exercise its powers of its own initiative the procedure set out in rule 4.3(2) to (6) applies.

(7) Directions of a court which are still in force immediately prior to the transfer of proceedings to another court will continue to apply following the transfer subject to –

PART II – Statutory Instruments

(a)   any changes of terminology which are required to apply those directions to the court to which the proceedings are transferred; and

(b)   any variation or revocation of the direction.

(8) The court or court officer will –

(a)   take a note of the giving, variation or revocation of a direction under this rule; and

(b)   as soon as practicable serve a copy of the note on every party.

(Rule 12.48 provides for directions in proceedings under the 1980 Hague Convention and the European Convention.)

12.13 Setting dates for hearings and setting or confirming the timetable and date for the final hearing

(1) At the –

(a)   transfer to a court of proceedings;

(b)   postponement or adjournment of any hearing; or

(c)   conclusion of any hearing at which the proceedings are not finally determined,

the court will set a date for the proceedings to come before the court again for the purposes of giving directions or for such other purposes as the court directs.

(2) At any hearing the court may –

(a)   confirm a date for the final hearing or the week within which the final hearing is to begin (where a date or period for the final hearing has already been set);

(b)   set a timetable for the final hearing unless a timetable has already been fixed, or the court considers that it would be inappropriate to do so; or

(c)   set a date for the final hearing or a period within which the final hearing of the application is to take place.

(3) The court officer will notify the parties of –

(a)   the date of a hearing fixed in accordance with paragraph (1);

(b)   the timetable for the final hearing; and

(c)   the date of the final hearing or the period in which it will take place.

(4) Where the date referred to in paragraph (1) is set at the transfer of proceedings, the date will be as soon as possible after the transfer.

(5) The requirement in paragraph (1) to set a date for the proceedings to come before the court again is satisfied by the court setting or confirming a date for the final hearing.

12.14 Attendance at hearings

(1) This rule does not apply to proceedings under Chapter 6 of this Part except for proceedings for a declaration under rule 12.71.

(2) Unless the court directs otherwise and subject to paragraph (3), the persons who must attend a hearing are –

- (a) any party to the proceedings;
- (b) any litigation friend for any party or legal representative instructed to act on that party's behalf; and
- (c) any other person directed by the court or required by Practice Directions 12A or 12B or any other practice direction to attend.

(3) Proceedings or any part of them will take place in the absence of a child who is a party to the proceedings if –

- (a) the court considers it in the interests of the child, having regard to the matters to be discussed or the evidence likely to be given; and
- (b) the child is represented by a children's guardian or solicitor.

(4) When considering the interests of the child under paragraph (3) the court will give –

- (a) the children's guardian;
- (b) the solicitor for the child; and
- (c) the child, if of sufficient understanding,

an opportunity to make representations.

(5) Subject to paragraph (6), where at the time and place appointed for a hearing, the applicant appears but one or more of the respondents do not, the court may proceed with the hearing.

(6) The court will not begin to hear an application in the absence of a respondent unless the court is satisfied that –

- (a) the respondent received reasonable notice of the date of the hearing; or
- (b) the circumstances of the case justify proceeding with the hearing.

(7) Where, at the time and place appointed for a hearing one or more of the respondents appear but the applicant does not, the court may –

- (a) refuse the application; or
- (b) if sufficient evidence has previously been received, proceed in the absence of the applicant.

(8) Where at the time and place appointed for a hearing neither the applicant nor any respondent appears, the court may refuse the application.

(9) Paragraphs (5) to (8) do not apply to a hearing where the court –

- (a) is considering –
  - (i) whether to make a contact activity direction or to attach a contact activity condition to a contact order; or
  - (ii) an application for a financial compensation order, an enforcement order or an order under paragraph 9 of Schedule A1 to the 1989 Act following a breach of an enforcement order; and

(b)   has yet to obtain sufficient evidence from, or in relation to, the person who may be the subject of the direction, condition or order to enable it to determine the matter.

(10) Nothing in this rule affects the provisions of Article 18 of the Council Regulation in cases to which that provision applies.

(The Council Regulation makes provision in Article 18 for the court to stay proceedings where the respondent is habitually resident in another Member State of the European Union and has not been adequately served with the proceedings as required by that provision.)

12.15 Steps taken by the parties

If –

(a)   the parties or any children's guardian agree proposals for the management of the proceedings (including a proposed date for the final hearing or a period within which the final hearing is to take place); and

(b)   the court considers that the proposals are suitable,

it may approve them without a hearing and give directions in the terms proposed.

12.16 Applications without notice

(1) This rule applies to –

(a)   proceedings for a section 8 order;

(b)   emergency proceedings; and

(c)   proceedings relating to the exercise of the court's inherent jurisdiction (other than an application for the court's permission to start such proceedings and proceedings for collection, location and passport orders where Chapter 6 applies).

(2) An application in proceedings referred to in paragraph (1) may, in the High Court or a county court, be made without notice in which case the applicant must file the application –

(a)   where the application is made by telephone, the next business day after the making of the application; or

(b)   in any other case, at the time when the application is made.

(3) An application in proceedings referred to in paragraph (1)(a) or (b) may, in a magistrates' court, be made with the permission of the court, without notice, in which case the applicant must file the application at the time when the application is made or as directed by the court.

(4) Where –

(a)   a section 8 order;

(b)   an emergency protection order;

(c)   an order for the disclosure of information as to the whereabouts of a child under section 33 of the 1986 Act; or

(d)   an order authorising the taking charge of and delivery of a child under section 34 of the 1986 Act,

is made without notice, the applicant must serve a copy of the application on each respondent within 48 hours after the order is made.

(5) Within 48 hours after the making of an order without notice, the applicant must serve a copy of the order on –

(a)   the parties, unless the court directs otherwise;

(b)   any person who has actual care of the child or who had such care immediately prior to the making of the order; and

(c)   in the case of an emergency protection order and a recovery order, the local authority in whose area the child lives or is found.

(6) Where the court refuses to make an order on an application without notice it may direct that the application is made on notice in which case the application will proceed in accordance with rules 12.3 to 12.15.

(7) Where the hearing takes place outside the hours during which the court office is normally open, the court or court officer will take a note of the proceedings.

(Practice Direction 12E (Urgent Business) provides further details of the procedure for out of hours applications. See also Practice Direction 12D (Inherent Jurisdiction (including Wardship Proceedings).)

(Rule 12.47 provides for without-notice applications in proceedings under Chapter 6, section 1 of this Part, (proceedings under the 1980 Hague Convention and the European Convention).)

12.17 Investigation under section 37 of the 1989 Act

(1) This rule applies where a direction is given to an appropriate authority by the court under section 37(1) of the 1989 Act.

(2) On giving the direction the court may adjourn the proceedings.

(3) As soon as practicable after the direction is given the court will record the direction.

(4) As soon as practicable after the direction is given the court officer will –

(a)   serve the direction on –
    (i)   the parties to the proceedings in which the direction is given; and
    (ii)   the appropriate authority where it is not a party;

(b)   serve any documentary evidence directed by the court on the appropriate authority.

(5) Where a local authority informs the court of any of the matters set out in section 37(3)(a) to (c) of the 1989 Act it will do so in writing.

PART II – Statutory Instruments

(6) Unless the court directs otherwise, the court officer will serve a copy of any report to the court under section 37 of the 1989 Act on the parties.

(Section 37 of the 1989 Act refers to the appropriate authority and section 37(5) of that Act sets out which authority should be named in a particular case.)

12.18 Disclosure of a report under section 14A(8) or (9) of the 1989 Act

(1) In proceedings for a special guardianship order, the local authority must file the report under section 14A(8) or (9) of the 1989 Act within the timetable fixed by the court.

(2) The court will consider whether to give a direction that the report under section 14A(8) or (9) of the 1989 Act be disclosed to each party to the proceedings.

(3) Before giving a direction for the report to be disclosed, the court must consider whether any information should be deleted from the report.

(4) The court may direct that the report must not be disclosed to a party.

(5) The court officer must serve a copy of the report in accordance with any direction under paragraph (2).

(6) In paragraph (3), information includes information which a party has declined to reveal under rule 29.1(1).

12.19 Additional evidence

(1) This rule applies to proceedings for a section 8 order or a special guardianship order.

(2) Unless the court directs otherwise, a party must not –

   (a)   file or serve any document other than in accordance with these rules or any practice direction;

   (b)   in completing a form prescribed by these rules or any practice direction, give information or make a statement which is not required or authorised by that form; or

   (c)   file or serve at a hearing –

      (i)   any witness statement of the substance of the oral evidence which the party intends to adduce; or

      (ii)   any copy of any document (including any experts' report) which the party intends to rely on.

(3) Where a party fails to comply with the requirements of this rule in relation to any witness statement or other document, the party cannot seek to rely on that statement or other document unless the court directs otherwise.

12.20 Expert evidence – examination of child

(1) No person may cause the child to be medically or psychiatrically examined, or otherwise assessed, for the purpose of preparation of expert evidence for use in the proceedings without the court's permission.

(2) Where the court's permission has not been given under paragraph (1), no evidence arising out of an examination or assessment referred to in that paragraph may be adduced without the court's permission.

12.21 Hearings

(1) The court may give directions about the order of speeches and the evidence at a hearing.

(2) Subject to any directions given under paragraph (1), the parties and the children's guardian must adduce their evidence at a hearing in the following order –

  (a) the applicant;
  (b) any party with parental responsibility for the child;
  (c) other respondents;
  (d) the children's guardian;
  (e) the child, if the child is a party to proceedings and there is no children's guardian.

Chapter 3
Special Provisions about Public Law Proceedings

12.22 Application of rules 12.23 to 12.26

Rules 12.23 to 12.26 apply to care and supervision proceedings and in so far as practicable other public law proceedings

12.23 Timetable for the Child

(1) The court will set the timetable for the proceedings in accordance with the Timetable for the Child.

(2) The 'Timetable for the Child' means the timetable set by the court in accordance with its duties under section 1 and 32 of the 1989 Act and will –

  (a) take into account dates of the significant steps in the life of the child who is the subject of the proceedings; and
  (b) be appropriate for that child.

12.24 Directions

The court will direct the parties to –

  (a) monitor compliance with the court's directions; and
  (b) tell the court or court officer about –
    (i)   any failure to comply with a direction of the court; and
    (ii) any other delay in the proceedings.

12.25 First Appointment, Case Management Conference and Issues Resolution Hearing

(1) The court may set the date for the First Appointment, Case Management Conference and Issues Resolution Hearing at the times and in the circumstances referred to in Practice Direction 12A.

(2) The matters which the court will consider at the hearings referred to in paragraph (1) are set out in Practice Direction 12A.

12.26 Discussion between advocates

(1) When setting a date for a Case Management Conference or an Issues Resolution Hearing the court will direct a discussion between the parties' advocates to –

  (a) discuss the provisions of a draft of the Case Management Order; and
  (b) consider any other matter set out in Practice Direction 12A.

(2) Where there is a litigant in person the court will give directions about how that person may take part in the discussions between the parties' advocates.

(3) The court will direct that following a discussion between advocates they must prepare or amend a draft of the Case Management Order for the court to consider.

(4) Where it is not possible for the advocates to agree the terms of a draft of the Case Management Order, the advocates should specify on a draft of the Case Management Order or on a separate document if more practicable –

  (a) those provisions on which they agree; and
  (b) those provisions on which they disagree.

(5) Unless the court directs otherwise –

  (a) any discussion between advocates must take place no later than 2 days; and
  (b) a draft of the Case Management Order must be filed with the court no later than 1 day,

before the Case Management Conference or the Issues Resolution Hearing whichever may be appropriate.

(6) For the purposes of this rule 'advocate' includes a litigant in person.

12.27 Matters prescribed for the purposes of the Act

(1) Proceedings for an order under any of the following provisions of the 1989 Act –

  (a) a secure accommodation order under section 25;
  (b) an order giving permission to change a child's surname or remove a child from the United Kingdom under section 33(7);

(c) an order permitting the local authority to arrange for any child in its care to live outside England and Wales under paragraph 19(1) of Schedule 2;

(d) the extension or further extension of a supervision order under paragraph 6(3) of Schedule 3;

(e) appeals against the determination of proceedings of a kind set out in sub-paragraphs (a) to (d);

are specified for the purposes of section 41 of that Act in accordance with section 41(6)(i) of that Act.

(2) The persons listed as applicants in the table set out in rule 12.3 to proceedings for the variation of directions made with interim care or interim supervision orders under section 38(8) of the 1989 Act are the prescribed class of persons for the purposes of that section.

(3) The persons listed as applicants in the table set out in rule 12.3 to proceedings for the variation of a direction made under section 44(6) of the 1989 Act in an emergency protection order are the prescribed class of persons for the purposes of section 44(9) of that Act.

12.28 Exclusion requirements: interim care orders and emergency protection orders

(1) This rule applies where the court includes an exclusion requirement in an interim care order or an emergency protection order.

(2) The applicant for an interim care order or emergency protection order must –

(a) prepare a separate statement of the evidence in support of the application for an exclusion requirement;

(b) serve the statement personally on the relevant person with a copy of the order containing the exclusion requirement (and of any power of arrest which is attached to it);

(c) inform the relevant person of that person's right to apply to vary or discharge the exclusion requirement.

(3) Where a power of arrest is attached to an exclusion requirement in an interim care order or an emergency protection order, the applicant will deliver –

(a) a copy of the order; and

(b) a statement showing that the relevant person has been served with the order or informed of its terms (whether by being present when the order was made or by telephone or otherwise),

to the officer for the time being in charge of the police station for the area in which the dwelling-house in which the child lives is situated (or such other police station as the court may specify).

(4) Rules 10.6(2) and 10.10 to 10.17 will apply, with the necessary modifications, for the service, variation, discharge and enforcement of any

PART II – Statutory Instruments

exclusion requirement to which a power of arrest is attached as they apply to an order made on an application under Part 4 of the 1996 Act.

(5) The relevant person must serve the parties to the proceedings with any application which that person makes for the variation or discharge of the exclusion requirement.

(6) Where an exclusion requirement ceases to have effect whether –

   (a)   as a result of the removal of a child under section 38A(10) or 44A(10) of the 1989 Act;

   (b)   because of the discharge of the interim care order or emergency protection order; or

   (c)   otherwise,

the applicant must inform –

   (i)   the relevant person;

   (ii)   the parties to the proceedings;

   (iii)   any officer to whom a copy of the order was delivered under paragraph (3); and

   (iv)   (where necessary) the court.

(7) Where the court includes an exclusion requirement in an interim care order or an emergency protection order of its own motion, paragraph (2) will apply with the omission of any reference to the statement of the evidence.

(8) In this rule, 'the relevant person' has the meaning assigned to it by sections 38A(2) and 44A(2) of the 1989 Act.

12.29 Notification of consent

(1) Consent for the purposes of the following provisions of the 1989 Act –

   (a)   section 16(3);

   (b)   section 38A(2)(b)(ii) or 44A(2)(b)(ii); or

   (c)   paragraph 19(3)(c) or (d) of Schedule 2,

(2) must be given either –

   (i)   orally to the court; or

   (ii)   in writing to the court signed by the person giving consent.

(3) Any written consent for the purposes of section 38A(2) or 44A(2) of the 1989 Act must include a statement that the person giving consent –

   (a)   is able and willing to give to the child the care which it would be reasonable to expect a parent to give; and

   (b)   understands that the giving of consent could lead to the exclusion of the relevant person from the dwelling-house in which the child lives.

12.30 Proceedings for secure accommodation orders: copies of reports

In proceedings under section 25 of the 1989 Act, the court will, if practicable, arrange for copies of all written reports filed in the case to be made available before the hearing to –

(a) the applicant;

(b) the parent or guardian of the child to whom the application relates;

(c) any legal representative of the child;

(d) the children's guardian; and

(e) the child, unless the court directs otherwise,

and copies of the reports may, if the court considers it desirable, be shown to any person who is entitled to notice of any hearing in accordance with Practice Direction 12C.

Chapter 4
Special Provisions about Private Law Proceedings

12.31 The First Hearing Dispute Resolution Appointment

(1) The court may set a date for the First Hearing Dispute Resolution Appointment after the proceedings have been issued.

(2) The court officer will give notice of any of the dates so fixed to the parties.

(Provisions relating to the timing of and issues to be considered at the First Hearing Dispute Resolution Appointment are contained in Practice Direction 12B.)

12.32 Answer

A respondent must file and serve on the parties an answer to the application for an order in private law proceedings within 14 days beginning with the date on which the application is served.

12.33 Applications for warning notices or applications to amend enforcement orders by reason of change of residence

(1) This rule applies in relation to an application to the High Court or a county court for –

(a) a warning notice to be attached to a contact order; or

(b) an order under paragraph 5 of Schedule A1 to the 1989 Act to amend an enforcement order by reason of change of residence.

(2) The application must be made without notice.

(3) The court may deal with the application without a hearing.

(4) If the court decides to deal with the application at a hearing, rules 12.5, 12.7 and 12.8 will apply.

12.34 Service of a risk assessment

(1) Where an officer of the Service or a Welsh family proceedings officer has filed a risk assessment with the court, subject to paragraph (2), the court officer will as soon as practicable serve copies of the risk assessment on each party.

PART II – Statutory Instruments

(2) Before serving the risk assessment, the court must consider whether, in order to prevent a risk of harm to the child, it is necessary for –

(a)   information to be deleted from a copy of the risk assessment before that copy is served on a party; or

(b)   service of a copy of the risk assessment (whether with information deleted from it or not) on a party to be delayed for a specified period,

and may make directions accordingly.

12.35 Service of enforcement orders or orders amending or revoking enforcement orders

(1) Paragraphs (2) and (3) apply where the High Court or a county court makes –

(a)   an enforcement order; or

(b)   an order under paragraph 9(2) of Schedule A1 to the 1989 Act (enforcement order made following a breach of an enforcement order).

(2) As soon as practicable after an order has been made, a copy of it must be served by the court officer on –

(a)   the parties, except the person against whom the order is made;

(b)   the officer of the Service or the Welsh family proceedings officer who is to comply with a request under section 11M of the 1989 Act to monitor compliance with the order; and

(c)   the responsible officer.

(3) Unless the court directs otherwise, the applicant must serve a copy of the order personally on the person against whom the order is made.

(4) The court officer must send a copy of an order made under paragraph 4, 5, 6 or 7 of Schedule A1 to the 1989 Act (revocation or amendment of an enforcement order) to –

(a)   the parties;

(b)   the officer of the Service or the Welsh family proceedings officer who is to comply with a request under section 11M of the 1989 Act to monitor compliance with the order;

(c)   the responsible officer; and

(d)   in the case of an order under paragraph 5 of Schedule A1 to the 1989 Act (amendment of enforcement order by reason of change of residence), the responsible officer in the former local justice area.

(5) In this rule, 'responsible officer' has the meaning given in paragraph 8(8) of Schedule A1 to the 1989 Act.

Chapter 5
Special Provisions about Inherent Jurisdiction Proceedings

12.36 Where to start proceedings

(1) An application for proceedings under the Inherent Jurisdiction of the court must be started in the High Court.

(2) Wardship proceedings, except applications for an order that a child be made or cease to be a ward of court, may be transferred to the county court unless the issues of fact or law make them more suitable for hearing in the High Court.

(The question of suitability for hearing in the High Court is explained in Practice Direction 12D (Inherent Jurisdiction (including Wardship Proceedings)).)

12.37 Child as respondent to wardship proceedings

(1) A child who is the subject of wardship proceedings must not be made a respondent to those proceedings unless the court gives permission following an application under paragraph (2).

2) Where nobody other than the child would be a suitable respondent to wardship proceedings, the applicant may apply without notice for permission to make the wardship application –

  (a)   without notice; or
  (b)   with the child as the respondent.

12.38 Registration requirements

The court officer will send a copy of every application for a child to be made a ward of court to the principal registry for recording in the register of wards.

12.39 Notice of child's whereabouts

(1) Every respondent, other than a child, must file with the acknowledgment of service a notice stating –

  (a)   the respondent's address; and
  (b)   either –
      (i)   the whereabouts of the child; or
      (ii)   that the respondent is unaware of the child's whereabouts if that is the case.

(2) Unless the court directs otherwise, the respondent must serve a copy of that notice on the applicant.

(3) Every respondent other than a child must immediately notify the court in writing of –

  (a)   any subsequent changes of address; or
  (b)   any change in the child's whereabouts,

PART II – Statutory Instruments

and, unless the court directs otherwise, serve a copy of that notice on the applicant.

(4) In this rule a reference to the whereabouts of a child is a reference to –

    (a)   the address at which the child is living;

    (b)   the person with whom the child is living; and

    (c)   any other information relevant to where the child may be found.

12.40 Enforcement of orders in wardship proceedings

The High Court may secure compliance with any direction relating to a ward of court by an order addressed to the tipstaff.

(The role of the tipstaff is explained in Practice Direction 12D (Inherent Jurisdiction (including Wardship Proceedings)).)

12.41 Child ceasing to be ward of court

(1) A child who, by virtue of section 41(2) of the Senior Courts Act 1981, automatically becomes a ward of court on the making of a wardship application will cease to be a ward on the determination of the application unless the court orders that the child be made a ward of court.

(2) Nothing in paragraph (1) affects the power of the court under section 41(3) of the Senior Courts Act 1981 to order that any child cease to be a ward of court.

Chapter 6
Proceedings under the 1980 Hague Convention, the European Convention, the Council Regulation, and the 1996 Hague Convention

12.43 Scope

This Chapter applies to –

    (a)   proceedings relating to children under the 1980 Hague Convention or the European Convention; and

    (b)   applications relating to the Council Regulation or the 1996 Hague Convention in respect of children.

Section 1
Proceedings under the 1980 Hague Convention or the European Convention

12.44 Interpretation

In this section –

'the 1985 Act' means the Child Abduction and Custody Act 1985;

'Central Authority' means, in relation to England and Wales, the Lord Chancellor;

'Contracting State' has the meaning given in –

(a) section 2 of the 1985 Act in relation to the 1980 Hague Convention; and

(b) section 13 of the 1985 Act in relation to the European Convention; and

'decision relating to custody' has the same meaning as in the European Convention.

('the 1980 Hague Convention' and the 'the European Convention' are defined in rule 2.3.)

12.45 Where to start proceedings

Every application under the 1980 Hague Convention or the European Convention must be –

(a) made in the High Court and issued in the principal registry; and
(b) heard by a Judge of the High Court unless the application is –
    (i)   to join a respondent; or
    (ii) to dispense with service or extend the time for acknowledging service.

12.46 Evidence in support of application

Where the party making an application under this section does not produce the documents referred to in Practice Direction 12F, the court may –

(a) fix a time within which the documents are to be produced;
(b) accept equivalent documents; or
(c) dispense with production of the documents if the court considers it has sufficient information.

12.47 Without-notice applications

(1) This rule applies to applications –

(a) commencing or in proceedings under this section;
(b) for interim directions under section 5 or 19 of the 1985 Act;
(c) for the disclosure of information about the child and for safeguarding the child's welfare, under rule 12.57;
(d) for the disclosure of relevant information as to where the child is, under section 24A of the 1985 Act; or
(e) for a collection order, location order or passport order.

(2) Applications under this rule may be made without notice, in which case the applicant must file the application –

(a) where the application is made by telephone, the next business day after the making of the application; or
(b) in any other case, at the time when the application is made.

(3) Where an order is made without notice, the applicant must serve a copy of the order on the other parties as soon as practicable after the making of the order, unless the court otherwise directs.

PART II – Statutory Instruments

(4) Where the court refuses to make an order on an application without notice, it may direct that the application is made on notice.

(5) Where any hearing takes place outside the hours during which the court office is usually open –

(a)   if the hearing takes place by telephone, the applicant's solicitors will, if practicable, arrange for the hearing to be recorded; and

(b)   in all other cases, the court or court officer will take a note of the proceedings.

(Practice Direction 12E (Urgent Business) provides further details of the procedure for out of hours applications. See also Practice Direction 12D (Inherent Jurisdiction (including Wardship Proceedings)).)

12.48 Directions

(1) As soon as practicable after an application to which this section applies has been made, the court may give directions as to the following matters, among others –

(a)   whether service of the application may be dispensed with;

(b)   whether the proceedings should be transferred to another court under rule 12.54;

(c)   expedition of the proceedings or any part of the proceedings (and any direction for expedition may specify a date by which the court must issue its final judgment in the proceedings or a specified part of the proceedings);

(d)   the steps to be taken in the proceedings and the time by which each step is to be taken;

(e)   whether the child or any other person should be made a party to the proceedings;

(f)   if the child is not made a party to the proceedings, the manner in which the child's wishes and feelings are to be ascertained, having regard to the child's age and maturity and in particular whether an officer of the Service or a Welsh family proceedings officer should report to the court for that purpose;

(g)   where the child is made a party to the proceedings, the appointment of a children's guardian for that child unless a children's guardian has already been appointed;

(h)   the attendance of the child or any other person before the court;

(i)   the appointment of a litigation friend for a child or for any protected party, unless a litigation friend has already been appointed;

(j)   the service of documents;

(k)   the filing of evidence including expert evidence; and

(l)   whether the parties and their representatives should meet at any stage of the proceedings and the purpose of such a meeting.

(Rule 16.2 provides for when the court may make the child a party to the proceedings and rule 16.4 for the appointment of a children's guardian for the child who is made a party. Rule 16.5 (without prejudice to rule 16.6) requires a child who is a party to the proceedings but not the subject of those proceedings to have a litigation friend.)

(2) Directions of a court which are in force immediately prior to the transfer of proceedings to another court under rule 12.54 will continue to apply following the transfer subject to –

(a) any changes of terminology which are required to apply those directions to the court to which the proceedings are transferred; and

(b) any variation or revocation of the directions.

(3) The court or court officer will –

(a) take a note of the giving, variation or revocation of directions under this rule; and

(b) as soon as practicable serve a copy of the directions order on every party.

12.49 Answer

(1) Subject to paragraph (2) and to any directions given under rule 12.48, a respondent must file and serve on the parties an answer to the application within 7 days beginning with the date on which the application is served.

(2) The court may direct a longer period for service where the respondent has been made a party solely on one of the following grounds –

(a) a decision relating to custody has been made in the respondent's favour; or

(b) the respondent appears to the court to have sufficient interest in the welfare of the child.

12.50 Filing and serving written evidence

(1) The respondent to an application to which ths section applies may file and serve with the answer a statement verified by a statement of truth, together with any further evidence on which the respondent intends to rely.

(2) The applicant may, within 7 days beginning with the date on which the respondent's evidence was served under paragraph (1), file and serve a statement in reply verified by a statement of truth, together with any further evidence on which the applicant intends to rely.

12.51 Adjournment

The court will not adjourn the hearing of an application to which this section applies for more than 21 days at any one time.

12.52 Stay of proceedings upon notification of wrongful removal etc.

(1) In this rule and in rule 12.53 –

(a)'relevant authority' means –

(i) the High Court;

PART II – Statutory Instruments

(ii)   a county court;

(iii)   a magistrates' court;

(iv)   the Court of Session;

(v)   a sheriff court;

(vi)   a children's hearing within the meaning of section 93 of the Children (Scotland) Act 1995;

(vii)   the High Court in Northern Ireland;

(viii)   a county court in Northern Ireland;

(ix)   a court of summary jurisdiction in Northern Ireland;

(x)   the Royal Court of Jersey;

(xi)   a court of summary jurisdiction in Jersey;

(xii)   the High Court of Justice of the Isle of Man;

(xiii)   a court of summary jurisdiction in the Isle of Man; or

(xiv)   the Secretary of State; and

(b)'rights of custody' has the same meaning as in the 1980 Hague Convention.

(2) Where a party to proceedings under the 1980 Hague Convention knows that an application relating to the merits of rights of custody is pending in or before a relevant authority, that party must file within the proceedings under the 1980 Hague Convention a concise statement of the nature of that application, including the relevant authority in or before which it is pending.

(3) On receipt of a statement filed in accordance with paragraph (2) above, a court officer will notify the relevant authority in or before which the application is pending and will subsequently notify the relevant authority of the result of the proceedings.

(4) On receipt by the relevant authority of a notification under paragraph (3) from the High Court or equivalent notification from the Court of Session, the High Court in Northern Ireland or the High Court of Justice of the Isle of Man –

(a)   all further proceedings in the action will be stayed(GL) unless and until the proceedings under the 1980 Hague Convention in the High Court, Court of Session, the High Court in Northern Ireland or the High Court of Justice of the Isle of Man are dismissed; and

(b)   the parties to the action will be notified by the court officer of the stay(GL) and dismissal.

12.53 Stay of proceedings where application made under s.16 of the 1985 Act (registration of decisions under the European Convention)

(1) A person who –

(a)   is a party to –

(i)   proceedings under section 16 of the 1985 Act; or

(ii)   proceedings as a result of which a decision relating to custody has been registered under section 16 of the 1985 Act; and

(b)   knows that an application is pending under –

(i)   section 20(2) of the 1985 Act;

(ii)   Article 21(2) of the Child Abduction and Custody (Jersey) Law 2005; or

(iii) section 42(2) of the Child Custody Act 1987 (an Act of Tynwald),

must file within the proceedings under section 16 of the 1985 Act a concise statement of the nature of the pending application.

(2) On receipt of a statement filed in accordance with paragraph (1) above, a court officer will notify the relevant authority in or before which the application is pending and will subsequently notify the relevant authority of the result of the proceedings.

(3) On receipt by the relevant authority of a notification under paragraph (2) from the High Court or equivalent notification from the Court of Session, the High Court in Northern Ireland or the High Court of Justice of the Isle of Man, the court officer will notify the parties to the action.

12.54 Transfer of proceedings

(1) At any stage in proceedings under the 1985 Act the court may –

(a)   of its own initiative; or

(b)   on the application of a party with a minimum of two days' notice;

order that the proceedings be transferred to a court listed in paragraph (4).

(2) Where the court makes an order for transfer under paragraph (1) –

(a)   the court will state its reasons on the face of the order;

(b)   a court officer will send a copy of the order, the application and the accompanying documents (if any) and any evidence to the court to which the proceedings are transferred; and

(c)   the costs of the proceedings both before and after the transfer will be at the discretion of the court to which the proceedings are transferred.

(3) Where proceedings are transferred to the High Court from a court listed in paragraph (4), a court officer will notify the parties of the transfer and the proceedings will continue as if they had been commenced in the High Court.

(4) The listed courts are the Court of Session, the High Court in Northern Ireland, the Royal Court of Jersey or the High Court of Justice of the Isle of Man.

12.55 Revocation and variation of registered decisions

(1) This rule applies to decisions which –

(a)   have been registered under section 16 of the 1985 Act; and

(b)   are subsequently varied or revoked by an authority in the Contracting State in which they were made.

(2) The court will, on cancelling the registration of a decision which has been revoked, notify –

(a)   the person appearing to the court to have care of the child;

(b)   the person on whose behalf the application for registration of the decision was made; and

(c)   any other party to the application.

(3) The court will, on being informed of the variation of a decision, notify –

(a)   the party appearing to the court to have care of the child; and

(b)   any party to the application for registration of the decision;

and any such person may apply to make representations to the court before the registration is varied.

(4) Any person appearing to the court to have an interest in the proceedings may apply for the registration of a decision for the cancellation or variation of the decision referred to in paragraph (1).

12.56 The central index of decisions registered under the 1985 Act

A central index of decisions registered under section 16 of the 1985 Act, together with any variation of those decisions made under section 17 of that Act, will be kept by the principal registry.

12.57 Disclosure of information in proceedings under the European Convention

At any stage in proceedings under the European Convention the court may, if it has reason to believe that any person may have relevant information about the child who is the subject of those proceedings, order that person to disclose such information and may for that purpose order that the person attend before it or file affidavit[(GL)] evidence

Section 2
Applications relating to the Council Regulation and the 1996 Hague Convention

12.58 Interpretation

(1) In this section –

'Central Authority' means, in relation to England and Wales, the Lord Chancellor;

'Contracting State' means a State party to the 1996 Hague Convention;

'judgment' has the meaning given in Article 2(4) of the Council Regulation;

'Member State' means a Member State bound by the Council Regulation or a country which has subsequently adopted the Council Regulation;

'parental responsibility' has the meaning given in –

(a)   Article 2(7) of the Council Regulation in relation to proceedings under that Regulation; and

(b)   Article 1(2) of the 1996 Hague Convention in relation to proceedings under that Convention; and

'seised' has the meaning given in Article 16 of the Council Regulation.

(2) In rules 12.59 to 12.70, references to the court of another member State or Contracting State include authorities within the meaning of 'court' in Article 2(1) of the Council Regulation, and authorities of Contracting States which have jurisdiction to take measures directed to the protection of the person or property of the child within the meaning of the 1996 Hague Convention.

12.59 Procedure under Article 11(6) of the Council Regulation where the court makes a non-return order under Article 13 of the 1980 Hague Convention

(1) Where the court makes an order for the non-return of a child under Article 13 of the 1980 Hague Convention, it must immediately transmit the documents referred to in Article 11(6) of the Council Regulation –

    (a)   directly to the court with jurisdiction or the central authority in the Member State where the child was habitually resident immediately before the wrongful removal to, or wrongful retention in, England and Wales; or

    (b)   to the Central Authority for England and Wales for onward transmission to the court with jurisdiction or the central authority in the other Member State mentioned in sub-paragraph (a).

(2) The documents required by paragraph (1) must be transmitted by a method which, in the case of direct transmission to the court with jurisdiction in the other Member State, ensures and, in any other case, will not prevent, their receipt by that court within one month of the date of the non-return order.

12.60 Procedure under Article 11(7) of the Council Regulation where the court receives a non-return order made under Article 13 of the 1980 Hague Convention by a court in another Member State

(1) This rule applies where the court receives an order made by a court in another Member State for the non-return of a child.

(2) In this rule, the order for non-return of the child and the papers transmitted with that order from the court in the other Member State are referred to as 'the non-return order'.

(3) Where, at the time of receipt of the non-return order, the court is already seised of a question of parental responsibility in relation to the child, –

    (a)   the court officer shall immediately –

        (i)   serve copies of the non-return order on each party to the proceedings in which a question of parental responsibility in relation to the child is at issue; and

        (ii)   where the non-return order was received directly from the court or the central authority in the other Member State, transmit to the Central Authority for England and Wales a copy of the non-return order.

    (b)   the court shall immediately invite the parties to the 1980 Hague Convention proceedings to file written submissions in respect of the question of custody by a specified date, or to attend a hearing to consider the future conduct of the proceedings in the light of the non-return order.

(4) Where, at the time of receipt of the non-return order, the court is not already seised of the question of parental responsibility in relation to the child, it shall immediately –

(a)   open a court file in respect of the child and assign a court reference to the file;

(b)   serve a copy of the non-return order on each party to the proceedings before the court in the Member State which made that order;

(c)   invite each party to file, within 3 months of notification to that party of receipt of the non-return order, submissions in the form of –
    (i)   an application for an order under –
        (aa) the 1989 Act; or
        (bb) (in the High Court only) an application under the inherent jurisdiction in respect of the child; or
    (ii) where permission is required to make an application for the order in question, an application for that permission;

(d)   where the non-return order was received directly from the court or central authority in the other Member State, transmit to the Central Authority for England and Wales a copy of the non-return order.

(5) In a case to which paragraph (4) applies where no application is filed within the 3 month period provided for by paragraph (4)(c) the court must close its file in respect of the child.

(Enforcement of a subsequent judgment requiring the return of the child, made under Article 11(8) by a court examining custody of the child under Article 11(7), is dealt with in Part 31 below.)

12.61 Transfer of proceedings under Article 15 of the Council Regulation or under Article 8 of the 1996 Hague Convention

(1) Where the court is considering the transfer of proceedings to the court of another Member State or Contracting State under rules 12.62 to 12.64 it will –

(a)   fix a date for a hearing for the court to consider the question of transfer; and

(b)   give directions as to the manner in which the parties may make representations.

(2) The court may, with the consent of all parties, deal with the question of transfer without a hearing.

(3) Directions which are in force immediately prior to the transfer of proceedings to a court in another Member State or Contracting State under rules 12.62 to 12.64 will continue to apply until the court in that other State accepts jurisdiction in accordance with the provisions of the Council Regulation or the 1996 Hague Convention (as appropriate), subject to any variation or revocation of the directions.

(4) The court or court officer will –

(a)   take a note of the giving, variation or revocation of directions under this rule; and

(b)   as soon as practicable serve a copy of the directions order on every party.

(5) A register of all applications and requests for transfer of jurisdiction to or from another Member State or Contracting State will be kept by the principal registry.

12.62 Application by a party for transfer of the proceedings

(1) A party may apply to the court under Article 15(1) of the Council Regulation or under Article 8(1) of the 1996 Hague Convention –

(a)   to stay$^{(GL)}$ the proceedings or a specified part of the proceedings and to invite the parties to introduce a request before a court of another Member State or Contracting State; or

(b)   to make a request to a court of another Member State or another Contracting State to assume jurisdiction for the proceedings, or a specified part of the proceedings.

(2) An application under paragraph (1) must be made –

(a)   to the court in which the relevant parental responsibility proceedings are pending; and

(b)   using the Part 18 procedure.

(3) The applicant must file the application notice and serve it on the respondents –

(a)   where the application is also made under Article 11 of the Council Regulation, not less than 5 days, and

(b)   in any other case, not less than 42 days,

before the hearing of the application.

12.63 Application by a court of another Member State or another Contracting State for transfer of the proceedings

(1) This rule applies where a court of another Member State or another Contracting State makes an application under Article 15(2)(c) of the Council Regulation or under Article 9 of the 1996 Hague Convention that the court having jurisdiction in relation to the proceedings transfer the proceedings or a specific part of the proceedings to the applicant court.

(2) When the court receives the application, the court officer will –

(a)   as soon as practicable, notify the Central Authority for England and Wales of the application; and

(b)   serve the application, and notice of the hearing on all other parties in England and Wales not less than 5 days before the hearing of the application.

PART II – Statutory Instruments

12.64 Exercise by the court of its own initiative of powers to seek to transfer the proceedings

(1) The court having jurisdiction in relation to the proceedings may exercise its powers of its own initiative under Article 15 of the Council Regulation or Article 8 of the 1996 Hague Convention in relation to the proceedings or a specified part of the proceedings.

(2) Where the court proposes to exercise its powers, the court officer will give the parties not less than 5 days' notice of the hearing.

12.65 Application to High Court to make request under Article 15 of the Council Regulation or Article 9 of the 1996 Hague Convention to request transfer of jurisdiction

(1) An application for the court to request transfer of jurisdiction in a matter concerning a child from another Member State or another Contracting State under Article 15 of the Council Regulation, or Article 9 of the 1996 Hague Convention (as the case may be) must be made to the principal registry and heard in the High Court.

(2) An application must be made without notice to any other person and the court may give directions about joining any other party to the application.

(3) Where there is agreement between the court and the court or competent authority to which the request under paragraph (1) is made to transfer the matter to the courts of England and Wales, the court will consider with that other court or competent authority the specific timing and conditions for the transfer.

(4) Upon receipt of agreement to transfer jurisdiction from the court or other competent authority in the Member State, or Contracting State to which the request has been made, the court officer will serve on the applicant a notice that jurisdiction has been accepted by the courts of England and Wales.

(5) The applicant must attach the notice referred to in subparagraph (3) to any subsequent application in relation to the child.

(6) Nothing in this rule requires an application with respect to a child commenced following a transfer of jurisdiction to be made to or heard in the High Court.

(7) Upon allocation, the court to which the proceedings are allocated must immediately fix a directions hearing to consider the future conduct of the case.

12.66 Procedure where the court receives a request from the authorities of another Member State or Contracting State to assume jurisdiction in a matter concerning a child

(1) Where any court other than the High Court receives a request to assume jurisdiction in a matter concerning a child from a court or other authority which has jurisdiction in another Member State or Contracting State, that

court must immediately refer the request to a Judge of the High Court for a decision regarding acceptance of jurisdiction to be made.

(2) Upon the High Court agreeing to the request under paragraph (1), the court officer will notify the parties to the proceedings before the other Member State or Contracting State of that decision, and the case must be allocated as if the application had been made in England and Wales.

(3) Upon allocation, the court to which the proceedings are allocated must immediatelt fix a directions hearing to consider the future conduct of the case.

(4) The court officer will serve notice of the directions hearing on all parties to the proceedings in the other Member State or Contracting State no later than 5 days before the date of that hearing.

12.67 Service of the court's order or request relating to transfer of jurisdiction under the Council Regulation or the 1996 Hague Convention

The court officer will serve an order or request relating to transfer of jurisdiction on all parties, the Central Authority of the other Member State or Contracting State, and the Central Authority for England and Wales.

12.68 Questions as to the court's jurisdiction or whether the proceedings should be stayed

(1) If at any time after issue of the application it appears to the court that under any of Articles 16 to 18 of the Council Regulation it does not or may not have jurisdiction to hear an application, or that under Article 19 of the Council Regulation or Article 13 of the 1996 Hague Convention it is or may be required to stay$^{(GL)}$ the proceedings or to decline jurisdiction, the court must –

(a) stay$^{(GL)}$ the proceedings; and
(b) fix a date for a hearing to determine jurisdiction or whether there should be a stay$^{(GL)}$ or other order.

(2) The court officer will serve notice of the hearing referred to at paragraph (1)(b) on the parties to the proceedings.

(3) The court must, in writing –

(a) give reasons for its decision under paragraph (1); and
(b) where it makes a finding of fact, state such finding.

(4) The court may with the consent of all the parties deal with any question as to the jurisdiction of the court, or as to whether the proceedings should be stayed$^{(GL)}$, without a hearing.

12.69 Request for consultation as to contemplated placement of child in England and Wales

(1) This rule applies to a request made –

(a) under Article 56 of the Council Regulation, by a court in another Member State; or

(b)   under Article 33 of the 1996 Hague Convention by a court in another Contracting State

for consultation on or consent to the contemplated placement of a child in England and Wales.

(2) Where the court receives a request directly from a court in another Member State or Contracting State, the court shall, as soon as practicable after receipt of the request, notify the Central Authority for England and Wales of the request and take the appropriate action under paragraph (4).

(3) Where it appears to the court officer that no proceedings relating to the child are pending before a court in England and Wales, the court officer must inform the Central Authority for England and Wales of that fact and forward to the Central Authority all documents relating to the request sent by the court in the other Member State or Contracting State.

(4) Where the court receives a request forwarded by the Central Authority for England and Wales, the court must, as soon as practicable after receipt of the request, either –

(a)   where proceedings relating to the child are pending before the court, fix a directions hearing; or
(b)   where proceedings relating to the child are pending before another court in England and Wales, send a copy of the request to that court.

12.70 Request made by court in England and Wales for consultation as to contemplated placement of child in another Member State or Contracting State

(1) This rule applies where the court is contemplating the placement of a child in another Member State under Article 56 of the Council Regulation or another Contracting State under Article 33 of the 1996 Hague Convention, and proposes to send a request for consultation with or for the consent of the central authority or other authority having jurisdiction in the other State in relation to the contemplated placement.

(2) In this rule, a reference to 'the request' includes a reference to a report prepared for purposes of Article 33 of the 1996 Hague Convention where the request is made under that Convention.

(3) Where the court sends the request directly to the central authority or other authority having jurisdiction in the other State, it shall at the same time send a copy of the request to the Central Authority for England and Wales.

(4) The court may send the request to the Central Authority for England and Wales for onward transmission to the central authority or other authority having jurisdiction in the other Member State.

(5) The court should give consideration to the documents which should accompany the request.

(See Chapters 1 to 3 of this Part generally, for the procedure governing applications for an order under paragraph 19(1) of Schedule 2 to the 1989 Act permitting a local authority to arrange for any child in its care to live outside England and Wales.)

(Part 14 sets out the procedure governing applications for an order under section 84 (giving parental responsibility prior to adoption abroad) of the Adoption and Children Act 2002.)

12.71 Application for a declaration as to the extent, or existence, of parental responsibility in relation to a child under Article 16 of the 1996 Hague Convention

(1) Any interested person may apply for a declaration –

    (a)   that a person has, or does not have, parental responsibility for a child; or

    (b)   as to the extent of a person's parental responsibility for a child,

where the question arises by virtue of the application of Article 16 of the 1996 Hague Convention.

(2) An application for a declaration as to the extent, or existence of a person's parental responsibility for a child by virtue of Article 16 of the 1996 Hague Convention must be made in the principal registry and heard in the High Court.

(3) An application for a declaration referred to in paragraph (1) may not be made where the question raised is otherwise capable of resolution in any other family proceedings in respect of the child.

Chapter 7
Communication of Information: Proceedings Relating to Children

12.72 Interpretation

In this Chapter 'independent reviewing officer' means a person appointed in respect of a child in accordance with regulation 2A of the Review of Children's Cases Regulations 1991, or regulation 3 of the Review of Children's Cases (Wales) Regulations 2007.

12.73 Communication of information: general

(1) For the purposes of the law relating to contempt of court, information relating to proceedings held in private (whether or not contained in a document filed with the court) may be communicated –

    (a)   where the communication is to –
        (i)   a party;
        (ii)   the legal representative of a party;
        (iii)   a professional legal adviser;
        (iv)   an officer of the service or a Welsh family proceedings officer;
        (v)   the welfare officer;

(vi)   the Legal Services Commission;

(vii)   an expert whose instruction by a party has been authorised by the court for the purposes of the proceedings;

(viii) a professional acting in furtherance of the protection of children;

(ix)   an independent reviewing officer appointed in respect of a child who is, or has been, subject to proceedings to which this rule applies;

(b)   where the court gives permission; or

(c)   subject to any direction of the court, in accordance with rule 12.75 and Practice Direction 12G.

(2) Nothing in this Chapter permits the communication to the public at large, or any section of the public, of any information relating to the proceedings.

(3) Nothing in rule 12.75 and Practice Direction 12G permits the disclosure of an unapproved draft judgment handed down by any court.

12.74 Instruction of experts

(1) No party may instruct an expert for any purpose relating to proceedings, including to give evidence in those proceedings, without the permission of the court.

(2) Where the permission of the court has not been given under paragraph (1), no evidence arising out of an unauthorised instruction may be introduced without permission of the court.

12.75 Communication of information for purposes connected with the proceedings

(1) A party or the legal representative of a party, on behalf of and upon the instructions of that party, may communicate information relating to the proceedings to any person where necessary to enable that party –

(a)   by confidential discussion, to obtain support, advice or assistance in the conduct of the proceedings;

(b)   to engage in mediation or other forms of alternative dispute resolution;

(c)   to make and pursue a complaint against a person or body concerned in the proceedings; or

(d)   to make and pursue a complaint regarding the law, policy or procedure relating to a category of proceedings to which this Part applies.

(2) Where information is communicated to any person in accordance with paragraph (1)(a) of this rule, no further communication by that person is permitted.

(3) When information relating to the proceedings is communicated to any person in accordance with paragraphs (1)(b), (c) or (d) of this rule –

(a)   the recipient may communicate that information to a further recipient, provided that –

(i) the party who initially communicated the information consents to that further communication; and

(ii) the further communication is made only for the purpose or purposes for which the party made the initial communication; and

(b) the information may be successively communicated to and by further recipients on as many occasions as may be necessary to fulfil the purpose for which the information was initially communicated, provided that on each such occasion the conditions in sub-paragraph (a) are met.

Practice Direction 12A –
Public Law Proceedings Guide to Case Management: April 2010

This Practice Direction supplements FPR Part 12

Scope

1.1 This Practice Direction applies to care and supervision proceedings. In so far as practicable, it is to be applied to all other Public Law Proceedings.

1.2 This Practice Direction replaces Practice Direction Guide to Case Management in Public Law Proceedings dated April 2008.

1.3 This Practice Direction will come into effect on 6th April 2010. The new form of application for a care or supervision order (Form C110) only applies to proceedings commenced on or after 6th April 2010. Subject to this it is intended that this Practice Direction should apply in so far as practicable to applications made and not disposed of before 6th April 2010. In relation to these applications –

(1) the Practice Direction Guide to Case Management in Public Law Proceedings dated April 2008 applies where it is not practicable to apply this Practice Direction; and

(2) the court may give directions relating to the application of this Practice Direction or the April 2008 Practice Direction. This is subject to the overriding objective below and to the proviso that such a direction will neither cause further delay nor involve repetition of steps already taken or decisions already made in the case.

1.4 This Practice Direction is to be read with the rules and is subject to them.

1.5 A Glossary of terms is at paragraph 26.

The overriding objective

2.1 This Practice Direction has the overriding objective of enabling the court to deal with cases justly, having regard to the welfare issues involved. Dealing with a case justly includes, so far as is practicable –

(1) ensuring that it is dealt with expeditiously and fairly;

(2)   dealing with the case in ways which are proportionate to the nature, importance and complexity of the issues;

(3)   ensuring that the parties are on an equal footing;

(4)   saving expense; and

(5)   allotting to it an appropriate share of the court's resources, while taking into account the need to allot resources to other cases.

APPLICATION BY THE COURT OF THE OVERRIDING OBJECTIVE

2.2 The court must seek to give effect to the overriding objective when it –

(1)   exercises the case management powers referred to in this Practice Direction; or

(2)   interprets any provision of this Practice Direction.

DUTY OF THE PARTIES

2.3 The parties are required to help the court further the overriding objective.

Court case management

The main principles

3.1 The main principles underlying court case management and the means of the court furthering the overriding objective in Public Law Proceedings are –

(1)   **Timetable for the Child**: each case will have a timetable for the proceedings set by the court in accordance with the Timetable for the Child;

(2)   **judicial continuity**: each case will be allocated to one or not more than two case management judges (in the case of magistrates' courts, case managers), who will be responsible for every case management stage in the proceedings through to the Final Hearing and, in relation to the High Court or county court, one of whom may be – and where possible should be – the judge who will conduct the Final Hearing;

(3)   **main case management tools**: each case will be managed by the court by using the appropriate main case management tools;

(4)   **active case management**: each case will be actively case managed by the court with a view at all times to furthering the overriding objective;

(5)   **consistency**: each case will, so far as compatible with the overriding objective, be managed in a consistent way and using the standardised steps provided for in this Direction.

The main case management tools

THE TIMETABLE FOR THE CHILD

3.2 The 'Timetable for the Child' is defined by the rules as the timetable set by the court in accordance with its duties under section 1 and 32 of the 1989 Act and shall –

(1)   take into account dates of the significant steps in the life of the child who is the subject of the proceedings; and

(2) be appropriate for that child. The court will set the timetable for the proceedings in accordance with the Timetable for the Child and review this Timetable regularly. Where adjustments are made to the Timetable for the Child, the timetable for the proceedings will have to be reviewed. The Timetable for the Child is to be considered at every stage of the proceedings and whenever the court is asked to make directions whether at a hearing or otherwise.

3.3 The steps in the child's life which are to be taken into account by the court when setting the Timetable for the Child include not only legal steps but also social, care, health and education steps.

3.4 Examples of the dates the court will record and take into account when setting the Timetable for the Child are the dates of –

(1) any formal review by the Local Authority of the case of a looked after child (within the meaning of section 22(1) of the 1989 Act);
(2) the child taking up a place at a new school;
(3) any review by the Local Authority of any statement of the child's special educational needs;
(4) any assessment by a paediatrician or other specialist;
(5) the outcome of any review of Local Authority plans for the child, for example, any plans for permanence through adoption, Special Guardianship or placement with parents or relatives;
(6) any change or proposed change of the child's placement.

3.5 Due regard should be paid to the Timetable for the Child to ensure that the court remains child-focused throughout the progress of Public Law Proceedings and that any procedural steps proposed under the Public Law Outline are considered in the context of significant events in the child's life.

3.6 The applicant is required to provide the information needed about the significant steps in the child's life in the Application Form and to update this information regularly taking into account information received from others involved in the child's life such as other parties, members of the child's family, the person who is caring for the child, the children's guardian and the child's key social worker.

3.7 Before setting the timetable for the proceedings the factors which the court will consider will include the need to give effect to the overriding objective and the timescales in the Public Law Outline by which the steps in the Outline are to be taken. Where possible, the timetable for the proceedings should be in line with those timescales. However, there will be cases where the significant steps in the child's life demand that the steps in the proceedings be taken at times which are outside the timescales set out in the Outline. In those cases the timetable for the proceedings may not adhere to one or more of the timescales set out in the Outline.

3.8 Where more than one child is the subject of the proceedings, the court should consider and may set a Timetable for the Child for each child. The children may not all have the same Timetable, and the court will consider the appropriate progress of the proceedings in relation to each child.

PART II – Statutory Instruments

3.9 Where there are parallel care proceedings and criminal proceedings against a person connected with the child for a serious offence against the child, linked directions hearings should where practicable take place as the case progresses. The timing of the proceedings in a linked care and criminal case should appear in the Timetable for the Child.

CASE MANAGEMENT DOCUMENTATION

3.10 Case Management Documentation includes the –

(1)   Application Form and Annex Documents;
(2)   Case Analysis and Recommendations provided by Cafcass or CAFCASS CYMRU;
(3)   Local Authority Case Summary;
(4)   Other Parties' Case Summaries.

3.11 The court will encourage the use of the Case Management Documentation which is not prescribed by the rules.

THE CASE MANAGEMENT RECORD

3.12 The court's filing system for the case will be known as the Case Management Record and will include the following main documents –

(1)   the Case Management Documentation;
(2)   Standard Directions on Issue and on First Appointment;
(3)   Case Management Orders approved by the court.

3.13 Parties or their legal representatives will be expected to retain their own record containing copies of the documents on the court's Case Management Record.

THE FIRST APPOINTMENT

3.14 The purpose of the First Appointment is to confirm allocation of the case and give initial case management directions.

THE CASE MANAGEMENT ORDER

3.15 The Case Management Order is an order which will be made by the court at the conclusion of the Case Management Conference, the Issues Resolution Hearing and any other case management hearing. It is designed to achieve active case management as defined in paragraph 3.20 below. The parties are required to prepare and submit to the court a draft of this order in accordance with paragraphs 5.8 to 5.10 below. The order will include such of the provisions referred to in the Glossary at paragraph 26(12) as are appropriate to the proceedings.

ADVOCATES' MEETING/DISCUSSION

3.16 The court will consider directing advocates to have discussions before the Case Management Conference and the Issues Resolution Hearing. Advocates may well find that the best way to have these discussions is to meet. Such discussion is intended to facilitate agreement and to narrow the issues for the court to consider. Advocates and litigants in person may take part in the Advocates' Meeting or discussions.

THE CASE MANAGEMENT CONFERENCE

3.17 In each case there will be a Case Management Conference to enable the case management judge or case manager, with the co-operation of the parties, actively to manage the case and, at the earliest practicable opportunity to –

(1) identify the relevant and key issues; and
(2) give full case management directions including confirming the Timetable for the Child.

THE ISSUES RESOLUTION HEARING

3.18 In each case there will be an Issues Resolution Hearing before the Final Hearing to –

(1) identify any remaining key issues; and
(2) as far as possible, resolve or narrow those issues.

ACTIVE CASE MANAGEMENT

3.19 The court must further the overriding objective by actively managing cases.

3.20 Active case management includes –

(1) identifying the Timetable for the Child;
(2) identifying the appropriate court to conduct the proceedings and transferring the proceedings as early as possible to that court;
(3) encouraging the parties to co-operate with each other in the conduct of the proceedings;
(4) retaining the Case Management Record;
(5) identifying all facts and matters that are in issue at the earliest stage in the proceedings and at each hearing;
(6) deciding promptly which issues need full investigation and hearing and which do not and whether a fact finding hearing is required;
(7) deciding the order in which issues are to be resolved;
(8) identifying at an early stage who should be a party to the proceedings;
(9) considering whether the likely benefits of taking a particular step justify any delay which will result and the cost of taking it;
(10) directing discussion between advocates and litigants in person before the Case Management Conference and Issues Resolution Hearing;
(11) requiring the use of the Case Management Order and directing advocates and litigants in person to prepare or adjust the draft of this Order where appropriate;
(12) standardising, simplifying and regulating –
    (a) the use of Case Management Documentation and forms;
    (b) the court's orders and directions;
(13) controlling –
    (a) the use and cost of experts;

PART II – Statutory Instruments

      (b)   the nature and extent of the documents which are to be disclosed to the parties and presented to the court;

      (c)   whether and, if so, in what manner the documents disclosed are to be presented to the court;

      (d)   the progress of the case;

(14) where it is demonstrated to be in the interests of the child, encouraging the parties to use an alternative dispute resolution procedure if the court considers such a procedure to be appropriate and facilitating the use of such procedure;

(15) helping the parties to reach agreement in relation to the whole or part of the case;

(16) fixing the dates for all appointments and hearings;

(17) dealing with as many aspects of the case as it can on the same occasion;

(18) where possible dealing with additional issues which may arise from time to time in the case without requiring the parties to attend at court;

(19) making use of technology; and

(20) giving directions to ensure that the case proceeds quickly and efficiently.

The Expectations

4.1 The expectations are that proceedings should be –

    (1)   conducted using the Case Management Tools and Case Management Documentation referred to in this Practice Direction in accordance with the Public Law Outline;

    (2)   finally determined within the timetable fixed by the court in accordance with the Timetable for the Child – the timescales in the Public Law Outline being adhered to and being taken as the maximum permissible time for the taking of the step referred to in the Outline unless the Timetable for the Child demands otherwise.

4.2 However, there may be cases where the court considers that the child's welfare requires a different approach from the one contained in the Public Law Outline. In those cases, the court will –

    (1)   determine the appropriate case management directions and timetable; and

    (2)   record on the face of the order the reasons for departing from the approach in the Public Law Outline.

How the parties should help court case management

Main methods of helping

Good case preparation

5.1 The applicant should prepare the case before proceedings are issued. In care and supervision proceedings the Local Authority should use the Pre-proceedings checklist.

THE TIMETABLE FOR THE CHILD

5.2 The applicant must state in the Application Form all information concerning significant steps in the child's life that are likely to take place during the proceedings. The applicant is to be responsible for updating this information regularly and giving it to the court. The applicant will need to obtain information about these significant steps and any variations and additions to them from others involved in the child's life such as other parties, members of the child's family, the person who is caring for the child, the children's guardian and the child's key social worker. When the other persons involved in the child's life become aware of a significant step in the child's life or a variation of an existing one, that information should be given to the applicant as soon as possible.

5.3 The information about the significant steps in the child's life will enable the court to set the Timetable for the Child and to review that Timetable in the light of new information. The Timetable for the Child will be included or referred to in the draft of a Case Management Order, the Case Management Order, Standard Directions on Issue and on First Appointment and the directions given at the Case Management Conference and Issues Resolution Hearing.

CASE MANAGEMENT DOCUMENTATION

5.4 The parties must use the Case Management Documentation.

CO-OPERATION

5.5 The parties and their representatives should co-operate with the court in case management, including the fixing of timetables to avoid unacceptable delay, and in the crystallisation and resolution of the issues on which the case turns.

DIRECTIONS

5.6 The parties will –

(1)   monitor compliance with the court's directions; and
(2)   tell the court or court officer about any failure to comply with a direction of the court or any other delay in the proceedings.

THE CASE MANAGEMENT RECORD

5.7 The parties are expected to retain a record containing copies of the documents on the court's Case Management Record.

DRAFTING THE CASE MANAGEMENT ORDER

5.8 Parties should start to consider the content of the draft of the Case Management Order at the earliest opportunity either before or in the course of completing applications to the court or the response to the application. They should in any event consider the drafting of a Case Management Order after the First Appointment.

PART II – Statutory Instruments

5.9 Only one draft of the Case Management Order should be filed with the court for each of the Case Management Conference and the Issues Resolution Hearing. It is the responsibility of the advocate for the applicant, which in care and supervision proceedings will ordinarily be the Local Authority, to prepare those drafts and be responsible for obtaining comments from the advocates and the parties.

5.10 There should be ongoing consideration of the Case Management Orders throughout the proceedings. The Case Management Orders should serve as an *aide memoire* to everyone involved in the proceedings of –

(1)   the Timetable for the Child;
(2)   the case management decisions;
(3)   the identified issues.

5.11 In paragraphs 5.4, 5.6 to 5.9 'parties' includes parties' legal representatives.

Findings of fact hearings

6 In a case where the court decides that a fact finding hearing is necessary, the starting point is that the proceedings leading to that hearing are to be managed in accordance with the case management steps in this Practice Direction.

Ethnicity, language, religion and culture

7 At each case management stage of the proceedings, particularly at the First Appointment and Case Management Conference, the court will consider giving directions regarding the obtaining of evidence about the ethnicity, language, religion and culture of the child and other significant persons involved in the proceedings. The court will subsequently consider the implications of this evidence for the child in the context of the issues in the case.

Adults who may be protected parties

8.1 The applicant must give details in the Application Form of any referral to or assessment by the local authority's Adult Learning Disability team (or its equivalent).The Local Authority should tell the court about other referrals or assessments if known such as a referral to Community Mental Health.

8.2 The court will investigate as soon as possible any issue as to whether an adult party or intended party to the proceedings lacks capacity (within the meaning of the Mental Capacity Act 2005) to conduct the proceedings. A representative (a litigation friend, next friend or guardian ad litem) is needed to conduct the proceedings on behalf of an adult who lacks capacity to do so ('a protected party'). The expectation of the Official Solicitor is that the Official Solicitor will only be invited to act for a protected party as guardian ad litem or litigation friend if there is no other person suitable and willing to act.

8.3 Any issue as to the capacity of an adult to conduct the proceedings must be determined before the court gives any directions relevant to that adult's role within the proceedings.

8.4 Where the adult is a protected party, that party's representative should be involved in any instruction of an expert, including the instruction of an expert to assess whether the adult, although a protected party, is competent to give evidence. The instruction of an expert is a significant step in the proceedings. The representative will wish to consider (and ask the expert to consider), if the protected party is competent to give evidence, their best interests in this regard. The representative may wish to seek advice about 'special measures'. The representative may put forward an argument on behalf of the protected party that the protected party should not give evidence.

8.5 If at any time during the proceedings, there is reason to believe that a party may lack capacity to conduct the proceedings, then the court must be notified and directions sought to ensure that this issue is investigated without delay.

Child likely to lack capacity to conduct the proceedings when aged 18

9 Where it appears that a child is –

(1)   a party to the proceedings and not the subject of them;
(2)   nearing age 18; and
(3)   considered likely to lack capacity to conduct the proceedings when 18, the court will consider giving directions relating to the investigation of a child's capacity in this respect.

Outline of the process and how to use the Main Case Management Tools

10.1 The Public Law Outline set out in the Table below contains an outline of

(1)   the order of the different stages of the process;
(2)   the purposes of the main case management hearings and matters to be considered at them;
(3)   the latest timescales within which the main stages of the process should take place.

10.2 In the Public Law Outline –

(1)'CMC' means the Case Management Conference;
(2)'FA' means the First Appointment;
(3)'IRH' means the Issues Resolution Hearing;
(4)'LA' means the Local Authority which is applying for a care or supervision order;
(5)'OS' means the Official Solicitor.

Public Law Outline

PRE-PROCEEDINGS

PRE-PROCEEDINGS CHECKLIST

Annex Documents (the documents specified in the Annex to the Application Form to be attached to that form where available):	Other Checklist Documents which already exist on LA's files which are to be disclosed in the event of proceedings normally before the day of the FA:
– Social Work Chronology	– Previous court orders & judgments/reasons
– Initial Social Work Statement	– Any relevant assessment materials
– Initial and Core Assessments	– Section 7 & 37 reports
– Letters Before Proceedings – Schedule of Proposed Findings	– Relatives & friends materials (e.g., a genogram)
– Care Plan	– Other relevant reports & records
	– Single, joint or inter-agency materials (e.g., health & education/Home Office & Immigration documents)
	– Records of discussions with the family
	– Key LA minutes & records for the child (including Strategy Discussion Record)
	– Pre-existing care plans (e.g., child in need plan, looked after child plan & child protection plan)

STAGE 1 – ISSUE AND THE FIRST APPOINTMENT	
ISSUE	FIRST APPOINTMENT
On DAY 1 and by DAY 3	By DAY 6
Objectives: To ensure compliance with pre-proceedings checklist; to allocate proceedings; to obtain the information necessary for initial case management at the FA	Objectives: To confirm allocation; to give initial case management directions

On Day 1:	
On Day 1: – The LA files the Application Form and Annex Documents where available – Court officer issues application	– LA normally serves Other Checklist Documents on the parties – Parties notify LA & court of need for a contested hearing
– Court nominates case manager(s) – Court gives Standard Directions on Issue including:	– Court makes arrangements for a contested hearing – Initial case management by court including:

– Pre-proceedings checklist compliance including preparation and service of any missing Annex Documents
    – Allocate and/or transfer
	– Confirm Timetable for the Child
	    – Confirm allocation or transfer
	    – Identify additional parties & representation (including allocation of children's guardian)

– Appoint children's guardian
    – Appoint solicitor for the child
	– Identify 'Early Final Hearing' cases
	    – Scrutinise Care Plan

– Case Analysis for FA	– Court gives Standard Directions on FA including:
– Appoint a guardian ad litem or litigation friend for a protected party or any non subject child who is a party, including the OS where appropriate	– Case Analysis and Recommendations for Stages 2 & 3 – Preparation and service of any missing Annex Documents
– List FA by Day 6	– What Other Checklist Documents are to be filed
– Make arrangements for contested hearing (if necessary)	– LA Case Summary – Other Parties' Case Summaries

By Day 3
– Cafcass/CAFCASS CYMRU expected to allocate case to children's guardian
– LA serves the Application Form and Annex Documents, on parties
	– Parties' initial witness statements
	    – For the Advocates' Meeting
	    – List CMC or (if appropriate) an Early Final Hearing
	    – Upon transfer

PART II – Statutory Instruments

STAGE 2 – CASE MANAGEMENT CONFERENCE	
ADVOCATES' MEETING	**CMC**
No later than 2 days before CMC	**No later than day 45**
Objectives: To prepare the Draft Case Management Order; to identify experts and draft questions for them	**Objectives: To identify issue(s); to give full case management directions**

– Consider information on the Application Form, all Other Parties' Case Summaries and Case Analysis and Recommendations
 	
– Identify proposed experts and draft questions in accordance with Experts Practice Direction
 	
– Draft Case Management Order
 	
– Notify court of need for a contested hearing
 	
– File draft of the Case Management Order with the case manager/case management judge by 11am one working day before the CMC
	– Detailed case management by the court
	
	   – Scrutinise compliance with directions
	   – Review and confirm Timetable for the Child
	   – Identify key issue(s)
	   – Confirm allocation or transfer
	   – Consider case management directions in the draft of the Case Management Order
	   – Scrutinise Care Plan
	
	   – Check compliance with Experts Practice Direction
	– Court issues Case Management Order
	– Court lists IRH and, where necessary, a warned period for Final Hearing

STAGE 3 – ISSUES RESOLUTION HEARING	
ADVOCATES' MEETING	**IRH**
Between 2 and 7 days before the IRH	**Between 16 & 25 weeks**
Objective: To prepare or update the draft Case Management Order	**Objectives: To resolve and narrow issue(s); to identify any remaining key issues**

– Consider all other parties' Case Summaries and Case Analysis and Recommendations	– Identification by the court of the key issue(s) (if any) to be determined
– Draft Case Management Order	– Final case management by the court:
– Notify court of need for a contested hearing/time for oral evidence to be given	– Scrutinise compliance with directions
– File Draft Case Management Order with the case manager/case management judge by 11am one working day before the IRH	– Review and confirm the Timetable for the Child
	– Consider case management directions in the draft of the Case Management Order
	– Scrutinise Care Plan
	– Give directions for Hearing documents:
	– Threshold agreement or facts/issues remaining to be determined
	– Final Evidence & Care Plan
	– Case Analysis and Recommendations
	– Witness templates
	– Skeleton arguments
	– Judicial reading list/reading time/judgment writing time
	– Time estimate
	– Bundles Practice Direction compliance
	– List or confirm Hearing
	– Court issues Case Management Order

PART II – Statutory Instruments

STAGE 4	
HEARING	
Hearing set in accordance with the Timetable for the Child	
Objective: To determine remaining issues	
– All file & serve updated Case Management Documentation & bundle – Draft final order(s) in approved form	– Judgment/Reasons – Disclose documents as required after hearing

Starting the proceedings

PRE-PROCEEDINGS CHECKLIST

11.1 The Pre-proceedings Checklist is to be used by the applicant to help prepare for the start of the proceedings.

11.2 The Pre-proceedings Checklist contains the documents which are specified in the Annex to the Application Form. The rules require those documents which are known as the 'Annex Documents' to be filed with the Application Form where available. The Annex Documents are –

    (1)   Social Work Chronology;
    (2)   Initial Social Work Statement;
    (3)   Initial and Core Assessments;
    (4)   Letters before Proceedings;
    (5)   Schedule of Proposed Findings; and
    (6)   Care Plan.

11.3 In addition, the Pre-proceedings Checklist contains examples of documents other than the Annex Documents which will normally be on the Local Authority file at the start of proceedings so that they can be served on parties in accordance with the Public Law Outline. These documents are known as the 'Other Checklist Documents' and are not to be filed with the court at the start of the proceedings but are to be disclosed to the parties normally before the day of the First Appointment or in accordance with the court's directions and to be filed with the court only as directed by the court.

COMPLIANCE WITH PRE-PROCEEDINGS CHECKLIST

11.4 It is recognised that in some cases the circumstances are such that the safety and welfare of the child may be jeopardised if the start of proceedings is delayed until all of the documents appropriate to the case and referred to in the Pre-proceedings Checklist are available. The safety and welfare of the child should never be put in jeopardy because of lack of documentation. (Nothing in this Practice Direction affects an application for an emergency protection order under section 44 of the 1989 Act).

11.5 The court recognises that the preparation may need to be varied to suit the circumstances of the case. In cases where any of the Annex Documents required to be attached to the Application Form are not available at the time of issue of the application, the court will consider making directions on issue about when any missing documentation is to be filed. The expectation is that there will be a good reason why one or more of the documents are not available. Further directions relating to any missing documentation are likely to be made at the First Appointment. The court also recognises that some documents on the Pre-proceedings Checklist may not exist and may never exist, for example, the Section 37 report, and that in urgent proceedings no Letter Before Proceedings may have been sent.

What the court will do at the issue of proceedings

OBJECTIVES

12.1 The objectives at this stage are for the court –

  (1) to identify the Timetable for the Child;
  (2) in care and supervision proceedings, to ensure compliance with the Pre-proceedings Checklist;
  (3) to allocate proceedings;
  (4) to obtain the information necessary to enable initial case management at the First Appointment.

12.2 The steps which the court will take once proceedings have been issued include those set out in paragraphs 12.3 to 12.5 below.

ALLOCATION

12.3 By reference to the Allocation Order, the court will consider allocation of the case and transfer to the appropriate level of court those cases which are obviously suitable for immediate transfer.

Other steps to be taken by the court

DIRECTIONS

12.4 The court will –

  (1) consider giving directions –
      (a) appropriate to the case including Standard Directions On Issue;
      (b) in care and supervision proceedings, relating to the preparation, filing and service of any missing Annex Documents and what Other Checklist Documents are to be filed and by when;
      (c) relating to the representation of any protected party or any child who is a party to, but is not the subject of, the proceedings by a guardian ad litem or litigation friend, including the Official Solicitor where appropriate;
  (2) appoint a children's guardian in specified proceedings (in relation to care and supervision proceedings the court will expect that Cafcass or CAFCASS CYMRU will have received notice from the Local Authority that proceedings were going to be started);

PART II – Statutory Instruments

(3)   appoint a solicitor for the child under section 41(3) of the 1989 Act where appropriate;

(4)   request the children's guardian or if appropriate another officer of the service or Welsh family proceedings officer to prepare a Case Analysis and Recommendations for the First Appointment;

(5)   make arrangements for a contested hearing, if necessary.

(A suggested form for the drafting of Standard Directions on Issue is Form PLO 8 which is available from HMCS)

SETTING A DATE FOR THE FIRST APPOINTMENT

12.5 The court will record the Timetable for the Child and set a date for the First Appointment normally no later than 6 days from the date of issue of the proceedings and in any event in line with the Timetable for the Child.

CASE MANAGERS IN THE MAGISTRATES' COURTS

12.6 In the magistrates' courts, the justices' clerk may nominate one but not more than two case managers.

The First Appointment objectives

13.1 The First Appointment is the first hearing in the proceedings. The main objectives of the First Appointment are to –

(1)   confirm allocation; and

(2)   give initial case management directions having regard to the Public Law Outline.

13.2 The steps which the court will take at the First Appointment include those set out in paragraphs 13.3 to 13.6 below.

STEPS TO BE TAKEN BY THE COURT

13.3 The court will –

(1)   confirm the Timetable for the Child;

(2)   make arrangements for any contested interim hearing such as an application for an interim care order;

(3)   confirm in writing the allocation of the case or, if appropriate, transfer the case;

(4)   request the children's guardian or if appropriate another officer of the service or Welsh family proceedings officer to prepare a Case Analysis and Recommendations for the Case Management Conference or Issues Resolution Hearing;

(5)   scrutinise the Care Plan;

(6)   consider giving directions relating to –

(a)   those matters in the Public Law Outline which remain to be considered including preparation, filing and service of any missing Annex Documents and what Other Checklist documents are to be filed and by when;

(b)   the joining of a person who would not otherwise be a respondent under the rules as a party to the proceedings;

(c)   where any person to be joined as a party may be a protected party, an investigation of that person's capacity to conduct the proceedings and the representation of that person by a guardian ad litem or litigation friend, including the Official Solicitor where appropriate;

(d)   the identification of family and friends as proposed carers and any overseas, immigration, jurisdiction and paternity issues;

(e)   any other documents to be filed with the court;

(f)   evidence to be obtained as to whether a parent who is a protected party is competent to make a statement.

(A suggested form for the drafting of Standard Directions on First Appointment is Form PLO 9 which is available from HMCS)

EARLY FINAL HEARING

13.4 Cases which are suitable for an early Final Hearing are those cases where all the evidence necessary to determine issues of fact and welfare is immediately or shortly available to be filed. Those cases are likely to include cases where the child has no parents, guardians, relatives who want to care for the child, or other carers. The court will –

(1)   identify at the First Appointment whether the case is one which is suitable for an early Final Hearing; and

(2)   set a date for that Final Hearing.

SETTING A DATE FOR THE CASE MANAGEMENT CONFERENCE.

13.5 The court will set a date for the Case Management Conference normally no later than 45 days from the date of issue of the proceedings and in any event in line with the Timetable for the Child.

ADVOCATES' MEETING/DISCUSSION AND THE DRAFTING OF THE CASE MANAGEMENT ORDER

13.6 The court will consider directing a discussion between the parties' advocates and any litigant in person and the preparation of a draft of the Case Management Order as outlined below.

EXPERTS

13.7 A party who wishes to instruct an expert should comply with the Experts Practice Direction. Where the parties are agreed on any matter relating to experts or expert evidence, the draft agreement must be submitted for the court's approval as early as possible in the proceedings.

Advocates' Meeting/discussion and the drafting of the Case Management Order

14.1 The main objective of the Advocates' Meeting or discussion is to prepare a draft of the Case Management Order for approval by the court.

PART II – Statutory Instruments

14.2 Where there is a litigant in person the court will consider the most effective way in which that person can be involved in the advocates discussions and give directions as appropriate including directions relating to the part to be played by any McKenzie Friend.

14.3 Timing of the discussions is of the utmost importance. Discussions of matters 'outside the court room door', which could have taken place at an earlier time, are to be avoided. Discussions are to take place no later than 2 days before the Case Management Conference or the Issues Resolution Hearing whichever is appropriate. The discussions may take place earlier than 2 days before those hearings, for example, up to 7 days before them.

14.4 Following discussion the advocates should prepare or adjust the draft of the Case Management Order. In practice the intention is that the advocate for the applicant, which in care and supervision proceedings will ordinarily be the Local Authority, should take the lead in preparing and adjusting the draft of the Case Management Order following discussion with the other advocates. The aim is for the advocates to agree a draft of the Case Management Order which is to be submitted for the approval of the court.

14.5 Where it is not possible for the advocates to agree the terms of the draft of the Case Management Order, the advocates should specify on the draft, or on a separate document if more practicable –

(1)   those provisions on which they agree; and
(2)   those provisions on which they disagree.

14.6 Unless the court directs otherwise, the draft of the Case Management Order must be filed with the court no later than 11am on the day before the Case Management Conference or the Issues Resolution Hearing whichever may be appropriate.

14.7 At the Advocates' Meeting or discussion before the Case Management Conference, the advocates should also try to agree the questions to be put to any proposed expert (whether jointly instructed or not) if not previously agreed. Under the Experts Practice Direction the questions on which the proposed expert is to give an opinion are a crucial component of the expert directions which the court is required to consider at the Case Management Conference.

Case Management Conference objectives

15.1 The Case Management Conference is the main hearing at which the court manages the case. The main objectives of the Conference are to –

(1)   identify key issues; and
(2)   give full case management directions.

15.2 The steps which the court will take at the Case Management Conference include those steps set out in paragraphs 15.3 to 15.5 below.

STEPS TO BE TAKEN BY THE COURT

15.3 The court will –

(1)　review and confirm the Timetable for the Child;

(2)　confirm the allocation or the transfer of the case;

(3)　scrutinise the Care Plan;

(4)　identify the key issues;

(5)　identify the remaining case management issues;

(6)　resolve remaining case management issues set out in the draft of the Case Management Order;

(7)　identify any special measures such as the need for access for the disabled or provision for vulnerable witnesses;

(8)　scrutinise the Case Management Record to check whether directions have been complied with and if not, consider making further directions as appropriate;

(9)　where expert evidence is required, check whether the parties have complied with the Experts Practice Direction, in particular the section on preparation for the relevant hearing and consider giving directions as appropriate.

CASE MANAGEMENT ORDER

15.4 The court will issue the approved Case Management Order. Parties or their legal representatives will be expected to submit in electronic form the final approved draft of the Case Management Order on the conclusion of, and the same day as, the Case Management Conference.

SETTING A DATE FOR THE ISSUES RESOLUTION HEARING/FINAL HEARING

15.5 The court will set –

(1)　a date for the Issues Resolution Hearing normally at any time between 16 and 25 weeks from the date of issue of the proceedings and in any event in line with the Timetable for the Child; and

(2)　if necessary, specify a period within which the Final Hearing of the application is to take place unless a date has already been set.

The Issues Resolution Hearing objectives

16.1 The objectives of this hearing are to –

(1)　resolve and narrow issues;

(2)　identify key remaining issues requiring resolution.

16.2 The Issues Resolution Hearing is likely to be the hearing before the Final Hearing. Final case management directions and other preparations for the Final Hearing will be made at this hearing.

STEPS TO BE TAKEN BY THE COURT

16.3 The court will –

(1)　identify the key issues (if any) to be determined;

(2)　review and confirm the Timetable for the Child;

(3)　consider giving case management directions relating to –

　　(a)　any outstanding matter contained in the draft of the Case Management Order;

PART II – Statutory Instruments

(b)   the preparation and filing of final evidence including the filing of witness templates;

(c)   skeleton arguments;

(d)   preparation and filing of bundles in accordance with the Bundles Practice Direction;

(e)   any agreement relating to the satisfaction of the threshold criteria under section 31 of the 1989 Act or facts and issues remaining to be determined in relation to it or to any welfare question which arises;

(f)   time estimates;

(g)   the judicial reading list and likely reading time and judgment writing time;

(4)   issue the Case Management Order.

16.4 For the avoidance of doubt the purpose of an Issues Resolution Hearing is to –

(1)   identify key issues which are not agreed;

(2)   examine if those key issues can be agreed; and

(3)   where those issues cannot be agreed, examine the most proportionate method of resolving those issues.

16.5 The expectation is that the method of resolving the key issues which cannot be agreed will be at a hearing (ordinarily the Final hearing) where there is an opportunity for the relevant oral evidence to be heard and challenged.

Attendance at the Case Management Conference and the Issues Resolution Hearing

17 An advocate who has conduct of the Final Hearing should ordinarily attend the Case Management Conference and the Issues Resolution Hearing. Where the attendance of this advocate is not possible, then an advocate who is familiar with the issues in the proceedings should attend.

Flexible powers of the court

18.1 Attention is drawn to the flexible powers of the court either following the issue of the application in that court, the transfer of the case to that court or at any other stage in the proceedings.

18.2 The court may give directions without a hearing including setting a date for the Final Hearing or a period within which the Final Hearing will take place. The steps, which the court will ordinarily take at the various stages of the proceedings provided for in the Public Law Outline, may be taken by the court at another stage in the proceedings if the circumstances of the case merit this approach.

18.3 The flexible powers of the court include the ability for the court to cancel or repeat a particular hearing. For example, if the issue on which the case turns can with reasonable practicability be crystallised and resolved by having an early Final Hearing, then in the fulfilment of the overriding objective, such a flexible approach must be taken to secure compliance with section 1(2) of the 1989 Act.

Alternative Dispute Resolution

19.1 The court will encourage the parties to use an alternative dispute resolution procedure and facilitate the use of such a procedure where it is –

(1)   readily available;
(2)   demonstrated to be in the interests of the child; and
(3)   reasonably practicable and safe.

19.2 At any stage in the proceedings, the parties can ask the court for advice about alternative dispute resolution.

19.3 At any stage in the proceedings the court itself will consider whether alternative dispute resolution is appropriate. If so, the court may direct that a hearing or proceedings be adjourned for such specified period as it considers appropriate –

(1)   to enable the parties to obtain information and advice about alternative dispute resolution; and
(2)   where the parties agree, to enable alternative dispute resolution to take place.

Co-operation

20.1 Throughout the proceedings the parties and their representatives should cooperate wherever reasonably practicable to help towards securing the welfare of the child as the paramount consideration.

20.2 At each court appearance the court will ask the parties and their legal representatives –

(1)   what steps they have taken to achieve co-operation and the extent to which they have been successful;
(2)   if appropriate the reason why co-operation could not be achieved; and
(3)   the steps needed to resolve any issues necessary to achieve co-operation.

Agreed directions

21.1 The parties, their advisers and the children's guardian, are encouraged to try to agree directions for the management of the proceedings.

21.2 To obtain the court's approval the agreed directions must –

(1)   set out a Timetable for the Child by reference to calendar dates for the taking of steps for the preparation of the case;
(2)   include a date when it is proposed that the next hearing will take place.

PART II – Statutory Instruments

Variation of case management timetable

22 It is emphasised that a party or the children's guardian must apply to the court at the earliest opportunity if they wish to vary by extending the dates set by the court for –

(1)   a directions appointment;

(2)   a First Appointment;

(3)   a Case Management Conference;

(4)   an Issues Resolution Hearing;

(5)   the Final Hearing;

(6)   the period within which the Final Hearing of the application is to take place; or

(7)   any Meeting/discussion between advocates or for the filing of the draft of the Case Management Orders.

Who performs the functions of the court

23.1 Where this Practice Direction provides for the court to perform case management functions, then except where any rule, practice direction, any other enactment or the Family Proceedings (Allocation to Judiciary) Directions ([2009] 2 FLR 51) provides otherwise, the functions may be performed –

(1)   in relation to proceedings in the High Court or in a district registry, by any judge or district judge of that Court including a district judge of the principal registry;

(2)   in relation to proceedings in the county court, by any judge or district judge including a district judge of the principal registry when the principal registry is treated as if it were a county court; and

(3)   in relation to proceedings in a magistrates' court by –

    (a)   any family proceedings court constituted in accordance with sections 66 and 67 of the 1980 Act;

    (b)   a single justice; or

    (c)   a justices' clerk.

23.2 The case management functions to be exercised by a justices' clerk may be exercised by an assistant justices' clerk provided that person has been specifically authorised by a justices' clerk to exercise case management functions. Any reference in this Practice Direction to a justices' clerk is to be taken to include an assistant justices' clerk so authorised. The justices' clerk may in particular appoint one but not more than two assistant justices' clerks as case managers for each case.

23.3 In proceedings in a magistrates' court, where a party considers that there are likely to be issues arising at a hearing (including the First Appointment, Case Management Conference and Issues Resolution Hearing) which need to be decided by a family proceedings court, rather than a justices' clerk, then that party should give the court written notice of that need at least 2 days before the hearing.

23.4 Family proceedings courts may consider making arrangements to ensure a court constituted in accordance with s 66 of the 1980 Act is available at the same time as Issues Resolution Hearings are being heard by a justices' clerk. Any delay as a result of the justices' clerk considering for whatever reason that it is inappropriate for a justices' clerk to perform a case management function on a particular matter and the justices' clerk's referring of that matter to the court should then be minimal.

Technology

24 Where the facilities are available to the court and the parties, the court will consider making full use of technology including electronic information exchange and video or telephone conferencing.

Other Practice Directions

25.1 This Practice Direction must be read with the Bundles Practice Direction.

25.2 The Bundles Practice Direction is applied to Public Law Proceedings in the High Court and county court with the following adjustments –

(1)   add 'except the First Appointment; Case Management Conference, and Issues Resolution Hearing referred to in the Practice Direction Public Law Proceedings Guide to Case Management: April 2010 where there are no contested applications being heard at those hearings' to paragraph 2.2;

(2)   the reference to –

   (a)   the 'Protocol for Judicial Case Management in Public law Children Act Cases [2003] 2 FLR 719' in paragraph 6.1;

   (b)   the 'Practice Direction: Care Cases: Judicial Continuity and Judicial Case Management' in paragraph 15; and

   (c)   'the Public Law Protocol' in paragraph 15, shall be read as if it were a reference to this Practice Direction.

25.3 Paragraph 1.9 of the Practice Direction: Experts in Family Proceedings Relating to Children dated April 2008 should be read as if 'Practice Direction: Guide to Case Management in Public law Proceedings, paragraphs 13.7, 14.3 and 25(29)' were a reference to 'Practice Direction Public Law Proceedings Guide to Case Management: April 2010, paragraphs 14.7, 15.3 and 26(33)'.

Glossary

26 In this Practice Direction –

(1)'the 1989 Act' means the Children Act 1989;

(2)'the 1980 Act' means the Magistrates' Courts Act 1980;

(3)'advocate' means a person exercising a right of audience as a representative of, or on behalf of, a party;

(4)'Allocation Order' means any order made by the Lord Chancellor under Part 1 of Schedule 11 to the 1989 Act;

(5)'alternative dispute resolution' means the methods of resolving a dispute other than through the normal court process;

(6)'Annex Documents' means the documents specified in the Annex to the Application Form;

(7)'Application Form' means Form C110 and Annex Documents;

(8)'assistant justices' clerk' has the meaning assigned to it by section 27(5) of the Courts Act 2003;

(9)'the Bundles Practice Direction' means the Practice Direction Family Proceedings: Court Bundles (Universal Practice to be Applied in all Courts other than Family Proceedings Court) of 27 July 2006;

(10)'Case Analysis and Recommendations' means a written or oral outline of the case from the child's perspective prepared by the children's guardian or other officer of the service or Welsh family proceedings officer at different stages of the proceedings requested by the court, to provide –

    (a)   an analysis of the issues that need to be resolved in the case including –

        (i)   any harm or risk of harm;

        (ii)   the child's own views;

        (iii)   the family context including advice relating to ethnicity, language, religion and culture of the child and other significant persons;

        (iv)   the Local Authority work and proposed care plan;

        (v)   advice about the court process including the Timetable for the Child; and

        (vi)   identification of work that remains to be done for the child in the short and longer term; and

    (b)   recommendations for outcomes, in order to safeguard and promote the best interests of the child in the proceedings;

(11)'Case Management Documentation' includes the documents referred to in paragraph 3.10;

(12)'Case Management Order' means an order made by the court which identifies the Timetable for the Child, any delay in the proceedings and the reason for such delay and the key issues in the proceedings and includes such of the following provisions as are appropriate to the proceedings –

    (a)   preliminary information –

        (i)   the names and dates of birth of the children who are the subject of the proceedings;

        (ii)   the names and legal representatives of the parties, and whether they attended the hearing;

        (iii)   any interim orders made in respect of the children and any provisions made for the renewal of those orders;

    (b)   any recitals that the court considers should be recorded in the order, including those relating to –

        (i)   any findings made by the court or agreed between the parties;

        (ii)   any other agreements or undertakings made by the parties;

    (c)   orders made at the hearing by way of case management relating to –

        (i)   the joinder of parties;

        (ii)   the determination of parentage of the children;

(iii) the appointment of a guardian ad litem or litigation friend (including the Official Solicitor where appropriate);

(iv) the transfer of the proceedings to a different court;

(v) the allocation of the proceedings to a case management judge;

(vi) the filing and service of threshold criteria documents;

(vii) the preparation and filing of assessments, including Core Assessments and parenting assessments;

(viii) in accordance with the Experts' Practice Direction, the preparation and filing of other expert evidence, and experts' meetings;

(ix) care planning and directions in any application for placement for adoption;

(x) the filing and service of evidence/further evidence on behalf of the local authority;

(xi) the filing and service of evidence/further evidence on behalf of the other parties;

(xii) the filing and service of the Case Analysis and Recommendations;

(xiii) the disclosure of documents into the proceedings held by third parties, including medical records, police records and Home Office information;

(xiv) the disclosure of documents and information relating to the proceedings to non-parties;

(xv) the listing of further hearings, and case management documentation to be prepared for those hearings;

(xvi) advocates' Meetings;

(xvii) the filing of bundles and other preparatory material for future hearings;

(xviii) technology/special measures;

(xix) media attendance and reporting;

(xx) linked or other proceedings;

(xxi) non-compliance with any court orders;

(xxii) such further or other directions as may be necessary for the purposes of case management;

(xxiii) attendance at court (including child/children's guardian);

(13)'Case Management Record' means the court's filing system for the case which includes the documents referred to at paragraph 3.12;

(14)'Case manager' means the justices' clerk or assistant justices' clerk who manages the case in the magistrates' courts;

(15)'Care Plan' means a 'section 31A plan' referred to in section 31A of the 1989 Act;

(16)'Core Assessment' means the assessment undertaken by the Local Authority in accordance with The Framework for the Assessment of Children in Need and their Families (Department of Health et al, 2000);

(17)'court' means the High Court, county court or the magistrates' court;

(18)'court officer' means –

     (a)   in the High Court or a county court, a member of court staff ; and

     (b)   in a magistrates' court, the designated officer;

(19)'Experts Practice Direction' means the Practice Direction regarding Experts in Family Proceedings relating to Children;

(20)'genogram' means a family tree, setting out in diagrammatic form the family's background;

(21)'hearing' includes a directions appointment;

(22)'Initial Assessment' means the assessment undertaken by the Local Authority in accordance with The Framework for the Assessment of Children in Need and their Families (Department of Health et al, 2000);

(23)'Initial Social Work Statement' means a statement prepared by the Local Authority strictly limited to the following evidence –

     (a)   the precipitating incident(s) and background circumstances relevant to the grounds and reasons for making the application including a brief description of any referral and assessment processes that have already occurred;

     (b)   any facts and matters that are within the social worker's personal knowledge limited to the findings sought by the Local Authority;

     (c)   any emergency steps and previous court orders that are relevant to the application;

     (d)   any decisions made by the Local Authority that are relevant to the application;

     (e)   information relevant to the ethnicity, language, religion, culture, gender and vulnerability of the child and other significant persons in the form of a 'family profile' together with a narrative description and details of the social care and other services that are relevant to the same;

     (f)   where the Local Authority is applying for an interim order: the Local Authority's initial proposals for the child (which are also to be set out in the Care Plan) including placement, contact with parents and other significant persons and the social care services that are proposed;

     (g)   the Local Authority's initial proposals for the further assessment of the parties during the proceedings including twin track /concurrent planning (where more than one permanence option for the child is being explored by the Local Authority);

(24)'legal representative' means a –

     (a)   barrister,

     (b)   solicitor,

     (c)   solicitor's employee,

     (d)   manager of a body recognised under section 9 of the Administration of Justice Act 1985, or

     (e)   person who, for the purposes of the Legal Services Act 2007, is an authorised person in relation to an activity which constitutes the conduct of litigation (within the meaning of that Act), who has been instructed to act for a party in relation to the proceedings;

(25)'Letter Before Proceedings' means any letter from the Local Authority containing written notification to the parents and others with parental responsibility for the child of the Local Authority's plan to apply to court for a care or supervision order and any related subsequent correspondence confirming the Local Authority's position;

(26)'Local Authority Case Summary' means a document prepared by the Local Authority advocate for all case management hearings including –

  (a) a recommended reading list and suggested reading time;

  (b) the key issues in the case;

  (c) any additional information relevant to the Timetable for the Child or for the conduct of the hearing or the proceedings;

  (d) a summary of updating information;

  (e) the issues and directions which the court will need to consider at the hearing in question, including any interim orders sought;

  (f) any steps which have not been taken or directions not complied with, an explanation of the reasons for non–compliance and the effect, if any, on the Timetable for the Child;

  (g) any relevant information relating to ethnicity, cultural or gender issues;

(27)'justices' clerk' has the meaning assigned to it by section 27(1) of the Courts Act 2003;

(28)'McKenzie Friend' means any person permitted by the court to sit beside an unrepresented litigant in court to assist the litigant by prompting, taking notes and giving advice to the litigant;

(29)'Other Checklist Documents' means the documents listed in the Pre-proceedings Checklist which will normally be on the local authority file prior to the start of proceedings but which are not –

  (a) to be filed with the court on issue; or

  (b) Annex Documents.

(30)'Other Parties' Case Summaries' means summaries by parties other than the Local Authority containing –

  (a) the party's proposals for the long term future of the child (to include placement and contact);

  (b) the party's reply to the Local Authority's Schedule of Proposed Findings;

  (c) any proposal for assessment / expert evidence; and

  (d) the names, addresses and contact details of any family or friends who it is suggested be approached in relation to long term care / contact or respite;

(31)'Pre-proceedings Checklist' means the Annex Documents and the Other Checklist Documents set out in the Public Law Outline;

(32)'Public Law Outline' means the Table contained in paragraph 10;

(33)'Public Law Proceedings' means proceedings for –

(a) a residence order under section 8 of the 1989 Act with respect to a child who is subject of a care order;

(b) a special guardianship order relating to a child who is subject of a care order;

(c) a secure accommodation order under section 25 of the 1989 Act;

(d) a care order under section 31(1)(a) of the 1989 Act or the discharge of such an order under section 39(1) of the 1989 Act;

(e) an order giving permission to change a child's surname or remove a child from the United Kingdom under section 33(7) of the 1989 Act;

(f) a supervision order under section 31(1)(b) of the 1989 Act, the discharge or variation of such an order under section 39(2) of that Act, or the extension or further extension of such an order under paragraph 6(3) of Schedule 3 to that Act;

(g) an order making provision for contact under section 34(2) to (4) of the 1989 Act or an order varying or discharging such an order under section 34(9) of that Act;

(h) an education supervision order, the extension of an education supervision order under paragraph 15(2) of Schedule 3 to the 1989 Act, or the discharge of such an order under paragraph 17(1) of Schedule 3 to that Act;

(i) an order varying directions made with an interim care order or interim supervision order under section 38(8)(b) of the 1989 Act;

(j) an order under section 39(3) of the 1989 Act varying a supervision order in so far as it affects a person with whom the child is living but who is not entitled to apply for the order to be discharged;

(k) an order under section 39(3A) of the 1989 Act varying or discharging an interim care order in so far as it imposes an exclusion requirement on a person who is not entitled to apply for the order to be discharged;

(l) an order under section 39(3B) of the 1989 Act varying or discharging an interim care order in so far as it confers a power of arrest attached to an exclusion requirement;

(m) the substitution of a supervision order for a care order under section 39(4) of the 1989 Act;

(n) a child assessment order or the variation or discharge of such an order under section 43(12) of the 1989 Act;

(o) an order permitting the Local Authority to arrange for any child in its care to live outside England and Wales under paragraph 19(1) of Schedule 2 to the 1989 Act;

(p) a contribution order, or the variation or revocation of such an order under paragraph 23(8), of Schedule 2 to the 1989 Act;

(q) an appeal under paragraph 8(1) of Schedule 8 to the 1989 Act.

(34) 'rules' means rules of court governing the practice and procedure to be followed in Public Law Proceedings;

(35)'Schedule of Proposed Findings' means the schedule of findings of fact prepared by the Local Authority sufficient to satisfy the threshold criteria under section 31(2) of the 1989 Act and to inform the Care Plan;

(36)'section 7 report' means any report under section 7 of the 1989 Act;

(37)'section 37 report' means any report by the Local Authority to the court as a result of a direction under section 37 of the 1989 Act;

(38)'Social Work Chronology' means a schedule containing –

    (a)   a succinct summary of the significant dates and events in the child's life in chronological order- a running record to be updated during the proceedings;

    (b)   information under the following headings –

        (i)   serial number;

        (ii) date;

        (iii) event-detail;

        (iv) witness or document reference (where applicable);

(39)'specified proceedings' has the meaning assigned to it by section 41(6) of the 1989 Act;

(40)'Standard Directions on Issue' mean directions made by the court which will include such of the directions set out in the Public Law Outline, Stage 1, column 1 as are appropriate to the proceedings;

(41)'Standard Directions on First Appointment' means directions made by the court which will include such of the directions set out in the Public Law Outline, Stage 1, column 2 and directions relating to the following as are appropriate to the proceedings –

    (a)   the Timetable for the Child;

    (b)   the joining of a party to the proceedings;

    (c)   the appointment of a guardian ad litem or litigation friend including the Official Solicitor where appropriate for a protected party or non subject child;

    (d)   allocation of the case to a case manager or case management judge;

    (e)   experts in accordance with the Experts Practice Direction;

    (f)   the interim care plan setting out details as to proposed placement and contact;

    (g)   any other evidence(such as evidence relating to vulnerability, ethnicity, culture, language, religion or gender) and disclosure of evidence between the parties;

    (h)   filing and service of the draft of the Case Management Order before the Case Management Conference;

    (i)   listing the Issues Resolution Hearing and Final Hearing;

    (j)   media attendance and reporting;

(42)'Strategy Discussion Record' means a note of the strategy discussion within the meaning of 'Working Together to Safeguard Children' (2006);

(43)'Timetable for the Child' has the meaning assigned to it by the rules (see paragraph 3.2 of this Practice Direction).

PART II – Statutory Instruments

Practice Direction 12B –
The Revised Private Law Programme

This Practice Direction supplements FPR Part 12

1 Introduction

1.1 The Private Law Programme has achieved marked success in enabling the resolution of the majority of cases by consent at the First Hearing Dispute Resolution Appointment ('FHDRA'). It has been revised to build on the successes of the initial programme and to take account of recent developments in the law and practice associated with private family law.

1.2 In particular, there have been several legislative changes affecting private family law. The Allocation and Transfer of Proceedings Order 2008 (the 'Allocation Order'), requires the transfer of cases from the County Court to the Family Proceedings Court (FPC). Sections 1 to 5 and Schedule 1 of the Children and Adoption Act 2006 which came into force on 8th December 2008, amends the Children Act 1989 by introducing Contact Activity Directions, Contact Activity Conditions, Contact Monitoring Requirements, Financial Compensation Orders and Enforcement Orders.

1.3 There has been growing recognition of the impact of domestic violence and abuse, drug and alcohol misuse and mental illness, on the proper consideration of the issues in private family law; this includes the acceptance that Court orders, even those made by consent, must be scrutinised to ensure that they are safe and take account of any risk factors. Coupled with this is the need to take account of the duty on Cafcass, pursuant to s 16A Children Act 1989, to undertake risk assessments where an officer of the Service ('Cafcass Officer') suspects that a child is at risk of harm. (References to Cafcass include CAFCASS CYMRU and references to the Cafcass Officer include the Welsh family proceedings officer in Wales).

1.4 There is awareness of the importance of involving children where appropriate in the decision making process.

1.5 The Revised Programme incorporates these developments. It also retains the essential feature of the FHDRA as the forum for the parties to be helped to reach agreement as to, and understanding of, the issues that divide them. It recognises that having reached agreement parties may need assistance in putting it into effect in a co-operative way.

1.6 The Revised Programme is designed to provide a framework for the consistent national approach to the resolution of the issues in private family law whilst enabling local practices and initiatives to be operated in addition and within the framework.

1.7 The Revised Programme is designed to assist parties to reach safe agreements where possible, to provide a forum in which to find the best way to resolve issues in each individual case and to promote outcomes that are sustainable, that are in the best interests of children and that take account of their perspectives.

2 Principles

2.1 Where an application is made to a court under Part II of the Children Act 1989, the child's welfare is the court's paramount concern. The court will apply the principle of the 'Overriding Objective' to enable it to deal with a case justly, having regard to the welfare principles involved. So far as practicable the Court will –

(a) Deal expeditiously and fairly with every case;
(b) Deal with a case in ways which are proportionate to the nature, importance and complexity of the issues;
(c) Ensure that the parties are on an equal footing;
(d) Save unnecessary expense;
(e) Allot to each case an appropriate share of the court's resources, while taking account of the need to allot resources to other cases.

2.2 The court will give effect to the overriding objective when applying this programme and when exercising its powers to manage cases.

The parties are required to help the court further the overriding objective and promote the welfare of the child by the application of the welfare principle, pursuant to s 1(1) of the Children Act 1989.

This Programme provides that consideration and discussion of all issues will not take place until the FHDRA when parties are on an equal footing and can hear what is said to and by each other. This excludes the safety checks and enquiries carried out by Cafcass before the first hearing that are required for that hearing and deal only with safety issues.

At the **FHDRA** the Court shall consider in particular –

(a) Whether and the extent to which the parties can safely resolve some or all of the issues with the assistance of the Cafcass Officer and any available mediator.
(b) Risk identification followed by active case management including risk assessment, and compliance with the Practice Direction 14th January 2009: 'Residence and Contact Orders: Domestic Violence and Harm'.
(c) Further dispute resolution.
(d) The avoidance of delay through the early identification of issues and timetabling, subject to the Allocation Order.
(e) Judicial scrutiny of the appropriateness of consent orders.
(f) Judicial consideration of the way to involve the child.
(g) Judicial continuity.

PART II – Statutory Instruments

3 Practical arrangements before the FHDRA

3.1 Applications shall be issued on the day of receipt in accordance with the appropriate Rules of Procedure. It is important that the form C100 is fully completed, especially on pages 1, 2, 3, 10 and 11 otherwise delay may be caused by requests for information.

3.2 If possible at the time of issue, and in any event by no later than 24 hours after issue, or in courts where applications are first considered on paper, by no later than 48 hours after issue, the court shall –

(i)   send or hand to the Applicant
(ii)   send to Cafcass

the following –

(a)   a copy of the Application Form C100, (together with Supplemental Information Form C1A) (if provided) (references to form C1A are to be read as form C100A following the introduction of this replacement form),
(b)   the Notice of Hearing,
(c)   the Acknowledgment Form C7,
(d)   a blank Form C1A,
(e)   the Certificate of Service Form C9,
(f)   information leaflets for the parties.

3.3 Save in urgent cases that require an earlier listing, the fully effective operation of this Practice Direction requires the FHDRA to take place within **4** weeks of the application. Where practicable, the first hearing must be listed to be heard in this period and in any event no later than within **6** weeks of the application. Where, at the time of introduction of this Programme, the Designated Family Judge/Justices' Clerk determines that it is not practicable to list the first hearing within 4 weeks, they should, in consultation with HMCS and Cafcass, formulate a timetable for revisiting the position and managing to list the FHDRA within 4 weeks.

3.4 Copies of each Application Form C100 and Notice of Hearing shall be sent by the court to Cafcass in accordance with 3.2 above.

3.5 The Respondent shall have at least 14 days notice of the hearing where practicable, but the court may abridge this time.

3.6 The Respondent should file a response on the Forms C7/C1A no later than 14 days before the hearing.

3.7 A copy of Forms C7/C1A shall be sent by the court to Cafcass on the day of receipt.

3.8 **NOTE:** This provision relates to cases that are placed in the FHDRA list for hearing other than by direct application in accordance with the procedure referred to in paragraph 3.1. Such listing may follow an application under the Family Law Act 1996, or a direction by the Court in other proceedings. In all such cases, or where the Court adjourns proceedings to a 'dispute resolution hearing' (sometimes called 'conciliation'), this will be treated as an adjournment to a FHDRA, and the documents referred to in para 3.2 must be filed and copied to parties and Cafcass for safety checks and enquiries, in the same way.

3.9 Before the FHDRA Cafcass shall identify any safety issues by the steps outlined below. Such steps shall be confined to matters of safety. Neither Cafcass nor a Cafcass Officer shall discuss with either party before the FHDRA any matter other than relates to safety. The Parties will not be invited to talk about other issues, for example relating to the substance of applications or replies or about issues concerning matters of welfare or the prospects of resolution. If such issues are raised by either party they will be advised that such matters will be deferred to the FHDRA when there is equality between the parties and full discussion can take place which will also be a time when any safety issues that have been identified also can be taken into account –

(a) In order to inform the court of possible risks of harm to the child in accordance with its safeguarding framework Cafcass will carry out safeguarding enquiries, including checks of local authorities and police, and telephone risk identification interviews with parties.

(b) If risks of harm are identified, Cafcass may invite parties to meet separately with the Cafcass Officer before the FHDRA to clarify any safety issue.

(c) Cafcass shall record and outline any safety issues for the court.

(d) The Cafcass Officer will not initiate contact with the child prior to the FHDRA. If contacted by a child, discussions relating to the issues in the case will be postponed to the day of the hearing or after when the Cafcass officer will have more knowledge of the issues.

(e) At least 3 days before the hearing the Cafcass Officer shall report the outcome of risk identification work to the court by completing the Form at Schedule 2.

4 The First Hearing Dispute Resolution Appointment.

4.1 The parties and Cafcass Officer shall attend this hearing. A mediator may attend where available.

4.2 At the hearing, which is not privileged, the court should have the following documents –

(a) C100 application, and C1A if any
(b) Notice of Hearing
(c) C7 response and C1A if any
(d) Schedule 2 safeguarding information

4.3 The detailed arrangements for the participation of mediators will be arranged locally. These will include –

(a) Arrangements for the mediator to ask the parties in a particular case to consent to the mediator seeing the papers in the case where it seems appropriate to do so.

PART II – Statutory Instruments

(b)   Arrangements for the mediator to ask the parties to waive privilege for the purpose of the first hearing where it seems to the mediator appropriate to do so in order to assist the work of the mediator and the outcome of the first hearing.

(c)   In all cases it is important that such arrangements are put in place in a way that avoids any pressure being brought to bear in this connection on the parties that is inconsistent with general good mediation practice.

4.4 At the FHDRA the Court, in collaboration with the Cafcass Officer, and with the assistance of any mediator present, will seek to assist the parties in conciliation and in resolution of all or any of the issues between them. Any remaining issues will be identified, the Cafcass Officer will advise the court of any recommended means of resolving such issues and directions will be given for the future resolution of such issues. At all times the decisions of the Court and the work of the Cafcass Officer will take account of any risk or safeguarding issues that have been identified.

4.5 The Cafcass Officer shall, where practicable, speak separately to each party at court and before the hearing.

4.6 In the County Court, the Court shall have available a telephone contact to the Family Proceedings Court listing manager, diary dates for the appropriate Family Proceedings Court, or other means by which the County Court, at the time of the hearing, will be able to list subsequent hearings in the Family Proceedings Court.

5 Conduct of the Hearing. The following matters shall be considered

5.1 Safeguarding –

(a)   The court shall inform the parties of the content of any screening report or other information which has been provided by Cafcass, unless it considers that to do so would create a risk of harm to a party or the child. The court may need to consider whether and how any information contained in the checks should be disclosed to the parties if Cafcass have not disclosed it.

(b)   Whether a risk assessment is required and when.

(c)   Whether a fact finding hearing is needed to determine allegations whose resolution is likely to affect the decision of the court.

5.2 Dispute Resolution –

(a)   There will be at every FHDRA a period in which the Cafcass Officer, with the assistance of any Mediator and in collaboration with the Court, will seek to conciliate and explore with the parties the resolution of all or some of the issues between them. The procedure to be followed in this connection at the hearing will be determined by local arrangements between the Cafcass manager, or equivalent in Wales, and the Designated Family Judge or the Justices' Clerk where appropriate.

(b)   What is the result of any such meeting at Court?

(c)   What other options there are for resolution e.g. may the case be suitable for further intervention by Cafcass; mediation by an external provider; collaborative law or use of a parenting plan?

(d)   Would the parties be assisted by attendance at Parenting Information Programmes or other activities, whether by formal statutory provision under section 11 Children Act 1989 as amended by Children and Adoption Act 2006 or otherwise?

5.3 **Consent Orders:**

Where agreement is reached at any hearing or submitted in writing to the court, no order will be made without scrutiny by the court. Where safeguarding checks or risk assessment work remain outstanding, the making of a final order may be deferred for such work. In such circumstances the court shall adjourn the case for no longer than 28 days to a fixed date. A written notification of this work is to be provided by Cafcass in accordance with the timescale specified by the court. If satisfactory information is then available, the order may be made at the adjourned hearing in the agreed terms without the need for attendance by the parties. If satisfactory information is not available, the order will not be made, and the case will be adjourned for further consideration with an opportunity for the parties to make further representations.

5.4 **Reports –**

(a)   Are there welfare issues or other specific considerations which should be addressed in a report by Cafcass or the Local Authority? Before a report is ordered, the court should consider alternative ways of working with the parties such as are referred to in paragraph 5.2 above. If a report is ordered in accordance with Section 7 of the Children Act 1989, it should be directed specifically towards and limited to those issues. General requests should be avoided and the Court should state in the Order the specific factual and other issues that are to be addressed in a focused report. In determining whether a request for a report should be directed to the relevant local authority or to Cafcass, the court should consider such information as Cafcass has provided about the extent and nature of the local authority's current or recent involvement with the subject of the application and the parties, and any relevant protocol between Cafcass and the Association of Directors of Children's Services.

(b)   Is there a need for an investigation under S 37 Children Act 1989?

(c)   A copy of the Order requesting the report and any relevant court documents are to be sent to Cafcass or, in the case of the Local Authority, to the Legal Adviser to the Director of the Local Authority Children's Services and, where known, to the allocated social worker by the court forthwith.

(d)   Is any expert evidence required in compliance with the Experts' Practice Direction?

5.5 **Wishes and feelings of the child –**

(a)   Is the child aware of the proceedings? How are the wishes and feelings of the child to be ascertained (if at all)?

(b)   How is the child to be involved in the proceedings, if at all, and whether at or after the FHDRA?

(c)   If consideration is given to the joining of the child as a party to the application, the court should consider the current Guidance from the President of the Family Division. Where the court is considering the appointment of a guardian ad litem, it should first seek to ensure that the appropriate Cafcass manager has been spoken to so as to consider any advice in connection with the prospective appointment and the timescale involved. In considering whether to make such an appointment the Court shall take account of the demands on the resources of Cafcass that such appointment would make.

(d)   Who will inform the child of the outcome of the case where appropriate?

5.6 **Case Management –**

(a)   What, if any, issues are agreed and what are the key issues to be determined?

(b)   Are there any interim orders which can usefully be made (e.g. indirect, supported or supervised contact) pending final hearing?

(c)   What directions are required to ensure the application is ready for final hearing – statements, reports etc?

(d)   List for final hearing, consider the need for judicial continuity (especially if there has been or is to be a fact finding hearing or a contested interim hearing).

5.7 **Transfer to FPC:**

The case should be transferred to the FPC, pursuant to the Allocation and Transfer of Proceedings Order 2008 unless one of the specified exceptions applies. The date should be fixed at court and entered on the order.

6 The Order

6.1 **The Order shall set out in particular –**

(a)   The issues about which the parties are agreed

(b)   The issues that remain to be resolved

(c)   The steps that are planned to resolve the issues

(d)   Any interim arrangements pending such resolution, including arrangements for the involvement of children.

(e)   The timetable for such steps and, where this involves further hearings, the date of such hearings.

(f)   A statement as to any facts relating to risk or safety; in so far as they are resolved the result will be stated and, in so far as not resolved, the steps to be taken to resolve them will be stated.

(g)   If it be the case, the fact of the transfer of the case to the Family Proceedings Court with the date and purpose of the next hearing (h)　If it be the case, the fact that the case cannot be transferred to the Family Proceedings Court and the reason for the decision.

(i)　Whether in the event of an order, by consent or otherwise, or pending such an order, the parties are to be assisted by participation in mediation, Parenting Information Programmes, or other types of parenting intervention, and to detail any contact activity directions or conditions imposed by the court.

6.2 A suggested template order is available as set out in Schedule 1 below.

7 Commencement and Implementation

7.1 This Practice Direction will come into effect on April 1st 2010. So that procedural changes can be made by all agencies, the requirement for full implementation of the provisions is postponed, but in any event it should be effected by no later than October 4th 2010.

SCHEDULE 1

The suggested form of Order which courts may wish to use is PLP10 which is available from Her Majesty's Court Service.

SCHEDULE 2

Report Form on outcome of safeguarding enquiries. See version for Cafcass in England and for CAFCASS CYMRU in Wales.

Practice Direction 12C –
Service of Application in Certain Proceedings Relating to Children

This Practice Direction supplements FPR Part 12 (Procedure Relating to Children except Parental Order Proceedings and Proceedings for Applications in Adoption, Placement and Related Proceedings), rule 12.8 (Service of the application)

Persons who receive copy of application form

1.1 In relation to the proceedings in column 1 of the following table, column 2 sets out the documentation which persons listed in column 3 are to receive –

Proceedings	Documentation	Who receives a copy of the documentation
1 Private law proceedings; public law proceedings; emergency proceedings (except those proceedings referred to in entries 2 and 3 of the Table below);	Application form (including any supplementary forms); Form C6 (Notice of proceedings); and in private law proceedings, the form of answer.	All the respondents to the application.

PART II – Statutory Instruments

Proceedings	Documentation	Who receives a copy of the documentation
proceedings for a declaration under rule 12.71 as to the existence, or extent, of parental responsibility under Article 16 of the 1996 Hague Convention; an order relating to the exercise of the court's inherent jurisdiction (including wardship proceedings).		
2 An enforcement order (section 11J of the 1989 Act); a financial compensation order (section 11O of the 1989 Act).	As above	All the respondents to the application; and where the child was a party to the proceedings in which the contact order was made – (a) the person who was the children's guardian or litigation friend in those proceedings; or (b) where there was no children's guardian or litigation friend, the person who was the legal representative of the child in those proceedings.
3 A care or a supervision order (section 31 of the 1989 Act).	As above and such of the documents specified in the Annex to Form C110 as are available.	All the respondents to the application; and Cafcass or CAFCASS CYMRU.

Proceedings	Documentation	Who receives a copy of the documentation
4 Proceedings for an order for the return of a child under the 1980 Hague Convention or registration of an order under the European Convention.	As above and the documents referred to in part 2 of the Practice Direction 12F (International Child Abduction).	All the respondents to the application.

(Rule 12.3 sets out who the parties to the proceedings are.)

1.2 When filing the documents referred to in column 2 of the Table in paragraph 1.1, the applicant must also file sufficient copies for one to be served on each respondent and Cafcass or CAFCASS CYMRU.

1.3 Where the application for an order in proceedings referred to in column 1 of the Table in paragraph 1.1 is made in respect of more than one child all the children must be included in the same application form.

1.4 The applicant will serve Form C6A (notice to non parties) on the persons referred to in the Table in paragraph 3.1 at the same time as serving the documents in column 2 of the Table in paragraph 1.1.

Time for serving application

2.1 In relation to the proceedings in column 1 of the following table, column 2 sets out the time period within which the application and accompanying documents must be served on each respondent –

Proceedings	Minimum number of days prior to hearing or directions appointment for service
1 Private law proceedings; and proceedings for – an order permitting the child's name to be changed or the removal of the child from the United Kingdom (33(7) of the 1989 Act); an order permitting the local authority to arrange for any child in its care to live outside England and Wales (Schedule 2, paragraph 19(1) of the 1989 Act); a contribution order (Schedule 2, paragraph 23(1) of the 1989 Act);	14 days.

Proceedings	Minimum number of days prior to hearing or directions appointment for service
an order revoking a contribution order (Schedule 2, paragraph 23(8) of the 1989 Act); an appeal under paragraph 8(1) of Schedule 8 to the 1989 Act; an order relating to the exercise of the court's inherent jurisdiction (including wardship proceedings); a declaration under rule 12.71 as to the existence, or extent, of parental responsibility under Article 16 of the 1996 Hague Convention.	
2 Proceedings for – a residence order under section 8 of the 1989 Act relating to a child who is the subject of a care order; a special guardianship order relating to a child who is the subject of a care order (section 14A of the 1989 Act); an education supervision order (section 36 of the 1989 Act); an order discharging a care order (section 39(1) of the 1989 Act); an order varying or discharging a supervision order (section 39(2) of the 1989 Act) or extending or further extending a supervision order under paragraph 6(3) of Schedule 3 to the 1989 Act; an order varying a supervision order in so far as it affects the person with whom the child is living (section 39(3) of the 1989 Act); an application to substitute a supervision order for a care order (section 39(4) of the 1989 Act); an order extending an education supervision order (Schedule 3, paragraph 15(2) to the 1989 Act);	7 days.

Proceedings	Minimum number of days prior to hearing or directions appointment for service
an order discharging an education supervision order (Schedule 3, paragraph 17(1) to the 1989 Act).	
3 Proceedings for – a care or supervision order (section 31 of the 1989 Act); an order making provision for contact under section 34(2) to (4) of the 1989 Act or an order varying or discharging such an order under section 34(9) of the 1989 Act; an order varying directions made with an interim care order or interim supervision order under section 38(8)(b) of the 1989 Act; an order under section 39(3A) of the 1989 Act varying or discharging an interim care order in so far as it imposes an exclusion requirement on a person who is not entitled to apply for the order to be discharged; an order under section 39(3B) of the 1989 Act varying or discharging an interim care order in so far as it confers a power of arrest attached to an exclusion requirement. a child assessment order (section 43(1) of the 1989 Act).	3 days.
4 Proceedings for an order for the return of a child under the 1980 Hague Convention or registration of an order under the European Convention.	4 days
5 An order varying or discharging a child assessment order (section 43(12) of the 1989 Act).	2 days

PART II – Statutory Instruments

Proceedings	Minimum number of days prior to hearing or directions appointment for service
6 Emergency proceedings; and proceedings for a secure accommodation order (section 25 of the 1989 Act);	1 day

2.2 The court may extend or shorten the time period referred to in column 2 of the table in paragraph 2.1 (see rule 4.1(3)(a)).

2.3 Where the application is to be served on a child, rule 6.33 provides that, in addition to the persons to be served in accordance with rules 6.28 and 6.32, the application must also be served on the persons or bodies listed in rule 6.33(3) unless the court orders otherwise.

Persons who receive a copy of Form C6A (Notice to Non-Parties)

3.1 In relation to each type of proceedings in column 1 of the following table, the persons listed in column 2 are to receive a copy of Form C6A (Notice of Proceedings/Hearing/Directions Appointment to Non-Parties) –

Proceedings	Persons to whom notice is to be given
1 All applications.	Subject to separate entries below: local authority providing accommodation for the child; persons who are caring for the child at the time when the proceedings are commenced; and in the case of proceedings brought in respect of a child who is alleged to be staying in a refuge which is certified under section 51(1) or (2) of the 1989 Act, the person who is providing the refuge.
2 An order appointing a guardian (section 5(1) of the 1989 Act).	As for all applications; and the father or parent (being a woman who is a parent by virtue of section 43 of the Human Fertilisation and Embryology Act 2008) of the child if that person does not have parental responsibility.
3 A section 8 order (section 8 of the 1989 Act).	As for all applications; and,

Proceedings	Persons to whom notice is to be given
	every person whom the applicant believes –
	(i) to be named in a court order with respect to the same child, which has not ceased to have effect;
	(ii) to be party to pending proceedings in respect of the same child; or
	(iii) to be a person with whom the child has lived for at least 3 years prior to the application,
	unless, in a case to which (i) or (ii) applies, the applicant believes that the court order or pending proceedings are not relevant to the application.
4 A special guardianship order (section 14A of the 1989 Act); variation or discharge of a special guardianship order (section 14D of the 1989 Act).	As for all applications; and every person whom the applicant believes –
	(i) to be named in a court order with respect to the same child, which has not ceased to have effect;
	(ii) to be party to pending proceedings in respect of the same child; or
	(iii) to be a person with whom the child has lived for at least 3 years prior to the application,
	unless, in a case to which (i) or (ii) applies, the applicant believes that the court order or pending proceedings are not relevant to the application;
	if the child is not being accommodated by the local authority, the local authority in whose area the applicant is ordinarily resident; and
	in the case of an application under section 14D of the 1989 Act, the local authority that prepared the report under section 14A(8) or (9) in the proceedings leading to the order which it is sought to have varied or discharged, if different from any local authority that will otherwise be notified.

PART II – Statutory Instruments

Proceedings	Persons to whom notice is to be given
5 An order permitting the local authority to arrange for any child in its care to live outside England and Wales (Schedule 2, paragraph 19(1) of the 1989 Act).	As for all applications; and the parties to the proceedings leading to the care order.
6 A care or supervision order (section 31 of the 1989 Act).	As for all applications; and every person whom the applicant believes to be a party to pending relevant proceedings in respect of the same child; and every person whom the applicant believes to be a parent without parental responsibility for the child.
7 A child assessment order (section 43(1) of the 1989 Act).	As for all applications; and every person whom the applicant believes to be a parent of the child; every person whom the applicant believes to be caring for the child; every person in whose favour a contact order is in force with respect to the child; and every person who is allowed to have contact with the child by virtue of an order under section 34 of the 1989 Act.
8 An order varying or discharging a child assessment order (section 43(12) of the 1989 Act).	The persons referred to in section 43(11)(a) to (e) of the 1989 Act who were not party to the application for the order which it is sought to have varied or discharged.
9 An emergency protection order (section 44(1) of the 1989 Act).	As for all applications above; and every person whom the applicant believes to be a parent of the child.
10 An order varying a direction under section 44(6) in an emergency protection order (section 44(9)(b) of the 1989 Act).	As for all applications; and the local authority in whose area the child is living; and

Proceedings	Persons to whom notice is to be given
	any person whom the applicant believes to be affected by the direction which it is sought to have varied.
11 A warrant authorising a constable to assist in the exercise of certain powers to search for children and inspect premises (section 102 of the 1989 Act).	The person referred to in section 102(1) of the 1989 Act; and any person preventing or likely to prevent such a person from exercising powers under enactments mentioned in subsection (6) of that section.
12 An enforcement order (section 11J of the 1989 Act); a financial compensation order (section 11O of the 1989 Act).	Any officer of the Service or Welsh family proceedings officer who is monitoring compliance with a contact order (in accordance with section 11H(2) of the 1989 Act).
13 An order revoking or amending an enforcement order (Schedule A1, paragraphs 4 to 7 of the 1989 Act) (rule 12.33 makes provision regarding applications under Schedule A1, paragraph 5 of the 1989 Act); an order following a breach of an enforcement order (Schedule A1, paragraph 9 of the 1989 Act).	Any officer of the Service or Welsh family proceedings officer who is monitoring compliance with the enforcement order (in accordance with section 11M(1) of the 1989 Act); the responsible officer (as defined in section 197 of the Criminal Justice Act 2003, as modified by Schedule A1 to the 1989 Act).
14 A declaration under rule 12.71 as to the existence, or extent, of parental responsibility under Article 16 of the 1996 Hague Convention.	A person who the applicant believes is a parent of the child.

PART II – Statutory Instruments

Practice Direction 12D –
Inherent Jurisdiction (including Wardship) Proceedings

This Practice Direction supplements FPR Part 12, Chapter 5

The nature of inherent jurisdiction proceedings

1.1 It is the duty of the court under its inherent jurisdiction to ensure that a child who is the subject of proceedings is protected and properly taken care of. The court may in exercising its inherent jurisdiction make any order or determine any issue in respect of a child unless limited by case law or statute.

Such proceedings should not be commenced unless it is clear that the issues concerning the child cannot be resolved under the Children Act 1989.

1.2 The court may under its inherent jurisdiction, in addition to all of the orders which can be made in family proceedings, make a wide range of injunctions for the child's protection of which the following are the most common –

(a)   orders to restrain publicity;

(b)   orders to prevent an undesirable association;

(c)   orders relating to medical treatment;

(d)   orders to protect abducted children, or children where the case has another substantial foreign element; and

(e)   orders for the return of children to and from another state.

1.3 The court's wardship jurisdiction is part of and not separate from the court's inherent jurisdiction. The distinguishing characteristics of wardship are that –

(a)   custody of a child who is a ward is vested in the court; and

(b)   although day to day care and control of the ward is given to an individual or to a local authority, no important step can be taken in the child's life without the court's consent.

Transfer of proceedings to county court

2.1 Whilst county courts do not have jurisdiction to deal with applications that a child be made or cease to be a ward of court, consideration should be given to transferring the case in whole or in part to a county court where a direction has been given confirming the wardship and directing that the child remain a ward of court during his minority or until further order.

2.2 The county court must transfer the case back to the High Court if a decision is required as to whether the child should remain a ward of court.

2.3 The following proceedings in relation to a ward of court will be dealt with in the High Court unless the nature of the issues of fact or law makes them more suitable for hearing in the county court –

(a)   those in which an officer of the Cafcass High Court Team or the Official Solicitor is or becomes the litigation friend or children's guardian of the ward or a party to the proceedings;

(b)   those in which a local authority is or becomes a party;

(c)   those in which an application for paternity testing is made;

(d)   those in which there is a dispute about medical treatment;

(e)   those in which an application is opposed on the grounds of lack of jurisdiction;

(f)   those in which there is a substantial foreign element;

(g)   those in which there is an opposed application for leave to take the child permanently out of the jurisdiction or where there is an application for temporary removal of a child from the jurisdiction and it is opposed on the ground that the child may not be duly returned.

Parties

3.1 Where the child has formed or is seeking to form an association, considered to be undesirable, with another person, that other person should not be made a party to the application. Such a person should be made a respondent only to an application within the proceedings for an injunction or committal. Such a person should not be added to the title of the proceedings nor allowed to see any documents other than those relating directly to the proceedings for the injunction or committal. He or she should be allowed time to obtain representation and any injunction should in the first instance extend over a few days only.

Removal from jurisdiction

4.1 A child who is a ward of court may not be removed from England and Wales without the court's permission. Practice Direction 12F (International Child Abduction) deals in detail with locating and protecting children at risk of unlawful removal.

Criminal Proceedings

5.1 Where a child has been interviewed by the police in connection with contemplated criminal proceedings and the child subsequently becomes a ward of court, the permission of the court deciding the wardship proceedings ('the wardship court') is not required for the child to be called as a witness in the criminal proceedings.

5.2 Where the police need to interview a child who is already a ward of court, an application must be made for permission for the police to do so. Where permission is given the order should, unless there is some special reason to the contrary, give permission for any number of interviews which may be required by the prosecution or the police. If a need arises to conduct any interview beyond the permission contained in the order, a further application must be made.

5.3 The above applications must be made with notice to all parties.

5.4 Where a person may become the subject of a criminal investigation and it is considered necessary for the child who is a ward of court to be interviewed without that person knowing that the police are making inquiries, the application for permission to interview the child may be made without notice to that party. Notice should, however, where practicable be given to the children's guardian.

5.5 There will be other occasions where the police need to deal with complaints, or alleged offences, concerning children who are wards of court where it is appropriate, if not essential, for action to be taken straight away without the prior permission of the wardship court, for example –

(a)   serious offences against the child such as rape, where a medical examination and the collection of forensic evidence ought to be carried out promptly;

(b)   where the child is suspected by the police of having committed a criminal act and the police wish to interview the child in respect of that matter;

(c)   where the police wish to interview the child as a potential witness.

5.6 In such instances, the police should notify the parent or foster parent with whom the child is living or another 'appropriate adult' (within the Police and Criminal Evidence Act 1984 – Code of Practice C for the Detention, Treatment and Questioning of Persons by Police Officers) so that that adult has the opportunity of being present when the police interview the child. Additionally, if practicable the child's guardian (if one has been appointed) should be notified and invited to attend the police interview or to nominate a third party to attend on the guardian's behalf. A record of the interview or a copy of any statement made by the child should be supplied to the children's guardian. Where the child has been interviewed without the guardian's knowledge, the guardian should be informed at the earliest opportunity of this fact and (if it be the case) that the police wish to conduct further interviews. The wardship court should be informed of the situation at the earliest possible opportunity thereafter by the children's guardian, parent, foster parent (through the local authority) or other responsible adult.

Applications to the Criminal Injuries Compensation Authority

6.1 Where a child who is a ward of court has a right to make a claim for compensation to the Criminal Injuries Compensation Authority ('CICA'), an application must be made by the child's guardian, or, if no guardian has been appointed, the person with care and control of the child, for permission to apply to CICA and disclose such documents on the wardship proceedings file as are considered necessary to establish whether or not the child is eligible for an award plus, as appropriate, the amount of the award.

6.2 Any order giving permission should state that any award made by CICA should normally be paid into court immediately upon receipt and, once that payment has been made, application should made to the court as to its management and administration. If it is proposed to invest the award in any other way, the court's prior approval must be sought

The role of the tipstaff

7.1 The tipstaff is the enforcement officer for all orders made in the High Court. The tipstaff's jurisdiction extends throughout England and Wales. Every applicable order made in the High Court is addressed to the tipstaff in children and family matters (eg 'The Court hereby directs the Tipstaff of the High Court of Justice, whether acting by himself or his assistants or a police officer as follows...').

7.2 The tipstaff may effect an arrest and then inform the police. Sometimes the local bailiff or police will detain a person in custody until the tipstaff arrives to collect that person or give further directions as to the disposal of the matter.

The tipstaff may also make a forced entry although there will generally be a uniformed police officer standing by to make sure there is no breach of the peace.

7.3 There is only one tipstaff (with two assistants) but the tipstaff can also call on any constable or bailiff to assist in carrying out the tipstaff's duties.

7.4 The majority of the tipstaff's work involves locating children and taking them into protective custody, including cases of child abduction abroad.

Practice Direction 12E –
Urgent Business

This Practice Direction supplements FPR Part 12

Introduction

1.1 This Practice Direction describes the procedure to be followed in respect of urgent and out of hours cases in the Family Division of the High Court. For the avoidance of doubt, it does not relate to cases in respect of adults.

1.2 Urgent or out of hours applications, particularly those which have become urgent because they have not been pursued sufficiently promptly, should be avoided. A judge who has concerns that the urgent or out of hours facilities may have been abused may require a representative of the applicant to attend at a subsequent directions hearing to provide an explanation.

1.3 Urgent applications should whenever possible be made within court hours. The earliest possible liaison is required with the Clerk of the Rules who will attempt to accommodate genuinely urgent applications (at least for initial directions) in the Family Division applications court, from which the matter may be referred to another judge.

1.4 When it is not possible to apply within court hours, contact should be made with the security office at the Royal Courts of Justice (020 7947 6000 or 020 7947 6260) who will refer the matter to the urgent business officer. The urgent business officer can contact the duty judge. The judge may agree to hold a hearing, either convened at court or elsewhere, or by telephone.

1.5 When the hearing is to take place by telephone it should, unless not practicable, be by tape-recorded conference call arranged (and paid for in the first instance) by the applicant's solicitors. Solicitors acting for potential applicants should consider having standing arrangements with their telephone service providers under which such conference calls can be arranged. All parties (especially the judge) should be informed that the call is being recorded by the service provider. The applicant's solicitors should order a transcript of the hearing from the service provider. Otherwise the applicant's legal representative should prepare a note for approval by the judge.

General Issues

2.1 Parents, carers or other necessary respondents should whenever possible be given the opportunity to have independent legal advice or at least to have access to support or counselling.

2.2 In suitable cases, application may be made for directions providing for anonymity of the parties and others involved in the matter in any order or subsequent listing of the case. Exceptionally, a reporting restriction order may be sought.

2.3 Either the Official Solicitor or Cafcass, or CAFCASS CYMRU, as the case may be, may be invited by the court to be appointed as advocate to the court.

Medical treatment and press injunction cases

3.1 It may be desirable for a child who is the subject of such proceedings to be made a party and represented through a children's guardian (usually an officer of Cafcass or a Welsh Family Proceedings Officer). Cafcass and CAFCASS CYMRU stand ready to arrange for an officer to accept appointment as a children's guardian. They should be contacted at the earliest opportunity where an urgent application is envisaged. For urgent out of hours applications, the urgent business officer will contact a representative of Cafcass. CAFCASS CYMRU is not able to deal with cases that arise out of office hours and those cases should be referred to Cafcass who will deal with the matter on behalf of CAFCASS CYMRU until the next working day. A child of sufficient understanding to instruct his or her own solicitor should be made a party and given notice of any application.

3.2 Interim declarations/orders under the wardship jurisdiction or Children Act 1989 may be made on application either by an NHS trust, a local authority, an interested adult (where necessary with the leave of the court) or by the child if he or she has sufficient understanding to make the application.

Consultation with Cafcass, CAFCASS CYMRU and Official Solicitor

4.1 Cafcass, CAFCASS CYMRU and members of the Official Solicitor's legal staff are prepared to discuss cases before proceedings are issued. In all cases in which the urgent and out of hours procedures are to be used it would be helpful if the Official Solicitor, Cafcass or CAFCASS CYMRU have had some advance notice of the application and its circumstances.

4.2 Enquiries about children cases should be directed to the duty lawyer:

Cafcass National Office
6th Floor, Sanctuary Buildings
Great Smith Street
London SW1P 3BT
Tel: 0844 353 3350
Fax: 0844 353 3351.

Enquiries should be marked 'FAO High Court Team or FAO HCT'.

4.3 Enquiries about children cases in Wales should be directed to:

Social Care Team
Legal Services
Welsh Assembly Government
Cathays Park
Cardiff
CF10 3NQ
Tel: 02920 823913
Fax: 02920 826727.

4.4 Medical and welfare cases relating to an adult lacking capacity in relation to their medical treatment or welfare are brought in the Court of Protection. Enquiries about adult medical and welfare cases should be addressed to a Court of Protection healthcare and welfare lawyer at the office of the Official Solicitor:
81 Chancery Lane
London
WC2A 1DD
Tel: 0207 911 7127
Fax: 0207 911 7105
Email: enquiries@offsol.gsi.gov.uk

Reference should also be made to Practice Direction E, accompanying Part 9 of the Court of Protection Rules 2007, and to Practice Direction B accompanying Part 10 of those Rules. Information for parties and practitioners is available on the website of the Ministry of Justice www.justice.gov.uk and general information for members of the public is available on www.direct.gov.uk.

Practice Direction 12F – International Child Abduction

This Practice Direction supplements FPR Part 12, Chapters 5 and 6

Part I – Introduction

1.1 This Practice Direction explains what to do if a child has been brought to, or kept in, England and Wales without the permission of anyone who has rights of custody in respect of the child in the country where the child was habitually resident immediately before the removal or retention. It also explains what to do if a child has been taken out of, or kept out of, England and Wales[a] without the permission of a parent or someone who has rights of custody in respect of the child. These cases are called 'international child abduction cases' and are dealt with in the High Court. This Practice Direction also explains what to do if you receive legal papers claiming that you have abducted a child. You can find the legal cases which are mentioned in this Practice Direction, and other legal material, on the website http://www.bailii. org (British and Irish Legal Information Institute).

PART II – Statutory Instruments

1.2 If you have rights of custody in respect of a child and the child has been brought to England or Wales without your permission, or has been brought here with your permission but the person your child is staying with is refusing to return the child, then you can apply to the High Court of Justice, which covers all of England and Wales, for an order for the return of the child.

1.3 How you make an application to the High Court, what evidence you need to provide and what orders you should ask the court to make are all explained in this Practice Direction.

1.4 If your child is under 16 years of age and has been brought to England or Wales from a country which is a party (a 'State party') to the 1980 Hague Convention on the Civil Aspects of International Child Abduction ('the 1980 Hague Convention') then you can make an application to the High Court for an order under that Convention for the return of your child to the State in which he or she was habitually resident immediately before being removed or being kept away. This is explained in Part 2 below.

1.5 If your child is over 16 years of age and under 18, or has been brought to England or Wales from a country which is not a State party to the 1980 Hague Convention, then you can make an application for the return of your child under the inherent jurisdiction of the High Court with respect to children. In exercising this jurisdiction over children, the High Court will make your child's welfare its paramount consideration. How to make an application under the inherent jurisdiction of the High Court with respect to children is explained in Part 3 below.

1.6 It might be necessary for you to make an urgent application to the court if you are not sure where your child is, or you think that there is a risk that the person who is keeping your child away from you might take the child out of the United Kingdom or hide them away. Part 4 below explains how to make an urgent application to the High Court for orders to protect your child until a final decision can be made about returning the child and also how to ask for help from the police and government agencies if you think your child might be taken out of the country.

Rights of Access

1.7 Rights of access to children (also called contact or visitation) may be enforced in England and Wales. Access orders made in other Member States of the European Union can be enforced under EU law, and the 1980 Hague Convention expects State parties to comply with orders and agreements concerning access as well as rights of custody. If you have an access order and you want to enforce it in England or Wales, you should read Part 5 below.

Part 2 – Hague Convention Cases

2.1 States which are party to the 1980 Hague Convention have agreed to return children who have been either wrongfully removed from, or wrongfully retained away from, the State where they were habitually resident immediately before the wrongful removal or retention. There are very limited exceptions to this obligation.

2.2 'Wrongfully removed' or 'wrongfully retained' means removed or retained in breach of rights of custody in respect of the child attributed to a person or a body or an institution. 'Rights of custody' are interpreted very widely (see paragraph 2.16 below).

2.3 The text of the 1980 Hague Convention and a list of Contracting States (that is, State parties) can be found on the website of the Hague Conference on Private International Law at http://www.hcch.net. All Member States of the European Union are State parties to the 1980 Hague Convention, and all but Denmark are bound by an EU Regulation which supplements the operation of the 1980 Hague Convention between the Member States of the EU (Council Regulation (EC) No 2201/2003, see paragraph 2.6).

2.4 In each State party there is a body called the Central Authority whose duty is to help people use the 1980 Hague Convention.

2.5 If you think that your child has been brought to, or kept in, England or Wales, and your State is a State party to the 1980 Hague Convention, then you should get in touch with your own Central Authority who will help you to send an application for the return of your child to the Central Authority for England and Wales. However, you are not obliged to contact your own Central Authority. You may contact the Central Authority for England and Wales directly, or you may simply instruct lawyers in England or Wales to make an application for you. The advantage of making your application through the Central Authority for England and Wales if you are applying from outside the United Kingdom is that you will get public funding ('legal aid') to make your application, regardless of your financial resources.

The Central Authority for England and Wales

2.6 The Child Abduction and Custody Act 1985 brings the 1980 Hague Convention into the law of England and Wales and identifies the Lord Chancellor as the Central Authority. His duties as the Central Authority are carried out by the International Child Abduction and Contact Unit (ICACU). ICACU also carries out the duties of the Central Authority for two other international instruments. These are the European Convention on Recognition and Enforcement of Decisions concerning Custody of Children signed at Luxembourg on 20 May 1980 (called 'the European Convention' in this Practice Direction but sometimes also referred to as 'the Luxembourg Convention') and the European Union Council Regulation (EC) No 2201/2003 of 27 November 2003 on jurisdiction and the recognition and enforcement of judgments in matrimonial matters and in matters of parental responsibility ('the Council Regulation[b]'). The Council Regulation has direct effect in the law of England and Wales.

(b) The Council Regulation (EC) No 2201/2003 of 27 November 2003 concerning jurisdiction and the recognition and enforcement of judgments in matrimonial matters and the matters of parental responsibility, repealing Regulation (EC) No 1347/2000 is also known as Brussels IIa, or Brussels II Revised, or Brussels II bis.

PART II – Statutory Instruments

2.7 ICACU is open Mondays to Fridays from 9.00 a.m. to 5.00 p.m. It is located in the Office of the Official Solicitor and Public Trustee and its contact details are as follows:

International Child Abduction and Contact Unit
81 Chancery Lane
London WC2A 1DD
DX 0012 London Chancery Lane
Tel: + 44 (0)20 7911 7045 / 7047
Fax: + 44 (0)20 7911 7248
Email: enquiries@offsol.gsi.gov.uk

In an emergency (including out of normal working hours) contact should be made with the Royal Courts of Justice on one of the following telephone numbers:
+ 44 (0)20 7947 6000, or
+ 44 (0) 20 7947 6260.

In addition, in an emergency or outside normal working hours advice on international child abduction can be sought from reunite International Child Abduction Centre on +44 (0)1162 556 234. Outside office hours you will be directed to the 24 hour emergency service. You can also see information on reunite's website http://www.reunite.org.

What ICACU Will Do

2.8 When ICACU receives your application for the return of your child, unless you already have a legal representative in England and Wales whom you want to act for you, it will send your application to a solicitor whom it knows to be experienced in international child abduction cases and ask them to take the case for you. You will then be the solicitor's client and the solicitor will make an application for public funding to meet your legal costs. The solicitor will then apply to the High Court for an order for the return of your child.

2.9 You can find out more about ICACU and about the 1980 Hague Convention and the other international instruments mentioned at paragraph 2.6 on two websites: Information for parties and practitioners is available on http://www.justice.gov.uk and general information for members of the public is available on http://www.direct.gov.uk.

Applying to the High Court – the Form and Content of Application

2.10 An application to the High Court for an order under the 1980 Hague Convention must be made in the Principal Registry of the Family Division in Form C67. If the Council Regulation applies, then the application must be headed both 'in the matter of the Child Abduction and Custody Act 1985' and 'in the matter of Council Regulation (EC) 2201/2003'. This is to ensure that the application is handled quickly (see paragraph 2.14 below) and to draw the court's attention to its obligations under the Council Regulation.

2.11 The application must include –

(a) the names and dates of birth of the children;

(b) the names of the children's parents or guardians;

(c) the whereabouts or suspected whereabouts of the children;

(d) the interest of the applicant in the matter (e.g. mother, father, or person with whom the child lives and details of any order placing the child with that person);

(e) the reasons for the application;

(f) details of any proceedings (including proceedings not in England or Wales, and including any legal proceedings which have finished) relating to the children;

(g) where the application is for the return of a child, the identity of the person alleged to have removed or retained the child and, if different, the identity of the person with whom the child is thought to be;

(h) in an application to which the Council Regulation also applies, any details of measures of which you are aware that have been taken by courts or authorities to ensure the protection of the child after its return to the Member State of habitual residence.

2.12 The application should be accompanied by all relevant documents including (but not limited to) –

(a) an authenticated copy of any relevant decision or agreement;

(b) a certificate or an affidavit from a Central Authority, or other competent authority of the State of the child's habitual residence, or from a qualified person, concerning the relevant law of that State.

2.13 As the applicant you may also file a statement in support of the application, although usually your solicitor will make and file a statement for you on your instructions. The statement must contain and be verified by a statement of truth in the following terms:

> 'I make this statement knowing that it will be placed before the court, and I confirm that to the best of my knowledge and belief its contents are true.'

(Further provisions about statements of truth are contained in Part 17 of these Rules and in Practice Direction 17A).

The Timetable for the Case

2.14 Proceedings to which the Council Regulation applies must be completed in 6 weeks 'except where exceptional circumstances make this impossible'. The following procedural steps are intended to ensure that applications under the 1980 Hague Convention and the Council Regulation are handled quickly –

(a) the application must be headed both 'in the matter of the Child Abduction and Custody Act 1985' and 'in the matter of Council Regulation (EC) 2201/2003';

(b) the court file will be marked to –

(i) draw attention to the nature of the application; and

(ii) state the date on which the 6 week period will expire (the 'hear-by date');

PART II – Statutory Instruments

(c)   listing priority will, where necessary, be given to such applications;

(d)   the trial judge will expedite the transcript of the judgment and its approval and ensure that it is sent to the Central Authority without delay.

(The above is taken from the judgment of the Court of Appeal, Civil Division in *Vigreux v Michel & anor* [2006] EWCA Civ 630, [2006] 2 FLR 1180).

Applications for Declarations

2.15 If a child has been taken from England and Wales to another State party, the judicial or administrative authorities of that State may ask for a declaration that the removal or retention of the child was wrongful. Or it might be thought that a declaration from the High Court that a child has been wrongfully removed or retained away from the United Kingdom would be helpful in securing his return. The High Court can make such declarations under section 8 of the Child Abduction and Custody Act 1985. An application for a declaration is made in the same way as an application for a return order, the only difference being that the details of relevant legal proceedings in respect of which the declaration is sought (if any), including a copy of any order made relating to the application, should be included in the documentation.

Rights of Custody

2.16 'Rights of custody' includes rights relating to the care of the person of the child and, in particular, the right to determine the child's place of residence. Rights of custody may arise by operation of law (that is, they are conferred on someone automatically by the legal system in which they are living) or by a judicial or administrative decision or as a result of an agreement having legal effect. The rights of a person, an institution or any other body are a matter for the law of the State of the child's habitual residence, but it is for the State which is being asked to return the child to decide: if those rights amount to rights of custody for the purposes of the 1980 Hague Convention; whether at the time of the removal or retention those rights were actually being exercised; and whether there has been a breach of those rights.

2.17 In England and Wales a father who is not married to the mother of their child does not necessarily have 'rights of custody' in respect of the child. An unmarried father in England and Wales who has parental responsibility for a child has rights of custody in respect of that child. In the case of an unmarried father without parental responsibility, the concept of rights of custody may include more than strictly legal rights and where immediately before the removal or retention of the child he was exercising parental functions over a substantial period of time as the only or main carer for the child he may have rights of custody. An unmarried father can ask ICACU or his legal representative for advice on this. It is important to remember that it will be for the State which is being asked to return the child to decide if the father's circumstances meet that State's requirements for the establishment of rights of custody.

2.18 Sometimes, court orders impose restrictions on the removal of children from the country in which they are living. These can be orders under the Children Act 1989 ('section 8' orders) or orders under the inherent jurisdiction of the High Court (sometimes called 'injunctions'). Any removal of a child in breach of an order imposing such a restriction would be wrongful under the 1980 Hague Convention.

2.19 The fact that court proceedings are in progress about a child does not of itself give rise to a prohibition on the removal of the child by a mother with sole parental responsibility from the country in which the proceedings are taking place unless –

(a)   the proceedings are Wardship proceedings in England and Wales (in which case removal would breach the rights of custody attributed to the High Court and fathers with no custody rights could rely on that breach); or

(b)   the court is actually considering the custody of the child, because then the court itself would have rights of custody.

Particular provisions for European Convention applications

2.20 The European Convention provides for the mutual recognition and enforcement of decisions relating to custody and access, so if a child has been brought here or retained here in breach of a custody order, then that order can be enforced. The European Convention has now been superseded to a very great extent by the Council Regulation. If however you want to make an application under the European Convention, then you make it in the same way as is described in paragraphs 2.10 and 2.11 above, but in addition you must include a copy of the decision relating to custody (or rights of access – see paragraph 5.1 below) which you are seeking to register or enforce, or about which you are seeking a declaration by the court.

Defending Abduction Proceedings

2.21 If you are served with an application – whether it is under the 1980 Hague or the European Convention or the inherent jurisdiction of the High Court – you must not delay. You must obey any directions given in any order with which you have been served, and you should seek legal advice at the earliest possible opportunity, although neither you nor the child concerned will automatically be entitled to legal aid.

2.22 It is particularly important that you tell the court where the child is, because the child will not be permitted to live anywhere else without the permission of the court, or to leave England and Wales, until the proceedings are finished.

2.23 It is also particularly important that you present to the court any defence to the application which you or the child might want to make at the earliest possible opportunity, although the orders with which you will have been served are likely to tell you the time by which you will have to do this.

PART II – Statutory Instruments

2.24 If the child concerned objects to any order sought in relation to them, and if the child is of an age and understanding at which the court will take account of their views, the court is likely to direct that the child is seen by an officer of the Children and Family Court Advisory and Support Service (Cafcass) or in Wales CAFCASS CYMRU. You should cooperate in this process. Children are not usually made parties to abduction cases, but in certain exceptional circumstances the court can make them parties so that they have their own separate legal representation. These are all matters about which you should seek legal advice.

(Provisions about the power of the court to join parties are contained in rule 12.3 and provisions about the joining and representation of children are contained in Part 16 of these Rules and the Practice Direction 16A (Representation of Children).

Part 3 – Non-Convention Cases

3.1 Applications for the return of children wrongfully removed or retained away from States which are not parties to the 1980 Hague Convention or in respect of children to whom that Convention does not apply, can be made to the High Court under its inherent jurisdiction with respect to children. Such proceedings are referred to as 'non-Convention' cases. In proceedings under the inherent jurisdiction of the High Court with respect to children, the child's welfare is the court's paramount consideration. The extent of the court's enquiry into the child's welfare will depend on the circumstances of the case; in some cases the child's welfare will be best served by a summary hearing and, if necessary, a prompt return to the State from which the child has been removed or retained. In other cases a more detailed enquiry may be necessary (see *Re J (Child Returned Abroad: Convention Rights)* [2005] UKHL 40; [2005] 2 FLR 802).

3.2 Every application for the return of a child under the inherent jurisdiction must be made in the Principal Registry of the Family Division and heard in the High Court.

Provision about the inherent jurisdiction is made at Chapter 5 of Part 12 of the Rules and in Practice Direction 12D (Inherent Jurisdiction (including Wardship) Proceedings).

The Form and content of the application

3.3 An application for the return of a child under the inherent jurisdiction must be made in Form C66 and must include the information in paragraph 2.11 above.

3.4 You must file a statement in support of your application, which must exhibit all the relevant documents. The statement must contain and be verified by a statement of truth in the following terms:

'I make this statement knowing that it will be placed before the court, and confirm that to the best of my knowledge and belief its contents are true.'

(Further provisions about statements of truth are contained in Part 17 of these Rules and Practice Direction 17A).

Timetable for Non-Convention Cases

3.5 While the 6 week deadline referred to in paragraph 2.14 is set out in the 1980 Hague Convention and in the Council Regulation, non-Convention child abduction cases must similarly be completed in 6 weeks except where exceptional circumstances make this impossible. Paragraph 2.14 applies to these cases as appropriate for a non-Convention case.

Part 4 – General Provisions

Urgent applications, or applications out of business hours

4.1 Guidance about urgent and out of hours applications is in Practice Direction 12E (Urgent Business).

Police assistance to prevent removal from England and Wales

4.2 The Child Abduction Act 1984 sets out the circumstances in which the removal of a child from this jurisdiction is a criminal offence. The police provide the following 24 hour service to prevent the unlawful removal of a child –

(a) they inform ports directly when there is a real and imminent threat that a child is about to be removed unlawfully from the country; and

(b) they liaise with Immigration Officers at the ports in an attempt to identify children at risk of removal.

4.3 Where the child is under 16, it is not necessary to obtain a court order before seeking police assistance. The police do not need an order to act to protect the child. If an order has already been obtained it should however be produced to the police. Where the child is between 16 and 18, an order must be obtained restricting or restraining removal before seeking police assistance.

4.4 Where the child is a ward of court (see Practice Direction 12D (Inherent Jurisdiction (including Wardship) Proceedings) the court's permission is needed to remove that child from the jurisdiction. When the court has not given that permission and police assistance is sought to prevent the removal of the ward, the applicant must produce evidence that the child is a ward such as –

(a) an order confirming wardship;

(b) an injunction; or

(c) where the matter is urgent and no order has been made, a certified copy of the wardship application.

4.5 The application for police assistance must be made by the applicant or his legal representative to the applicant's local police station except that applications may be made to any police station –

(a) in urgent cases;

(b) where the wardship application has just been issued; or

(c) where the court has just made the order relied on.

4.6 The police will, if they consider it appropriate, institute the 'port alert' system (otherwise known as 'an all ports warning') to try to prevent removal from the jurisdiction where the danger of removal is –

(a) real (ie not being sought merely by way of insurance); and

(b) imminent (ie within 24 to 48 hours).

4.7 The request for police assistance must be accompanied by as much of the following information as possible –

(a) *the child:* the name, sex, date of birth, physical description, nationality and passport number; if the child has more than one nationality or passport, provide details;

(b) *the person likely to remove:* the name, age, physical description, nationality, passport number, relationship to the child, and whether the child is likely to assist him or her; if the person has more than one nationality or passport, provide details;

(c) *person applying for a port alert:* the name, relationship to the child, nationality, telephone number and (if appropriate) solicitor's or other legal representative's name and contact details; if the person has more than one nationality, provide details;

(d) likely destination;

(e) likely time of travel and port of embarkation and, if known, details of travel arrangements;

(f) grounds for port alert (as appropriate) –

   (i) suspected offence under section 1 or section 2 of the Child Abduction Act 1984;

   (ii) the child is subject to a court order.

(g) details of person to whom the child should be returned if intercepted.

4.8 If the police decide that the case is one in which the port-alert system should be used, the child's name will remain on the stop list for **four weeks**. After that time it will be removed automatically unless a further application is made.

The Identity and Passport Service

4.9 Where the court makes an order prohibiting or otherwise restricting the removal of a child from the United Kingdom, or from any specified part of it, or from a specified dependent territory, the court may make an order under section 37 of the Family Law Act 1986 requiring any person to surrender any UK passport which has been issued to, or contains particulars of, the child.

4.10 The Identity and Passport Service ('IPS') will take action to prevent a United Kingdom passport or replacement passport being issued only where the IPS has been served with a court order expressly requiring a United Kingdom passport to be surrendered, or expressly prohibiting the issue of any further United Kingdom passport facilities to the child without the consent of the court, or the holder of such an order. Accordingly, in every case in which such an order has been made, the IPS must be served the same day if possible, or at the latest the following day, with a copy of the order. It is the responsibility of the applicant to do this. The specimen form of letter set out below should be used and a copy of the court order must be attached to the letter. Delay in sending the letter to the IPS must be kept to an absolute minimum.

'The Caveat Officer

Fraud and Intelligence Unit

Identity and Passport Service

Globe House

89 Eccleston Square

London SW1V 1PN

Dear Sir/Madam

. . . .

v . . . .

Case

no: . . . .

This is to inform you that the court has today made an order

*prohibiting the issue of a passport/passports to [name(s)] [date of birth (if known)] of [address] without the consent of the holder of the order.

*requiring [name(s)] [date of birth (if known)] of [address] to surrender the passport(s) issued to him/her/them/the following child[ren] / or which contain(s) particulars of the following child[ren]:

Name   Date of Birth

*and has granted an injunction/*made an order restraining the removal of the child[ren] from the jurisdiction.

(*Delete as appropriate)

Please add these names to your records to prevent the issue of further passport facilities for the child[ren]. I enclose a copy of the court order.

Yours faithfully

Applicant's name / Applicant's Solicitor's name'

4.11 Following service on the IPS of an order either expressly requiring a United Kingdom passport to be surrendered by, or expressly prohibiting the issue of any further United Kingdom passport facilities to the child, the IPS will maintain a prohibition on issuing a passport, or further passport facilities until the child's 16th birthday. The order should state that a passport must not be granted/applied for without the consent of the court or the holder of the order.

Note: These requests may also be sent to any of the regional Passport Offices.

4.12 Further information on communicating with the IPS where the court has made a request of, or an order against, the IPS, may be found in the Protocol: Communicating with the Identity and Passport Service in Family Proceedings of August 2003.

4.13 Information about other circumstances, in which the IPS will agree not to issue a passport to a child if the IPS receives an application, or an order in more general terms than set out at 4.11 above, from a person who claims to have parental responsibility for the child, is available from the IPS or at www.direct.gov.uk.

The Home Office

4.14 Information about communicating with the Home Office, where a question of the immigration status of a party arises in family proceedings, may be found in the Protocol: Communicating with the Home Office in Family Proceedings (revised and re-issued October 2010).

Press Reporting

4.15 When a child has been abducted and a judge considers that publicity may help in tracing the child, the judge may adjourn the case for a short period to enable representatives of the Press to attend to give the case the widest possible publicity.

4.16. If a Child Rescue Alert has been used concerning a child, within the UK or abroad, it will give rise to media publicity. The court should be informed that this has happened. If there are already court proceedings concerning a child, it is advisable to obtain the agreement of the court before there is publicity to trace a missing child. If the court has not given its permission for a child who is the subject of children proceedings to be identified as the subject of proceedings, to do so would be contempt of court.

Other Assistance

4.17 The Missing Persons Bureau will be participating for the UK in the European Union wide 116 000 hotline for missing children. Parents and children can ring this number for assistance. (It is primarily intended to deal with criminal matters, for example stranger kidnapping.)

4.18 It may also be possible to trace a child by obtaining a court order under the inherent jurisdiction or the wardship jurisdiction of the High Court addressed to certain government departments, as set out in Practice Direction 6C.

Part 5 – Applications about rights of access

5.1 Access orders made in another Member State of the European Union (except Denmark) can be enforced in England or Wales under the Council Regulation.

5.2 Chapter III of the Council Regulation sets out provision for recognition and enforcement of parental responsibility orders, which include orders for custody and access (residence and contact) between Member States. Under

Article 41 of the Council Regulation you can enforce an access order in your favour from another Member State directly, provided you produce the certificate given under Article 41(2) by the court which made the order. This is a quick procedure. The unsuccessful party is not allowed to oppose recognition of the order.

5.3 The rules on recognition and enforcement of parental responsibility orders are in Part 31. You should apply to the High Court using Form C69. Rule 31.8 covers applications for Article 41 of the Council Regulation. You can make the application without notice.

5.4 If the Council Regulation does not apply, and the access order was made by a State party to the European Convention, an application can be made to enforce the order under Article 11 of the European Convention. Paragraph 2.20 above gives further information about how to make the application.

5.5 Article 21 of the 1980 Hague Convention requires the States parties to respect rights of access. However, in the case of *Re G (A Minor) (Hague Convention: Access)* [1993] 1 FLR 669, the Court of Appeal took the view that Article 21 conferred no jurisdiction to determine matters relating to access, or to recognise or enforce foreign access orders (see Practice Note of 5 March 1993: Child Abduction Unit: Lord Chancellor's Department set out in the Annex to this Practice Direction). (The Child Abduction Unit is now called ICACU see paragraph 2.6.) An access order which does not fall within the Council Regulation or the (very limited) application of the European Convention may only be enforced by applying for a 'contact order' under section 8 of the Children Act 1989.

5.6 This means that if, during the course of proceedings under the 1980 Hague Convention for a return order, the applicant decides to ask for access (contact) instead of the return of the child, but no agreement can be reached, a separate application for a contact order will have to be made, or the court invited to make a contact order without an application being made (Children Act 1989, s 10(1)(b)).

Part 6 – Child abduction cases between the United Kingdom and Pakistan

6.1 A consensus was reached in January 2003 between the President of the Family Division and the Hon. Chief Justice of Pakistan as to the principles to be applied in resolving child abduction cases between the UK and Pakistan.

The Protocol setting out that consensus can be accessed at:

http://www.fco.gov.uk/resources/en/pdf/2855621/3069133

ANNEX

See paragraph 5.5

Practice Note

5 March 1993

Citations: [1993] 1 FLR 804

Child Abduction Unit: Lord Chancellor's Department

Duties of the Central Authority for England and Wales under Article 21 of the Hague Convention on the Civil Aspects of International Child Abduction

CHILD ABDUCTION AND CUSTODY ACT 1985

In the case of *R G (A Minor) (Hague Convention: Access)* [1993] 1 FLR 669 the Court of Appeal considered the duties of the Central Authority for England and Wales on receiving an application in respect of rights of access under Art 21 of the Hague Convention.

The Court of Appeal took the view that Art 21 conferred no jurisdiction to determine matters relating to access, or to recognise or enforce foreign access orders. It provides, however, for executive co-operation in the enforcement of such recognition as national law allows.

Accordingly, the duty of the Central Authority is to make appropriate arrangements for the applicant by providing solicitors to act on his behalf in applying for legal aid and instituting proceedings in the High Court under s 8 of the Children Act 1989.

If, during the course of proceedings under Art 21 of the Convention, the applicant decides to seek access instead of the return of the child, but no agreement can be reached and the provisions of the European Convention on the Recognition and Enforcement of Decisions Concerning Custody of Children and on Restoration of Custody of Children are not available, a separate application under s 8 of the Children Act 1989 will have to be made.

Central Authority for England and Wales

NOTES

NB. The Child Abduction Unit is now called ICACU, see paragraph 2.6.

Practice Direction 12G –
Communication of Information

This Practice Direction supplements FPR Part 12, Chapter 7

1.1 Chapter 7 deals with the communication of information (whether or not contained in a document filed with the court) relating to proceedings which relate to children.

1.2 Subject to any direction of the court, information may be communicated for the purposes of the law relating to contempt in accordance with paragraphs 2.1, 3.1 or 4.1.

Communication of information by a party etc. for other purposes

2.1 A person specified in the first column of the following table may communicate to a person listed in the second column such information as is specified in the third column for the purpose or purposes specified in the fourth column –

A party	A lay adviser, a McKenzie Friend, or a person arranging or providing pro bono legal services	Any information relating to the proceedings	To enable the party to obtain advice or assistance in relation to the proceedings
A party	A health care professional or a person or body providing counselling services for children or families	To enable the party or any child of the party to obtain health care or counselling	
A party	The Child Maintenance and Enforcement Commission, a McKenzie Friend, a lay adviser or the First-tier Tribunal dealing with an appeal made under section 20 of the Child Support Act 1991	For the purposes of making or responding to an appeal under section 20 of the Child Support Act 1991 or the determination of such an appeal	
A party	An adoption panel	To enable the adoption panel to discharge its functions as appropriate	

A party	The European Court of Human Rights	For the purpose of making an application to the European Court of Human Rights	
A party or any person lawfully in receipt of information	The Children's Commissioner or the Children's Commissioner for Wales	To refer an issue affecting the interests of children to the Children's Commissioner or the Children's Commissioner for Wales	
A party, any person lawfully in receipt of information or a proper officer	A person or body conducting an approved research project	For the purpose of an approved research project	
A legal representative or a professional legal adviser	A person or body responsible for investigating or determining complaints in relation to legal representatives or professional legal advisers	For the purposes of the investigation or determination of a complaint in relation to a legal representative or a professional legal adviser	
A legal representative or a professional legal adviser	A person or body assessing quality assurance systems	To enable the legal representative or professional legal adviser to obtain a quality assurance assessment	

A legal representative or a professional legal adviser	An accreditation body	Any information relating to the proceedings providing that it does not, or is not likely to, identify any person involved in the proceedings	To enable the legal representative or professional legal adviser to obtain accreditation
A party	A police officer	The text or summary of the whole or part of a judgment given in the proceedings	For the purpose of a criminal investigation
A party or any person lawfully in receipt of information	A member of the Crown Prosecution Service	To enable the Crown Prosecution Service to discharge its functions under any enactment	

Communication for the effective functioning of Cafcass and CAFCASS CYMRU

3.1 An officer of the Service or a Welsh family proceedings officer, as appropriate, may communicate to a person listed in the second column such information as is specified in the third column for the purpose or purposes specified in the fourth column –

A Welsh family proceedings officer	A person or body exercising statutory functions relating to inspection of CAFCASS CYMRU	Any information relating to the proceedings which is required by the person or body responsible for the inspection	For the purpose of an inspection of CAFCASS CYMRU by a body or person appointed by the Welsh Ministers

An officer of the Service or a Welsh family proceedings officer	The General Social Care Council or the Care Council for Wales	Any information relating to the proceedings providing that it does not, or is not likely to, identify any person involved in the proceedings	For the purpose of initial and continuing accreditation as a social worker of a person providing services to Cafcass or CAFCASS CYMRU in accordance with section 13(2) of the Criminal Justice and Courts Services Act 2000 or section 36 of the Children Act 2004 as the case may be
An officer of the Service or a Welsh family proceedings officer	A person or body providing services relating to professional development or training to Cafcass or CAFCASS CYMRU	Any information relating to the proceedings providing that it does not, or is not likely to, identify any person involved in the proceedings without that person's consent	To enable the person or body to provide the services, where the services cannot be effectively provided without such disclosure

An officer of the Service or a Welsh family proceedings officer	A person employed by or contracted to Cafcass or CAFCASS CYMRU for the purposes of carrying out the functions referred to in column 4 of this row	Any information relating to the proceedings	Engagement in processes internal to Cafcass or CAFCASS CYMRU which relate to the maintenance of necessary records concerning the proceedings, or to ensuring that Cafcass or CAFCASS CYMRU functions are carried out to a satisfactory standard

Communication to and by Ministers of the Crown and Welsh Ministers

4.1 A person specified in the first column of the following table may communicate to a person listed in the second column such information as is specified in the third column for the purpose or purposes specified in the fourth column –

A party or any person lawfully in receipt of information relating to the proceedings	A Minister of the Crown with responsibility for a government department engaged, or potentially engaged, in an application before the European Court of Human Rights relating to the proceedings	Any information relating to the proceedings of which he or she is in lawful possession	To provide the department with information relevant, or potentially relevant, to the proceedings before the European Court of Human Rights

A Minister of the Crown	The European Court of Human Rights	For the purpose of engagement in an application before the European Court of Human Rights relating to the proceedings	
A Minister of the Crown	Lawyers advising or representing the United Kingdom in an application before the European Court of Human Rights relating to the proceedings	For the purpose of receiving advice or for effective representation in relation to the application before the European Court of Human Rights.	
A Minister of the crown or a Welsh Minister	Another Minister, or Ministers, of the Crown or a Welsh Minister	For the purpose of notification, discussion and the giving or receiving of advice regarding issues raised by the information in which the relevant departments have, or may have, an interest	

5.1 This paragraph applies to communications made in accordance with paragraphs 2.1, 3.1 and 4.1 and the reference in this paragraph to 'the table' means the table in the relevant paragraph.

5.2 A person in the second column of the table may only communicate information relating to the proceedings received from a person in the first column for the purpose or purposes –

    (a)   for which he or she received that information; or

    (b)   of professional development or training, providing that any communication does not, or is not likely to, identify any person involved in the proceedings without that person's consent.

6.1 In this Practice Direction –

'accreditation body' means –
  (a)   The Law Society,
  (b)   Resolution, or
  (c)   The Legal Services Commission;

'adoption panel' means a panel established in accordance with regulation 3 of the Adoption Agencies Regulations 2005 or regulation 3 of the Adoption Agencies (Wales) Regulations 2005;

'approved research project' means a project of research –
  (a)   approved in writing by a Secretary of State after consultation with the President of the Family Division,
  (b)   approved in writing by the President of the Family Division, or
  (c)   conducted under section 83 of the Act of 1989 or section 13 of the Criminal Justice and Court Services Act 2000;

'body assessing quality assurance systems' includes –
  (a)   The Law Society,
  (b)   The Legal Services Commission, or
  (c)   The General Council of the Bar;

'body or person responsible for investigating or determining complaints in relation to legal representatives or professional legal advisers' means –
  (a)   The Law Society,
  (b)   The General Council of the Bar,
  (c)   The Institute of Legal Executives,
  (d)   The Legal Services Ombudsman; or
  (e)   The Office of Legal Complaints.

'Cafcass' has the meaning assigned to it by section 11 of the Criminal Justice and Courts Services Act 2000;

'CAFCASS CYMRU' means the part of the Welsh Assembly Government exercising the functions of Welsh Ministers under Part 4 of the Children Act 2004;

'criminal investigation' means an investigation conducted by police officers with a view to it being ascertained –
  (a)   whether a person should be charged with an offence, or
  (b)   whether a person charged with an offence is guilty of it;

'health care professional' means –
  (a)   a registered medical practitioner,
  (b)   a registered nurse or midwife,
  (c)   a clinical psychologist, or
  (d)   a child psychotherapist;

'lay adviser' means a non-professional person who gives lay advice on behalf of an organisation in the lay advice sector;

'McKenzie Friend' means any person permitted by the court to sit beside an unrepresented litigant in court to assist that litigant by prompting, taking notes and giving him advice; and

PART II – Statutory Instruments

'social worker' has the meaning assigned to it by section 55 of the Care Standards Act 2000.

Practice Direction 12H –
Contribution Orders

This Practice Direction supplements FPR Part 12

1.1 Paragraph 23(6) of Schedule 2 to the 1989 Act provides that where –

(a)   a contribution order is in force;

(b)   the local authority serve another contribution notice; and

(c)   the contributor and the local authority reach an agreement under paragraph 22(7) in respect of that other contribution notice,

the effect of the agreement shall be to discharge the order from the date on which it is agreed that the agreement shall take effect.

1.2 Where a local authority notifies the court of an agreement reached under paragraph 23(6) of Schedule 2 to the 1989 Act, the notification must be sent in writing to the designated officer of the court.

Practice Direction 12I –
Applications for Reporting Restriction Orders

This Practice Direction supplements FPR Part 12

1 This direction applies to any application in the Family Division founded on Convention rights for an order restricting publication of information about children or incapacitated adults.

2 Applications to be heard in the High Court

Orders can only be made in the High Court and are normally dealt with by a Judge of the Family Division. If the need for an order arises in existing proceedings in the county court, judges should either transfer the application to the High Court or consult their Family Division Liaison Judge. Where the matter is urgent, it can be heard by the Urgent Applications Judge of the Family Division (out of hours contact number 020 7947 6000).

3 Service of application on the national news media

Section 12(2) of the Human Rights Act 1998 means that an injunction restricting the exercise of the right to freedom of expression must not be granted where the person against whom the application is made is neither present nor represented unless the court is satisfied (a) that the applicant has taken all practicable steps to notify the respondent, or (b) that there are compelling reasons why the respondent should not be notified.

Service of applications for reporting restriction orders on the national media can now be effected via the Press Association's CopyDirect service, to which national newspapers and broadcasters subscribe as a means of receiving notice of such applications.

The court will bear in mind that legal advisers to the media (i) are used to participating in hearings at very short notice where necessary; and (ii) are able to differentiate between information provided for legal purposes and information for editorial use. Service of applications via the CopyDirect service should henceforth be the norm.

The court retains the power to make without notice orders, but such cases will be exceptional, and an order will always give persons affected liberty to apply to vary or discharge it at short notice.

4 Further guidance

The *Practice Note Applications for Reporting Restriction Orders* dated 18 March 2005 and issued jointly by the Official Solicitor and the Deputy Director of Legal Services, provides valuable guidance and should be followed.

5 Issued with the concurrence and approval of the Lord Chancellor.

Practice Direction 12J –
Residence and Contact Orders: Domestic Violence and Harm

This Practice Direction supplements FPR Part 12

1 This Practice Direction applies to any family proceedings in the High Court, a county court or a magistrates' court in which an application is made for a residence order or a contact order in respect of a child under the Children Act 1989 ("the 1989 Act") or the Adoption and Children Act 2002 ("the 2002 Act") or in which any question arises about residence or about contact between a child and a parent or other family member.

2 The practice set out in this Direction is to be followed in any case in which it is alleged, or there is otherwise reason to suppose, that the subject child or a party has experienced domestic violence perpetrated by another party or that there is a risk of such violence. For the purpose of this Direction, the term 'domestic violence' includes physical violence, threatening or intimidating behaviour and any other form of abuse which, directly or indirectly, may have caused harm to the other party or to the child or which may give rise to the risk of harm.

> ('Harm' in relation to a child means ill-treatment or the impairment of health or development, including, for example, impairment suffered from seeing or hearing the ill-treatment of another: Children Act 1989, ss 31(9), 105(1))

PART II – Statutory Instruments

General principles

3 The court must, at all stages of the proceedings, consider whether domestic violence is raised as an issue, either by the parties or otherwise, and if so must:

- identify at the earliest opportunity the factual and welfare issues involved;
- consider the nature of any allegation or admission of domestic violence and the extent to which any domestic violence which is admitted, or which may be proved, would be relevant in deciding whether to make an order about residence or contact and, if so, in what terms;
- give directions to enable the relevant factual and welfare issues to be determined expeditiously and fairly.

4 In all cases it is for the court to decide whether an order for residence or contact accords with Section 1(1) of the 1989 Act or section 1(2) of the 2002 Act, as appropriate; any proposed residence or contact order, whether to be made by agreement between the parties or otherwise must be scrutinised by the court accordingly. The court shall not make a consent order for residence or contact or give permission for an application for a residence or contact order to be withdrawn, unless the parties are present in court, except where it is satisfied that there is no risk of harm to the child in so doing.

5 In considering, on an application for a consent order for residence or contact, whether there is any risk of harm to the child, the court shall consider all the evidence and information available. The court may direct a report under Section 7 of the 1989 Act either orally or in writing before it makes its determination; in such a case, the court may ask for information about any advice given by the officer preparing the report to the parties and whether they or the child have been referred to any other agency, including local authority children's services. If the report is not in writing, the court shall make a note of its substance on the court file.

Issue

6 Immediately on receipt of an application for a residence order or a contact order, or of the acknowledgement of the application, the court shall send a copy of it, together with any accompanying documents, to Cafcass or Cafcass Cymru, as appropriate, to enable Cafcass or Cafcass Cymru to undertake initial screening in accordance with their safeguarding policies.

Liaison

7 The Designated Family Judge, or in the magistrates' court the Justices' Clerk, shall take steps to ensure that arrangements are in place for:

- the prompt delivery of documents to Cafcass or Cafcass Cymru in accordance with paragraph 6
- any information obtained by Cafcass or Cafcass Cymru as a result of initial screening or otherwise and any risk assessments prepared by

Cafcass or Cafcass Cymru under section 16A of the 1989 Act to be placed before the appropriate court for consideration and directions

- a copy of any record of admissions or findings of fact made pursuant to paragraphs 12 & 21 below to be made available as soon as possible to any Officer of Cafcass or Welsh family proceedings officer or local authority officer preparing a report under section 7 of the 1989 Act.

Response of the court on receipt of information

8 Where any information provided to the court before the first hearing, whether as a result of initial screening by Cafcass or Cafcass Cymru or otherwise, indicates that there are issues of domestic violence which may be relevant to the court's determination, the court may give directions about the conduct of the hearing and for written evidence to be filed by the parties before the hearing.

9 If at any stage the court is advised by Cafcass or Cafcass Cymru or otherwise that there is a need for special arrangements to secure the safety of any party or child attending any hearing, the court shall ensure that appropriate arrangements are made for the hearing and for all subsequent hearings in the case, unless it considers that these are no longer necessary.

First hearing

10 At the first hearing, the court shall inform the parties of the content of any screening report or other information which has been provided by Cafcass or Cafcass Cymru, unless it considers that to do so would create a risk of harm to a party or the child.

(Specific provision about service of a risk assessment under section 16A of the 1989 Act is made by rule 12.34 of the Family Procedure Rules 2010.)

11 The court must ascertain at the earliest opportunity whether domestic violence is raised as an issue and must consider the likely impact of that issue on the conduct and outcome of the proceedings. In particular, the court should consider whether the nature and effect of the domestic violence alleged is such that, if proved, the decision of the court is likely to be affected.

Admissions

12 Where at any hearing an admission of domestic violence to another person or the child is made by a party, the admission should be recorded in writing and retained on the court file.

Directions for a fact-finding hearing

13 The court should determine as soon as possible whether it is necessary to conduct a fact-finding hearing in relation to any disputed allegation of domestic violence before it can proceed to consider any final order(s) for residence or contact. Where the court determines that a finding of fact hearing is not necessary, the order shall record the reasons for that decision.

PART II – Statutory Instruments

14 Where the court considers that a fact-finding hearing is necessary, it must give directions to ensure that the matters in issue are determined expeditiously and fairly and in particular it should consider:

- directing the parties to file written statements giving particulars of the allegations made and of any response in such a way as to identify clearly the issues for determination;
- whether material is required from third parties such as the police or health services and may give directions accordingly;
- whether any other evidence is required to enable the court to make findings of fact in relation to the allegations and may give directions accordingly.

15 Where the court fixes a fact-finding hearing, it must at the same time fix a further hearing for determination of the application. The hearings should be arranged in such a way that they are conducted by the same judge or, in the magistrates' court, by at least the same chairperson of the justices.

Reports under Section 7

16 In any case where domestic violence is raised as an issue, the court should consider directing that a report on the question of contact, or any other matters relating to the welfare of the child, be prepared under section 7 of the 1989 Act by an Officer of Cafcass or a Welsh family proceedings officer (or local authority officer if appropriate), unless the court is satisfied that it is not necessary to do so in order to safeguard the child's interests. If the court so directs, it should consider the extent of any enquiries which can properly be made at this stage and whether it is appropriate to seek information on the wishes and feelings of the child before findings of fact have been made.

Representation of the child

17 Subject to the seriousness of the allegations made and the difficulty of the case, the court shall consider whether it is appropriate for the child who is the subject of the application to be made a party to the proceedings and be separately represented. If the case is proceeding in the magistrates' court and the court considers that it may be appropriate for the child to be made a party to the proceedings, it may transfer the case to the relevant county court for determination of that issue and following such transfer the county court shall give such directions for the further conduct of the case as it considers appropriate.

Interim orders before determination of relevant facts

18 Where the court gives directions for a fact-finding hearing, the court should consider whether an interim order for residence or contact is in the interests of the child; and in particular whether the safety of the child and the residential parent can be secured before, during and after any contact.

19 In deciding any question of interim residence or contact pending a full hearing the court should: –

(*a*)   take into account the matters set out in section 1(3) of the 1989 Act or section 1(4) of the 2002 Act ('the welfare check-list'), as appropriate;

(*b*)   give particular consideration to the likely effect on the child of any contact and any risk of harm, whether physical, emotional or psychological, which the child is likely to suffer as a consequence of making or declining to make an order;

20 Where the court is considering whether to make an order for interim contact, it should in addition consider

(*a*)   the arrangements required to ensure, as far as possible, that any risk of harm to the child is minimised and that the safety of the child and the parties is secured; and in particular:

    (i)   whether the contact should be supervised or supported, and if so, where and by whom; and

    (ii)   the availability of appropriate facilities for that purpose

(*b*)   if direct contact is not appropriate, whether it is in the best interests of the child to make an order for indirect contact.

The fact-finding hearing

21 At the fact-finding hearing, the court should, wherever practicable, make findings of fact as to the nature and degree of any domestic violence which is established and its effect on the child, the child's parents and any other relevant person. The court shall record its findings in writing, and shall serve a copy on the parties. A copy of any record of findings of fact or of admissions must be sent to any officer preparing a report under Section 7 of the 1989 Act.

22 At the conclusion of any fact-finding hearing, the court shall consider, notwithstanding any earlier direction for a section 7 report, whether it is in the best interests of the child for the court to give further directions about the preparation or scope of any report under section 7; where necessary, it may adjourn the proceedings for a brief period to enable the officer to make representations about the preparation or scope of any further enquiries. The court should also consider whether it would be assisted by any social work, psychiatric, psychological or other assessment of any party or the child and if so (subject to any necessary consent) make directions for such assessment to be undertaken and for the filing of any consequent report.

23 Where the court has made findings of fact on disputed allegations, any subsequent hearing in the proceedings should be conducted by the same judge or, in the magistrates' court, by at least the same chairperson of the justices. Exceptions may be made only where observing this requirement would result in delay to the planned timetable and the judge or chairperson is satisfied, for reasons recorded in writing, that the detriment to the welfare of the child would outweigh the detriment to the fair trial of the proceedings.

PART II – Statutory Instruments

In all cases where domestic violence has occurred

24 The court should take steps to obtain (or direct the parties or an Officer of Cafcass or a Welsh family proceedings officer to obtain) information about the facilities available locally to assist any party or the child in cases where domestic violence has occurred.

25 Following any determination of the nature and extent of domestic violence, whether or not following a fact-finding hearing, the court should consider whether any party should seek advice or treatment as a precondition to an order for residence or contact being made or as a means of assisting the court in ascertaining the likely risk of harm to the child from that person, and may (with the consent of that party) give directions for such attendance and the filing of any consequent report.

Factors to be taken into account when determining whether to make residence or contact orders in all cases where domestic violence has occurred

26 When deciding the issue of residence or contact the court should, in the light of any findings of fact, apply the individual matters in the welfare checklist with reference to those findings; in particular, where relevant findings of domestic violence have been made, the court should in every case consider any harm which the child has suffered as a consequence of that violence and any harm which the child is at risk of suffering if an order for residence or contact is made and should only make an order for contact if it can be satisfied that the physical and emotional safety of the child and the parent with whom the child is living can, as far as possible, be secured before during and after contact.

27 In every case where a finding of domestic violence is made, the court should consider the conduct of both parents towards each other and towards the child; in particular, the court should consider;

(a) the effect of the domestic violence which has been established on the child and on the parent with whom the child is living;

(b) the extent to which the parent seeking residence or contact is motivated by a desire to promote the best interests of the child or may be doing so as a means of continuing a process of violence, intimidation or harassment against the other parent;

(c) the likely behaviour during contact of the parent seeking contact and its effect on the child;

(d) the capacity of the parent seeking residence or contact to appreciate the effect of past violence and the potential for future violence on the other parent and the child;

(e) the attitude of the parent seeking residence or contact to past violent conduct by that parent; and in particular whether that parent has the capacity to change and to behave appropriately.

Directions as to how contact is to proceed

28 Where the court has made findings of domestic violence but, having applied the welfare checklist, nonetheless considers that direct contact is in the best interests of the child, the court should consider what if any directions or conditions are required to enable the order to be carried into effect and in particular should consider:

(*a*)   whether or not contact should be supervised, and if so, where and by whom;

(*b*)   whether to impose any conditions to be complied with by the party in whose favour the order for contact has been made and if so, the nature of those conditions, for example by way of seeking advice or treatment (subject to any necessary consent);

(*c*)   whether such contact should be for a specified period or should contain provisions which are to have effect for a specified period;

(*d*)   whether or not the operation of the order needs to be reviewed; if so the court should set a date for the review and give directions to ensure that at the review the court has full information about the operation of the order.

29 Where the court does not consider direct contact to be appropriate, it shall consider whether it is in the best interests of the child to make an order for indirect contact.

The reasons of the court

30 In its judgment or reasons the court should always make clear how its findings on the issue of domestic violence have influenced its decision on the issue of residence or contact. In particular, where the court has found domestic violence proved but nonetheless makes an order, the court should always explain, whether by way of reference to the welfare check-list or otherwise, why it takes the view that the order which it has made is in the best interests of the child.

31 This Practice Direction is issued by the President of the Family Division, as the nominee of the Lord Chief Justice, with the agreement of the Lord Chancellor.

Practice Direction 12K – Children Act 1989: Exclusion Requirement

This Practice Direction supplements FPR Part 12

Under s 38A(5) and s 44A(5) of the Children Act 1989 the court may attach a power of arrest to an exclusion requirement included in an interim care order or an emergency protection order. In cases where an order is made which includes an exclusion requirement, the following shall apply:

(1)   If a power of arrest is attached to the order then unless the person to whom the exclusion requirement refers was given notice of the hearing

and attended the hearing, the name of that person and that an order has been made including an exclusion requirement to which a power of arrest has been attached shall be announced in open court at the earliest opportunity. This may be either on the same day when the court proceeds to hear cases in open court or where there is no further business in open court on that day at the next listed sitting of the court.

(2)   When a person arrested under a power of arrest cannot conveniently be brought before the relevant judicial authority sitting in a place normally used as a courtroom within 24 hours after the arrest, he may be brought before the relevant judicial authority at any convenient place but, as the liberty of the subject is involved, the press and the public should be permitted to be present, unless security needs make this impracticable.

(3)   Any order of committal made otherwise than in public or in a courtroom open to the public, shall be announced in open court at the earliest opportunity. This may be either on the same day when the court proceeds to hear cases in open court or where there is no further business in open court on that day at the next listed sitting of the court. The announcement shall state –

(*a*) the name of the person committed,

(*b*) in general terms the nature of the contempt of the court in respect of which the order of committal has been made and

(*c*) the length of the period of committal.

Practice Direction 12L –
Children Act 1989: Risk Assessments under Section 16A

This Practice Direction supplements FPR Part 12

1 This Practice Direction applies to any family proceedings in the High Court, a county court or a magistrates' court in which a risk assessment is made under section 16A of the Children Act 1989 ("the 1989 Act"). It has effect from 1 October 2007.

2 Section 16A(2) of the 1989 Act provides that, if in carrying out any function to which the section applies (as set out in section 16A(1)), an officer of the Service or a Welsh family proceedings officer is given cause to suspect that the child concerned is at risk of harm, the officer must make a risk assessment in relation to the child and provide the risk assessment to the court.

3 The duty to provide the risk assessment to the court arises irrespective of the outcome of the assessment. Where an officer is given cause to suspect that the child concerned is at risk of harm and makes a risk assessment in accordance with section 16A(2), the officer must provide the assessment to the court, even if he or she reaches the conclusion that there is no risk of harm to the child.

4 The fact that a risk assessment has been carried out is a material fact that should be placed before the court, whatever the outcome of the assessment. In

reporting the outcome to the court, the officer should make clear the factor or factors that triggered the decision to carry out the assessment.

5 Issued by the President of the Family Division, as the nominee of the Lord Chief Justice, with the agreement of the Lord Chancellor.

Practice Direction 12M –
Family Assistance Orders: Consultation

This Practice Direction supplements FPR Part 12

1 This Practice Direction applies to any family proceedings in the High Court, a county court or a magistrates' court in which the court is considering whether to make a family assistance order under section 16 of the Children Act 1989, as amended ("the 1989 Act"). It has effect from 1 October 2007.

2 Before making a family assistance order the court must have obtained the opinion of the appropriate officer about whether it would be in the best interests of the child in question for a family assistance order to be made and, if so, how the family assistance order could operate and for what period.

3 The appropriate officer will be an officer of the Service, a Welsh family proceedings officer or an officer of a local authority, depending on the category of officer the court proposes to require to be made available under the family assistance order.

4 The opinion of the appropriate officer may be given orally or in writing (for example, it may form part of a report under section 7 of the 1989 Act).

5 Before making a family assistance order the court must give any person whom it proposes be named in the order an opportunity to comment upon any opinion given by the appropriate officer.

6 Issued by the President of the Family Division, as the nominee of the Lord Chief Justice, with the agreement of the Lord Chancellor

Practice Direction 12N –
Enforcement of Children Act 1989 Contact Orders: Disclosure of Information to Officers of the National Probation Service (High Court and County Court)

This Practice Direction supplements FPR Part 12

1 This Practice Direction applies to proceedings in the High Court or a county court where:

(*a*) the court is considering an application for an enforcement order[1] or for an order following an alleged breach of an enforcement order[2] and asks an officer of the Service or a Welsh family proceedings officer to provide information to the court in accordance with section 11L(5) of the Children Act 1989; or

PART II – Statutory Instruments

1   Under section 11J of the Children Act 1989.
2   Under paragraph 9 of Schedule A1 to the Children Act 1989.

(b)   the court makes an enforcement order or an order following an alleged breach of an enforcement order and asks an officer of the Service or a Welsh family proceedings officer to monitor compliance with that order and to report to the court in accordance with section 11M of the Children Act 1989.

2 In all cases in which paragraph 1 applies, the officer of the Service or Welsh family proceedings officer will need to discuss aspects of the court case with an officer of the National Probation Service.

3 In order to ensure that the officer of the Service or Welsh family proceedings officer will not potentially be in contempt of court by virtue of such discussions, the court should, when making a request under section 11L(5) or section 11M of the Children Act 1989, give leave to that officer to disclose to the National Probation Service such information (whether or not contained in a document filed with the court) in relation to the proceedings as is necessary.

4 This Practice Direction comes into force on 8 December 2008.

Practice Direction 12O –
Arrival of Child in England by Air

This Practice Direction supplements FPR Part 12

Where a person seeks an order for the return to him of children about to arrive in England by air and desires to have information to enable him to meet the aeroplane, the judge should be asked to include in his order a direction that the airline operating the flight, and, if he has the information, the immigration officer at the appropriate airport, should supply such information to that person.

To obtain such information in such circumstances in a case where a person already has an order for the return to him of children, that person should apply to a judge ex parte for such a direction.

Practice Direction 12P –
Removal from Jurisdiction: Issue of Passports

This Practice Direction supplements FPR Part 12

1 Removal from jurisdiction

The President has directed that on application for leave to remove from the jurisdiction for holiday periods a ward of court who has been placed by a local authority with foster-parents whose identity the court considers should remain confidential, for example because they are prospective adopters, it is important that such foster-parents should not be identified in the court's order. In such cases the order should be expressed as giving leave to the local authority to arrange for the child to be removed from England and Wales for the purpose of holidays.

It is also considered permissible, where care and control has been given to a local authority, or to an individual, for the court to give general leave to make such arrangements in suitable cases, thereby obviating the need to make application for leave each time it is desired to remove the child from the jurisdiction.

2 Issue of passports

It is the practice of the Passport Department of the Home Office to issue passports for wards in accordance with the court's direction. This frequently results in passports being restricted to the holiday period specified in the order giving leave. It is the President's opinion that it is more convenient for wards' passports to be issued without such restriction.

The Passport Department has agreed to issue passports on this basis unless the court otherwise directs. It will, of course, still be necessary for the leave of the court to be obtained for the child's removal.

****

PART 14
PROCEDURE FOR APPLICATIONS IN ADOPTION, PLACEMENT AND RELATED PROCEEDINGS

14.1 Application of this Part and interpretation

(1) The rules in this Part apply to the following proceedings –

    (a)   adoption proceedings;

    (b)   placement proceedings; and

    (c)   proceedings for –

        (i)   the making of a contact order under section 26 of the 2002 Act;

        (ii)   the variation or revocation of a contact order under section 27 of the 2002 Act;

        (iii)   an order giving permission to change a child's surname or remove a child from the United Kingdom under section 28(2) and (3) of the 2002 Act;

        (iv)   a section 84 order;

        (v)   a section 88 direction;

        (vi)   a section 89 order; or

        (vii)   any other order that may be referred to in a practice direction.

(2) In this Part –

    'Central Authority' means –

        (a)   in relation to England, the Secretary of State; and

        (b)   in relation to Wales, the Welsh Ministers;

'Convention adoption order' means an adoption order under the 2002 Act which, by virtue of regulations under section 1 of the Adoption (Intercountry Aspects) Act 1999 (regulations giving effect to the Convention on Protection of Children and Co-operation in Respect of Intercountry Adoption, concluded at the Hague on 29th May 1993), is made as a Convention adoption order;

'guardian' means –

> (a)   a guardian (other than the guardian of the estate of a child) appointed in accordance with section 5 of the 1989 Act; and
>
> (b)   a special guardian within the meaning of section 14A of the 1989 Act;

'provision for contact' means a contact order under section 8 or 34 of the 1989 Act or a contact order under section 26 of the 2002 Act;

'section 88 direction' means a direction given by the High Court under section 88 of the 2002 Act that section 67(3) of that Act (status conferred by adoption) does not apply or does not apply to any extent specified in the direction.

14.2 Application for a serial number

(1) This rule applies to any application in proceedings by a person who intends to adopt the child.

(2) If, before the proceedings have started, the applicant requests a court officer to assign a serial number to identify the applicant in connection with the proceedings in order for the applicant's identity to be kept confidential in those proceedings, a serial number will be so assigned.

(3) The court may at any time direct that a serial number identifying the applicant in the proceedings referred to in paragraph (2) must be removed.

(4) If a serial number has been assigned to a person under paragraph (2) –

> (a)   the court officer will ensure that any application form or application notice sent in accordance with these rules does not contain information which discloses, or is likely to disclose, the identity of that person to any other party to that application who is not already aware of that person's identity; and
>
> (b)   the proceedings on the application will be conducted with a view to securing that the applicant is not seen by or made known to any party who is not already aware of the applicant's identity except with the applicant's consent.

14.3 Who the parties are

(1) In relation to the proceedings set out in column 1 of the following table, column 2 sets out who the application may be made by and column 3 sets out who the respondents to those proceedings will be.

Proceedings for	Applicants	Respondents
An adoption order (section 46 of the 2002 Act).	The prospective adopters (sections 50 and 51 of the 2002 Act).	Each parent who has parental responsibility for the child unless that parent has given notice under section 20(4)(a) of the 2002 Act (statement of wish not to be informed of any application for an adoption order) which has effect; any guardian of the child unless that guardian has given notice under section 20(4)(a) of the 2002 Act (statement of wish not to be informed of any application for an adoption order) which has effect; any person in whose favour there is provision for contact; any adoption agency having parental responsibility for the child under section 25 of the 2002 Act; any adoption agency which has taken part at any stage in the arrangements for adoption of the child; any local authority to whom notice under section 44 of the 2002 Act (notice of intention to adopt or apply for a section 84 order) has been given;

PART II – Statutory Instruments

Proceedings for	Applicants	Respondents
		any local authority or voluntary organisation which has parental responsibility for, is looking after or is caring for, the child; and the child where –
		– permission has been granted to a parent or guardian to oppose the making of the adoption order (section 47(3) or 47(5) of the 2002 Act);
		– the child opposes the making of an adoption order;
		– a children and family reporter recommends that it is in the best interests of the child to be a party to the proceedings and that recommendation is accepted by the court;
		– the child is already an adopted child;
		– any party to the proceedings or the child is opposed to the arrangements for allowing any person contact with the child, or a person not being allowed contact with the child after the making of the adoption order;
		– the application is for a Convention adoption order or a section 84 order;

Proceedings for	Applicants	Respondents
		– the child has been brought into the United Kingdom in the circumstances where section 83(1) of the 2002 Act applies (restriction on bringing children in); – the application is for an adoption order other than a Convention adoption order and the prospective adopters intend the child to live in a country or territory outside the British Islands after the making of the adoption order; or – the prospective adopters are relatives of the child.
A section 84 order.	The prospective adopters asking for parental responsibility prior to adoption abroad.	As for an adoption order.
A placement order (section 21 of the 2002 Act).	A local authority (section 22 of the 2002 Act).	Each parent who has parental responsibility for the child: any guardian of the child; any person in whose favour an order under the 1989 Act is in force in relation to the child; any adoption agency or voluntary organisation which has parental responsibility for, is looking after, or is caring for, the child; the child; and

PART II – Statutory Instruments

Proceedings for	Applicants	Respondents
		the parties or any persons who are or have been parties to proceedings for a care order in respect of the child where those proceedings have led to the application for the placement order.
An order varying a placement order (section 23 of the 2002 Act).	The joint application of the local authority authorised by the placement order to place the child for adoption and the local authority which is to be substituted for that authority (section 23 of the 2002 Act).	The parties to the proceedings leading to the placement order which it is sought to have varied except the child who was the subject of those proceedings; and any person in whose favour there is provision for contact.
An order revoking a placement order (section 24 of the 2002 Act).	The child; the local authority authorised to place the child for adoption; or where the child is not placed for adoption by the authority, any other person who has the permission of the court to apply (section 24 of the 2002 Act).	The parties to the proceedings leading to the placement order which it is sought to have revoked; and any person in whose favour there is provision for contact.
A contact order (section 26 of the 2002 Act).	The child; the adoption agency; any parent, guardian or relative;	The adoption agency authorised to place the child for adoption or which has placed the child for adoption;

Proceedings for	Applicants	Respondents
	any person in whose favour there was provision for contact under the 1989 Act which ceased to have effect on an adoption agency being authorised to place a child for adoption, or placing a child for adoption who is less than six weeks old (section 26(1) of the 2002 Act); a person in whose favour there was a residence order in force immediately before the adoption agency was authorised to place the child for adoption or placed the child for adoption at a time when the child was less than six weeks old;

a person who by virtue of an order made in the exercise of the High Court's inherent jurisdiction with respect to children had care of the child immediately before that time; or any person who has the permission of the court to make the application (section 26 of the 2002 Act). | the person with whom the child lives or is to live; each parent with parental responsibility for the child; any guardian of the child; and the child where – – the adoption agency authorised to place the child for adoption or which has placed the child for adoption or a parent with parental responsibility for the child opposes the making of the contact order under section 26 of the 2002 Act; – the child opposes the making of the contact order under section 26 of the 2002 Act;

– existing provision for contact is to be revoked; – relatives of the child do not agree to the arrangements for allowing any person contact with the child, or a person not being allowed contact with the child; or – the child is suffering or is at risk of suffering harm within the meaning of the 1989 Act. |

Proceedings for	Applicants	Respondents
An order varying or revoking a contact order (section 27 of the 2002 Act).	The child; the adoption agency; or any person named in the contact order (section 27(1) of the 2002 Act).	The parties to the proceedings leading to the contact order which it is sought to have varied or revoked; and any person named in the contact order.
An order permitting the child's name to be changed or the removal of the child from the United Kingdom (section 28(2) and (3) of the 2002 Act).	Any person including the adoption agency or the local authority authorised to place, or which has placed, the child for adoption (section 28(2) of the 2002 Act).	The parties to proceedings leading to any placement order; the adoption agency authorised to place the child for adoption or which has placed the child for adoption; any prospective adopters with whom the child is living; each parent with parental responsibility for the child; and any guardian of the child.
A section 88 direction.	The adopted child; the adopters; any parent; or any other person.	The adopters; the parents; the adoption agency; the local authority to whom notice under section 44 of the 2002 Act (notice of intention to apply for a section 84 order) has been given; and the Attorney-General.

Proceedings for	Applicants	Respondents
A section 89 order.	The adopters; the adopted person; any parent; the relevant Central Authority; the adoption agency; the local authority to whom notice under section 44 of the 2002 Act (notice of intention to adopt or apply for a section 84 order) has been given; the Secretary of State for the Home Department; or any other person.	The adopters; the parents; the adoption agency; and the local authority to whom notice under section 44 of the 2002 Act (notice of intention to adopt or apply for a section 84 order) has been given.

(2) The court may at any time direct that a child, who is not already a respondent to proceedings, be made a respondent to proceedings where –

    (a)   the child –
        (i)   wishes to make an application; or
        (ii)   has evidence to give to the court or a legal submission to make which has not been given or made by any other party; or
    (b)   there are other special circumstances.

(3) The court may at any time direct that –

    (a)   any other person or body be made a respondent to proceedings; or
    (b)   a party be removed.

(4) If the court makes a direction for the addition or removal of a party, it may give consequential directions about –

    (a)   serving a copy of the application form on any new respondent;
    (b)   serving relevant documents on the new party; and
    (c)   the management of the proceedings.

14.4 Notice of proceedings to person with foreign parental responsibility

(1) This rule applies where a child is subject to proceedings to which this Part applies and –

(a)   a parent of the child holds or is believed to hold parental responsibility for the child under the law of another State which subsists in accordance with Article 16 of the 1996 Hague Convention following the child becoming habitually resident in a territorial unit of the United Kingdom; and

(b)   that parent is not otherwise required to be joined as a respondent under rule 14.3.

(2) The applicant shall give notice of the proceedings to any parent to whom the applicant believes paragraph (1) applies in any case in which a person who was a parent with parental responsibility under the 1989 Act would be a respondent to the proceedings in accordance with rule 14.3.

(3) The applicant and every respondent to the proceedings shall provide such details as they possess as to the identity and whereabouts of any parent they believe to hold parental responsibility for the child in accordance with paragraph (1) to the court officer, upon making, or responding to the application as appropriate.

(4) Where the existence of such a parent only becomes apparent to a party at a later date during the proceedings, that party must notify the court officer of those details at the earliest opportunity.

(5) Where a parent to whom paragraph (1) applies receives notice of proceedings, that parent may apply to the court to be joined as a party using the Part 18 procedure.

14.5 Who is to serve

(1) The general rules about service in Part 6 are subject to this rule.

(2) In proceedings to which this Part applies, a document which has been issued or prepared by a court officer will be served by the court officer except where –

(a)   a practice direction provides otherwise; or
(b)   the court directs otherwise.

(3) Where a court officer is to serve a document, it is for the court to decide which of the methods of service specified in rule 6.23 is to be used

14.6 What the court or a court officer will do when the application has been issued

(1) As soon as practicable after the application has been issued in proceedings –

(a)   the court will –
    (i)   if section 48(1) of the 2002 Act (restrictions on making adoption orders) applies, consider whether it is proper to hear the application;
    (ii)   subject to paragraph (4), set a date for the first directions hearing;

  (iii) appoint a children's guardian in accordance with rule 16.3(1);

  (iv) appoint a reporting officer in accordance with rule 16.30;

  (v) consider whether a report relating to the welfare of the child is required, and if so, request such a report in accordance with rule 16.33;

  (vi) set a date for the hearing of the application; and

  (vii) do anything else that may be set out in a practice direction; and

(b) a court officer will –

  (i) subject to receiving confirmation in accordance with paragraph (2)(b)(ii), give notice of any directions hearing set by the court to the parties and to any children's guardian, reporting officer or children and family reporter;

  (ii) serve a copy of the application form (but, subject to sub-paragraphs (iii) and (iv), not the documents attached to it) on the persons referred to in Practice Direction 14A;

  (iii) send a copy of the certified copy of the entry in the register of live-births or Adopted Children Register and any health report attached to an application for an adoption order to –

   (aa) any children's guardian, reporting officer or children and family reporter; and

   (bb) the local authority to whom notice under section 44 of the 2002 Act (notice of intention to adopt or apply for a section 84 order) has been given;

  (iv) if notice under rule 14.9(2) has been given (request to dispense with consent of parent or guardian), in accordance with that rule inform the parent or guardian of the request and send a copy of the statement of facts to –

   (aa) the parent or guardian;

   (bb) any children's guardian, reporting officer or children and family reporter;

   (cc) any local authority to whom notice under section 44 of the 2002 Act (notice of intention to adopt or apply for a section 84 order) has been given; and

   (dd) any adoption agency which has placed the child for adoption; and

  (v) do anything else that may be set out in a practice direction.

(2) In addition to the matters referred to in paragraph (1), as soon as practicable after an application for an adoption order or a section 84 order has been issued the court or the court officer will –

(a) where the child is not placed for adoption by an adoption agency –

  (i) ask either the Service or the Assembly to file any relevant form of consent to an adoption order or a section 84 order; and

  (ii) ask the local authority to prepare a report on the suitability of the prospective adopters if one has not already been prepared; and

(b) where the child is placed for adoption by an adoption agency, ask the adoption agency to –

> (i) file any relevant form of consent to –
>   (aa) the child being placed for adoption;
>   (bb) an adoption order;
>   (cc) a future adoption order under section 20 of the 2002 Act; or
>   (dd) a section 84 order;
> (ii) confirm whether a statement has been made under section 20(4)(a) of the 2002 Act (statement of wish not to be informed of any application for an adoption order) and if so, to file that statement;
> (iii) file any statement made under section 20(4)(b) of the 2002 Act (withdrawal of wish not to be informed of any application for an adoption order) as soon as it is received by the adoption agency; and
> (iv) prepare a report on the suitability of the prospective adopters if one has not already been prepared.

(3) In addition to the matters referred to in paragraph (1), as soon as practicable after an application for a placement order has been issued –

> (a) the court will consider whether a report giving the local authority's reasons for placing the child for adoption is required, and if so, will direct the local authority to prepare such a report; and
> (b) the court or the court officer will ask either the Service or the Assembly to file any form of consent to the child being placed for adoption.

(4) Where it considers it appropriate the court may, instead of setting a date for a first directions hearing, give the directions provided for by rule 14.8.

14.7 Date for first directions hearing

Unless the court directs otherwise, the first directions hearing must be within 4 weeks beginning with the date on which the application is issued.

14.8 The first directions hearing

(1) At the first directions hearing in the proceedings the court will –

> (a) fix a timetable for the filing of –
>   (i) any report relating to the suitability of the applicants to adopt a child;
>   (ii) any report from the local authority;
>   (iii) any report from a children's guardian, reporting officer or children and family reporter;
>   (iv) if a statement of facts has been filed, any amended statement of facts;
>   (v) any other evidence, and
>   (vi) give directions relating to the reports and other evidence;

(b) consider whether the child or any other person should be a party to the proceedings and, if so, give directions in accordance with rule 14.3(2) or (3) joining that child or person as a party;

(c) give directions relating to the appointment of a litigation friend for any protected party or child who is a party to, but not the subject of, proceedings unless a litigation friend has already been appointed;

(d) consider whether the case needs to be transferred to another court and, if so, give directions to transfer the proceedings to another court in accordance with any order made by the Lord Chancellor under Part 1 of Schedule 11 to the 1989 Act;

(e) give directions about –
   (i) tracing parents or any other person the court considers to be relevant to the proceedings;
   (ii) service of documents;
   (iii) subject to paragraph (2), disclosure as soon as possible of information and evidence to the parties; and
   (iv) the final hearing.

(By rule 3.3 the court may also direct that the case be adjourned if it considers that alternative dispute resolution is appropriate.)

(2) Rule 14.13(2) applies to any direction given under paragraph (1)(e)(iii) as it applies to a direction given under rule 14.13(1).

(3) In addition to the matters referred to in paragraph (1), the court will give any of the directions listed in Practice Direction 14B in proceedings for –

(a) a Convention adoption order;
(b) a section 84 order;
(c) a section 88 direction;
(d) a section 89 order; or
(e) an adoption order where section 83(1) of the 2002 Act applies (restriction on bringing children in).

(4) The parties or their legal representatives must attend the first directions hearing unless the court directs otherwise.

(5) Directions may also be given at any stage in the proceedings –

(a) of the court's own initiative; or
(b) on the application of a party or any children's guardian or, where the direction concerns a report by a reporting officer or children and family reporter, the reporting officer or children and family reporter.

(6) For the purposes of giving directions or for such purposes as the court directs –

(a) the court may set a date for a further directions hearing or other hearing; and
(b) the court officer will give notice of any date so fixed to the parties and to any children's guardian, reporting officer or children and family reporter.

(7) After the first directions hearing the court will monitor compliance by the parties with the court's timetable and directions.

14.9 Requesting the court to dispense with the consent of any parent or guardian

(1) This rule applies where the applicant wants to ask the court to dispense with the consent of any parent or guardian of a child to –

(a)   the child being placed for adoption;

(b)   the making of an adoption order except a Convention adoption order; or

(c)   the making of a section 84 order.

(2) The applicant requesting the court to dispense with the consent must –

(a)   give notice of the request in the application form or at any later stage by filing a written request setting out the reasons for the request; and

(b)   file a statement of facts setting out a summary of the history of the case and any other facts to satisfy the court that –

(i)   the parent or guardian cannot be found or is incapable of giving consent; or

(ii)   the welfare of the child requires the consent to be dispensed with.

(3) If a serial number has been assigned to the applicant under rule 14.2, the statement of facts supplied under paragraph (2)(b) must be framed so that it does not disclose the identity of the applicant.

(4) On receipt of the notice of the request –

(a)   a court officer will –

(i)   inform the parent or guardian of the request unless the parent or guardian cannot be found; and

(ii)   send a copy of the statement of facts filed in accordance with paragraph (2)(b) to –

(aa)   the parent or guardian unless the parent or guardian cannot be found;

(bb)   any children's guardian, reporting officer or children and family reporter;

(cc)   any local authority to whom notice under section 44 of the 2002 Act (notice of intention to adopt or apply for a section 84 order) has been given; and

(dd)   any adoption agency which has placed the child for adoption; and

(b)   if the applicant considers that the parent or guardian is incapable of giving consent, the court will consider whether to –

(i)   appoint a litigation friend for the parent or guardian under rule 15.6(1); or

(ii)   give directions for an application to be made under rule 15.6(3)

(iii)   unless a litigation friend is already appointed for that parent or guardian.

14.10 Consent

(1) Consent of any parent or guardian of a child –

    (a)   under section 19 of the 2002 Act, to the child being placed for adoption; and

    (b)   under section 20 of the 2002 Act, to the making of a future adoption order,

must be given in the form referred to in Practice Direction 5A or a form to the like effect.

(2) Subject to paragraph (3), consent –

    (a)   to the making of an adoption order; or

    (b)   to the making of a section 84 order,

may be given in the form referred to in Practice Direction 5A or a form to the like effect or otherwise as the court directs.

(3) Any consent to a Convention adoption order must be in a form which complies with the internal law relating to adoption of the Convention country of which the child is habitually resident.

(4) Any form of consent executed in Scotland must be witnessed by a Justice of the Peace or a Sheriff.

(5) Any form of consent executed in Northern Ireland must be witnessed by a Justice of the Peace.

(6) Any form of consent executed outside the United Kingdom must be witnessed by –

    (a)   any person for the time being authorised by law in the place where the document is executed to administer an oath for any judicial or other legal purpose;

    (b)   a British Consular officer;

    (c)   a notary public; or

    (d)   if the person executing the document is serving in any of the regular armed forces of the Crown, an officer holding a commission in any of those forces.

14.11 Reports by the adoption agency or local authority

(1) The adoption agency or local authority must file the report on the suitability of the applicant to adopt a child within the timetable fixed by the court.

(2) A local authority that is directed to prepare a report on the placement of the child for adoption must file that report within the timetable fixed by the court.

(3) The reports must cover the matters specified in Practice Direction 14C.

(4) The court may at any stage request a further report or ask the adoption agency or local authority to assist the court in any other manner.

PART II – Statutory Instruments

(5) A court officer will send a copy of any report referred to in this rule to any children's guardian, reporting officer or children and family reporter.

(6) A report to the court under this rule is confidential.

14.12 Health reports

(1) Reports by a registered medical practitioner ('health reports') made not more than 3 months earlier on the health of the child and of each applicant must be attached to an application for an adoption order or a section 84 order except where –

  (a)   the child was placed for adoption with the applicant by an adoption agency;
  (b)   the applicant or one of the applicants is a parent of the child; or
  (c)   the applicant is the partner of a parent of the child.

(2) Health reports must contain the matters set out in Practice Direction 14D.

(3) A health report is confidential

14.13 Confidential reports to the court and disclosure to the parties

(1) The court will consider whether to give a direction that a confidential report be disclosed to each party to the proceedings.

(2) Before giving such a direction the court will consider whether any information should be deleted including information which –

  (a)   discloses, or is likely to disclose, the identity of a person who has been assigned a serial number under rule 14.2(2); or
  (b)   discloses the particulars referred to in rule 29.1(1) where a party has given notice under rule 29.1(2) (disclosure of personal details).

(3) The court may direct that the report will not be disclosed to a party

14.14 Communication of information relating to proceedings

For the purposes of the law relating to contempt of court, information (whether or not it is recorded in any form) relating to proceedings held in private may be communicated –

  (a)   where the court gives permission;
  (b)   unless the court directs otherwise, in accordance with Practice Direction 14E; or
  (c)   where the communication is to –
    (i)   a party;
    (ii)   the legal representative of a party;
    (iii) a professional legal adviser;
    (iv)   an officer of the service or a Welsh family proceedings officer;
    (v)   a welfare officer;
    (vi)   the Legal Services Commission;
    (vii) an expert whose instruction by a party has been authorised by the court for the purposes of the proceedings; or

(viii) a professional acting in furtherance of the protection of children.

14.15 Notice of final hearing

A court officer will give notice to the parties, any children's guardian, reporting officer or children and family reporter and to any other person to whom a practice direction may require such notice to be given –

(a) of the date and place where the application will be heard; and

(b) of the fact that, unless the person wishes or the court requires, the person need not attend.

14.16 The final hearing

(1) Any person who has been given notice in accordance with rule 14.15 may attend the final hearing and, subject to paragraph (2), be heard on the question of whether an order should be made.

(2) A person whose application for the permission of the court to oppose the making of an adoption order under section 47(3) or (5) of the 2002 Act has been refused is not entitled to be heard on the question of whether an order should be made.

(3) Any member or employee of a party which is a local authority, adoption agency or other body may address the court at the final hearing if authorised to do so.

(4) The court may direct that any person must attend a final hearing.

(5) Paragraphs (6) and (7) apply to –

(a) an adoption order;

(b) a section 84 order; or

(c) a section 89 order.

(6) Subject to paragraphs (7) and (8), the court cannot make an order unless the applicant and the child personally attend the final hearing.

(7) The court may direct that the applicant or the child need not attend the final hearing.

(8) In a case of adoption by a couple under section 50 of the 2002 Act, the court may make an adoption order after personal attendance of one only of the applicants if there are special circumstances.

(9) The court cannot make a placement order unless a legal representative of the applicant attends the final hearing.

14.17 Proof of identity of the child

(1) Unless the contrary is shown, the child referred to in the application will be deemed to be the child referred to in the form of consent –

(a) to the child being placed for adoption;

(b) to the making of an adoption order; or

PART II – Statutory Instruments

(c)   to the making of a section 84 order,

where the conditions in paragraph (2) apply.

(2) The conditions are –

(a)   the application identifies the child by reference to a full certified copy of an entry in the registers of live-births;

(b)   the form of consent identifies the child by reference to a full certified copy of an entry in the registers of live-births attached to the form; and

(c)   the copy of the entry in the registers of live-births referred to in sub-paragraph (a) is the same or relates to the same entry in the registers of live-births as the copy of the entry in the registers of live-births attached to the form of consent.

(3) Where the child is already an adopted child paragraph (2) will have effect as if for the references to the registers of live-births there were substituted references to the Adopted Children Register.

(4) Subject to paragraph (7), where the precise date of the child's birth is not proved to the satisfaction of the court, the court will determine the probable date of birth.

(5) The probable date of the child's birth may be specified in the placement order, adoption order or section 84 order as the date of the child's birth.

(6) Subject to paragraph (7), where the child's place of birth cannot be proved to the satisfaction of the court –

(a)   the child may be treated as having been born in the registration district of the court where it is probable that the child may have been born in –
(i)   the United Kingdom;
(ii)   the Channel Islands; or
(iii)   the Isle of Man; or

(b)   in any other case, the particulars of the country of birth may be omitted from the placement order, adoption order or section 84 order.

(7) A placement order identifying the probable date and place of birth of the child will be sufficient proof of the date and place of birth of the child in adoption proceedings and proceedings for a section 84 order.

14.18 Disclosing information to an adopted adult

(1) The adopted person has the right, on request, to receive from the court which made the adoption order a copy of the following –

(a)   the application form for an adoption order (but not the documents attached to that form);

(b)   the adoption order and any other orders relating to the adoption proceedings;

(c)   orders allowing any person contact with the child after the adoption order was made; and

(d)   any other document or order referred to in Practice Direction 14F.

(2) The court will remove any protected information from any copy of a document or order referred to in paragraph (1) before the copies are given to the adopted person.

(3) This rule does not apply to an adopted person under the age of 18 years.

(4) In this rule 'protected information' means information which would be protected information under section 57(3) of the 2002 Act if the adoption agency gave the information and not the court.

14.19 Translation of documents

(1) Where a translation of any document is required for the purposes of proceedings for a Convention adoption order the translation must –

    (a)   unless the court directs otherwise, be provided by the applicant; and
    (b)   be signed by the translator to certify that the translation is accurate.

(2) This rule does not apply where the document is to be served in accordance with the Service Regulation.

14.20 Application for recovery orders

(1) An application for any of the orders referred to in section 41(2) of the 2002 Act (recovery orders) may –

    (a)   in the High Court or a county court, be made without notice in which case the applicant must file the application –
        (i)   where the application is made by telephone, the next business day after the making of the application; or
        (ii)   in any other case, at the time when the application is made; and
    (b)   in a magistrates' court, be made, with the permission of the court, without notice in which case the applicant must file the application at the time when the application is made or as directed by the court.

(2) Where the court refuses to make an order on an application without notice it may direct that the application is made on notice in which case the application will proceed in accordance with rules 14.1 to 14.17.

(3) The respondents to an application under this rule are –

    (a)   in a case where –
        (i)   placement proceedings;
        (ii)   adoption proceedings; or
        (iii)   proceedings for a section 84 order,
    are pending, all parties to those proceedings;
    (b)   any adoption agency authorised to place the child for adoption or which has placed the child for adoption;
    (c)   any local authority to whom notice under section 44 of the 2002 Act (notice of intention to adopt or apply for a section 84 order) has been given;
    (d)   any person having parental responsibility for the child;
    (e)   any person in whose favour there is provision for contact;

(f)   any person who was caring for the child immediately prior to the making of the application; and

(g)   any person whom the applicant alleges to have effected, or to have been or to be responsible for, the taking or keeping of the child.

14.21 Inherent jurisdiction and fathers without parental responsibility

Where no proceedings have started an adoption agency or local authority may ask the High Court for directions on the need to give a father without parental responsibility notice of the intention to place a child for adoption.

14.22 Timing of applications for section 89 order

An application for a section 89 order must be made within 2 years beginning with the date on which –

(a)   the Convention adoption or Convention adoption order; or

(b)   the overseas adoption or determination under section 91 of the 2002 Act,

to which it relates was made.

14.23 Custody of documents

All documents relating to proceedings under the 2002 Act must, while they are in the custody of the court, be kept in a place of special security.

14.24 Documents held by the court not to be inspected or copied without the court's permission

Subject to the provisions of these rules, any practice direction or any direction given by the court –

(a)   no document or order held by the court in proceedings under the 2002 Act will be open to inspection by any person; and

(b)   no copy of any such document or order, or of an extract from any such document or order, will be taken by or given to any person.

14.25 Orders

(1) An order takes effect from the date when it is made, or such later date as the court may specify.

(2) In proceedings in Wales a party may request that an order be drawn up in Welsh as well as English.

14.26 Copies of orders

(1) Within 7 days beginning with the date on which the final order was made in proceedings, or such shorter time as the court may direct, a court officer will send –

(a)   a copy of the order to the applicant;

(b)   a copy, which is sealed$^{(GL)}$, authenticated with the stamp of the court or certified as a true copy, of –
  (i)   an adoption order;
  (ii)   a section 89 order; or
  (iii)   an order quashing or revoking an adoption order or allowing an appeal against an adoption order,
  to the Registrar General;

(c)   a copy of a Convention adoption order to the relevant Central Authority;

(d)   a copy of a section 89 order relating to a Convention adoption order or a Convention adoption to the –
  (i)   relevant Central Authority;
  (ii)   adopters;
  (iii)   adoption agency; and
  (iv)   local authority;

(e)   unless the court directs otherwise, a copy of a contact order under section 26 of the 2002 Act or a variation or revocation of a contact order under section 27 of the 2002 Act to the –
  (i)   person with whom the child is living;
  (ii)   adoption agency; and
  (iii)   local authority; and

(f)   a notice of the making or refusal of –
  (i)   the final order; or
  (ii)   an order quashing or revoking an adoption order or allowing an appeal against an order in proceedings,
  to every respondent and, with the permission of the court, any other person.

(2) The court officer will also send notice of the making of an adoption order or a section 84 order to –

(a)   any court in Great Britain which appears to the court officer to have made any such order as is referred to in section 46(2) of the 2002 Act (order relating to parental responsibility for, and maintenance of, the child); and

(b)   the principal registry, if it appears to the court officer that a parental responsibility agreement has been recorded at the principal registry.

(3) A copy of any final order may be sent to any other person with the permission of the court.

(4) The court officer will send a copy of any order made during the course of the proceedings to the following persons or bodies, unless the court directs otherwise –

(a)   all the parties to those proceedings;
(b)   any children and family reporter appointed in those proceedings;
(c)   any adoption agency or local authority which has prepared a report on the suitability of an applicant to adopt a child;
(d)   any local authority which has prepared a report on placement for adoption.

PART II – Statutory Instruments

(5) If an order has been drawn up in Welsh as well as English in accordance with rule 14.25(2) any reference in this rule to sending an order is to be taken as a reference to sending both the Welsh and English orders.

14.27 Amendment and revocation of orders

(1) Subject to paragraph (2), an application under –

(a)   section 55 of the 2002 Act (revocation of adoptions on legitimation); or

(b)   paragraph 4 of Schedule 1 to the 2002 Act (amendment of adoption order and revocation of direction),

may be made without serving a copy of the application notice.

(2) The court may direct that an application notice be served on such persons as it thinks fit.

(3) Where the court makes an order granting the application, a court officer will send the Registrar General a notice –

(a)   specifying the amendments; or

(b)   informing the Registrar General of the revocation,

giving sufficient particulars of the order to enable the Registrar General to identify the case.

14.28 Keeping registers in the family proceedings court

(1) A magistrates' court officer will keep a register in which there will be entered a minute or memorandum of every adjudication of the court in proceedings to which this Part applies.

(2) The register may be stored in electronic form on the court computer system and entries in the register will include, where relevant, the following particulars –

(a)   the name and address of the applicant;

(b)   the name of the child including, in adoption proceedings, the name of the child prior to, and after, adoption;

(c)   the age and sex of the child;

(d)   the nature of the application; and

(e)   the minute of adjudication.

(3) The part of the register relating to adoption proceedings will be kept separately to any other part of the register and will –

(a)   not contain particulars of any other proceedings; and

(b)   be kept by the court in a place of special security.

Practice Direction 14A –
Who Receives a Copy of the Application Form for Orders in Proceedings

This Practice Direction supplements FPR Part 14, rule 14.6(1)(b)(ii)

Persons who receive copy of application form

1 In relation to each type of proceedings in column 1 of the following table, column 2 sets out which persons are to receive a copy of the application form:

Proceeding for	Who Receives a Copy of the Application Form
An adoption order (section 46 of the Act); or a section 84 order	Any appointed children's guardian, children and family reporter and reporting officer; the local authority to whom notice under section 44 (notice of intention to apply to adopt or apply for a section 84 order) has been given; the adoption agency which placed the child for adoption with the applicants; any other person directed by the court to receive a copy.
A placement order (section 21 of the Act); or an order varying a placement order (section 23 of the Act)	Each parent with parental responsibility for the child or guardian of the child; any appointed children's guardian, children and family reporter and reporting officer; any other person directed by the court to receive a copy.
An order revoking a placement order (section 24 of the Act)	Each parent with parental responsibility for the child or guardian of the child; any appointed children's guardian and children and family reporter; the local authority authorised by the placement order to place the child for adoption; any other person directed by the court to receive a copy.

Proceeding for	Who Receives a Copy of the Application Form
A contact order (section 26 of the Act); an order varying or revoking a contact order (section 27 of the Act); an order permitting the child's name to be changed or the removal of the child from the United Kingdom (section 28(2) of the Act); a recovery order (section 41(2) of the Act); a section 89 order; and a section 88 direction	All the parties; any appointed children's guardian and children and family reporter; any other person directed by the court to receive a copy.

Practice Direction 14B –
The First Directions Hearing – Adoptions with a Foreign Element

This Practice Direction supplements FPR Part 14, rule 14.8(3)

Application

1 This Practice Direction applies to proceedings for:

(a)   a Convention adoption order;
(b)   a section 84 order;
(c)   a section 88 direction;
(d)   a section 89 order; and
(e)   an adoption order where the child has been brought into the United Kingdom in the circumstances where section 83(1) of the Act applies.

The first directions hearing

2 At the first directions hearing the court will, in addition to any matters referred to in rule 14.8(1) –

(a)   consider whether the requirements of the Act and the Adoptions with a Foreign Element Regulations 2005 (S.I. 2005/392) appear to have been complied with and, if not, consider whether or not it is appropriate to transfer the case to the High Court;

(b)   consider whether all relevant documents are translated into English and, if not, fix a timetable for translating any outstanding documents;

(c)   consider whether the applicant needs to file an affidavit setting out the full details of the circumstances in which the child was brought to the United Kingdom, of the attitude of the parents to the application and confirming compliance with the requirements of The Adoptions with A Foreign Element Regulations 2005;

(d)   give directions about –

(i)   the production of the child's passport and visa;

(ii)   the need for the Official Solicitor and a representative of the Home Office to attend future hearings; and

(iii)   personal service on the parents (via the Central Authority in the case of an application for a Convention Adoption Order) including information about the role of the Official Solicitor and availability of legal aid to be represented within the proceedings; and

(e)   consider fixing a further directions appointment no later than 6 weeks after the date of the first directions appointment and timetable a date by which the Official Solicitor should file an interim report in advance of that further appointment.

Practice Direction 14C –
Reports by the Adoption Agency or Local Authority

This Practice Direction supplements FPR Part 14, rule 14.11(3)

Matters to be contained in reports

1.1 The matters to be covered in the report on the suitability of the applicant to adopt a child are set out in Annex A to this Practice Direction.

1.2 The matters to be covered in a report on the placement of the child for adoption are set out in Annex B to this Practice Direction.

1.3 Where a matter to be covered in the reports set out in Annex A and Annex B does not apply to the circumstances of a particular case, the reasons for not covering the matter should be given.

ANNEX A – REPORT TO THE COURT WHERE THERE HAS BEEN AN APPLICATION FOR AN ADOPTION ORDER OR AN APPLICATION FOR A SECTION 84 ORDER

Section A: The Report and Matters for the Proceedings

Section B: The Child and the Birth Family

Section C: The Prospective Adopter of the Child

Section D: The Placement

Section E: Recommendations

PART II – Statutory Instruments

Section F: Further information for proceedings relating to Convention Adoption Orders, Convention adoptions, section 84 Orders or adoptions where section 83(1) of the 2002 Act applies.

Section A: The Report and Matters for the Proceedings

Part 1 – The report

For each of the principal author/s of the report:

(i)   name;

(ii)   role in relation to this case;

(iii)   sections completed in this report;

(iv)   qualifications and experience;

(v)   name and address of the adoption agency; and

(vi)   adoption agency case reference number.

Part 2 – Matters for the proceedings

(a)   Whether the adoption agency considers that any other person should be made a respondent or a party to the proceedings, including the child.

(b)   Whether any of the respondents is under the age of 18.

(c)   Whether a respondent is a person who, by reason of mental disorder within the meaning of the Mental Health Act 1983, is incapable of managing and administering his or her property and affairs. If so, medical evidence should be provided with particular regard to the effect on that person's ability to make decisions in the proceedings.

Section B: The Child and the Birth Family

Part 1

(i) Information about the child

(a)   Name, sex, date and place of birth and address including local authority area.

(b)   Photograph and physical description.

(c)   Nationality.

(d)   Racial origin and cultural and linguistic background.

(e)   Religious persuasion (including details of baptism, confirmation or equivalent ceremonies).

(f)   Details of any siblings, half-siblings and step-siblings, including dates of birth.

(g)   Whether the child is looked after by a local authority.

(h)   Whether the child has been placed for adoption with the prospective adopter by a UK adoption agency.

(i)   Whether the child was being fostered by the prospective adopter.

(j)   Whether the child was brought into the UK for adoption, including date of entry and whether an adoption order was made in the child's country of origin.

(k)   Personality and social development, including emotional and behavioural development and any related needs.

(l)   Details of interests, likes and dislikes.

(m)   A summary, written by the agency's medical adviser, of the child's health history, his current state of health and any need for health care which is anticipated, and date of the most recent medical examination.

(n)   Any known learning difficulties or known general medical or mental health factors which are likely to have, or may have, genetic implications.

(o)   Names, addresses and types of nurseries or schools attended, with dates.

(p)   Educational attainments.

(q)   Any special needs in relation to the child (whether physical, learning, behavioural or any other) and his emotional and behavioural development.

(r)   Whether the child is subject to a statement under the Education Act 1996.

(s)   Previous orders concerning the child –
    (i)   the name of the court;
    (ii)   the order made; and
    (iii)   the date of the order.

(t)   Inheritance rights and any claim to damages under the Fatal Accidents Act 1976 the child stands to retain or lose if adopted.

(u)   Any other relevant information which might assist the court.

ii) *Information about each parent of the child*

(a)   Name, date and place of birth and address (date on which last address was confirmed current) including local authority area.

(b)   Photograph, if available, and physical description.

(c)   Nationality.

(d)   Racial origin and cultural and linguistic background.

(e)   Whether the mother and father were married to each other at the time of the child's birth or have subsequently married.

(f)   Where the parent has been previously married or entered into a civil partnership, dates of those marriages or civil partnerships.

(g)   Where the mother and father are not married, whether the father has parental responsibility and, if so, how it was acquired.

(h)   If the identity or whereabouts of the father are not known, the information about him that has been ascertained and from whom, and the steps that have been taken to establish paternity.

(i)   Past and present relationship with the other parent.

(j)   Other information about the parent, where available –
    (i)   health, including any known learning difficulties or known general medical or mental health factors which are likely to have, or may have, genetic implications;
    (ii)   religious persuasion;
    (iii)   educational history;
    (iv)   employment history; and
    (v)   personality and interests.

(k)   Any other relevant information which might assist the court.

PART II – Statutory Instruments

Part 2

Relationships, contact arrangements and views.

THE CHILD

(a)   If the child is in the care of a local authority or voluntary organisation, or has been, details (including dates) of any placements with foster parents, or other arrangements in respect of the care of the child, including particulars of the persons with whom the child has had his home and observations on the care provided.

(b)   The child's wishes and feelings (if appropriate, having regard to the child's age and understanding) about adoption, the application and its consequences, including any wishes in respect of religious and cultural upbringing.

(c)   The child's wishes and feelings in relation to contact (if appropriate, having regard to the child's age and understanding).

(d)   The child's wishes and feelings recorded in any other proceedings.

(e)   Date when the child's views were last ascertained.

THE CHILD'S PARENTS (OR GUARDIAN) AND RELATIVES

(a)   The parents' wishes and feelings before the placement, about the placement and about adoption, the application and its consequences, including any wishes in respect of the child's religious and cultural upbringing.

(b)   Each parent's (or guardian's) wishes and feelings in relation to contact.

(c)   Date/s when the views of each parent or guardian were last ascertained.

(d)   Arrangements concerning any siblings, including half-siblings and step-siblings, and whether any are the subject of a parallel application or have been the subject of any orders. If so, for each case give –
  (i)   the name of the court;
  (ii)   the order made, or (if proceedings are pending) the order applied for; and
  (iii) the date of order, or date of next hearing if proceedings are pending.

(e)   Extent of contact with the child's mother and father and, in each case, the nature of the relationship enjoyed.

(f)   The relationship which the child has with relatives, and with any other person considered relevant, including –
  (i)   the likelihood of any such relationship continuing and the value to the child of its doing so; and
  (ii)   the ability and willingness of any of the child's relatives, or of any such person, to provide the child with a secure environment in which the child can develop, and otherwise to meet the child's needs.

(g)   The wishes and feelings of any of the child's relatives, or of any such person, regarding the child.

(h)   Whether the parents (or members of the child's family) have met or are likely to meet the prospective adopter and, if they have met, the effect on all involved of such meeting.

(i)   Dates when the views of members of the child's wider family and any other relevant person were last ascertained.

Part 3

A summary of the actions of the adoption agency

(a)   Brief account of the agency's actions in the case, with particulars and dates of all written information and notices given to the child and his parents and any person with parental responsibility.

(b)   If consent has been given for the child to be placed for adoption, and also consent for the child to be adopted, the names of those who gave consent and the date such consents were given. If such consents were subsequently withdrawn, the dates of these withdrawals.

(c)   If any statement has been made under section 20(4)(a) of the Adoption and Children Act 2002 (the '2002 Act') that a parent or guardian does not wish to be informed of any application for an adoption order, the names of those who have made such statements and the dates the statements were made. If such statements were subsequently withdrawn, the dates of these withdrawals.

(d)   Whether an order has been made under section 21 of the 2002 Act, section 18 of the Adoption (Scotland) Act 1978 or Article 17(1) or 18(1) of the Northern Ireland Order 1987.

(e)   Details of the support and advice given to the parents and any services offered or taken up.

(f)   If the father does not have parental responsibility, details of the steps taken to inform him of the application for an adoption order.

(g)   Brief details and dates of assessments of the child's needs, including expert opinions.

(h)   Reasons for considering that adoption would be in the child's best interests (with date of relevant decision and reasons for any delay in implementing the decision).

Section C: The Prospective Adopter of the Child

Part 1

Information about the prospective adopter, including suitability to adopt

(a)   Name, date and place of birth and address (date on which last address was confirmed current) including local authority area.

(b)   Photograph and physical description.

(c)   Whether the prospective adopter is domiciled or habitually resident in a part of the British Islands and, if habitually resident, for how long they have been habitually resident.

(d)   Racial origin and cultural and linguistic background.

(e)   Marital status or civil partnership status, date and place of most recent marriage (if any) or civil partnership (if any).

(f)   Details of any previous marriage, civil partnership, or relationship where the prospective adopter lived with another person as a partner in an enduring family relationship.

(g)   Relationship (if any) to the child.

(h)   Where adopters wish to adopt as a couple, the status of the relationship and an assessment of the stability and permanence of their relationship.

(i)   If a married person or a civil partner is applying alone, the reasons for this.

(j)   Description of how the prospective adopter relates to adults and children.

(k)   Previous experience of caring for children (including as a step-parent, foster parent, child-minder or prospective adopter) and assessment of ability in this respect, together where appropriate with assessment of ability in bringing up the prospective adopter's own children.

(l)   A summary, written by the agency's medical adviser, of the prospective adopter's health history, current state of health and any need for health care which is anticipated, and date of most recent medical examination.

(m)   Assessment of ability and suitability to bring up the child throughout his childhood.

(n)   Details of income and comments on the living standards of the household with particulars of the home and living conditions (and particulars of any home where the prospective adopter proposes to live with the child, if different).

(o)   Details of other members of the household, including any children of the prospective adopter even if not resident in the household.

(p)   Details of the parents and any siblings of the prospective adopter, with their ages or ages at death.

(q)   Other information about the prospective adopter –
    (i)   religious persuasion;
    (ii)   educational history;
    (iii)   employment history; and
    (iv)   personality and interests.

(r)   Confirmation that the applicants have not been convicted of, or cautioned for, a specified offence within the meaning of regulation 23(3) of the Adoption Agencies Regulations 2005 (S.I. 2005/389).

(s)   Confirmation that the prospective adopter is still approved.

(t)   Confirmation that any referees have been interviewed, with a report of their views and opinion of the weight to be placed thereon and whether they are still valid.

(u)   Details of any previous family court proceedings in which the prospective adopter has been involved (which have not been referred to elsewhere in this report.)

Part 2

Wishes, views and contact arrangements

PROSPECTIVE ADOPTER

(a) Whether the prospective adopter is willing to follow any wishes of the child or his parents or guardian in respect of the child's religious and cultural upbringing.

(b) The views of other members of the prospective adopter's household and wider family in relation to the proposed adoption.

(c) Reasons for the prospective adopter wishing to adopt the child and extent of understanding of the nature and effect of adoption. Whether the prospective adopter has discussed adoption with the child.

(d) Any hope and expectations the prospective adopter has for the child's future.

(e) The prospective adopter's wishes and feelings in relation to contact.

Part 3

Actions of the adoption agency

(a) Brief account of the Agency's actions in the case, with particulars and dates of all written information and notices given to the prospective adopter.

(b) The Agency's proposals for contact, including options for facilitating or achieving any indirect contact or direct contact.

(c) The Agency's opinion on the likely effect on the prospective adopter and on the security of the placement of any proposed contact.

(d) Where the prospective adopter has been approved by an agency as suitable to be an adoptive parent, the agency's reasons for considering that the prospective adopter is suitable to be an adoptive parent for this child (with dates of relevant decisions).

Section D: The Placement

(a) Where the child was placed for adoption by an adoption agency (section 18 of the 2002 Act), the date and circumstances of the child's placement with prospective adopter.

(b) Where the child is living with persons who have applied for the adoption order to be made (section 44 of the 2002 Act), the date when notice of intention to adopt was given.

(c) Where the placement is being provided with adoption support, this should be summarised and should include the plan and timescales for continuing the support beyond the making of the adoption order.

(d) Where the placement is not being provided with adoption support, the reasons why.

(e) A summary of the information obtained from the Agency's visits and reviews of the placement, including whether the child has been seen separately to the prospective adopter and whether there has been sufficient opportunity to see the family group and the child's interaction in the home environment.

(f)   An assessment of the child's integration within the family of the prospective adopter and the likelihood of the child's full integration into the family and community.

(g)   Any other relevant information that might assist the court.

Section E: Recommendations

(a)   The relative merits of adoption and other orders with an assessment of whether the child's long term interests would be best met by an adoption order or by other orders (such as residence and special guardianship orders).

(b)   Recommendations as to whether or not the order sought should be made (and, if not, alternative proposals).

(c)   Recommendations as to whether there should be future contact arrangements (or not).

Section F: Further Information for Proceedings Relating to Convention Adoption Orders, Convention Adoptions, Section 84 Orders or an Adoption where Section 83(1) of the 2002 Act applies.

(a)   The child's knowledge of their racial and cultural origin.

(b)   The likelihood of the child's adaptation to living in the country he/she is to be placed.

(c)   Where the UK is the State of origin, reasons for considering that, after possibilities for placement of the child within the UK have been given due consideration, intercountry adoption is in the child's best interests.

(d)   Confirmation that the requirements of regulations made under sections 83(4), (5), (6) and (7) and 84(3) and (6) of the 2002 Act have been complied with.

(e)   For a Convention adoption or a Convention Adoption Order where the United Kingdom is either the State of origin or the receiving State, confirmation that the Central Authorities of both States have agreed that the adoption may proceed.

(f)   Where the State of origin is not the United Kingdom, the documents supplied by the Central Authority of the State of origin should be attached to the report, together with translation if necessary.

(g)   Where a Convention adoption order is proposed, details of the arrangements which were made for the transfer of the child to the UK and that they were in accordance with the Adoptions with a Foreign Element Regulations 2005 (S.I. 2005/392).

ANNEX B – REPORT TO THE COURT WHERE THERE HAS BEEN AN APPLICATION FOR A PLACEMENT ORDER

Section A: The Report and Matters for the Proceedings

Section B: The Child and the Birth Family

Section C: Recommendations

Section A: The Report and Matters for the Proceedings

Part 1

The report

For each of the principal author/s of the report:

(i) name;

(ii) role in relation to this case;

(iii) section completed in this report;

(iv) qualifications and experience;

(v) name and address of the adoption agency; and

(vi) adoption agency case reference number.

Part 2

Matters for the proceedings

(a) Whether the adoption agency considers that any other person should be made a respondent or a party to the proceedings.

(b) Whether any of the respondents is under the age of 18.

(c) Whether a respondent is a person who, by reason of mental disorder within the meaning of the Mental Health Act 1983, is incapable of managing and administering his or her property and affairs. If so, medical evidence should be provided with particular regard to the effect on that person's ability to make decisions in the proceedings.

Section B: The child and the birth family

Part 1

(i) Information about the child

(a) Name, sex, date and place of birth and address including local authority area.

(b) Photograph and physical description.

(c) Nationality.

(d) Racial origin and cultural and linguistic background.

(e) Religious persuasion (including details of baptism, confirmation or equivalent ceremonies).

(f) Details of any siblings, half-siblings and step-siblings, including dates of birth.

(g) Whether the child is looked after by a local authority.

(h) Personality and social development, including emotional and behavioural development and any related needs.

(i) Details of interests, likes and dislikes.

(j) A summary, written by the agency's medical adviser, of the child's health history, his current state of health and any need for health care which is anticipated, and date of the most recent medical examination.

(k) Any known learning difficulties or known general medical or mental health factors which are likely to have, or may have, genetic implications.

PART II – Statutory Instruments

(l) Names, addresses and types of nurseries or schools attended, with dates.

(m) Educational attainments.

(n) Any special needs in relation to the child (whether physical, learning, behavioural or any other) and his emotional and behavioural development.

(o) Whether the child is subject to a statement under the Education Act 1996.

(p) Previous orders concerning the child:
    (i) the name of the court;
    (ii) the order made; and
    (ii) the date of the order.

(q) Inheritance rights and any claim to damages under the Fatal Accidents Act 1976 the child stands to retain or lose if adopted.

(r) Any other relevant information which might assist the court.

(ii) Information about each parent of the child

(a) Name, date and place of birth and address (date on which last address was confirmed current) including local authority area.

(b) Photograph, if available, and physical description.

(c) Nationality.

(d) Racial origin and cultural and linguistic background.

(e) Whether the mother and father were married to each other at the time of the child's birth, or have subsequently married.

(f) Where the parent has been previously married or entered into a civil partnership, dates of those marriages or civil partnerships.

(g) Where the mother and father are not married, whether the father has parental responsibility and, if so, how it was acquired.

(h) If the identity or whereabouts of the father are not known, the information about him that has been ascertained and from whom, and the steps that have been taken to establish paternity.

(i) Past and present relationship with the other parent.

(j) Other information about the parent, where available –
    (i) health, including any known learning difficulties or known general medical or mental health factors which are likely to have, or may have, genetic implications;
    (ii) religious persuasion;
    (iii) educational history;
    (iv) employment history; and
    (v) personality and interests.

(k) Any other relevant information which might assist the court.

Part 2

Relationships, contact arrangements and views

THE CHILD

(a) If the child is in the care of a local authority or voluntary organisation, or has been, details (including dates) of any placements with foster parents, or other arrangements in respect of the care of the child, including particulars of the persons with whom the child has had his home and observations on the care provided.

(b) The child's wishes and feelings (if appropriate, having regard to the child's age and understanding) about the application, its consequences, and adoption, including any wishes in respect of religious and cultural upbringing.

(c) The child's wishes and feelings in relation to contact (if appropriate, having regard to the child's age and understanding).

(d) The child's wishes and feelings recorded in any other proceedings.

(e) Date when the child's views were last ascertained.

THE CHILD'S PARENTS (OR GUARDIAN) AND RELATIVES

(a) The parents' wishes and feelings about the application, its consequences, and adoption, including any wishes in respect of the child's religious and cultural upbringing.

(b) Each parent's (or guardian's) wishes and feelings in relation to contact.

(c) Date/s when the views of each parent or guardian were last ascertained.

(d) Arrangements concerning any siblings, including half-siblings and step-siblings, and whether any are the subject of a parallel application or have been the subject of any orders. If so, for each case give –
  (i)   the name of the court;
  (ii) the order made, or (if proceedings are pending) the order applied for; and
  (iii) the date of order, or date of next hearing if proceedings are pending.

(e) Extent of contact with the child's mother and father and in each case the nature of the relationship enjoyed.

(f) The relationship which the child has with relatives, and with any other person considered relevant, including –
  (i)   the likelihood of any such relationship continuing and the value to the child of its doing so; and
  (ii) the ability and willingness of any of the child's relatives, or of any such person, to provide the child with a secure environment in which the child can develop, and otherwise to meet the child's needs.

(g) The wishes and feelings of any of the child's relatives, or of any such person, regarding the child.

(h) Dates when the views of members of the child's wider family and any other relevant person were last ascertained.

Part 3

Summary of the actions of the adoption agency

(a) Brief account of the Agency's actions in the case, with particulars and dates of all written information and notices given to the child and his parents and any person with parental responsibility.

PART II – Statutory Instruments

(b)   If consent has been given for the child to be placed for adoption, and also consent for the child to be adopted, the names of those who gave consent and the date such consents were given. If such consents were subsequently withdrawn, the dates of these withdrawals.

(c)   If any statement has been made under section 20(4)(a) of the 2002 Act that a parent or guardian does not wish to be informed of any application for an adoption order, the names of those who have made such statements and the dates the statements were made. If such statements were subsequently withdrawn, the dates of these withdrawals.

(d)   Details of the support and advice given to the parents and any services offered or taken up.

(e)   If the father does not have parental responsibility, details of the steps taken to inform him of the application for a placement order.

(f)   Brief details and dates of assessments of the child's needs, including expert opinions.

(g)   Reasons for considering that adoption would be in the child's best interests (with date of relevant decision and reasons for any delay in implementing the decision).

Section C: Recommendations

(a)   The relative merits of a placement order and other orders (such as a residence or special guardianship order) with an assessment of why the child's long term interests are likely to be best met by a placement order rather than by any other order.

(b)   Recommendations as to whether there should be future contact arrangements (or not), including whether a contact order under section 26 of the 2002 Act should be made.

Practice Direction 14D –
Reports by a Registered Medical Practitioner
('Health Reports')

This Practice Direction supplements FPR Part 14, rule 14.12(2)

Matters to be contained in health reports

1.1 Rule 14.12(1) requires that health reports must be attached to an application for an adoption order or a section 84 order except where –

(a)   the child was placed for adoption with the applicant by an adoption agency;

(b)   the applicant or one of the applicants is a parent of the child; or

(c)   the applicant is the partner of a parent of the child.

1.2 The matters to be contained in the health reports are set out in the Annex to this Practice Direction.

1.3 Where a matter to be contained in the health report does not apply to the circumstances of a particular case, the reasons for not covering the matter should be given.

ANNEX – CONTENTS OF HEALTH REPORTS

This information is required for reports on the health of children and their prospective adopter(s). Its purpose is to build up a full picture of each child's health history and current state of health, including strengths and weaknesses. This will enable local authorities' medical adviser to base their advice to the court on the fullest possible information when commenting on the health implications of the proposed adoption. The reports made by the examining doctor should cover, as far as practicable, the following matters.

1 The child

Name, date of birth, sex, weight and height.

A A health history of each natural parent, so far as is possible, including –

(i)   name, date of birth, sex, weight and height;
(ii) a family health history, covering the parents, the brothers and sisters and the other children of the natural parent, with details of any serious physical or mental illness and inherited and congenital disease;
(iii) past health history, including details of any serious physical or mental illness, disability, accident, hospital admission or attendance at an out-patient department, and in each case any treatment given;
(iv) a full obstetric history of the mother, including any problems in the ante-natal, labour and post-natal periods, with the results of any tests carried out during or immediately after pregnancy;
(v)   details of any present illness including treatment and prognosis;
(vi) any other relevant information which might assist the medical adviser; and
(vii) the name and address of any doctor(s) who might be able to provide further information about any of the above matters.

B A neo-natal report on the child, including –

(i)   details of the birth, and any complications;
(ii) results of a physical examination and screening tests;
(iii) details of any treatment given;
(iv) details of any problem in management and feeding;
(v)   any other relevant information which might assist the medical adviser; and
(vi) the name and address of any doctor(s) who might be able to provide further information about any of the above matters.

C A full health history and examination of the child, including –

(i)   details of any serious illness, disability, accident, hospital admission or attendance at an out-patient department, and in each case any treatment given;
(ii) details and dates of immunisations;

PART II – Statutory Instruments

(iii)   a physical and developmental assessment according to age, including an assessment of vision and hearing and of neurological, speech and language development and any evidence of emotional or conduct disorder;

(iv)   details, if relevant, of the impact of any addiction or substance use on the part of the natural mother before, during or following the pregnancy, and its impact or likely future impact on the child;

(v)   the impact, if any, on the child's development and likely future development of any past exposure to physical, emotional or sexual abuse or neglectful home conditions and/or any non-organic failure to thrive;

(vi)   for a child of school age, the school health history (if available);

(vii)   any other relevant information which might assist the medical adviser; and

(viii) the name and address of any doctor(s) who might be able to provide further information about any of the above matters.

D The signature, name, address and qualifications of the registered medical practitioner who prepared the report, and the date of the report and of the examinations carried out.

2 The applicant

(If there is more than one applicant, a report on each applicant should be supplied covering all the matters listed below.)

A –

(i)   name, date of birth, sex, weight and height;

(ii)   a family health history, covering the parents, the brothers and sisters and the children of the applicant, with details of any serious physical or mental illness and inherited and congenital disease;

(iii)   marital history, including (if applicable) reasons for inability to have children, and any history of domestic violence;

(iv)   past health history, including details of any serious physical or mental illness, disability, accident, hospital admission or attendance at an out-patient department, and in each case any treatment given;

(v)   obstetric history (if applicable);

(vi)   details of any present illness, including treatment and prognosis;

(vii)   a full medical examination;

(viii) details of any consumption of alcohol, tobacco and habit-forming drugs;

(ix)   any other relevant information which might assist the medical adviser; and

(x)   the name and address of any doctor(s) who might be able to provide further information about any of the above matters.

B The signature, name, address and qualifications of the registered medical practitioner who prepared the report, and the date of the report and of the examinations carried out.

Practice Direction 14E –
Communication of Information Relating to Proceedings

This Practice Direction supplements FPR Part 14, rule 14.14(b)

Communication of information relating to proceedings

1.1 Rule 14.14 deals with the communication of information (whether or not it is recorded in any form) relating to proceedings.

1.2 Subject to any direction of the court, information may be communicated for the purposes of the law relating to contempt in accordance with paragraphs 1.3 or 1.4.

1.3 A person specified in the first column of the following table may communicate to a person listed in the second column such information as is specified in the third column for the purpose or purposes specified in the fourth column.

Communication of information without permission of the court

Communicated by	To	Information	Purpose
A party	A lay adviser or a McKenzie Friend	Any information relating to the proceedings	To enable the party to obtain advice or assistance in relation to the proceedings.
A party	The party's spouse, civil partner, cohabitant or close family member		For the purpose of confidential discussions enabling the party to receive support from his spouse, civil partner, cohabitant or close family member.
A party	A health care professional or a person or body providing counselling services for children or families		To enable the party or any child of the party to obtain health care or counselling.

Communicated by	To	Information	Purpose
A party	The Secretary of State, a McKenzie Friend, a lay adviser or an appeal tribunal dealing with an appeal made under section 20 of the Child Support Act 1991[1]		For the purposes of making or responding to an appeal under section 20 of the Child Support Act 1991 or the determination of such an appeal.
A party	An adoption panel		To enable the adoption panel to discharge its functions as appropriate.
A party or any person lawfully in receipt of information	The Children's Commissioner or the Children's Commissioner for Wales		To refer an issue affecting the interests of children to the Children's Commissioner or the Children's Commissioner for Wales.
A party or a legal representative	A mediator		For the purpose of mediation in relation to the proceedings.
A party, any person lawfully in receipt of information or a proper officer	A person or body conducting an approved research project		For the purpose of an approved research project.

Communicated by	To	Information	Purpose
A party, a legal representative or a professional legal adviser	A person or body responsible for investigating or determining complaints in relation to legal representatives or professional legal advisers		For the purposes of making a complaint or the investigation or determination of a complaint in relation to a legal representative or a professional legal adviser.
A legal representative or a professional legal adviser	A person or body assessing quality assurance systems		To enable the legal representative or professional legal adviser to obtain a quality assurance assessment.
A legal representative or a professional legal adviser	An accreditation body	Any information relating to the proceedings providing that it does not, or is not likely to, identify any person involved in the proceedings	To enable the legal representative or professional legal adviser to obtain accreditation.
A party	An elected representative or peer	The text or summary of the whole or part of a judgment given in the proceedings	To enable the elected representative or peer to give advice, investigate any complaint or raise any question of policy or procedure.
A party	The General Medical Council		For the purpose of making a complaint to the General Medical Council.

PART II – Statutory Instruments

Communicated by	To	Information	Purpose
A party	A police officer		For the purpose of a criminal investigation.
A party or any person lawfully in receipt of information	A member of the Crown Prosecution Service		To enable the Crown Prosecution Service to discharge its functions under any enactment.

1.4 A person in the second column of the table in paragraph 1.3 may only communicate information relating to the proceedings received from a person in the first column for the purpose or purposes –

(a)   for which he received that information, or

(b)   of professional development or training, providing that any communication does not, or is not likely to, identify any person involved in the proceedings without that person's consent.

1.5 In this Practice Direction

(1)   'accreditation body' means –
    (a)   The Law Society,
    (b)   Resolution, or
    (c)   The Legal Services Commission;

(1A) 'adoption panel' means a panel established in accordance with regulation 3 of the Adoption Agencies Regulations 2005[2] or regulation 3 of the Adoption Agencies (Wales) Regulations 2005[3];

(2)   'approved research project' means a project of research –
    (a)   approved in writing by a Secretary of State after consultation with the President of the Family Division,
    (b)   approved in writing by the President of the Family Division, or
    (c)   conducted under section 83 of the Act of 1989 or section 13 of the Criminal Justice and Court Services Act 2000;

(3)   'body assessing quality assurance systems' includes –
    (a)   The Law Society,
    (b)   The Legal Services Commission, or
    (c)   The General Council of the Bar;

(4)   'body or person responsible for investigating or determining complaints in relation to legal representatives or professional legal advisers' means –
    (a)   The Law Society,
    (b)   The General Council of the Bar,
    (c)   The Institute of Legal Executives, or
    (d)   The Legal Services Ombudsman;

(5) 'cohabitant' means one of two persons who are neither married to each other nor civil partners of each other but are living together as husband and wife or as if they were civil partners;

(6) 'criminal investigation' means an investigation conducted by police officers with a view to it being ascertained –
 (a) whether a person should be charged with an offence, or
 (b) whether a person charged with an offence is guilty of it;

(7) 'elected representative' means –
 (a) a member of the House of Commons,
 (b) a member of the National Assembly for Wales, or
 (c) a member of the European Parliament elected in England and Wales;

(8) 'health care professional' means –
 (a) a registered medical practitioner,
 (b) a registered nurse or midwife,
 (c) a clinical psychologist, or
 (d) a child psychotherapist;

(9) 'lay adviser' means a non-professional person who gives lay advice on behalf of an organisation in the lay advice sector;

(10) 'McKenzie Friend' means any person permitted by the court to sit beside an unrepresented litigant in court to assist that litigant by prompting, taking notes and giving him advice;

(11) 'mediator' means a family mediator who is –
 (a) undertaking, or has successfully completed, a family mediation training course approved by the United Kingdom College of Family Mediators, or
 (b) a member of the Law Society's Family Mediation Panel;

(12) 'peer' means a member of the House of Lords as defined by the House of Lords Act 1999.

Practice Direction 14F –
Disclosing Information to an Adopted Adult

This Practice Direction supplements FPR Part 14, rule 14.18(1)(d)

How to request for information

1.1 Rule 14.18 states that an adopted person who is over the age of 18 has the right to receive from the court which made the adoption order a copy of –

(a) the application form for an adoption order (but not the documents attached to that form);

(b) the adoption order and any other orders relating to the adoption proceedings; and

(c) orders allowing any person contact with the child after the adoption order was made.

PART II – Statutory Instruments

1.2 An application under rule 14.18 must be made in form A64 which is contained in the practice direction supplementing rule 5 and must have attached to it a full certified copy of the entry in the Adopted Children Register relating to the applicant.

1.3 The completed application form must be taken to the court which made the adoption order along with evidence of the applicant's identity showing a photograph and signature, such as a passport or driving licence.

Additional documents that the adopted person is also entitled to receive from the court

2 The adopted adult is also entitled to receive the following documents –

    (a)   any transcript or written reasons of the court's decision; and
    (b)   a report made to the court by –
        (i)   a children's guardian, reporting officer or children and family reporter;
        (ii)   a local authority; or
        (iii)   an adoption agency.

Before the documents are sent to the adopted adult

3 The court will remove protected information from documents before they are sent to the adopted adult.

****

PART 16
REPRESENTATION OF CHILDREN AND REPORTS IN PROCEEDINGS INVOLVING CHILDREN

Chapter 1
Application of this Part

16.1 Application of this Part

This Part –

    (a)   sets out when the court will make a child a party in family proceedings; and
    (b)   contains special provisions which apply in proceedings involving children.

Chapter 2
Child as Party in Family Proceedings

16.2 When the court may make a child a party to proceedings

(1) The court may make a child a party to proceedings if it considers it is in the best interests of the child to do so.

(2) This rule does not apply to a child who is the subject of proceedings –

(a)   which are specified proceedings; or

(b)   to which Part 14 applies.

(The Practice Direction 16A sets out the matters which the court will take into consideration before making a child a party under this rule.)

Chapter 3
When a Children's Guardian or Litigation Friend will be Appointed

16.3 Appointment of a children's guardian in specified proceedings or proceedings to which Part 14 applies

(1) Unless it is satisfied that it is not necessary to do so to safeguard the interests of the child, the court must appoint a children's guardian for a child who is –

(a)   the subject of; and

(b)   a party to,

proceedings –

(i)   which are specified proceedings; or

(ii)   to which Part 14 applies.

(Rules 12.6 and 14.6 set out the point in the proceedings when the court will appoint a children's guardian in specified proceedings and proceedings to which Part 14 respectively.)

(2) At any stage in the proceedings –

(a)   a party may apply, without notice to the other parties unless the court directs otherwise, for the appointment of a children's guardian; or

(b)   the court may of its own initiative appoint a children's guardian.

(3) Where the court refuses an application under paragraph (2)(a) it will give reasons for the refusal and the court or a court officer will –

(a)   record the refusal and the reasons for it; and

(b)   as soon as practicable, notify the parties and either the Service or the Assembly of a decision not to appoint a children's guardian.

(4) When appointing a children's guardian the court will consider the appointment of anyone who has previously acted as a children's guardian of the same child.

(5) Where the court appoints a children's guardian in accordance with this rule, the provisions of Chapter 6 of this Part apply.

16.4 Appointment of a children's guardian in proceedings not being specified proceedings or proceedings to which Part 14 applies

(1) Without prejudice to rule 8.42 or 16.6, the court must appoint a children's guardian for a child who is the subject of proceedings, which are not proceedings of a type referred to in rule 16.3(1), if –

(a)   the child is an applicant in the proceedings;

(b   a provision in these rules provides for the child to be a party to the proceedings; or

(c)   the court has made the child a party in accordance with rule 16.2.

(2) The provisions of Chapter 7 of this Part apply where the appointment of a children's guardian is required in accordance with paragraph (1).

('children's guardian' is defined in rule 2.3.)

16.5 Requirement for a litigation friend

(1) Without prejudice to rule 16.6, where a child is –

(a)   a party to proceedings; but

(b)   not the subject of those proceedings,

the child must have a litigation friend to conduct proceedings on the child's behalf.

(2) The provisions of Chapter 5 of this Part apply where a litigation friend is required in accordance with paragraph (1).

Chapter 4
Where a Children's Guardian or Litigation Friend is not Required

16.6 Circumstances in which a child does not need a children's guardian or litigation friend

(1) Subject to paragraph (2), a child may conduct proceedings without a children's guardian or litigation friend where the proceedings are proceedings –

(a)   under the 1989 Act;

(b)   to which Part 11 (applications under Part 4A of the Family Law Act 1996) or Part 14 (applications in adoption, placement and related proceedings) of these rules apply; or

(c)   relating to the exercise of the court's inherent jurisdiction with respect to children,

and one of the conditions set out in paragraph (3) is satisfied.

(2) Paragraph (1) does not apply where the child is the subject of and a party to proceedings –

(a)   which are specified proceedings; or

(b)   to which Part 14 applies.

(3) The conditions referred to in paragraph (1) are that either –

(a)   the child has obtained the court's permission; or

(b)   a solicitor –

(i)   considers that the child is able, having regard to the child's understanding, to give instructions in relation to the proceedings; and

(ii)   has accepted instructions from that child to act for that child in the proceedings and, if the proceedings have begun, the solicitor is already acting.

(4) An application for permission under paragraph (3)(a) may be made by the child without notice.

(5) Where a child –

(a)   has a litigation friend or children's guardian in proceedings to which this rule applies; and

(b)   wishes to conduct the remaining stages of the proceedings without the litigation friend or children's guardian,

the child may apply to the court, on notice to the litigation friend or children's guardian, for permission for that purpose and for the removal of the litigation friend or children's guardian.

(6) The court will grant an application under paragraph (3)(a) or (5) if it considers that the child has sufficient understanding to conduct the proceedings concerned or proposed without a litigation friend or children's guardian.

(7) In exercising its powers under paragraph (6) the court may require the litigation friend or children's guardian to take such part in the proceedings as the court directs.

(8) The court may revoke any permission granted under paragraph (3)(a) where it considers that the child does not have sufficient understanding to participate as a party in the proceedings concerned without a litigation friend or children's guardian.

(9) Where a solicitor is acting for a child in proceedings without a litigation friend or children's guardian by virtue of paragraph (3)(b) and either of the conditions specified in paragraph (3)(b)(i) or (ii) cease to be fulfilled, the solicitor must inform the court immediately.

(10) Where –

(a)   the court revokes any permission under paragraph (8); or

(b)   either of the conditions specified in paragraph (3)(b)(i) or (ii) is no longer fulfilled,

the court may, if it considers it necessary in order to protect the interests of the child concerned, appoint a person to be that child's litigation friend or children's guardian.

Chapter 5
Litigation Friend

16.7 Application of this Chapter

This Chapter applies where a child must have a litigation friend to conduct proceedings on the child's behalf in accordance with rule 16.5.

PART II – Statutory Instruments

16.8 Stage of proceedings at which a litigation friend becomes necessary

(1) This rule does not apply in relation to a child who is conducting proceedings without a litigation friend in accordance with rule 16.6.

(2) A person may not without the permission of the court take any step in proceedings except –

    (a)   filing an application form; or
    (b)   applying for the appointment of a litigation friend under rule 16.11,

until the child has a litigation friend.

(3) Any step taken before a child has a litigation friend has no effect unless the court orders otherwise.

16.9 Who may be a litigation friend for a child without a court order

(1) This rule does not apply if the court has appointed a person to be a litigation friend.

(2) A person may act as a litigation friend if that person –

    (a)   can fairly and competently conduct proceedings on behalf of the child;
    (b)   has no interest adverse to that of the child; and
    (c)   subject to paragraph (3), undertakes to pay any costs which the child may be ordered to pay in relation to the proceedings, subject to any right that person may have to be repaid from the assets of the child.

(3) Paragraph (2)(c) does not apply to the Official Solicitor, an officer of the Service or a Welsh family proceedings officer.

16.10 How a person becomes a litigation friend without a court order

(1) If the court has not appointed a litigation friend, a person who wishes to act as such must file a certificate of suitability stating that that person satisfies the conditions specified in rule 16.9(2).

(2) The certificate of suitability must be filed at the time when the person who wishes to act as litigation friend first takes a step in the proceedings on behalf of the child.

(3) A court officer will send the certificate of suitability to every person on whom, in accordance with rule 6.28, the application form should be served.

(4) This rule does not apply to the Official Solicitor, an officer of the Service or a Welsh family proceedings officer.

16.11 Appointment of litigation friend by the court

(1) The court may, if the person to be appointed consents, make an order appointing as a litigation friend –

    (a)   the Official Solicitor;
    (b)   an officer of the Service or a Welsh family proceedings officer; or
    (c)   some other person.

(2) An order appointing a litigation friend may be made by the court of its own initiative or on the application of –

(a)   a person who wishes to be a litigation friend; or
(b)   a party to the proceedings.

(3) The court may at any time direct that a party make an application for an order under paragraph (2).

(4) An application for an order appointing a litigation friend must be supported by evidence.

(5) Unless the court directs otherwise, a person appointed under this rule to be a litigation friend for a child will be treated as a party for the purpose of any provision in these rules requiring a document to be served on, or sent to, or notice to be given to, a party to the proceedings.

(6) Subject to rule 16.9(3), the court may not appoint a litigation friend under this rule unless it is satisfied that the person to be appointed complies with the conditions specified in rule 16.9(2).

(7) This rule is without prejudice to rule 16.6.

16.12 Court's power to change litigation friend and to prevent person acting as litigation friend

(1) The court may –

(a)   direct that a person may not act as a litigation friend;
(b)   terminate a litigation friend's appointment; or
(c)   appoint a new litigation friend in substitution for an existing one.

(2) An application for an order or direction under paragraph (1) must be supported by evidence.

(3) Subject to rule 16.9(3), the court may not appoint a litigation friend under this rule unless it is satisfied that the person to be appointed complies with the conditions specified in rule 16.9(2).

16.13 Appointment of litigation friend by court order – supplementary

(1) A copy of the application for an order under rule 16.11 or 16.12 must be sent by a court officer to every person on whom, in accordance with rule 6.28, the application form should be served.

(2) A copy of an application for an order under rule 16.12 must also be sent to –

(a)   the person who is the litigation friend, or who is purporting to act as the litigation friend when the application is made; and
(b)   the person, if not the applicant, who it is proposed should be the litigation friend.

16.14 Powers and duties of litigation friend

(1) The litigation friend –

    (a)   has the powers and duties set out in Practice Direction 16A; and

    (b)   must exercise those powers and duties in accordance with Practice Direction 16A.

(2) Where the litigation friend is an officer of the Service or a Welsh family proceedings officer, rule 16.20 applies as it applies to a children's guardian appointed in accordance with Chapter 6.

16.15 Procedure where appointment of litigation friend comes to an end

(1) When a child who is not a protected party reaches the age of 18, a litigation friend's appointment comes to an end.

(2) A court officer will send a notice to the other parties stating that the appointment of the child's litigation friend to act has ended.

Chapter 6
Children's Guardian Appointed under Rule 16.3

16.16 Application of this Chapter

This Chapter applies where the court must appoint a children's guardian in accordance with rule 16.3.

16.17 Who may be a children's guardian

Where the court is appointing a children's guardian under rule 16.3 it will appoint an officer of the Service or a Welsh family proceedings officer.

16.18 What the court or a court officer will do once the court has made a decision about appointing a children's guardian

(1) Where the court appoints a children's guardian under rule 16.3 a court officer will record the appointment and, as soon as practicable, will –

    (a)   inform the parties and either the Service or the Assembly; and

    (b)   unless it has already been sent, send the children's guardian a copy of the application and copies of any document filed with the court in the proceedings.

(2) A court officer has a continuing duty to send the children's guardian a copy of any other document filed with the court during the course of the proceedings.

16.19 Termination of the appointment of the children's guardian

(1) The appointment of a children's guardian under rule 16.3 continues for such time as is specified in the appointment or until terminated by the court.

(2) When terminating an appointment in accordance with paragraph (1), the court will give reasons for doing so, a note of which will be taken by the court or a court officer.

16.20 Powers and duties of the children's guardian

(1) The children's guardian is to act on behalf of the child upon the hearing of any application in proceedings to which this Chapter applies with the duty of safeguarding the interests of the child.

(2) The children's guardian must also provide the court with such other assistance as it may require.

(3) The children's guardian, when carrying out duties in relation to specified proceedings, other than placement proceedings, must have regard to the principle set out in section 1(2) and the matters set out in section 1(3)(a) to (f) of the 1989 Act as if for the word 'court' in that section there were substituted the words 'children's guardian'.

(4) The children's guardian, when carrying out duties in relation to proceedings to which Part 14 applies, must have regard to the principle set out in section 1(3) and the matters set out in section 1(4)(a) to (f) of the 2002 Act as if for the word 'court' in that section there were substituted the words 'children's guardian'.

(5) The children's guardian's duties must be exercised in accordance with Practice Direction 16A.

(6) A report to the court by the children's guardian is confidential.

16.21 Where the child instructs a solicitor or conducts proceedings on the child's own behalf

(1) Where it appears to the children's guardian that the child –

  (a)   is instructing a solicitor direct; or
  (b)   intends to conduct and is capable of conducting the proceedings on that child's own behalf,

the children's guardian must inform the court of that fact.

(2) Where paragraph (1) applies the children's guardian –

  (a)   must perform such additional duties as the court may direct;
  (b)   must take such part in the proceedings as the court may direct; and
  (c)   may, with the permission of the court, have legal representation in the conduct of those duties.

PART II – Statutory Instruments

Chapter 7
Children's Guardian Appointed under Rule 16.4

16.22 Application of this Chapter

This Chapter applies where the court must appoint a children's guardian under rule 16.4.

16.23 Stage of proceedings at which a children's guardian becomes necessary

(1) This rule does not apply in relation to a child who is conducting proceedings without a children's guardian in accordance with rule 16.6.

(2) A person may not without the permission of the court take any step in proceedings except –

   (a)   filing an application form; or
   (b)   applying for the appointment of a children's guardian under rule 16.24,

until the child has a children's guardian.

(3) Any step taken before a child has a children's guardian has no effect unless the court orders otherwise.

16.24 Appointment of a children's guardian

(1) The court may make an order appointing as a children's guardian, an officer of the Service or a Welsh family proceedings officer or, if the person to be appointed consents –

   (a)   a person other than the Official Solicitor; or
   (b)   the Official Solicitor.

(2) An order appointing a children's guardian may be made by the court of its own initiative or on the application of –

   (a)   a person who wishes to be a children's guardian; or
   (b)   a party to the proceedings.

(3) The court may at any time direct that a party make an application for an order under paragraph (2).

(4) An application for an order appointing a children's guardian must be supported by evidence.

(5) The court may not appoint a children's guardian under this rule unless it is satisfied that that person –

   (a)   can fairly and competently conduct proceedings on behalf of the child;
   (b)   has no interest adverse to that of the child; and
   (c)   subject to paragraph (6), undertakes to pay any costs which the child may be ordered to pay in relation to the proceedings, subject to any right that person may have to be repaid from the assets of the child.

(6) Paragraph (5)(c) does not apply to the Official Solicitor, an officer of the Service or a Welsh family proceedings officer.

(7) This rule is without prejudice to rule 16.6 and rule 9.11.

(Rule 9.11 provides for a child to be separately represented in certain applications for a financial remedy.)

16.25 Court's power to change children's guardian and to prevent person acting as children's guardian

(1) The court may –

    (a)   direct that a person may not act as a children's guardian;

    (b)   terminate the appointment of a children's guardian; or

    (c)   appoint a new children's guardian in substitution for an existing one.

(2) An application for an order or direction under paragraph (1) must be supported by evidence.

(3) Subject to rule 16.24(6), the court may not appoint a children's guardian under this rule unless it is satisfied that the person to be appointed complies with the conditions specified in rule 16.24(5).

16.26 Appointment of children's guardian by court order – supplementary

(1) A copy of the application for an order under rule 16.24 or 16.25 must be sent by a court officer to every person on whom, in accordance with rule 6.28, the application form should be served.

(2) A copy of an application for an order under rule 16.25 must also be sent to –

    (a)   the person who is the children's guardian, or who is purporting to act as the children's guardian when the application is made; and

    (b)   the person, if not the applicant, who it is proposed should be the children's guardian.

16.27 Powers and duties of children's guardian

(1) The children's guardian –

    (a)   has the powers and duties set out in Practice Direction 16A; and

    (b)   must exercise those powers and duties in accordance with Practice Direction 16A.

(2) Where the children's guardian is an officer of the Service or a Welsh family proceedings officer, rule 16.20 applies to a children's guardian appointed in accordance with this Chapter as it applies to a children's guardian appointed in accordance with Chapter 6.

16.28 Procedure where appointment of children's guardian comes to an end

(1) When a child reaches the age of 18, the appointment of a children's guardian comes to an end.

PART II – Statutory Instruments

(2) A court officer will send a notice to the other parties stating that the appointment of the child's children's guardian to act has ended.

Chapter 8
Duties of Solicitor Acting for the Child

16.29 Solicitor for child

(1) Subject to paragraphs (2) and (4), a solicitor appointed –

    (a)   under section 41(3) of the 1989 Act; or
    (b)   by the children's guardian in accordance with the Practice Direction 16A,

must represent the child in accordance with instructions received from the children's guardian.

(2) If a solicitor appointed as mentioned in paragraph (1) considers, having taken into account the matters referred to in paragraph (3), that the child –

    (a)   wishes to give instructions which conflict with those of the children's guardian; and
    (b)   is able, having regard to the child's understanding, to give such instructions on the child's own behalf,

the solicitor must conduct the proceedings in accordance with instructions received from the child.

(3) The matters the solicitor must take into account for the purposes of paragraph (2) are –

    (a)   the views of the children's guardian; and
    (b)   any direction given by the court to the children's guardian concerning the part to be taken by the children's guardian in the proceedings.

(4) Where –

    (a)   no children's guardian has been appointed; and
    (b)   the condition in section 41(4)(b) of the 1989 Act is satisfied,

a solicitor appointed under section 41(3) of the 1989 Act must represent the child in accordance with instructions received from the child.

(5) Where a solicitor appointed as mentioned in paragraph (1) receives no instructions under paragraphs (1), (2) or (4), the solicitor must represent the child in furtherance of the best interests of the child.

(6) A solicitor appointed under section 41(3) of the 1989 Act or by the children's guardian in accordance with Practice Direction 16A must serve documents, and accept service of documents, on behalf of the child in accordance with rule 6.31 and, where the child has not been served separately and has sufficient understanding, advise the child of the contents of any document so served.

(7) Where the child wishes an appointment of a solicitor –

(a) under section 41(3) of the 1989 Act; or

(b) by the children's guardian in accordance with the Practice Direction 16A,

to be terminated –

(i) the child may apply to the court for an order terminating the appointment; and

(ii) the solicitor and the children's guardian will be given an opportunity to make representations.

(8) Where the children's guardian wishes an appointment of a solicitor under section 41(3) of the 1989 Act to be terminated –

(a) the children's guardian may apply to the court for an order terminating the appointment; and

(b) the solicitor and, if of sufficient understanding, the child, will be given an opportunity to make representations.

(9) When terminating an appointment in accordance with paragraph (7) or (8), the court will give its reasons for so doing, a note of which will be taken by the court or a court officer.

(10) The court or a court officer will record the appointment under section 41(3) of the 1989 Act or the refusal to make the appointment.

Chapter 9
Reporting Officer

16.30 When the court appoints a reporting officer

In proceedings to which Part 14 applies, the court will appoint a reporting officer where –

(a) it appears that a parent or guardian of the child is willing to consent to the placing of the child for adoption, to the making of an adoption order or to a section 84 order; and

(b) that parent or guardian is in England or Wales.

16.31 Appointment of the same reporting officer in respect of two or more parents or guardians

The same person may be appointed as the reporting officer for two or more parents or guardians of the child.

16.32 The duties of the reporting officer

(1) The reporting officer must witness the signature by a parent or guardian on the document in which consent is given to –

(a) the placing of the child for adoption;

(b) the making of an adoption order; or

(c) the making of a section 84 order.

PART II – Statutory Instruments

(2) The reporting officer must carry out such other duties as are set out in Practice Direction 16A.

(3) A report to the court by the reporting officer is confidential.

(4) The reporting officer's duties must be exercised in accordance with Practice Direction 16A.

Chapter 10
Children and Family Reporter and Welfare Officer

16.33 Request by court for a welfare report in respect of the child

(1) Where the court is considering an application for an order in proceedings, the court may ask –

    (a)   in proceedings to which Parts 12 and 14 apply, a children and family reporter; or

    (b)   in proceedings to which Part 12 applies, a welfare officer,

to prepare a report on matters relating to the welfare of the child, and, in this rule, the person preparing the report is called 'the officer'.

(2) It is the duty of the officer to –

    (a)   comply with any request for a report under this rule; and

    (b)   provide the court with such other assistance as it may require.

(3) A report to the court under this rule is confidential.

(4) The officer, when carrying out duties in relation to proceedings under the 1989 Act, must have regard to the principle set out in section 1(2) and the matters set out in section 1(3)(a) to (f) of that Act as if for the word 'court' in that section there were substituted the words 'children and family reporter' or 'welfare officer' as the case may be.

(5) A party may question the officer about oral or written advice tendered by that officer to the court.

(6) The court officer will notify the officer of a direction given at a hearing at which –

    (a)   the officer is not present; and

    (b)   the welfare report is considered.

(7) The officer's duties must be exercised in accordance with Practice Direction 16A

    ('children and family reporter' and 'welfare officer' are defined in rule 2.3)

****

Chapter 12
Supplementary Appointment Provisions

16.36 Persons who may not be appointed as children's guardian, reporting officer or children and family reporter

(1) In adoption proceedings or proceedings for a section 84 order or a section 89 order, no person may be appointed as a children's guardian, reporting officer or children and family reporter who –

    (a)   is a member, officer or servant of a local authority which is a party to the proceedings;

    (b)   is, or has been, a member, officer or servant of a local authority or voluntary organisation who has been directly concerned in that capacity in arrangements relating to the care, accommodation or welfare of the child during the 5 years prior to the start of the proceedings; or

    (c)   is a serving probation officer who has, in that capacity, been previously concerned with the child or the child's family.

(2) In placement proceedings, a person described in paragraph (1)(b) or (c) may not be appointed as a children's guardian, reporting officer or children and family reporter.

16.37 Appointment of the same person as children's guardian, reporting officer and children and family reporter

The same person may be appointed to act as one or more of the following –

    (a)   the children's guardian;
    (b)   the reporting officer; and
    (c)   the children and family reporter.

Chapter 13
Officers of the Service, Welsh Family Proceedings Officers and Local Authority Officers: Further Duties

16.38 Officers of the Service, Welsh family proceedings officers and local authority officers acting under certain duties

(1) This rule applies when –

    (a)   an officer of the Service or a Welsh family proceedings officer is acting under a duty in accordance with –

        (i)   section 11E(7) of the 1989 Act (providing the court with information as to the making of a contact activity direction or a contact activity condition);

        (ii)   section 11G(2) of the 1989 Act (monitoring compliance with a contact activity direction or a contact activity condition);

        (iii)   section 11H(2) of the 1989 Act (monitoring compliance with a contact order);

PART II – Statutory Instruments

      (iv)   section 11L(5) of the 1989 Act (providing the court with information as to the making of an enforcement order);

      (v)   section 11M(1) of the 1989 Act (monitoring compliance with an enforcement order);

      (vi)   section 16(6) of the 1989 Act (providing a report to the court in accordance with a direction in a family assistance order); and

      (vii) section 16A of the 1989 Act (making a risk assessment); and

  (b)   a local authority officer is acting under a duty in accordance with section 16(6) of the 1989 Act (providing a report to the court in accordance with a direction in a family assistance order).

(2) In this rule, –

  (a)   'contact activity direction', 'contact activity condition' and 'enforcement order' have the meanings given in rule 12.2; and

  (b)   references to 'the officer' are to the officer of the Service, Welsh family proceedings officer or local authority officer referred to in paragraph (1).

(3) In exercising the duties referred to in paragraph (1), the officer must have regard to the principle set out in section 1(2) of the 1989 Act and the matters set out in section 1(3)(a) to (f) of the 1989 Act as if for the word 'court' in that section there were substituted the words 'officer of the Service, Welsh family proceedings officer or local authority officer'.

(4) The officer's duties referred to in paragraph (1) must be exercised in accordance with Practice Direction 16A.

Chapter 14
Enforcement Orders and Financial Compensation Orders: Persons Notified

16.39 Application for enforcement orders and financial compensation orders: duties of the person notified

(1) This rule applies where a person who was the child's children's guardian, litigation friend or legal representative in the proceedings in which a contact order was made has been notified of an application for an enforcement order or for a financial compensation order as required by Practice Direction 12C.

(2) The person who has been notified of the application must –

  (a)   consider whether it is in the best interests of the child for the child to be made a party to the proceedings for an enforcement order or a financial compensation order (as applicable); and

  (b)   before the date fixed for the first hearing in the case notify the court, orally or in writing, of the opinion reached on the question, together with the reasons for this opinion.

(3) In this rule, 'enforcement order' and 'financial compensation order' have the meanings given in rule 12.2.

Practice Direction 16A –
Representation of Children

This Practice Direction supplements FPR Part 16

Part 1
General

Reference in title of proceedings

1.1 Where a litigation friend represents a child in family proceedings in accordance with rule 16.5 and Chapter 5 of Part 16, the child should be referred to in the title of the proceedings as 'A.B. (a child by C.D. his/her litigation friend).

1.2 Where a children's guardian represents a child in family proceedings in accordance with rule 16.4 and Chapter 7 of Part 16, the child should be referred to in the title as 'A.B. (a child by C.D. his/her children's guardian).

1.3 A child who is conducting proceedings on that child's own behalf should be referred to in the title as 'A.B. (a child).'

Part 2
Litigation Friend

Duties of the litigation friend

2.1 It is the duty of a litigation friend fairly and competently to conduct proceedings on behalf of the child. The litigation friend must have no interest in the proceedings adverse to that of the child and all steps and decisions the litigation friend takes in the proceedings must be taken for the benefit of the child.

2.2 A litigation friend who is an officer of the Service or a Welsh family proceedings officer has, in addition, the duties set out in Part 3 of this Practice Direction and must exercise those duties as set out in that Part.

Becoming a litigation friend without a court order

3.1 In order to become a litigation friend without a court order the person who wishes to act as litigation friend must file a certificate of suitability –

(a)   stating that the litigation friend consents to act;

(b)   stating that the litigation friend knows or believes that the [applicant][respondent] is a child to whom rule 16.5 and Chapter 5 of Part 16 apply;

(c)   stating that the litigation friend can fairly and competently conduct proceedings on behalf of the child and has no interest adverse to that of the child;

(d)   undertaking to pay any costs which the child may be ordered to pay in relation to the proceedings, subject to any right the litigation friend may have to be repaid from the assets of the child; and

(e)   which the litigation friend has verified by a statement of truth.

PART II – Statutory Instruments

3.2 Paragraph 3.1 does not apply to the Official Solicitor, an officer of the Service or a Welsh family proceedings officer.

3.3 The court officer will send the certificate of suitability to one of the child's parents or guardians or, if there is no parent or guardian, to the person with whom the child resides or in whose care the child is.

3.4 The litigation friend must file the certificate of suitability at a time when the litigation friend first takes a step in the proceedings on behalf of the child.

Application for a court order appointing a litigation friend

4.1 An application for a court order appointing a litigation friend should be made in accordance with Part 18 and must be supported by evidence.

4.2 The court officer must serve the application notice on the persons referred to in paragraph 3.3.

4.3 The evidence in support must satisfy the court that the proposed litigation friend –

  (a)   consents to act;
  (b)   can fairly and competently conduct proceedings on behalf of the child;
  (c)   has no interest adverse to that of the child; and
  (d)   undertakes to pay any costs which the child may be ordered to pay in relation to the proceedings, subject to any right the litigation friend may have to be repaid from the assets of the child.

4.4 Paragraph 4.3(d) does not apply to the Official Solicitor, an officer of the Service of a Welsh family proceedings officer.

4.5 The proposed litigation friend may be one of the persons referred to in paragraph 3.3 where appropriate, or otherwise may be the Official Solicitor, an officer of the Service or a Welsh family proceedings officer. Where it is sought to appoint the Official Solicitor, an officer of the Service or a Welsh family proceedings officer, provision should be made for payment of that person's charges.

Change of litigation friend and prevention of person acting as litigation friend.

5.1 Where an application is made for an order under rule 16.12, the application must set out the reasons for seeking it and the application must be supported by evidence.

5.2 Subject to paragraph 4.4, if the order sought is substitution of a new litigation friend for an existing one, the evidence must satisfy the court of the matters set out in paragraph 4.3.

5.3 The court officer will serve the application notice on –

  (a)   the persons referred to in paragraph 3.3; and
  (b)   the litigation friend or person purporting to act as litigation friend.

Part 3
Children's Guardian Appointed under Rule 16.3

How the children's guardian exercises duties – investigations and appointment of solicitor

6.1 The children's guardian must make such investigations as are necessary to carry out the children's guardian's duties and must, in particular –

(a) contact or seek to interview such persons as the children's guardian thinks appropriate or as the court directs; and

(b) obtain such professional assistance as is available which the children's guardian thinks appropriate or which the court directs be obtained.

6.2 The children's guardian must –

(a) appoint a solicitor for the child unless a solicitor has already been appointed;

(b) give such advice to the child as is appropriate having regard to that child's understanding; and

(c) where appropriate instruct the solicitor representing the child on all matters relevant to the interests of the child arising in the course of proceedings, including possibilities for appeal.

6.3 Where the children's guardian is authorised in the terms mentioned by and in accordance with section 15(1) of the Criminal Justice and Court Services Act 2000 or section 37(1) of the Children Act 2004 (right of officer of the Service or Welsh family proceedings officer to conduct litigation or exercise a right of audience), paragraph 6.2(a) will not apply if the children's guardian intends to have conduct of the proceedings on behalf of the child unless –

(a) the child wishes to instruct a solicitor direct; and

(b) the children's guardian or the court considers that the child is of sufficient understanding to do so.

6.4 Where rule 16.21 (Where the child instructs a solicitor or conducts proceedings on the child's own behalf) applies, the duties set out in paragraph 6.2(a) and (c) do not apply.

How the children's guardian exercises duties – attendance at court, advice to the court and reports

6.5 The children's guardian or the solicitor appointed under section 41(3) of the 1989 Act or in accordance with paragraph 6.2(a) must attend all directions hearings unless the court directs otherwise.

6.6 The children's guardian must advise the court on the following matters –

(a) whether the child is of sufficient understanding for any purpose including the child's refusal to submit to a medical or psychiatric examination or other assessment that the court has the power to require, direct or order;

(b) the wishes of the child in respect of any matter relevant to the proceedings including that child's attendance at court;

(c)   the appropriate forum for the proceedings;

(d)   the appropriate timing of the proceedings or any part of them;

(e)   the options available to it in respect of the child and the suitability of each such option including what order should be made in determining the application; and

(f)   any other matter on which the court seeks advice or on which the children's guardian considers that the court should be informed.

6.7 The advice given under paragraph 6.6 may, subject to any direction of the court, be given orally or in writing. If the advice is given orally, a note of it must be taken by the court or the court officer.

6.8 The children's guardian must –

(a)   unless the court directs otherwise, file a written report advising on the interests of the child in accordance with the timetable set by the court; and

(b)   in proceedings to which Part 14 applies, where practicable, notify any person the joining of whom as a party to those proceedings would be likely, in the opinion of the children's guardian, to safeguard the interests of the child, of the court's power to join that person as a party under rule 14.3 and must inform the court –

(i)   of any notification;

(ii)   of anyone whom the children's guardian attempted to notify under this paragraph but was unable to contact; and

(iii)   of anyone whom the children's guardian believes may wish to be joined to the proceedings.

(Part 18 sets out the procedure for making an application to be joined as a party in proceedings.)

How the children's guardian exercises duties – service of documents and inspection of records

6.9 The children's guardian must serve and accept service of documents on behalf of the child in accordance with rule 6.31 and, where the child has not himself been served and has sufficient understanding, advise the child of the contents of any document so served.

6.10 Where the children's guardian inspects records of the kinds referred to in –

(a)   section 42 of the 1989 Act (right to have access to local authority records); or

(b)   section 103 of the 2002 Act (right to have access to adoption agency records)

the children's guardian must bring all records and documents which may, in the opinion of the children's guardian, assist in the proper determination of the proceedings to the attention of –

(i)   the court; and

(ii)   unless the court directs otherwise, the other parties to the proceedings.

How the children's guardian exercises duties – communication of a court's decision to the child

6.11 The children's guardian must ensure that, in relation to a decision made by the court in the proceedings –

    (a)   if the children's guardian considers it appropriate to the age and understanding of the child, the child is notified of that decision; and

    (b)   if the child is notified of the decision, it is explained to the child in a manner appropriate to that child's age and understanding.

Part 4
Appointment of Children's Guardian under Rule 16.4

Section 1 – When a child should be made a party to proceedings

7.1 Making the child a party to the proceedings is a step that will be taken only in cases which involve an issue of significant difficulty and consequently will occur in only a minority of cases. Before taking the decision to make the child a party, consideration should be given to whether an alternative route might be preferable, such as asking an officer of the Service or a Welsh family proceedings officer to carry out further work or by making a referral to social services or, possibly, by obtaining expert evidence.

7.2 The decision to make the child a party will always be exclusively that of the court, made in the light of the facts and circumstances of the particular case. The following are offered, solely by way of guidance, as circumstances which may justify the making of such an order –

    (a)   where an officer of the Service or Welsh family proceedings officer has notified the court that in the opinion of that officer the child should be made a party;

    (b)   where the child has a standpoint or interest which is inconsistent with or incapable of being represented by any of the adult parties;

    (c)   where there is an intractable dispute over residence or contact, including where all contact has ceased, or where there is irrational but implacable hostility to contact or where the child may be suffering harm associated with the contact dispute;

    (d)   where the views and wishes of the child cannot be adequately met by a report to the court;

    (e)   where an older child is opposing a proposed course of action;

    (f)   where there are complex medical or mental health issues to be determined or there are other unusually complex issues that necessitate separate representation of the child;

    (g)   where there are international complications outside child abduction, in particular where it may be necessary for there to be discussions with overseas authorities or a foreign court;

    (h)   where there are serious allegations of physical, sexual or other abuse in relation to the child or there are allegations of domestic violence not capable of being resolved with the help of an officer of the Service or Welsh family proceedings officer;

PART II – Statutory Instruments

(i)   where the proceedings concern more than one child and the welfare of the children is in conflict or one child is in a particularly disadvantaged position;

(j)   where there is a contested issue about scientific testing.

7.3 It must be recognised that separate representation of the child may result in a delay in the resolution of the proceedings. When deciding whether to direct that a child be made a party, the court will take into account the risk of delay or other facts adverse to the welfare of the child. The court's primary consideration will be the best interests of the child.

7.4 When a child is made a party and a children's guardian is to be appointed –

(a)   consideration should first be given to appointing an officer of the Service or Welsh family proceedings officer. Before appointing an officer, the court will cause preliminary enquiries to be made of Cafcass or CAFCASS CYMRU. For the relevant procedure, reference should be made to the practice note issued by Cafcass in June 2006 and any modifications of that practice note.

(b)   If Cafcass or CAFCASS CYMRU is unable to provide a children's guardian without delay, or if for some other reason the appointment of an officer of the Service of Welsh family proceedings officer is not appropriate, rule 16.24 makes further provision for the appointment of a children's guardian.

7.5 The court may, at the same time as deciding whether to join a child as a party, consider whether the proceedings should be transferred to another court taking into account the provisions of Part 3 of the Allocation and Transfer of Proceedings Order 2008.

Section 2 – Children's guardian appointed under rule 16.4

DUTIES OF THE CHILDREN'S GUARDIAN

7.6 It is the duty of a children's guardian fairly and competently to conduct proceedings on behalf of the child. The children's guardian must have no interest in the proceedings adverse to that of the child and all steps and decisions the children's guardian takes in the proceedings must be taken for the benefit of the child.

7.7 A children's guardian who is an officer of the Service or a Welsh family proceedings officer has, in addition, the duties set out in Part 3 of this Practice Direction and must exercise those duties as set out in that Part.

BECOMING A CHILDREN'S GUARDIAN WITHOUT A COURT ORDER

7.8 In order to become a children's guardian without a court order the person who wishes to act as children's guardian must file a certificate of suitability –

(a)   stating that the children's guardian consents to act;

(b)   stating that the children's guardian knows or believes that the [applicant][respondent] is a child to whom rule 16.4 and Chapter 7 of Part 16 apply;

(c) stating that the children's guardian can fairly and competently conduct proceedings on behalf of the child and has no interest adverse to that of the child;

(d) undertaking to pay any costs which the child may be ordered to pay in relation to the proceedings, subject to any right the children's guardian may have to be repaid from the assets of the child; and

(e) which the children's guardian has verified by a statement of truth.

7.9 Paragraph 7.8 does not apply to the Official Solicitor, an officer of the Service or a Welsh family proceedings officer.

7.10 The court officer will send the certificate of suitability to one of the child's parents or guardians or, if there is no parent or guardian, to the person with whom the child resides or in whose care the child is.

7.11 The children's guardian must file either the certificate of suitability at a time when the children's guardian first takes a step in the proceedings on behalf of the child.

APPLICATION FOR A COURT ORDER APPOINTING A CHILDREN'S GUARDIAN

7.12 An application for a court order appointing a children's guardian should be made in accordance with Part 18 and must be supported by evidence.

7.13 The court officer must serve the application notice on the persons referred to in paragraph 7.10.

7.14 The evidence in support must satisfy the court that the proposed children's guardian –

(a) consents to act;

(b) can fairly and competently conduct proceedings on behalf of the child;

(c) has no interest adverse to that of the child; and

(d) undertakes to pay any costs which the child may be ordered to pay in relation to the proceedings, subject to any right the children's guardian may have to be repaid from the assets of the child.

7.15 Paragraph 7.14 does not apply to the Official Solicitor, an officer of the Service of a Welsh family proceedings officer.

7.16 The proposed children's guardian may be one of the persons referred to in paragraph 7.10 where appropriate, or otherwise may be the Official Solicitor, an officer of the Service or a Welsh family proceedings officer. Where it is sought to appoint the Official Solicitor, an officer of the Service or a Welsh family proceedings officer, provision should be made for payment of that person's charges.

CHANGE OF CHILDREN'S GUARDIAN AND PREVENTION OF PERSON ACTING AS CHILDREN'S GUARDIAN.

7.17 Where an application is made for an order under rule 16.25, the application must set out the reasons for seeking it and must be supported by evidence.

PART II – Statutory Instruments

7.18 Subject to paragraph 7.15, if the order sought is substitution of a new children's guardian for an existing one, the evidence must satisfy the court of the matters set out in paragraph 7.14.

7.19 The court officer will serve the application notice on –

(a)   the persons referred to in paragraph 7.10; and

(b)   the children's guardian or person purporting to act as children's guardian.

Part 5
Reporting Officer

How the reporting officer exercises duties

8.1 The reporting officer must –

(a)   ensure so far as reasonably practicable that the parent or guardian is –

    (i)   giving consent unconditionally to the placing of the child for adoption or to the making of an adoption order (as defined in section 46 of the Adoption and Children Act 2002) or a section 84 order; and

    (ii)   with full understanding of what is involved;

(b)   investigate all the circumstances relevant to a parent's or guardian's consent; and

(c)   on completing the investigations the reporting officer must –

    (i)   make a report in writing to the court in accordance with the timetable set by the court, drawing attention to any matters which, in the opinion of the reporting officer, may be of assistance to the court in considering the application; or

    (ii)   make an interim report to the court if a parent or guardian of the child is unwilling to consent to the placing of the child for adoption or to the making of an adoption order or section 84 order.

8.2 On receipt of an interim report under paragraph 8.1(1)(c)(ii) a court officer must inform the applicant that a parent or guardian of the child is unwilling to consent to the placing of the child for adoption or to the making of an adoption order or section 84 order.

8.3 The reporting officer may at any time before the final hearing make an interim report to the court if the reporting officer considers it necessary and ask the court for directions.

8.4 The reporting officer must attend hearings as directed by the court.

Part 6
Children and Family Reporter and Welfare Officer

How the children and family reporter or welfare officer exercises powers and duties

9.1 In this Part, the person preparing the welfare report in accordance with rule 16.33 is called 'the officer'.

9.2 The officer must make such investigations as may be necessary to perform the officer's powers and duties and must, in particular –

(a) contact or seek to interview such persons as appear appropriate or as the court directs; and

(b) obtain such professional assistance as is available which the children and family reporter thinks appropriate or which the court directs be obtained.

9.3 The officer must –

(a) notify the child of such contents of the report (if any) as the officer considers appropriate to the age and understanding of the child, including any reference to the child's own views on the application and the recommendation; and

(b) if the child is notified of any contents of the report, explain them to the child in a manner appropriate to the child's age and understanding.

9.4 The officer must –

(a) attend hearings as directed by the court;

(b) advise the court of the child's wishes and feelings;

(c) advise the court if the officer considers that the joining of a person as a party to the proceedings would be likely to safeguard the interests of the child;

(d) consider whether it is in the best interests of the child for the child to be made a party to the proceedings, and if so, notify the court of that opinion together with the reasons for that opinion; and

(e) where the court has directed that a written report be made –

(i) file the report; and

(ii) serve a copy on the other parties and on any children's guardian,

in accordance with the timetable set by the court.

Part 7
Parental Order Reporter

How the parental order reporter exercises duties – investigations and reports

10.1 The parental order reporter must make such investigations as are necessary to carry out the parental order reporter's duties and must, in particular –

(a) contact or seek to interview such persons as the parental order reporter thinks appropriate or as the court directs; and

(b) obtain such professional assistance as is available which the parental order reporter thinks appropriate or which the court directs be obtained.

How the parental order reporter exercises duties – attendance at court, advice to the court and reports

10.2 The parental order reporter must attend all directions hearings unless the court directs otherwise.

PART II – Statutory Instruments

10.3 The parental order reporter must advise the court on the following matters –

(a)   the appropriate forum for the proceedings;

(b)   the appropriate timing of the proceedings or any part of them;

(c)   the options available to it in respect of the child and the suitability of each such option including what order should be made in determining the application; and

(d)   any other matter on which the court seeks advice or on which the parental order reporter considers that the court should be informed.

10.4 The advice given under paragraph 10.3 may, subject to any direction of the court, be given orally or in writing. If the advice is given orally, a note of it must be taken by the court or the court officer.

10.5 The parental order reporter must –

(a)   unless the court directs otherwise, file a written report advising on the interests of the child in accordance with the timetable set by the court; and

(b)   where practicable, notify any person the joining of whom as a party to those proceedings would be likely, in the opinion of the parental order reporter, to safeguard the interests of the child, of the court's power to join that person as a party under rule 13.3 and must inform the court –

(i)   of any notification;

(ii)   of anyone whom the parental order reporter attempted to notify under this paragraph but was unable to contact; and

(iii)   of anyone whom the parental order reporter believes may wish to be joined to the proceedings.

(Part 18 sets out the procedure for making an application to be joined as a party in proceedings.)

Part 8
Officers of the Service, Welsh Family Proceedings Officers and Local Authority Officers: Further Duties

How officers of the Service, Welsh family proceedings officers and local authority officers exercise certain further duties

11.1 This Part applies when an officer of the Service, a Welsh family proceedings officer or a local authority officer is acting under a duty referred to in rule 16.38(1). In this Part, the person acting under a duty referred to in rule 16.38(1) is referred to as 'the officer'.

11.2 The officer must make such investigations as may be necessary to perform the officer's duties and must, in particular –

(a)   contact or seek to interview such persons as the officer thinks appropriate or as the court directs; and

(b)   obtain such professional assistance as the officer thinks appropriate or which the court directs.

11.3 The officer must –

(a) notify the child of such (if any) of the contents of any report or risk assessment as the officer considers appropriate to the age and understanding of the child;

(b) if the child is notified of any contents of a report or risk assessment, explain them to the child in a manner appropriate to the child's age and understanding;

(c) consider whether to recommend in any report or risk assessment that the court lists a hearing for the purposes of considering the report or risk assessment;

(d) consider whether it is in the best interests of the child for the child to be made a party to the proceedings, and, if so, notify the court of that opinion together with the reasons for that opinion.

11.4 When making a risk assessment, the officer must, if of the opinion that the court should exercise its discretion under rule 12.34(2), state in the risk assessment –

(a) the way in which the officer considers the court should exercise its discretion (including the officer's view on the length of any suggested delay in service); and

(b) the officer's reasons for that reaching that view.

11.5 The officer must file any report or risk assessment with the court –

(a) at or by the time directed by the court;

(b) in the absence of any direction, at least 14 days before a relevant hearing; or

(c) where there has been no direction from the court and there is no relevant hearing listed, as soon as possible following the completion of the report or risk assessment.

11.6 In paragraph 11.5, a hearing is relevant if the court officer has given the officer notice that a report prepared by the officer is to be considered at it.

11.7 A copy of any report prepared as a result of acting under a duty referred to in rule 16.38(1)(a)(i) to (vi) or (b) (but not any risk assessment) must, as soon as practicable, be served by the officer on the parties.

(Rule 12.34 makes provision for the service of risk assessments.)

****

PART 18
PROCEDURE FOR OTHER APPLICATIONS IN PROCEEDINGS

18.1 Types of application for which Part 18 procedure may be followed

(1) The Part 18 procedure is the procedure set out in this Part.

(2) An applicant may use the Part 18 procedure if the application is made –

(a) in the course of existing proceedings;

(b)   to start proceedings except where some other Part of these rules prescribes the procedure to start proceedings; or

(c)   in connection with proceedings which have been concluded.

(3) Paragraph (2) does not apply –

(a)   to applications where any other rule in any other Part of these rules sets out the procedure for that type of application;

(b)   if a practice direction provides that the Part 18 procedure may not be used in relation to the type of application in question.

18.2 Applications for permission to start proceedings

An application for permission to start proceedings must be made to the court where the proceedings will be started if permission is granted.

18.3 Respondents to applications under this Part

The following persons are to be respondents to an application under this Part –

(a)   where there are existing proceedings or the proceedings have been concluded –

(i)   the parties to those proceedings; and

(ii)   if the proceedings are proceedings under Part 11, the person who is the subject of those proceedings;

(b)   where there are no existing proceedings –

(i)   if notice has been given under section 44 of the 2002 Act (notice of intention to adopt or apply for an order under section 84 of that Act), the local authority to whom notice has been given; and

(ii)   if an application is made for permission to apply for an order in proceedings, any person who will be a party to the proceedings brought if permission is granted; and

(c)   any other person as the court may direct.

18.4 Application notice to be filed

(1) Subject to paragraph (2) the applicant must file an application notice.

(2) An applicant may make an application without filing an application notice if –

(a)   this is permitted by a rule or practice direction; or

(b)   the court dispenses with the requirement for an application notice.

18.5 Notice of an application

(1) Subject to paragraph (2), a copy of the application notice must be served on –

(a)   each respondent;

(b)   in relation to proceedings under Part 11, the person who is, or, in the case of an application to start proceedings, it is intended will be, the subject of the proceedings; and

(c)   in relation to proceedings under Parts 12 and 14, the children's guardian (if any).

(2) An application may be made without serving a copy of the application notice if this is permitted by –

(a)   a rule;
(b)   a practice direction; or
(c)   the court.

(Rule 18.8 deals with service of a copy of the application notice.)

18.6 Time when an application is made

When an application must be made within a specified time, it is so made if the court receives the application notice within that time.

18.7 What an application notice must include

(1) An application notice must state –

(a)   what order the applicant is seeking; and
(b)   briefly, why the applicant is seeking the order.

(2) A draft of the order sought must be attached to the application notice.

(Part 17 requires an application notice to be verified by a statement of truth if the applicant wishes to rely on matters set out in his application as evidence.)

18.8 Service of a copy of an application notice

(1) Subject to rule 2.4, a copy of the application notice must be served in accordance with the provisions of Part 6 –

(a)   as soon as practicable after it is filed; and
(b)   in any event –
    (i)   where the application is for an interim order under rule 9.7 at least 14 days; and
    (ii)   in any other case, at least 7 days;
    before the court is to deal with the application.

(2) The applicant must, when filing the application notice, file a copy of any written evidence in support.

(3) If a copy of an application notice is served by a court officer it must be accompanied by –

(a)   a notice of the date and place where the application will be heard;
(b)   a copy of any witness statement in support; and
(c)   a copy of the draft order which the applicant has attached to the application.

(4) If –

(a)   an application notice is served; but

PART II – Statutory Instruments

(b)   the period of notice is shorter than the period required by these rules or a practice direction,

the court may direct that, in the circumstances of the case, sufficient notice has been given and hear the application.

(5) This rule does not require written evidence –

(a)   to be filed if it has already been filed; or
(b)   to be served on a party on whom it has already been served.

18.9 Applications which may be dealt with without a hearing

(1) The court may deal with an application without a hearing if –

(a)   the court does not consider that a hearing would be appropriate; or
(b)   the parties agree as to the terms of the order sought or the parties agree that the court should dispose of the application without a hearing and the court does not consider that a hearing would be appropriate.

(2) Where –

(a)   an application is made for permission to make an application in proceedings under the 1989 Act; and
(b)   the court refuses the application without a hearing in accordance with paragraph (1)(a),

the court must, at the request of the applicant, re-list the application and fix a date for a hearing.

(3) Paragraph (2) does not apply to magistrates' courts.

18.10 Service of application notice following court order where application made without notice

(1) This rule applies where the court has disposed of an application which it permitted to be made without service of a copy of the application notice.

(2) Where the court makes an order, whether granting or dismissing the application, a copy of the application notice and any evidence in support must unless the court orders otherwise, be served with the order on –

(a)   all the parties in proceedings; and
(b)   in relation to proceedings under Part 11, the person who is, or, in the case of an application to start proceedings, it is intended will be, the subject of the proceedings.

(3) The order must contain a statement of the right to make an application to set aside$^{(GL)}$ or vary the order under rule 18.11.

18.11 Application to set aside or vary order made without notice

(1) A person who was not served with a copy of the application notice before an order was made under rule 18.10 may apply to have the order set aside(GL) or varied.

(2) An application under this rule must be made within 7 days beginning with the date on which the order was served on the person making the application.

18.12 Power of the court to proceed in the absence of a party

(1) Where the applicant or any respondent fails to attend the hearing of an application, the court may proceed in the absence of that person.

(2) Where –

    (a)   the applicant or any respondent fails to attend the hearing of an application; and

    (b)   the court makes an order at the hearing,

the court may, on application or of its own initiative, re-list the application.

(3) Paragraph (2) does not apply to magistrates' courts.

18.13 Dismissal of totally without merit applications

If the High Court or a county court dismisses an application (including an application for permission to appeal) and it considers that the application is totally without merit –

    (a)   the court's order must record that fact; and

    (b)   the court must at the same time consider whether it is appropriate to make a civil restraint order.

Practice Direction 18A –
Other Applications in Proceedings

This Practice Direction supplements FPR Part 18

Application of Part 18

1.1 Part 18 makes general provision for a procedure for making applications. All applications for the court's permission should be made under this Part, with the exception of applications for permission for which specific provision is made in other Parts of the FPR, in which case the application should be made under the specific provision. Examples of where specific provision has been made in another Part of the FPR for applications for permission are rule 11.3 (Permission to apply for a forced marriage protection order) and rule 30.3 (Permission to appeal).

PART II – Statutory Instruments

Reference to a judge

2.1 In the High Court or a county court a district judge may refer to a judge any matter which the district judge thinks should properly be decided by a judge, and the judge may either dispose of the matter or refer it back to the district judge.

Additional requirements in relation to application notices

3.1 In addition to the requirements set out in rule 18.7, the following requirements apply to the applications to which the respective paragraph refers.

3.2 An application notice must be signed and include –

(a)   the title of the case (if available);
(b)   the reference number of the case (if available);
(c)   the full name of the applicant;
(d)   where the applicant is not already a party, the applicant's address for service, including a postcode. Postcode information may be obtained from www.royalmail.com or the Royal Mail Address Management Guide; and
(e)   either a request for a hearing or a request that the application be dealt with without a hearing.

3.3 An application notice relating to an application under section 42(6) of the Adoption and Children Act 2002 (permission to apply for an adoption order) must include –

(a)   the child's name, sex, date of birth and nationality;
(b)   in relation to each of the child's parents or guardians, their name, address and nationality;
(c)   the length of time that the child has had his or her home with the applicant;
(d)   the reason why the child has had his or her home with the applicant;
(e)   details of any local authority or adoption agency involved in placing the child in the applicant's home; and
(f)   if there are or have been other court proceedings relating to the child, the nature of those proceedings, the name of the court in which they are being or have been dealt with, the date and type of any order made and, if the proceedings are still ongoing, the date of the next hearing.

3.4 An application notice relating to an application in the High Court by a local authority for permission under section 100(3) of the Children Act 1989 must include a draft of the application form.

3.5 Where permission is required to take any step under the Children Act 1989 (for example an application to be joined as a party to the proceedings) the application notice must include a draft of the application for the making of which permission is sought together with sufficient copies for one to be served on each respondent.

3.6 In an application for permission to bring proceedings under Schedule 1 of the Children Act 1989, the draft application for the making of which permission is sought must be accompanied by a statement setting out the financial details which the person seeking permission believes to be relevant to the request and contain a declaration that it is true to the maker's best knowledge and belief, together with sufficient copies for one to be served on each respondent.

3.7 The provisions in Schedule 1 which require an application for permission to bring proceedings are –

(a)   paragraph 7(2) – permission is required to make an application for variation of a secured periodical payments order after the death of the parent liable to make the payments if a period of 6 months has passed from the date on which representation in regard to that parent's estate is first taken out; and

(b)   paragraph 11(3) – permission is required to make an application to alter a maintenance agreement following the death of one of the parties if a period of 6 months has passed beginning with the day on which representation in regard to the estate of the deceased is first taken out.

Other provisions in relation to application notices

4.1 On receipt of an application notice containing a request for a hearing, unless the court considers that the application is suitable for consideration without a hearing, the court officer will, if serving a copy of the application notice, notify the applicant of the time and date fixed for the hearing of the application.

4.2 On receipt of an application notice containing a request that the application be dealt with without a hearing, the court will decide whether the application is suitable for consideration without a hearing.

4.3 Where the court –

(a)   considers that the application is suitable for consideration without a hearing; but

(b)   is not satisfied that it has sufficient material to decide the application immediately,

it may give directions for the filing of evidence and will inform the applicant and the respondent(s) of its decision. (Rule 18.11 enables a party to apply for an order made without notice to be set aside or varied.)

4.4 Where the court does not consider that the application is suitable for consideration without a hearing –

(a)   it may give directions as to the filing of evidence; and

(b)   the court officer will notify the applicant and the respondent of the time, date and place for the hearing of the application and any directions given.

4.5 In the High Court or a county court if the application is intended to be made to a judge, the application notice should so state. In that case, paragraphs 4.2, 4.3 and 4.4 will apply as though references to the court were references to a judge.

4.6 Every application should be made as soon as it becomes apparent that it is necessary or desirable to make it.

4.7 Applications should, wherever possible, be made so that they are considered at any directions hearing or other hearing for which a date has been fixed or for which a date is about to be fixed.

4.8 The parties must anticipate that at any hearing (including any directions hearing) the court may wish to review the conduct of the case as a whole and give any necessary directions. They should be ready to assist the court in doing so and to answer questions the court may ask for this purpose.

4.9 Where a date for a hearing has been fixed, a party who wishes to make an application at that hearing but does not have sufficient time to file an application notice should as soon as possible inform the court (if possible in writing) and, if possible, the other parties of the nature of the application and the reason for it. That party should then make the application orally at the hearing.

Applications without service of application notice

5.1 An application may be made without service of an application notice only –

    (a)   where there is exceptional urgency;
    (b)   where the overriding objective is best furthered by doing so;
    (c)   by consent of all parties;
    (d)   with the permission of the court;
    (e)   where paragraph 4.9 applies; or
    (f)   where a court order, rule or practice direction permits.

Giving notice of an application

6.1 Unless the court otherwise directs or paragraph 5.1 of this practice direction applies, the application notice must be served as soon as practicable after it has been issued and, if there is to be a hearing, at least 7 days before the hearing date.

6.2 Where an application notice should be served but there is not sufficient time to do so, informal notification of the application should be given unless the circumstances of the application require no notice of the application to be given.

Pre-action applications

7.1 All applications made before proceedings are commenced should be made under this Part.

Telephone hearings

8.1 The court may direct that an application be dealt with by a telephone hearing.

8.2 The applicant should, if seeking a direction under paragraph 8.1, indicate this on the application notice. Where the applicant has not indicated such an intention but nevertheless wishes to seek a direction the request should be made as early as possible.

8.3 A direction under paragraph 8.1 will not normally be made unless every party entitled to be given notice of the application and to be heard at the hearing has consented to the direction.

8.4 No representative of a party to an application being heard by telephone may attend the court in person while the application is being heard unless the other party to the application has agreed that the representative may do so.

8.5 If an application is to be heard by telephone the following directions will apply, subject to any direction to the contrary –

    (a)   the applicant's legal representative is responsible for arranging the telephone conference for precisely the time fixed by the court. The telecommunications provider used must be one of the approved panel of service providers (see HMCS website at www.hmcourts-service.gov.uk);

    (b)   the applicant's legal representative must tell the operator the telephone numbers of all those participating in the conference call and the sequence in which they are to be called;

    (c)   it is the responsibility of the applicant's legal representative to ascertain from all the other parties whether they have instructed counsel and, if so the identity of counsel, and whether the legal representative and counsel will be on the same or different telephone numbers;

    (d)   the sequence in which those involved are to be called will be –

        (i)   the applicant's legal representative and (if on a different number) his counsel;

        (ii)   the legal representative (and counsel) for all other parties; and

        (iii)   the judge or justices, as the case may be;

    (e)   each speaker is to remain on the line after being called by the operator setting up the conference call. The call may be 2 or 3 minutes before the time fixed for the application;

    (f)   when the judge has or justices have been connected the applicant's legal representative (or counsel) will introduce the parties in the usual way;

    (g)   if the use of a 'speakerphone' by any party causes the court or any other party any difficulty in hearing what is said the judge or justices may require that party to use a hand held telephone;

    (h)   the telephone charges debited to the account of the party initiating the conference call will be treated as part of the costs of the application.

Video conferencing

9.1 Where the parties to a matter wish to use video conferencing facilities, and those facilities are available in the relevant court, the parties should apply to the court for directions. (Practice Direction 22A provides guidance on the use of video conferencing)

Note of proceedings

10.1 The court or court officer should keep, either by way of a note or a tape recording, brief details of all proceedings before the court, including the dates of the proceedings and a short statement of the decision taken at each hearing.

Evidence

11.1 The requirement for evidence in certain types of applications is set out in some of the rules in the FPR and practice directions. Where there is no specific requirement to provide evidence it should be borne in mind that, as a practical matter, the court will often need to be satisfied by evidence of the facts that are relied on in support of or for opposing the application.

11.2 The court may give directions for the filing of evidence in support of or opposing a particular application. The court may also give directions for the filing of evidence in relation to any hearing that it fixes on its own initiative. The directions may specify the form that evidence is to take and when it is to be served.

11.3 Where it is intended to rely on evidence which is not contained in the application itself, the evidence, if it has not already been served, should be served with the application.

11.4 Where a respondent to an application wishes to rely on evidence, that evidence must be filed in accordance with any directions the court may have given and a court officer will serve the evidence on the other parties, unless the court directs otherwise.

11.5 If it is necessary for the applicant to serve any evidence in reply the court officer will serve it on the other parties unless the court directs otherwise.

11.6 Evidence must be filed with the court as well as served on the parties.

11.7 The contents of an application notice may be used as evidence provided the contents have been verified by a statement of truth.

Consent orders

12.1 The parties to an application for a consent order must ensure that they provide the court with any material it needs to be satisfied that it is appropriate to make the order. Subject to any rule in the FPR or practice direction a letter will generally be acceptable for this purpose.

12.2 Where a judgment or order has been agreed in respect of an application where a hearing date has been fixed, the parties must inform the court immediately.

Other applications considered without a hearing

13.1 Where rule 18.9(1)(b) applies the court will treat the application as if it were proposing to make an order on its own initiative.

13.2 Where the parties agree that the court should dispose of the application without a hearing they should so inform the court in writing and each should confirm that all evidence and other material on which he or she relies has been disclosed to the other parties to the application.

Miscellaneous

14.1 If the case is proceeding in the High Court and the draft order is unusually long or complex it should also be supplied in electronic form on such storage medium as shall be agreed with the judge or court staff, for use by the court office.

14.2 Where rule 18.12 applies the power to re-list the application in rule 18.12(2) is in addition to any other powers of the court with regard to the order (for example to set aside, vary, discharge or suspend the order).

Costs

15.1 Attention is drawn to the CPR costs practice direction and, in particular, to the court's power to make a summary assessment of costs.

15.2 Attention is also drawn to rule 44.13(1) of the CPR which provides that if an order makes no mention of costs, none are payable in respect of the proceedings to which it relates.

PART 19
ALTERNATIVE PROCEDURE FOR APPLICATIONS

19.1 Types of application for which Part 19 procedure may be followed

(1) The Part 19 procedure is the procedure set out in this Part.

(2) An applicant may use the Part 19 procedure where the Part 18 procedure does not apply and –

    (a)   there is no form prescribed by a rule or referred to in Practice Direction 5A in which to make the application;

    (b)   the applicant seeks the court's decision on a question which is unlikely to involve a substantial dispute of fact; or

    (c)   paragraph (5) applies.

(3) The court may at any stage direct that the application is to continue as if the applicant had not used the Part 19 procedure and, if it does so, the court may give any directions it considers appropriate.

(4) Paragraph (2) does not apply if a practice direction provides that the Part 19 procedure may not be used in relation to the type of application in question.

(5) A rule or practice direction may, in relation to a specified type of proceedings –

(a)   require or permit the use of the Part 19 procedure; and
(b)   disapply or modify any of the rules set out in this Part as they apply to those proceedings.

19.2 Applications for which the Part 19 procedure must be followed

(1) The Part 19 procedure must be used in an application made in accordance with –

(a)   section 60(3) of the 2002 Act (order to prevent disclosure of information to an adopted person);
(b)   section 79(4) of the 2002 Act (order for Registrar General to give any information referred to in section 79(3) of the 2002 Act); and
(c)   rule 14.21 (directions of High Court regarding fathers without parental responsibility).

(2) The respondent to an application made in accordance with para-graph (1)(b) is the Registrar General.

19.3 Contents of the application

Where the applicant uses the Part 19 procedure, the application must state –

(a)   that this Part applies;
(b)   either –
    (i)   the question which the applicant wants the court to decide; or
    (ii)   the order which the applicant is seeking and the legal basis of the application for that order;
(c)   if the application is being made under an enactment, what that enactment is;
(d)   if the applicant is applying in a representative capacity, what that capacity is; and
(e)   if the respondent appears or is to appear in a representative capacity, what that capacity is.

(Part 17 requires a statement of case to be verified by a statement of truth.)

19.4 Issue of application without naming respondents

(1) A practice direction may set out circumstances in which an application may be issued under this Part without naming a respondent.

(2) The practice direction may set out those cases in which an application for permission must be made by application notice before the application is issued.

(3) The application for permission –

(a)   need not be served on any other person; and
(b)   must be accompanied by a copy of the application which the applicant proposes to issue.

(4) Where the court gives permission, it will give directions about the future management of the application.

19.5 Acknowledgment of service

(1) Subject to paragraph (2), each respondent must –

    (a)   file an acknowledgment of service within 14 days beginning with the date on which the application is served; and

    (b)   serve the acknowledgment of service on the applicant and any other party.

(2) If the application is to be served out of the jurisdiction, the respondent must file and serve an acknowledgment of service within the period set out in Practice Direction 6B.

(3) The acknowledgment of service must –

    (a)   state whether the respondent contests the application;

    (b)   state, if the respondent seeks a different order from that set out in the application, what that order is; and

    (c)   be signed by the respondent or the respondent's legal representative.

19.6 Consequence of not filing an acknowledgment of service

(1) This rule applies where –

    (a)   the respondent has failed to file an acknowledgment of service; and

    (b)   the time period for doing so has expired.

(2) The respondent may attend the hearing of the application but may not take part in the hearing unless the court gives permission.

19.7 Filing and serving written evidence

(1) The applicant must, when filing the application, file the written evidence on which the applicant intends to rely.

(2) The applicant's evidence must be served on the respondent with the application.

(3) A respondent who wishes to rely on written evidence must file it when filing the acknowledgment of service.

(4) A respondent who files written evidence must also, at the same time, serve a copy of that evidence on the other parties.

(5) Within 14 days beginning with the date on which a respondent's evidence was served on the applicant, the applicant may file further written evidence in reply.

(6) An applicant who files further written evidence must also, within the same time limit, serve a copy of that evidence on the other parties.

PART II – Statutory Instruments

19.8 Evidence – general

(1) No written evidence may be relied on at the hearing of the application unless –

    (a)   it has been served in accordance with rule 19.7; or

    (b)   the court gives permission.

(2) The court may require or permit a party to give oral evidence at the hearing.

(3) The court may give directions requiring the attendance for cross-examination(GL) of a witness who has given written evidence.

    (Rule 22.1 contains a general power for the court to control evidence.)

19.9 Procedure where respondent objects to use of the Part 19 procedure

(1) A respondent who contends that the Part 19 procedure should not be used because –

    (a)   there is a substantial dispute of fact; and

    (b)   the use of the Part 19 procedure is not required or permitted by a rule or practice direction,

must state the reasons for that contention when filing the acknowledgment of service.

(2) When the court receives the acknowledgment of service and any written evidence, it will give directions as to the future management of the case.

    (Rule 19.7 requires a respondent who wishes to rely on written evidence to file it when filing the acknowledgment of service.)

    (Rule 19.1(3) allows the court to make an order that the application continue as if the applicant had not used the Part 19 procedure.)

Practice Direction 19A –
Alternative Procedure for Applications

This Practice Direction supplements FPR Part 19

Types of application in which Part 19 procedure must be used

1.1 An applicant must use the Part 19 procedure if the application is for an order under –

    (a)   section 60(3) of the 2002 Act, to prevent disclosure of information to an adopted person;

    (b)   section 79(4) of the 2002 Act, to require the Registrar General to provide information; or

    (c)   rule 14.21 (Inherent jurisdiction and fathers without parental responsibility) in Part 14, to request directions of the High Court regarding fathers without parental responsibility.

Types of application in which Part 19 procedure may be used

1.2 An applicant may use the Part 19 procedure if Part 18 does not apply and if –

(a)   there is no prescribed form in which to make the application; or

(b)   the applicant seeks the court's decision on a question which is unlikely to involve a substantial dispute of fact.

1.3 An applicant may also use the Part 19 procedure if a practice direction permits or requires its use for the type of proceedings concerned.

1.4 The practice directions referred to in paragraph 1.3 may in some respects modify or disapply the Part 19 procedure and, where that is so, it is those practice directions, rather than this one, which must be complied with.

1.5 The types of application for which the Part 19 procedure may be used include an application for an order or direction which is unopposed by each respondent before the commencement of the proceedings and the sole purpose of the application is to obtain the approval of the court to the agreement.

1.6 Where it appears to a court officer that an applicant is using the Part 19 procedure inappropriately, the officer may refer the application to the court for consideration of the point.

1.7 The court may at any stage order the application to continue as if the applicant had not used the Part 19 procedure and, if it does so, the court will give such directions as it considers appropriate (see rule 19.1(3)).

The application

2.1 Where an applicant uses the Part 19 procedure, the application form referred to in Practice Direction 5A should be used and must state the matters set out in rule 19.3 and, if paragraphs 1.3 and 1.4 apply, must comply with the requirements of the practice direction in question. In particular, the application form must state that Part 19 applies. A Part 19 application form means an application form which so states.

2.2 An application –

(a)   in accordance with rule 19.4, to ask the High Court for directions on the need to give a father without parental responsibility notice of the intention to place a child for adoption; or

(b)   under section 60(3) of the 2002 Act for an order to prevent disclosure of information to an adopted person,

may be issued without naming a respondent.

Responding to the application

3.1 Where a respondent who wishes to respond to a Part 19 application is required to file an acknowledgement of service, that acknowledgement of service should be in form FP5 which is referred to in Practice Direction 5A but can, alternatively be given in an informal document such as a letter.

PART II – Statutory Instruments

3.2 Rule 19.5 sets out provisions relating to an acknowledgement of service of a Part 19 application.

3.3 Rule 19.6 sets out the consequence of failing to file an acknowledgement of service.

3.4 A respondent who believes that the Part 19 procedure should not be used because there is a substantial dispute of fact or, as the case may be, because its use is not authorised by any rule in the FPR or any practice direction, must state the reasons for that belief in writing when filing the acknowledgement of service (see rule 19.9). If the statement of reasons includes matters of evidence, it should be verified by a statement of truth.

Managing the application

4.1 The court may give directions immediately a Part 19 application is issued either on the application of a party or of its own initiative. The directions may include fixing a hearing date where –

(a)   there is no dispute; or

(b)   where there may be a dispute, but a hearing date could conveniently be given.

4.2 Where the court does not fix a hearing date when the application is issued, it will give directions for the disposal of the application as soon as practicable after the respondent has acknowledged service of the application or, as the case may be, after the period for acknowledging service has expired.

4.3 Certain applications may not require a hearing.

4.4 The court may convene a directions hearing before giving directions.

Evidence

5.1 An applicant wishing to rely on written evidence should file it when the Part 19 application form is issued.

5.2 Evidence will normally be in the form of a witness statement or an affidavit but an applicant may rely on the matters set out in the application form provided it has been verified by a statement of truth.

(For information about statements of truth see Part 7 and Practice Direction 17A, and about written evidence see Part 22 and Practice Direction 22A.)

5.3 A respondent wishing to rely on written evidence should file it with the acknowledgement of service (see rule 19.7(3)).

5.4 Rule 19.7 sets out the times and provisions for filing and serving written evidence.

5.5 A party may apply to the court for an extension of time to serve and file evidence under rule 19.7 or for permission to serve and file additional evidence under rule 19.8(1).

(For information about applications see Part 18 and Practice Direction 18A.)

5.6 The parties may, subject to paragraphs 5.7 and 5.8, agree in writing on an extension of time for serving and filing evidence under rule 19.7(3) or rule 19.7(5).

5.7 An agreement extending time for a respondent to file evidence in reply under rule 19.7(3) –

(a) must be filed by the respondent at the same time as the acknowledgement of service; and

(b) must not extend time by more than 17 days after the respondent files the acknowledgement of service.

5.8 An agreement extending time for an applicant to file evidence in reply under rule 19.7(5) must not extend time to more than 28 days after service of the respondent's evidence on the applicant.

Hearing

6.1 The court may on the hearing date –

(a) proceed to hear the case and dispose of the application;

(b) give case management directions.

****

PART 25
EXPERTS AND ASSESSORS

25.1 Duty to restrict expert evidence

Expert evidence will be restricted to that which is reasonably required to resolve the proceedings.

25.2 Interpretation

(1) A reference to an 'expert' in this Part –

(a) is a reference to a person who has been instructed to give or prepare expert evidence for the purpose of family proceedings; and

(b) does not include –

(i) a person who is within a prescribed description for the purposes of section 94(1) of the 2002 Act (persons who may prepare a report for any person about the suitability of a child for adoption or of a person to adopt a child or about the adoption, or placement for adoption, of a child); or

(ii) an officer of the Service or a Welsh family proceedings officer when acting in that capacity.

(Regulation 3 of the Restriction on the Preparation of Adoption Reports Regulations 2005 (S.I. 2005/1711) sets out which persons are within a prescribed description for the purposes of section 94(1) of the 2002 Act.)

(2) 'Single joint expert' means an expert instructed to prepare a report for the court on behalf of two or more of the parties (including the applicant) to the proceedings.

25.3 Experts – overriding duty to the court

(1) It is the duty of experts to help the court on matters within their expertise.

(2) This duty overrides any obligation to the person from whom experts have received instructions or by whom they are paid.

25.4 Court's power to restrict expert evidence

(1) No party may call an expert or put in evidence an expert's report without the court's permission.

(2) When parties apply for permission they must identify –

(a) the field in which the expert evidence is required; and
(b) where practicable, the name of the proposed expert.

(3) If permission is granted it will be in relation only to the expert named or the field identified under paragraph (2).

(4) The court may limit the amount of a party's expert's fees and expenses that may be recovered from any other party.

25.5 General requirement for expert evidence to be given in a written report

(1) Expert evidence is to be given in a written report unless the court directs otherwise.

(2) The court will not direct an expert to attend a hearing unless it is necessary to do so in the interests of justice.

25.6 Written questions to experts

(1) A party may put written questions about an expert's report (which must be proportionate) to –

(a) an expert instructed by another party; or
(b) a single joint expert appointed under rule 25.7.

(2) Written questions under paragraph (1) –

(a) may be put once only;
(b) must be put within 10 days beginning with the date on which the expert's report was served; and
(c) must be for the purpose only of clarification of the report,

unless in any case –
    (i) the court directs otherwise; or
    (ii) a practice direction provides otherwise.

(3) An expert's answers to questions put in accordance with paragraph (1) are treated as part of the expert's report.

(4) Where –

(a) a party has put a written question to an expert instructed by another party; and

(b) the expert does not answer that question,

the court may make use of one or both of the following orders in relation to the party who instructed the expert –

(i) that the party may not rely on the evidence of that expert; or

(ii) that the party may not recover the fees and expenses of that expert from any other party.

25.7 Court's power to direct that evidence is to be given by a single joint expert

(1) Where two or more parties wish to submit expert evidence on a particular issue, the court may direct that the evidence on that issue is to be given by a single joint expert.

(2) Where the parties who wish to submit the evidence ('the relevant parties') cannot agree who should be the single joint expert, the court may –

(a) select the expert from a list prepared or identified by the instructing parties; or

(b) direct that the expert be selected in such other manner as the court may direct.

25.8 Instructions to a single joint expert

(1) Where the court gives a direction under rule 25.7(1) for a single joint expert to be used, the instructions are to be contained in a jointly agreed letter unless the court directs otherwise.

(2) Where the instructions are to be contained in a jointly agreed letter, in default of agreement the instructions may be determined by the court on the written request of any relevant party copied to the other relevant parties.

(3) Where the court permits the relevant parties to give separate instructions to a single joint expert, each instructing party must, when giving instructions to the expert, at the same time send a copy of the instructions to the other relevant parties.

(4) The court may give directions about –

(a) the payment of the expert's fees and expenses; and

(b) any inspection, examination or assessments which the expert wishes to carry out.

(5) The court may, before an expert is instructed, limit the amount that can be paid by way of fees and expenses to the expert.

(6) Unless the court directs otherwise, the relevant parties are jointly and severally liable for the payment of the expert's fees and expenses.

PART II – Statutory Instruments

25.9 Power of court to direct a party to provide information

(1) Subject to paragraph (2), where a party has access to information which is not reasonably available to another party, the court may direct the party who has access to the information to prepare, file and serve a document recording the information.

(2) In proceedings under Part 14 (procedure for applications in adoption, placement and related proceedings) –

- (a)   the court may direct the party with access to the information to prepare and file a document recording the information; and
- (b)   a court officer will send a copy of that document to the other party.

25.10 Contents of report

(1) An expert's report must comply with the requirements set out in Practice Direction 25A.

(2) At the end of an expert's report there must be a statement that the expert understands and has complied with their duty to the court.

(3) The instructions to the expert are not privileged against disclosure.

(Rule 21.1 explains what is meant by disclosure.)

25.11 Use by one party of expert's report disclosed by another

Where a party has disclosed an expert's report, any party may use that expert's report as evidence at any relevant hearing.

25.12 Discussions between experts

(1) The court may, at any stage, direct a discussion between experts for the purpose of requiring the experts to –

- (a)   identify and discuss the expert issues in the proceedings; and
- (b)   where possible, reach an agreed opinion on those issues.

(2) The court may specify the issues which the experts must discuss.

(3) The court may direct that following a discussion between the experts they must prepare a statement for the court setting out those issues on which –

- (a)   they agree; and
- (b)   they disagree,

with a summary of their reasons for disagreeing.

25.13 Expert's right to ask court for directions

(1) Experts may file written requests for directions for the purpose of assisting them in carrying out their functions.

(2) Experts must, unless the court directs otherwise, provide copies of the proposed request for directions under paragraph (1) –

    (a)   to the party instructing them, at least 7 days before they file the requests; and

    (b)   to all other parties, at least 4 days before they file them.

(3) The court, when it gives directions, may also direct that a party be served with a copy of the directions.

25.14 Assessors

(1) This rule applies where the court appoints one or more persons under section 70 of the Senior Courts Act 1981 or section 63 of the County Courts Act 1984 as an assessor

(2) An assessor will assist the court in dealing with a matter in which the assessor has skill and experience.

(3) The assessor will take such part in the proceedings as the court may direct and in particular the court may direct an assessor to –

    (a)   prepare a report for the court on any matter at issue in the proceedings; and

    (b)   attend the whole or any part of the hearing to advise the court on any such matter.

(4) If the assessor prepares a report for the court before the hearing has begun –

    (a)   the court will send a copy to each of the parties; and

    (b)   the parties may use it at the hearing.

(5) Unless the court directs otherwise, an assessor will be paid at the daily rate payable for the time being to a fee-paid deputy district judge of the principal registry and an assessor's fees will form part of the costs of the proceedings.

(6) The court may order any party to deposit in the court office a specified sum in respect of an assessor's fees and, where it does so, the assessor will not be asked to act until the sum has been deposited.

(7) Paragraphs (5) and (6) do not apply where the remuneration of the assessor is to be paid out of money provided by Parliament.

Practice Direction 25A –
Experts and Assessors in Family Proceedings

This Practice Direction supplements FPR Part 25

Introduction

1.1 Sections 1 to 9 of this Practice Direction deal with the use of expert evidence and the instruction of experts, and section 10 deals with the appointment of assessors, in all types of family proceedings. The guidance incorporates and supersedes the *Practice Direction on Experts in Family Proceedings relating to Children* (1 April 2008) and other relevant guidance with effect on and from 6 April 2011.

Where the guidance refers to 'an expert' or 'the expert', this includes a reference to an expert team.

1.2 For the purposes of this guidance, the phrase ' proceedings relating to children' is a convenient description. It is not a legal term of art and has no statutory force. In this guidance it means –

    (a)   placement and adoption proceedings; or

    (b)   family proceedings which –

        (i)   relate to the exercise of the inherent jurisdiction of the High Court with respect to children;

        (ii)   are brought under the Children Act 1989 in any family court; or

        (iii)   are brought in the High Court and county courts and 'otherwise relate wholly or mainly to the maintenance or upbringing of a minor'.

AIMS OF THE GUIDANCE ON EXPERTS AND EXPERT EVIDENCE

1.3 The aim of the guidance in sections 1 to 9 is to –

    (a)   provide the court with early information to determine whether expert evidence or assistance will help the court;

    (b)   help the court and the parties to identify and narrow the issues in the case and encourage agreement where possible;

    (c)   enable the court and the parties to obtain an expert opinion about a question that is not within the skill and experience of the court;

    (d)   encourage the early identification of questions that need to be answered by an expert; and

    (e)   encourage disclosure of full and frank information between the parties, the court and any expert instructed.

1.4 The guidance does not aim to cover all possible eventualities. Thus it should be complied with so far as consistent in all the circumstances with the just disposal of the matter in accordance with the rules and guidance applying to the procedure in question.

PERMISSION TO INSTRUCT AN EXPERT OR TO USE EXPERT EVIDENCE

1.5 The general rule in family proceedings is that the court's permission is required to call an expert or to put in evidence an expert's report: see rule 25.4(1). In addition, in proceedings relating to children, the court's permission is required to instruct an expert: see rule 12.74(1).

1.6 Thee court and the parties must have regard in particular to the following considerations –

    (a)   Proceedings relating to children are confidential and, in the absence of the court's permission, disclosure of information and documents relating to such proceedings may amount to a contempt of court or contravene statutory provisions protecting this confidentiality.

(b) For the purposes of the law of contempt of court, information relating to such proceedings (whether or not contained in a document filed with the court or recorded in any form) may be communicated only to an expert whose instruction by a party has been permitted by the court (see rules 12.73 and 14.14).

(c) In proceedings to which Part 12 of the FPR applies, the court's permission is required to cause the child to be medically or psychiatrically examined or otherwise assessed for the purpose of the preparation of expert evidence for use in the proceedings; where the court's permission has not been given, no evidence arising out of such an examination or assessment may be adduced without the court's permission (see rule 12.20).

1.7 In practice, the need to have the court's permission to disclose information or documents to an expert, or (under rule 12.20) to have the child examined or assessed, means that in proceedings relating to children the court strictly controls the number, fields of expertise and identity of the experts who may be first instructed and then called.

1.8 Before permission is obtained from the court to instruct an expert in proceedings relating to children, it will be necessary for the party seeking permission to make enquiries of the expert in order to provide the court with information to enable it to decide whether to give permission. In practice, enquiries may need to be made of more than one expert for this purpose. This will in turn require each expert to be given sufficient information about the case to decide whether or not he or she is in a position to accept instructions. Such preliminary enquiries, and the disclosure of information about the case which is a necessary part of such enquiries, will not require the court's permission and will not amount to a contempt of court: see sections 4.1 and 4.2 (Preliminary Enquiries of the Expert and Expert's Response to Preliminary Enquiries).

1.9 Section 4 (Proceedings relating to children) gives guidance on applying for the court's permission to instruct an expert, and on instructing the expert, in proceedings relating to children. The court, when granting permission to instruct an expert, will also give directions about the preparation and filing of the expert's report and the attendance of the expert give evidence: see section 4.4 (Draft Order for the relevant hearing).

1.10 In proceedings other than those relating to children, the court's permission is not required to instruct an expert. Section 5 (Proceedings other than those relating to children) gives guidance on instructing an expert, and on seeking the court's permission to use expert evidence, prior to and in such proceedings. Section 5 emphasises that the use of a single joint expert should be considered in all cases where expert evidence is required.

PART II – Statutory Instruments

WHEN SHOULD THE COURT BE ASKED FOR PERMISSION?

1.11 Any application (or proposed application) for permission to instruct an expert or to use expert evidence should be raised with the court – and, where appropriate, with the other parties – as soon as possible. This will normally mean –

(a)   in public law proceedings under the Children Act 1989, by or at the Case Management Conference: see rule 12.25;

(b)   in private law proceedings under the Children Act 1989, by or at the First Hearing Dispute Resolution Appointment: see rule 12.31;

(c)   in placement and adoption proceedings, by or at the First Directions Hearing: see rule 14.8;

(d)   in financial proceedings, by or at the First Appointment: see rule 9.15;

(e)   in defended matrimonial and civil partnership proceedings, by or at the Case Management Hearing: see rules 7.20 and 7.22.

In this practice direction the 'relevant hearing' means any hearing at which the court's permission is sought to instruct an expert or to use expert evidence.

General matters

SCOPE OF THE GUIDANCE

2.1 Sections 1 to 9 of this guidance apply to all experts who are or may be instructed to give or prepare evidence for the purpose of family proceedings in a court in England and Wales. The guidance also applies to those who instruct, or propose to instruct, an expert for such a purpose. Section 10 applies to the appointment of assessors in family proceedings in England and Wales.

2.2 This guidance does not apply to proceedings issued before 6 April 2011 but in any such proceedings the court may direct that this guidance will apply either wholly or partly. This is subject to the overriding objective for the type of proceedings, and to the proviso that such a direction will neither cause further delay nor involve repetition of steps already taken or of decisions already made in the case.

PRE-APPLICATION INSTRUCTION OF EXPERTS

2.3 When experts' reports are commissioned before the commencement of proceedings, it should be made clear to the expert that he or she may in due course be reporting to the court and should therefore consider himself or herself bound by this guidance. A prospective party to family proceedings relating to children (for example, a local authority) should always write a letter of instruction when asking a potential witness for a report or an opinion, whether that request is within proceedings or pre-proceedings (for example, when commissioning specialist assessment materials, reports from a treating expert or other evidential materials); and the letter of instruction should conform to the principles set out in this guidance.

EMERGENCY AND URGENT CASES

2.4 In emergency or urgent cases – for example, where, before formal issue of proceedings, a without-notice application is made to the court during or out of business hours; or where, after proceedings have been issued, a previously unforeseen need for (further) expert evidence arises at short notice – a party may wish to call expert evidence without having complied with all or any part of this guidance. In such circumstances, the party wishing to call the expert evidence must apply forthwith to the court – where possible or appropriate, on notice to the other parties – for directions as to the future steps to be taken in respect of the expert evidence in question.

ORDERS

2.5 Where an order or direction requires an act to be done by an expert, or otherwise affects an expert, the party instructing that expert – or, in the case of a jointly instructed expert, the lead solicitor – must serve a copy of the order or direction on the expert forthwith upon receiving it.

ADULTS WHO MAY BE PROTECTED PARTIES

2.6 The court will investigate as soon as possible any issue as to whether an adult party or intended party to family proceedings lacks capacity (within the meaning of the Mental Capacity Act 2005) to conduct the proceedings. An adult who lacks capacity to act as a party to the proceedings is a protected party and must have a litigation friend to conduct the proceedings on their behalf. The expectation of the Official Solicitor is that the Official Solicitor will only be invited to act for the protected party as litigation friend if there is no other person suitable or willing to act.

2.7 Any issue as to the capacity of an adult to conduct the proceedings must be determined before the court gives any directions relevant to that adult's role in the proceedings.

2.8 Where the adult is a protected party, that party's representative should be involved in any instruction of an expert, including the instruction of an expert to assess whether the adult, although a protected party, is competent to give evidence. The instruction of an expert is a significant step in the proceedings. The representative will wish to consider (and ask the expert to consider), if the protected party is competent to give evidence, their best interests in this regard. The representative may wish to seek advice about 'special measures'. The representative may put forward an argument on behalf of the protected party that the protected party should not give evidence.

2.9 If at any time during the proceedings there is reason to believe that a party may lack capacity to conduct the proceedings, then the court must be notified and directions sought to ensure that this issue is investigated without delay.

CHILD LIKELY TO LACK CAPACITY TO CONDUCT THE PROCEEDINGS ON WHEN HE OR SHE REACHES 18

2.10 Where it appears that a child is –

PART II – Statutory Instruments

(a)   a party to the proceedings and not the subject of them;

(b)   nearing age 18; and

(c)   considered likely to lack capacity to conduct the proceedings when 18,

the court will consider giving directions for the child's capacity in this respect to be investigated.

The Duties of Experts

OVERRIDING DUTY

3.1 An expert in family proceedings has an overriding duty to the court that takes precedence over any obligation to the person from whom the expert has received instructions or by whom the expert is paid.

PARTICULAR DUTIES

3.2 An expert shall have regard to the following, among other, duties –

(a)   to assist the court in accordance with the overriding duty;

(b)   to provide advice to the court that conforms to the best practice of the expert's profession;

(c)   to provide an opinion that is independent of the party or parties instructing the expert;

(d)   to confine the opinion to matters material to the issues between the parties and in relation only to questions that are within the expert's expertise (skill and experience);

(e)   where a question has been put which falls outside the expert's expertise, to state this at the earliest opportunity and to volunteer an opinion as to whether another expert is required to bring expertise not possessed by those already involved or, in the rare case, as to whether a second opinion is required on a key issue and, if possible, what questions should be asked of the second expert;

(f)   in expressing an opinion, to take into consideration all of the material facts including any relevant factors arising from ethnic, cultural, religious or linguistic contexts at the time the opinion is expressed;

(g)   to inform those instructing the expert without delay of any change in the opinion and of the reason for the change.

CONTENT OF THE EXPERT'S REPORT

3.3 The expert's report shall be addressed to the court and prepared and filed in accordance with the court's timetable and shall –

(a)   give details of the expert's qualifications and experience;

(b)   include a statement identifying the document(s) containing the material instructions and the substance of any oral instructions and, as far as necessary to explain any opinions or conclusions expressed in the report, summarising the facts and instructions which are material to the conclusions and opinions expressed;

(c)   state who carried out any test, examination or interview which the expert has used for the report and whether or not the test, examination or interview has been carried out under the expert's supervision;

(d) give details of the qualifications of any person who carried out the test, examination or interview;

(e) in expressing an opinion to the court –

    (i) take into consideration all of the material facts including any relevant factors arising from ethnic, cultural, religious or linguistic contexts at the time the opinion is expressed, identifying the facts, literature and any other material including research material that the expert has relied upon in forming an opinion;

    (ii) describe their own professional risk assessment process and process of differential diagnosis, highlighting factual assumptions, deductions from the factual assumptions, and any unusual, contradictory or inconsistent features of the case;

    (iii) indicate whether any proposition in the report is an hypothesis (in particular a controversial hypothesis), or an opinion deduced in accordance with peer-reviewed and tested technique, research and experience accepted as a consensus in the scientific community;

    (iv) indicate whether the opinion is provisional (or qualified, as the case may be), stating the qualification and the reason for it, and identifying what further information is required to give an opinion without qualification;

(f) where there is a range of opinion on any question to be answered by the expert –

    (i) summarise the range of opinion;

    (ii) identify and explain, within the range of opinions, any 'unknown cause', whether arising from the facts of the case (for example, because there is too little information to form a scientific opinion) or from limited experience or lack of research, peer review or support in the relevant field of expertise;

    (iii) give reasons for any opinion expressed: the use of a balance sheet approach to the factors that support or undermine an opinion can be of great assistance to the court;

(g) contain a summary of the expert's conclusions and opinions;

(h) contain a statement that the expert –

    (i) has no conflict of interest of any kind, other than any conflict disclosed in his or her report;

    (ii) does not consider that any interest disclosed affects his or her suitability as an expert witness on any issue on which he or she has given evidence;

    (iii) will advise the instructing party if, between the date of the expert's report and the final hearing, there is any change in circumstances which affects the expert's answers to (i) or (ii) above;

    (iv) understands their duty to the court and has complied with that duty; and

    (v) is aware of the requirements of Part 25 and this practice direction;

PART II – Statutory Instruments

(i)   be verified by a statement of truth in the following form –

'I confirm that I have made clear which facts and matters referred to in this report are within my own knowledge and which are not. Those that are within my own knowledge I confirm to be true. The opinions I have expressed represent my true and complete professional opinions on the matters to which they refer.'

(Part 17 deals with statements of truth. Rule 17.6 sets out the consequences of verifying a document containing a false statement without an honest belief in its truth.)

Proceedings relating to children

Preparation for the relevant hearing

PRELIMINARY ENQUIRIES OF THE EXPERT

4.1 In good time for the information requested to be available for the relevant hearing or for the advocates' meeting or discussion where one takes place before the relevant hearing, the solicitor for the party proposing to instruct the expert (or lead solicitor or solicitor for the child if the instruction proposed is joint) shall approach the expert with the following information –

(a)   the nature of the proceedings and the issues likely to require determination by the court;

(b)   the questions about which the expert is to be asked to give an opinion (including any ethnic, cultural, religious or linguistic contexts);

(c)   the date when the court is to be asked to give permission for the instruction (or if –– unusually – permission has already been given, the date and details of that permission);

(d)   whether permission is to be asked of the court for the instruction of another expert in the same or any related field (that is, to give an opinion on the same or related questions);

(e)   the volume of reading which the expert will need to undertake;

(f)   whether or not permission has been applied for or given for the expert to examine the child;

(g)   whether or not it will be necessary for the expert to conduct interviews – and, if so, with whom;

(h)   the likely timetable of legal and social work steps;

(i)   in care and supervision proceedings, any dates in the Timetable for the Child which would be relevant to the proposed timetable for the assessment;

(j)   when the expert's report is likely to be required;

(k)   whether and, if so, what date has been fixed by the court for any hearing at which the expert may be required to give evidence (in particular the Final Hearing); and whether it may be possible for the expert to give evidence by telephone conference or video link: see section 8 (Arrangements for experts to give evidence) below;

(l)   the possibility of making, through their instructing solicitors, representations to the court about being named or otherwise identified in any public judgment given by the court.

It is essential that there should be proper co-ordination between the court and the expert when drawing up the case management timetable: the needs of the court should be balanced with the needs of the expert whose forensic work is undertaken as an adjunct to his or her main professional duties.

EXPERT'S RESPONSE TO PRELIMINARY ENQUIRIES

4.2 In good time for the relevant hearing or for the advocates' meeting or discussion where one takes place before the relevant hearing, the solicitors intending to instruct the expert shall obtain confirmation from the expert –

(a)   that acceptance of the proposed instructions will not involve the expert in any conflict of interest;

(b)   that the work required is within the expert's expertise;

(c)   that the expert is available to do the relevant work within the suggested time scale;

(d)   when the expert is available to give evidence, of the dates and times to avoid and, where a hearing date has not been fixed, of the amount of notice the expert will require to make arrangements to come to court (or to give evidence by telephone conference or video link) without undue disruption to his or her normal professional routines;

(e)   of the cost, including hourly or other charging rates, and likely hours to be spent, attending experts' meetings, attending court and writing the report (to include any examinations and interviews);

(f)   of any representations which the expert wishes to make to the court about being named or otherwise identified in any public judgment given by the court.

Where parties have not agreed on the appointment of a single joint expert before the relevant hearing, they should obtain the above confirmations in respect of all experts whom they intend to put to the court for the purposes of rule 25.7(2)(a) as candidates for the appointment.

THE PROPOSAL TO INSTRUCT AN EXPERT

4.3 Any party who proposes to ask the court for permission to instruct an expert shall, by 11 a.m. on the business day before the relevant hearing, file and serve a written proposal to instruct the expert, in the following detail –

(a)   the name, discipline, qualifications and expertise of the expert (by way of C.V. where possible);

(b)   the expert's availability to undertake the work;

(c)   the relevance of the expert evidence sought to be adduced to the issues in the proceedings and the specific questions upon which it is proposed that the expert should give an opinion (including the relevance of any ethnic, cultural, religious or linguistic contexts);

(d)   the timetable for the report;

(e)   the responsibility for instruction;

PART II – Statutory Instruments

(f)   whether or not the expert evidence can properly be obtained by the joint instruction of the expert by two or more of the parties;

(g)   whether the expert evidence can properly be obtained by only one party (for example, on behalf of the child);

(h)   why the expert evidence proposed cannot be given by social services undertaking a core assessment or by the Children's Guardian in accordance with their respective statutory duties;

(i)   the likely cost of the report on an hourly or other charging basis: where possible, the expert's terms of instruction should be made available to the court;

(j)   the proposed apportionment (at least in the first instance) of any jointly instructed expert's fee; when it is to be paid; and, if applicable, whether public funding has been approved.

DRAFT ORDER FOR THE RELEVANT HEARING

4.4 Any party proposing to instruct an expert shall, by **11 a.m. on the business day before the relevant hearing**, submit to the court a draft order for directions dealing in particular with –

(a)   the party who is to be responsible for drafting the letter of instruction and providing the documents to the expert;

(b)   the issues identified by the court and the questions about which the expert is to give an opinion;

(c)   the timetable within which the report is to be prepared, filed and served;

(d)   the disclosure of the report to the parties and to any other expert;

(e)   the organisation of, preparation for and conduct of an experts' discussion;

(f)   the preparation of a statement of agreement and disagreement by the experts following an experts' discussion;

(g)   making available to the court at an early opportunity the expert reports in electronic form;

(h)   the attendance of the expert at court to give oral evidence (alternatively, the expert giving his or her evidence in writing or remotely by video link), whether at or for the Final Hearing or another hearing; unless agreement about the opinions given by the expert is reached at or before the Issues Resolution Hearing ('IRH') or, if no IRH is to be held, by a specified date prior to the hearing at which the expert is to give oral evidence ('the specified date').

Letter of Instruction

4.5 The solicitor or party instructing the expert shall, **within 5 business days after the relevant hearing**, prepare (in agreement with the other parties where appropriate), file and serve a letter of instruction to the expert which shall –

(a)   set out the context in which the expert's opinion is sought (including any ethnic, cultural, religious or linguistic contexts);

(b)   set out the specific questions which the expert is required to answer, ensuring that they –

(i) are within the ambit of the expert's area of expertise;

(ii) do not contain unnecessary or irrelevant detail;

(iii) are kept to a manageable number and are clear, focused and direct; and

(iv) reflect what the expert has been requested to do by the court.

(The Annex to this guidance sets out suggested questions in letters of instruction to (1) child mental health professionals or paediatricians, and (2) adult psychiatrists and applied psychologists, in Children Act 1989 proceedings.)

(c) list the documentation provided, or provide for the expert an indexed and paginated bundle which shall include –

(i) a copy of the order (or those parts of the order) which gives permission for the instruction of the expert, immediately the order becomes available;

(ii) an agreed list of essential reading; and

(iii) a copy of this guidance;

(d) identify any materials provided to the expert which have not been produced either as original medical (or other professional) records or in response to an instruction from a party, and state the source of that material (such materials may contain an assumption as to the standard of proof, the admissibility or otherwise of hearsay evidence, and other important procedural and substantive questions relating to the different purposes of other enquiries, for example, criminal or disciplinary proceedings);

(e) identify all requests to third parties for disclosure and their responses, to avoid partial disclosure, which tends only to prove a case rather than give full and frank information;

(f) identify the relevant people concerned with the proceedings (for example, the treating clinicians) and inform the expert of his or her right to talk to them provided that an accurate record is made of the discussions;

(g) identify any other expert instructed in the proceedings and advise the expert of their right to talk to the other experts provided that an accurate record is made of the discussions;

(h) subject to any public funding requirement for prior authority, define the contractual basis upon which the expert is retained and in particular the funding mechanism including how much the expert will be paid (an hourly rate and overall estimate should already have been obtained), when the expert will be paid, and what limitation there might be on the amount the expert can charge for the work which they will have to do. In cases where the parties are publicly funded, there should also be a brief explanation of the costs and expenses excluded from public funding by Funding Code criterion 1.3 and the detailed assessment process.

ASKING THE COURT TO SETTLE THE LETTER OF INSTRUCTION TO A SINGLE
JOINT EXPERT

4.6 Where possible, the written request for the court to consider the letter of
instruction referred to in rule 25.8(2) should be set out in an e-mail to the court
(or, by prior arrangement, directly to the judge dealing with the proceedings)
and copied by e-mail to the other instructing parties. In the Family Proceedings
Court, the request should be sent to the legal adviser who will refer it to the
appropriate judge or justices, if necessary). The court will settle the letter of
instruction, usually without a hearing to avoid delay; and will send (where
practicable, by e-mail) the settled letter to the lead solicitor for transmission
forthwith to the expert, and copy it to the other instructing parties for
information.

KEEPING THE EXPERT UP TO DATE WITH NEW DOCUMENTS

4.7 As often as may be necessary, the expert should be provided promptly with
a copy of any new document filed at court, together with an updated document
list or bundle index.

Proceedings other than those relating to children

5.1 Wherever possible, expert evidence should be obtained from a single joint
expert instructed by both or all the parties ('SJE'). To that end, a party wishing
to instruct an expert should first give the other party or parties a list of the
names of one or more experts in the relevant speciality whom they consider
suitable to be instructed.

5.2 Within 10 days after receipt of the list of proposed experts, the other party
or parties should indicate any objection to one or more of the named experts
and, if so, supply the name(s) of one or more experts whom they consider
suitable.

5.3 Each party should disclose whether they have already consulted any of the
proposed experts about the issue(s) in question.

5.4 Where the parties cannot agree on the identity of the expert, each party
should think carefully before instructing their own expert because of the costs
implications. Disagreements about the use and identity of an expert may be
better managed by the court in the context of an application for directions (see
paragraphs 5.8 and 5.9 below).

AGREEMENT TO INSTRUCT SEPARATE EXPERTS

5.5 If the parties agree to instruct separate experts –

   (a)   they should agree in advance that the reports will be disclosed; and
   (b)   the instructions to each expert should comply, so far as appropriate,
          with paragraphs 4.5 to 4.7 above (Letter of instruction).

AGREEMENT TO INSTRUCT AN SJE

5.6 If there is agreement to instruct an SJE, **before instructions are given** the
parties should –

(a)	so far as appropriate, comply with the guidance in paragraphs 4.1 (Preliminary inquiries of the expert) and 4.2 (Expert's confirmation in response to preliminary enquiries) above;

(b)	have agreed in what proportion the SJE's fee is to be shared between them (at least in the first instance) and when it is to be paid; and

(c)	if applicable, have obtained agreement for public funding.

4.7 The instructions to the SJE should comply, so far as appropriate, with paragraphs 4.5 to 4.7 above (Letter of instruction).

SEEKING THE COURT'S DIRECTIONS FOR THE USE OF AN SJE

5.8 Where the parties seek the court's directions for the use of an SJE, they should comply, so far as appropriate, with paragraphs 4.1 to 4.4 (Preparation for the relevant hearing) above.

5.9 The instructions to the SJE should comply, so far as appropriate, with paragraphs 4.5 to 4.7 above (Letter of instruction).

The Court's control of expert evidence: consequential issues

WRITTEN QUESTIONS

6.1 Where –

(a)	written questions are put to an expert in accordance with rule 25.6, the court will specify the timetable according to which the expert is to answer the written questions;

(b)	a party sends a written question or questions under rule 25.6 direct to an expert, a copy of the questions must, at the same time, be sent to the other party or parties.

EXPERTS' DISCUSSION OR MEETING: PURPOSE

6.2 In accordance with rule 25.12, the court may, at any stage, direct a discussion between experts for the purpose outlined in paragraph (1) of that rule. Rule 25.12(2) provides that the court may specify the issues which the experts must discuss. The expectation is that those issues will include –

(a)	the reasons for disagreement on any expert question and what, if any, action needs to be taken to resolve any outstanding disagreement or question;

(b)	explanation of existing evidence or additional evidence in order to assist the court to determine the issues.

One of the aims of the specification of those issues for discussion is to limit, wherever possible, the need for the experts to attend court to give oral evidence.

EXPERTS' DISCUSSION OR MEETING: ARRANGEMENTS

6.3 Subject to the directions given by the court under rule 25.12, the solicitor or other professional who is given the responsibility by the court ('the nominated professional') shall – **within 15 business days after the experts' reports have been filed and copied to the other parties** – make arrangements for the experts to meet or communicate. Subject to any specification by the court of the issues which experts must discuss under rule 25.12(2), the following matters should be considered as appropriate –

(a) where permission has been given for the instruction of experts from different disciplines, a global discussion may be held relating to those questions that concern all or most of them;

(b) separate discussions may have to be held among experts from the same or related disciplines, but care should be taken to ensure that the discussions complement each other so that related questions are discussed by all relevant experts;

(c) **5 business days prior to a discussion or meeting**, the nominated professional should formulate an agenda including a list of questions for consideration. The agenda should, subject always to the provisions of rule 25.12(1), focus on those questions which are intended to clarify areas of agreement or disagreement.

Questions which repeat questions asked in the letter of instruction or which seek to rehearse cross-examination in advance of the hearing should be rejected as likely to defeat the purpose of the meeting.

The agenda may usefully take the form of a list of questions to be circulated among the other parties in advance and should comprise all questions that each party wishes the experts to consider.

The agenda and list of questions should be sent to each of the experts **not later than 2 business days before the discussion**;

(d) the nominated professional may exercise his or her discretion to accept further questions after the agenda with list of questions has been circulated to the parties. **Only in exceptional circumstances should questions be added to the agenda within the 2-day period before the meeting. Under no circumstances should any question received on the day of or during the meeting be accepted**. This does not preclude questions arising during the meeting for the purposes of clarification. Strictness in this regard is vital, for adequate notice of the questions enables the parties to identify and isolate the expert issues in the case before the meeting so that the experts' discussion at the meeting can concentrate on those issues;

(e) the discussion should be chaired by the nominated professional. A minute must be taken of the questions answered by the experts. Where the court has given a direction under rule 25.12(3) and subject to that direction, a Statement of Agreement and Disagreement must be prepared which should be agreed and signed by each of the experts who participated in the discussion. In accordance with rule 25.12(3) the statement must contain a summary of the experts' reasons for disagreeing. The statement should be served and filed **not later than 5 business days after the discussion has taken place**;

(f) in each case, whether some or all of the experts participate by telephone conference or video link to ensure that minimum disruption is caused to professional schedules and that costs are minimised.

MEETINGS OR CONFERENCES ATTENDED BY A JOINTLY INSTRUCTED EXPERT

6.4 Jointly instructed experts should not attend any meeting or conference which is not a joint one, unless all the parties have agreed in writing or the court has directed that such a meeting may be held, and it is agreed or directed who is to pay the expert's fees for the meeting or conference. Any meeting or conference attended by a jointly instructed expert should be proportionate to the case.

COURT-DIRECTED MEETINGS INVOLVING EXPERTS IN PUBLIC LAW CHILDREN ACT CASES

6.5 In public law Children Act proceedings, where the court gives a direction that a meeting shall take place between the local authority and any relevant named experts for the purpose of providing assistance to the local authority in the formulation of plans and proposals for the child, the meeting shall be arranged, chaired and minuted in accordance with the directions given by the court.

Positions of the Parties

7.1 Where a party refuses to be bound by an agreement that has been reached at an experts' discussion or meeting, that party must inform the court and the other parties in writing, **within 10 business days after the discussion or meeting or, where an IRH is to be held, not less than 5 business days before the IRH**, of his or her reasons for refusing to accept the agreement.

Arrangements for Experts to give evidence

PREPARATION

8.1 Where the court has directed the attendance of an expert witness, the party who is responsible for the instruction of the expert shall, **by the specified date or, where an IRH is to be held, by the IRH**, ensure that –

(a) a date and time (if possible, convenient to the expert) are fixed for the court to hear the expert's evidence, substantially in advance of the hearing at which the expert is to give oral evidence and no later than a specified date prior to that hearing or, where an IRH is to be held, than the IRH;

(b) if the expert's oral evidence is not required, the expert is notified as soon as possible;

(c) the witness template accurately indicates how long the expert is likely to be giving evidence, in order to avoid the inconvenience of the expert being delayed at court;

(d) consideration is given in each case to whether some or all of the experts participate by telephone conference or video link, or submit their evidence in writing, to ensure that minimum disruption is caused to professional schedules and that costs are minimised.

PART II – Statutory Instruments

EXPERTS ATTENDING COURT

8.2 Where expert witnesses are to be called, all parties shall, **by the specified date or, where an IRH is to be held, by the IRH**, ensure that –

- (a)   the parties' advocates have identified (whether at an advocates' meeting or by other means) the issues which the experts are to address;
- (b)   wherever possible, a logical sequence to the evidence is arranged, with experts of the same discipline giving evidence on the same day;
- (c)   the court is informed of any circumstance where all experts agree but a party nevertheless does not accept the agreed opinion, so that directions can be given for the proper consideration of the experts' evidence and opinion and of the party's reasons for not accepting the agreed opinion;
- (d)   in the exceptional case the court is informed of the need for a witness summons.

Action after the Final Hearing

9.1 **Within 10 business days after the Final Hearing**, the solicitor instructing the expert shall inform the expert in writing of the outcome of the case, and of the use made by the court of the expert's opinion.

9.2 Where the court directs preparation of a transcript, it may also direct that the solicitor instructing the expert shall send a copy to the **expert within 10 business days after receiving the transcript**.

9.3 After a Final Hearing in the Family Proceedings Court, the (lead) solicitor instructing the expert shall send the expert a copy of the court's written reasons for its decision **within 10 business days after receiving the written reasons**.

Appointment of assessors in family proceedings

10.1 The power to appoint one or more assessors to assist the court is conferred on the High Court by section 70(1) of the Senior Courts Act 1981, and on a county court by section 63(1) of the County Courts Act 1984. In practice, these powers have been used in appeals from a district judge or costs judge in costs assessment proceedings – although, in principle, the statutory powers permit one or more assessors to be appointed in any family proceedings where the High Court or a county court sees fit.

10.2 **Not less than 21 days before making any such appointment**, the court will notify each party in writing of the name of the proposed assessor, of the matter in respect of which the assistance of the assessor will be sought and of the qualifications of the assessor to give that assistance.

10.3 Any party may object to the proposed appointment, either personally or in respect of the proposed assessor's qualifications.

10.4 Any such objection must be made in writing and filed and served **within 7 business days of receipt of the notification from the court of the proposed appointment**, and will be taken into account by the court in deciding whether or not to make the appointment.

ANNEX

(drafted by the Family Justice Council)

Suggested questions in letters of instruction to child mental health professional or paediatrician in Children Act 1989 proceedings

A The Child(ren)

1 Please describe the child(ren)'s current health, development and functioning (according to your area of expertise), and identify the nature of any significant changes which have occurred –

- Behavioural
- Emotional
- Attachment organisation
- Social/peer/sibling relationships
- Cognitive/educational
- Physical –
  - Growth, eating, sleep
  - Non-organic physical problems (including wetting and soiling)
  - Injuries
  - Paediatric conditions

2 Please comment on the likely explanation for/aetiology of the child(ren)'s problems/difficulties/injuries –

- History/experiences (including intrauterine influences, and abuse and neglect)
- Genetic/innate/developmental difficulties
- Paediatric/psychiatric disorders

3 Please provide a prognosis and risk if difficulties not addressed above.

4 Please describe the child(ren)'s needs in the light of the above –

- Nature of care-giving
- Education
- Treatment

in the short and long term (subject, where appropriate, to further assessment later).

B The parents/primary carers

5 Please describe the factors and mechanisms which would explain the parents' (or primary carers) harmful or neglectful interactions with the child(ren) (if relevant).

6 What interventions have been tried and what has been the result?

7 Please assess the ability of the parents or primary carers to fulfil the child(ren)'s identified needs now.

8 What other assessments of the parents or primary carers are indicated?

PART II – Statutory Instruments

- Adult mental health assessment
- Forensic risk assessment
- Physical assessment
- Cognitive assessment

9 What, if anything, is needed to assist the parents or primary carers now, within the child(ren)'s time scales and what is the prognosis for change?

- Parenting work
- Support
- Treatment/therapy

C. Alternatives

10 Please consider the alternative possibilities for the fulfilment of the child(ren)'s needs

- What sort of placement
- Contact arrangements

Please consider the advantages, disadvantages and implications of each for the child(ren).

Suggested questions in letters of instruction to adult psychiatrists and applied psychologists in Children Act 1989 proceedings –

1 Does the parent/adult have – whether in his/her history or presentation – a mental illness/disorder (including substance abuse) or other psychological/ emotional difficulty and, if so, what is the diagnosis?
2 How do any/all of the above (and their current treatment if applicable) affect his/her functioning, including interpersonal relationships?
3 If the answer to Q1 is yes, are there any features of either the mental illness or psychological/emotional difficulty or personality disorder which could be associated with risk to others, based on the available evidence base (whether published studies or evidence from clinical experience)?
4 What are the experiences/antecedents/aetiology which would explain his/her difficulties, if any, (taking into account any available evidence base or other clinical experience)?
5 What treatment is indicated, what is its nature and the likely duration?
6 What is his/her capacity to engage in/partake of the treatment/therapy?
7 Are you able to indicate the prognosis for, time scales for achieving, and likely durability of, change?
8 What other factors might indicate positive change?

(It is assumed that this opinion will be based on collateral information as well as interviewing the adult).

****

PART 27
HEARINGS AND DIRECTIONS APPOINTMENTS

27.1 Application of this Part

This Part is subject to any enactment, any provision in these rules or a practice direction.

(Rule 27.4(7) makes additional provision in relation to requirements to stay proceedings where the respondent does not appear and a relevant European regulation or international convention applies)

27.2 Reasons for a decision of the magistrates' courts

(1) This rule applies to proceedings in a magistrates' court.

(2) After a hearing, the court will make its decision as soon as is practicable.

(3) The court must give written reasons for its decision.

(4) Paragraphs (5) and (6) apply where the functions of the court are being performed by –

    (a)   two or three lay justices; or

    (b)   by a single lay justice in accordance with these rules and Practice Direction 2A.

(5) The justices' clerk must, before the court makes an order or refuses an application or request, make notes of –

    (a)   the names of the justice or justices constituting the court by which the decision is made; and

    (b)   in consultation with the justice or justices, the reasons for the court's decision.

(6) The justices' clerk must make a written record of the reasons for the court's decision.

(7) When making an order or refusing an application, the court, or one of the justices constituting the court by which the decision is made, will announce its decision and –

    (a)   the reasons for that decision; or

    (b)   a short explanation of that decision.

(8) Subject to any other rule or practice direction, the court officer will supply a copy of the order and the reasons for the court's decision to the persons referred to in paragraph (9) –

    (a)   by close of business on the day when the court announces its decision; or

    (b)   where that time is not practicable and the proceedings are on notice, no later than 72 hours from the time when the court announced its decision.

(9) The persons referred to in paragraph (8) are –

PART II – Statutory Instruments

(a)   the parties (unless the court directs otherwise);

(b)   any person who has actual care of a child who is the subject of proceedings, or who had such care immediately prior to the making of the order;

(c)   in the case of an emergency protection order and a recovery order, the local authority in whose area the child lives or is found;

(d)   in proceedings to which Part 14 applies –

    (i)   an adoption agency or local authority which has prepared a report on the suitability of the applicant to adopt a child;

    (ii)   a local authority which has prepared a report on the placement of the child for adoption;

(e)   any other person who has requested a copy if the court is satisfied that it is required in connection with an appeal or possible appeal.

(10) In this rule, 'lay justice' means a justice of the peace who is not a District Judge (Magistrates' Courts).

(Rule 12.16(5) provides for the applicant to serve a section 8 order and an order in emergency proceedings made without notice within 48 hours after the making of the order. Rule 10.6(1) provides for the applicant to serve the order in proceedings under Part 4 of the 1996 Act. Rule 4.1(3)(a) permits the court to extend or shorten the time limit for compliance with any rule. Rule 6.33 provides for other persons to be supplied with copy documents under paragraph (8).)

27.3 Attendance at hearing or directions appointment

Unless the court directs otherwise, a party shall attend a hearing or directions appointment of which that party has been given notice.

27.4 Proceedings in the absence of a party

(1) Proceedings or any part of them shall take place in the absence of any party, including a party who is a child, if –

(a)   the court considers it in the interests of the party, having regard to the matters to be discussed or the evidence likely to be given; and

(b)   the party is represented by a children's guardian or solicitor,

and when considering the interests of a child under sub-paragraph (a) the court shall give the children's guardian, the solicitor for the child and, if of sufficient understanding and the court thinks it appropriate, the child, an opportunity to make representations.

(2) Subject to paragraph (3), where at the time and place appointed for a hearing or directions appointment the applicant appears but one or more of the respondents do not, the court may proceed with the hearing or appointment.

(3) The court shall not begin to hear an application in the absence of a respondent unless –

(a)   it is proved to the satisfaction of the court that the respondent received reasonable notice of the date of the hearing; or

(b)   the court is satisfied that the circumstances of the case justify proceeding with the hearing.

(4) Where, at the time and place appointed for a hearing or directions appointment, one or more of the respondents appear but the applicant does not, the court may refuse the application or, if sufficient evidence has previously been received, proceed in the absence of the applicant.

(5) Where, at the time and place appointed for a hearing or directions appointment, neither the applicant nor any respondent appears, the court may refuse the application.

(6) Paragraphs (2) to (5) do not apply to a hearing to which paragraphs (5) to (8) of rule 12.14 do not apply by virtue of paragraph (9) of that rule.

(7) Nothing in this rule affects any provision of a European regulation or international convention by which the United Kingdom is bound which requires a court to stay proceedings where a respondent in another State has not been adequately served with proceedings in accordance with the requirements of that regulation or convention.

27.5 Application to set aside judgment or order following failure to attend

(1) Where a party does not attend a hearing or directions appointment and the court gives judgment or makes an order against him, the party who failed to attend may apply for the judgment or order to be set aside^(GL).

(2) An application under paragraph (1) must be supported by evidence.

(3) Where an application is made under paragraph (1), the court may grant the application only if the applicant –

(a)   acted promptly on finding out that the court had exercised its power to enter judgment or make an order against the applicant;

(b)   had a good reason for not attending the hearing or directions appointment; and

(c)   has a reasonable prospect of success at the hearing or directions appointment.

(4) This rule does not apply to magistrates' courts.

27.6 Court bundles and place of filing of documents and bundles

(1) The provisions of Practice Direction 27A must be followed for the preparation of court bundles and for other related matters in respect of hearings and directions appointments.

(2) Paragraph (3) applies where the file of any family proceedings has been sent from one designated county court or registry to another for the purpose of a hearing or for some other purpose.

PART II – Statutory Instruments

(3) A document needed for the purpose for which the proceedings have been sent to the other court or registry must be filed in that court or registry.

(Practice Direction 27A (Family Proceedings: Court Bundles (Universal Practice to be applied in All Courts other than the Family Proceedings Courts)) does not apply to magistrates' courts.)

27.7 Representation of companies or other corporations

A company or other corporation may be represented at a hearing or directions appointment by an employee if –

(a)   the employee has been authorised by the company or corporation to appear at the hearing or directions appointment on its behalf; and

(b)   the court gives permission.

27.8 Impounded documents

(1) Documents impounded by order of the court must not be released from the custody of the court except in compliance with –

(a)   a court order; or

(b)   a written request made by a Law Officer or the Director of Public Prosecutions.

(2) A document released from the custody of the court under paragraph (1)(b) must be released into the custody of the person who requested it.

(3) Documents impounded by order of the court, while in the custody of the court, may not be inspected except by a person authorised to do so by a court order.

27.9 Official shorthand note etc of proceedings

(1) Unless the judge directs otherwise, an official shorthand note will be taken at the hearing in open court of proceedings pending in the High Court.

(2) An official shorthand note may be taken of any other proceedings before a judge if directions for the taking of such a note are given by the Lord Chancellor.

(3) The shorthand writer will sign the note and certify it to be a correct shorthand note of the proceedings and will retain the note unless directed by the district judge to forward it to the court.

(4) On being so directed, the shorthand writer will furnish the court with a transcript of the whole or such part of the shorthand note as may be directed.

(5) Any party, any person who has intervened in the proceedings, the Queen's Proctor or, where a declaration of parentage has been made under section 55A of the 1986 Act, the Registrar General is entitled to require from the shorthand writer a transcript of the shorthand note, and the shorthand writer will, at the request of any person so entitled, supply that person with a transcript of the

whole or any part of the note on payment of the shorthand writer's charges authorised by any scheme in force providing for the taking of official shorthand notes of legal proceedings.

(6) Save as permitted by this rule, the shorthand writer will not, without the permission of the court, furnish the shorthand note or a transcript of the whole or any part of it to anyone.

(7) In these rules, references to a shorthand note include references to a record of the proceedings made by mechanical means and in relation to such a record references to the shorthand writer include the person responsible for transcribing the record.

27.10 Hearings in private

(1) Proceedings to which these rules apply will be held in private, except –

    (a)   where these rules or any other enactment provide otherwise;

    (b)   subject to any enactment, where the court directs otherwise.

(2) For the purposes of these rules, a reference to proceedings held 'in private' means proceedings at which the general public have no right to be present.

27.11 Attendance at private hearings

(1) This rule applies when proceedings are held in private, except in relation to –

    (a)   hearings conducted for the purpose of judicially assisted conciliation or negotiation;

    (b)   proceedings to which the following provisions apply –

        (i)   Part 13 (proceedings under section 54 of the Human Fertilisation and Embryology Act 2008);

        (ii)   Part 14 (procedure for applications in adoption, placement and related proceedings); and

        (iii)   any proceedings identified in a practice direction as being excepted from this rule.

(2) When this rule applies, no person shall be present during any hearing other than –

    (a)   an officer of the court;

    (b)   a party to the proceedings;

    (c)   a litigation friend for any party, or legal representative instructed to act on that party's behalf;

    (d)   an officer of the service or Welsh family proceedings officer;

    (e)   a witness;

    (f)   duly accredited representatives of news gathering and reporting organisations; and

    (g)   any other person whom the court permits to be present.

PART II – Statutory Instruments

(3) At any stage of the proceedings the court may direct that persons within paragraph (2)(f) shall not attend the proceedings or any part of them, where satisfied that –

(a)   this is necessary –
    (i)   in the interests of any child concerned in, or connected with, the proceedings;
    (ii)   for the safety or protection of a party, a witness in the proceedings, or a person connected with such a party or witness; or
    (iii)   for the orderly conduct of the proceedings; or
(b)   justice will otherwise be impeded or prejudiced.

(4) The court may exercise the power in paragraph (3) of its own initiative or pursuant to representations made by any of the persons listed in paragraph (5), and in either case having given to any person within paragraph (2)(f) who is in attendance an opportunity to make representations.

(5) At any stage of the proceedings, the following persons may make representations to the court regarding restricting the attendance of persons within paragraph (2)(f) in accordance with paragraph (3) –

(a)   a party to the proceedings;
(b)   any witness in the proceedings;
(c)   where appointed, any children's guardian;
(d)   where appointed, an officer of the service or Welsh family proceedings officer, on behalf of the child the subject of the proceedings;
(e)   the child, if of sufficient age and understanding.

(6) This rule does not affect any power of the court to direct that witnesses shall be excluded until they are called for examination.

(7) In this rule 'duly accredited' refers to accreditation in accordance with any administrative scheme for the time being approved for the purposes of this rule by the Lord Chancellor.

Practice Direction 27A –
Family Proceedings: Court Bundles (Universal Practice to be applied in All Courts other than the Family Proceedings Court)

This Practice Direction supplements FPR Part 27

1 The President of the Family Division has issued this practice direction to achieve consistency across the country in all family courts (other than the Family Proceedings Court) in the preparation of court bundles and in respect of other related matters.

Application of the practice direction

2.1 Except as specified in para 2.4, and subject to specific directions given in any particular case, the following practice applies to –

(a) all hearings of whatever nature (including but not limited to hearings in family proceedings, Civil Procedure Rules 1998 Part 7 and Part 8 claims and appeals) before a judge of the Family Division of the High Court wherever the court may be sitting;

(b) all hearings in family proceedings in the Royal Courts of Justice (RCJ);

(c) all hearings in the Principal Registry of the Family Division (PRFD) at First Avenue House; and

(d) all hearings in family proceedings in all other courts except for Family Proceedings Courts.

2.2 'Hearings' includes all appearances before a judge or district judge, whether with or without notice to other parties and whether for directions or for substantive relief.

2.3 This practice direction applies whether a bundle is being lodged for the first time or is being re-lodged for a further hearing (see para 9.2).

2.4 This practice direction does not apply to –

(a) cases listed for one hour or less at a court referred to in para 2.1(c) or 2.1(d); or

(b) the hearing of any urgent application if and to the extent that it is impossible to comply with it.

2.5 The designated family judge responsible for any court referred to in para 2.1(c) or 2.1(d) may, after such consultation as is appropriate (but in the case of hearings in the PRFD at First Avenue House only with the agreement of the Senior District Judge), direct that in that court this practice direction shall apply to all family proceedings irrespective of the length of hearing.

Responsibility for the preparation of the bundle

3.1 A bundle for the use of the court at the hearing shall be provided by the party in the position of applicant at the hearing (or, if there are cross-applications, by the party whose application was first in time) or, if that person is a litigant in person, by the first listed respondent who is not a litigant in person.

3.2 The party preparing the bundle shall paginate it. If possible the contents of the bundle shall be agreed by all parties.

Contents of the bundle

4.1 The bundle shall contain copies of all documents relevant to the hearing, in chronological order from the front of the bundle, paginated and indexed, and divided into separate sections (each section being separately paginated) as follows –

PART II – Statutory Instruments

(a)   preliminary documents (see para 4.2) and any other case management documents required by any other practice direction;

(b)   applications and orders;

(c)   statements and affidavits (which must be dated in the top right corner of the front page);

(d)   care plans (where appropriate);

(e)   experts' reports and other reports (including those of a guardian, children's guardian or litigation friend); and

(f)   other documents, divided into further sections as may be appropriate.

Copies of notes of contact visits should normally not be included in the bundle unless directed by a judge.

4.2 At the commencement of the bundle there shall be inserted the following documents (the preliminary documents) –

(i)   an up to date summary of the background to the hearing confined to those matters which are relevant to the hearing and the management of the case and limited, if practicable, to one A4 page;

(ii)   a statement of the issue or issues to be determined (1) at that hearing and (2) at the final hearing;

(iii)   a position statement by each party including a summary of the order or directions sought by that party (1) at that hearing and (2) at the final hearing;

(iv)   an up to date chronology, if it is a final hearing or if the summary under (i) is insufficient;

(v)   skeleton arguments, if appropriate, with copies of all authorities relied on; and

(vi)   a list of essential reading for that hearing.

4.3 Each of the preliminary documents shall state on the front page immediately below the heading the date when it was prepared and the date of the hearing for which it was prepared.

4.4 The summary of the background, statement of issues, chronology, position statement and any skeleton arguments shall be cross-referenced to the relevant pages of the bundle.

4.5 The summary of the background, statement of issues, chronology and reading list shall in the case of a final hearing, and shall so far as practicable in the case of any other hearing, each consist of a single document in a form agreed by all parties. Where the parties disagree as to the content the fact of their disagreement and their differing contentions shall be set out at the appropriate places in the document.

4.6 Where the nature of the hearing is such that a complete bundle of all documents is unnecessary, the bundle (which need not be repaginated) may comprise only those documents necessary for the hearing, but –

(i)   the summary (para 4.2(i)) must commence with a statement that the bundle is limited or incomplete; and

(ii) the bundle shall if reasonably practicable be in a form agreed by all parties.

4.7 Where the bundle is re-lodged in accordance with para 9.2, before it is re-lodged –

(a) the bundle shall be updated as appropriate; and

(b) all superseded documents (and in particular all outdated summaries, statements of issues, chronologies, skeleton arguments and similar documents) shall be removed from the bundle.

Format of the bundle

5.1 The bundle shall be contained in one or more A4 size ring binders or lever arch files (each lever arch file being limited to 350 pages).

5.2 All ring binders and lever arch files shall have clearly marked on the front and the spine –

(a) the title and number of the case;

(b) the court where the case has been listed;

(c) the hearing date and time;

(d) if known, the name of the judge hearing the case; and

(e) where there is more than one ring binder or lever arch file, a distinguishing letter (A, B, C etc).

Timetable for preparing and lodging the bundle

6.1 The party preparing the bundle shall, whether or not the bundle has been agreed, provide a paginated index to all other parties not less than 4 working days before the hearing (in relation to a case management conference to which the provisions of the *Protocol for Judicial Case Management in Public Law Children Act Cases* [2003] 2 FLR 719 apply, not less than 5 working days before the case management conference).

6.2 Where counsel is to be instructed at any hearing, a paginated bundle shall (if not already in counsel's possession) be delivered to counsel by the person instructing that counsel not less than 3 working days before the hearing.

6.3 The bundle (with the exception of the preliminary documents if and insofar as they are not then available) shall be lodged with the court not less than 2 working days before the hearing, or at such other time as may be specified by the judge.

6.4 The preliminary documents shall be lodged with the court no later than 11 am on the day before the hearing and, where the hearing is before a judge of the High Court and the name of the judge is known, shall at the same time be sent by email to the judge's clerk.

Lodging the bundle

7.1 The bundle shall be lodged at the appropriate office. If the bundle is lodged in the wrong place the judge may –

(a) treat the bundle as having not been lodged; and

PART II – Statutory Instruments

(b)   take the steps referred to in para 12.

7.2 Unless the judge has given some other direction as to where the bundle in any particular case is to be lodged (for example a direction that the bundle is to be lodged with the judge's clerk) the bundle shall be lodged –

(a)   for hearings in the RCJ, in the office of the Clerk of the Rules, Room TM 9.09, Royal Courts of Justice, Strand, London WC2A 2LL (DX 44450 Strand);

(b)   for hearings in the PRFD at First Avenue House, at the List Office counter, 3rd floor, First Avenue House, 42/49 High Holborn, London, WC1V 6NP (DX 396 Chancery Lane); and

(c)   for hearings at any other court, at such place as may be designated by the designated family judge or other judge at that court and in default of any such designation at the court office of the court where the hearing is to take place.

7.3 Any bundle sent to the court by post, DX or courier shall be clearly addressed to the appropriate office and shall show the date and place of the hearing on the outside of any packaging as well as on the bundle itself.

Lodging the bundle – additional requirements for cases being heard at First Avenue House or at the RCJ

8.1 In the case of hearings at the RCJ or First Avenue House, parties shall –

(a)   if the bundle or preliminary documents are delivered personally, ensure that they obtain a receipt from the clerk accepting it or them; and

(b)   if the bundle or preliminary documents are sent by post or DX, ensure that they obtain proof of posting or despatch.

The receipt (or proof of posting or despatch, as the case may be) shall be brought to court on the day of the hearing and must be produced to the court if requested. If the receipt (or proof of posting or despatch) cannot be produced to the court the judge may: (i) treat the bundle as having not been lodged; and (ii) take the steps referred to in para 12.

8.2 For hearings at the RCJ –

(a)   bundles or preliminary documents delivered after 11 am on the day before the hearing will not be accepted by the Clerk of the Rules and shall be delivered –

(i)   in a case where the hearing is before a judge of the High Court, directly to the clerk of the judge hearing the case;

(ii)   in a case where the hearing is before a Circuit Judge, Deputy High Court Judge or Recorder, directly to the messenger at the Judge's entrance to the Queen's Building (with telephone notification to the personal assistant to the Designated Family Judge, 020 7947 7155, that this has been done).

(b)   upon learning before which judge a hearing is to take place, the clerk to counsel, or other advocate, representing the party in the position of applicant shall no later than 3 pm the day before the hearing –

(i)   in a case where the hearing is before a judge of the High Court, telephone the clerk of the judge hearing the case;

(ii) in a case where the hearing is before a circuit judge, deputy high court judge or recorder, telephone the personal assistant to the designated family judge;

to ascertain whether the judge has received the bundle (including the preliminary documents) and, if not, shall organise prompt delivery by the applicant's solicitor.

Removing and re-lodging the bundle

9.1 Following completion of the hearing the party responsible for the bundle shall retrieve it from the court immediately or, if that is not practicable, shall collect it from the court within 5 working days. Bundles which are not collected in due time may be destroyed.

9.2 The bundle shall be re-lodged for the next and any further hearings in accordance with the provisions of this practice direction and in a form which complies with para 4.7.

Time estimates

10.1 In every case a time estimate (which shall be inserted at the front of the bundle) shall be prepared which shall so far as practicable be agreed by all parties and shall –

(a)   specify separately: (i) the time estimated to be required for judicial pre-reading; and (ii) the time required for hearing all evidence and submissions; and (iii) the time estimated to be required for preparing and delivering judgment; and

(b)   be prepared on the basis that before they give evidence all witnesses will have read all relevant filed statements and reports.

10.2 Once a case has been listed, any change in time estimates shall be notified immediately by telephone (and then immediately confirmed in writing) –

(a)   in the case of hearings in the RCJ, to the Clerk of the Rules;

(b)   in the case of hearings in the PRFD at First Avenue House, to the List Officer at First Avenue House; and

(c)   in the case of hearings elsewhere, to the relevant listing officer.

Taking cases out of the list

11 As soon as it becomes known that a hearing will no longer be effective, whether as a result of the parties reaching agreement or for any other reason, the parties and their representatives shall immediately notify the court by telephone and by letter. The letter, which shall wherever possible be a joint letter sent on behalf of all parties with their signatures applied or appended, shall include –

(a)   a short background summary of the case;

(b)   the written consent of each party who consents and, where a party does not consent, details of the steps which have been taken to obtain that party's consent and, where known, an explanation of why that consent has not been given;

(c)   a draft of the order being sought; and

(d)   enough information to enable the court to decide (i) whether to take the case out of the list and (ii) whether to make the proposed order.

Penalties for failure to comply with the practice direction

12 Failure to comply with any part of this practice direction may result in the judge removing the case from the list or putting the case further back in the list and may also result in a 'wasted costs' order in accordance with CPR, Part 48.7 or some other adverse costs order.

Commencement of the practice direction and application of other practice directions

13 This practice direction replaces *Practice Direction (Family Proceedings: Court Bundles) (10 March 2000)* [2000] 1 WLR 737, [2000] 1 FLR 536 and shall have effect from 2 October 2006.

14 Any reference in any other practice direction to *Practice Direction (Family Proceedings: Court Bundles) (10 March 2000)* shall be read as if substituted by a reference to this practice direction.

15 This practice direction should where appropriate be read in conjunction with *Practice Direction (Family Proceedings: Human Rights)* [2000] 1 WLR 1782, [2000] 2 FLR 429 and with *Practice Direction (Care Cases: Judicial Continuity and Judicial Case Management)* appended to the *Protocol for Judicial Case Management in Public Law Children Act Cases*. In particular, nothing in this practice direction is to be read as removing or altering any obligation to comply with the requirements of the *Public Law Protocol*.

This Practice Direction is issued –

(i)   in relation to family proceedings, by the President of the Family Division, as the nominee of the Lord Chief Justice, with the agreement of the Lord Chancellor; and

(ii)   to the extent that it applies to proceedings to which s 5 of the Civil Procedure Act 1997 applies, by the Master of the Rolls as the nominee of the Lord Chief Justice, with the agreement of the Lord Chancellor.

Practice Direction 27B –
Attendance of Media Representatives at Hearings in Family Proceedings (High Court and County Courts)

This Practice Direction supplements FPR Part 27

1 Introduction

1.1 This Practice Direction supplements rule 27.11 of the Family Procedure Rules 2010 ('FPR 2010') and deals with the right of representatives of news gathering and reporting organisations ('media representatives') to attend at hearings of family proceedings which take place in private subject to the discretion of the court to exclude such representatives from the whole or part of any hearing on specified grounds[1] It takes effect on 27 April 2009.

2 Matters unchanged by the rule

2.1 Rule 27.11(1) contains an express exception in respect of hearings which are conducted for the purpose of judicially assisted conciliation or negotiation and media representatives do not have a right to attend these hearings. Financial Dispute Resolution hearings will come within this exception. First Hearing Dispute Resolution appointments in private law Children Act cases will also come within this exception to the extent that the judge plays an active part in the conciliation process. Where the judge plays no part in the conciliation process or where the conciliation element of a hearing is complete and the judge is adjudicating upon the issues between the parties, media representatives should be permitted to attend, subject to the discretion of the court to exclude them on the specified grounds. Conciliation meetings or negotiation conducted between the parties with the assistance of an officer of the service or a Welsh Family Proceedings officer, and without the presence of the judge, are not 'hearings' within the meaning of this rule and media representatives have no right to attend such appointments.

The exception in rule 27.11(1) does not operate to exclude media representatives from –

- Hearings to consider applications brought under Parts IV and V of the Children Act 1989, including Case Management Conferences and Issues Resolution Hearings
- Hearings relating to findings of fact
- Interim hearings
- Final hearings.

The rights of media representatives to attend such hearings are limited only by the powers of the court to exclude such attendance on the limited grounds and subject to the procedures set out in paragraphs (3)–(5) of rule 27.11.

2.2 During any hearing, courts should consider whether the exception in rule 27.11(1) becomes applicable so that media representatives should be directed to withdraw.

2.3 The provisions of the rules permitting the attendance of media representatives and the disclosure to third parties of information relating to the proceedings do not entitle a media representative to receive or peruse court documents referred to in the course of evidence, submissions or judgment without the permission of the court or otherwise in accordance with Part 12, Chapter 7 of the Family Procedure Rules 2010 and Practice Direction 12G (rules relating to disclosure to third parties). (This is in contrast to the position

PART II – Statutory Instruments

in civil proceedings, where the court sits in public and where members of the public are entitled to seek copies of certain documents[1]).

1   See *GIO Services Ltd v Liverpool and London Ltd* [1999] 1 WLR 984.

2.4 The question of attendance of media representatives at hearings in family proceedings to which rule 27.11 and this guidance apply must be distinguished from statutory restrictions on publication and disclosure of information relating to proceedings, which continue to apply and are unaffected by the rule and this guidance.

2.5 The prohibition in section 97(2) of the Children Act 1989, on publishing material intended to or likely to identify a child as being involved in proceedings or the address or school of any such child, is limited to the duration of the proceedings[1]. However, the limitations imposed by section 12 of the Administration of Justice Act 1960 on publication of information relating to certain proceedings in private[2] apply during and after the proceedings. In addition, in proceedings to which s 97(2) of the Children Act 1989 applies the court should continue to consider at the conclusion of the proceedings whether there are any outstanding welfare issues which require a continuation of the protection afforded during the course of the proceedings by that provision.

1   See *Clayton v Clayton* [2006] EWCA Civ 878.
2   In particular proceedings which –
    (a)   relate to the exercise of the inherent jurisdiction of the High Court with respect to minors;
    (b)   are brought under the Children Act 1989; or
    (c)   otherwise relate wholly or mainly to the maintenance or upbringing of a minor.

3 Aims of the guidance

3.1 This Practice Direction is intended to provide guidance regarding –

- the handling of applications to exclude media representatives from the whole or part of a hearing; and
- the exercise of the court's discretion to exclude media representatives whether upon the court's own motion or any such application.

3.2 While the guidance does not aim to cover all possible eventualities, it should be complied with so far as consistent in all the circumstances with the just determination of the proceedings.

4 Identification of media representatives as 'accredited'

4.1 Media representatives will be expected to carry with them identification sufficient to enable court staff, or if necessary the court itself, to verify that they are 'accredited' representatives of news gathering or reporting organisations within the meaning of the rule.

4.2 By virtue of paragraph (7) of the rule, it is for the Lord Chancellor to approve a scheme which will provide for accreditation. The Lord Chancellor has decided that the scheme operated by the UK Press Card Authority provides sufficient accreditation; a card issued under that scheme will be the expected form of identification, and production of the Card will be both necessary and sufficient to demonstrate accreditation.

4.3 A media representative unable to demonstrate accreditation in accordance with the UK Press Card Authority scheme, so as to be able to attend by virtue of paragraph (2)(f) of the rule, may nevertheless be permitted to attend at the court's discretion under paragraph (2)(g).

5 Exercise of the discretion to exclude media representatives from all or part of the proceedings

5.1 The rule anticipates and should be applied on the basis that media representatives have a right to attend family proceedings throughout save and to the extent that the court exercises its discretion to exclude them from the whole or part of any proceedings on one or more of the grounds set out in paragraph (3) of the rule.

5.2 When considering the question of exclusion on any of the grounds set out in paragraph (3) of the rule the court should –

- specifically identify whether the risk to which such ground is directed arises from the mere fact of media presence at the particular hearing or hearings the subject of the application or whether the risk identified can be adequately addressed by exclusion of media representatives from a part only of such hearing or hearings;
- consider whether the reporting or disclosure restrictions which apply by operation of law, or which the court otherwise has power to order will provide sufficient protection to the party on whose behalf the application is made or any of the persons referred to in paragraph (3)(a) of the rule;
- consider the safety of the parties in cases in which the court considers there are particular physical or health risks against which reporting restrictions may be inadequate to afford protection;
- in the case of any vulnerable adult or child who is unrepresented before the court, consider the extent to which the court should of its own motion take steps to protect the welfare of that adult or child.

5.3 Paragraph (3)(a)(iii) of the rule permits exclusion where necessary 'for the orderly conduct of proceedings'. This enables the court to address practical problems presented by media attendance. In particular, it may be difficult or even impossible physically to accommodate all (or indeed any) media representatives who wish to attend a particular hearing on the grounds of the restricted size or layout of the court room in which it is being heard. Court staff will use their best efforts to identify more suitable accommodation in advance of any hearing which appears likely to attract particular media attention, and to move hearings to larger court rooms where possible. However, the court should not be required to adjourn a hearing in order for larger accommodation to be sought where this will involve significant disruption or delay in the proceedings.

PART II – Statutory Instruments

5.4 Paragraph (3)(b) of the rule permits exclusion where, unless the media are excluded, justice will be impeded or prejudiced for some reason other than those set out in sub-paragraph (a). Reasons of administrative inconvenience are not sufficient. Examples of circumstances where the impact on justice of continued attendance might be sufficient to necessitate exclusion may include –

- a hearing relating to the parties' finances where the information being considered includes price sensitive information (such as confidential information which could affect the share price of a publicly quoted company); or
- any hearing at which a witness (other than a party) states for credible reasons that he or she will not give evidence in front of media representatives, or where there appears to the court to be a significant risk that a witness will not give full or frank evidence in the presence of media representatives.

5.5 In the event of a decision to exclude media representatives, the court should state brief reasons for the decision.

6 Applications to exclude media representatives from all or part of proceedings

6.1 The court may exclude media representatives on the permitted grounds of its own motion or after hearing representations from the interested persons listed at paragraph (5) of the rule. Where exclusion is proposed, any media representatives who are present are entitled to make representations about that proposal. There is, however, no requirement to adjourn proceedings to enable media representatives who are not present to attend in order to make such representations, and in such a case the court should not adjourn unless satisfied of the necessity to do so having regard to the additional cost and delay which would thereby be caused.

6.2 Applications to exclude media representatives should normally be dealt with as they arise and by way of oral representations, unless the court directs otherwise.

6.3 When media representatives are expected to attend a particular hearing (for example, where a party is encouraging media interest and attendance) and a party intends to apply to the court for the exclusion of the media, that party should, if practicable, give advance notice to the court, to the other parties and (where appointed) any children's guardian, officer of the service or Welsh Family Proceedings officer, NYAS or other representative of the child of any intention to seek the exclusion of media representatives from all or part of the proceedings. Equally, legal representatives and parties should ensure that witnesses are aware of the right of media representatives to attend and should notify the court at an early stage of the intention of any witness to request the exclusion of media representatives

6.4 Prior notification by the court of a pending application for exclusion will not be given to media interests unless the court so directs. However, where such an application has been made, the applicant must where possible, notify the relevant media organisations [and should do so by means of the Press

Association CopyDirect service, following the procedure set out in the Official Solicitor/CAFCASS *Practice Note* dated 18 March 2005][1].

NOTES

Amendments.[1] The additional words were added by the President in *Re Child X* (above), paragraph 87.

Practice Direction 27C –
Attendance of Media Representatives at Hearings in Family Proceedings (Family Proceedings Court)

This Practice Direction supplements FPR Part 27

1 Introduction

1.1 This Practice Direction supplements rule 27.11 of the Family Procedure Rules 2010 ('the Rules') and deals with the right of representatives of news gathering and reporting organisations ('media representatives') to attend at hearings of relevant proceedings[1] subject to the discretion of the court to exclude such representatives from the whole or part of any hearing on specified grounds.[2] It takes effect on 27th April 2009. References to a 'hearing' within this Practice Direction include reference to a directions appointment, whether conducted by the justices, a district judge or a justices' clerk.

1 'relevant proceedings' are defined in rule 1 of the Rules by reference to section 93(3) of the Children Act 1989.
2 It does not, accordingly, apply where hearings are held in open court where the general public including media representatives attend as of right.

2 Matters unchanged by the rule

2.1 Rule 27.11(1) contains an express exception in respect of hearings which are conducted for the purpose of judicially assisted conciliation or negotiation and media representatives do not have a right to attend these hearings. First Hearing Dispute Resolution appointments in private law Children Act cases will come within this exception to the extent that the justices, a district judge or a justices' clerk play an active part in the conciliation process. Where the justices, a district judge or a justices' clerk play no part in the conciliation process or where the conciliation element of a hearing is complete and the court is adjudicating upon the issues between the parties, media representatives should be permitted to attend subject to the discretion of the court to exclude them on the specified grounds. Conciliation meetings or negotiation conducted between the parties with the assistance of an officer of the service or a Welsh Family Proceedings officer, and without the presence of the justices, a district judge or a justices' clerk, are not 'hearings' within the meaning of this rule and media representatives have no right to attend such appointments.

The exception in rule 27.11(1) does not operate to exclude media representatives from –

- Hearings to consider applications brought under Parts IV and V of the Children Act 1989, including Case Management Conferences and Issues Resolution Hearings
- Hearings relating to findings of fact
- Interim hearings
- Final hearings.

The rights of media representatives to attend such hearings are limited only by the powers of the court to exclude such attendance on the limited grounds and subject to the procedures set out in paragraphs (3) to (5) of rule 27.11.

2.2 During any hearing, the court should consider whether the exception in rule 27.11(1) becomes applicable so that media representatives should be directed to withdraw.

2.3 The provisions of the rules permitting the attendance of media representatives and the disclosure to third parties of information relating to the proceedings do not entitle a media representative to receive or peruse court documents referred to in the course of evidence, submissions or decisions of the court (in particular, written reasons) without the permission of the court or otherwise in accordance with Part 12, Chapter 7 of the Family Procedure Rules 2010 and Practice Direction 12G.

2.4 The question of attendance of media representatives at hearings in family proceedings to which rule 27.11 and this guidance apply must be distinguished from statutory restrictions on publication and disclosure of information relating to proceedings, which continue to apply and are unaffected by the rule and this guidance.

2.5 The prohibition in section 97(2) of the Children Act 1989, on publishing material intended to or likely to identify a child as being involved in proceedings or the address or school of any such child, is limited to the duration of the proceedings[1]. However, the limitations imposed by section 12 of the Administration of Justice Act 1960 on publication of information relating to certain proceedings in private[2] apply during and after the proceedings. In addition, in the course of proceedings to which s 97(2) of the Children Act 1989 applies the court should consider whether at the conclusion of the proceedings there may be outstanding welfare issues which may require a continuation of the protection afforded during the course of the proceedings by s 97 (2) of the Children Act 1989 and which are not fully met by a direction under section 39 Children and Young Persons Act 1933,[3] so that any party seeking such protection has an opportunity to apply to the county court or High Court for the appropriate order before the proceedings are finally concluded.

1   See *Clayton v Clayton* [2006] EWCA Civ 878
2   In particular proceedings which –
    (a)   relate to the exercise of the inherent jurisdiction of the High Court with respect to minors;
    (b)   are brought under the Children Act 1989; or
    (c)   otherwise relate wholly or mainly to the maintenance or upbringing of a minor

3   Power of court to prohibit publication of certain matters in newspapers

3 Aims of the guidance

3.1 This Practice Direction is intended to provide guidance regarding –

- the handling of applications to exclude media representatives from the whole or part of a hearing: and
- the exercise of the court's discretion to exclude media representatives whether upon the court's own motion or any such application.

3.2 While the guidance does not aim to cover all possible eventualities, it should be complied with so far as consistent in all the circumstances with the just determination of the proceedings.

4 Identification of media representatives as 'accredited'

4.1 Media representatives will be expected to carry with them identification sufficient to enable court staff, or if necessary the court itself, to verify that they are 'accredited' representatives of news gathering or reporting organisations within the meaning of the rule.

4.2 By virtue of paragraph (7) of the rule, it is for the Lord Chancellor to approve a scheme which will provide for accreditation. The Lord Chancellor has decided that the scheme operated by the UK Press Card Authority provides sufficient accreditation: a card issued under that scheme will be the expected form of identification, and production of the Card will be both necessary and sufficient to demonstrate accreditation.

4.3 A media representative unable to demonstrate accreditation in accordance with the UK Press Card Authority scheme so as to be able to attend by virtue of paragraph (2)(f) of the rule may nevertheless be permitted to attend at the court's discretion under paragraph (2)(g).

5 Exercise of the discretion to exclude media representatives from all or part of the proceedings.

5.1 The rule anticipates and should be applied on the basis that media representatives have a right to attend family proceedings throughout save and to the extent that the court exercises its discretion to exclude them from the whole or part of any proceedings on one or more of the grounds set out in paragraph (3) of the rule.

5.2 When considering the question of exclusion on any of the grounds set out in paragraph (3) of the rule the court should –

- specifically identify whether the risk to which such ground is directed arises from the mere fact of media presence at the particular hearing or hearings the subject of the application or whether the risk identified can be adequately addressed by exclusion of media representatives from a part only of such hearing or hearings;
- consider whether the reporting or disclosure restrictions which apply by operation of law, or which the court otherwise has power to order

will provide sufficient protection to the party on whose behalf the application is made or any of the persons referred to in paragraph (3)(a) of the rule;

- consider the safety of the parties in cases in which the court considers there are particular physical or health risks against which reporting restrictions may be inadequate to afford protection;

- in the case of any vulnerable adult or child who is unrepresented before the court, consider the extent to which the court should of its own motion take steps to protect the welfare of that adult or child.

5.3 Paragraph (3)(a)(iii) of the rule permits exclusion where necessary 'for the orderly conduct of proceedings'. This enables the court to address practical problems presented by media attendance. In particular, it may be difficult or even impossible physically to accommodate all (or indeed any) media representatives who wish to attend a particular hearing on the grounds of the restricted size or layout of the court room in which it is being heard. Court staff will use their best efforts to identify more suitable accommodation in advance of any hearing which appears likely to attract particular media attention, and to move hearings to larger court rooms where possible. However, the court should not be required to adjourn a hearing in order for larger accommodation to be sought where this will involve significant disruption or delay in the proceedings.

5.4 Paragraph (3)(b) of the rule permits exclusion where, unless the media are excluded, justice will be impeded or prejudiced for some reason other than those set out in sub-paragraph (a). Reasons of administrative inconvenience are not sufficient. An example of circumstances where the impact on justice of continued attendance might be sufficient to necessitate exclusion would be any hearing at which a witness (other than a party) states for credible reasons that he or she will not give evidence in front of media representatives, or where there appears to the court to be a significant risk that a witness will not give full or frank evidence in the presence of media representatives.

5.5 In the event of a decision to exclude media representatives, the court should state brief reasons for the decision.

6 Applications to exclude media representatives from all or part of proceedings.

6.1 The court may exclude media representatives on the permitted grounds of its own motion or after hearing representations from the interested persons listed at paragraph (5) of the rule. Where exclusion is proposed, any media representatives who are present are entitled to make representations about that proposal. There is, however, no requirement to adjourn proceedings to enable media representatives who are not present to attend in order to make such representations, and in such a case the court should not adjourn unless satisfied of the necessity to do so having regard to the additional cost and delay which would thereby be caused.

6.2 Applications to exclude media representatives should normally be dealt with as they arise and by way of oral representations, unless the court directs otherwise.

6.3 When media representatives are expected to attend a particular hearing (for example, where a party is encouraging media interest and attendance) and a party intends to apply to the court for the exclusion of the media, such party should, if practicable, give advance notice to the court, to the other parties and (where appointed) any children's guardian, officer of the service or Welsh Family Proceedings officer, NYAS or other representative of the child of any intention to seek the exclusion of media representatives from all or part of the proceedings. Equally, legal representatives and parties should ensure that witnesses are aware of the right of media representatives to attend and should notify the court at an early stage of the intention of any witness to request the exclusion of media representatives.

6.4 Prior notification by the court of a pending application for exclusion will not be given to media interests unless the court so directs. However, where such an application has been made, the applicant must where possible, notify the relevant media organisations [and should do so by means of the Press Association CopyDirect service, following the procedure set out in the Official Solicitor/CAFCASS Practice Note dated 18 March 2005][1].

NOTES

Amendments.[1] The additional words were added by the President in *Re Child X* (above), paragraph 87.

PART 28
COSTS

28.1 Costs

The court may at any time make such order as to costs as it thinks just.

28.2 Application of other rules

(1) Subject to rule 28.3 and to paragraph (2), Parts 43, 44 (except rules 44.3(2) and (3), 44.9 to 44.12C, 44.13(1A) and (1B) and 44.18 to 20), 47 and 48 and rule 45.6 of the CPR apply to costs in proceedings, with the following modifications –

    (a)   in rule 43.2(1)(c)(ii), 'district judge' includes a district judge of the principal registry;

    (b)   in rule 48.7(1) after 'section 51(6) of the Senior Courts Act 1981' insert 'or section 145A of the Magistrates' Courts Act 1980';

    (c)   in accordance with any provisions in Practice Direction 28A; and

    (d)   any other necessary modifications.

(2) Part 47 and rules 44.3C and 45.6 of the CPR do not apply to proceedings in a magistrates' court.

28.3 Costs in financial remedy proceedings

(1) This rule applies in relation to financial remedy proceedings.

(2) Rule 44.3(1), (4) and (5) of the CPR do not apply to financial remedy proceedings.

(3) Rule 44.3(6) to (9) of the CPR apply to an order made under this rule as they apply to an order made under rule 44.3 of the CPR.

(4) In this rule –

'costs' has the same meaning as in rule 43.2(1)(a) of the CPR; and
'financial remedy proceedings' means proceedings for –

    (a) a financial order except an order for maintenance pending suit, an order for maintenance pending outcome of proceedings, an interim periodical payments order or any other form of interim order for the purposes of rule 9.7(1)(a), (b), (c) and (e);

    (b) an order under Part 3 of the 1984 Act;

    (c) an order under Schedule 7 to the 2004 Act;

    (d) an order under section 10(2) of the 1973 Act;

    (e) an order under section 48(2) of the 2004 Act.

(5) Subject to paragraph (6), the general rule in financial remedy proceedings is that the court will not make an order requiring one party to pay the costs of another party.

(6) The court may make an order requiring one party to pay the costs of another party at any stage of the proceedings where it considers it appropriate to do so because of the conduct of a party in relation to the proceedings (whether before or during them).

(7) In deciding what order (if any) to make under paragraph (6), the court must have regard to –

    (a) any failure by a party to comply with these rules, any order of the court or any practice direction which the court considers relevant;

    (b) any open offer to settle made by a party;

    (c) whether it was reasonable for a party to raise, pursue or contest a particular allegation or issue;

    (d) the manner in which a party has pursued or responded to the application or a particular allegation or issue;

    (e) any other aspect of a party's conduct in relation to proceedings which the court considers relevant; and

    (f) the financial effect on the parties of any costs order.

(8) No offer to settle which is not an open offer to settle is admissible at any stage of the proceedings, except as provided by rule 9.17.

28.4 Wasted costs orders in the magistrates' court : appeals

A legal or other representative against whom a wasted costs order is made in the magistrates' court may appeal to the Crown Court.

Practice Direction 28A –
Costs

This Practice Direction supplements FPR Part 28

Application and modification of the CPR

1.1 Rule 28.2 provides that subject to rule 28.3 of the FPR and to paragraph (2) of rule 28.2, Parts 43, 44 (except rules 44.3(2) and (3), 44.9 to 44.12C, 44.13(1A) and (1B) and 44.18 to 20), 47 and 48 and rule 45.6 of the CPR apply to costs in family proceedings with the modifications listed in rule 28.2(1)(a) to (d). Rule 28.2(1)(c) refers to modifications in accordance with this Practice Direction.

1.2 In addition to the modifications to the CPR listed in rule 28.2(1), in rule 48.1(1)(b) after paragraph (ii) insert '(iii) section 68A of the Magistrates' Courts Act 1980.'.

1.3 Rule 28.2(2) provides that Part 47 and rules 44.3C and 45.6 of the CPR do not apply to proceedings in a magistrates' court.

Application and modification of the Practice Direction supplementing
CPR Parts 43 to 48

2.1 For the purpose of proceedings to which these Rules apply, the Practice Direction about costs which supplements Parts 43 to 48 of the CPR ('the costs practice direction') will apply, but with the exclusions and modifications explained below to reflect the exclusions and modifications to those Parts of the CPR as they are applied by Part 28 of these Rules.

2.2 Rule 28.2(1) applies, with modifications and certain exceptions, Parts 43 to 48 of the CPR to costs in family proceedings. Paragraph 1.2 of this Practice Direction modifies rule 48.1(1)(b) when it applies to family proceedings. Rule 28.2(2), by way of exception, disapplies Part 47, rules 44.3C and 45.6 of the CPR in the case of family proceedings in a magistrates' court. Rule 28.3, again by way of exception, additionally disapplies CPR rule 44.3(1), (4) and (5) in the case of financial remedy proceedings, regardless of court.

2.3 The costs practice direction does not, therefore, apply in its entirety but with the exclusion of certain sections reflecting the non-application of certain rules of the CPR which those sections supplement.

2.4 The costs practice direction applies as follows –

- to family proceedings generally, other than in magistrates' courts, with the exception of sections 6, 15, 16 ,17 and 23A;
- to family proceedings generally, in magistrates' courts only, with the exception of sections 6, 15, 16 ,17,23A and sections 28–49A;
- to financial remedy proceedings, other than in magistrates' courts, with the exception of section 6, paragraphs 8.1 to 8.4 of section 8 and sections 15, 16, 17 and 23A;

PART II – Statutory Instruments

- to a financial remedy proceedings, in magistrates' courts only, with the exception of section 6, paragraphs 8.1 to 8.4 of section 8, sections 15, 16, 17, 23A and sections 28–49A.

2.5 All subsequent editions of the costs practice direction as and when they are published and come into effect shall in the same way extend to all family proceedings.

2.6 The costs practice direction includes provisions applicable to proceedings following changes in the manner in which legal services are funded pursuant to the Access to Justice Act 1999. It should be noted that although the cost of the premium in respect of legal costs insurance (section 29) or the cost of funding by a prescribed membership organisation (section 30) may be recoverable, family proceedings (within section 58A(2) of the Courts and Legal Services Act 1990) cannot be the subject of an enforceable conditional fee agreement.

2.7 Paragraph 1.4 of section 1 of the costs practice direction shall be modified as follows –

in the definition of 'counsel' for 'High court or in the county courts' substitute 'High Court, county courts or in a magistrates' court'.

General interpretation of references in CPR

3.1 References in the costs practice direction to 'claimant' and 'defendant' are to be read as references to equivalent terms used in proceedings to which these Rules apply and other terms and expressions used in the costs practice direction shall be similarly treated.

3.2 References in CPR Parts 43 to 48 to other rules or Parts of the CPR shall be read, where there is an equivalent rule or Part in these Rules, to that equivalent rule or Part.

Costs in financial remedy proceedings

4.1 Rule 28.3 relates to the court's power to make costs orders in financial remedy proceedings. For the purposes of rule 28.3, 'financial remedy proceedings' are defined in accordance with rule 28.3(4)(b). That definition, which is more limited than the principal definition in rule 2.3(1), includes –

(a) an application for a financial order, except –
 (i) an order for maintenance pending suit or an order for maintenance pending outcome of proceedings;
 (ii) an interim periodical payments order or any other form of interim order for the purposes of rule 9.7(1)(a),(b),(c) and (e);
(b) an application for an order under Part 3 of the Matrimonial and Family Proceedings Act 1984 or Schedule 7 to the Civil Partnership Act 2004; and
(c) an application under section 10(2) of the Matrimonial Causes Act 1973 or section 48(2) of the Civil Partnership Act 2004.

4.2 Accordingly, it should be noted that –

(a) while most interim financial applications are excluded from rule 28.3, the rule does apply to an application for an interim variation order within rule 9.7(1)(d),

(b) rule 28.3 does not apply to an application for any of the following financial remedies –

  (i) an order under Schedule 1 to the Children Act 1989;

  (ii) an order under section 27 of the Matrimonial Causes Act 1973 or Part 9 of Schedule 5 to the Civil Partnership Act 2004;

  (iii) an order under section 35 of the Matrimonial Causes Act 1973 or paragraph 69 of Schedule 5 to the Civil Partnership Act 2004; or

  (iv) an order under Part 1 of the Domestic Proceedings and Magistrates' Courts Act 1978 or Schedule 6 to the Civil Partnership Act 2004.

4.3 Under rule 28.3 the court only has the power to make a costs order in financial remedy proceedings when this is justified by the litigation conduct of one of the parties. When determining whether and how to exercise this power the court will be required to take into account the list of factors set out in that rule. The court will not be able to take into account any offers to settle expressed to be 'without prejudice' or 'without prejudice save as to costs' in deciding what, if any, costs orders to make.

4.4 In considering the conduct of the parties for the purposes of rule 28.3(6) and (7) (including any open offers to settle), the court will have regard to the obligation of the parties to help the court to further the overriding objective (see rules 1.1 and 1.3) and will take into account the nature, importance and complexity of the issues in the case. This may be of particular significance in applications for variation orders and interim variation orders or other cases where there is a risk of the costs becoming disproportionate to the amounts in dispute.

4.5 Parties who intend to seek a costs order against another party in proceedings to which rule 28.3 applies should ordinarily make this plain in open correspondence or in skeleton arguments before the date of the hearing. In any case where summary assessment of costs awarded under rule 28.3 would be appropriate parties are under an obligation to file a statement of costs in CPR Form N260.

4.6 An interim financial order which includes an element to allow a party to deal with legal fees (see *A v A (maintenance pending suit: provision for legal fees)* [2001] 1 WLR 605; *G v G (maintenance pending suit; costs)* [2002] EWHC 306 (Fam); *McFarlane v McFarlane, Parlour v Parlour* [2004] EWCA Civ 872; *Moses-Taiga v Taiga* [2005] EWCA Civ 1013; *C v C (Maintenance Pending Suit: Legal Costs)* [2006] Fam Law 739; *Currey v Currey (No 2)* [2006] EWCA Civ 1338) is an order made pursuant to section 22 of the Matrimonial Causes Act 1973 or an order under paragraph 38 of Schedule 5 of the 2004 Act, and is not a 'costs order' within the meaning of rule 28.3.

PART II – Statutory Instruments

4.7 By virtue of rule 28.2(1), where rule 28.3 does not apply, the exercise of the court's discretion as to costs is governed by the relevant provisions of the CPR and in particular rule 44.3 (excluding r 44.3(2) and (3)).

PART 29
MISCELLANEOUS

29.1 Personal details

(1) Unless the court directs otherwise, a party is not required to reveal –

   (a)   the party's home address or other contact details;
   (b)   the address or other contact details of any child;
   (c)   the name of a person with whom the child is living, if that person is not the applicant; or
   (d)   in relation to an application under section 28(2) of the 2002 Act (application for permission to change the child's surname), the proposed new surname of the child.

(2) Where a party does not wish to reveal any of the particulars in paragraph (1), that party must give notice of those particulars to the court and the particulars will not be revealed to any person unless the court directs otherwise.

(3) Where a party changes home address during the course of proceedings, that party must give notice of the change to the court.

29.2 Disclosure of information under the 1991 Act

Where the Commission requires a person mentioned in regulation 3(1), 4(2) or 6(2)(a) of the Child Support Information Regulations 2008 to furnish information or evidence for a purpose mentioned in regulation 4(1) of those Regulations, nothing in these rules will –

   (a)   prevent that person from furnishing the information or evidence sought; or
   (b)   require that person to seek permission of the court before doing so.

29.3 Method of giving notice

(1) Unless directed otherwise, a notice which is required by these rules to be given to a person must be given –

   (a)   in writing; and
   (b)   in a manner in which service may be effected in accordance with Part 6.

(2) Rule 6.33 applies to a notice which is required by these rules to be given to a child as it applies to a document which is to be served on a child.

29.4 Withdrawal of applications in proceedings

(1) This rule applies to applications in proceedings –

(a) under Part 7;
(b) under Parts 10 to 14 or under any other Part where the application relates to the welfare or upbringing of a child or;
(c) where either of the parties is a protected party.

(2) Where this rule applies, an application may only be withdrawn with the permission of the court.

(3) Subject to paragraph (4), a person seeking permission to withdraw an application must file a written request for permission setting out the reasons for the request.

(4) The request under paragraph (3) may be made orally to the court if the parties are present.

(5) A court officer will notify the other parties of a written request.

(6) The court may deal with a written request under paragraph (3) without a hearing if the other parties, and any other persons directed by the court, have had an opportunity to make written representations to the court about the request.

29.5 The Human Rights Act 1998

(1) In this rule –

'the 1998 Act' means the Human Rights Act 1998;
'Convention right' has the same meaning as in the 1998 Act; and
'declaration of incompatibility' means a declaration of incompatibility under section 4 of the 1998 Act.

(2) A party who seeks to rely on any provision of or right arising under the 1998 Act or seeks a remedy available under that Act must inform the court in that party's application or otherwise in writing specifying –

(a) the Convention right which it is alleged has been infringed and details of the alleged infringement; and
(b) the relief sought and whether this includes a declaration of incompatibility.

(3) The High Court may not make a declaration of incompatibility unless 21 days' notice, or such other period of notice as the court directs, has been given to the Crown.

(4) Where notice has been given to the Crown, a Minister, or other person permitted by the 1998 Act, will be joined as a party on giving notice to the court.

(5) Where a claim is made under section 7(1) of the 1998 Act (claim that public authority acted unlawfully) in respect of a judicial act –

(a) that claim must be set out in the application form or the appeal notice; and
(b) notice must be given to the Crown.

(6) Where paragraph (4) applies and the appropriate person (as defined in section 9(5) of the 1998 Act) has not applied within 21 days, or such other period as the court directs, beginning with the date on which the notice to be joined as a party was served, the court may join the appropriate person as a party.

(7) On any application concerning a committal order, if the court ordering the release of the person concludes that that person's Convention rights have been infringed by the making of the order to which the application or appeal relates, the judgment or order should so state, but if the court does not do so, that failure will not prevent another court from deciding the matter.

(8) Where by reason of a rule, practice direction or court order the Crown is permitted or required –

(a)   to make a witness statement;
(b)   to swear an affidavit[GL];
(c)   to verify a document by a statement of truth; or
(d)   to discharge any other procedural obligation,

that function will be performed by an appropriate officer acting on behalf of the Crown, and the court may if necessary nominate an appropriate officer.

(Practice Direction 29A (Human Rights – Joining the Crown) makes provision for the notices mentioned in this rule.)

****

29.8 Applications for relief which is precluded by the 1991 Act

(1) This rule applies where an application is made for an order which, in the opinion of the court, it would be prevented from making under section 8 or 9 of the 1991 Act and in this rule, 'the matter' means the question of whether or not the court would be so prevented.

(2) The court will consider the matter without holding a hearing.

(3) Where the court officer receives the opinion of the court, as mentioned in paragraph (1), the court officer must send a notice to the applicant of that opinion.

(4) Paragraphs (5) to (11) apply where the court officer sends a notice under paragraph (3).

(5) Subject to paragraph (6), no requirement of these rules apply except the requirements –

(a)   of this rule;
(b)   as to service of the application by the court officer; and
(c)   as to any procedural step to be taken following the making of an application of the type in question.

(6) The court may direct that the requirements of these rules apply, or apply to such extent or with such modifications as are set out in the direction.

(7) If the applicant informs the court officer, within 14 days of the date of the notice, that the applicant wishes to persist with the application, the court will give appropriate directions for the matter to be heard and determined and may provide for the hearing to be without notice.

(8) Where directions are given in accordance with paragraph (7), the court officer must –

    (a)   inform the applicant of the directions;

    (b)   send a copy of the application to the other parties;

    (c)   if the hearing is to be without notice, inform the other parties briefly –

        (i)   of the nature and effect of the notice given to the applicant under paragraph (3);

        (ii)   that the matter is being resolved without a hearing on notice; and

        (iii)   that they will be notified of the result; and

    (d)   if the hearing is to be on notice, inform the other parties of –

        (i)   the circumstances which led to the directions being given; and

        (ii)   the directions.

(9) If the applicant does not inform the court officer as mentioned in paragraph (7), the application shall be treated as having been withdrawn.

(10) Where –

    (a)   the matter is heard in accordance with directions given under paragraph (7); and

    (b)   the court determines that it would be prevented, under section 8 or 9 of the 1991 Act, from making the order sought by the applicant,

the court will dismiss the application.

(11) Where the court dismisses the application –

    (a)   the court must give its reasons in writing; and

    (b)   the court officer must send a copy of the reasons to the parties.

29.9 Modification of rule 29.8 where the application is not freestanding

(1) Where the court officer sends a notice under rule 29.8(3) in relation to an application which is contained in another document ('the document') which contains material extrinsic to the application –

    (a)   subject to paragraph (2), the document will be treated as if it did not contain the application in respect of which the notice was served; and

    (b)   the court officer, when sending copies of the documents to the respondents under any provision of these rules, must attach –

        (i)   a copy of the notice under rule 29.8(3); and

        (ii)   a notice informing the respondents of the effect of paragraph (1)(a).

(2) If the court determines that it is not prevented by section 8 or 9 of the 1991 Act from making the order sought by the application, the court –

PART II – Statutory Instruments

(a)   must direct that the document shall be treated as if it contained the application; and

(b)   may give such directions as it considers appropriate for the subsequent conduct of the proceedings.

****

Practice Direction 29A – Human Rights, Joining the Crown

This Practice Direction supplements FPR Part 29, rule 29.5 (The Human Rights Act 1998)

Section 4 of the Human Rights Act 1998

1.1 Where a party has informed the court about –

(a)   a claim for a declaration of incompatibility in accordance with section 4 of the Human Rights Act 1998; or

(b)   an issue for the court to decide which may lead to the court considering making a declaration,

then the court may at any time consider whether notice should be given to the Crown as required by that Act and give directions for the content and service of the notice. The rule allows a period of 21 days before the court will make the declaration but the court may vary this period of time.

1.2 The court will normally consider the issues and give the directions referred to in paragraph 1.1 at a directions hearing.

1.3 The notice must be served on the person named in the list published under section 17 of the Crown Proceedings Act 1947.

1.4 The notice will be in the form directed by the court and will normally include the directions given by the court. The notice will also be served on all the parties.

1.5 The court may require the parties to assist in the preparation of the notice.

1.6 Unless the court orders otherwise, the Minister or other person permitted by the Human Rights Act 1998 to be joined as a party must, if he or she wishes to be joined, give notice of his or her intention to be joined as a party to the court and every other party. Where the Minister has nominated a person to be joined as a party the notice must be accompanied by the written nomination.

(Section 5(2)(a) of the Human Rights Act 1998 permits a person nominated by a Minister of the Crown to be joined as a party. The nomination may be signed on behalf of the Minister.)

Section 9 of the Human Rights Act 1998

2.1 The procedure in paragraphs 1.1 to 1.6 also applies where a claim is made under sections 7(1)(a) and 9(3) of the Human Rights Act 1998 for damages in respect of a judicial act.

2.2 Notice must be given to the Lord Chancellor and should be served on the Treasury Solicitor on his behalf.

2.3 The notice will also give details of the judicial act, which is the subject of the claim for damages, and of the court that made it.

(Section 9(4) of the Human Rights Act 1998 provides that no award of damages may be made against the Crown as provided for in section 9(3) unless the appropriate person is joined in the proceedings. The appropriate person is the Minister responsible for the court concerned or a person or department nominated by him or her (section 9(5) of the Act).

Practice Direction 29B – Human Rights Act 1998

This Practice Direction supplements FPR Part 29

1 It is directed that the following practice shall apply as from 2 October 2000 in all family proceedings:

Citation of authorities

2 When an authority referred to in s 2 of the Human Rights Act 1998 ('the Act') is to be cited at a hearing –

(a)   the authority to be cited shall be an authoritative and complete report;

(b)   the court must be provided with a list of authorities it is intended to cite and copies of the reports –

    (i)   in cases to which *Practice Direction (Family Proceedings: Court Bundles)* (10 March 2000) [2000] 1 FLR 536 applies, as part of the bundle;

    (ii)   otherwise, not less than 2 clear days before the hearing; and

(c)   copies of the complete original texts issued by the European Court and Commission, either paper based or from the Court's judgment database (HUDOC) which is available on the internet, may be used.

Allocation to judges

3

(1)   The hearing and determination of the following will be confined to a High Court judge –

    (*a*)   a claim for a declaration of incompatibility under s 4 of the Act; or

    (*b*)   an issue which may lead to the court considering making such a declaration.

(2)   The hearing and determination of a claim made under the Act in respect of a judicial act shall be confined in the High Court to a High Court judge and in county courts to a circuit judge.

PART 30
APPEALS

30.1 Scope and interpretation

(1) The rules in this Part apply to appeals to –

(a)   the High Court; and
(b)   a county court.

(2) This Part does not apply to an appeal in detailed assessment proceedings against a decision of an authorised court officer.

(Rules 47.20 to 47.23 of the CPR deal with appeals against a decision of an authorised court officer in detailed assessment proceedings.)

(3) In this Part –

'appeal court' means the court to which an appeal is made;
'appeal notice' means an appellant's or respondent's notice;
'appellant' means a person who brings or seeks to bring an appeal;
'lower court' means the court from which, or the person from whom, the appeal lies; and
'respondent' means –

(*a*)   a person other than the appellant who was a party to the proceedings in the lower court and who is affected by the appeal; and

(*b*)   a person who is permitted by the appeal court to be a party to the appeal.

(4) This Part is subject to any rule, enactment or practice direction which sets out special provisions with regard to any particular category of appeal.

30.2 Parties to comply with the practice direction

All parties to an appeal must comply with Practice Direction 30A.

30.3 Permission

(1) An appellant or respondent requires permission to appeal –

(a)   against a decision in proceedings where the decision appealed against was made by a district judge or a costs judge, unless paragraph (2) applies; or
(b)   as provided by Practice Direction 30A.

(2) Permission to appeal is not required where the appeal is against –

(a)   a committal order; or
(b)   a secure accommodation order under section 25 of the 1989 Act.

(3) An application for permission to appeal may be made –

(a) to the lower court at the hearing at which the decision to be appealed was made; or

(b) to the appeal court in an appeal notice.

(Rule 30.4 sets out the time limits for filing an appellant's notice at the appeal court. Rule 30.5 sets out the time limits for filing a respondent's notice at the appeal court. Any application for permission to appeal to the appeal court must be made in the appeal notice (see rules 30.4(1) and 30.5(3).)

(4) Where the lower court refuses an application for permission to appeal, a further application for permission to appeal may be made to the appeal court.

(5) Where the appeal court, without a hearing, refuses permission to appeal, the person seeking permission may request the decision to be reconsidered at a hearing.

(6) A request under paragraph (5) must be filed within 7 days beginning with the date on which the notice that permission has been refused was served.

(7) Permission to appeal may be given only where –

(a) the court considers that the appeal would have a real prospect of success; or

(b) there is some other compelling reason why the appeal should be heard.

(8) An order giving permission may –

(a) limit the issues to be heard; and

(b) be made subject to conditions.

(9) In this rule 'costs judge' means a taxing master of the Senior Courts.

30.4 Appellant's notice

(1) Where the appellant seeks permission from the appeal court it must be requested in the appellant's notice.

(2) Subject to paragraph (3), the appellant must file the appellant's notice at the appeal court within –

(a) such period as may be directed by the lower court (which may be longer or shorter than the period referred to in sub-paragraph (b)); or

(b) where the court makes no such direction, 21 days after the date of the decision of the lower court against which the appellant wishes to appeal.

(3) Where the appeal is against an order under section 38(1) of the 1989 Act, the appellant must file the appellant's notice within 7 days beginning with the date of the decision of the lower court.

(4) Unless the appeal court orders otherwise, an appellant's notice must be served on each respondent and the persons referred to in paragraph (5) –

PART II – Statutory Instruments

(a)   as soon as practicable; and

(b)   in any event not later than 7 days,

after it is filed.

(5) The persons referred to in paragraph (4) are –

(a)   any children's guardian, welfare officer, or children and family reporter;

(b)   a local authority who has prepared a report under section 14A(8) or (9) of the 1989 Act;

(c)   an adoption agency or local authority which has prepared a report on the suitability of the applicant to adopt a child;

(d)   a local authority which has prepared a report on the placement of the child for adoption; and

(e)   where the appeal is from a magistrates' court, the court officer.

30.5 Respondent's notice

(1) A respondent may file and serve a respondent's notice.

(2) A respondent who –

(a)   is seeking permission to appeal from the appeal court; or

(b)   wishes to ask the appeal court to uphold the order of the lower court for reasons different from or additional to those given by the lower court,

must file a respondent's notice.

(3) Where the respondent seeks permission from the appeal court it must be requested in the respondent's notice.

(4) A respondent's notice must be filed within –

(a)   such period as may be directed by the lower court; or

(b)   where the court makes no such direction, 14 days beginning with the date referred to in paragraph (5).

(5) The date referred to in paragraph (4) is –

(a)   the date on which the respondent is served with the appellant's notice where –
permission to appeal was given by the lower court; or
permission to appeal is not required;

(b)   the date on which the respondent is served with notification that the appeal court has given the appellant permission to appeal; or

(c)   the date on which the respondent is served with notification that the application for permission to appeal and the appeal itself are to be heard together.

(6) Unless the appeal court orders otherwise, a respondent's notice must be served on the appellant, any other respondent and the persons referred to in rule 30.4(5) –

    (a)   as soon as practicable; and

    (b)   in any event not later than 7 days,

after it is filed.

(7) Where there is an appeal against an order under section 38(1) of the 1989 Act –

    (a)   a respondent may not, in that appeal, bring an appeal from the order or ask the appeal court to uphold the order of the lower court for reasons different from or additional to those given by the lower court; and

    (b)   paragraphs (2) and (3) do not apply.

30.6 Grounds of appeal

The appeal notice must state the grounds of appeal.

30.7 Variation of time

(1) An application to vary the time limit for filing an appeal notice must be made to the appeal court.

(2) The parties may not agree to extend any date or time limit set by –

    (a)   these rules;

    (b)   Practice Direction 30A; or

    (c)   an order of the appeal court or the lower court.

(Rule 4.1(3)(a) provides that the court may extend or shorten the time for compliance with a rule, practice direction or court order (even if an application for extension is made after the time for compliance has expired).)

(Rule 4.1(3)(c) provides that the court may adjourn or bring forward a hearing.)

30.8 Stay

Unless the appeal court or the lower court orders otherwise, an appeal does not operate as a stay[GL] of any order or decision of the lower court.

30.9 Amendment of appeal notice

An appeal notice may not be amended without the permission of the appeal court.

30.10 Striking out appeal notices and setting aside or imposing conditions on permission to appeal

(1) The appeal court may –

    (a)   strike out[GL] the whole or part of an appeal notice;

    (b)   set aside[GL] permission to appeal in whole or in part;

    (c)   impose or vary conditions upon which an appeal may be brought.

PART II – Statutory Instruments

(2) The court will only exercise its powers under paragraph (1) where there is a compelling reason for doing so.

(3) Where a party was present at the hearing at which permission was given that party may not subsequently apply for an order that the court exercise its powers under paragraphs (1)(b) or (1)(c).

30.11 Appeal court's powers

(1) In relation to an appeal the appeal court has all the powers of the lower court.

> (Rule 30.1(4) provides that this Part is subject to any enactment that sets out special provisions with regard to any particular category of appeal.)

(2) The appeal court has power to –

(a)   affirm, set aside$^{(GL)}$ or vary any order or judgment made or given by the lower court;
(b)   refer any application or issue for determination by the lower court;
(c)   order a new hearing;
(d)   make orders for the payment of interest;
(e)   make a costs order.

(3) The appeal court may exercise its powers in relation to the whole or part of an order of the lower court.

> (Rule 4.1 contains general rules about the court's case management powers.)

(4) If the appeal court –

(a)   refuses an application for permission to appeal;
(b)   strikes out an appellant's notice; or
(c)   dismisses an appeal,

and it considers that the application, the appellant's notice or the appeal is totally without merit, the provisions of paragraph (5) must be complied with.

(5) Where paragraph (4) applies –

(a)   the court's order must record the fact that it considers the application, the appellant's notice or the appeal to be totally without merit; and
(b)   the court must at the same time consider whether it is appropriate to make a civil restraint order.

30.12 Hearing of appeals

(1) Every appeal will be limited to a review of the decision of the lower court unless –

(a)   an enactment or practice direction makes different provision for a particular category of appeal; or
(b)   the court considers that in the circumstances of an individual appeal it would be in the interests of justice to hold a re-hearing.

(2) Unless it orders otherwise, the appeal court will not receive –

(a) oral evidence; or

(b) evidence which was not before the lower court.

(3) The appeal court will allow an appeal where the decision of the lower court was –

(a) wrong; or

(b) unjust because of a serious procedural or other irregularity in the proceedings in the lower court.

(4) The appeal court may draw any inference of fact which it considers justified on the evidence.

(5) At the hearing of the appeal a party may not rely on a matter not contained in that party's appeal notice unless the appeal court gives permission.

30.13 Assignment of appeals to the Court of Appeal

(1) Where the court from or to which an appeal is made or from which permission to appeal is sought ('the relevant court') considers that –

(a) an appeal which is to be heard by a county court or the High Court would raise an important point of principle or practice; or

(b) there is some other compelling reason for the Court of Appeal to hear it,

the relevant court may order the appeal to be transferred to the Court of Appeal.

(2) This rule does not apply to proceedings in a magistrates' court.

30.14 Reopening of final appeals

(1) The High Court will not reopen a final determination of any appeal unless –

(a) it is necessary to do so in order to avoid real injustice;

(b) the circumstances are exceptional and make it appropriate to reopen the appeal; and

(c) there is no alternative effective remedy.

(2) In paragraphs (1), (3), (4) and (6), 'appeal' includes an application for permission to appeal.

(3) This rule does not apply to appeals to a county court.

(4) Permission is needed to make an application under this rule to reopen a final determination of an appeal.

(5) There is no right to an oral hearing of an application for permission unless, exceptionally, the judge so directs.

(6) The judge will not grant permission without directing the application to be served on the other party to the original appeal and giving that party an opportunity to make representations.

PART II – Statutory Instruments

(7) There is no right of appeal or review from the decision of the judge on the application for permission, which is final.

(8) The procedure for making an application for permission is set out in Practice Direction 30A.

Practice Direction 30A – Appeals

This Practice Direction supplements FPR Part 30

1.1 This practice direction applies to all appeals to which Part 30 applies.

Routes of appeal

2.1 The following table sets out to which court or judge an appeal is to be made (subject to obtaining any necessary permission) –

Decision of:	Appeal made to:
Magistrates' Court	Circuit judge
District judge of a county court	Circuit judge
District judge of the High Court	High Court judge
District judge of the principal registry of the Family Division	High Court judge
Costs judge	High Court Judge
Circuit judge or recorder	Court of Appeal
High Court judge	Court of Appeal

(Provisions setting out routes of appeal include section 16(1) of the Senior Courts Act 1981 (as amended); section 77(1) of the County Courts Act 1984 (as amended) and the Access to Justice Act 1999 (Destination of Appeals) (Family Proceedings) Order 2009 (see paragraphs 9.1 to 9.12 below. The Family Proceedings (Allocation to Judiciary) (Appeals) Directions 2009 provide for an appeal from a magistrates' court to be heard by a Circuit judge.

The routes of appeal from an order or decision relating to contempt of court of a magistrates' court under section 63(3) of the Magistrates' Courts Act 1980 and of a county court and the High Court are set out in section 13(2) of the Administration of Justice Act 1960. Appeals under section 8(1) of the Gender Recognition Act 2004 lie to the High Court (see section 8 of the 2004 Act). The procedure for appeals to the Court of Appeal is governed by the Civil Procedure Rules 1998, in particular CPR Part 52.).

2.2 Where the decision to be appealed is a decision in a Part 19 (Alternative Procedure For Applications) application on a point of law in a case which did not involve any substantial dispute of fact, the court to which the appeal lies, where that court is the High Court or a county court and unless the appeal would lie to the Court of Appeal in any event, must consider whether to order the appeal to be transferred to the Court of Appeal under rule 30.13 (Assignment of Appeals to the Court of Appeal).

Grounds for appeal

3.1 Rule 30.12 (hearing of appeals) sets out the circumstances in which the appeal court will allow an appeal.

3.2 The grounds of appeal should –

    (a)   set out clearly the reasons why rule 30.12 (3)(a) or (b) is said to apply; and

    (b)   specify in respect of each ground, whether the ground raises an appeal on a point of law or is an appeal against a finding of fact.

Permission to appeal

4.1 Rule 30.3 (Permission) sets out the circumstances when permission to appeal is required. At present permission to appeal is required where the decision appealed against was made by a district judge or a costs judge. However, no permission is required where rule 30.3(2) (appeals against a committal order or a secure accommodation order under section 25 of the Children Act 1989) applies.

    (The requirement of permission to appeal may be imposed by a practice direction – see rule 30.3(1)(b) (Permission).).

Court to which permission to appeal application should be made

4.2 An application for permission should be made orally at the hearing at which the decision to be appealed against is made.

4.3 Where –

    (a)   no application for permission to appeal is made at the hearing; or

    (b)   the lower court refuses permission to appeal,

an application for permission to appeal may be made to the appeal court in accordance with rules 30.3(3) and (4) (Permission).

    (Rule 30.1(3) defines 'lower court'.)

4.4 Where no application for permission to appeal has been made in accordance with rule 30.3(3)(a) (Permission) but a party requests further time to make such an application the court may adjourn the hearing to give that party an opportunity to do so.

4.5 There is no appeal from a decision of the appeal court to allow or refuse permission to appeal to that court (although where the appeal court, without a hearing, refuses permission to appeal, the person seeking permission may

PART II – Statutory Instruments

request that decision to be reconsidered at a hearing- see section 54(4) of the Access to Justice Act 1999 and rule 30.3(5) (Permission)).

Material omission from a judgment of the lower court

4.6 Where a party's advocate considers that there is a material omission from a judgment of the lower court or, in a magistrates' court, the written reasons for the decision of the lower court (including inadequate reasons for the lower court's decision), the advocate should before the drawing of the order give the lower court which made the decision the opportunity of considering whether there is an omission and should not immediately use the omission as grounds for an application to appeal.

4.7 Paragraph 4.8 below applies where there is an application to the lower court for permission to appeal on the grounds of a material omission from a judgment of the lower court. Paragraph 4.9 below applies where there is an application for permission to appeal to the appeal court on the grounds of a material omission from a judgment of the lower court. Paragraphs 4.8 and 4.9 do not apply where the lower court is a magistrates' court.

4.8 Where the application for permission to appeal is made to the lower court, the court which made the decision must –

   (a)   consider whether there is a material omission and adjourn for that purpose if necessary; and

   (b)   where the conclusion is that there has been such an omission, provide additions to the judgment.

4.9 Where the application for permission to appeal is made to the appeal court, the appeal court –

   (a)   must consider whether there is a material omission; and

   (b)   where the conclusion is that there has been such an omission, may adjourn the application and remit the case to the lower court with an invitation to provide additions to the judgment.

Consideration of Permission without a hearing

4.10 An application for permission to appeal may be considered by the appeal court without a hearing.

4.11 If permission is granted without a hearing the parties will be notified of that decision and the procedure in paragraphs 6.1 to 6.8 will then apply.

4.12 If permission is refused without a hearing the parties will be notified of that decision with the reasons for it. The decision is subject to the appellant's right to have it reconsidered at an oral hearing. This may be before the same judge.

4.13 A request for the decision to be reconsidered at an oral hearing must be filed at the appeal court within 7 days after service of the notice that permission has been refused. A copy of the request must be served by the appellant on the respondent at the same time.

Permission hearing

4.14 Where an appellant, who is represented, makes a request for a decision to be reconsidered at an oral hearing, the appellant's advocate must, at least 4 days before the hearing, in a brief written statement –

(a)   inform the court and the respondent of the points which the appellant proposes to raise at the hearing;

(b)   set out the reasons why permission should be granted notwithstanding the reasons given for the refusal of permission; and

(c)   confirm, where applicable, that the requirements of paragraph 4.17 have been complied with (appellant in receipt of services funded by the Legal Services Commission).

4.15 The respondent will be given notice of a permission hearing, but is not required to attend unless requested by the court to do so.

4.16 If the court requests the respondent's attendance at the permission hearing, the appellant must supply the respondent with a copy of the appeal bundle (see paragraph 5.9) within 7 days of being notified of the request, or such other period as the court may direct. The costs of providing that bundle shall be borne by the appellant initially, but will form part of the costs of the permission application.

Appellants in receipt of services funded by the Legal Services Commission applying for permission to appeal

4.17 Where the appellant is in receipt of services funded by the Legal Services Commission (or legally aided) and permission to appeal has been refused by the appeal court without a hearing, the appellant must send a copy of the reasons the appeal court gave for refusing permission to the relevant office of the Legal Services Commission as soon as it has been received from the court. The court will require confirmation that this has been done if a hearing is requested to re-consider the question of permission.

Limited permission

4.18 Where a court under rule 30.3 (Permission) gives permission to appeal on some issues only, it will –

(a)   refuse permission on any remaining issues; or

(b)   reserve the question of permission to appeal on any remaining issues to the court hearing the appeal.

4.19 If the court reserves the question of permission under paragraph 4.18(b), the appellant must, within 14 days after service of the court's order, inform the appeal court and the respondent in writing whether the appellant intends to pursue the reserved issues. If the appellant does intend to pursue the reserved issues, the parties must include in any time estimate for the appeal hearing, their time estimate for the reserved issues.

4.20 If the appeal court refuses permission to appeal on the remaining issues without a hearing and the applicant wishes to have that decision reconsidered

PART II – Statutory Instruments

at an oral hearing, the time limit in rule 30.3(6) (Permission) shall apply. Any application for an extension of this time limit should be made promptly. The court hearing the appeal on the issues for which permission has been granted will not normally grant, at the appeal hearing, an application to extend the time limit in rule 30.3(6) for the remaining issues.

4.21 If the appeal court refuses permission to appeal on remaining issues at or after an oral hearing, the application for permission to appeal on those issues cannot be renewed at the appeal hearing (see section 54(4) of the Access to Justice Act 1999).

Respondents' costs of permission applications

4.22 In most cases, applications for permission to appeal will be determined without the court requesting –

(a)   submissions from; or
(b)   if there is an oral hearing, attendance by,

the respondent.

4.23 Where the court does not request submissions from or attendance by the respondent, costs will not normally be allowed to a respondent who volunteers submissions or attendance.

4.24 Where the court does request –

(a)   submissions from; or
(b)   attendance by the respondent,

the court will normally allow the costs of the respondent if permission is refused.

Appellant's notice

5.1 An appellant's notice must be filed and served in all cases. Where an application for permission to appeal is made to the appeal court it must be applied for in the appellant's notice.

Human Rights

5.2 Where the appellant seeks –

(a)   to rely on any issue under the Human Rights Act 1998; or
(b)   a remedy available under that Act,

for the first time in an appeal the appellant must include in the appeal notice the information required by rule 29.5(2).

5.3 Practice Direction 29A (Human Rights, Joining the Crown) will apply as if references to the directions hearing were to the application for permission to appeal.

Extension of time for filing appellant's notice

5.4. If an extension of time is required for filing the appellant's notice the application must be made in that notice. The notice should state the reason for the delay and the steps taken prior to the application being made.

5.5 Where the appellant's notice includes an application for an extension of time and permission to appeal has been given or is not required the respondent has the right to be heard on that application and must be served with a copy of the appeal bundle (see paragraph 5.9). However, a respondent who unreasonably opposes an extension of time runs the risk of being ordered to pay the appellant's costs of that application.

5.6 If an extension of time is given following such an application the procedure at paragraphs 6.1 to 6.8 applies.

Applications

5.7 Notice of an application to be made to the appeal court for a remedy incidental to the appeal (e.g. an interim injunction under rule 20.2 (Orders for interim remedies)) may be included in the appeal notice or in a Part 18 (Procedure For Other Applications in Proceedings) application notice.

(Paragraph 13 of this practice direction contains other provisions relating to applications.).

Documents

5.8 The appellant must file the following documents together with an appeal bundle (see paragraph 5.9) with his or her appellant's notice –

(a) two additional copies of the appellant's notice for the appeal court;
(b) one copy of the appellant's notice for each of the respondents;
(c) one copy of the appellant's skeleton argument for each copy of the appellant's notice that is filed;
(d) a sealed or stamped copy of the order being appealed or a copy of the notice of the making of an order;
(e) a copy of any order giving or refusing permission to appeal, together with a copy of the court's reasons for allowing or refusing permission to appeal;
(f) any witness statements or affidavits in support of any application included in the appellant's notice.

5.9 An appellant must include the following documents in his or her appeal bundle –

(a) a sealed or stamped copy of the appellant's notice;
(b) a sealed or stamped copy of the order being appealed, or a copy of the notice of the making of an order;
(c) a copy of any order giving or refusing permission to appeal, together with a copy of the court's reasons for allowing or refusing permission to appeal;

(d)   any affidavit or witness statement filed in support of any application included in the appellant's notice;

(e)   where the appeal is against a consent order, a statement setting out the change in circumstances since the order was agreed or other circumstances justifying a review or re-hearing;

(f)   a copy of the appellant's skeleton argument;

(g)   a transcript or note of judgment or, in a magistrates' court, written reasons for the court's decision (see paragraph 5.23), and in cases where permission to appeal was given by the lower court or is not required those parts of any transcript of evidence which are directly relevant to any question at issue on the appeal;

(h)   the application form;

(i)   any application notice (or case management documentation) relevant to the subject of the appeal;

(j)   any other documents which the appellant reasonably considers necessary to enable the appeal court to reach its decision on the hearing of the application or appeal; and

(k)   such other documents as the court may direct.

5.10 All documents that are extraneous to the issues to be considered on the application or the appeal must be excluded. The appeal bundle may include affidavits, witness statements, summaries, experts' reports and exhibits but only where these are directly relevant to the subject matter of the appeal.

5.11 Where the appellant is represented, the appeal bundle must contain a certificate signed by the appellant's solicitor, counsel or other representative to the effect that the appellant has read and understood paragraph 5.10 and that the composition of the appeal bundle complies with it.

5.12 Where it is not possible to file all the above documents, the appellant must indicate which documents have not yet been filed and the reasons why they are not currently available. The appellant must then provide a reasonable estimate of when the missing document or documents can be filed and file them as soon as reasonably practicable.

Skeleton arguments

5.13 The appellant's notice must, subject to paragraphs 5.14 and 5.15, be accompanied by a skeleton argument. Alternatively the skeleton argument may be included in the appellant's notice. Where the skeleton argument is so included it will not form part of the notice for the purposes of rule 30.9 (Amendment of appeal notice).

5.14 Where it is impracticable for the appellant's skeleton argument to accompany the appellant's notice it must be filed and served on all respondents within 14 days of filing the notice.

5.15 An appellant who is not represented need not file a skeleton argument but is encouraged to do so since this will be helpful to the court.

5.16 A skeleton argument must contain a numbered list of the points which the party wishes to make. These should both define and confine the areas of controversy. Each point should be stated as concisely as the nature of the case allows.

5.17 A numbered point must be followed by a reference to any document on which the party wishes to rely.

5.18 A skeleton argument must state, in respect of each authority cited –

(a) the proposition of law that the authority demonstrates; and
(b) the parts of the authority (identified by page or paragraph references) that support the proposition.

5.19 If more than one authority is cited in support of a given proposition, the skeleton argument must briefly state the reason for taking that course.

5.20 The statement referred to in paragraph 5.19 should not materially add to the length of the skeleton argument but should be sufficient to demonstrate, in the context of the argument –

(a) the relevance of the authority or authorities to that argument; and
(b) that the citation is necessary for a proper presentation of that argument.

5.21 The cost of preparing a skeleton argument which –

(a) does not comply with the requirements set out in this paragraph; or
(b) was not filed within the time limits provided by this Practice Direction (or any further time granted by the court),

will not be allowed on assessment except to the extent that the court otherwise directs.

5.22 The appellant should consider what other information the appeal court will need. This may include a list of persons who feature in the case or glossaries of technical terms. A chronology of relevant events will be necessary in most appeals.

Suitable record of the judgment

5.23 Where the judgment to be appealed has been officially recorded by the court, an approved transcript of that record should accompany the appellant's notice. Photocopies will not be accepted for this purpose. However, where there is no officially recorded judgment, the following documents will be acceptable –

Written judgments – Where the judgment was made in writing a copy of that judgment endorsed with the judge's signature.
Written reasons – in a magistrates' court, a copy of the written reasons for the court's decision.
Note of judgment – When judgment was not officially recorded or made in writing a note of the judgment (agreed between the appellant's and respondent's advocates) should be submitted for approval to the judge whose decision is being appealed. If the parties cannot agree on a single note of the

PART II – Statutory Instruments

judgment, both versions should be provided to that judge with an explanatory letter. For the purpose of an application for permission to appeal the note need not be approved by the respondent or the lower court judge.

Advocates' notes of judgments where the appellant is unrepresented – When the appellant was unrepresented in the lower court it is the duty of any advocate for the respondent to make the advocate's note of judgment promptly available, free of charge to the appellant where there is no officially recorded judgment or if the court so directs. Where the appellant was represented in the lower court it is the duty of the appellant's own former advocate to make that advocate's note available in these circumstances. The appellant should submit the note of judgment to the appeal court.

5.24 An appellant may not be able to obtain an official transcript or other suitable record of the lower court's decision within the time within which the appellant's notice must be filed. In such cases the appellant's notice must still be completed to the best of the appellant's ability on the basis of the documentation available. However it may be amended subsequently with the permission of the appeal court in accordance with rule 30.9 (Amendment of appeal notice).

Advocates' notes of judgments

5.25 Advocates' brief (or, where appropriate, refresher) fee includes –

(a)   remuneration for taking a note of the judgment of the court;
(b)   having the note transcribed accurately;
(c)   attempting to agree the note with the other side if represented;
(d)   submitting the note to the judge for approval where appropriate;
(e)   revising it if so requested by the judge,
(f)   providing any copies required for the appeal court, instructing solicitors and lay client; and
(g)   providing a copy of the note to an unrepresented appellant.

Appeals from decision made by a family proceedings court under Parts 4 and 4A of the Family Law Act 1996

5.26 Where the appeal is brought against the making of a hospital order or a guardianship order under the Mental Health Act 1983, the court officer for the court from which the appeal is brought must send a copy of any written evidence considered by the magistrates under section 37(1)(a) of that Act to the appeal court.

Appeals under section 8(1) of the Gender Recognition Act 2004

5.27 Paragraph 5.28 to 5.30 apply where the appeal is brought under section 8(1) of the Gender Recognition Act 2004 to the High Court on a point of law against a decision by the Gender Recognition Panel to reject the application under sections 1(1), 5(2), 5(a)(2) or 6(1) of the 2004 Act.

5.28 The appeal notice must be –

(a)   filed in the principal registry of the Family Division; and
(b)   served on the Secretary of State and the President of the Gender Recognition Panels.

5.29 The Secretary of State may appear and be heard in the proceedings on the appeal.

5.30 Where the High Court issues a gender recognition certificate under section 8(3)(a) of the Gender Recognition Act 2004, the court officer must send a copy of that certificate to the Secretary of State.

Transcripts or Notes of Evidence

5.31 When the evidence is relevant to the appeal an official transcript of the relevant evidence must be obtained. Transcripts or notes of evidence are generally not needed for the purpose of determining an application for permission to appeal.

Notes of evidence

5.32 If evidence relevant to the appeal was not officially recorded, a typed version of the judge's (including a district judge (magistrates' courts) or justices' clerk's /assistant clerk's notes of evidence must be obtained.

Transcripts at public expense

5.33 Where the lower court or the appeal court is satisfied that –

(a)   an unrepresented appellant; or
(b)   an appellant whose legal representation is provided free of charge to the appellant and not funded by the Community Legal Service,

is in such poor financial circumstances that the cost of a transcript would be an excessive burden the court may certify that the cost of obtaining one official transcript should be borne at public expense.

5.34 In the case of a request for an official transcript of evidence or proceedings to be paid for at public expense, the court must also be satisfied that there are reasonable grounds for appeal. Whenever possible a request for a transcript at public expense should be made to the lower court when asking for permission to appeal.

Filing and service of appellant's notice

5.35 Rule 30.4 (Appellant's notice) sets out the procedure and time limits for filing and serving an appellant's notice. Subject to paragraph 5.36, the appellant must file the appellant's notice at the appeal court within such period as may be directed by the lower court, which should not normally exceed 14 days or, where the lower court directs no such period within 21 days of the date of the decision that the appellant wishes to appeal.

5.36 Rule 30.4(3) (Appellant's notice) provides that unless the appeal court orders otherwise, where the appeal is against an order under section 38(1) of the 1989 Act, the appellant must file the appellant's notice within 7 days beginning with the date of the decision of the lower court.

5.37 Where the lower court announces its decision and reserves the reasons for its judgment or order until a later date, it should, in the exercise of powers under rule 30.4(2)(a))(Appellant's notice), fix a period for filing the appellant's notice at the appeal court that takes this into account.

5.38 Except where the appeal court orders otherwise a sealed or stamped copy of the appellant's notice, including any skeleton arguments must be served on all respondents and other persons referred to in rule 30.4(5) (Appellant's notice) in accordance with the timetable prescribed by rule 30.4(4)) (Appellant's notice) except where this requirement is modified by paragraph 5.14 in which case the skeleton argument should be served as soon as it is filed.

5.39 Where the appellant's notice is to be served on a child, then rule 6.33 (supplementary provision relating to service on children) applies and unless the appeal court orders otherwise a sealed or stamped copy of the appellant's notice, including any skeleton arguments must be served on the persons or bodies mentioned in rule 6.33(2). For example, the appeal notice must be served on any children's guardian, welfare officer or children and family reporter who is appointed in the proceedings.

5.40 Unless the court otherwise directs, a respondent need not take any action when served with an appellant's notice until such time as notification is given to the respondent that permission to appeal has been given.

5.41 The court may dispense with the requirement for service of the notice on a respondent.

5.42 Unless the appeal court directs otherwise, the appellant must serve on the respondent the appellant's notice and skeleton argument (but not the appeal bundle),where the appellant is applying for permission to appeal in the appellant's notice.

5.43 Where permission to appeal –

(a)   has been given by the lower court; or
(b)   is not required,

the appellant must serve the appeal bundle on the respondent and the persons mentioned in paragraph 5.39 with the appellant's notice.

Amendment of Appeal Notice

5.44 An appeal notice may be amended with permission. Such an application to amend and any application in opposition will normally be dealt with at the hearing unless that course would cause unnecessary expense or delay in which case a request should be made for the application to amend to be heard in advance.

Procedure after permission is obtained

6.1 This paragraph sets out the procedure where –

(a)   permission to appeal is given by the appeal court; or
(b)   the appellant's notice is filed in the appeal court and –

    (i)   permission was given by the lower court; or

    (ii)   permission is not required.

6.2 If the appeal court gives permission to appeal, the appeal bundle must be served on each of the respondents within 7 days of receiving the order giving permission to appeal.

6.3 The appeal court will send the parties –

   (a)   notification of the date of the hearing or the period of time (the 'listing window') during which the appeal is likely to be heard;

   (b)   where permission is granted by the appeal court a copy of the order giving permission to appeal; and

   (c)   any other directions given by the court.

6.4 Where the appeal court grants permission to appeal, the appellant must add the following documents to the appeal bundle –

   (a)   the respondent's notice and skeleton argument (if any);

   (b)   those parts of the transcripts of evidence which are directly relevant to any question at issue on the appeal;

   (c)   the order granting permission to appeal and, where permission to appeal was granted at an oral hearing, the transcript (or note) of any judgment which was given; and

   (d)   any document which the appellant and respondent have agreed to add to the appeal bundle in accordance with paragraph 7.16.

6.5 Where permission to appeal has been refused on a particular issue, the appellant must remove from the appeal bundle all documents that are relevant only to that issue.

Time estimates

6.6 If the appellant is legally represented, the appeal court must be notified, in writing, of the advocate's time estimate for the hearing of the appeal.

6.7 The time estimate must be that of the advocate who will argue the appeal. It should exclude the time required by the court to give judgment.

6.8 A court officer will notify the respondent of the appellant's time estimate and if the respondent disagrees with the time estimate the respondent must inform the court within 7 days of the notification. In the absence of such notification the respondent will be deemed to have accepted the estimate proposed on behalf of the appellant.

Respondent

7.1 A respondent who wishes to ask the appeal court to vary the order of the lower court in any way must appeal and permission will be required on the same basis as for an appellant.

(Paragraph 3.2 applies to grounds of appeal by a respondent.).

PART II – Statutory Instruments

7.2 A respondent who wishes to appeal or who wishes to ask the appeal court to uphold the order of the lower court for reasons different from or additional to those given by the lower court must file a respondent's notice.

7.3 A respondent who does not file a respondent's notice will not be entitled, except with the permission of the court, to rely on any reason not relied on in the lower court. This paragraph and paragraph 7.2 do not apply where the appeal is against an order under section 38(1) of the 1989 Act (see rule 30.5(7) (Respondent's notice)).

7.4 Paragraphs 5.3 (Human Rights and extension for time for filing appellant's notice) and 5.4 to 5.6 (extension of time for filing appellant's notice) of this practice direction also apply to a respondent and a respondent's notice.

Time limits

7.5 The time limits for filing a respondent's notice are set out in rule 30.5(4) and (5) (Respondent's notice).

7.6 Where an extension of time is required the extension must be requested in the respondent's notice and the reasons why the respondent failed to act within the specified time must be included.

7.7 Except where paragraphs 7.8 and 7.10 apply, the respondent must file a skeleton argument for the court in all cases where the respondent proposes to address arguments to the court. The respondent's skeleton argument may be included within a respondent's notice. Where a skeleton argument is included within a respondent's notice it will not form part of the notice for the purposes of rule 30.9 (Amendment of appeal notice).

7.8 A respondent who –

(a)   files a respondent's notice; but
(b)   does not include a skeleton argument with that notice,

must file the skeleton argument within 14 days of filing the notice.

7.9 A respondent who does not file a respondent's notice but who files a skeleton argument must file that skeleton argument at least 7 days before the appeal hearing.

(Rule 30.5(4) (Respondent's notice) sets out the period for filing a respondent's notice.).

7.10 A respondent who is not represented need not file a skeleton argument but is encouraged to do so in order to assist the court.

7.11 The respondent must serve the skeleton argument on –

(*a*)   the appellant; and
(*b*)   any other respondent;

at the same time as the skeleton argument is filed at court. Where a child is an appellant or respondent the skeleton argument must also be served on the persons listed in rule 6.33(2) unless the court directs otherwise.

7.12 A respondent's skeleton argument must conform to the directions at paragraphs 5.16 to 5.22 with any necessary modifications. It should, where appropriate, answer the arguments set out in the appellant's skeleton argument.

Applications within respondent's notices

7.13 A respondent may include an application within a respondent's notice in accordance with paragraph 5.7.

Filing respondent's notices and skeleton arguments

7.14 The respondent must file the following documents with the respondent's notice in every case –

(a) two additional copies of the respondent's notice for the appeal court; and

(b) one copy each for the appellant, any other respondents and any persons referred to in paragraph 5.39.

7.15 The respondent may file a skeleton argument with the respondent's notice and –

(*a*) where doing so must file two copies; and

(*b*) where not doing so must comply with paragraph 7.8.

7.16 If the respondent considers documents in addition to those filed by the appellant to be necessary to enable the appeal court to reach its decision on the appeal and wishes to rely on those documents, any amendments to the appeal bundle should be agreed with the appellant if possible.

7.17 If the representatives for the parties are unable to reach agreement, the respondent may prepare a supplemental bundle.

7.18 The respondent must file any supplemental bundle so prepared, together with the requisite number of copies for the appeal court, at the appeal court –

(a) with the respondent's notice; or

(b) if a respondent's notice is not filed, within 21 days after the respondent is served with the appeal bundle.

7.19 The respondent must serve –

(a) the respondent's notice;

(b) the skeleton argument (if any); and

(c) the supplemental bundle (if any),

on –

(i) the appellant; and

(ii) any other respondent;

at the same time as those documents are filed at the court. Where a child is an appellant or respondent the documents referred to in paragraphs (a) to (c) above must also be served on the persons listed in rule 6.33(2) unless the court directs otherwise.

PART II – Statutory Instruments

Appeals to the High Court

Application

8.1 The appellant's notice must be filed in –

(a)   the principal registry of the Family Division; or

(b)   the district registry which is nearest to the court from which the appeal lies.

8.2 A respondent's notice must be filed at the court where the appellant's notice was filed.

8.3 In the case of appeals from district judges of the High Court, applications for permission and any other applications in the appeal, appeals may be heard and directions in the appeal may be given by a High Court Judge or by any person authorised under section 9 of the Senior Courts Act 1981 to act as a judge of the High Court.

Appeals to a county court

Appeals to a judge of a county court from a district judge

9.1 The Designated Family Judge in consultation with the Family Division Liaison Judges has responsibility for the allocation of appeals from decisions of district judges to circuit judges.

Appeals to a county court from a magistrates' court

Appeals under section 111A of the Magistrates' Courts Act 1980 ('the 1980 Act') from a magistrates' court to a county court on the ground that the decision is wrong in law or in excess of jurisdiction

9.2 As a result of an amendment to section 111 of the 1980 Act by the Access to Justice Act 1999 (Destination of Appeals) (Family Proceedings) Order 2009 ('the Destination Order') an application to have a case stated for the opinion of the High Court under section 111 of that Act may not be made in relation to family proceedings. Family proceedings for those purposes are defined as –

(a)   proceedings which, by virtue of section 65 of the 1980 Act, are or may be treated as family proceedings for the purposes of that Act; and

(b)   proceedings under the Child Support Act 1991.

9.3 Section 111A of the 1980 Act, which is inserted by article 4(3) of the Destination Order, provides that in family proceedings as defined in paragraph 9.2 above a person may appeal to a county court on the ground that a decision is wrong in law or is in excess of jurisdiction; this appeal to a county court replaces the procedure for making an application to have a case stated. Section 111A(3)(a) provides that no appeal may be brought under section 111A if there is a right of appeal to a county court against the decision otherwise than under that section.

9.4 Subject to section 111A of the 1980 Act and any other enactment, the following rules in Part 30 apply to appeals under section 111A of the 1980 Act –

(a) 30.1 (scope and interpretation);
(b) 30.2 (parties to comply with the practice direction);
(c) 30.4 (appellant's notice);
(d) 30.6 (grounds of appeal);
(e) 30.8 (stay); and
(f) 30.9 (amendment of appeal notice).

9.5 Section 111A(4) of the 1980 Act provides that the notice of appeal must be filed within 21 days after the day on which the decision of the magistrates' court was given. The notice of appeal should also be served within this period of time. The time period for filing the appellant's notice in rule 30.4(2) does not apply. There can be no extension of this 21 day time limit under rule 4.1(3)(a).

Other statutory rights of appeal from a magistrates' court and the court at which the appellant's notice is to be filed-provisions applying to those appeals and appeals under section 111A of the 1980 Act

9.6 The effect of the Destination Order is that appeals against decisions of magistrates' courts in family proceedings shall lie to a county court instead of to the High Court. In addition to replacing appeals by way of case stated by amending the 1980 Act as outlined above, the Destination Order amends the statutory provisions listed in paragraph 9.7 below to provide for the appeals under those provisions to lie to a county court instead of to the High Court. Paragraph 9.7 also refers to the amendment to the 1980 Act for completeness.

9.7 Paragraph 9.8 and 9.9 below apply to appeals under –

(a) section 4(7) of the Maintenance Orders Act 1958;
(b) section 29 of the Domestic Proceedings and Magistrates' Courts Act 1978;
(c) section 60(5) of the Family Law 1986;
(d) section 94(1) to (9) of the Children Act 1989;
(e) section 61 of the Family Law Act 1996;
(f) sections 10(1)(a) to (3) and 13 (1) and (2) of the Crime and Disorder Act 1998; or
(g) section 111A of the 1980 Act.

9.8 Subject to any enactment or to any directions made by the President of the Family Division in exercise of the powers conferred on him under section 9 of the Courts and Legal Services Act 1990, a district judge may –

(a) dismiss an appeal –
   (i) for want of prosecution; or
   (ii) with the consent of the parties; or
(b) give leave for the appeal to be withdrawn,
and may deal with any question of costs arising out of the dismissal or withdrawal.

Unless the court directs otherwise, any interlocutory application in an appeal under the statutory provisions listed in paragraph 9.7 may be made to a district judge.

PART II – Statutory Instruments

9.9 Subject to paragraph 9.10 below, the appellant's notice and other documents required to be filed by rule 30.4 and this practice direction shall where the appeal is against the making by a magistrates' court of any order or any refusal by a magistrates' court to make such an order –

(a)   in proceedings listed in Schedule 1 to this Practice Direction, be filed in a care centre within the meaning of article 2(b) of the Allocation and Transfer of Proceedings Order 2008;

(b)   in proceedings under the Adoption and Children Act 2002, be filed in an adoption centre or an intercountry adoption centre within the meaning of article 2(c) and (d) of the Allocation and Transfer of Proceedings Order 2008; and

(c)   in any other case, be filed in a family hearing centre within the meaning of article 2(a) of that Order.

9.10 Where the appeal is an appeal from a decision of a magistrates' court under section 94 of the 1989 Act or section 61 of the Family Law Act 1996, the documents required to be filed by rule 30.4 and this practice direction may be filed in the principal registry of the Family Division of the High Court.

9.11 Article 11 of the Destination Order amends article 3 of the Allocation and Transfer of Proceedings Order 2008 to provide that the principal registry of the Family Division of the High Court is treated as a county court for the purposes of appeals from decisions of a magistrates' court under section 94 of the Children Act 1989 and section 61 of the Family Law Act 1996.

9.12 This practice direction applies to appeals under the statutory provisions listed in paragraph 9.7 with the following modifications and any other necessary modifications –

(a)   after paragraph 5.6 insert –

'5.6A Paragraphs 5.4 to 5.6 do not apply to an appeal to a county court under section 111A of the Magistrates' Courts Act 1980.'

(b)   in paragraph 5.35, insert 'and 5.36A' after ' subject to paragraph 5.36';
(c)   after paragraph 5.36 insert –

'5.36A Where the appeal is to a judge of a county court under section 111A of the Magistrates' Courts Act 1980, the appellant's notice must be filed and served within 21 days after the day on which the decision of the lower court was given.'.

Appeals to a county court from the Child Maintenance and Enforcement Commission ('the Commission'): Deduction order appeals

9.13 A 'deduction order appeal' is an appeal under regulation 25AB(1)(a) to (d) of the Child Support (Collection and Enforcement) Regulations 1992 (S.I. 1992/1989)('the Collection and Enforcement Regulations').A deduction order appeal is an appeal against –

(a)   the making of a regular deduction order under section 32A of the Child Support Act 1991 ('the 1991 Act');
(b)   a decision on an application to review a regular deduction order;

(c)   a decision to withhold consent to the disapplication of sections 32G(1) and 32H(2)(b) of the 1991 Act which has the effect of unfreezing funds in the liable person's account; or

(d)   the making of a final lump sum deduction order under section 32F of the 1991 Act.

A deduction order appeal lies to a county court from the Commission as a result of regulation 25AB(1) of the Collection and Enforcement Regulations.

9.14 The rules in Part 30 apply to deduction order appeals with the amendments set out in paragraphs 9.15 to 9.27 and 9.29 and 9.30 below. The rules in Part 30 also apply to appeals against the decision of a district judge in proceedings relating to a deduction order appeal with the amendments set out in paragraph 9.28 below.

9.15 'The respondent' means –

(a)   the Commission and any person other than the appellant who was served with an order under section 32A(1), 32E(1) or 32F(1) of the 1991 Act; and

(b)   a person who is permitted by the appeal court to be a party to the appeal.

9.16 The appellant will serve the appellant's notice on the Commission and any other respondent.

9.17 The appellant shall file and serve the appellant's notice, within 21 days of –

(a)   where the appellant is a deposit-taker, service of the order;

(b)   where the appellant is a liable person, receipt of the order; or

(c)   where the appellant is either a deposit-taker or a liable person, the date of receipt of notification of the decision.

9.18 For the purposes of paragraph 9.17 –

(a)   references to 'liable person' and 'deposit-taker' are to be interpreted in accordance with section 32E of the 1991 Act and regulation 25A(2) of the Collection and Enforcement Regulations and section 54 of the 1991 Act, respectively; and

(b)   the liable person is to be treated as having received the order or notification of the decision 2 days after it was posted by the Commission.

9.19 Rule 4.1(3)(a) (court's power to extend or shorten the time for compliance with a rule, practice direction or court order) does not apply to an appeal against the making of a lump sum deduction order under section 32F of the 1991 Act in so far as that rule gives the court power to extend the time set out in paragraph 9.17 for filing and serving an appellant's notice after the time for filing and serving the that notice set out in paragraph 9.17 has expired.

PART II – Statutory Instruments

9.20 The Commission shall provide to the court and serve on all other parties to the appeal any information and evidence relevant to the making of the decision or order being appealed, within 14 days of receipt of the appellant's notice.

9.21 Subject to paragraph 9.23, a respondent who wishes to ask the appeal court to uphold the order or decision of the Commission for reasons different from or in additional to those given by the Commission must file a respondent's notice.

9.22 A respondent's notice must be filed within 14 days of receipt of the appellant's notice.

9.23 Where the Commission as a respondent, wishes to contend that its order or decision should be –

(a)   varied, either in any event or in the event of the appeal being allowed in whole or in part; or

(b)   affirmed on different grounds from those on which it relied when making the order or decision,

it shall, within 14 days of receipt of the appellant's notice, file and serve on all other parties to the appeal a respondent's notice.

9.24 In so far as rule 30.7(Variation of time) may permit any application for variation of the time limit for filing an appellant's notice after the time for filing the appellant's notice has expired, that rule shall not apply to an appeal made against an order under section 32F(1) of the Act of 1991.

9.25 Rule 30.8 (stay) shall not apply to an appeal made against an order under section 32F(1) of the Act of 1991.

9.26 A district judge may hear a deduction order appeal.

9.27 Rule 30.11 (appeal court's powers) does not apply to deduction order appeals.

9.28 Rule 30.11(2)(d) (making orders for payment of interest) does not apply in the case of an appeal against a decision of a district judge in proceedings relating to a deduction order appeal.

9.29 In the case of a deduction order appeal –

(a)   the appeal court has power to –
   (i)   affirm or set aside the order or decision;
   (ii)   remit the matter to the Commission for the order or decision to be reconsidered, with appropriate directions;
   (iii) refer any application or issue for determination by the Commission;
   (iv)   make a costs order; and

(b)   the appeal court may exercise its powers in relation to the whole or part of an order or decision of the Commission.

9.30 In rule 30.12 (Hearing of appeals) –

(a) at the beginning of paragraph (1), for 'Every' substitute 'Subject to paragraph (2A), every';

(b) at the beginning of paragraph (2), for 'Unless' substitute 'Subject to paragraph (2A), unless';

(c) after paragraph (2), insert –

'(2A) In the case of a deduction order appeal, the appeal will be a re-hearing, unless the appeal court orders otherwise.';

(d) in paragraph (3), after 'lower court' insert 'or, in a deduction order appeal, the order or decision of the Commission'; and

(e) for sub-paragraph (b) of paragraph (3), substitute –
    '(b) unjust because of a serious procedural or other irregularity in –
        (i) the proceedings in the lower court; or
        (ii) the making of an order or decision by the Commission.'

Information about the Commission's decision

9.31 In relation to the deduction order appeals listed in column 1 of the table in Schedule 2 to this Practice Direction –

(a) the documents to be filed and served by the appellant include the documents set out in Column 3; and

(b) the relevant information to be provided by the Commission in accordance with paragraph 9.20 above includes the information set out in Column 4.

The court at which the appeal notice is to be filed

9.32 In relation to a deduction order appeal, the appellant's notice and other documents required to be filed with that notice shall be filed in a county court (the Collection and Enforcement Regulations 25AB(1)).

The Commission's address for service

9.33 For the purposes of a deduction order appeal the Commission's address for service is –

Commission Legal Adviser
Deduction Order Team
Legal Enforcement (Civil)
Antonine House
Callendar Road
Falkirk
FK1 1XT

All notices or other documents for CMEC relating to a deduction order appeal should be sent to the above address.

9.34 This practice direction applies to deduction order appeals and appeals against the decision of a district judge in proceedings relating to a deduction order appeal with the following modifications and any other necessary modifications –

(a)   in paragraph 5.35, insert 'and 5.36B' after ' subject to paragraph 5. 36A';

(b)   after paragraph 5.36A insert –

'5.36A Where the appeal is a deduction order appeal, the appellant's notice must be filed and served within 21 days of –

(a)   where the appellant is a deposit-taker, service of the order;

(b)   where the appellant is a liable person, receipt of the order; or

(c)   where the appellant is either a deposit-taker or a liable person, the date of receipt of notification of the decision the lower court was given.'.

Appeal against the court's decision under rules 31.10, 31.11 or 31.14

10.1 The rules in Part 30 apply to appeals against the court's decision under rules 31.10, 31.11 or 31.14 with the amendments set out in paragraphs 10.2 to 10.5 below. Rules 31.15 and 31.16 apply to these appeals. These modifications do not apply to appeals against the decision made on appeal under rule 31.15.

10.2 Rule 30.3 (permission to appeal) does not apply.

10.3 The time for filing an appellant's notice at the appeal court in rule 30.4(2) does not apply. Rule 31.15 sets out the time within which an appeal against the court's decision under rules 31.10, 31.11 or 31.14 must be made to a judge of the High Court.

10.4 Rule 4.1(3)(a) (court's power to extend or shorten the time for compliance with a rule, practice direction or court order) does not apply to an appeal against the court's decision under rules 31.10, 31.11 or 31.14 in so far as that rule gives the court power to extend the time set out in rules 31.15 for filing an appellant's notice.

10.5 Rules 30.7 (variation), 30.8 (stay of proceedings), 30.10 (striking out appeal notices, setting aside or imposing conditions on permission to appeal) and 30.12 (hearing of appeals) do not apply.

Appeals against pension orders and pension compensation sharing orders

11.1 Paragraph 11.2 below applies to appeals against –

(a)   a pension sharing order under section 24B of the Matrimonial Causes Act 1973 or the variation of such an order under section 31 of that Act;

(b)   a pension sharing order under Part 4 of Schedule 5 to the Civil Partnership Act 2004 or the variation of such an order under Part 11 of Schedule 5 to that Act;

(c)   a pension compensation sharing order under section 24E of the Matrimonial Causes Act 1973 or a variation of such an order under section 31 of that Act; and

(d)   a pension compensation sharing order under Part 4 of Schedule 5 to the Civil Partnership Act 2004 or a variation of such an order under Part 11 of Schedule 5 to that Act.

11.2 Rule 4.1(3)(a) (court's power to extend or shorten the time for compliance with a rule, practice direction or court order) does not apply to an appeal against the making of the orders referred to in paragraph 11.1 above in so far as that rule gives the court power to extend the time set out in rule 30.4 for filing and serving an appellant's notice after the time for filing and serving that notice has expired .

11.3 In so far as rule 30.7 (Variation of time) may permit any application for variation of the time limit for filing an appellant's notice after the time for filing the appellant's notice has expired, that rule shall not apply to an appeal made against the orders referred to in paragraph 11.1 above.

Appeals to a court under section 20 of the 1991 Act (appeals in respect of parentage determinations)

12.1 The rules in Chapters 1 and 5 of Part 8 will apply as appropriate to an appeal under section 20(1) of the 1991 Act where that appeal must be made to a court in accordance with the Child Support Appeals (Jurisdiction of Courts) Order 2002.

12.2 The respondent to such an appeal will be the Child Maintenance and Enforcement Commission.

12.3 Where the justices' clerk or the court is considering whether or not to transfer appeal proceedings under section 20(1) of the 1991 Act, rules 12.9 to 12.11 will apply as appropriate.

Applications

13.1 Where a party to an appeal makes an application whether in an appeal notice or by Part 18 (Procedure For Other Applications in Proceedings) application notice, the provisions of Part 18 will apply.

13.2 The applicant must file the following documents with the notice –

    (a)   one additional copy of the application notice for the appeal court, one copy for each of the respondents and the persons referred to in paragraph 5.39;

    (b)   where applicable a sealed or stamped copy of the order which is the subject of the main appeal or a copy of the notice of the making of an order;

    (c)   a bundle of documents in support which should include –

        (i)   the Part 18 application notice; and

        (ii)   any witness statements and affidavits filed in support of the application notice.

Appeals against consent orders

14.1 The rules in Part 30 and the provisions of this Practice Direction apply to appeals relating to orders made by consent in addition to orders which are not made by consent. An appeal is the only way in which a consent order can be challenged.

PART II – Statutory Instruments

Disposing of applications or appeals by consent

15.1 An appellant who does not wish to pursue an application or an appeal may request the appeal court for an order that the application or appeal be dismissed. Such a request must state whether the appellant is a child, or a protected person.

15.2 The request must be accompanied by a consent signed by the other parties stating whether the respondent is a child, or a protected person and consents to the dismissal of the application or appeal.

Allowing unopposed appeals or applications on paper

16.1 The appeal court will not normally make an order allowing an appeal unless satisfied that the decision of the lower court was wrong, but the appeal court may set aside or vary the order of the lower court with consent and without determining the merits of the appeal, if it is satisfied that there are good and sufficient reasons for doing so. Where the appeal court is requested by all parties to allow an application or an appeal the court may consider the request on the papers. The request should state whether any of the parties is a child, or protected person and set out the relevant history of the proceedings and the matters relied on as justifying the proposed order and be accompanied by a copy of the proposed order.

Summary assessment of costs

17.1 Costs are likely to be assessed by way of summary assessment at the following hearings –

(a)   contested directions hearings;
(b)   applications for permission to appeal at which the respondent is present;
(c)   appeals from case management decisions or decisions made at directions hearings; and
(d)   appeals listed for one day or less.

(Provision for summary assessment of costs is made by section 13 of the Practice Direction supplementing CPR Part 44)

17.2 Parties attending any of the hearings referred to in paragraph 17.1 should be prepared to deal with the summary assessment.

Reopening of final appeals

18.1 This paragraph applies to applications under rule 30.14 (Reopening of final appeals) for permission to reopen a final determination of an appeal.

18.2 In this paragraph, 'appeal' includes an application for permission to appeal.

18.3 Permission must be sought from the court whose decision the applicant wishes to reopen.

18.4 The application for permission must be made by application notice and supported by written evidence, verified by a statement of truth.

18.5 A copy of the application for permission must not be served on any other party to the original appeal unless the court so directs.

18.6 Where the court directs that the application for permission is to be served on another party, that party may within 14 days of the service on him or her of the copy of the application file a written statement either supporting or opposing the application.

18.7 The application for permission, and any written statements supporting or opposing it, will be considered on paper by a single judge, and will be allowed to proceed only if the judge so directs.

SCHEDULE 1

Description of proceedings

(1) Proceedings under section 25 of the Children Act 1989;

(2) Proceedings under Parts IV and V of the Children Act 1989;

(3) Proceedings under Schedules 2 and 3 to the Children Act 1989;

(4) Applications for leave under section 91(14),(15) or (17) of the Children Act 1989;

(5) Proceedings under section 102 of the Children Act 1989 or section 79 of the Childcare Act 2006;

(6) Proceedings for a residence order under section 8 of the Children Act 1989 or for a special guardianship order under section 14A of the Children Act 1989 with respect to a child who is the subject of a care order.

(7) Proceedings for a residence order under section 8 of the Children Act 1989 where either section 28(1)(child placed for adoption) or 29(4) (placement order in force) of the Adoption and Children Act 2002 applies;

(8) Proceedings for a special guardianship order under section 14A of the Children Act 1989 where either section 28(1)(child placed for adoption) or section 29(5) (placement order in force) of the Adoption and Children Act 2002 applies.

PART II – Statutory Instruments

SCHEDULE 2

Appeal	Relevant legisation	Appellant information	Commission information
Appeal against the making of a regular deduction order (under section 32A of the 1991 Act)	Section 32C(4)(a) of the 1991 Act The Collection and Enforcement Regulations 25AB(1)(a) (appeals)	A copy of the order; A covering letter explaining that the order has been made and the reasons for the order namely that there are arrears of child maintenance and/or no other arrangements have been made for the payment of child maintenance, including arrears	The amount of the current maintenance calculation, the period of debt and the total amount of arrears (including account breakdown if appropriate) and the reasons for the Commission's decision, details of all previous attempts to negotiate payment i.e. phone calls and letters to the non resident parent, details of any previous enforcement action taken
Appeal against a decision on an application for a review of a regular deduction order	Sections 32C(4)(b) 32C(2)(k) of the 1991 Act The Collection and Enforcement Regulations 25G (review of a regular deduction order) and 25AB(1)(b) (appeals)	A decision notification setting out whether or not the review has been agreed by the Commission and the resulting action to be taken if agreed; with an enclosure setting out the specific reasons for the Commission's decision	The reasons for the Commission's decision in respect of the application for review and any evidence supporting that decision

Appeal	Relevant legisation	Appellant information	Commission information
Appeal against the withholding of consent to the disapplication of sections 32G(1) and 32H(2)(b) of the 1991 Act	Section 32I(4) of the 1991 Act The Collection and Enforcement Regulations 25N (disapplication of sections 32G(1) and 32H(2)(b) of the 1991 Act) and 25AB(1)(c) (appeals)	A decision notification setting out that either: *a*) consent has been refused; or *b*) consent has been given in relation to part of the application i.e. that only some of the funds which were requested to be released have been agreed to be released (the right of appeal will lie in respect of the part of the application which has been refused). There will be an enclosure with the notification setting out the reasons for the decision on the application.	The reasons for the Commission's decision in respect of the application for consent and any evidence supporting that decision

PART II – Statutory Instruments

Appeal	Relevant legisation	Appellant information	Commission information
Appeal against the making of a final lump sum deduction order (under section 32F of the 1991 Act)	Section 32J(5) of the 1991 Act Collection and Enforcement Regulations 25AB(1)(d) (appeals)	A copy of the order; A covering letter explaining that the order has been made and the reasons for the order namely that there are arrears of child maintenance and/or no other arrangements have been made for the payment of child maintenance, including arrears	The amount of the current maintenance calculation (if applicable), the period of debt and the total amount of arrears (including account breakdown if appropriate) and the reasons for the Commission's decision, details of all previous attempts to negotiate payment i.e. phone calls and letters to the non resident parent, details of any previous enforcement action taken.

PART 31
REGISTRATION OF ORDERS UNDER THE COUNCIL REGULATION, THE CIVIL PARTNERSHIP (JURISDICTION AND RECOGNITION OF JUDGMENTS) REGULATIONS 2005 AND UNDER THE HAGUE CONVENTION 1996

31.1 Scope

This Part applies to proceedings for the recognition, non-recognition and registration of –

(a) judgments to which the Council Regulation applies;

(b) measures to which the 1996 Hague Convention applies; and

(c) judgments to which the Jurisdiction and Recognition of Judgments Regulations apply, and which relate to dissolution or annulment of overseas relationships entitled to be treated as a civil partnership, or legal separation of the same.

31.2 Interpretation

(1) In this Part –

(a) 'judgment' is to be construed –
    (i) in accordance with the definition in Article 2(4) of the Council Regulation where it applies;
    (ii) in accordance with regulation 6 of the Jurisdiction and Recognition of Judgments Regulations where those Regulations apply; or
    (iii) as meaning any measure taken by an authority with jurisdiction under Chapter II of the 1996 Hague Convention where that Convention applies;

(b) 'the Jurisdiction and Recognition of Judgments Regulations' means the Civil Partnership (Jurisdiction and Recognition of Judgments) Regulations 2005;

(c) 'Member State' means –
    (i) where registration, recognition or non-recognition is sought of a judgment under the Council Regulation, a Member State of the European Union which is bound by that Regulation or a country which has subsequently adopted it;
    (ii) where recognition is sought of a judgment to which the Jurisdiction and Recognition of Judgments Regulations apply, a Member State of the European Union to which Part II of those Regulations applies;

(d) 'Contracting State' means a State, other than a Member State within the meaning of (c) above, in relation to which the 1996 Hague Convention is in force as between that State and the United Kingdom; and

(e) 'parental responsibility' –
    (i) where the Council Regulation applies, has the meaning given in Article 2(7) of that Regulation; and
    (ii) where the 1996 Hague Convention applies, has the meaning given in Article 1(2) of that Convention.

(2) References in this Part to registration are to the registration of a judgment in accordance with the provisions of this Part.

31.3 Where to start proceedings

(1) Every application under this Part, except for an application under rule 31.18 for a certified copy of a judgment, or under rule 31.20 for rectification of a certificate issued under Articles 41 or 42, must be made to the principal registry.

(2) Nothing in this rule prevents the determination of an issue of recognition as an incidental question by any court in proceedings, in accordance with Article 21(4) of the Council Regulation.

(3) Notwithstanding paragraph (1), where recognition of a judgment is raised as an incidental question in proceedings under the 1996 Hague Convention or the Jurisdiction and Recognition of Judgments Regulations the court hearing those proceedings may determine the question of recognition.

PART II – Statutory Instruments

31.4 Application for registration, recognition or non-recognition of a judgment

(1) Any interested person may apply to the court for an order that the judgment be registered, recognised or not recognised.

(2) Except for an application under rule 31.7, an application for registration, recognition or non-recognition must be –

    (a)   made to a district judge of the principal registry; and

    (b)   in the form, and supported by the documents and the information required by a practice direction.

31.5 Documents – supplementary

(1) Except as regards a copy of a judgment required by Article 37(1)(a) of the Council Regulation, where the person making an application under this Part does not produce the documents required by rule 31.4(2)(b) the court may –

    (a)   fix a time within which the documents are to be produced;

    (b)   accept equivalent documents; or

    (c)   dispense with production of the documents if the court considers it has sufficient information.

(2) This rule does not apply to applications under rule 31.7.

31.6 Directions

(1) As soon as practicable after an application under this Part has been made, the court may (subject to the requirements of the Council Regulation) give such directions as it considers appropriate, including as regards the following matters –

    (a)   whether service of the application may be dispensed with;

    (b)   expedition of the proceedings or any part of the proceedings (and any direction for expedition may specify a date by which the court must give its decision);

    (c)   the steps to be taken in the proceedings and the time by which each step is to be taken;

    (d)   the service of documents; and

    (e)   the filing of evidence.

(2) The court or court officer will –

    (a)   record the giving, variation or revocation of directions under this rule; and

    (b)   as soon as practicable serve a copy of the directions order on every party.

31.7 Recognition and enforcement under the Council Regulation of a judgment given in another Member State relating to rights of access or under Article 11(8) for the return of the child to that State

(1) This rule applies where a judgment has been given in another Member State –

(a)   relating to rights of access: or

(b)   under Article 11(8) of the Council Regulation for the return of a child to that State,

which has been certified, in accordance with Article 41(2) or 42(2) as the case may be, by the judge in the court of origin.

(2) An application for recognition or enforcement of the judgment must be –

(a)   made in writing to a district judge of the principal registry; and

(b)   accompanied by a copy of the certificate issued by the judge in the court of origin.

(3) The application may be made without notice.

(4) Rules 31.5 and 31.8 to 31.17 do not apply to an application made under this rule.

(5) Nothing in this rule shall prevent a holder of parental responsibility from seeking recognition and enforcement of a judgment in accordance with the provisions of rules 31.8 to 31.17.

31.8 Registration for enforcement or order for non-recognition of a judgment

(1) This rule applies where an application is made for an order that a judgment given in another Member State, or a Contracting State, should be registered, or should not be recognised, except where rule 31.7 applies.

(2) Where the application is made for an order that the judgment should be registered –

(a)   upon receipt of the application, and subject to any direction given by the court under rule 31.6 the court officer will serve the application on the person against whom registration is sought;

(b)   the court will not accept submissions from either the person against whom registration is sought or any child in relation to whom the judgment was given.

(3) Where the application is for an order that the judgment should not be recognised –

(a)   upon receipt of the application, and subject to any direction given by the court under rule 31.6, the court officer will serve the application on the person in whose favour judgment was given;

(b)   the person in whose favour the judgment was given must file an answer to the application and serve it on the applicant –

  (i)   within 1 month of service of the application; or

  (ii)   if the applicant is habitually resident in another Member State, within two months of service of the application.

(4) In cases to which the 1996 Hague Convention applies and the Council Regulation does not apply, the court may extend the time set out in subparagraph (3)(b)(ii) on account of distance.

(5) The person in whose favour the judgment was given may request recognition or registration of the judgment in their answer, and in that event must comply with 31.4(2)(b) to the extent that such documents, information and evidence are not already contained in the application for non-recognition.

(6) If, in a case to which the Council Regulation applies, the person in whose favour the judgment was given fails to file an answer as required by paragraph (3), the court will act in accordance with the provisions of Article 18 of the Council Regulation.

(7) If, in a case to which the 1996 Hague Convention applies and the Service Regulation does not, the person in whose favour the judgment was given fails to file an answer as required by paragraph (3) –

(a)   where the Hague Convention of 15th November 1965 on the service abroad of judicial and extrajudicial documents in civil or commercial matters applies, the court shall apply Article 15 of that Convention; and

(b)   in all other cases, the court will not consider the application unless –

   (i)   it is proved to the satisfaction of the court that the person in whose favour judgment was given was served with the application within a reasonable period of time to arrange his or her response; or

   (ii)   the court is satisfied that the circumstances of the case justify proceeding with consideration of the application.

(8) In a case to which the Jurisdiction and Recognition of Judgments Regulations apply, if the person in whose favour judgment was given fails to file an answer as required by paragraph (3), the court will apply the Service Regulation where that regulation applies, and if it does not –

(a)   where the Hague Convention of 15th November 1965 on the service abroad of judicial and extrajudicial documents in civil or commercial matters applies, the court shall apply Article 15 of that Convention; and

(b)   in all other cases, the court will apply the provisions of paragraph (7)(b).

31.9 Stay of recognition proceedings by reason of an appeal

Where recognition or non-recognition of a judgment given in another Member State or Contracting State is sought, or is raised as an incidental question in other proceedings, the court may stay the proceedings –

(a)   if an ordinary appeal against the judgment has been lodged; or

(b)   if the judgment was given in the Republic of Ireland, if enforcement of the judgment is suspended there by reason of an appeal.

31.10 Effect of refusal of application for a decision that a judgment should not be recognised

Where the court refuses an application for a decision that a judgment should not be recognised, the court may –

(a) direct that the decision to refuse the application is to be treated as a decision that the judgment be recognised; or

(b) treat the answer under paragraph (3)(b) of rule 31.8 as an application that the judgment be registered for enforcement if paragraph (5) of that rule is complied with and order that the judgment be registered for enforcement in accordance with rule 31.11.

31.11 Notification of the court's decision on an application for registration or non-recognition

(1) Where the court has –

(a) made an order on an application for an order that a judgment should be registered for enforcement; or

(b) refused an application that a judgment should not be recognised and ordered under rule 31.10 that the judgment be registered for enforcement,

the court officer will as soon as practicable take the appropriate action under paragraph (2) or (3).

(2) If the court refuses the application for the judgment to be registered for enforcement, the court officer will serve the order on the applicant and the person against whom judgment was given in the state of origin.

(3) If the court orders that the judgment should be registered for enforcement, the court officer will –

(a) register the judgment in the central index of judgments kept by the principal registry;

(b) confirm on the order that the judgment has been registered; and

(c) serve on the parties the court's order endorsed with the court officer's confirmation that the judgment has been registered.

(4) A sealed order of the court endorsed in accordance with paragraph (3)(b) will constitute notification that the judgment has been registered under Article 28(2) of the Council Regulation or under Article 26 of the 1996 Hague Convention, as the case may be, and in this Part 'notice of registration' means a sealed order so endorsed.

(5) The notice of registration must state –

(a) full particulars of the judgment registered and the order for registration;

(b) the name of the party making the application and his address for service within the jurisdiction;

(c) the right of the person against whom judgment was given to appeal against the order for registration; and

(d)   the period within which an appeal against the order for registration may be made.

31.12 Effect of registration under rule 31.11

Registration of a judgment under rule 31.11 will serve for the purpose of Article 21(3) of the Council Regulation, Article 24 of the 1996 Hague Convention, or regulation 7 of the Jurisdiction and Recognition of Judgments Regulations (as the case may be) as a decision that the judgment is recognised.

31.13 The central index of judgments registered under rule 31.11

The central index of judgments registered under rule 31.11 will be kept by the principal registry.

31.14 Decision on recognition of a judgment only

(1) Where an application is made seeking recognition of a judgment only, the provisions of rules 31.8 and 31.9 apply to that application as they do to an application for registration for enforcement.

(2) Where the court orders that the judgment should be recognised, the court officer will serve a copy of the order on each party as soon as practicable.

(3) A sealed order of the court will constitute notification that the judgment has been recognised under Article 21(3) of the Council Regulation, Article 24 of the 1996 Hague convention or regulation 7 of the Jurisdiction and Recognition of Judgments Regulations, as the case may be.

(4) The sealed order shall indicate –

(a)   full particulars of the judgment recognised;
(b)   the name of the party making the application and his address for service within the jurisdiction;
(c)   the right of the person against whom judgment was given to appeal against the order for recognition; and
(d)   the period within which an appeal against the order for recognition may be made.

31.15 Appeal against the court's decision under rules 31.10, 31.11 or 31.14

(1) An appeal against the court's decision under rules 31.10, 31.11 or 31.14 must be made to a judge of the High Court –

(a)   within one month of the date of service of the notice of registration; or
(b)   if the party bringing the appeal is habitually resident in another Member State, or a Contracting State, within two months of the date of service.

(2) The court may not extend time for an appeal on account of distance unless the matter is one to which the 1996 Hague Convention applies and the Council Regulation does not apply.

(3) If, in a case to which the 1996 Hague Convention applies and the Service Regulation does not, the appeal is brought by the applicant for a declaration of enforceability or registration and the respondent fails to appear –

    (a)   where the Hague Convention of 15th November 1965 on the service abroad of judicial and extrajudicial documents in civil or commercial matters applies, the court shall apply Article 15 of that Convention; and

    (b)   in all other cases, the court will not consider the appeal unless –

        (i)   it is proved to the satisfaction of the court that the respondent was served with notice of the appeal within a reasonable period of time to arrange his or her response; or

        (ii)   the court is satisfied that the circumstances of the case justify proceeding with consideration of the appeal.

(4) This rule is subject to rule 31.16.

(The procedure for applications under rule 31.15 is set out in Practice Direction 30A (Appeals).)

31.16 Stay of enforcement where appeal pending in state of origin

(1) A party against whom enforcement is sought of a judgment which has been registered under rule 31.11 may apply to the court with which an appeal is lodged under rule 31.15 for the proceedings to be stayed where –

    (a)   that party has lodged an ordinary appeal in the Member State or Contracting State of origin; or

    (b)   the time for such an appeal has not yet expired.

(2) Where an application for a stay is filed in the circumstances described in paragraph (1)(b), the court may specify the time within which an appeal must be lodged.

31.17 Enforcement of judgments registered under rule 31.11

(1) The court will not enforce a judgment registered under rule 31.11 until after –

    (a)   the expiration of any applicable period under rules 31.15 or 31.16; or

    (b)   if that period has been extended by the court, the expiration of the period so extended.

(2) A party applying to the court for the enforcement of a registered judgment must produce to the court a certificate of service of –

    (a)   the notice of registration of the judgment; and

    (b)   any order made by the court in relation to the judgment.

(Service out of the jurisdiction, including service in accordance with the Service Regulation, is dealt with in chapter 4 of Part 6 and in Practice Direction 6B.)

31.18 Request for a certificate or a certified copy of a judgment

(1) An application for a certified copy of a judgment, or for a certificate under Articles 39, 41 or 42 of the Council Regulation, must be made to the court which made the order and without giving notice to any other party.

(2) The application must be made in the form, and supported by the documents and information required by a practice direction.

(3) The certified copy of the judgment will be an office copy sealed with the seal of the court and signed by the district judge, or by the court where the application is made to the Magistrates' Court. It will be issued with a certified copy of any order which has varied any of the terms of the original order.

(4) Where the application is made for the purposes of applying for recognition or recognition and enforcement of the order in another Contracting State, the court must indicate on the certified copy of the judgment the grounds on which it based its jurisdiction to make the order, for the purposes of Article 23(2)(a) of the 1996 Hague Convention.

31.19 Certificates issued in England and Wales under Articles 41 and 42 of the Council Regulation

The court officer will serve –

    (a)   a certificate issued under Article 41 or 42; or
    (b)   a certificate rectified under rule 31.20,

on all parties and will transmit a copy to the Central Authority for England and Wales.

31.20 Rectification of certificate issued under Article 41 or 42 of the Council Regulation

(1) Where there is an error in a certificate issued under Article 41 or 42, an application to rectify that error must be made to the court which issued the certificate.

(2) A rectification under paragraph (1) may be made –

    (a)   by the court of its own initiative; or
    (b)   on application by –
        (i)   any party to the proceedings; or
        (ii)   the court or Central Authority of another Member State.

(3) An application under paragraph (2)(b) may be made without notice being served on any other party.

31.21 Authentic instruments and agreements under Article 46 of the Council Regulation

This Chapter applies to an authentic instrument and an agreement to which Article 46 of the Council Regulation applies as it applies to a judgment.

31.22 Application for provisional, including protective measures

An application for provisional, including protective, measures under Article 20 of the Council Regulation or Articles 11 or 12 of the 1996 Hague Convention may be made notwithstanding that the time for appealing against an order for registration of a judgment has not expired or that a final determination of any issue relating to enforcement of the judgment is pending.

Practice Direction 31A –
Registration of orders under the Council Regulation, the Civil Partnership (Jurisdiction and Recognition of Judgments) Regulations 2005 and under the 1996 Hague Convention

This Practice Direction supplements FPR Part 31

Form of application

1.1 An application under rule 31.4 must be made using the Part 19 procedure, except that the provisions of rules 31.8 to 31.14 and of this Practice Direction shall apply in place of rules 19.4 to 19.9.

1.2 Where the application is for recognition only of an order, it should be made clear that the application does not extend to registration for enforcement.

Evidence in support of all applications for registration, recognition or non-recognition

2.1 The requirements for information and evidence for applications differ according to whether the application is made under the Council Regulation, the Jurisdiction and Recognition of Judgments Regulations, or the 1996 Hague Convention.

2.2 All applications to which rule 31.4(2) applies must be supported by a statement that is sworn to be true or an affidavit, exhibiting the judgment, or a verified, certified or otherwise duly authenticated copy of the judgment. In the case of an application under the Jurisdiction and Recognition of Judgments Regulations or under the 1996 Hague Convention, a translation of the judgment should be supplied.

2.3 Where any other document required by this Practice Direction or by direction of the court under rule 31.5 is not in English, the applicant must supply a translation of that document into English certified by a notary public or a person qualified for the purpose, or accompanied by witness statement or affidavit confirming that the translation is accurate.

Evidence required in support of application for registration, recognition or non-recognition of a judgment under the Council Regulation

3.1 An application for a judgment to be registered, recognised or not recognised under the Council Regulation must be accompanied by a witness

PART II – Statutory Instruments

statement or an affidavit exhibiting the following documents and giving the information required by 3.2 or 3.3 below, as appropriate.

3.2 In the case of an application for recognition or registration –

(a)   the certificate in the form set out in Annex I or Annex II of the Council Regulation, issued by the Member State in which judgment was given;

(b)   in the case of a judgment given in default, the documents referred to in Article 37(2);

(c)   whether the judgment provides for the payment of a sum or sums of money;

(d)   whether interest is recoverable on the judgment or part of the judgment in accordance with the law of the State in which the judgment was given, and if that is the case, the rate of interest, the date from which interest is recoverable, and the date on which interest ceases to accrue;

(e)   an address within the jurisdiction of the court for service of process on the party making the application and stating, in so far as is known to the applicant, the name and usual or last known address or place of business of the person against whom judgment was given; and

(f)   where appropriate, whether Article 56 has been complied with, and the identity and address of the authority or authorities from whom consent has been obtained, together with evidence of that consent.

3.3 In the case of an application for an order that a judgment should not be recognised under Article 21(3) –

(a)   the certificate referred to at paragraph 3.2(a);

(b)   in relation to the documents identified at paragraph 3.2(b), those documents or a statement that no such service or acceptance occurred if that is the case;

(c)   an address within the jurisdiction of the court for service of process on the applicant and stating, in so far as is known to the applicant, the name and usual or last known address or place of business of the person in whose favour judgment was given; and

(d)   a statement of the ground or grounds under Articles 22 or 23 (as the case may be) on which it is requested that the judgment should not be recognised, the reasons why the applicant asserts that such ground or grounds is, or are, made out, and any documentary evidence on which the applicant relies.

Evidence required in support of an application for registration, recognition or non-recognition of a judgment under the 1996 Hague Convention.

4.1 An application for an order for a judgment to be registered under Article 26 or not recognised under Article 24 of the 1996 Hague Convention must be accompanied by a witness statement or affidavit exhibiting the following documents and giving the information required by 4.2, 4.3 or 4.4 below as appropriate.

4.2 In the case of an application for registration –

(a) those documents necessary to show that the judgment is enforceable according to the law of the Contracting State in which it was given;

(b) a description of the opportunities provided by the authority which gave the judgment in question for the child to be heard, except where that judgment was given in a case of urgency;

(c) where the judgment was given in a case of urgency, a statement as to the circumstances of the urgency that led to the child not having the opportunity to be heard;

(d) details of any measures taken in the non-Contracting State of the habitual residence of the child, if applicable, specifying the nature and effect of the measure, and the date on which it was taken;

(e) in as far as not apparent from the copy of the judgment provided, a statement of the grounds on which the authority which gave the judgment based its jurisdiction, together with any documentary evidence in support of that statement;

(f) where appropriate, a statement regarding whether Article 33 of the 1996 Hague Convention has been complied with, and the identity and address of the authority or authorities from which consent has been obtained, together with evidence of that consent; and

(g) the information referred to at 3.2(c) to (e) above.

4.3 In the case of an application for an order that a judgment should not be recognised –

(a) a statement of the ground or grounds under Article 23 of the 1996 Hague Convention on which it is requested that the judgment be not recognised, the reasons why the applicant asserts that such ground or grounds is or are made out, and any documentary evidence on which the Applicant relies; and

(b) an address within the jurisdiction of the court for service of process on the applicant and stating, in so far as is known to the applicant, the name and usual or last known address or place of business of the person in whose favour judgment was given.

4.4 Where is it sought to apply for recognition only of a judgment under the 1996 Hague Convention, the provisions of paragraph 4.2 apply with the exception that the applicant is not required to produce the document referred to in subparagraph 4.2(a).

Evidence required in support of an application for recognition or non-recognition of a judgment under the Jurisdiction and Recognition of Judgments Regulations

5.1 An application for recognition of a judgment under regulation 7 of the Jurisdiction and Recognition of Judgments Regulations or for non-recognition of a judgment under regulation 8 must be accompanied by a witness statement or affidavit exhibiting the following documents and giving the information at 5.2 or 5.3 below, as appropriate.

5.2 In the case of an application for recognition of a judgment –

(a)   where applicable, details of any decision determining the question of the substance or validity of the civil partnership previously given by a court of civil jurisdiction in England and Wales, or by a court elsewhere;

(b)   where the judgment was obtained otherwise than by means of proceedings –

    (i)   an official document certifying that the judgment is effective under the law of the country in which it was obtained;

    (ii)   where either civil partner was domiciled in another country from that in which the judgment was obtained at the relevant date, an official document certifying that the judgment is recognised as valid under the law of that country; or

    (iii)   a verified, certified or otherwise duly authenticated copy of the document at (i) or (ii) above, as appropriate;

(c)   in relation to a judgment obtained by means of proceedings and given in default, the original or a certified true copy of the document which establishes that the party who did not respond was served with the document instituting the proceedings or with an equivalent document, or any document indicating that the respondent has accepted the judgment unequivocally; and

(d)   the information referred to at paragraph 3.2(c) to (e) above.

5.3 In the case of an application for non-recognition of a judgment –

(a)   an address within the jurisdiction of the court for service of process on the applicant and stating, in so far as is known to the applicant, the name and usual or last known address or place of business of the person in whose favour judgment was given;

(b)   a statement of the ground or grounds under regulation 8 of the Jurisdiction and Recognition of Judgments Regulations on which it is requested that the judgment should not be recognised together with any documentary evidence on which the applicant relies; and

(c)   where the judgment was obtained by means of proceedings, the document referred to at paragraph 5.2(c) or a statement that no such service or acceptance occurred if that is the case.

Evidence in support of application for a certificate under Articles 39, 41 or 42 of the Council Regulation, or for a certified copy of a judgment

6.1 The procedure described in the following paragraphs should be used where the application for the certified copy of the judgment or relevant certificate under the Council Regulation has not been made at the conclusion of the proceedings to which it relates.

6.2 An application for a certified copy of a judgment, or for a certificate under Articles 39, 41 or 42 of the Council Regulation must be made by witness statement or affidavit, containing the information and attaching the documents required under paragraph 6.3, and paragraphs 6.4, 6.5 or 6.6 below, as appropriate.

6.3 All applications must –

(a)   provide details of the proceedings in which the judgment was obtained;

(b)   attach a copy of the application by which the proceedings were begun;

(c)   attach a copy of all statements of case filed in the proceedings; and

(d)   state –

   (i)   whether the judgment provides for the payment of a sum of money; and

   (ii)   whether interest is recoverable on the judgment or part of it and if so, the rate of interest, the date from which interest is recoverable, and the date on which interest ceases to accrue.

Further, where the application relates to the Council Regulation, the applicant must attach a document showing that he or she benefitted from legal aid in the proceedings to which the judgment relates, if that is the case.

6.4 An application for a certified copy of the judgment and a certificate under Article 41 or 42 of the Council Regulation must –

(a)   contain a statement of whether the certificate is sought under Article 41 or Article 42;

(b)   attach a document evidencing the service of the application by which the proceedings were begun on all respondents, and if no such service occurred, details of all opportunities provided to each respondent to put their case before the court;

(c)   provide information regarding the age of the child at the time of the judgment and the opportunities given during the proceedings, if any, for the child's wishes and feelings to be ascertained;

(d)   state the full names, addresses and dates and places of birth (where available) of all persons holding parental responsibility in relation to the child or children to whom the judgment relates; and

(e)   state the full names and dates of birth of each child to whom the judgment relates.

6.5 An application for a certified copy of the judgment and a certificate under Article 39 of the Council Regulation must –

(a)   state whether the certificate sought relates to a parental responsibility matter or a matrimonial matter;

(b)   in relation to a parental responsibility matter, attach evidence that the judgment has been served on the respondent;

(c)   in the case of a judgment given in default, attach a document which establishes that the respondent was served with the petition or application by which the proceedings were commenced, or a document indicating that the respondent accepted the judgment unequivocally;

(d)   state that the time for appealing has expired, or give the date on which it will expire, as appropriate, and state whether a notice of appeal against the judgment has been given;

(e)   in relation to a matrimonial matter, give the full name, address, country and place of birth, and date of birth of each party, and the country, place and date of the marriage;

(f)   in relation to a parental responsibility matter, give the full name, address, place and date of birth of each person who holds parental responsibility ;

(g)   as appropriate, give the name, address, and date and place of birth of the person with access rights, or to whom the child is to be returned.

6.6 An application for a certified copy of a judgment for the purposes of recognition and enforcement of the judgment under the 1996 Hague Convention must –

(a)   provide a statement of the grounds on which the court based its jurisdiction to make the orders in question;

(b)   indicate the age of the child at the time of the judgment and the measures taken, if any, for the child's wishes and feelings to be ascertained; and

(c)   indicate which persons were provided with notice of the proceedings and, where such persons were served with the proceedings, attach evidence of such service.

PART 32
REGISTRATION AND ENFORCEMENT OF ORDERS

****

Chapter 4
Registration and Enforcement of Custody Orders under the 1986 Act

32.23 Interpretation

In this Chapter –

'appropriate court' means, in relation to –
(a)   Scotland, the Court of Session;
(b)   Northern Ireland, the High Court in Northern Ireland; and
(c)   a specified dependent territory, the corresponding court in that territory;

'appropriate officer' means, in relation to –
(a)   the Court of Session, the Deputy Principal Clerk of Session;
(b)   the High Court in Northern Ireland, the Master (Care and Protection) of that court; and
(c)   the appropriate court in a specified dependent territory, the corresponding officer of that court;

'Part 1 order' means an order under Part 1 of the 1986 Act;
'the register' means the register kept for the purposes of Part 1 of the 1986 Act; and
'specified dependent territory' means a dependent territory specified in column 1 of Schedule 1 to the Family Law Act 1986 (Specified Dependent Territories) Order 1991.

32.24 Prescribed officer and functions of the court

(1) The prescribed officer for the purposes of sections 27(4) and 28(1) of the 1986 Act is the family proceedings department manager of the principal registry.

(2) The function of the court under sections 27(3) and 28(1) of the 1986 Act shall be performed by a court officer.

32.25 Application for the registration of an order made by the High Court or a county court

(1) An application under section 27 of the 1986 Act for the registration of an order made in the High Court or a county court may be made by sending to a court officer at the court which made the order –

    (a)   a certified copy of the order;

    (b)   a copy of any order which has varied the terms of the original order;

    (c)   a statement which –

        (i)   contains the name and address of the applicant and the applicant's interest under the order;

        (ii)   contains –

            (aa)   the name and date of birth of the child in respect of whom the order was made;

            (bb)   the whereabouts or suspected whereabouts of the child; and

            (cc)   the name of any person with whom the child is alleged to be;

        (iii)   contains the name and address of any other person who has an interest under the order and states whether the order has been served on that person;

        (iv)   states in which of the jurisdictions of Scotland, Northern Ireland or a specified dependent territory the order is to be registered;

        (v)   states that to the best of the applicant's information and belief, the order is in force;

        (vi)   states whether, and if so where, the order is already registered;

        (vii)   gives details of any order known to the applicant which affects the child and is in force in the jurisdiction in which the order is to be registered;

        (viii)   annexes any document relevant to the application; and

        (ix)   is verified by a statement of truth; and

    (d)   a copy of the statement referred to in paragraph (c).

(2) On receipt of the documents referred to in paragraph (1), the court officer will, subject to paragraph (4) –

    (a)   keep the original statement and send the other documents to the appropriate officer;

    (b)   record in the court records the fact that the documents have been sent to the appropriate officer; and

    (c)   file a copy of the documents.

PART II – Statutory Instruments

(3) On receipt of a notice that the document has been registered in the appropriate court the court officer will record that fact in the court records.

(4) The court officer will not send the documents to the appropriate officer if it appears to the court officer that –

(a)   the order is no longer in force; or
(b)   the child has reached the age of 16.

(5) Where paragraph (4) applies –

(a)   the court officer must, within 14 days of the decision, notify the applicant of the decision of the court officer in paragraph (4) and the reasons for it; and
(b)   the applicant may apply to a judge, but not a district judge, in private for an order that the documents be sent to the appropriate court.

32.26 Registration of orders made in Scotland, Northern Ireland or a specified dependent territory

(1) This rule applies where the prescribed officer receives, for registration, a certified copy of an order made in Scotland, Northern Ireland or a specified dependent territory.

(2) The prescribed officer will –

(a)   enter in the register –
  (i)   the name and address of the applicant and the applicant's interest under the order;
  (ii)   the name and date of birth of the child and the date the child will attain the age of 16;
  (iii)   the whereabouts or suspected whereabouts of the child; and
  (iv)   the terms of the order, its date and the court which made it;
(b)   file the certified copy and accompanying documents; and
(c)   notify –
  (i)   the court which sent the order; and
  (ii)   the applicant,
  that the order has been registered.

32.27 Revocation and variation of an order made in the High Court or a county court

(1) Where a Part 1 order, registered in an appropriate court, is varied or revoked, the court officer of the court making the order of variation or revocation will –

(a)   send a certified copy of the order of variation or revocation to –
  (i)   the appropriate officer; and
  (ii)   if a different court, the court which made the Part 1 order;
(b)   record in the court records the fact that a copy of the order has been sent; and
(c)   file a copy of the order.

(2) On receipt of notice from the appropriate court that its register has been amended, this fact will be recorded by the court officer of –

(a)   the court which made the order of variation or revocation; and

(b)   if different, the court which made the Part 1 order.

32.28 Registration of varied, revoked or recalled orders made in Scotland, Northern Ireland or a specified dependent territory

(1) This rule applies where the prescribed officer receives a certified copy of an order made in Scotland, Northern Ireland or a specified dependent territory which varies, revokes or recalls a registered Part 1 order.

(2) The prescribed officer shall enter particulars of the variation, revocation or recall in the register and give notice of the entry to –

(a)   the court which sent the certified copy;

(b)   if different, the court which made the Part 1 order;

(c)   the applicant for registration; and

(d)   if different, the applicant for the variation, revocation of recall of the order.

(3) An application under section 28(2) of the 1986 Act must be made in accordance with the Part 19 procedure.

(4) The applicant for the Part 1 order, if not the applicant under section 28(2) of the 1986 Act, must be made a defendant to the application.

(5) Where the court cancels a registration under section 28(2) of the 1986 Act, the court officer will amend the register and give notice of the amendment to the court which made the Part 1 order.

32.29 Interim directions

The following persons will be made parties to an application for interim directions under section 29 of the 1986 Act –

(a)   the parties to the proceedings for enforcement; and

(b)   if not a party to those proceedings, the applicant for the Part 1 order.

32.30 Staying and dismissal of enforcement proceedings

(1) The following persons will be made parties to an application under section 30(1) or 31(1) of the 1986 Act –

(a)   the parties to the proceedings for enforcement which are sought to be stayed[(GL)]; and

(b)   if not a party to those proceedings, the applicant for the Part 1 order.

(2) Where the court makes an order under section 30(2) or (3) or section 31(3) of the 1986 Act, the court officer will amend the register and give notice of the amendment to –

(a)   the court which made the Part 1 order; and

(b)   the applicants for –

PART II – Statutory Instruments

       (i)   registration;

      (ii)   enforcement; and

    (iii)   stay$^{(GL)}$or dismissal of the enforcement proceedings.

32.31 Particulars of other proceedings

A party to proceedings for or relating to a Part 1 order who knows of other proceedings which relate to the child concerned (including proceedings out of the jurisdiction and concluded proceedings) must file a witness statement which –

(a)   states in which jurisdiction and court the other proceedings were begun;

(b)   states the nature and current state of the proceedings and the relief claimed or granted;

(c)   sets out the names of the parties to the proceedings and their relationship to the child;

(d)   if applicable and if known, states the reasons why relief claimed in the proceedings for or relating to the Part 1 order was not claimed in the other proceedings; and

(e)   is verified by a statement of truth.

32.32 Inspection of register

The following persons may inspect any entry in the register relating to a Part 1 order and may request copies of the order any document relating to it –

(a)   the applicant for registration of the Part 1 order;

(b)   a person who, to the satisfaction of a district judge, has an interest under the Part 1 order; and

(c)   a person who obtains the permission of a district judge.

PART 33
ENFORCEMENT

Chapter 1
General Rules

33.1 Application

(1) The rules in this Part apply to an application made in the High Court and a county court to enforce an order made in family proceedings.

(2) Part 50 of, and Schedules 1 and 2 to, the CPR apply, as far as they are relevant and with necessary modification (including the modifications referred to in rule 33.7), to an application made in the High Court and a county court to enforce an order made in family proceedings.

Section 1
Enforcement of orders for the payment of money

33.2 Application of the Civil Procedure Rules

Part 70 of the CPR applies to proceedings under this Section as if –

(a)   in rule 70.1, in paragraph (2)(d), 'but does not include a judgment or order for the payment of money into court' is omitted; and

(b)   rule 70.5 is omitted.

33.3 How to apply

(1) Except where a rule or practice direction otherwise requires, an application for an order to enforce an order for the payment of money must be made in a notice of application accompanied by a statement which must –

(a)   state the amount due under the order, showing how that amount is arrived at; and

(b)   be verified by a statement of truth.

(2) The notice of application may either –

(a)   apply for an order specifying the method of enforcement; or

(b)   apply for an order for such method of enforcement as the court may consider appropriate.

(3) If an application is made under paragraph (2)(b), an order to attend court will be issued and rule 71.2 (6) and (7) of the CPR will apply as if the application had been made under that rule.

33.4 Transfer of orders

(1) This rule applies to an application for the transfer –

(a)   to the High Court of an order made in a designated county court; and

(b)   to a designated county court of an order made in the High Court.

(2) The application must be –

(a)   made without notice; and

(b)   accompanied by a statement which complies with rule 33.3(1).

(3) The transfer will have effect upon the filing of the application.

(4) Where an order is transferred from a designated county court to the High Court –

(a)   it will have the same force and effect; and

(b)   the same proceedings may be taken on it,

as if it were an order of the High Court.

(5) This rule does not apply to the transfer of orders for periodical payments or for the recovery of arrears of periodical payments.

Section 2
Committal and injunction

33.5 General rule – committal hearings to be in public

(1) The general rule is that proceedings in the High Court for an order of committal will be heard in public.

(2) An order of committal may be heard in private where this is permitted by rule 6 of Order 52 of the RSC (cases in which a court may sit in private).

33.6 Proceedings in the principal registry treated as pending in a designated county court

(1) This rule applies where an order for the warrant of committal of any person to prison has been made or issued in proceedings which are –

   (a)   in the principal registry; and
   (b)   treated as pending in a designated county court or a county court.

(2) The person subject to the order will, wherever located, be treated for the purposes of section 122 of the County Courts Act 1984 as being out of the jurisdiction of the principal registry.

(3) Where –

   (a)   a committal is for failure to comply with the terms of an injunction(GL); or
   (b)   an order or warrant for the arrest or committal of any person is made or issued in proceedings under Part 4 of the 1996 Act in the principal registry which are treated as pending in a county court,

the order or warrant may, if the court so directs, be executed by the tipstaff within any county court.

33.7 Specific modifications of the CCR

(1) CCR Order 29, rule 1 (committal for breach of an order or undertaking) applies to –

   (a)   section 8 orders, except those referred to in paragraph (2)(a); and
   (b)   orders under the following sections of the 1989 Act –
       (i)   section 14A (special guardianship orders);
       (ii)   14B(2)(b) (granting of permission on making a special guardianship order to remove a child from the United Kingdom);
       (iii) section 14C(3)(b) (granting of permission to remove from the United Kingdom a child who is subject to a special guardianship order); and
       (iv)   section 14D (variation or discharge of a special guardianship order),

as if paragraph (3) of that rule were substituted by the following paragraph –

'(3) In the case of a section 8 order (within the meaning of section 8(2) of the Children Act 1989) or an order under section 14A, 14B(2)(b), 14C(3)(b) or 14D of the Children Act 1989 enforceable by committal order under paragraph (1), the judge or the district judge may, on the application of the person entitled to enforce the order, direct that the proper officer issue a copy of the order, endorsed with or incorporating a notice as to the consequences of disobedience, for service in accordance with paragraph (2), and no copy of the order shall be issued with any such notice endorsed or incorporated save in accordance with such a direction.'.

(2) CCR Order 29, rule 1 applies to –

(a)   contact orders to which a notice has been attached under section 11I of the 1989 Act or under section 8(2) of the Children and Adoption Act 2006;

(b)   orders under section 11J of the 1989 Act (enforcement orders); and

(c)   orders under paragraph 9 of Schedule A1 to the 1989 Act (orders following breach of enforcement orders),

as if paragraph (3) were omitted.

33.8 Section 118 County Courts Act 1984 and the tipstaff

For the purposes of section 118 of the County Courts Act 1984 in its application to the hearing of family proceedings at the Royal Courts of Justice or the principal registry, the tipstaff is deemed to be an officer of the court.

Practice Direction 33A –
Enforcement of Undertakings

This Practice Direction supplements FPR Part 33

Enforcement of undertaking to do or abstain from doing any act other than the payment of money

1.1 Rule 33.1(2) provides that Part 50 of, and Schedules 1 and 2 to, the CPR (which contain the Rules of the Supreme Court (RSC) and County Court Rules (CCR) respectively) apply, as far as they are relevant and with necessary modification, to an application made in the High Court and a county court to enforce an order made in family proceedings.

1.2 Subject to the Debtors Act 1869 (which makes provision in relation to orders for the payment of money), RSC Order 45.5 and CCR Order 29.1 enable a judgment or order to be enforced by committal for contempt of court where –

(a)   a person who is required by a judgment or order to do an act has refused or neglected to do that act within the specified time; or

(b)   a person disobeys a judgment or order requiring him to abstain from doing an act.

1.3 These Rules apply to undertakings as they apply to orders, with necessary modifications.

1.4 The form of an undertaking to do or abstain from doing any act must be endorsed with a notice setting out the consequences of disobedience, as follows –

> 'You may be sent to prison for contempt of court if you break the promises that you have given to the court'.

1.5 The person giving the undertaking must make a signed statement to the effect that he or she understands the terms of the undertaking being given and the consequences of failure to comply with it, as follows –

> 'I understand the undertaking that I have given, and that if I break any of my promises to the court I may be sent to prison for contempt of court'.

1.6 The statement need not be given before the court in person. It may be endorsed on the court copy of the undertaking or may be filed in a separate document such as a letter.

Enforcement of undertaking for the payment of money

2.1 Any undertaking for the payment of money that has effect as if it was an order made under Part 2 of the Matrimonial Causes Act 1973 may be enforced as if it was an order and Part 33 applies accordingly.

2.2 The form of an undertaking for the payment of money that has effect as if it were an order under Part 2 of the Matrimonial Causes Act 1973 must be endorsed with a notice setting out the consequences of disobedience, as follows –

> 'If you fail to pay any sum of money which you have promised the court that you would pay, a person entitled to enforce the undertaking may apply to the court for an order. If it is proved that you have had the means to pay the sum but you have refused or neglected to pay that sum, you may be sent to prison.'

2.3 The person giving the undertaking must make a signed statement to the effect that he or she understands the terms of the undertaking being given and the consequences of failure to comply with it, as follows –

> 'I understand the undertaking that I have given, and that if I break my promise to the court to pay any sum of money, I may be sent to prison'.

2.4 The statement need not be given before the court in person. It may be endorsed on the court copy of the undertaking or may be filed in a separate document such as a letter.

****

PART 36
TRANSITIONAL ARRANGEMENTS AND PILOT SCHEMES

36.1 Transitional provisions

Practice Direction 36A shall make provision for the extent to which these rules shall apply to proceedings started before the day on which they come into force.

36.2 Pilot schemes

Practice directions may modify or disapply any provision of these rules –

(a)   for specified periods; and

(b)   in relation to proceedings in specified courts,

during the operation of pilot schemes for assessing the use of new practices and procedures in connection with proceedings.

GLOSSARY

Scope

This glossary is a guide to the meaning of certain legal expressions as used in these rules, but it does not give the expressions any meaning in the rules which they do not otherwise have in the law.

Expression	Meaning
Affidavit	A written, sworn, statement of evidence.
Cross-examination	Questioning of a witness by a party other than the party who called the witness.
Evidence in chief	The evidence given by a witness for the party who called him.
Injunction	A court order prohibiting a person from doing something or requiring a person to do something.
Official copy	A copy of an official document, supplied and marked as such by the office which issued the original.
Pre-action protocol	Statements of best practice about pre-action conduct which have been approved by the President of the Family Division and which are annexed to a Practice Direction.
Privilege	The right of a party to refuse to disclose a document or produce a document or to refuse to answer questions on the ground of some special interest recognised by law.

PART II – Statutory Instruments

Expression	Meaning
Seal	A seal is a mark which the court puts on document to indicate that the document has been issued by the court.
Service	Steps required by rules of court to bring documents used in court proceedings to a person's attention.
Set aside	Cancelling a judgment or order or a step taken by a party in the proceedings.
Stay	A stay imposes a halt on proceedings, apart from the taking of any steps allowed by the rules or the terms of the stay. Proceedings can be continued if a stay is lifted.
Strike out	Striking out means the court ordering written material to be deleted so that it may no longer be relied upon.
Without prejudice	Negotiations with a view to settlement are usually conducted 'without prejudice' which means that the circumstances in which the content of those negotiations may be revealed to the court are very restricted.

Practice Direction 36A –
Transitional Arrangements

This Practice Direction supplements FPR Part 36

Content of this Practice Direction

1.1 This Practice Direction deals with the application of the FPR to proceedings started before 6th April 2011 ('existing proceedings').

1.2 In this Practice Direction 'the previous rules' means, as appropriate, the Rules of the Supreme Court 1965 and County Court Rules 1981 as in force immediately before 26 April 1999, and –

the Maintenance Orders (Facilities for Enforcement) Rules 1922;
the Magistrates' Courts (Guardianship of Minors) Rules 1974;
the Magistrates' Courts (Reciprocal Enforcement of Maintenance Orders) Rules 1974;
the Magistrates' Courts (Reciprocal Enforcement of Maintenance Orders) (Republic of Ireland) Rules 1975;
the Magistrates' Courts (Reciprocal Enforcement of Maintenance Orders) (Hague Convention Countries) Rules 1980;
the Magistrates' Courts (Child Abduction and Custody) Rules 1986;

the Magistrates' Courts (Civil Jurisdiction and Judgments Act 1982) Rules 1986;

the Family Proceedings Rules 1991;

the Family Proceedings Courts (Children Act 1989) Rules 1991;

the Family Proceedings Courts (Matrimonial Proceedings etc.) Rules 1991 (in so far as those rules do not relate to enforcement or variation of orders);

the Magistrates' Courts (Costs Against Legal Representatives in Civil Proceedings) Rules 1991 (in so far as those rules relate to family proceedings);

the Family Proceedings Courts (Child Support Act 1991) Rules 1993;

the Magistrates' Courts (Reciprocal Enforcement of Maintenance Orders) (United States of America) Rules 1995 (subject to the saving in paragraph 3.6 of this Practice Direction);

the Magistrates' Courts (Hearsay Evidence in Civil Proceedings) Rules 1999 (in so far as those rules relate to family proceedings); and

the Family Procedure (Adoption) Rules 2005,

as in force immediately before 6th April 2011.

General scheme of transitional arrangements

2.1 The general scheme is –

(a) to apply the FPR to existing proceedings so far as is practicable; but

(b) where this is not practicable, to apply the previous rules to such proceedings.

Where the previous rules will normally apply

General principle

3.1 Where an initiating step has been taken in a case before 6th April 2011, in particular a step using forms or other documentation required by the previous rules, the case will proceed in the first instance under the previous rules. Where a party must take a step in response to something done by another party in accordance with the previous rules, that step must also be in accordance with those rules.

Responding to old process

3.2 A party who is served with an old type of originating process (for example, an originating summons) on or after 6th April 2011 must respond in accordance with the previous rules and the instructions on any forms received.

Filing and service of pleadings where old process served

3.3 Where a case has been begun by an old type of originating process (whether served before or after 6th April 2011), filing and service of pleadings will continue according to the previous rules.

Pre-commencement order inconsistent with FPR

3.4 Where a court order has been made before 6th April 2011, that order must still be complied with on or after that date.

Steps taken before commencement

3.5 Where a party has, before 6th April 2011, taken any step in the proceedings in accordance with the previous rules, that step will remain valid on or after that date, and a party will not normally be required to take any action that would amount to taking such a step again under the FPR.

Saving – Reciprocal enforcement of maintenance orders (United States of America)

3.6 Where, by virtue of article 6(2) of the Reciprocal Enforcement of Maintenance Orders (United States of America) Order 2007, the Reciprocal Enforcement of Maintenance (United States of America) Order 1995 continues in full force and effect, the Magistrates' Courts (Reciprocal Enforcement of Maintenance Orders) (United States of America) Rules 1995 shall, notwithstanding any provision in the FPR, continue to apply as if they had not been amended by the Magistrates' Courts (Reciprocal Enforcement of Maintenance Orders) (Miscellaneous Amendment) Rules 2007.

Where the FPR will normally apply

General principle

4.1 Where a new step is to be taken in any existing proceedings on or after 6th April 2011, it is to be taken under the FPR.

Part 1 (Overriding objective) to apply

4.2 Part 1 of the FPR (Overriding objective) will apply to all existing proceedings from 6th April 2011 onwards.

Issuing of application forms after the FPR come into force

4.3

    (1) The general rule is that –
        (a)   only application forms under the FPR will be issued by the court on or after 6th April 2011; and
        (b)   if a request to issue an old type of form or originating process (summons, etc.) is received at the court on or after 6th April 2011, it will be returned unissued.

    (2) By way of exception to the general rule, the court may in cases of urgency direct that the form or process is to be issued as if the request to issue it had been a request to issue an application form under the FPR and, if it does so, the court may make such supplementary directions as it considers appropriate.

First time before a court on or after 6th April 2011

4.4

(1) When proceedings come before a court (whether at a hearing or on paper) for the first time on or after 6th April 2011, the court may direct how the FPR are to apply to the proceedings and may disapply certain provisions of the FPR. The court may also give case management directions.

(2) The general presumption will be that the FPR will apply to the proceedings from then on unless the court directs or this practice direction provides otherwise.

(3) If an application has been issued before 6th April 2011 and the hearing of the application has been set on or after that date, the general presumption is that the application will be decided having regard to the FPR.

(4) When the first occasion on which existing proceedings are before a court on or after 6th April 2011 is a hearing of a substantive issue, the general presumption is that the hearing will be conducted according to the FPR.

Costs

4.5

(1) Any assessment of costs that takes place on or after 6th April 2011 will be in accordance with FPR Part 28 and the provisions of the Civil Procedure Rules as applied by that Part.

(2) However, the general presumption is that no costs for work undertaken before 6th April 2011 will be disallowed if those costs would have been allowed on detailed assessment before that date.

(3) The decision as to whether to allow costs for work undertaken on or after 6th April 2011 will generally be taken in accordance with FPR Part 28 and the provisions of the Civil Procedure Rules as applied by that Part.

****

Part III

PRACTICE DIRECTIONS AND GUIDANCE

PRACTICE DIRECTION
3 NOVEMBER 2008

Citation: [2009] 1 FLR 365

ALLOCATION AND TRANSFER OF PROCEEDINGS

1.1 This Practice Direction is given by the President of the Family Division under the powers delegated to him by the Lord Chief Justice under paragraph 2(2) of part 1 of Schedule 2 to the Constitutional Reform Act 2005 and is agreed by the Lord Chancellor.

1.2 The objective of this Practice Direction is to ensure that the criteria for the transfer of proceedings are applied in such a way that proceedings are heard at the appropriate level of court, that the capacity of magistrates' courts is properly utilised and that proceedings are only dealt with in the High Court if the relevant criteria are met.

1.3 This Practice Direction will come into effect on 25 November 2008. Where practicable, it applies to proceedings started before but not concluded by 25 November. The Practice Directions of 5 June 1992 (distribution of business) and 22 February 1993 (applications under the Children Act 1989 by children) are revoked except that they will continue to apply to any proceedings to which it is not practicable to apply this Practice Direction.

1.4 A reference to an article is a reference to the article so numbered in the Allocation and Transfer of Proceedings Order 2008.

Part 1

2 This Part of this Practice Direction applies to all family proceedings (whether or not the Allocation and Transfer of Proceedings Order 2008 applies to such proceedings).

Timing and continuing review of decision on appropriate venue

3.1 The issue as to which court is the most appropriate hearing venue must be addressed by the court speedily as soon as there is sufficient information to determine whether the case meets the criteria for hearing in that court. This information may come to light before, during or after the first hearing. It must then be kept under effective review at all times; it should not be assumed that proceedings will necessarily remain in the court in which they were started or to which they have been transferred. For example proceedings that have been transferred to a county court because one or more of the criteria in article 15 applies should be transferred back to the magistrates' court if the reason for transfer falls away. Conversely, an unforeseen late complication may require a transfer from a magistrates' court to a county court.

3.2 Where a court is determining where the proceedings ought to be heard it will consider all relevant information including that given by the applicant either in the application form or otherwise, for example in any request for proceedings to be transferred to another magistrates' court or to a county court under rule 6 of the Family Proceedings Courts (Children Act 1989) Rules 1991.

Timeliness

4.1 Article 13 and paragraph 12.1 require the court to have regard to delay. Therefore the listing availability of the court in which the proceedings have been started and in neighbouring magistrates' courts and county courts must always be ascertained before deciding where proceedings should be heard.

4.2 If a magistrates' court is considering transferring proceedings to a county court or a county court is considering transferring proceedings to the High Court but that decision is finely balanced, the proceedings should not be transferred if the transfer would lead to delay. Conversely, if the High Court is considering transferring proceedings to a county court or a county court is considering transferring proceedings to a magistrates' court but that decision is finely balanced, the proceedings should be transferred if retaining them would lead to delay.

4.3 Transferring proceedings may mean that there will be a short delay in the proceedings being heard since the papers may need to be sent to the court to which they are being transferred. The court will determine whether the delay is significant, taking into account the circumstances of the case and with reference to the interests of the child.

4.4 While there is no express reference in the Allocation and Transfer of Proceedings Order 2008 or in Part 3 of this Practice Direction to the length of the hearing or to judicial continuity such issues may be relevant.

Transfer of proceedings to or from the High Court

5.1 A court will take into account the following factors (which are not exhaustive) when considering whether the criteria in articles 7 or 18 or paragraph 11.2 or 12.3 apply, such that the proceedings ought to be heard in the High Court –

(1)   there is alleged to be a risk that a child concerned in the proceedings will suffer serious physical or emotional harm in the light of –
       (a)   the death of another child in the family, a parent or any other material person; or
       (b)   the fact that a parent or other material person may have committed a grave crime, for example, murder, manslaughter or rape,

in particular where the essential factual framework is in dispute or there are issues over the causation of injuries or a material conflict of expert evidence;

(2)   the application concerns medical treatment for a child which involves a risk to the child's physical or emotional health which goes beyond the normal risks of routine medical treatment;

(3)   an adoption order is sought in relation to a child who has been adopted abroad in a country whose adoption orders are not recognised in England and Wales;

(4)   an adoption order is sought in relation to a child who has been brought into the United Kingdom in circumstances where section 83 of the Adoption and Children Act 2002 applies and

    (a)   the person bringing the child, or causing the child to be brought –

        (i)   has not complied with any requirement imposed by regulations made under section 83(4); or

        (ii)   has not met any condition required to be met by regulations made under section 83(5) within the required time; or

    (b)   there are complicating features in relation to the application;

(5)   it is likely that the proceedings will set a significant new precedent or alter existing principles of common law;

(6)   where periodical payments, a lump sum or transfer of property are an issue –

    (a)   the capital value of the assets involved and the extent to which they are available for, or susceptible to, distribution or adjustment;

    (b)   any substantial allegations of fraud or deception or non-disclosure;

    (c)   any substantial contested allegations of conduct.

5.2 The following proceedings are likely to fall within the criteria for hearing in the High Court unless the nature of the issues of fact or law raised in the proceedings may make them more suitable to be dealt with in a county court –

(1)   proceedings involving a contested issue of domicile;

(2)   applications to restrain a respondent from taking or continuing with foreign proceedings;

(3)   suits in which the Queen's Proctor intervenes or shows cause and elects trial in the High Court;

(4)   proceedings in which an application is opposed on the grounds of want of jurisdiction;

(5)   proceedings in which there is a complex foreign element or where the court has invited submissions to be made under Article 11(7) of Council Regulation (EC) No 2201/2003 of 27 November 2003 concerning jurisdiction and the recognition and enforcement of judgments in matrimonial matters and the matters of parental responsibility;

(6)   proceedings in which there is an application to remove a child permanently or temporarily from the jurisdiction to a non-Hague Convention country.

(7)   interlocutory applications involving –

PART III – Practice Directions and Guidance

(a)   search orders; or

(b)   directions as to dealing with assets out of the jurisdiction.

5.3 Proceedings will not normally be suitable to be dealt with in the High Court merely because of any of the following –

(1)   intractable problems with regard to contact;

(2)   sexual abuse;

(3)   injury to a child which is neither life-threatening nor permanently disabling;

(4)   routine neglect, even if it spans many years and there is copious documentation;

(5)   temporary or permanent removal to a Hague Convention country;

(6)   standard human rights issues;

(7)   uncertainty as to immigration status;

(8)   the celebrity of the parties;

(9)   the anticipated length of the hearing;

(10)   the quantity of evidence;

(11)   the number of experts;

(12)   the possible availability of a speedier hearing.

5.4 A substantial reason for starting proceedings in the High Court will only exist where the nature of the proceedings or the issues raised are such that they ought to be heard in the High Court. Where proceedings have been started in the High Court under article 7(c) or paragraph 11.2(4) and the High Court considers that there is no substantial reason for them to have been started there, the High Court will transfer the proceedings to a county court or a magistrates' court and may make any orders about costs which it considers appropriate.

Part 2

6 This Part of this Practice Direction applies to family proceedings to which the Allocation and Transfer of Proceedings Order 2008 applies.

Transfer of proceedings from one magistrates' court to another or from one county court to another

7.1 Where a magistrates' court is considering transferring proceedings to another magistrates' court or a county court is considering transferring proceedings to another county court, the court will take into account the following factors (which are not exhaustive) when considering whether it would be more convenient for the parties for the proceedings to be dealt with by the other court –

(1)   the fact that a party is ill or suffers a disability which could make it inconvenient to attend at a particular court;

(2)   the fact that the child lives in the area of the other court;

(3)   the need to avoid delay.

Transfer of proceedings from a magistrates' court to a county court

8.1 Where a magistrates' court is considering whether one or more of the criteria in article 15(*1*) (except article 15(1)(*g*) and (*h*)) apply such that the proceedings ought to be heard in the county court, the magistrates' court will first consider whether another magistrates' court would have suitable experience to deal with the issues which have given rise to consideration of article 15. If so, the magistrates' court will then consider whether the proceedings could be dealt with more quickly or within the same time if they were transferred to the other magistrates' court rather than a county court. If so, the magistrates' court will transfer the proceedings to the other magistrates' court rather than a county court.

8.2 A magistrates' court may only transfer proceedings to a county court under article 15(1)(*a*) if it considers that the transfer will significantly accelerate the determination of the proceedings. Before considering a transfer on this ground, the magistrates' court must obtain information about the hearing dates available in other magistrates' courts and in the relevant county court. The fact that a hearing could be arranged in a county court at an earlier date than in any appropriate magistrates' court does not by itself justify the transfer of proceedings under article 15(1)(*a*); the question of whether the determination of the proceedings would be significantly accelerated must be considered in the light of all the circumstances.

Transfer of proceedings from a county court to a magistrates' court

9.1 A county court must transfer to a magistrates' court under article 16(1) proceedings that have previously been transferred under article 15(1) where the county court considers that none of the criteria in article 15(1) apply. In particular, proceedings transferred to a county court by a magistrates' court for resolution of a single issue, for example, use of the inherent powers of the High Court in respect of medical testing of a child or disclosure of information by HM Revenue and Customs, should be transferred back to the magistrates' court once the issue has been resolved.

9.2 Subject to articles 5(3), 6, 8 and 13 and paragraphs 4 and 12.1, straightforward proceedings for –

(1)　a residence order;
(2)　a contact order;
(3)　a prohibited steps order;
(4)　a specific issue order;
(5)　a special guardianship order; or
(6)　an order under Part 4 of the Family Law Act 1996

which are started in a county court should be transferred to a magistrates' court if the county court considers that none of the criteria in article 15(1)(*b*) to (*i*) apply to those proceedings.

PART III – Practice Directions and Guidance

Part 3

10 This Part of this Practice Direction applies to any family proceedings to which the Allocation and Transfer of Proceedings Order 2008 does not apply.

Starting proceedings

11.1 Subject to paragraph 11.2, family proceedings must be started in a county court.

11.2 Family proceedings may be started in the High Court only if –

(1)   the proceedings are exceptionally complex;
(2)   the outcome of the proceedings is important to the public in general;
(3)   an enactment or rule requires the proceedings to be started in the High Court; or
(4)   there is another substantial reason for starting the proceedings in the High Court.

Transferring proceedings

12.1 When making any decision about the transfer of proceedings the court must have regard to the need to avoid delay in the proceedings.

12.2 A county court will take into account the following factors (which are not exhaustive) when considering whether to transfer proceedings to another county court –

(1)   whether the transfer will significantly accelerate the determination of the proceedings;
(2)   whether it is more convenient for the parties for the proceedings to be dealt with by another county court; and
(3)   whether there is another good reason for the proceedings to be transferred.

12.3 A county court will take into account the following factors (which are not exhaustive) when considering whether to transfer proceedings to the High Court –

(1)   whether the proceedings are exceptionally complex;
(2)   whether the outcome of the proceedings is important to the public in general;
(3)   whether an enactment or rule requires the proceedings to be dealt with in the High Court; and
(4)   whether there is another substantial reason for the proceedings to be transferred.

12.4 The High Court will also take into account the factors in paragraph 12.3 when considering whether to transfer proceedings to a county court.

The Right Honourable
Sir Mark Potter
The President of the Family Division

The Right Honourable
Jack Straw MP
The Lord Chancellor

FAMILY PROCEEDINGS (ALLOCATION TO JUDICIARY) DIRECTIONS 2009

Citation: [2009] All ER (D) 98 (Feb); [2009] 2 FLR 51

The President of the Family Division, in exercise of the powers conferred on him by section 9 of the Courts and Legal Services Act 1990 and having consulted the Lord Chancellor, gives the following Directions:

1 These Directions shall come into force on 16 February 2009.

2 In these Directions, in the absence of a contrary implication–

'adoption centre' means a court designated as an adoption centre by the Allocation and Transfer of Proceedings Order 2008;

'family proceedings' and 'judge' have the meanings assigned to them in section 9 of the Courts and Legal Services Act 1990;

'nominated' in relation to a judge means a judge who has been approved as one to whom family proceedings may be allocated by the President of the Family Division;

'Schedule' means the Schedule to these Directions.

3 Any reference in these Directions to the Allocation and Transfer of Proceedings Order 2008 ('the 2008 Order') is to be read as a reference to the Children (Allocation of Proceedings) Order 1991, the Children (Allocation of Proceedings) (Appeals) Order 1991 or the Family Law Act 1996 (Part IV) (Allocation of Proceedings) Order 1997, as appropriate, where any of those Orders applies as a result of Article 29 of the 2008 Order (transitional provisions).

4 These Directions apply to any family proceedings (except proceedings on appeal from an order or decision made by a magistrates' court) which are pending in a county court or which, by virtue of section 42 of the Matrimonial and Family Proceedings Act 1984 or of a provision of the Allocation and Transfer of Proceedings Order 2008, are treated as pending in a county court in the Principal Registry of the Family Division of the High Court.

5(1) These Directions apply, so far as practicable, to proceedings started before but not concluded by 16 February 2009.

(2) Where, by reason of paragraph (1), these Directions do not apply to particular proceedings which have been started but not concluded before 16 February 2009, the Family Proceedings (Allocation to Judiciary) Directions 1999 continue to apply to those proceedings.

6 Subject to the following paragraphs of these Directions, the proceedings described in the Schedule shall be allocated to a judge or to a specified description of judge in accordance with the following Table, by reference to the categories shown in column (b) of the Table and described in the Schedule and subject to the limitations specified in column (c) of the Table.

(a) Judge or specified description of judge	(b) Categories of proceedings by reference to the Schedule	(c) Categories of proceedings by reference to the Schedule
A circuit judge, deputy circuit judge or recorder nominated for public family law proceedings	All categories of proceedings	
A circuit judge, deputy circuit judge or recorder nominated for private family law proceedings	B, D, E	
A district judge of the Principal Registry[1]	A, B, C, D	D Interlocutory matters only
A district judge nominated for public family law proceedings	A, B, C, D	D Interlocutory matters only
A district judge nominated for private family law proceedings	B, D	D Interlocutory matters only
A judge not referred to in any of the preceding entries in this table.	B(i), B(iii), B(vii)	B(i) Only: (1) proceedings in which an order under section 8 of the Children Act 1989 is sought at a without notice hearing where (a) no nominated judge is available to hear the proceedings; and (b) any order is limited in time until a hearing before a nominated judge; and (2) proceedings under section 15 of and Schedule 1 to the Children Act 1989. B(iii) In the case of a deputy district judge, all proceedings except enforcement

7 Without prejudice to the provisions of paragraph 6, any proceedings to which these Directions apply, including any appeal referred to in paragraph 10, may be allocated to–

(a) a judge of the Family Division of the High Court;

(b) a person acting as a judge of the Family Division of the High Court in pursuance of a request made under section 9(1) of the Supreme Court Act 1981 other than a former judge of the Court of Appeal or a former puisne judge of the High Court; but proceedings in categories A and C of the Schedule shall be allocated only to a judge who has been nominated for them;

(c) a person sitting as a recorder who has been authorised to act as a judge of the Family Division of the High Court under section 9(4) of the Supreme Court Act 1981;

(d) a person sitting as a recorder who is a District Judge (Magistrates' Courts) and is nominated for public family law proceedings in the County Court;

(e) a person sitting as a Recorder who is a District Judge of the Principal Registry of the Family Division.

8 When a person sitting as a recorder is also a district judge nominated for public family law proceedings, any proceedings may be allocated to him which, under these Directions, may be allocated to a district judge nominated for public family law proceedings.

9 A circuit judge or district judge nominated for private family law proceedings who is sitting at an adoption centre may, with the agreement of the Family Division Liaison Judge for the relevant region, hear proceedings in category C of the Schedule, limited in the case of a district judge to interlocutory matters only.

10 Where in any proceedings to which these Directions apply an appeal may be heard by a circuit judge, deputy circuit judge or recorder, it may be heard by any judge of that description who under these Directions would have been able to hear the proceedings at first instance.

The Right Honourable Sir Mark Potter

President of the Family Division and Head of Family Justice

SCHEDULE

Category	Description of proceedings
A	(i) Proceedings under section 25 of the Children Act 1989; (ii) Proceedings under Parts IV and V of the Children Act 1989; (iii) Proceedings under Schedules 2 and 3 to the Children Act 1989; (iv) Applications for leave under section 91(14),(15) or (17) of the Children Act 1989; (v) Proceedings under section 102 of the 1989 Act or section 79 of the Childcare Act 2006; (vi) Proceedings for a residence order under section 8 of the Children Act 1989 or for a special guardianship order under section 14A of the Children Act 1989 with respect to a child who is the subject of a care order.
B	(i) Proceedings under Parts I and II of the Children Act 1989, except where the proceedings come within Category A(vi), C(iii) or C(iv) of this Schedule; (ii) Proceedings under sections 33,34 and 37 of the Family Law Act 1986; (iii) Proceedings under Part 4 of the Family Law Act 1996; (iv) Proceedings under Part 4A of the Family Law Act 1996; (v) Proceedings under section 20 of the Child Support Act 1990; (vi) Proceedings under section 30 of the Human Fertilisation and Embryology Act 1990; (vii) Family proceedings for which no express provision is made in this Schedule.
C	(i) Proceedings under section 21 of the Adoption Act 1976; (ii) Proceedings under the Adoption and Children Act 2002; (iii) Proceedings for a residence order under section 8 of the Children Act 1989 where either section 28(1)(child placed for adoption) or 29(4)(placement order in force) of the Adoption and Children Act 2002 applies; (iv) Proceedings for a special guardianship order under section 14A of the Children Act 1989 where either section 28(1)(child placed for adoption) or section 29(5)(placement order in force) of the Adoption and Children Act 2002 applies.
D	Proceedings under sections 55,55A, 56 and 57 of the Family Law Act 1986

E	The hearing of contested proceedings for
	(i) a decree of divorce, nullity or judicial separation; or
	(ii) an order for dissolution or nullity of civil partnership or a separation order.

PRESIDENT'S GUIDANCE
22 APRIL 2009

Citation: [2009] 2 FLR 167

APPLICATIONS CONSEQUENT UPON THE ATTENDANCE OF THE MEDIA IN FAMILY PROCEEDINGS

1 The Government's announcement about the attendance of the media at hearings in family proceedings (see *Family Justice in View* Cm 7502, December 2008) has been implemented by a change to the Family Proceedings Rules made by *The Family Proceedings (Amendment) (No 2) Rules 2009* SI 2009 No 857 (county court and High Court) and *The Family Proceedings Courts (Miscellaneous Amendments) Rules 2009* SI 2009 No 858 (magistrates' courts) and two Practice Directions *Attendance of Media Representatives at Hearings in Family Proceedings* dated 20th April 2009 made by the President to support the rule changes in the respective courts.

2 In the county court and High Court media attendance is implemented by the change to FPR Rule 10.28. (to which the Practice Direction applies). Change regarding media attendance in the family proceedings courts is introduced through amendment to the Family Proceedings Courts (Children Act 1989) Rules 1991, with the insertion of rule 16A.

3 In broad terms the changes for the county court and the High Court relating to media attendance permit duly accredited representatives of news gathering and reporting organisations, and any other unaccredited person whom the court permits, to be present at hearings of all family proceedings (defined by s 32 Matrimonial and Family Proceedings Act 1984) except hearings conducted for the purposes of judicially assisted conciliation or negotiation. They also provide that the court can exclude media representatives

4 For the county court and the High Court, the change relates to most of the proceedings which are for the time being heard in private. It therefore covers a wide range of proceedings including for example public and private law proceedings under the Children Act 1989 and claims for ancillary relief under the Matrimonial Causes Act 1973.

5 Representatives of newspapers or news agencies are admitted to the family proceedings courts under section 69 (2) Magistrates' Courts Act 1980. Media attendance will now be regulated by the insertion of rule '16A Restrictions on presence of persons at directions appointment and hearing'. Duly accredited representatives of news gathering and reporting organisations are not entitled to be present at hearings conducted for the purposes of judicially assisted conciliation or negotiation. They may also be excluded for reasons set out in rule 16A(3).

6 In respect of the county court and the High Court the new Part 11 of the FPR, and in respect of the family proceedings court the new Part 11C of the

Family Proceedings Courts (Children Act 1989) Rules 1991 as amended, regarding communication of information only apply to proceedings concerning children. In particular, they do not apply to proceedings for ancillary relief. Nor do they <u>expressly</u> cover communication of information to representatives of the media.

7 As appears from the Practice Direction governing the county court and High Court, it is a premise of the change for these courts that the proceedings remain proceedings held in private and that therefore the existing position relating to the publication of matters relating to proceedings which are so heard continues to apply, both whilst the proceedings continue and when they have ended (see the Practice Direction paras 2.4 and 2.5)

8 Useful summaries of the position relating to the publication of matters relating to proceedings heard in private can be found in: *Clayton v Clayton* [2006] EWCA Civ 878 [2007] 1 FLR 11 (in particular at paragraphs 23 to 60, 82 to 85, 92 to 104 and 118 to 136 and *Re B (A Child) (Disclosure)* [2004] EWHC 411 (Fam), [2004] 2 FLR 142 (in particular at paragraphs 62 to 82 (on s 12 AJA 1960) and 83 to 107 (on the jurisdiction to relax or increase the statutory restrictions on publication). Other useful cases are listed in the footnote to this paragraph.[1]

9 It is to be noted that the above decisions all concern the interests and welfare of children and that the approach in ancillary relief proceedings (which are also likely to be productive of media applications) has not been the subject of similar judicial consideration and guidance.

10 The new Rules and the Practice Directions include provisions relating to the exclusion of media representatives but are silent on the approach to be taken by the courts to the exercise of their discretion in respect of other issues which may well arise as a consequence of the attendance of media representatives at hearings in family proceedings. In this respect the Government declined to adopt the recommendation of the High Court judges to address the detail of such issues when introducing the change. It is therefore left to the courts to determine how such issues are to be approached and decided. It is clear that a principled approach to such issues should be applied by the courts and that this can only properly be developed by the courts with the benefit of full argument from the interested parties.

11 The change to admit media representatives to hearings in family proceedings in county courts and the High Court is likely to give rise to a number of issues relating to the exercise of discretion by all levels of court. In particular it is likely that courts will quickly be faced with applications for the provision of documents to media representatives present in court to enable them the better to follow the substance of the proceedings. If minded to grant such application, the court will need to consider the terms of any restriction relating to the use (and in particular the publication) of information contained in any such documents provided to media representatives as a condition of their being so provided.

PART III – Practice Directions and Guidance

12 In cases involving children, applications, whether by the media or the parties, are also likely to raise issues as to

(i)   The proper application of the existing statutory provisions restricting the publication of the identity of children and information relating to proceedings heard in private;

(ii) the adequacy of the protection afforded in children cases by Section 12 of the Administration of Justice Act 1960 ('AJA 1960') which, inter alia, does not extend to the identity of the parties or witnesses;

(iii) the effect of the publication of any anonymised judgment;

and whether or not injunctive relief may be required upon a wider basis.

13 In relation to the need for injunctive relief in cases affecting children, particularly in local courts, it may be necessary to consider how far it is appropriate to protect from identification not only the children and the parties, but also witnesses and others whose identities will be known locally as associated with the child or his family.

14 Finally, there will be issues over the need on child welfare grounds for protection to extend beyond the end of the hearing (see paragraph 2.5 of the respective Practice Directions).

15 No doubt the basic opposing arguments in relation to the question of access to documents will be, on the one hand, that the Government has sought to retain the basic structure and rationale of the long standing policy of privacy in relation to children proceedings, while at the same time admitting the press, to avoid charges of 'secret justice' and to promote better understanding of the working of the family courts. For these purposes, however, access to court documents is not generally necessary or desirable having regard to their confidential nature.

16 On the other hand, the media may argue that, particularly in those cases where there is not a formal oral opening, they should be enabled to see statements and documents filed in order fully to understand the nature and progress of the proceedings, and so as to be able to publish articles, within appropriate reporting constraints, about the cases which they attend. In this connection, it is likely, if not inevitable, that in individual cases of high interest to the media, courts at all levels and all over the country will be faced with detailed legal argument relating to rival Convention Rights, public and private interests, the welfare of children, and the construction and application of the primary and secondary legislation.

17 Inconsistency of approach in children cases as to the principles to be applied to the determination of such issues on the part of the courts, parties, witnesses, other persons involved in the relevant events (eg social workers and doctors) and the media could well give rise to justified criticism on grounds of uncertainty. It would not promote the public interest in the proper administration of justice and could be damaging to children.

18 So far as ancillary relief proceedings are concerned, policy, privacy and Convention issues may also arise for decision, albeit the interests of children may not be engaged.

19 The purpose of this guidance is therefore to try to avoid, or at least to minimise, inconsistency by providing that decisions are made by the High Court (and the Appellate Courts) as soon as possible as to the principled approach to be taken. Its purpose is also to provide that, until that is done, delay in decision making in individual cases, (particularly those concerning children) should be avoided. It is to be hoped that the media will co-operate in these aims.

20 Pending the availability of formal judicial guidance from the High Court or Court of Appeal as to the principled approach to be adopted, all County Courts and Magistrates' Courts hearing family proceedings should carefully consider adopting the following course:

   (i)   The court should deal in accordance with the Rules and Practice Directions with any application made for exclusion of the media from the proceedings or any part of them on any of the grounds set out in the Practice Directions.

  (ii)   Where a representative of the media in attendance at the proceedings applies to be shown court documents, the court should seek the consent of the parties to such representative being permitted (subject to appropriate conditions as to anonymity and restrictions upon onward disclosure) to see such summaries, position statements and other documents as appear reasonably necessary to a broad understanding of the issues in the case.

 (iii)   If the objection of any of the parties is maintained, then in any case where the objecting party demonstrates reasonably arguable grounds for resisting disclosure of the document or documents sought, no order for disclosure should be made, but the following course of action should be considered.

 (iv)   If considered necessary or appropriate the court should transfer (or, in the case of a family proceedings court, take the first step to bring about an urgent transfer of) the proceedings to the High Court for the determination of any disclosure and/or reporting issues.

  (v)   Alternatively, in order to avoid delay in decision making on the substantive issues in the case, the court should adjourn determination of any disclosure and/or reporting issues pending a decision by the High Court (or the Appellate Courts) on the principled approach to be taken to them and should make any necessary interim orders in accordance with the argument mentioned in paragraph 15 above in order to secure the position meanwhile.

 (vi)   Similarly, if a representative of the media applies for reporting restrictions to be lifted during the currency of a case, in the absence of agreement between the parties the court should consider following one or the other of the alternative steps set out in sub-paragraphs (iv)–(v) above.

PART III – Practice Directions and Guidance

(vii) If injunctive relief is sought restraining publication based on Convention rights rather than statutory provisions, the matter should in any event be transferred to the High Court to be dealt with under the *President's Practice Direction (Applications for Reporting Restriction Orders)* 18 March 2005 and the *Practice Note (Official Solicitor: Deputy Director of Legal Services CAFCASS: Applications for Reporting Restriction Orders* [2005] 2 FLR 111 and, if interim injunctive relief appears necessary under threat of publication before such application can be dealt with by a High Court judge, the county court should comply with s 12(2) of Human Rights Act 1998.

21 The underlying aim of this guidance is to seek to ensure that the principled approach to be taken is determined by the High Court (and the Appellate Courts) as soon as possible and that in the interim changes of practice do not take place which may not accord with that principled approach. Though this may result in delayed rulings on some early contested applications involving arguments such as those mentioned in paragraphs 15 and 16 above, it may be considered desirable, in the absence of legislative guidance, that such rulings should only be made on the basis of authoritative judicial guidance following proper determination, with the benefit of full argument, of the relevant principled approach for the longer term.

22 To assist in the early determination of the principled approach:

(i)   Arrangements will be made in the High Court to identify appropriate test cases and for their early determination, and

(ii) Arrangements will be made to seek to ensure that directions are given as soon as is practicable in any proceedings that are transferred to the High Court because they raise substantial issues arising from the attendance of media representatives

(iii) Proceedings which are transferred to the High Court other than in the PRFD should be put before a family High Court Judge on circuit or, failing the presence on circuit of a High Court Judge, before the Family Division Liaison Judge as an urgent application for directions.

Sir Mark Potter
President of the Family Division

Part IV

MISCELLANEOUS

2009

JANUARY

M	T	W	T	F	S	S
			1	2	3	4
5	6	7	8	9	10	11
12	13	14	15	16	17	18
19	20	21	22	23	24	25
26	27	28	29	30	31	

FEBRUARY

M	T	W	T	F	S	S
						1
2	3	4	5	6	7	8
9	10	11	12	13	14	15
16	17	18	19	20	21	22
23	24	25	26	27	28	

MARCH

M	T	W	T	F	S	S
						1
2	3	4	5	6	7	8
9	10	11	12	13	14	15
16	17	18	19	20	21	22
23	24	25	26	27	28	29
30	31					

APRIL

M	T	W	T	F	S	S
		1	2	3	4	5
6	7	8	9	10	11	12
13	14	15	16	17	18	19
20	21	22	23	24	25	26
27	28	29	30			

MAY

M	T	W	T	F	S	S
				1	2	3
4	5	6	7	8	9	10
11	12	13	14	15	16	17
18	19	20	21	22	23	24
25	26	27	28	29	30	31

JUNE

M	T	W	T	F	S	S
1	2	3	4	5	6	7
8	9	10	11	12	13	14
15	16	17	18	19	20	21
22	23	24	25	26	27	28
29	30					

JULY

M	T	W	T	F	S	S
		1	2	3	4	5
6	7	8	9	10	11	12
13	14	15	16	17	18	19
20	21	22	23	24	25	26
27	28	29	30	31		

AUGUST

M	T	W	T	F	S	S
					1	2
3	4	5	6	7	8	9
10	11	12	13	14	15	16
17	18	19	20	21	22	23
24	25	26	27	28	29	30
31						

SEPTEMBER

M	T	W	T	F	S	S
	1	2	3	4	5	6
7	8	9	10	11	12	13
14	15	16	17	18	19	20
21	22	23	24	25	26	27
28	29	30				

OCTOBER

M	T	W	T	F	S	S
			1	2	3	4
5	6	7	8	9	10	11
12	13	14	15	16	17	18
19	20	21	22	23	24	25
26	27	28	29	30	31	

NOVEMBER

M	T	W	T	F	S	S
						1
2	3	4	5	6	7	8
9	10	11	12	13	14	15
16	17	18	19	20	21	22
23	24	25	26	27	28	29
30						

DECEMBER

M	T	W	T	F	S	S
	1	2	3	4	5	6
7	8	9	10	11	12	13
14	15	16	17	18	19	20
21	22	23	24	25	26	27
28	29	30	31			

2010

JANUARY

M	T	W	T	F	S	S
				1	2	3
4	5	6	7	8	9	10
11	12	13	14	15	16	17
18	19	20	21	22	23	24
25	26	27	28	29	33	31

FEBRUARY

M	T	W	T	F	S	S
1	2	3	4	5	6	7
8	9	10	11	12	13	14
15	16	17	18	19	20	21
22	23	24	25	26	27	28

MARCH

M	T	W	T	F	S	S
1	2	3	4	5	6	7
8	9	10	11	12	13	14
15	16	17	18	19	20	21
22	23	24	25	26	27	28
29	30	31				

APRIL

M	T	W	T	F	S	S
			1	2	3	4
5	6	7	8	9	10	11
12	13	14	15	16	17	18
19	20	21	22	23	24	25
26	27	28	29	30		

MAY

M	T	W	T	F	S	S
					1	2
3	4	5	6	7	8	9
10	11	12	13	14	15	16
17	18	19	20	21	22	23
24	25	26	27	28	29	30
31						

JUNE

M	T	W	T	F	S	S
	1	2	3	4	5	6
7	8	9	10	11	12	13
14	15	16	17	18	19	20
21	22	23	24	25	26	27
28	29	30				

JULY

M	T	W	T	F	S	S
			1	2	3	4
5	6	7	8	9	10	11
12	13	14	15	16	17	18
19	20	21	22	23	24	25
26	27	28	29	30	31	

AUGUST

M	T	W	T	F	S	S
						1
2	3	4	5	6	7	8
9	10	11	12	13	14	15
16	17	18	19	20	21	22
23	24	25	26	27	28	29
30	31					

SEPTEMBER

M	T	W	T	F	S	S
		1	2	3	4	5
6	7	8	9	10	11	12
13	14	15	16	17	18	19
20	21	22	23	24	25	26
27	28	29	30			

OCTOBER

M	T	W	T	F	S	S
				1	2	3
4	5	6	7	8	9	10
11	12	13	14	15	16	17
18	19	20	21	22	23	24
25	26	27	28	29	30	31

NOVEMBER

M	T	W	T	F	S	S
1	2	3	4	5	6	7
8	9	10	11	12	13	14
15	16	17	18	19	20	21
22	23	24	25	26	27	28
29	30					

DECEMBER

M	T	W	T	F	S	S
		1	2	3	4	5
6	7	8	9	10	11	12
13	14	15	16	17	18	19
20	21	22	23	24	25	26
27	28	29	30	31		

2011

JANUARY

M	T	W	T	F	S	S
					1	2
3	4	5	6	7	8	9
10	11	12	13	14	15	16
17	18	19	20	21	22	23
24	25	26	27	28	29	30
31						

FEBRUARY

M	T	W	T	F	S	S
	1	2	3	4	5	6
7	8	9	10	11	12	13
14	15	16	17	18	19	20
21	22	23	24	25	26	27
28						

MARCH

M	T	W	T	F	S	S
	1	2	3	4	5	6
7	8	9	10	11	12	13
14	15	16	17	18	19	20
21	22	23	24	25	26	27
28	29	30	31			

APRIL

M	T	W	T	F	S	S
				1	2	3
4	5	6	7	8	9	10
11	12	13	14	15	16	17
18	19	20	21	22	23	24
25	26	27	28	29	30	

MAY

M	T	W	T	F	S	S
						1
2	3	4	5	6	7	8
9	10	11	12	13	14	15
16	17	18	19	20	21	22
23	24	25	26	27	28	29
30	31					

JUNE

M	T	W	T	F	S	S
		1	2	3	4	5
6	7	8	9	10	11	12
13	14	15	16	17	18	19
20	21	22	23	24	25	26
27	28	29	30			

JULY

M	T	W	T	F	S	S
				1	2	3
4	5	6	7	8	9	10
11	12	13	14	15	16	17
18	19	20	21	22	23	24
25	26	27	28	29	30	31

AUGUST

M	T	W	T	F	S	S
1	2	3	4	5	6	7
8	9	10	11	12	13	14
15	16	17	18	19	20	21
22	23	24	25	26	27	28
29	30	31				

SEPTEMBER

M	T	W	T	F	S	S
			1	2	3	4
5	6	7	8	9	10	11
12	13	14	15	16	17	18
19	20	21	22	23	24	25
26	27	28	29	30		

OCTOBER

M	T	W	T	F	S	S
					1	2
3	4	5	6	7	8	9
10	11	12	13	14	15	16
17	18	19	20	21	22	23
24	25	26	27	28	29	30
31						

NOVEMBER

M	T	W	T	F	S	S
	1	2	3	4	5	6
7	8	9	10	11	12	13
14	15	16	17	18	19	20
21	22	23	24	25	26	27
28	29	30				

DECEMBER

M	T	W	T	F	S	S
			1	2	3	4
5	6	7	8	9	10	11
12	13	14	15	16	17	18
19	20	21	22	23	24	25
26	27	28	29	30	31	

2012

JANUARY

M	T	W	T	F	S	S
						1
2	3	4	5	6	7	8
9	10	11	12	13	14	15
16	17	18	19	20	21	22
23	24	25	26	27	28	29
30	31					

FEBRUARY

M	T	W	T	F	S	S
		1	2	3	4	5
6	7	8	9	10	11	12
13	14	15	16	17	18	19
20	21	22	23	24	25	26
27	28	29				

MARCH

M	T	W	T	F	S	S
			1	2	3	4
5	6	7	8	9	10	11
12	13	14	15	16	17	18
19	20	21	22	23	24	25
26	27	28	29	30	31	

APRIL

M	T	W	T	F	S	S
						1
2	3	4	5	6	7	8
9	10	11	12	13	14	15
16	17	18	19	20	21	22
23	24	25	26	27	28	29
30						

MAY

M	T	W	T	F	S	S
	1	2	3	4	5	6
7	8	9	10	11	12	13
14	15	16	17	18	19	20
21	22	23	24	25	26	27
28	29	30	31			

JUNE

M	T	W	T	F	S	S
				1	2	3
4	5	6	7	8	9	10
11	12	13	14	15	16	17
18	19	20	21	22	23	24
25	26	27	28	29	30	

JULY

M	T	W	T	F	S	S
						1
2	3	4	5	6	7	8
9	10	11	12	13	14	15
16	17	18	19	20	21	22
23	24	25	26	27	28	29
30	31					

AUGUST

M	T	W	T	F	S	S
		1	2	3	4	5
6	7	8	9	10	11	12
13	14	15	16	17	18	19
20	21	22	23	24	25	26
27	28	29	30	31		

SEPTEMBER

M	T	W	T	F	S	S
					1	2
3	4	5	6	7	8	9
10	11	12	13	14	15	16
17	18	19	20	21	22	23
24	25	26	27	28	29	30

OCTOBER

M	T	W	T	F	S	S
1	2	3	4	5	6	7
8	9	10	11	12	13	14
15	16	17	18	19	20	21
22	23	24	25	26	27	28
29	30	31				

NOVEMBER

M	T	W	T	F	S	S
			1	2	3	4
5	6	7	8	9	10	11
12	13	14	15	16	17	18
19	20	21	22	23	24	25
26	27	28	29	30		

DECEMBER

M	T	W	T	F	S	S
					1	2
3	4	5	6	7	8	9
10	11	12	13	14	15	16
17	18	19	20	21	22	23
24	25	26	27	28	29	30
31						

HOLIDAYS AND NOTABLE DATES

	2011
New Year's Day UK IRL USA CDN AUS NZ	Jan 1
St David's Day WAL	Mar 1
St Patrick's Day IRL	Mar 17
British Summer Time begins	Mar 27
Mothering Sunday	Apr 3
Good Friday UK CDN AUS NZ	Apr 22
St George's Day ENG	Apr 23
Easter Monday UK IRL CDN AUS NZ	Apr 25
May Day Holiday UK	May 1
Spring Bank Holiday UK	May 30
Father's Day	Jun 19
August Bank Holiday UK	Aug 29
British Summer Time ends	Oct 30
St Andrew's Day SCO	Nov 30
Christmas Day UK IRL USA CDN AUS NZ	Dec 25
Boxing Day/St Stephen's Day UK IRL CDN AUS NZ	Dec 26

	2012
New Year's Day UK IRL USA CDN AUS NZ	Jan 1
St David's Day WAL	Mar 1
St Patrick's Day IRL	Mar 17
British Summer Time begins	Mar 25
Mothering Sunday	Mar 18
Good Friday UK CDN AUS NZ	Apr 6
St George's Day ENG	Apr 23
Easter Monday UK IRL CDN AUS NZ	Apr 9
May Day Holiday UK	May 7
Spring Bank Holiday UK	Jun 4
Diamond Jubilee Holiday UK	Jun 5
Father's Day	Jun 17
August Bank Holiday UK	Aug 27
British Summer Time ends	Oct 28
St Andrew's Day SCO	Nov 30

PART 4 – Miscellaneous

Christmas Day UK IRL USA CDN AUS NZ	Dec 25
Boxing Day/St Stephen's Day UK IRL CDN AUS NZ	Dec 26